The Wars of Yesterday

THE WARS OF YESTERDAY

THE BALKAN WARS AND THE EMERGENCE OF MODERN MILITARY CONFLICT, 1912–13

Edited by Katrin Boeckh and Sabine Rutar

berghahn
NEW YORK • OXFORD
www.berghahnbooks.com

First published in 2018 by
Berghahn Books
www.berghahnbooks.com

© 2018, 2020 Katrin Boeckh and Sabine Rutar
First paperback edition published in 2020

All rights reserved. Except for the quotation of short passages for the purposes of criticism and review, no part of this book may be reproduced in any form or by any means, electronic or mechanical, including photocopying, recording, or any information storage and retrieval system now known or to be invented, without written permission of the publisher.

Library of Congress Cataloging-in-Publication Data
A C.I.P. cataloging record is available from the Library of Congress

British Library Cataloguing in Publication Data
A catalogue record for this book is available from the British Library

ISBN 978-1-78533-774-1 hardback
ISBN 978-1-78920-843-6 paperback
ISBN 978-1-78533-775-8 ebook

Contents

List of Tables   vii

Acknowledgements   viii

Part I. Introductions

The Wars of Yesterday: The Balkan Wars and the Emergence of   3
Modern Military Conflict, 1912/13. An Introduction.
Katrin Boeckh and Sabine Rutar

Chapter 1   'Modern Wars' and 'Backward Societies': The   19
Balkan Wars in the History of Twentieth-Century
European Warfare
Wolfgang Höpken

Part II. Beyond the Balkans: Diplomatic and Geopolitical Aspects

Chapter 2   Ottoman Diplomacy on the Origins of the Balkan   93
Wars
Gül Tokay

Chapter 3   Austria-Hungary, Germany and the Balkan Wars: 113
A Diplomatic Struggle for Peace, Influence and
Supremacy
Alma Hannig

Chapter 4   Not Just a Prelude: The First Balkan War Crisis as   137
the Catalyst of Final European War Preparations
Michael Hesselholt Clemmesen

Part III. Armies, Soldiers, Irregulars

Chapter 5   The Ottoman Mobilization in the Balkan War: 163
Failure and Reorganization
Mehmet Beşikçi

Chapter 6   The Thracian Theatre of War 1912   190
Richard C. Hall

Chapter 7	Morale, Ideology and the Barbarization of Warfare among Greek Soldiers *Spyridon Tsoutsoumpis*	206
Chapter 8	A Forgotten Lesson: The Romanian Army between the Campaign in Bulgaria (1913) and the Tutrakan Debacle (1916) *Claudiu-Lucian Topor*	240
Chapter 9	Serbian Chetniks: Traditions of Irregular Warfare *Alexey Timofeev*	258

Part IV. Civilians, Wounded, Invalids

Chapter 10	The Future Enemy's Soldiers-To-Be: Fear of War in Trieste, Austria-Hungary *Sabine Rutar*	285
Chapter 11	The Plight of the Muslim Population in Salonica and Surrounding Areas *Vera Goseva and Natasha Kotlar-Trajkova*	312
Chapter 12	Cleansing the Nation: War-Related Demographic Changes in Macedonia *Iakovos D. Michailidis*	326
Chapter 13	Jewish Philanthropy and Mutual Assistance Between Ottomanism and Communal Identities *Eyal Ginio*	344
Chapter 14	The Assistance of the British Red Cross to the Ottoman Empire *Oya Dağlar Macar*	373
Chapter 15	War Neurosis and Psychiatry in the Aftermath of the Balkan Wars *Heike Karge*	392
Conclusion	Bringing the Balkan Wars into Historiographic Debates *Katrin Boeckh and Sabine Rutar*	416
Index		425

Tables

Table 5.1.	Amount of manpower planned to be mobilized for the Ottoman armies before the Balkan War	165
Table 5.2.	Manpower actually mobilized for the Ottoman armies in the Balkan War (at the start of the war)	166
Table 5.3.	Comparison of manpower mobilization figures: Ottomans and Balkan Alliance	167
Table 5.4.	Comparison of manpower mobilization throughout the First World War	177

Acknowledgements

Without the help of many good spirits, this volume would not have seen the light of day. We would like to acknowledge the assistance of the colleagues and institutions that actively supported the publication of this book, and to express our sincere gratitude. Dr Wolfgang Levermann of the *Volkswagen* Foundation has been sympathetic to the project from our initial proposal to the completion of the present volume, the Foundation supporting us by generous funding. Prof. Dr Mehmet Hacısalihoğlu of the Center for Balkan and Black Sea Studies at Yıldız Technical University and his student assistants provided a congenial infrastructure and a perfect setting for fruitful discussions in beautiful Istanbul.

Aiveen Donnelly, Jim Gibbons, Christian Mady, Alexander Legler, Kathleen Luft, Zoe Roth and Joanna Wiesler assisted us in the preparation of the manuscript. We are grateful to the Leibniz Institute for East and Southeast European Studies (IOS) in Regensburg, which generously funded the volume's editing process. A final thank you is due to Chris Chappell, Amanda Horn and Charlotte Mosedale, as well as Berghahn's production team, who assiduously supported and assisted us from the publisher's side.

Part I
Introductions

The Wars of Yesterday

THE BALKAN WARS AND THE EMERGENCE OF MODERN MILITARY CONFLICT, 1912/13

An Introduction

Katrin Boeckh and Sabine Rutar

The Balkan Wars of 1912/13 and their outcomes have shaped much of the military and political thinking of the Balkan elites during the last century. At the same time, these wars were intimations of what was to become the bloodiest, most violent century in Europe's and indeed humankind's history. Wars often lead to other wars. Yet this process of contagion happened in a particularly gruesome manner during the twentieth century. In Europe, the Balkan Wars marked the beginning of the twentieth century's history of warfare.

In the First Balkan War (October 1912–May 1913), Serbia, Montenegro, Greece and Bulgaria declared war on the Ottoman Empire; in the Second Balkan War (June–August 1913), Bulgaria fought Serbia, Montenegro and Greece over the Ottoman territories they had each just gained. From July onwards, Serbia, Montenegro and Greece were supported by Romania, who entered the war hoping to seize the southern Dobruja from Bulgaria. These hopes were realized. Albania, declared an independent state in November 1912, was thus a product of the First Balkan War. The borders of other territories were changed and obtained features that partially remain valid up to the present: the historical region of Macedonia, a main theatre of the wars, was divided among Greece (Aegean Macedonia), Bulgaria (Pirin Macedonia) and Serbia (Vardar Macedonia, corresponding largely to today's Republic of Macedonia, established in 1991). The Ottoman Empire's loss of most of its European territories in the conflict was one more warning sign of its inner weakness; it ceased to exist in the aftermath of the First World War, and was succeeded by the Republic of Turkey in 1923.

As this enumeration of territorial and political changes makes plain, the states existing today in the area can hardly offer a satisfactory framework for exploring the history of the two Balkan Wars, which in many ways exerted a more profound impact on the region than even the Great War. And yet, in Southeastern Europe, scholars addressing and researching these first European wars of the twentieth century have long adopted a traditional military and/or political history perspective, firmly rooted in the respective national master narratives of the former belligerents. Among the tasks of our volume is to challenge these master narratives.

The second war was not succeeded by much of a postwar period, for only slightly more than a year after the fighting ended, the First World War broke out. Once more, the Balkan countries engaged in war to pursue territorial claims that had remained unsatisfied. Territorial aspirations continued to be at stake in both the Second World War and, in yet another manner, the Yugoslav wars of the 1990s. As a result, the local populations in the region faced unstable living conditions, in both a social and a political sense, throughout nearly the full span of the twentieth century, interspersed with only a few decades that lacked violent conflict. All the wars caused destruction, displacement and death. State borders remained contested, and all too often the region's political regimes ignored the rights of ethnic minorities.

These conflicts happened in the shadow of global events. Western scholars in particular have tended to interpret the two Balkan Wars of 1912/13 as a mere prelude to the Great War, a marginal event in the context of great power politics, hardly worth mentioning. Labelled 'regional wars', they quickly faded into the background as the echo of the shots fired in Sarajevo on 28 June 1914 rippled across the globe.[1] Unsurprisingly, the attention directed to the centennials of these events followed the same pattern. Remarkably, recent histories of the origins of the First World War that do include the Balkan crises and even grant that they are worth focusing on in the narrative offer no comprehensive interpretation of the events. The Balkan peninsula, and Serbia in particular, retain the attributes that have invariably been ascribed to the region and have been used with greater frequency since the Yugoslav wars of the 1990s: the region is a powder keg, an accumulation of rogue states, a stage for melodramatic, squalid and bloody sequences.[2] On the other hand, scholars in Southeastern Europe have built upon their respective national master narratives, in which the Balkan Wars are firmly rooted.

Thus, the Balkan Wars, the conflicts that intimated so many features of future wars, have yet to find their appropriate interpretative place within the European historiography of twentieth-century warfare. Christopher Clark, in his book *The Sleepwalkers*, has effected a remarkable integration of the diplomatic efforts of the European powers during the Balkan Wars into the immediate prehistory of the Great War. Referring to the political and psychological culture of the leading European politicians and to the question of how war entered their backroom discussions, Clark has transcended the European historiographies that have centred on the nation-state, adding to them a multilateral, comparative approach.[3] And yet, among the responses he received were critical assessments, especially by scholars from Serbia, who noticed how, for example, his description of the gruesome details of the assassination of the Serbian King Aleksandar in 1903 reiterated many negative stereotypes about the Balkans.[4] To be sure, the centenary in 2012/13 brought forth several noteworthy efforts to adopt comprehensive and comparative historical perspectives;[5] these have given some fresh impetus to the few previous studies on the Balkan Wars.[6]

To achieve an open scholarly dialogue on the issues connected to the Balkan Wars of 1912/13, several of which remain quite sensitive, collaboration among historians from Southeastern Europe and Turkey as well as other countries needs to intensify. Such dialogue can transcend the boundaries of nation-state-centred historiographies and can place the wars in a genuinely European and global perspective. To foster such dialogue is one central aim of this volume. Its roots lie in the lively discussions at Yıldız Technical University İstanbul during the October 2012 centennial of the outbreak of war, generously supported by the Volkswagen Foundation (*VolkswagenStiftung*).[7]

The common methodological reference for all the authors in this volume is the field of New Military History, which, over the last two decades, has produced considerable discussion on how to study war and societies at war in a way that goes beyond the military and political spheres and aims at making war an integral part of social and cultural history.[8] In this vein, going beyond the historical tropes that have long characterized the historiography of the Balkan Wars, the authors in this volume explore these wars in their sociopolitical and sociocultural contexts, placing societal, political and military actors at the centre of attention. In so doing, our book is of interest to academic fields beyond war history and military history. The core subject is social and political history, surveyed from varying angles that make for a comprehensive whole, though one that is rooted in the specific. Not least, our book is highly relevant to anyone interested in the First World War and its prehistory.

Equally importantly, the authors move beyond the national frameworks within which these wars have largely been researched; they entangle events and use microhistorical tools to examine local contexts.[9] Given the traditional historiographic tropes related to the Balkan Wars, this methodological renewal can be achieved *only* through the collective framework offered in this volume, which overcomes the nationally organized settings of the writing of war history.

The volume is divided into four parts. Following Wolfgang Höpken's vigorous demonstration of how the Balkan Wars should be placed within the broader framework of the European history of wars in the twentieth century, in Part II, Alma Hannig, Gül Tokay and Michael Hesselholt Clemmesen set the frame of diplomacy, international relations and domestic politics in the face of war breaking out on the Southeastern European periphery. They apply the tools of new diplomatic and geopolitical history to explore sources pertaining to Austria-Hungary, the Ottoman Empire and the periphery 'at the other end', the Nordic countries.

Part III focuses on the social history of military life, of the 'Armies, Soldiers, Irregulars'. Mehmet Beşikçi discusses Ottoman recruitment practices and pays particular attention to the lessons the Empire learned from failures in the Balkan Wars, which were applied in the subsequent world war. Richard Hall gives a vivid account of one of the central battlefields of the First Balkan War, the Thracian war theatre, in today's Bulgaria, Greece and Turkey. Spyridon Tsoutsoumpis provides in-depth insights into how Greek soldiers experienced war and violence. Claudiu-Lucian Topor focuses on the hubris with which the victorious Romanian army exited the Second Balkan War, which led to its all-too-confident conduct in the First World War, with catastrophic consequences. Alexey Timofeev recapitulates the traditions of Serbian guerrilla warfare and investigates how these practices were effectively used during the Balkan Wars.

In the fourth part, the authors turn to civilian lives during wartime ('Civilians, Wounded, Invalids'). Sabine Rutar assesses the increased fear of rank-and-file soldiers-to-be in the multinational Austrian port city of Trieste in the face of war breaking out in the city's 'backyard'. Hers is a vivid microhistorical example of the final phase of what would soon become Stefan Zweig's 'world of yesterday', a milieu ridden by feelings of existential threat and difficult loyalties.[10] Vera Goseva and Natasha Kotlar-Trajkova trace the sufferings of the Muslim population in Salonica and its hinterland; and Iakovos Michailidis examines the effects of forced population transfers and displacement on the local population in one of the key disputed areas of the wars, Macedonia. Eyal

Ginio considers Jewish philanthropy and assistance, focusing on aspects of loyalty to both Ottomanism and communal identities. Oya Dağlar Macar discusses the support provided by the British Red Cross to the Ottoman Empire. Heike Karge concludes the volume with a pioneering study on war neuroses suffered by participants in the Balkan Wars.

Recently, Raymond Detrez maintained that the 'feeling of commonality and solidarity it [the Orthodox Christian or Romaic community] created was irreparably damaged during the Second Balkan War; what has remained of it is a masked unanimity vis-à-vis the real or imagined threat of Islam'.[11] Nation-centred historiographies have contributed to such divisiveness by continuously re-digging the imaginary trenches between the belligerents after the fact. Thus, a major task of the authors in the present volume has been to engage with the military and civilian agency of all belligerents and make visible their parallel experiences: conscripted soldiers and their commanders as well as irregular fighters on the one hand; and on the other the civilian population, which was involved in the war to an extent previously unacknowledged. Violence in the form of mass expulsions and atrocities, as well as the demonization of the 'other', are among the miseries the war brought to civilians living in the contested regions. Methodologically, Reinhart Koselleck's 'spaces of experience' and 'horizons of expectation' have paved the way for the collective exploring of such commonalities in this volume.[12]

So what makes these wars *the* Balkan Wars? And what makes them an integral part of the history of twentieth-century warfare in Europe? The authors look at a complex set of features to establish answers to these questions, such as the military procedures, the military technology, the equipment of the armies and of their irregular allies, the efforts of territorial ethnic homogenization, and the abounding propaganda intended to legitimize territorial conquest. Authors examine the utterances of specialists and intermediaries who were on location, along with local and international non-military observers such as medical and auxiliary personnel, among others. Astonishingly, observers from elsewhere in Europe and even further abroad reported from the region while the war was being waged: French aid workers for the Greek army and Dutch aid workers for the Bulgarian and Serbian armies, as well as Indian medical staff serving with British aid personnel for the Ottoman troops. As Oya Dağlar Macar and Wolfgang Höpken conclude in exploring sources of different parties involved, the medical knowledge about war injuries they brought back home proved to be highly useful during the First World War.

A special feature of the Balkan Wars were the guerrilla troops whose actions were much more dependent on those of the regular forces – and vice versa – than has been assumed. Their traditional arena was Macedonia, bringing a particularly tragic fate to this region's population, as Natasha Kotlar-Trajkova and Vera Goseva as well as Iakovos Michailidis elaborate, studying several locations and focusing on different angles of (forced) demographic changes in their respective chapters.

Here, partisan groups from all the future war parties were already active ahead of the outbreak of war. The weapons they used, such as the *makedonka*, were later exported to the Russian battlefields in the First World War, as Alexey Timofeev points out. His chapter proves how guerrilla troops are emblematic for weak states, especially in regions without effective state government, lacking administrative and institutional capacities. During the Balkan Wars, this connection between the political weakness of states and their military actions was conspicuous. After losing the First Balkan War, the Ottoman state proved capable of learning from that defeat and the loss of territories. According to Mehmet Beşikçi, it introduced a new and, as would soon become clear, more effective military law by May 1914. On the other side, the Balkan states drew no military lessons from their victory over the Ottoman Empire, forfeiting any advantage by going to war against one another. By 1914, Serbia, Bulgaria, Greece and Montenegro were exhausted, and the newly belligerent Romania would prove to be blinded by feelings of heroic glory, as Richard Hall and Claudiu-Lucian Topor point out in their respective chapters.

The ethnic composition of the belligerent armies mattered. While the Balkan armies were ethnically rather homogeneous, the rank and file of the imperial Ottoman army included ethnic Serbs, Bulgarians and Greeks, who confronted their co-nationals in the trenches. In an attempt to control them, these men were mobilized in so-called labour battalions – special units to support the fighting squads. And, as Mehmet Beşikçi shows, these potentially unreliable groups helped to weaken the seemingly overwhelming Ottoman military force from within.

The wars stirred up the international political scene in a substantially different way than the local European wars of earlier decades, such as the Russian-Ottoman war of 1877/78 or the Serbian-Bulgarian war of 1885/86. By the early twentieth century, Europe was gripped by fears of a more general conflagration. On the basis of little-explored Ottoman sources, Gül Tokay assesses how the triangular relationship of the Balkan states, the foreign powers and the Ottoman administration reached a deadlock in the summer of 1912, making war seem the only alternative for all parties.

When the First Balkan War broke out in October 1912, the Western European powers, signatories of the Treaty of Berlin (1878), hoped for an Ottoman victory and the preservation of the Ottoman Empire.[13] Diplomatic meetings, such as the Ambassadors' Conferences in London and Saint Petersburg, were organized with the aim of arranging a peaceful solution to the issue of the Ottoman territories in the Balkans. Alma Hannig shows how the war's outbreak led to important turning points in the diplomatic efforts of both Austria-Hungary and Germany, which changed their positions within the system of European great powers and deeply affected their future cooperation and reputations. The great powers refrained from any kind of military engagement in favour of the Ottomans, however.[14] Little known is the fact that the military conflict in the Balkan peninsula considerably reinforced the war preparations undertaken by the European states. Michael Hesselholt Clemmesen provides empirical evidence of how societies as far away from the battlefields as the Nordic countries became strongly militarized as a reaction to the outbreak of war on the southeastern periphery, without knowing, of course, what would happen in the summer of 1914.

Sentiments ranged from nationalist enthusiasm to bleak fear and the desperate wish to maintain peace. More than ever, the publics of various European countries sensed the imminent danger of a broader conflagration. Sabine Rutar exemplifies this sense of dread as it took hold in the Austrian port city of Trieste, where, perhaps more intensely than elsewhere, the outbreak of war in the Balkans caused fears of a huge war – even an imminent 'world war' – to spread to the common people. The anti-war gathering of Europe's socialists in Basel in November 1912, mere weeks after the outbreak of war in the Balkans, was a political expression of this widespread European fear.[15] The Balkan Wars thus acutely intensified both the perceptions of a general European crisis and the hopes that peace would ultimately prevail throughout the continent.[16] This, again, testifies to the larger European dimension of the Balkan Wars.

On the battlefields, the physical and psychological distress was immense. The permanent sense of insecurity, the rumours, the growing gap between war propaganda and real warfare fed anxieties and ultimately triggered atrocities not only against the military enemy but also against allegedly dangerous co-nationals. Spyridon Tsoutsoumpis vividly assesses this process among Greek soldiers. The result was no different from what happens in other wars: stricken individuals were affected not only physically, but also psychologically by post-traumatic stress disorders *ante litteram*. Because this is a thoroughly underresearched topic, Heike Karge's chapter is a pioneering effort.[17]

Religiosity and religious practice, as a means of coming to terms with the war, found new ways of expression among both the soldiers on the fronts and civilians. As Eyal Ginio shows, in the political arena, religious bonds were often instrumentalized: Jews prayed for an Ottoman victory in Antwerp; Orthodox Christians – for example in the Russian Empire – celebrated masses for the victory of the Christian allies in the Balkans; Balkan monarchs legitimized the war against the Ottoman Empire as a 'crusade' against non-Christians. Analysing communicative networks has revealed that religious minorities showed not only a high degree of loyalty to their countries of residence but also an effective connection to their co-religious communities in neighbouring states – even if these were opponents in the wars – in more distant European countries and even in Africa and the Americas.

To be sure, classical military histories, concerned with military units – their strategies and moves, their victories and defeats – and diplomatic correspondence, retain their value. Yet they need to be enhanced via the integration of a cluster of archival materials representing perspectives drawn from regional and local contexts. Probably the best example in this regard is one of the most frequently cited documents concerning the Balkan Wars, the famous report of the Carnegie Endowment for International Peace.[18] While it reveals atrocities committed by all belligerent parties, the legal effects of this first international initiative undertaken shortly before the Great War have nearly gone unnoticed, as has the report's influence on the development of international law and the punishment of war crimes.[19]

To achieve a comprehensive knowledge of the Balkan Wars that would effectively entangle them with the huge field of research on the history of twentieth-century European warfare, much remains to be explored in the archives; nevertheless, the authors in this volume together have taken a significant step towards this goal. They examine recollections of former soldiers and former members of irregular units as well as those of politicians and other public figures; in their sources, they go beyond the mainstream media and scrutinize, for example, medical journals as a source that reflects the great interest medical doctors took in the war and specifically in the effects of the new weapons on the human body. In doing so, the authors reveal the conflicts' entangled web of international significance and, at the same time, advance the social history of local war experiences. In this way, the wars are seen no longer as a mere prelude to world war but rather as an intimation of that war – and, in fact, of what was to become one of the most violent centuries in the history of humankind. They were the wars that signalled the demise of the world as it was known, the world that Stefan Zweig, in his 'memories of a European', so aptly referred to as the 'world of yesterday'.[20]

No longer exclusively national stories of victories and defeats, the wars become an emblem of lives torn by violence, displacement, political destabilization and imperial demise. No longer cast as an event relevant within the heroic stories of national master narratives, the wars become the guideposts of a horrific European twentieth century. They have shaped mental maps until today, and not only in the societies that are the legacies of the belligerents. The Balkan Wars gave root to the forceful image of the Balkans as a powder keg, last revitalized during the Yugoslav wars of the 1990s. In fact, it has been with a symbolic if not political consideration that these have frequently, and wrongly, been labelled 'Balkan Wars', even by scholars.[21]

The descriptions of the atrocities committed during the Balkan Wars, as compiled and disseminated forcefully but not only by the Carnegie Report, turned 'the Balkans' into a symbol for savagery, barbarism and terror. Such symbolism lives on, as became obvious during the Yugoslav wars of the 1990s. While the descriptions of mass expulsions and violence in the international press and by the belligerents themselves draw an unequivocal picture, it takes a specific communicative dynamic to turn this depiction into a persistent negative stereotype and suspicion of 'inborn' cruelty – a dynamic that aims at 'othering', at outsourcing evil, as it were, to divert attention away from the atrocities of one's own country.[22] After all, it is well known that war crimes and crimes against humanity were committed on a large scale by the belligerents in both world wars and various colonial conflicts.[23]

To reject national master narratives is to enable the weaving together of many impressively analogous war histories. Writing their *histoire croisée* leads to a complex perspective that, at the very least, displays the parallel experiences of loyalty crises and antagonistic constructions of the enemy and the self.[24] Such a perspective increases the understanding of both the idiosyncrasies of Balkan nationalization patterns and the course of de-imperialization in the region, comprehensible only if framed as part of a wider, global scenario.

Katrin Boeckh is Senior Researcher at the Leibniz Institute for East and Southeast European Studies in Regensburg and Professor for East and Southeast European History at the LMU Munich. She is the author of a volume on the Balkan Wars (*Von den Balkankriegen zum Ersten Weltkrieg: Kleinstaatenpolitik und ethnische Selbstbestimmung auf dem Balkan*, Oldenbourg, 1996) and co-editor, with Sabine Rutar, of *The Balkan Wars* *from Contemporary Perception to Historic Memory* (Palgrave, 2017). Her further monographs cover the political history of Ukraine and Serbia.

Sabine Rutar is Senior Researcher at the Leibniz Institute for East and Southeast European Studies in Regensburg. She is Editor-in-Chief of the quarterly *Südosteuropa. Journal of Politics and Society*; author of *Kultur – Nation – Milieu: Sozialdemokratie in Triest vor dem Ersten Weltkrieg* (Klartext, 2004); and editor of several academic collections, including *Violence in Late Socialist Public Spheres* (special issue of *European History Quarterly*, 2015) and *Beyond the Balkans: Towards an Inclusive History of Southeastern Europe* (Lit, 2014). Recently, she co-edited (with Katrin Boeckh) *The Balkan Wars from Contemporary Perception to Historic Memory* (Palgrave, 2017).

Notes

1 Cf. the otherwise convincing narratives of William Mulligan, *The Origins of the First World War* (Cambridge/New York: Cambridge University Press, 2010); Jürgen Angelow, *Der Weg in die Urkatastrophe: Der Zerfall des alten Europas 1900–1914* (Berlin: be.bra, 2010).
2 On the Balkans as a 'negative alter ego' of 'the West', see Maria Todorova, *Imagining the Balkans* (New York: Oxford University Press, 2009 [updated version of the original edition of 1997]).
3 Christopher Clark, *The Sleepwalkers: How Europe Went to War in 1914* (London: Penguin, 2012).
4 Ibid., 3–5, quotation on p. 4. Cf., for example, the review by Bojan Aleksov, in *Slavonic and East European Review* 92(2) (April 2014), 363–64, http://www.jstor.org/stable/10.5699/slaveasteurorev2.92.2.0363.
5 Cf. the thematic issue 'The Balkan Wars' of Études Balkaniques, 49(2) (2013), edited by Svetlozar Eldarov; M. Hakan Yavuz and Isa Blumi (eds), *War and Nationalism: The Balkan Wars, 1912–1913, and Their Sociopolitical Implications* (Salt Lake City, UT: University of Utah Press, 2013); Igor Despot, *Balkanski Ratovi 1912–1913 i njihov odjek u Hrvatskoj* [The Balkan Wars 1912–1913 and Their Reflection in Croatia] (Zagreb: Plejada, 2013), focusing on perceptions and political implications; Catherine Durandin and Cécile Folschweiller (eds), *Alerte en Europe: la guerre dans les Balkans (1912–1913)* (Paris: L'Harmattan, 2014); Catherine Horel (ed.), *Les guerres balkaniques (1912–1913): Conflits, enjeux, mémoires* (Brussels: P.I.E. Peter Lang, 2014); Jean-Paul Bled and Jean-Pierre Deschodt (eds), *Les guerres balkaniques 1912–1913* (Paris: PUPS, 2014); James Pettifer and Tom Buchanan (eds), *War in the Balkans: Conflict and Diplomacy before World War I* (London: Tauris, 2016).
6 Cf. Egidio Ivetic, *Le guerre balcaniche* (Bologna: Il Mulino, 2007); Richard C. Hall, *The Balkan Wars 1912–1913: Prelude to the First World War* (London:

Routledge, 2000); Katrin Boeckh, *Von den Balkankriegen zum Ersten Weltkrieg: Kleinstaatenpolitik und ethnische Selbstbestimmung auf dem Balkan* (Munich: Oldenbourg, 1996).
7 Cf. the conference report 'The Balkan Wars 1912/13. Experience, Perception, Remembrance. International Conference on the Occasion of the 100th Anniversary', 11–13 October 2012, Istanbul, *H-Soz-Kult*, 28 March 2013, http://hsozkult.geschichte.hu-berlin.de/tagungsberichte/id=4734.
8 Cf., for example, Stephen Morillo and Michael F. Pavkovic, *What Is Military History?* (Cambridge: Polity, 2013); Jörg Echternkamp, Wolfgang Schmidt and Thomas Vogel (eds), *Perspektiven der Militärgeschichte, Raum, Gewalt und Repräsentation in historischer Forschung und Bildung* (Munich: Oldenbourg, 2010); Rolf-Dieter Müller, *Militärgeschichte* (Vienna/Cologne/Weimar: Böhlau, 2009); Jeremy Black, *Rethinking Military History* (New York: Routledge, 2004); Jutta Nowosadtko, *Krieg, Gewalt und Ordnung: Einführung in die Militärgeschichte* (Tübingen: edition diskord, 2002); Richard Holmes (ed.), *The Oxford Companion to Military History* (Oxford: Oxford University Press, 2001); Thomas Kühne and Benjamin Ziemann (eds), *Was ist Militärgeschichte?* (Paderborn: Schöningh, 2000).
9 As a more immediate reference, see the pioneering work on the First World War by Benjamin Ziemann, *War Experiences in Rural Germany, 1914–1923* (Oxford/New York: Berg, 2007) (German original *Front und Heimat: Ländliche Kriegserfahrungen im südlichen Bayern 1914–1923* [Essen: Klartext, 1997]); cf. also Sönke Neitzel, *Blut und Eisen: Deutschland im Ersten Weltkrieg* (Zürich: Pendo, 2003); and Bernd Ulrich and Benjamin Ziemann (eds), *German Soldiers in the Great War: Letters and Eyewitness Accounts* (Barnsley: Pen & Sword Military, 2010). With a focus on the region at stake here, Southeastern Europe, the Second World War has also drawn renewed attention recently. Hannes Grandits (Berlin), Xavier Bougarel (Berlin/Paris) and Nathalie Clayer (Paris) in 2015 and 2016 led an international network project of senior and junior researchers that, precisely, transcended nation-state frameworks and fostered (comparative) local approaches in the vein of the New Military History. Cf. the network's gatherings in Berlin (October 2015) and Athens (March 2016), https://www.tu-berlin.de/fileadmin/i65/Veranstaltungen/2015/10/Humbold_Folder_-_FINAL.pdf; http://www.ciera.fr/de/node/13086; and http://www.resefe.fr/node/51.
10 Stefan Zweig, *The World of Yesterday: An Autobiography* (London et al: Cassell, 1943).
11 Cf. Raymond Detrez, 'Pre-national Identities in the Balkans', in Roumen Daskalov and Tchavdar Marinov (eds), *Entangled Histories of the Balkans*, Vol. I: *National Ideologies and Language Policies* (Leiden: Brill, 2013) (Balkans Studies Library, 9), 13–65, here 63.
12 Reinhart Koselleck, '"Space of Experience" and "Horizon of Expectation": Two Historical Categories', in Koselleck, *Futures Past: On the Semantics of Historical Time* (New York: Columbia University Press, 2004), 255–311.
13 Cf. Holger Afflerbach, *Der Dreibund: Europäische Großmacht- und Allianzpolitik vor dem Ersten Weltkrieg* (Vienna/Cologne/Weimar: Böhlau, 2002), 725.

14 See Katrin Boeckh, 'Buts de guerre et conférences de la paix: les guerres balkaniques de 1912/13 furent-elles pour les États du Sud-Est de l'Europe un prélude à la Première Guerre mondiale?', in Daniel Baric (ed.), *Les guerres balkaniques* [forthcoming]. Nikolaus Faulstroh, *Die Balkankrisen von 1908–1914 und die Jugoslawienkonflikte von 1991–1999 im Beziehungsgeflecht der Großmächte: Das Verhalten von internationalen Akteuren bei der Ausbreitung von Konflikten auf dem Balkan* (Baden-Baden: Nomos, 2015), underscores analogies between the international non-involvement in the Balkan Wars and in the Yugoslav wars of the 1990s.

15 Sandrine Mayoraz, Frithjof B. Schenk and Ueli Mäder (eds), *Hundert Jahre Basler Friedenskongress (1912–2012): Die erhoffte 'Verbrüderung der Völker'* (Basel/Zurich: Schweizerisches Sozialarchiv, 2015), http://sozarch7.uzh.ch/daten/Friedenskongress_Gesamtwerk.pdf.

16 Cf. Mulligan, *The Origins of the First World War*, 1–2; Clark, *The Sleepwalkers*, depicts the 'road to war' in a slightly more 'belligerent' manner.

17 One of the best assessments of how violence is triggered and perpetuated remains Heinrich Popitz, 'Gewalt', in Popitz, *Phänomene der Macht: Autorität – Herrschaft – Gewalt* (Tübingen: Mohr, 1986), 68–106.

18 Carnegie Endowment for International Peace, *Report of the International Commission to Inquire into the Causes and Conduct of the Balkan Wars* (Washington, DC: The Endowment, 1914).

19 For a deconstruction of the qualitative value of the Carnegie Report, cf. Roumen Daskalov, 'Bulgarian-Greek Dis/Entanglements', in Daskalov and Marinov, *Entangled Histories of the Balkans*, Vol. 1, 149–239, here 233–34. Daskalov points out that 'the belligerents argued their claims on different grounds and based their statistics on different criteria' (p. 233). See also the critical assessments of the report and its reception in Dietmar Müller and Stefan Troebst (eds), *Der 'Carnegie Report on the Causes and Conduct of the Balkan Wars 1912/13'. Wirkungs- und Rezeptionsgeschichte im Völkerrecht und in der Historiographie* [*Comparativ* 24 (2014), 6] (Leipzig: Leipziger Universitätsverlag, 2015).

20 Zweig, *The World of Yesterday*. In the German original, the subtitle is 'Memories of a European': Stefan Zweig, *Die Welt von gestern: Erinnerungen eines Europäers* (Stockholm: Bermann-Fischer, 1942).

21 For example, it was no coincidence that a new edition of the Carnegie Report was published in 1993, in the face of war breaking out in the former Yugoslavia: *The Other Balkan Wars: A 1913 Carnegie Endowment Inquiry in Retrospect with a New Introduction and Reflections on the Present Conflict by George F. Kennan* (Washington, DC: Carnegie Endowment for International Peace, 1993). Cf. also Misha Glenny, *The Fall of Yugoslavia: The Third Balkan War* (London: Penguin, 1996); Hannes Hofbauer, *Balkankrieg: Zehn Jahre Zerstörung Jugoslawiens* (Vienna: Promedia, 2001 [5th ed. 2015]); Johannes Grotzky, *Balkankrieg: Der Zerfall Jugoslawiens und die Folgen für Europa* (Munich: Pieper, 1993).

22 In the sense of Todorova, *Imagining the Balkans*.

23 Cf., for example, Benjamin Ziemann, 'Der Erste Weltkrieg als ein Laboratorium der Gewalt: Einleitung', in B. Ziemann (ed.), *Gewalt im Ersten Weltkrieg: Töten – Überleben – Verweigern* (Essen: Klartext, 2013), 7–21, for

an analytically convincing assessment of the practices and the meaning of violence in the Great War.
24 Cf. the similar analytical vein in Daskalov and Marinov, *Entangled Histories of the Balkans*, Vol. 1.

Bibliography

Afflerbach, Holger. *Der Dreibund: Europäische Großmacht- und Allianzpolitik vor dem Ersten Weltkrieg*. Vienna/Cologne/Weimar: Böhlau, 2002.
Aleksov, Bojan. 'Review: The Sleepwalkers: How Europe Went to War in 1914 by Clark, Christopher'. *Slavonic and East European Review* 92(2) (April 2014), 363–64, http://www.jstor.org/stable/10.5699/slaveasteurorev2.92.2.0363.
Angelow, Jürgen. *Der Weg in die Urkatastrophe: Der Zerfall des alten Europas 1900–1914*. Berlin: be.bra, 2010.
Black, Jeremy. *Rethinking Military History*. New York: Routledge, 2004.
Bled, Jean-Paul, and Jean-Pierre Deschodt (eds). *Les guerres balkaniques 1912–1913*. Paris: PUPS, 2014.
Boeckh, Katrin. *Von den Balkankriegen zum Ersten Weltkrieg: Kleinstaatenpolitik und ethnische Selbstbestimmung auf dem Balkan*. Munich: Oldenbourg, 1996.
Boeckh, Katrin. 'Buts de guerre et conférences de la paix: les guerres balkaniques de 1912/13 furent-elles pour les États du Sud-Est de l'Europe un prélude à la Première Guerre mondiale?', in Daniel Baric (ed.), *Les guerres balkaniques* [forthcoming].
Carnegie Endowment for International Peace. *Report of the International Commission to Inquire into the Causes and Conduct of the Balkan Wars*. Washington, DC: The Endowment, 1914.
Clark, Christopher. *The Sleepwalkers: How Europe Went to War in 1914*. London: Penguin, 2012.
Daskalov, Roumen. 'Bulgarian-Greek Dis/Entanglements', in Roumen Daskalov and Tchavdar Marinov (eds), *Entangled Histories of the Balkans*, Vol. 1: *National Ideologies and Language Policies* (Balkans Studies Library, 9) (Leiden: Brill, 2013), 149–239.
Daskalov, Roumen, and Tchavdar Marinov (eds). *Entangled Histories of the Balkans*, Vol. 1: *National Ideologies and Language Policies* (Balkans Studies Library, 9). Leiden: Brill, 2013.
Despot, Igor. *Balkanski Ratovi 1912–1913. i njihov odjek u Hrvatskoj* [The Balkan Wars 1912–1913 and Their Reflection in Croatia]. Zagreb: Plejada, 2013.
Detrez, Raymond. 'Pre-national Identities in the Balkans', in Roumen Daskalov and Tchavdar Marinov (eds), *Entangled Histories of the Balkans*, Vol. I: *National Ideologies and Language Policies* (Balkans Studies Library, 9) (Leiden: Brill, 2013), 13–65.
Durandin, Catherine, and Cécile Folschweiller (eds). *Alerte en Europe: la guerre dans les Balkans (1912–1913)*. Paris: L'Harmattan, 2014.
Echternkamp, Jörg, Wolfgang Schmidt and Thomas Vogel (eds). *Perspektiven der Militärgeschichte, Raum, Gewalt und Repräsentation in historischer Forschung und Bildung*. Munich: Oldenbourg, 2010.

Eldarov, Svetlozar (ed.). 'The Balkan Wars', special issue of Études Balkaniques 49(2) (2013).
Faulstroh, Nikolaus. *Die Balkankrisen von 1908–1914 und die Jugoslawienkonflikte von 1991–1999 im Beziehungsgeflecht der Großmächte: Das Verhalten von internationalen Akteuren bei der Ausbreitung von Konflikten auf dem Balkan.* Baden-Baden: Nomos, 2015.
Glenny, Misha. *The Fall of Yugoslavia: The Third Balkan War.* London: Penguin, 1996.
Grotzky, Johannes. *Balkankrieg: Der Zerfall Jugoslawiens und die Folgen für Europa.* Munich: Pieper, 1993.
Hall, Richard C. *The Balkan Wars 1912–1913: Prelude to the First World War.* London: Routledge, 2000.
Hofbauer, Hannes. *Balkankrieg: Zehn Jahre Zerstörung Jugoslawiens.* Vienna: Promedia, 2001 [5th ed. 2015].
Holmes, Richard (ed.). *The Oxford Companion to Military History.* Oxford: Oxford University Press, 2001.
Horel, Catherine (ed.). *Les guerres balkaniques (1912–1913): Conflits, enjeux, mémoires.* Brussels: P.I.E. Peter Lang, 2014.
Ivetic, Egidio. *Le guerre balcaniche.* Bologna: Il Mulino, 2007.
Koselleck, Reinhart. '"Space of Experience" and "Horizon of Expectation": Two Historical Categories', in Reinhart Koselleck, *Futures Past: On the Semantics of Historical Time* (New York: Columbia University Press, 2004), 255–311.
Kühne, Thomas, and Benjamin Ziemann (eds). *Was ist Militärgeschichte?* Paderborn: Schöningh, 2000.
Mayoraz, Sandrine, Frithjof B. Schenk and Ueli Mäder (eds). *Hundert Jahre Basler Friedenskongress (1912–2012): Die erhoffte 'Verbrüderung der Völker'.* Basel/Zurich: Schweizerisches Sozialarchiv, 2015.
Morillo, Stephen, and Michael F. Pavkovic. *What Is Military History?* Cambridge: Polity, 2013.
Müller, Dietmar, and Stefan Troebst (eds). *Der 'Carnegie Report on the Causes and Conduct of the Balkan Wars 1912/13'. Wirkungs- und Rezeptionsgeschichte im Völkerrecht und in der Historiographie* [Comparativ 24 (2014), 6]. Leipzig: Leipziger Universitätsverlag, 2015.
Müller, Rolf-Dieter. *Militärgeschichte.* Vienna/Cologne/Weimar: Böhlau, 2009.
Mulligan, William. *The Origins of the First World War.* Cambridge/New York: Cambridge University Press, 2010.
Neitzel, Sönke. *Blut und Eisen: Deutschland im Ersten Weltkrieg.* Zurich: Pendo, 2003.
Nowosadtko, Jutta. *Krieg, Gewalt und Ordnung: Einführung in die Militärgeschichte.* Tübingen: edition diskord, 2002.
The Other Balkan Wars: A 1913 Carnegie Endowment Inquiry in Retrospect with a New Introduction and Reflections on the Present Conflict by George F. Kennan. Washington, DC: Carnegie Endowment for International Peace, 1993.
Pettifer, James, and Tom Buchanan (eds). *War in the Balkans: Conflict and Diplomacy before World War I.* London: Tauris, 2016.
Popitz, Heinrich. 'Gewalt', in H. Popitz, *Phänomene der Macht: Autorität – Herrschaft – Gewalt* (Tübingen: Mohr, 1986), 68–106.

Todorova, Maria. *Imagining the Balkans*. New York: Oxford University Press, 2009 [updated version of the original edition of 1997].
Ulrich, Bernd, and Benjamin Ziemann (eds). *German Soldiers in the Great War: Letters and Eyewitness Accounts*. Barnsley: Pen & Sword Military, 2010.
Yavuz, M. Hakan, and Isa Blumi (eds). *War and Nationalism: The Balkan Wars, 1912–1913, and Their Sociopolitical Implications*. Salt Lake City, UT: University of Utah Press, 2013.
Ziemann, Benjamin. *War Experiences in Rural Germany, 1914–1923*. Oxford/New York: Berg, 2007. [German original *Front und Heimat: Ländliche Kriegserfahrungen im südlichen Bayern 1914–1923*. Essen: Klartext, 1997].
Ziemann, Benjamin. 'Der Erste Weltkrieg als ein Laboratorium der Gewalt. Einleitung', in B. Ziemann (ed.), *Gewalt im Ersten Weltkrieg: Töten – Überleben – Verweigern* (Essen: Klartext, 2013), 7–21.

1

'Modern Wars' and 'Backward Societies'
The Balkan Wars in the History of Twentieth-Century European Warfare

Wolfgang Höpken

The Balkan Wars have been perceived in ambivalent and contradictory ways, both among the general public and in scholarly works. Whereas in the Balkan countries they have generally long been glorified as 'wars of liberation', with little attention given to their violence and social consequences,[1] the European public and historiography often described them, as Enika Abazi has recently put it, 'exclusively in terms of atrocities'.[2] The contemporary European public was divided about the wars. Some observers reaffirmed what Maria Todorova has termed the 'orientalist' perception of the region,[3] attributing the extremely violent character of the wars to the 'semi-culture of the Balkan tribes',[4] while others acknowledged or even welcomed the Balkan Wars, in particular the first, as a legitimate fight for 'the nation'.[5] In addition, while many considered the wars to be 'traditional' and 'typically Balkan', others, such as military experts, who travelled in great numbers to the Balkan theatre, viewed the conflicts at the same time as 'modern', and foreshadowing many of the experiences that Europe could anticipate in its next war.

Scholars in military history no less have yet to reach a consensus about how to deal with the Balkan Wars and where to situate them in the history of twentieth-century European warfare. Some, like the doyens of military historiography John Keegan and Michael Howard, downplay their significance to a footnote, viewing them as totally overshadowed by the Great War.[6] Others have placed the wars outside the traditions of 'European' warfare. In their view, to quote the German-Israeli historian Dan Diner, these wars 'in their intensity and cruelty were alien to the regulated military wars between states in the European continent'[7] and, to quote another German historian, therefore should be placed in the category of colonial warfare.[8] It is only recently that the violence of the Balkan Wars has been considered in the broader context of what happened in other parts of Europe during the 'age of extremes'.[9] Reflecting upon the Yugoslav wars of the 1990s and trying to save the region and its people from the 'orientalist' accusation of being inherently violent, authors like Mark Biondich have regarded the wars and violence in the Balkans as an integral part of the 'dark' European twentieth century.[10]

It seems that these disparate perspectives in fact reflect the deeply ambivalent character of the two Balkan Wars. On the one hand, they were rather 'conventional' small-scale and local conflicts, by all criteria far removed from the dimension of warfare that the Great War would bring two years later. They can also scarcely be categorized as 'total war', neither in terms of their intensity and resources nor in their consequences for society. However, on the other hand, the Balkan Wars were also a watershed, at least in the history of wars in the Balkans. They were 'the last Turkish wars' in the tradition of the eighteenth- and nineteenth-century 'Oriental Question', but at the same time they went very much beyond the kind of warfare that the region had witnessed during the previous centuries. The Balkan Wars were hybrid in nature, a blend of traditional warfare with many of the features that would characterize the subsequent twentieth-century European conflicts. In the following, I illustrate this hybrid character by focusing mainly on four aspects of the wars: the relationship between war and society; the changing experiences of war; the intensity and extensity of war; and, finally, the question of the character of violence during the wars.

'Modern Warfare' and 'Backward Societies'

The armies that were involved in the Balkan Wars already reflect a tension between 'modernity' and 'backwardness'. In Serbia and Bulgaria in particular, and to a lesser degree and with a certain delay in Greece, the armies of the last quarter of the nineteenth century had developed into military formations that were 'modern' by almost all criteria. In Serbia, for example, military reform had been stimulated by the many deficits that the Serbian army had revealed during the war against the Ottomans in 1876 and, in particular, in Serbia's disastrous defeat by Bulgaria in 1885. Reform had transformed the army from 'peasants in arms' into a well-organized, well-trained and disciplined military force.¹¹ The first attempts to replace the traditional way of fighting in local and decentralized *četa* by a centrally commanded, 'standing' army had been undertaken during the 'First Serbian Uprising' in 1808 and 1811, but had failed. Nor had they materialized after the Serbian state had been established.¹² Demands for a professionalized standing army arose in particular during the 1860s, inspired by the French idea of a 'nation in arms' and guided by French concepts and advisers, but these demands were not satisfied, mainly because of the lack of financial resources. No more than a small prince's 'guard' of up to 4,000 standing soldiers came into being, while the bulk of the army of up to 100,000 men consisted of largely untrained peasants.¹³

The defeat in the first Serbian-Ottoman war of 1876 had revealed the flaws of the army, and even victory in the second war of 1877–78 could not hide the limitations of the 'peasant in arms'. The army was ill-equipped in technological terms, and it lacked clear command structures and often discipline as well. It had been more the weakness of the Ottoman army and the favourable international conditions than the quality of the army that had made Serbian military victory possible.¹⁴ Nationalist ambitions, which in political terms became more concrete during the last quarter of the nineteenth century, could hardly be achieved in the long run with such a 'premodern' army. A fundamental restructuring of the Serbian army therefore took place in 1883 and 1897. The *narodna vojska* (people's army) was abolished in favour of a standing professional army, based on regular conscriptions and a two-year period of service.¹⁵ The number of soldiers under arms grew constantly after the 1880s. The command structures were professionalized, and for the first time a regular general staff was established as a permanent body after 1876, in line with overall European practice.¹⁶ While the wars of the nineteenth century had been fought without any real strategic preparation, the war against the Ottoman Empire in 1912 had been prepared for professionally since the turn of the century.¹⁷ In particular, officers' education and qualifications were improved. After early attempts to establish a specific military education during the 1830s and 1840s had seen only unstable results, since the mid-century specific officers' schools, combining general education and military qualification, had been opened, finally leading to the foundation of a higher military academy in 1880.¹⁸ While in 1880 only 187 candidates enrolled in the higher military academy, on the eve of the Balkan Wars the number had risen to more than 1,700.¹⁹ The officers' material conditions had improved considerably with the turn of the century, and pensions had made the military profession particularly attractive. More importantly, the officer's social status had been enhanced, and as a result the officer corps had become a part of the urban and educated elite.[20] Just as in other European countries, as General Mišić noted in 1907, the Serbian state began to secure the social position of the officer as a major representative of the state and the nation.[21] The qualifications and regular training of the ordinary soldiers improved no less. Military manoeuvres were held, involving between 10,000 and 30,000 soldiers, numbers unknown in former times.[22] In 1909, the Serbian journal *Srpski Kniževni Glasnik* published statistical data, indicating that the Serbian army had even fewer disciplinary cases than the German army.[23]

Parallel to these institutional reforms, the army's technical equipment, which in 1877–78 and in 1885 had proven to be outdated, was substantially renewed by importing up-to-date weaponry, mainly from France and Germany.[24] Certainly the project of military modernization had not been accomplished when the war started, as foreign military attachés observed. Only the first army contingent was equipped with the most modern weaponry, while the second contingent lagged behind and the third contingent resembled the old peasant militia.[25] And despite the fact that the government had taken up substantial loans and almost plundered its treasury, the equipment did not allow more than a relatively short war.[26] In general, however, both diplomats and military specialists considered the Serbian army to be 'a well-conceived and well-functioning institution',[27] unprecedented in its size, restructured according to European standards, updated in its technological capabilities and well prepared in strategic terms.

Bulgaria, too, had taken a similar route towards 'military modernization'. Having been dependent largely on Russian equipment, know-how and officers after the 'liberation' of 1878, beginning with the era of Stefan Stambulov the Bulgarian army replaced the strong Russian influence with a more diverse system of institutional models, contacts and technical supply, relying in particular on France. The Japanese victory in the Russo-Japanese war of 1905, which left a great impression on the Bulgarian military, had an especially deep impact on the country's reorientation as far as military education, strategy and equipment were concerned.[28] Since that time, the country had established what the correspondent of the German *Kölnische Zeitung*, Richard von Mach, called a 'well-conceptualized and excellent organization of the army ... [based on] substantial financial means'.[29] Regular conscriptions, which had been introduced after the establishment of the Bulgarian state in 1878 and which were implemented, unlike in Greece, with few exceptions, gave the army a strong numerical basis. The number of officers increased constantly, reaching more than 2,200 on the eve of the wars.[30] They became qualified through a close network of military schools and academies and held, even more than in Serbia, a highly respected social status, being considered part of the country's *intelligentsia*.[31] Because officers were almost the only civil servants who had job security, higher military service became an important avenue of upward social mobility.

In terms of technology, the late 1890s also witnessed the transition in Bulgaria from an army relying on traditional warfare to one relying on machine-led warfare, much like industry had gone from artisan or manufacture production to machine production. Modern weapons were imported, mostly from Germany, and up-to-date artillery was obtained from France.[32] As the Bulgarian ambassador to Russia told the Russian prime minister on the eve of the Balkan Wars, for more than thirty years his country had concentrated all its energy and power on bringing the army to the highest level possible.[33] Even an airplane department was established in the Bulgarian War Ministry as early as 1906, and the first airplanes for the army were bought shortly thereafter. In the efforts of military preparation, officers were sent to France for training. Still, most of the airplanes were flown by foreign pilots, particularly Russians.[34] The actual military effect of aircraft during the Balkan Wars, as was also the case for the Ottoman Empire or Serbia,[35] was more than limited. The twenty-nine airplanes – among them eighteen that had been imported from Russia, six from France and four from Germany – flew 230 operations in both Balkan Wars, but only 79 of them in combat. The remaining flights served to provide supplies or intelligence, or to drop leaflets to the general population. Only four aircraft carried bombs, which were employed, among others, during the attack on Adrianople. They caused more psychological stress than military damage. Often planes were out of order, or operations had to be cancelled due to supply or weather problems.[36] Nevertheless, Bulgarian airpower drew considerable attention both domestically and internationally. It was seen as a striking sign of the country's military modernizing efforts.[37]

Military reform took root much later in Greece's army, which in the late nineteenth century was limited in size and weak in organizational capacity. Even decades after the country's independence in 1830, the army had minor military importance in comparison with the many irregular units, which often operated under the control of local 'warlords'.[38] The numerical strength of the army in the middle of the nineteenth century was not more than 10,000. It fluctuated between 15,000 and 25,000 soldiers during the following decades, until just before the Balkan Wars. Conscription, introduced only in 1880, was enforced with many exceptions, so that only a small percentage of those formally subject to conscription were actually drafted.[39] Lagging behind Bulgaria and Serbia, and despite severe financial limitations, military reforms in Greece nevertheless took shape after the turn of the century, improving the army's professionalization, equipment and qualifications, largely on the basis of French concepts and with France's support. On the side of the Balkan Alliance, only the tiny Montenegrin army remained at the beginning of its transformation from a militia-type *plemenska vojska* into an army with professional structure by the time of the Balkan Wars.[40] Command structures, however, were in practice still unregulated, and even the Montenegrin military leaders would complain of the lack of discipline among the soldiers and the lack of military education among the officers.[41]

All in all, the military in the Balkan states was surely one of the most successful arenas of 'modernization'. The cost was high, however. Given that none of the countries was able to produce much of the necessary military equipment by itself – not even ammunition for the new weapons – imports required huge financial resources. Military expenditures, reaching more than a quarter of the entire budget and exceeding, on a per capita basis, even those of industrialized Western European countries like Great Britain and Germany, constantly overstretched the budgets and contributed to the indebtedness of all the Balkan states at the turn of the century. Short-term loans and plundering the reserves in foreign currency to finance the purchase of weapons and ammunition had exhausted the countries' financial resources even before the war had started.[42] Even if this 'expensive army' was consuming more than a quarter of the Bulgarian budget, as the politician Stojan Danev, at that time head of the Bulgarian parliament, explained to the Austrian ambassador in early 1912, this was an 'inevitable sacrifice' in order to fulfil the country's 'national aspirations'.[43]

Foreign observers usually spoke with high esteem of most of the Balkan armies. The Bulgarian army in particular was praised for being familiar with 'the most modern practices of the most important European armies' and being 'comparable with the armies of the great European countries, which were long since used to wars'. The British Major P. Howell, who visited the Bulgarian army between the First and Second Balkan Wars, compared it to that of Japan – 'a highly successful army ... created ab ovo in one generation'. The Serbian army also, in terms of 'organization, weaponry and equipment [was considered to be] absolutely modern'.[44] The allied victories during the First Balkan War confirmed the Western perception that Serbia had proved able 'to form a well-equipped and disciplined army within a short period of time'.[45] The high opinion of the Allies' armies contrasted starkly with the rather sceptical views of foreign witnesses concerning the Ottoman army, which at the outbreak of the wars in 1912 was still in the middle of a German-guided modernization and reform process. While these usually were full of recognition for the ordinary Turkish soldier, not without reproducing conventional European stereotypes about the 'fanatic' Muslim warrior,[46] many observations by correspondents and diplomatic observers painted a more unfavourable picture of the army's outlook and preparation.[47] German advisers to the Ottoman Empire themselves noted positive effects in this effort, but they were generally frustrated by the slow pace of reform and sceptical of the army's quality.[48]

Owing not least to the apparently highly developed character of the Balkan armies, the many European military experts who witnessed the theatre of war in 1912–13 expected the Balkan War to be a 'modern one', one that offered even for their own countries insights from which they might learn. As one of them remarked, while the experiences of the Franco-German War of 1870–71 had already lost their importance, the war in the Balkans could offer conclusions for the next European war to come.[49] Prussian and Bavarian officers serving in the Ottoman Empire even asked for the opportunity to participate in the war on the Ottoman side as commanders in order to update their knowledge, requests that met with reluctance not only on the part of the Ottoman authorities, but also among the German ones. Although the German military was eager to have first-hand reports, the Ministry of Foreign Affairs hesitated to give the officers permission in view of possible diplomatic frictions. Indeed, only a few managed to serve in the field, after they relinquished their German citizenship for the duration of the war. Their reports to the war ministries of Prussia and Bavaria were well received as a source of valuable information.[50] At the centre of their interest were questions not only of military theory and strategy, but also of military technology, such as the new weaponry. The new ammunition and artillery used in the wars had 'stood the test' for future wars, in the words of a German military officer describing the Serbian army and its campaigns.[51] Because the warring parties had obtained their new weaponry from Germany, as was the case for the Ottoman Empire, or from France, as Serbia did, or from both Germany and France, as was true of Bulgaria, the Balkan Wars were also seen as a competition between German and French military technology.[52]

In the end, the conclusions that the foreign military experts drew from the theatre of war were mixed. Some of them, like the Bavarian Major Endres, saw 'little [that] could be learned from'.[53] And while his British colleague Major Howell, witnessing the Bulgarian warfare, saw little benefit for upcoming European wars, experiences from a war like that in Thrace, being fought more 'under Asian than under European conditions', could well offer something for 'colonial wars' such as in Afghanistan or Northern India.[54] Others, like his colleague Lossow, who served with Endres in the Ottoman army, saw valuable experiences insofar as the efficacy of the new, modern weapons was concerned. Even though the wars had offered a limited experience in strategic and technological terms, and had merely confirmed the military and strategic concepts their countries had developed,[55] they had demonstrated, at least, as German and Austrian observers noted, the importance of what was called the 'moral preparation' for war. More than ever, as a German officer pointed out, future wars could be won only if the soldiers were driven by a strong moral impetus to fight, and the Balkan soldiers had shown that 'a belligerent spirit' is nothing 'reprehensible', as was often heard among the German public, but an asset that must be constantly reaffirmed within the society.[56]

Adoption of the European principle of a standing and professional army, however, was not consistent, and the result was an element of 'hybridity', even in the military's organizational structure. Specifically, the traditional concept of a 'peasant nation in arms' had not been totally abandoned. Paramilitaries and 'armed civilians', forces that during the nineteenth century had been the backbone of the countries' military resources – and for some of them, such as Greece and Montenegro, even the most important resources – continued to play their role during wartime even after the establishment of regular armies. In Serbia, the idea of abolishing the *narodna vojska* in 1883 had met with resistance from the influential Radical Party, which considered a standing army a contradiction to the party's concept of an egalitarian and patriarchal Serbian society. Militia-type units were therefore kept up, albeit under the army's control. Četnik warfare was part of the military education, and their operational activities during military conflicts were seen as an auxiliary force, acting behind the front lines and in combination with the regular troops.[57] More than that, in Serbia as well as in Bulgaria, the irregular armed groups, the *četa* and *komitadži*, which had already played an important role in former wars and, since the turn of the century, had become crucial military actors in Macedonia in particular,[58] became an important and integral part of military campaigns during the Balkan Wars as well. Since 1910–11, četnik units increasingly were trained and the general staff of the Serbian army systematically began to organize their equipment and supply. When the war against the Ottoman Empire started, their activities were coordinated by the general staff.[59] Although they were increasingly subordinated to the regular army, they nonetheless continued to act on their own, blurring and undermining the army's monopoly on violence.[60] The traditional dualism between regular and irregular forces, which had never been eliminated during the Balkan countries' state-building process, was thus maintained, with dire consequences for the nature and, in particular, the level of violence during the Balkan Wars.

An even more striking expression of the armies' 'hybrid modernity' was the obvious contradiction between their relatively high standard in terms of number and technology and the general backwardness of the infrastructure and limited organizational capacities of their respective states. When the Balkan governments summoned their male citizens to arms in 1912 in then-unprecedented numbers, mobilization in Serbia, Bulgaria and Greece impressed foreign observers,[61] but was nevertheless accompanied by many logistical shortcomings. Transport facilities in particular were inadequate for the tremendous number of mobilized soldiers. Only roughly a quarter of them could be transported by rail. Motor vehicle transport was still in its early stages anyway, and had little impact on the conduct of the war.[62] The bulk of soldiers had to be transported by horse and oxcart or travelled on foot.[63] Though 'modern' in terms of the number of soldiers involved, the campaigns were thus as slow as those of the nineteenth-century wars. Soldiers, as it was reported from the Ottoman side, often were not familiar with the new and modern weapons or badly prepared to dig adequate trenches, and the newly imported heavy artillery were hard to transport on the badly prepared roads and bridges during the rainy autumn campaigns.[64] In addition, important items of equipment such as field kitchens, sometimes even uniforms and boots, were lacking, leaving soldiers often unprepared for bad weather conditions during the First Balkan War.[65] The supply of food also failed to 'meet the standards of a modern army', as observers noticed with regard to the Bulgarian army, leading to insufficient nutrition and even hunger among many soldiers in the course of the wars.[66] Although all Balkan governments had invested in communication facilities, not least for military reasons, as the Russo-Japanese war had been instructive in this respect, telegraph lines were less than half the length of those in Western European countries of comparable size. Finally, all the belligerents were prepared for an intensive but short war. As a result, there was a shortage of ammunition throughout the war,[67] which (fortunately) limited the effect of the modern weapons with which the armies were supplied.

Most dramatic and most painful, however, was the almost total lack of medical support during the wars. None of the Balkan states had provided for medical care, at least not in relation to the increased military capacities they had built up. In Serbia, serious ideas concerning medical care of the army had appeared only in the 1860s. They had been promoted largely by Vladan Djordjević, a physician who had tried to introduce the Prussian-style practice of military medicine in Serbia.[68] His ideas, however, were not put into effect during the following decades. As a result, Serbia entered the Serbian-Ottoman wars of 1876 and 1877–78 with about sixty doctors for more than 100,000 soldiers, less than a quarter of the number that would have been appropriate.[69] A foreign observer noted that 'the history of warfare in the last 25 years affords no example of an outright undersupply of medical personnel, in relation to what was actually required, that is commensurate with the situation in the recent Serbian-Turkish war'.[70] The picture had not changed in 1885, when only twenty-two military doctors were responsible for the care of Serbian soldiers during the war with Bulgaria.[71]

With the military modernization and expansion of the Serbian army, the number of doctors, both civilian and military, increased substantially over the following two decades. Considering the tremendous increase in troop strength and the army's technological progress, however, the roughly 290 doctors for more than 350,000 soldiers at the beginning of the Balkan Wars represented a proportion as insufficient as thirty years earlier.[72] Nurses were also lacking, both in numbers and still more in terms of qualifications. Women's organizations, which appeared on the scene during the second half of the nineteenth century, such as the *Kolo srpskih sestara* (Ring of Serbian Sisters), had taken it as one of their primary tasks to prepare young women as volunteers for wars to come.[73] But the 'ladies from all strata of society' who joined the hospitals in great numbers during the Balkan Wars, and were described by contemporary witnesses as well as later historians as having been inspired by a high patriotic passion,[74] had totally inadequate qualifications. Foreign doctors serving in the Balkan states complained almost unanimously about the lack of skill of the nurses, who sometimes worsened rather than improved the condition of the wounded.[75]

Medical supply in Bulgaria also was considered to be 'generally deficient'.[76] Despite 'preparing for the war for such a long time', as remembered by the German doctor Kirschner, who served during the war in Bulgarian hospitals, preparations in the medical field had been almost totally neglected,[77] and, following Bulgarian figures, there was a lack of about six hundred medical doctors to cope with the increasing number of wounded soldiers, not counting in international assistance.[78] Indeed, it was in part the disastrous experience of the Balkan Wars that finally led to the decision in Bulgaria as well as Serbia to open a medical faculty at the universities in Sofia and Belgrade, something that had been discussed since the 1890s and long demanded by the military.[79]

Montenegro had no institutionalized system of medical care for the army at all. It had four doctors for 40,000 soldiers.[80] When the war quickly involved more losses than expected, it became clear to the Montenegrin public, as the Austrian delegate to Cetinje reported, that fighting had been started 'with a carelessness recalling barbaric times'.[81]

In the Ottoman Empire, the situation, particularly at the beginning of the war, encountered just as many difficulties.[82] Here, the growing number of refugees who, in addition to wounded soldiers, poured into the cities in poor health made the situation even worse.[83] The situation became disastrous when cholera hit the armies in November 1912. For the Ottoman army, the disease proved to be 'an opponent more dangerous than the enemy'. With little professional and efficient treatment, many of the infected were left alone or sent behind the front lines, where San Stefano became a real 'cholera camp', causing up to 6,000 deaths.[84] The situation was only little better among the Bulgarian army, severely affecting its military capacities. Neither the medical personnel nor the institutional facilities were prepared to cope with the epidemic, at least not at the front.[85]

It was the many foreign doctors and nurses who came to the battlefields of the Balkan Wars who eased the situation, although they could hardly compensate for the numerous structural deficits. Immediately after the outbreak of hostilities, the International Red Cross, the national Red Cross organizations, governments and universities sent doctors to the individual warring countries. This had been a practice in former wars, but participants reached unprecedented numbers during the Balkan Wars,[86] thus also reflecting the new dimension of the war. While for some, like the experienced British Red Cross nurse Claire Stobart, their service was motivated by Christian compassion,[87] others had a combination of altruistic and practical motives. Like many military men, foreign doctors saw the Balkan Wars as an opportunity to gain first-hand experience for future wars. The last first-hand experience of war in Europe had occurred in 1870–71; the Russo-Japanese war and Second Boer War had offered only limited opportunity for practical observations, owing to the distance of the theatres of war from Europe. Thus, it was the Balkan Wars that enabled medical personnel to gain expertise in contemporary battlefield medicine. In particular, they could learn the effects of the new weaponry and ammunition. The usage of chloroform and bacteriological issues were also of interest.[88] Alfred Exner, the leading expert among military surgeons, went to the Balkan Wars to study new opportunities to perform field surgery near the front line,[89] and the annual congress of the German Society for Surgery dedicated a specific panel in 1913 to experiences during the Balkan Wars. Anton Waldmann, who in the 1920s would become one of the leading military medical specialists in the *Reichswehr*, praised the experience that German doctors had gained during the Balkan Wars.[90] Even American military doctors made use of more than one thousand X-ray images of wounded Turkish soldiers from the Balkan Wars to study the effects of new weapons and ammunition used during combat.[91] For all of them, as for the military experts, the Balkan Wars were not an expression of an apparently 'archaic' violence, but the first example of a new type of warfare they expected in the future. The Balkan Wars, as the Austrian medical doctor Josef Hamburger concluded from his service in the Bulgarian army, had shown not only the necessity to professionalize medical support for future wars to come; the medical competences that were demonstrated during the wars by foreign doctors could also help soldiers to better master their fear of combat when it took over their former feelings of 'honour and patriotism'. As Hamburger said of his experiences in the Balkans, not only did the current 'modern ammunition' produce injuries that were easy to cure, but experts should also think about how to produce more efficient bullets that could 'put the wounded out of action'.[92] Even if most medical doctors did not bring home anything 'totally new', the Balkan Wars nonetheless for them had 'great significance as a school of practical action'.[93]

In the Balkan Wars, the effects of inadequate medical care were disastrous on all sides. 'No treatment at all on the field would have been preferable to the well-intended but shocking ignorance', as the American war correspondent Fred Fox wrote from the Thracian battlefield.[94] The insufficient number and equipment of field hospitals left many wounded soldiers without quick and appropriate treatment.[95] Ivan Popov, a young reserve-officer, even writes in his war memories about 'marauding first-aid attendants', about witnessing wounded men who had not been treated but 'whose pockets had been turned upside-down'.[96] Because the new military technology meant that battles lasted much longer than in former wars, the wounded often lay on the battlefield for hours or even an entire day before they could be cared for after the fighting ended.[97]

The major problem, however, was the lack of adequate transportation facilities. Trains to transport wounded soldiers to the hospitals were lacking and the few transport facilities were badly organized.[98] Just as in the other countries and just as during the wars of 1877–78, the bulk of the wounded had to be transported by oxcart over bad roads, taking sometimes a week or even longer to reach a hospital.[99] This delay led to a high number of casualties among the wounded, particularly during the early weeks of the campaign.[100] There was, as foreign medical observers correctly recognized, 'a striking disproportion between the great number of heavily wounded as a result of the modern weaponry on the one hand, and the insufficient and primitive facilities for their transport on the other',[101] thus illustrating again the dichotomy between 'modernity' and 'backwardness' that characterized the entire war. As the historian Béla Király has put it, 'the Balkan Wars were wars in which the soldiers of underdeveloped societies operated technology far above their own developmental level'.[102]

Experiencing 'Modern Wars'

Technological modernization also produced new experiences of warfare, not only for the ordinary soldier, but also for society as a whole. The Balkan soldiers certainly did not face the 'industrialized warfare' their European companions would experience during the Great War just two years later. They were not confronted with the apocalyptic experience of trench warfare lasting for months on end, the nerve-racking alternation between silence and continuous fire, and the trauma of shell shock, as were soldiers on the Western Front during the First World War. Even some of the nineteenth-century wars, like the Crimean War, which Orlando Figes, for good reason, has recently labelled as an early example of 'total war',[103] were far larger in scope and intensity than the Balkan Wars. For the Balkan combatants, however, the two wars of 1912–13 produced a new sense of warfare. For many soldiers, combat differed from everything they had experienced in previous military confrontations.

To begin with, the sheer number of soldiers involved in the war overall and during the battles gave the war a new character. Serbia, which in 1876–78 in its last two wars against the Ottoman Empire had mobilized 124,000 and 82,000 soldiers, respectively, and in 1885 against Bulgaria just 52,000, called to arms almost 400,000 men, 14 per cent of the entire Serbian population.[104] Bulgaria mobilized almost 600,000 soldiers during the two wars, almost 12 per cent of the entire population – 'a nation in weapons' and 'something never seen before', as the leading army general Radko Dimitriev remembered.[105] Greece, which had never had an army exceeding 25,000 men, mobilized its biggest army ever, with more than 150,000 soldiers. During the Second Balkan War, Greece even recruited orphans, expatriates and men who originally were found unfit for service at the front.[106] In fact, the Balkan Wars were the first to be fought as a true *levée en masse* in Europe.

Still more importantly, battles were often fought for a much longer time, sometimes over days, or even during the night, something that soldiers had rarely confronted in earlier wars. Reporting from his service with the Bulgarian army, the Austrian medical doctor Bertold Reder wrote about soldiers who had been confronted with constant attacks for seven days without any opportunity to leave the trench.[107] In addition, the new weapons created a new experience of organized violence. In particular, the widely used shrapnel shells of the artillery confronted the soldiers not only with new kinds of physical damage; while 'traditional' gunshot wounds still prevailed, the number of combatants wounded by artillery fire rose substantially in comparison with former wars, and accounted for more than 20 per cent of all casualties.[108] The sound of cannon fire made the earth tremble and resonated throughout the body, as one soldier described his impressions of the battle of Lüle Burgas. Many soldiers were unsure how to behave in the face of such force.[109] But it was predominantly the psychological impact of these weapons that created the feeling of a new kind of war among the soldiers. Even foreign military specialists grasped this dimension of combat. Albin Kutschbach, a German officer who had been with the Serbian army, spoke about the 'unpleasant music' of the new artillery, which with its constant fire created an 'unbearable situation' from which soldiers continued to suffer long after the battle had ended, and several even 'went insane'.[110] The German doctor Ludwig Schliep, who claimed to have been one of the few working very close to the front lines, spoke about a 'concert of hell' when artillery guns were shaking the air, and 'pictures of horror, one never could forget'.[111] While the artillery fire was far from the continuous and hours-long bombings the First World War would bring, diplomats who witnessed the siege of the city of Scutari noticed the 'disastrous effect the new generation of artillery' had on the local population.[112] Anyone who might have thought that the new modern weapons would be 'more humane', the German war correspondent Colin Ross wrote, should visit the battlefields of Eastern Thrace: 'horrible is the effect of the modern artillery'.[113] While the new weapons were often rather inefficient in military terms, as military specialists recognized, the psychological effects were 'very demanding for the soldiers',[114] often producing what military doctors called 'traumatic neuroses', a term that would become common two years later during the Great War.[115]

Furthermore, according to military observers, the machine gun, which in the Russo-Japanese war had played merely the role of an 'additional weapon', in the Balkan Wars 'turned into an indispensable one' and produced what military and medical observers called a 'strong moral impression' among the soldiers, in particular those who were confronted with it for the first time.[116] In contrast to the Great War, we have relatively few soldiers' diaries from the Balkan Wars, simply because many soldiers were still illiterate, particularly on the Ottoman side but to a lesser extent also on the Serbian side. The little that was published, however, confirms the sense of the ordinary soldier that the Balkan Wars had brought a new experience of being confronted with death. 'All the time fire, it was horrible', the Bulgarian soldier Raicho Maidovski wrote in his diary from the Second Balkan War, 'for ten days now we have been constantly in a fight, without any rest, without any sleep'.[117] In particular, the Bulgarian siege of Adrianople in the spring of 1913 with its constant shelling was perceived as an unknown experience. The 'power of the artillery ... [and] the light effects of the flash-lightning thunder of the guns', as the Austrian consul von Herzfeld described, 'were an apotheosis of what we had seen and heard during the months before'.[118] The constant presence of death was also noted by others as something new for the soldiers, reflecting the new forms of warfare.[119]

Even the way of fighting was often perceived by soldiers as something novel and unusual. While the Balkan Wars in general were still characterized by conventional face-to-face killing, the new weaponry also produced a new experience of killing and dying. Not being familiar with the 'modern' weaponry, soldiers often fired without interruption, using up their supplies of ammunition.[120] Ottoman soldiers in particular, many of them insufficiently trained, often had problems handling the unfamiliar weapons.[121] Serbian soldiers, another source reports, initially hesitated to dig trenches to protect themselves against the enemy's artillery fire, because they considered this 'cowardly' behaviour.[122] Some voiced mixed feelings about this new way of fighting. 'Many discussions among us were raised by the question of the importance of the bayonet and the fire', the Bulgarian officer Dimităr Azmanov wrote in his memoirs. 'And many of our officers preferred the bayonet, as a material expression of moral energy, over the new weaponry.'[123] With the new weaponry, the experience of death also changed. 'Death has become invisible', wrote Colin Ross, expressing a feeling that would become a common notion during the Great War.[124] Even the environment suffered the repercussions of the new and much more intense way of fighting. Destruction of houses and whole villages turned entire landscapes into devastated areas. The British nurse Claire Stobart saw a 'depopulated wilderness' when she entered the Thracian battlefield after the fighting had ended. 'The land wore an eerie aspect', the American war photographer Herbert Baldwin wrote from the same area,[125] and the Czech pacifist and socialist Emanuel Skátula was reminded of a 'Dantesque disaster' when, as a young journalist, he visited the region around Lozengrad, where one of the fiercest battles had been fought.[126] The many casualties, which also reached unprecedented numbers, the new forms of physical disabilities, the pictures of totally destroyed and burned villages, all confronted both soldiers and civilians with a kind of war they had not known before, and with which their abilities to cope were inadequate.

On the Way to 'Total War'?

A third aspect of this 'new character' of the Balkan Wars that made them different from nineteenth-century experiences was the impact of the conflicts on the respective societies. Again, in comparison with the Great War, the differences are striking. During the First World War, as Roger Chickering wrote, it was not only the new *intensity* of warfare that turned the war into a 'total' war, but more than that, its new *extensity*, which subordinated the entire society to the necessities of the war.[127] This was not the case in the Balkan Wars. In some respects, particularly the effects upon the economy, the Balkan Wars by no means reached the same level of 'socialized warfare' as the Great War did. Yet never before had European society been so affected and involved as during the two Balkan Wars. In this sense, too, they can be seen as the 'prelude' to the First World War, as Richard Hall has called them.[128]

The much deeper impact of the wars on the societies concerned can be seen first of all in the new dimension of mobilization, mentioned above, which left virtually no family unaffected. 'The war', as a member of the Austrian Red Cross Mission to Bulgaria remembered of his impressions when entering the Bulgarian capital Sofia during the early weeks of the war, 'was not only felt in each home, it had become a dictator, whom the entire engine of the people's and the state's life had to serve'.[129] Almost all areas of economic life were interrupted when mobilization began.[130] Mobilization extended deep into society, and not only in quantitative terms. It affected social groups that in former times had not really been touched by war. Now, in contrast to previous wars, governments, in particular the Greek one, tried to call their emigrants back from abroad.[131] Bulgaria, with the silent support of the Russian government, even recruited compatriots from Odessa and Bessarabia who were not formally Bulgarian citizens.[132] For the first time, the Ottoman Empire called non-Muslim citizens to arms in substantial numbers, a measure that later caused a debate as to whether this had contributed to the country's disastrous defeat.[133] While the contribution of the non-Muslims to the conduct of the war was probably of minor significance, whether in 'positive' or 'negative' terms,[134] recruiting non-Muslims for the Ottoman army was certainly an example of the new dimensions of mobilization that were reached in the Balkan Wars. Women had been recruited for medical support in former wars, for example in 1877–78 or 1885, but during the Balkan Wars their inclusion became more widespread than ever before. In some countries, particularly the Ottoman Empire, recruitment of women as volunteers for the military medical service opened the door to hitherto unknown professions for young Muslim women. According to a recent author, the Balkan Wars 'played a pivotal role in the orientation of Turkish women toward nursing'.[135] Sometimes the role of women was even extended into semi-military activities, as women were involved in the military supply of paramilitary units or were even trained to use weapons.[136] With this new dimension of mobilization and inclusion in mind, Eyal Ginio, from the perspective of the Ottoman Empire, has spoken of the Balkan Wars as the 'first total war'.[137] Mindful of the scholarly debate on the criteria for a 'totality' of warfare, I would not go that far, but clearly the wars of 1912–13 were a watershed for the Balkan societies in this respect as well.[138]

Another facet of the new dimension of 'socializing the war' was the intensive and systematic preparation of society for war, both emotionally and ideologically. The decade before the outbreak of the Balkan Wars had witnessed an outburst of nationalist sentiments in all the countries of the region, in forms ranging from public discourse to textbooks and poetry. In Serbia, this intellectual mobilization centred on the idea of finally 'liberating' the Serbs in Kosovo. In Bulgaria, it was the aim of 'uniting' Macedonia and Thrace with the 'motherland'. Historian Stanoje Stanojević described the public mood during the last years before the war: 'All Serbia was turned into a workshop for the education of the people in one direction … that Kosovo had to be revenged'.[139] In Bulgaria, poets like Kyrill Hristov and the 'literary father of the nation', Ivan Vazov, became ardent advocates of waging war with the Ottomans to fulfil the dream of an 'integral' Bulgaria. In Greece also, the nationalist discourse had gained new momentum since the late nineteenth century.[140]

Intellectual mobilization for the war became not only more intensive but also rhetorically sharper, particularly in terms of its semantic radicalness. The official legitimation for war by the respective monarchs and governments still followed the semantic pattern of the former 'Turkish wars'. For example, Ferdinand I of Bulgaria called his subjects to arms to 'help our oppressed Christian brothers'[141] and thus turned the war into a *nouvelle croisade*. King George I of Greece spoke about the war as 'le cours sacré de l'orthodoxie'.[142] King Peter I of Serbia not only referred to the romantic claim of the Serbian 'medieval heritage' and the battle of Kosovo, but also employed a 'modern' human rights rhetoric, recalling the French Revolution's catchwords of 'liberté, egalité, fraternité' as a rationale for war,[143] thus turning it into a kind of *mission civilisatrice*. In the Ottoman Empire, too, the Balkan Wars produced an unprecedented level of emotionalizing war propaganda, which referred mostly to the atrocities committed by the Balkan allies against the Muslim population in the Balkans.[144] Differing from the Balkan opponents, however, the Ottoman Sultan refrained from making use of religious arguments. No 'jihad' was declared. The 'imperial idea', however, was obviously losing ground, even among the Empire's Muslim citizens. Among the Anatolian soldiers, as the commander in chief Mahmud Muhtar Paşa remembered after the wars, 'a strange emotional state of mind' had been increasingly recognizable: 'Four Anatolian vilayets [for them] were absolutely sufficient, and [they thought that] there was no need to shed blood for Rumelia'.[145]

Ethnic arguments also played an important part. Here, in particular, scholarly expertise was given a new role in the preparations for war, for example in the case of the Serbian ethnographer Jovan Cvijić or the linguist Aleksandar Belić, who provided 'academic' arguments to legitimize Serbian territorial claims.[146] Moreover, war was given a strong cultural connotation, and portrayed as a kind of final struggle between 'European civilization' and 'Muslim' and 'Asian barbarism'. An issue of a Serbian journal dedicated to the outbreak of the Balkan Wars spoke of a 'war for freedom and civilization',[147] and Cvijić saw the Serbian conquest of Kosovo as 'recovering a new area for European culture'.[148] Viewing the war as a decisive clash between 'culture' and 'barbarism' in a sense foreshadowed the intellectual battles two years later between French and German intellectuals, who described the Great War as a fight between 'German culture' and 'French civilization'. Sometimes this culturalist discourse slipped into a semi-racist rhetoric that explicitly dehumanized the opponent. The anti-Albanian rhetoric within Serbian public discourse, as in Vladan Djordjević's crypto-racist description of the Albanians, is a striking example of this.[149] As another example, the Serbian writer Veljko Petrović saw Serbia's military successes as proof of 'the significance of the Serbian race and its historical mission'.[150] In Greece, after the short alliance with Bulgaria during the First Balkan

War, it was 'the Bulgarian' who during the Second Balkan War became the symbol of 'the barbarian' in 'a fusion of ideas of cultural and racial backwardness', as Keith Brown has put it.[151] As for the Ottoman public, the constant experience of military defeat, foreign intervention and most of all the expulsion and flight of Turks and Muslims from the Balkans during the decade before the war radicalized the discourse and the perception of the Balkans as well, giving them more and more an essentialist and sometimes even racist undertone.[152] Finally, Romania, having been absent from the First Balkan War, rationalized its short-term participation in the Second Balkan War with the idea of combat against the Bulgarian as a symbol of the *Barbari balcanilor*.[153] 'Revenge', which became a popular keyword in Serbian war propaganda with regard to Kosovo,[154] might also be taken as an example of this new kind of radicalized semantics, going beyond the traditional romantic and nationalist rhetoric of the nineteenth century and turning 'the other' into what Carl Schmitt has labelled the 'absolute enemy' and the war into a kind of existentialist necessity, excluding all compromise and justifying all means.[155]

In addition, the perspective on war and the characterization of violence changed in public and intellectual discourse. While much of the belligerent rhetoric still followed a traditional nineteenth-century nationalism, as in Ivan Vazov's poems about *Makedonija*, others began to style the wars as an expression of existential heroism, praising the 'beauty of the soldier's body' or the aesthetic and the dramatic pathos of battle. Examples include some of Jordan Jovkov's poems, not to mention Kyrill Hristov's belligerent poetry.[156] Even a poet like Isidora Sekulić in Serbia, who later moved much more to the political left, was caught up in nationalist euphoria on the eve of the Balkan Wars: '[we] might be seen as not being reasonable', Sekulić wrote in 1912, 'because we speak about gallows and revenge and because we like cannons, fire, and blood'.[157] Certainly this was not yet the 'fire and blood' rhetoric of the First World War, such as that produced by Ernst Jünger, but it was a literary belligerency that very much resembled the fascination with war that would obsess certain German and French intellectuals on the eve of the Great War. Praising, as a Serbian journal did, the 'terrible, the merciless, the great dead' for which soldiers now were ready to sacrifice themselves[158] came close to expressing the morbid fascination with war that was typical of *fin de siècle* Europe. The French historians Stéphane Audoin-Rouzeau and Annette Becker have spoken, with respect to the First World War, about a 'culture of war' as a 'crystallized corpus of imagination, which gave the war a deeper meaning'.[159] Something very similar can be found in the Balkans before and during the Balkan Wars.

Ideological preparation for war, also something unknown in previous wars, became somewhat institutionalized. In Bulgaria, almost the entire intellectual elite participated in various institutions that distributed propaganda, engaged in censorship or offered moral support to the soldiers.[160] Intellectuals in Serbia were also involved in expressing and justifying Serbia's war aims by crafting ethnographic or historical arguments,[161] an activity that would be repeated two years later during the Great War, when they were energetically involved in drafting peace terms.[162] More than ever, churches took part in the ideological mobilization of the soldiers and the civilian population.[163] The effort to influence international public opinion was not new either, but it took hold during the Balkan Wars more intensely and systematically than ever, producing the many 'documentations' on all sides accusing the opponent of war crimes and atrocities.[164] For the first time, and again thanks to a lesson learned from the Russo-Japanese war in 1905, strict rules of censorship were applied, making unbiased information flows close to nonexistent. This pertained to journalists,[165] but with very few exceptions also to foreign military attachés.[166] 'The Serbians allowed the correspondents to see nothing', Fred Fox wrote in his reports from the Balkan Wars, 'the Bulgarian idea was to allow nothing to be seen ... It was an aggravation of the Japanese censorship ...'.[167] Reporting from close to the battlefield and playing the role of an authentic eyewitness had been part of the professionalization of the 'modern' war correspondent since the Crimean War.[168] With the Balkan Wars this had come to a halt. The *Times* correspondent Reginald Rankin expressed his frustration: 'Having travelled thousands of miles, and spent hundreds of pounds on our paper's account ... within ten miles from an epoch-making siege, yet forbidden to travel those last essential kilometres! ... The war correspondent as we have known him is no more; fugit Carthago.'[169]

While foreign press coverage was strongly restricted, the wars found an unprecedented representation in all kinds of local media. In Serbia alone, in addition to the daily press, four periodicals during 1912 and 1913 dedicated their thematic scope almost entirely to the wars, most of all the twice-weekly *Ilustrovana ratna kronika* (Illustrated War Chronicle). Making use not only of reports from the war theatre, but also of paintings, photos and poetry, this journal did not evade the reality of warfare, but nevertheless 'successfully suppressed any potentially disturbing reference to the actual suffering and slaughter'. Instead, it reaffirmed the mythical discourse of the Balkan Wars as the fulfilment of the heritage of the legacy of the battle of Kosovo, and of Dušan's empire.[170] In particular, photography and even film became new instruments widely used to bring the war closer to the public. The Bulgarian illustrated magazine *Iljustracija Svetlina*, which during the early stages of the war dedicated almost two-thirds of its pages to the war, for the first time made use of photographs not only from the front line, but also from the 'home front' in order to represent the war as a 'war of the entire nation'. The still modest film production industry also got an important stimulus from the wars. The Balkan Wars thus contributed to what Karl Kaser has called the 'visual modernization in the Balkans'.[171]

The effects of this intensive ideological preparation for war within the Balkan societies require further research. Official sources and local observers time and again gave witness to the overall euphoria with which the decision for war was greeted by the public.[172] Foreign correspondents were fascinated by the amount of emotional support for war, and sometimes they wondered with palpable regret whether this could be possible in their own society.[173] 'Would the Austrian-Hungarian soldier react in the same way?' asked Ladislaus von Fényes, a pacifist who had served in the Hungarian Red Cross mission in Serbia.[174] He suspected that the Austrian soldier would do his duty, but without the 'spiritual energy' that he had witnessed among Serbian troops. The military officer Major Felix Wagner, who had witnessed the war in Thrace, thought that, lacking all 'national euphoria', Austrian soldiers probably could be motivated at best by discipline and loyalty to the emperor.[175] Despite the many descriptions in memoirs and official sources, the presence of this kind of *August-Erlebnis* (August experience)[176] in the Balkan societies has been called into question. Lancelot L. Farrar, Jr., in an article in 2003, tried to show that in the Balkans, war euphoria was more an emotion cleverly staged by the political elites, one that at best struck root among the urban *inteligencija*, than the widespread condition reported by the official sources.[177] Indeed, some reports, including those by certain foreign diplomats and observers, portrayed a different state of affairs. While the German major Hochwaechter, one of the very few German military advisers who took part in Ottoman military operations, saw a 'great enthusiasm' for the war in Istanbul,[178] diplomatic reports from the provinces of the Ottoman Empire, particularly Anatolia, indicated that there was little enthusiasm among the population, and that not only Christians but also many among the Muslim population made use of the opportunity to buy an exemption from military service.[179] In the European parts of the Empire, the response to the outbreak of war and to mobilization was ambivalent at best.[180] For Serbia, usually described as full of enthusiasm for the war, Alfred Vischer, a Swiss doctor who witnessed the declaration of war in Belgrade, described less a nationalist euphoria than a calm, if supportive response among the population.[181] The Austrian military attaché in Belgrade also reported to Vienna that one could hardly speak of real euphoria in the streets, despite the propaganda campaign orchestrated by the press, and reports from outside the capital witnessed 'noisy rallies', but also 'indifference' among the local population.[182] The peasant was more interested in his harvest than in the war, a German diplomat pointed out, questioning whether the urban euphoria had really reached the countryside.[183] In a similar way, reports from Montenegro, at least for the year 1913, spoke of 'bitter reactions' among the peasants when the government ordered a new conscription in June, when they had to work in the fields.[184] Enthusiasm among the population was 'sufficient', but no war is ever really popular, a Bulgarian officer noted in his diary.[185] In Greece, where the public remembered the bitter defeat of 1897 in the Greco-Ottoman war, there was a mixed feeling of 'pride and apprehension', yet no substantial 'anti-war feeling'.[186] Further research may lead to a more balanced picture, analogous to what has occurred in research on the Great War. Even if there was enthusiasm at the beginning of the war, the daily experiences of fighting increasingly undermined nationalist feelings. Sometimes, for example within the Bulgarian army, frustration due to the deteriorating wartime conditions during the Second Balkan War even led to mutinies.[187] Confronted with the new dimensions of warfare, soldiers lost much of their nationalist sentiment, and even if they were not questioning the 'just cause' of 'their' war, they increasingly perceived it simply as 'bloodthirsty' and 'cruel'.[188]

Finally, death and physical disability resulting from the war were more common than ever. Casualties reached unprecedented numbers. Serbia had lost 6,000 soldiers in 1876 and 2,400 in 1878; 4,750 were killed or wounded during the war against Bulgaria in 1885.[189] During the Balkan Wars, the number climbed to 43,000 dead or wounded during the first war and 44,500 during the second war. Bulgaria lost 65,000 soldiers, dead or wounded, during the First and almost 80,000 during the short Second Balkan War; more than 30,000 died of diseases.[190] Battles like those at Çatalça, Lozengrad and Kumanovo produced casualties on a scale never experienced before.[191] Totals were still small in comparison with the 37 per cent of soldiers that Serbia would lose two years later during the Great War and the more than 22 per cent casualty rate that Bulgaria suffered during the same war, but the Balkan Wars were a departure from previous conflicts. Widows and disabled persons became visible in the cities and villages and could no longer be 'hidden' within families, as in previous wars.[192] Hundreds of thousands of refugees confronted the societies still more with the war's human consequences. For the first time, the Balkan societies felt that the war was not over when the fighting stopped.

'Modern Wars' and/or 'Archaic Violence'

The Balkan Wars without any doubt featured a particular kind of violence. It is exactly the degree and the nature of the violence that have been treated time and again as evidence that the Balkan Wars in fact were a kind of 'archaic war', rooted in a traditional regional 'cult of violence' and deviating from the 'regulated' warfare to which 'Europe' was accustomed, at least at home. (In the colonies, it was a different story.) Indeed, there is an abundant mass of sources that describe, often in detail, all kinds of extreme violence committed during the wars by all warring parties. These sources, however, are often of dubious nature. The Balkan governments themselves time and again raised the topic through public media and diplomacy. All addressed the international powers in pointing out their enemies' deeds, accusing them of what by all international criteria amounted to war crimes.[193] The numerous documentations produced by the warring parties to convict their opponents of war crimes, and published mostly for an international audience,[194] are also of little value, precisely because of their political agenda. Local communities presented petitions and accusations to the international powers and their representatives, providing information that was often detailed but hard to prove.[195] War correspondence, often accepted as first-hand evidence even in academic literature, must be treated with equal care. Most of the journalists, including the famous Leon Trotsky, who, rather because of his name than his real first-hand informative value, has become a major source, never came close to the front line.[196] The reports of journalists, noted Richard von Mach, the experienced Balkan correspondent of the German *Kölnische Zeitung*, were almost without exception the product of third-hand information, if not 'even pure fiction'.[197] Other writers, like Carl Pauli, based their information on unnamed 'witnesses' or collected detailed evidence concerning war crimes from the press, such as the impressive notes Leo Freundlich recorded about the events in the Albanian theatre of war in 1913–14, with a deep empathy for the victims. Such notes are certainly not without significance, but their details can hardly be taken for granted.[198] Even the famous Carnegie Report, which became a kind of key witness for the prosecution and has been quoted time and again, cannot be read without a due deconstructive effort on the part of the historian.[199] Finally, the members of the various diplomatic missions constantly sent reports with news and rumours about acts of violence on all sides, yet even they repeatedly complained of being cut off from first-hand information.[200] Being suspicious of the reports' and complaints' authenticity, it was not only the British government that was reluctant to take any serious political action.[201] Even the Austrians, who, due to their own tense political relations with Serbia, were particularly interested in collecting news about Serbian atrocities,[202] were critical towards their sources and attempted to secure the reliability of their informants.[203] They acknowledged that often there was 'a great deal of exaggeration' in the pieces of information they received.[204] Still, information based on witnesses who were deemed to be reliable left no doubt about the excessive violence that was happening – the killing of civilians, including women and children; the burning down of houses and entire villages; the wholesale looting and plundering. Consulate officials, for example, confirmed having personally observed such violations.[205] Non-partisan witnesses, such as foreign railway engineers and workers at the 'Oriental Railway', reported what they had witnessed; priests, both foreign and domestic, testified to their experiences.[206] The widespread acts of 'ethnic cleansing' raised suspicions among some observers of a strategy of systematic extermination.[207] This, however, does not find sufficient backing in the sources. Yet certainly they radicalized the already ongoing process of ethnic homogenization.[208] Sexual violence against women is also reported time and again in the sources, usually in a very general way, which makes it difficult to understand its dimensions and perpetrators.[209]

In fact, information based on personal observations or provided by 'non-partisan' and 'reliable' witnesses left no doubt about the excessive violence committed against civilians on all sides, about the burning down of houses and entire villages, about a systematic 'ethnic cleansing' in conquered territories. And also going beyond the suspicious 'slaughter narratives' of second- and third-hand reports, medical doctors and nurses confirmed from what they saw in the hospitals that the warfare had gone beyond all rules and regulations.[210]

Part of this excessive violence was certainly the result of the 'traditional' dualism of regular and irregular actors, of a longstanding absence of a strict line between 'combatants' and 'civilians'. Stefan Papaioannou, in his unpublished Ph.D. dissertation, provides abundant evidence attesting that, on all sides, the combatants, both regular and irregular, were responsible for all kinds of atrocities against the local population,[211] and often acting jointly in a coordinated manner.[212] Papaioannou's source collection confirms what the Austrian consul in Üsküb (Skopje) reported from the battlefield in Macedonia, namely that the violence against the civilian population in that area 'had not been acts of spontaneous brutality, committed in the heat of the battle by a gang of crude and embittered soldiers, but in cold blood and obviously by order'.[213] Even Balkan politicians acknowledged the excessive nature of the violence from time to time, usually attributing it to 'uncontrolled' irregular forces.[214] Taking account of the fact that the violence sometimes decreased when the regular army replaced the irregulars in a given occupied area,[215] there still can be no doubt that the armies and their leaders were responsible for atrocities as well, either by direct participation or simply by not intervening in the activities of irregular forces. Describing in a long and very personal *Stimmungsbericht* (report on the atmosphere) what he saw after the Serbian occupation of Üsküb, the Austrian consul Heimroth wrote that the Serbian troops had to be held responsible at the very least for not having stopped the excessive violence directed against the city's Muslim population after they had entered the town.[216] In another report, Heimroth added that not even in the Russo-Japanese war had he heard so many complaints about violence as was committed in a war that had begun under the slogan of liberating the Christian brothers and apparently ended with the suppression and attempted extermination of the whole non-Orthodox population.[217] Occasionally, even some of the soldiers' diaries note acts of violence that they witnessed or even took part in during the fighting.[218]

Blaming irregular forces and the army, Papaioannou on the other hand explicitly exonerates the civilian population from any accusation of having played an active role in this violence. He maintains that civilians were neither willing to kill their neighbours nor were they willing to die over ethnic and religious differences.[219] While he presents some good evidence, I still wonder to what extent such a generalization is appropriate. Indeed, Christians and Muslims time and again tried to prevent violence against each other when the military situation changed and a new army arrived.[220] On the other hand, the Balkan Wars created what Jörg Baberowski in a different context has called 'spaces of opportunity' (*Ermöglichungsräume*) for committing violence without the danger of being penalized.[221] Considerable evidence is available that 'ordinary people', too, were drawn into the dynamics of violence, not only as victims but also as bystanders and even perpetrators. Peasants took part in the fights, thus contributing to the blurring of the front lines.[222] The population distributed the land of their expelled neighbours among themselves,[223] took part in plundering or helped the troops and paramilitaries to identify the ethnic 'other'.[224] What appears as 'the mob' in diplomatic reports about the plundering of houses, in particular those left by the Muslim population, was nothing other than 'ordinary citizens', sometimes 'among the better families', making use of the situation.[225] During the conquest of the city of Ioannina/Janina by the Greek army, the report of the Austrian consulate-general tells us that 'the local population was affected literally by a kind of fever' and committed atrocities that 'are totally incompatible with the cultural mission the Balkan states claim to pursue in their fight'.[226] While it was certainly the armies and particularly the irregular groups that carried the violence into the local communities, it seems that the disappearance of the boundary between 'the civilian' and 'the soldier', so typical of the Balkan Wars, makes it difficult to draw any sharp line between soldiers, paramilitaries and civilians. 'The three categories merge into one', Heimroth wrote, summarizing his experiences in Üsküb. 'It seems that the liberator and the liberated join forces, acting jointly against the hated Muslims.'[227]

In other respects also, rules of warfare were obviously ignored. Wounded soldiers, it seems, were mistreated or even killed, albeit obviously not on a large scale and not in a systematic way. Foreign doctors observed that wounded enemy soldiers often arrived at the hospital with clear signs of physical mistreatment. 'Did you not recognize that there was not a single Turk among the wounded?', Ladislaus von Fényes asked his colleague in the hospital. 'What has happened to them?'[228] And Stojan Christov Kamburov, a senior officer with the 7th Preslav regiment, describes in his diary how his commander simply shot a wounded Turkish soldier who had asked the bypassing Bulgarians for some water.[229] There were also rumours among diplomatic representatives about the mistreatment or even killing of prisoners of war.[230] As a matter of fact, the totally new dimension of general mobilization confronted the warring parties with an unprecedented number of prisoners.[231] All sides, in particular during the Second Balkan War, blamed the others for not respecting international rules as far as the treatment of prisoners of war was concerned.[232] The sources, however, present a highly inconsistent picture and do not allow a generalized interpretation. Prisoners were certainly held under bad conditions, particularly in the conquered territories. After the conquest of the city of Adrianople by the allied forces, Turkish prisoners were kept for days without sufficient food supplies or medical treatment, which caused substantial casualties. Similar pieces of information were given by the Austrian consulate official from Niš.[233] Complaints about widespread and systematic mistreatment of prisoners of war or even large-scale murder,[234] however, met with some scepticism even among the Western powers.[235] Admitting the lack of precise information and not denying cases of bad supply or maltreatment, German diplomatic sources from Bulgaria for example considered Ottoman complaints still 'heavily exaggerated'. At least from the cases about which they had received direct evidence, they saw no grave violations of international standards.[236] And while the German Red Cross did notice a 'rough treatment' of the prisoners, leaving them with insufficient food, shelter and medical care,[237] the International Red Cross saw no evidence of any systematic mistreatment, either.[238]

Much of what in contemporary literature was described as a disturbingly 'Balkan' violence actually found its equivalents in other European wars, and particularly in the Great War. Generally, Papaioannou's conclusion is correct that this violence, in many respects, represented 'practices the Balkan armies shared with their contemporaries in Western and Central Europe'.[239] Indeed, it is questionable whether the idea of a regulated 'Bellona', where 'the soldier is characterized by a maximum of regulated violence, limiting violence to combatants',[240] has ever been a reality in a war, European or otherwise.[241] The Balkan Wars in this sense can hardly be seen as exceptional. What is more, the Balkan Wars and the First World War cannot be distinguished in terms of their violence. John Horne and Alan Kramer have given abundant examples of German war crimes at the Belgian front that do not essentially differ from many of the atrocities committed during the Balkan Wars.[242] Joanne Bourke has found examples of 'carnevalesque rites of killing'[243] that differ little from the excesses of the Balkan Wars. Mistreatment and even the killing of prisoners of war took place not only in the colonial wars outside Europe[244] but during the Great War as well.[245] 'Ethnic cleansing', apparently so typical of Balkan history and certainly more systematically carried out during the Balkan Wars than ever before, saw many parallels on the Eastern Front during the First World War.[246]

Conclusion

Following Maria Todorova's influential paradigm of the 'imagining of the Balkans', scholars have warned about debating the Balkan Wars in terms of 'a 'typification' of differences between Europe and the Balkan 'other'.[247] Indeed, in placing the Balkan Wars within European war history, one should not 'exoticize' them as 'un-European' wars deviating from the traditions of 'regulated' European warfare, nor should one simply see them as 'typical' of what Mark Mazower has called the 'dark continent'. To refer to Reinhart Koselleck's term *Sattelzeit* (a time of transition), they should be seen in their deep vacillation between being 'traditional' and 'modern'.[248] Highly modernized armies and an unprecedented mobilization of manpower came up against the limited institutional and organizational capacities of 'premodern' states and societies. Contemporary military observers indeed already noticed these ambiguities. The wars, as the British Major Howell acknowledged, 'cannot in every sense be classed as modern; only to a limited extent can they convey to us the impression of what modern European warfare really means .... The armament was up to date; but, as in Manchuria [in the Russo-Japanese war 1904–5], the general state of the country, in which all the operations took place, was a hundred or five hundred years behind the times'.[249]

The destructive capabilities of 'modern' armies merged with a 'tradition' of warfare that was not based on a clear distinction between 'regular' and 'irregular' actors. The result was a hitherto unknown level of violence and the overturning of experiences and skills that people had derived from the experiences of previous wars. In their ideological dimensions, the wars no less show their deeply ambivalent character, being fuelled by the 'traditional' romantic nationalism of the nineteenth-century 'Oriental Question', but also by the 'new' twentieth-century rhetoric of 'culturalism' and 'racism'. The wars were legitimized with conventional religious arguments, but at the same time seen by intellectuals as a field for new existential experiences. If 'modernity and primitive archaism coexisted [even] in the Great War',[250] as Stéphane Audoin-Rouzeau and Annette Becker have remarked, then the Balkan Wars surely are to be considered an integral part of the history of twentieth-century European wars.

Wolfgang Höpken is Professor for East and Southeast European History at Leipzig University. He recently published 'Inszenierungen des Imperiums: Imperiale Herrschaftslegitimierung in Österreich-Ungarn, Russland und dem Osmanischen Reich 1850–1914', in Eva Kowollik et al. (ed). *(Südost-)Europa: Narrative der Bewegtheit. Festschrift für Angela Richter* (Frank & Timme, 2017); and co-edited, with Wim van Meurs, *Der Erste Weltkrieg auf dem Balkan: Ereignis, Erfahrung, Erinnerung* (Otto Sagner, 2017). Currently he is a Senior Research Fellow within the Humanities Centre for Advanced Studies 'Multiple Secularities – Beyond the West, Beyond Modernities' at Leipzig University.

Notes

1. Cf., for example, for the Bulgarian historiography, Ivan Ilchev, 'The Balkan Wars in Recent Bulgarian Historiography and Textbooks', in Council of Europe (ed.), *Crossroads of European Histories: Multiple Outlooks on Five Key Moments in the History of Europe* (Strasbourg: Council of Europe Publ., 2006), 111–18. Ilchev concludes that communist rule had no great impact on the interpretation of the Balkan Wars, nor did the end of communism, despite some new questions raised by younger scholars, 'change the scope of scholarly interest' much. There remained 'a general inability to let go of pomp and traditional rhetoric' (p. 118).
2. Enika Abazi, 'Between Facts and Interpretations: Three Images of the Balkan Wars of 1912–13', in James Pettifer and Tom Buchanan (eds), *War in the Balkans: Conflict and Diplomacy before World War I* (London: Tauris, 2016), 203–25, here 217.
3. Maria Todorova, *Imagining the Balkans* (Oxford/New York: Oxford University Press, 1997).
4. Cf., as just one of many similar examples, Friedrich Immanuel, *Der Balkankrieg 1912: Vol. 4* (Berlin: Mittler, 1913), 79.
5. Cf. in this sense, for example, the Irish perceptions: Florian Keisinger, *Unzivilisierte Kriege im zivilisierten Europa? Die Balkankriege und die öffentliche Meinung in Deutschland, England und Irland 1876–1913* (Paderborn: Schöningh, 2008). Antje Weber in her dissertation on the view of German, Austrian and French war correspondents on the Balkan Wars also stresses the generally favourable perception of the First Balkan War as a war of 'liberation', but also in defence of Christian and European principles against an 'Asiatic' Ottoman Empire: Antje Weber, *Die Balkankriege 1912–1913 und das Ende der 'Türkei in Europa'*, Ph.D. dissertation (Tübingen: University of Tübingen, 2012). The picture was also highly divergent among the Swedish public: Johannes Tangeberg, 'Semi-Barbarians, Courageous Patriots, Orientalists: Swedish Views of the Balkan Wars in 1912/13', *Godišnjak za društvenu istoriju* 11(1) (2004), 55–71. Tangeberg concludes that 'the image of the Balkans as particularly cruel or violent seems not to have been present among Swedes' (p. 67). Also going beyond Todorova's approach and stressing the heterogeneous view on the Balkans is Eugene Michail, 'Western Attitudes to War in the Balkans and the Shifting Meanings of Violence, 1912–1991', *Journal of Contemporary History* 47(2) (2012), 219–39.
6. Michael Howard, *War in European History* (Oxford: Oxford University Press, 1976); John Keegan, *Die Kultur des Krieges* (Reinbek: Rowohlt, 1995); see also Geoffrey Wawro, *Warfare and Society in Europe 1792–1914* (London/New York: Routledge, 2000). The Balkan Wars are also absent from Dietrich Beyrau et al. (eds), *Formen des Krieges: Von der Antike bis zur Gegenwart* (Paderborn: Schöningh, 2007) and Rolf-Dieter Müller, *Militärgeschichte* (Cologne/Vienna/Weimar: Böhlau, 2009).
7. Dan Diner, *Das Jahrhundert verstehen: Eine universalhistorische Deutung* (Frankfurt/M.: Fischer Taschenbuchverlag, 2000), 33.

8   Dietrich Beyrau, 'Einführende Bemerkungen', in Bruno Thoß and Hans-Erich Volkmann (eds), *Erster Weltkrieg – Zweiter Weltkrieg: Ein Vergleich* (Paderborn: Schöningh, 2002), 729.
9   Cf., for example, Mark Mazower, *Dark Continent: Europe's Twentieth Century* (New York: Vintage Books, 1998) or Niall Ferguson, *The War of the World: Twentieth-Century Conflict and the Descent of the West* (London: Penguin Books, 2007).
10 Mark Biondich, *The Balkans: Revolutions, Wars and Political Violence since 1878* (Oxford: Oxford University Press, 2011).
11 Cf. Slavica Ratković-Kostić, *Evropeizacija srpske vojske 1878–1903* [The Europeanization of the Serbian Army 1878–1903] (Belgrade: Vojnoistorijski institut, 2007).
12 Mile Djurdjeva, 'Narodna vojska u Srbiji 1861–1889' [The National Army in Serbia 1861–1889], *Vojnoistorijski glasnik* 10(4) (1959), 78–93.
13 Slavica Ratković-Kostić, 'Srpska vojska u XIX. veku' [The Serbian Army in the Nineteenth Century], *Vojnoistorijski glasnik* 41(1–2) (1993), 25–45; Draga Vuksanović-Anić, *Stvaranje moderne srpske vojske* [The Formation of the Modern Serbian Army] (Belgrade: Srpska književna zadruga, 1993), 45–74.
14 Cf. the memoirs of the leading Serbian general, Živojin Mišić, *Moje uspomene* [My Memories] (Belgrade: BIGZ, 1978), 81.
15 Slobodan Jovanović, *Vlada Milana Obrenovića* [The Reign of Milan Obrenovich] (Sabrana dela, 5) (Belgrade: BIGZ, 1990), 72; Slobodan Jovanović, *Vlada Aleksandra Obrenovića* [The Reign of Alexander Obrenovich] (Sabrana dela, 7) (Belgrade: BIGZ, 1990), 46–47.
16 Slavica Ratković-Kostić, 'Generalštab srpske vojske 1876–1903' [The General Staff of the Serbian Army 1876–1903], *Vojnoistorijski glasnik* 41(1–2) (2003), 11–32.
17 Aleksandar Stojičević, *Istorija naših ratova za oslobodjenje i ujedinjenje* [The History of Our Wars of Liberation and Unification] (Belgrade: Štamparija Gl. Saveza Srpskih Zemljorad Zadruga, 1936), 70.
18 Miloje Pršić, 'Stvaranje i razvoj vojnog školstva u Srbiji od 1830 do 1919 godine' [The Creation and the Development of Military Schools in Serbia between 1830 and 1919], *Vojno Delo* 50(2) (1998), 115–47; Milić Milićević, *Reforma vojske Srbije 1897–1900* [The Reform of the Serbian Army 1897–1900] (Belgrade: Vojnoizdavački Zavod, 2002), 99–102.
19 Milić Milićević, 'Vitalni činioci razvoja srpske vojske tokom XIX. veka' [Vital Factors of the Development of the Serbian Army during the Nineteenth Century], *Vojnoistorijski glasnik* 41(1–2) (1993), 46–55.
20 Milić Milićević, 'Socijalno poreklo oficirskog kadra školovanog u Srbiji od 1850 do 1901 godine' [The Social Background of the Officer Cadre Educated in Serbia from 1850 to 1901], *Godišnjak za društvenu istoriju* 2(2) (1995), 194–201.
21 Živojin Mišić, *Strategija* [Strategy] (Belgrade: Vojnoizdavački i novinski centar, 1907 [reprint 1993]), 117.
22 Milićević, *Reforma vojske Srbije*, 147; Slavica Ratković-Kostić, 'Razvoj doctrine u vojsci Kraljevine Srbije 1882–1903' [The Development of the

Military Doctrine in the Kingdom of Serbia], *Vojnoistoriski glasnik* 45(1–2) (2007), 65–82.
23 *Srpski Kniževni Glasnik* 22(9) (1909), 704–13.
24 Slavica Ratković-Kostić, 'Usvojavanje savremenih sistema naoružanja u srpskoj vojsci krajem XIX. veka' [The Adoption of the Modern System of Armament in the Serbian Army at the End of the Nineteenth Century], *Vojnoistorijski glasnik* 43(1–2) (2005), 11–43; Dalibor Denda, 'Tajni raport putnika Damjana Vlajića 1907 godine o naoružanju i opremi srpske vojske' [The Secret Report of the Traveller Damjan Vlajich in 1907 about the Armament and Gear of the Serbian Army], *Vojnoistorijski glasnik* 46(2) (2008), 213–30; Miličević, *Reforma vojske Srbije*, 61. For intimate knowledge of the European military-technological developments among the Serbian military, cf. Ivan Mijatovič, 'Šesdeset godina Vojnotechničkog glasnika: Ishodište vojnotehničke misli u vojnoj štampi Kneževine/Kraljevine Srbije' [Sixty Years of the Military-Technical Journal: The Starting Point of Military-Technical Thinking in the Army Press of the Principality/Kingdom of Serbia], *Vojnotehnički glasnik* 60(2) (2012), 7–25, here 20.
25 Cf. the observations by Austrian diplomats in Österreichisches Staatsarchiv, Haus-, Hof- und Staatsarchiv (OeStA, HHStA) P.A. XII 385. Liasse XLV/3: Balkankrieg, k.u.k. Militärattaché Belgrad, no. 197, 6 October 1912: Stimmung in Belgrad; ibid., v. Ugron an Berchtold, no. 114, Belgrad, 22 October 1912: Militärische Nachrichten.
26 OeStA, HHStA P.A. XIX Serbien 63: Berichte, Weisungen, Varia 1912, v. Ugron an Berchtold no. 62 B, Belgrad, 24 June 1912: Projektierte Waffenbestellungen.
27 OeStA, HHStA P.A. XII 386. Liasse XLV/3: Balkankrieg, Abschrift pro actis k.u.k. Militärattaché Belgrad, no. 269; ibid., 440, Liasse XLV/22 ad Liasse XLV/3: Balkankrieg Evidenzbureau des k.u.k. Generalstabes Tagesbericht, 26 November 1912, B. no. 1500 res., 26 November 1912: Serbien: Die Ursachen der serbischen Erfolge. Cf. also 'Die serbische Armee', *Österreichische Illustrierte Zeitung* 23(44) (9 August 1913), 1228; similarly, 'Heerwesen der Balkanstaaten', *Streffleur's Militärische Zeitschrift* 50(2) (1909), 303–20; 'Die Armeen der Balkanstaaten', *Fremdenblatt*, 1 October 1912 (all sources from newspapers are based on HHStA Zeitungsarchiv 94).
28 Richard C. Hall, 'The Next War: The Influence of the Russo-Japanese War on Southeastern Europe and the Balkan Wars of 1912–1913', *Journal of Slavic Military Studies* 17(3) (2004), 563–77.
29 Richard von Mach, *Briefe aus dem Balkankrieg 1912–1913* (Berlin: Eisenschmidt, 1913), 14.
30 Cf. the statistical figures in Georgiev Velichko and Staiko Trifonov (eds), *Istoriia na Bŭlgarite 1878–1912 v dokumenti* [History of Bulgaria 1878–1912 in Documents], Vol. II, *1912–1918* (Sofia: Prosveta, 1996), 37.
31 On the social role of the Bulgarian officers, cf. Jordan Kolev, *Bălgarskata inteligentsiia 1878–1912* [The Bulgarian Inteligentsia 1878–1912] (Sofia: Univ. Izdat. Sv. Kl. Okhridski, 1992), 274–87.
32 On the modernization of the Bulgarian army since the 1890s, cf. the memoirs by the Bulgarian officer Dimităr Azmanov, *Moiata epokha 1878–1918* [My

Era 1878–1918] (Sofia: Izdat. na Ministerstvoto na Otbranata Sv. Georgi Pobedonosets, 1995), 83.
33 OeStA, HHStA P.A. XII 386. Liasse XLV/3: Balkankrieg, Thun an Berchtold, no. 45, St. Petersburg, 12 November 1912: Aeusserungen der hiesigen Vertreter der Türkei und Bulgariens seit Beginn des Krieges über die respektiven Chancen.
34 N.P. Mamontov, *S bolgarskimi voiskami ot Balkan' do Chataldzhi: Zapiski voennago korrespondenta* [With the Bulgarian Armies from the Balkan to Chataldzha: Notes of a War Correspondent] (Moscow: Tovar. Tipogr. A. I. Mamontova, 1913), 79; A.A. Riabinin, *Balkanskaia voina* [The Balkan War] (St. Peterburg, 1913), 16.
35 For the Ottoman military aircraft, which due to the lack of pilots and technical problems had almost no impact during the First and a very limited impact during the Second Balkan War, cf. Bülent Yilmazer, 'Ottoman Aviation, Prelude to Military Use of Aircraft', in Edward J. Erickson (ed.), *Defeat in Detail: The Ottoman Army in the Balkans 1912–13* (Westport, CT: Praeger, 2003), Appendix A, 347–70, here 356–63; for Serbia, Austrian military experts reported from the beginning of the war that Serbian aircraft could hardly be used for military activitites: OeStA, HHStA P.A. XII 440. Evidenzbureau des k.u.k. Generalstabes, Tagesbericht, 29 November 1912: B. no. 1549, 29 November 1912: Serbien. Bericht des k.u.k. Militärattachés Major Gellinek in Belgrad, 24 November 1912.
36 On the Bulgarian aircraft, cf. Dimităr Nedialkov, *Văzdushnata mosht na Carstvo Bălgariia. Chast I* [The Airpower of the Bulgarian Kingdom, Part I] (Sofia: Fark OOD, 2001), 11–59; Mamontov, *S bolgarskimi voiskami*, 80; Heinrich Meyer, *Der Balkankrieg 1912/13 und seine Lehren* (Munich: Meyer, 1913), 97–99. Their actual military importance is exaggerated by Georgi Marin, 'Prinosăt na bălgarskata aviaciia văv voennoto delo prez balkanskata voina 1912–1913' [The Contribution of Bulgarian Aviation to Military Activities during the Balkan Wars 1912–1913], in Bălgarsko Istorichesko Druzhestvo (ed), *Bălgariia 1300: Institutsiia i dărzhavnata traditsiia* [Bulgaria 1300: Institutions and State Traditions], Vol. III (Sofia: Bălgarsko Istorichesko Druzhestvo, 1983), 649–57.
37 Cf., for example, the public image as represented in photos and postcards in *Vojnata – takava, kakvato beshe: Bălgariia v Părvata Balkanska Voina 1912–1913 g.* [The War as It Really Was: Bulgaria during the First Balkan War 1912–1913] (Sofia: Univ. Izd. Sv. Kliment Okhridski, 2012), 168.
38 John Koliopulos, *Brigands with a Cause* (Oxford: Clarendon Press, 1987), 155, 196; Dimitris Michalopoulos, 'The Evolution of the Greek Army (1828–1868)', in Béla K. Király (ed.), *The Crucial Decade: East Central European Society and National Defense, 1859–1870* (New York: Columbia University Press, 1984), 317–30.
39 'Die Griechische Armee 1909', *Streffleur's Militärische Zeitschrift* 2 (1909), 1113–20. Cf. also Thanos Veremis, 'The Officer Corps in Greece 1912–1936', *Byzantine and Modern Greek Studies* 2(1) (1976), 113–33, here 113.
40 Novica Rakočević, 'The Organization and the Character of the Montenegrin Army in the First Balkan War', in Béla K. Király and Dimitrije Djordjević

(eds), *East Central European Society and the Balkan Wars* (War and Society in East Central Europe, XVIII) (New York: Columbia University Press, 1987), 112–25.
41 OeStA, HHStA P.A. XII 440. Liasse XLV/22 ad Liasse XLV/3: Balkankrieg, Evidenzbureau des k.u.k. Generalstabes, Tagesbericht, 26 December 1912, B. no. 1930 res., 26 December 1912: Militärische Situation in Montenegro; ibid., Evidenzbureau des k.u.k. Generalstabes Evidenz über den Balkankrieg, 23 November 1912, B. no. 1450 Montenegro (describing the command structure as 'patriarchaic' rather than 'professional' in the sense of modern armies); ibid., P.A. XII 441. Liasse XLV/3: Balkankrieg, Evidenzbureau des k.u.k. Generalstabes: Evb.Res. 683 v 1913: Eindrücke und Erfahrungen auf dem montenegrinisch-türkischen Kriegsschauplatz 1912/13 vom k.u.k. Militärattache in Cetinje, Hauptmann des Gen. Stabskorps Gustav Hupka; ibid., P.A. XII 388. Liasse XLV/3: Balkankrieg, Ledinegg an Berchtold, vertraulich, Antivari, 10 January 1913.
42 OeStA, HHStA P.A. XIX Serbien 63: Berichte, Weisungen, Varia 1912, Geheime Denkschrift über die Lage in Serbien, ddo. 25 June 1912; ibid., v. Ugron an Berchtold, no. 123 B: Über die serbischen Staatsfinanzen, Belgrad, 1 November 1912; ibid., P.A. XII 440. Liasse XLV/22 ad Liasse XLV/3: Balkankrieg, Evidenzbureau des k.u.k. Generalstabes: Evidenz über den Balkankrieg, 14 November 1912; *Neue Freie Presse*, 1 October 1912. For the financial dimension, cf. also Čedomir Antić, 'Crisis and Armament: Economic Relations between Great Britain and Serbia 1910–1912', *Balcanica* 36 (2005), 151–63.
43 OeStA, HHStA P.A. XV Bulgarien 74: Berichte, Weisungen 1912: Tarnowski an Aehrenthal no. 8c, Sofia, 9 February 1912: Unterredung mit Herrn Daneff.
44 'Die Mobilmachung der Balkan-Armeen', *Österreichische Illustrierte Zeitung* 22(2) (13 October 1912), 45; 'Heerwesen der Balkanstaaten', *Streffleur's Militärische Zeitschrift* 50(2) (1909), 303–32; *Streffleur's Militärische Zeitschrift* 50(3) (1909), 449–504; Major P. Howell, *The Campaign in Thrace: Six Lectures* (London: H. Rees, 1913), 152. Similar in its positive evaluation on the part of the German General Staff: *Kriegsgeschichtliche Einzelschriften, hg. vom Großen Generalstabe. Kriegsgeschichtliche Abteilung I: Heft 50: Der Balkankrieg 1912/13, Erstes Heft Die Ereignisse auf dem thrazischen Kriegsschauplatz bis zum Waffenstillstand* (Berlin, 1914), 11–13; and, from a Swiss perspective, Oberstleutnant Julius Meyer, *CVIII. Neujahrsblatt der Feuerwerker-Gesellschaft (Artillerie-Kollegium) in Zürich auf das Jahr 1913: Aus den Balkan-Kriegen* (Zurich: Kommissionsverlag Beer und Co., 1913), 49.
45 OeStA, HHStA P.A. XII 440. Liasse XLV/22 ad Liasse XLV/3: Balkankrieg, Evidenzbureau des k.u.k. Generalstabes: Tagesbericht, 13 December 1912: Serbien. Der Zustand der serbischen Armee im Felde.
46 Cf. the examples from the German, Austrian and French press in Weber, *Die Balkankriege*, 54–56.
47 Cf., for example, Lionel James, *With the Conquered Turk: The Story of a Latter-Day Adventurer* (Boston, MA: Small, Mayard and Comp., 1913), 19, 50, 99. The Austrian consul-general from Üsküb (Skopje) reported in January 1911 that the local army units were making 'a rather unfavourable

impression for European standards' ['... auf ein an europäische Verhältnisse gewöhntes Auge einen sehr ungünstigen Eindruck']. OeStA, HHStA P.A. XXXVIII Konsulate 441. Üsküb 1911–1913, Dr von Heimroth an Aehrenthal: Truppen-Dislokation und militärische Vorkommnisse, no. 7 Geheim, Uesküb, 9 January 1911.

48 Jan Christoph Reichmann, *'Tapfere Askers' und 'Feige Araber': der osmanische Verbündete aus der Sicht deutscher Soldaten im Orient 1914–1918*, Ph.D. dissertation (Münster: University of Münster, 2009), 71. More balanced in his evaluation than most of the contemporary witnesses is Erickson, *Defeat in Detail*, 332–37. Erickson acknowledges the many organizational, logistic and educational deficits of an army still 'professional unready' for a new war (p. 59), but he also sees the Ottoman army as having been able in a remarkable way to 'adapt', to 'learn' and to 'correct its mistakes'.

49 Hans Rohde, *Unsere Gefechtsvorschriften und der Balkankrieg* (Berlin: Eisenschmidt, 1915), 4.

50 Jehuda Wallach, *Anatomie einer Militärhilfe: Die preußisch-deutschen Militärmissionen in der Türkei 1835–1919* (Düsseldorf: Droste, 1976), 114; Michael Unger, *Die bayerischen Militärbeziehungen zur Türkei vor und im Ersten Weltkrieg* (Frankfurt/M.: Peter Lang, 2003), 116.

51 Albin Kutschbach, *Die Serben im Balkankrieg* (Stuttgart: Franckh, 1913), 137.

52 'Die Artillerie der Balkanstaaten nach dem Stande der heutigen Geschützausrüstung', *Militärzeitung* 36(30) (26 July 1913), 476–78; the Balkan Wars were viewed as proof of the superiority of French military technology by the French diplomat in Bulgaria, Camille Louis de Matharel, *Balkanskata voina prez pogled na edin frantsuzin* [The Balkan Wars as Viewed by a Frenchman] (Sofia: Voenno izdatelstvo, 1977), 247.

53 Quoted in Reichmann, *'Tapfere Askers' und 'Feige Araber'*, 71: 'Der Krieg ist im Großen und Ganzen aus naheliegenden Gründen nicht lehrhaft gewesen'.

54 Howell, *The Campaign in Thrace*, 142, 144.

55 German General Staff, *Kriegsgeschichtliche Einzelschriften, Heft 50: Der Balkankrieg 1912/13, Erstes Heft*, 139: 'Auf taktischem Gebiete brachte der Krieg zwar keine neuen Erkenntnisse von grundlegender Bedeutung, aber doch manche wertvolle Lehre für die Durchführung des Kampfes der Infanterie und Artillerie und insbesondere für das Zusammenwirken der Waffen'. Similarly, Rohde, *Unsere Gefechtsvorschriften*, 4–5, 15, 125–26.

56 Meyer, *Der Balkankrieg*, 101.

57 Milićević, *Reforma vojske Srbije*, 52; Milan Mijalkovski, 'Četničke (gerilske) jedinice Kraljevine Srbije – borci protiv terora turskog okupatora' [Chetnik (Guerrilla) Units in the Kingdom of Serbia – Fighters against the Terror of the Turkish Occupational Forces], *Zbornik radova Instituta za savremenu istoriju* 9 (2007), 59–81, here 63–71.

58 David McKenzie, 'Officer Conspirators and Nationalism in Serbia 1901–1914', in Stephen Fischer-Galațaţi and Béla K. Király (eds), *Essays on War and Society in East Central Europe, 1740–1920* (Boulder, CO: Social Science Monographs, 1987), 128.

59 Aleksandar Životić, 'Srpski gerilski odredi na prostoru stare Srbije 1911–1912' [Serbian Guerrilla Units in Old Serbia 1911–1912], *Zbornik radova Instituta za savremenu istoriju* 9 (2007), 119–36, here 121–33.

60 For a good analysis of the social and military role of those *četa* in Serbia, see Alexey Timofeev, 'Serbskie chetniki nakanune i v chode Balkanskih voin: sotsial'nyi fenomen, natsional'naia traditsiia i voennaia taktika' [The Serbian Chetniks before and during the Balkan Wars: Social Phenomenon, National Tradition and Military Tactic], in Rita Grishina (ed.), *Modernizaciia vs. voina: Chelovek na Balkanach nakanune i vo vremia Balkanskych voin (1912–1913)* [Modernization vs. War: Man in the Balkans before and during the Balkan Wars in 1912–1913] (Moscow: Institut slavianovedeniia Rossiiskoi akademii nauk, 2012), 102–22. Cf. also his contribution to this volume.

61 Cf., for Bulgaria, the reports by the French diplomat Matharel, *Balkanskata voina*, 24; and Colonel breveté Desbriere, *Aperçu sur la Campagne de Thrace* (Paris: Librairie Chapelot, 1913), 9, who calls the Bulgarian mobilization efforts 'très simples et très effectifs'. For Serbia, OeStA, HHStA P.A. XII 385. Liasse XLV/3: Balkankrieg, v. Ugron an Berchtold, no. 114, 23 October 1912: Militärische Nachrichten. Reports were more ambivalent for the Ottoman Empire, where, following a report by the Austrian military attaché from Istanbul, mobilization obviously met with organizational difficulties and even resistance from soldiers, who had only been released from service shortly before: OeStA, HHStA P.A. XII 440. Evidenzbureau des k.u.k. Generalstabes: Evidenz über den Balkankrieg, 11 November 1912, T. no. 1470 Türkei. Bericht des k.u.k. Militärattachés in Konstantinopel Obersten Pomjankowski.

62 Cf., for Serbia, Dalibor Denda, *Automobili u srpskoj vojsci 1908–1918* [Automobiles in the Serbian Army] (Belgrade: Institut za strategijska istraživanja, 2008). The Greek army claimed to have had access to 128 cars in Macedonia and 1,300 in Epirus; most of them, however, were small ones: OeStA, HHStA P.A. XII 380. Liasse XLV/3: Balkankrieg, Kral an Berchtold, no. 23, Salonica, 26 January 1913: Betreffend das Automobilwesen im griechischen Heer.

63 Cf., for the Bulgarian army, Nikola Ivanov, *Spomeni 1861–1918* [Memoirs 1861–1918], Vol. II (Sofia: Izdat. na Ministerstvoto na Otbranata Sv. Georgi Pobedonosets, 1997), 75; 'Dokumentalen razkaz za Balkanskata voina: Iz nepublikovanata kniga na Petăr Stoilov' [Documentary Narrative on the Balkan War: From the Unpublished Book of Petăr Stoilov], *Istorichesko bădeshte* 1–2 (2003), 254. For Serbia, Borislav Ratković, 'Mobilization of the Serbian Army for the First Balkan War', in Király and Djordjević, *East Central European Society and the Balkan Wars*, 146–57, here 146. The British parliamentarian Noel Buxton, otherwise full of praise for the standard of the Bulgarian army, gives an illustrative description of the slow pace with which the army was moving towards the Thracian war theatre: Noel Buxton, *With the Bulgarian Staff* (New York: The Macmillan Comp., 1913), 11.

64 Mahmud Muhtar Paşa, *Meine Führung im Balkankriege 1912* (Berlin: Mittler, 1913), 117, 172–73; Günter von Hochwaechter, *Mit den Türken in der Front*

im Stabe Mahmud Muchtar Pashas – Mein Kriegstagebuch über die Kämpfe bei Kirk Kilisse, Lüle Burgas und Cataldza (Berlin: Mittler, 1913), 68, 71. See also Maurice Baring, *Letters from the Near East 1909 and 1912* (London: Smith, Elder and Co., 1913), 128.

65 Cf., for example, the record of the proceedings of the preparation committee of the Bulgarian army, criticizing the lack of many basic supplies in mid September 1912, in Georgiev and Trifonov, *Istoriia na Bŭlgarite*, 22. See also the diary of Nikola Dodov, who, being drafted in September 1912, recognized that 'many of the soldiers were not equipped with full clothes': Nikola Dodov, *Dnevnik na Balkanskata voina* (Sofia: Voenno izdat., 2006), 12. Vasil Kolarov, later one of the leading figures in the Bulgarian Communist Party, took part in the Balkan Wars as a soldier. In his diary, he too notes that his regiment gave the impression of a 'half-naked army', with many soldiers marching without any real uniform: Vasil Kolarov, *Pobedi i porazheniia: Dnevnik* [Victories and Defeats: Diary] (Sofia: Christo Botev, 2001), 24. For the Ottoman army and their deficits in equipment and ammunition, see Hochwaechter, *Mit den Türken in der Front*, 12, 69.

66 OeStA, HHStA P.A. XII 387. Liasse XLV/3: Balkankrieg, Tarnowski an Berchtold, Sofia, no. 93, 27 December 1912: Zum bulgarisch-türkischen Feldzug; ibid., P.A. XII 440. Liasse XLV/22 ad Liasse XLV/3: Balkankrieg: Evidenzbureau des k.u.k. Generalstabes Tagesbericht, 20 December 1912: B. no. 1870 res. Bulgarien.

67 Shortage of ammunition and a lack of supply were identified by a governmental commission as among the reasons for Bulgaria's defeat in the Second Balkan War: OeStA, HHStA P.A. XV Bulgarien 75: Berichte, Weisungen, Varia 1913, Freiherr von Mittag an Berchtold, no. 75 A-J, Sofia, 6 November 1913: Zur Lage. On the Ottoman army, cf. OeStA, HHStA P.A. XII 440. Liasse XLV/22 ad Liasse XLV/3: Balkankrieg, Evidenzbureau des k.u.k. Generalstabes: Evidenz über den Balkankrieg, 11 November 1912; T. no. 1470 Türkei. Bericht des k.u.k. Militärattachés in Konstantinopel Obersten Pomjankowski; Hochwaechter, *Mit den Türken in der Front*, 25, 56, 69.

68 Vladan Gjordjewitj [Djordjević], *Die Entwicklung der öffentlichen Gesundheitspflege im serbischen Königreich vom XII. Jahrhundert bis 1883* (Berlin: Pasch, 1883), 23–39. In 1870–71, Djordjević had tried to study Prussian practices during the German-French war first-hand; he was not allowed to enter the battlefields but was restricted to visits to the military hospitals behind the front lines.

69 Mile Ignjatović, 'Srpsko ratno hirurško iskustvo, I. deo: Ratna hirurgija u vreme srpskih-turskih ratova' [Serbian Military Surgery I: Military Surgery during the Serbian-Turkish Wars], *Vojnosanitetski pregled* 60(5) (2003), 631–40.

70 Emil Knorr, *Entwicklung und Gestaltung des Heeres-Sanitätswesens der europäischen Staaten* (Hannover: Helwig, 1880), 913.

71 Mile Ignjatović, 'Srpsko ratno hirurško iskustvo, II. deo: Ratna hirurgija u Srbiji u vreme Srpsko-bugarskog rata' [Serbian Military Surgery II: Military Surgery during the Serbian-Bulgarian War], *Vojnosanitetski*

pregled 60(6) (2003), 757–62; Pavle Jović, 'Vojni lekari – prvi državni pitomci za studije medicine u inostranstvu' [Medical Doctors – the First State Sponsored Students for Medicine Abroad], *Vojnosanitetski pregled* 59(2) (2002), 215–16.

72 Mile Ignjatović, 'Srpsko ratno hirurško iskustvo, IV. deo: Ratna hirurgija u Srbiji u vreme balkanskih ratova' [Serbian Military Surgery IV: Military Surgery during the Balkan Wars], *Vojnosanitetski pregled* 61(2) (2004), 217–29; Vladimir Stanojević, *Istorija srpskog vojnog saniteta* [History of Serbian Military Medicine] (Belgrade: Vojnoizdavački i novinski centar, 1992), 70, 93.

73 On the role of women and women's organizations in medical preparations for war, cf. Svetlana Stefanović, *Nation und Geschlecht: Frauen in Serbien von der Mitte des 19. Jahrhunderts bis zum Zweiten Weltkrieg*, Ph.D. dissertation (Leipzig: University of Leipzig, 2011), 181; Vera Gavrilović, 'Žene lekari u Prvom Balkanskom ratu' [Women Doctors in the First Balkan War], in SANU (ed.), *Prvi Balkanski rat: Okrugli sto povodom 75. godišnjice 1912–1987* [The First Balkan War: Round Table on the Occasion of the 75th Anniversary 1912–1987] (Belgrade: SANU, 1991), 98.

74 'In jedem Verwundeten sah die Mutter ihren eigenen Sohn, die Tochter ihren Vater oder ihren Bruder oder ihren Geliebten, die alle ebenfalls in den Dienst des Vaterlandes sich gestellt …': Catherina Sturzenegger, *Serbisches Rotes Kreuz und internationale Liebestätigkeit während der Balkankriege 1912/13* (Zurich: Orell Füssli, 1914), 25.

75 Cf., with regard to Serbia, Fritz Tintner, 'Kriegschirurgische Erfahrungen im Bulgarisch-Türkischen Feldzug', *Der Militärarzt* 47(4) (1 March 1913), 54; Burghard Breitner [Bruno Sturm], *Kriegstagebuch: Balkankrieg 1913* (Vienna/Leipzig: Braumüller, 1913), 114–16, 123. For Bulgaria, see *Klinisch-therapeutische Wochenschrift Wien* 20(10) (10 March 1913), 312; 'Schlachtenbummlerinnen', *Das Rote Kreuz: Zentralorgan für alle Wohlfahrts- und Wohltätigkeitsbestrebungen* 38(5) (1913), 4.

76 Clyde Sinclair Ford, *The Balkan Wars: Being a Series of Lectures Delivered at the Army Service Schools* (Washington, DC: Press of the Army Service Schools, 1915), 138; the author had served in Turkish as well as Bulgarian hospitals during both wars.

77 Cf. the speech by Dr Kirschner in *Verhandlungen der Deutschen Gesellschaft für Chirurgie: 42. Congress, abgehalten zu Berlin, 26.–28. März 1913* (Berlin, 1913), 214: '… kann man ihnen den Vorwurf nicht ersparen, daß sie, obwohl sie sich erwiesener Maßen seit Jahren planmäßig auf den Krieg vorbereiten, für die Bereitstellung geeigneter Transportmittel sehr wenig gethan haben'.

78 OeStA, HHStA P.A. XII 441. Liasse XLV/3: Balkankrieg, Evidenzbureau des k.u.k. Generalstabes: Tagesbericht, 7 February 1913: Bulgarien. Eindrücke von der bulgarischen Armee im Feldzuge 1912. Instead of the 1,300 to 1,400 doctors that would have been needed, the army disposed only 680; cf. Konstantin Trošev, *Češkí lěkaři v Bulharsku v době Balkánských válek (1912–1913)* [Czech Doctors in Bulgaria during the Balkan Wars 1912–1913] (Varna: Slavena, 2003 [Prague: Univerzita Karlowa, 1984]), 131.

79 Michail Arnaudov, *Istoriia na Sofiiskiia univerzitet Sv. Kliment Okhridski prez părvoto mu polustoletie 1888–1938* [History of the University of Sofia St. Kliment of Ohrid during Its First 50 Years 1888–1939] (Sofia: Prodvorna pechatnitsa, 1939), 355–60. For Serbia, see Milan Jovanović-Batut, *Medicinski fakultet srpskog univerziteta* [The Medical Faculty of the Serbian University] (Belgrade, 1899); *Zdravlje* 8 (1912), 233.

80 'Aus den ärztlichen Gesellschaften Österreichs: Erfahrungen und Erlebnisse aus dem Balkankriege', *Klinisch-therapeutische Wochenschrift Wien* 20(10) (10 March 1913), 310; 'Im Feldlazarett von Podgoritza', *Österreichische Illustrierte Zeitung* 22(7) (17 November 1912), 181.

81 OeStA, HHStA P.A. XII 389. Liasse XLV/3: Balkankrieg, Weinzetl an Berchtold, no. 14 A-C, Cetinje, 19 February 1913: Der Angriff auf Scutari: 'Die alten Klagen, dass der Krieg ohne genügende Vorbereitung und insbesondere was das Sanitätswesen anbelangt, mit an barbarischen Zeiten erinnernder Sorglosigkeit begonnen wurde, werden wieder lauter denn je'. Cf. also for the early weeks of the war, ibid., 385, Frh. von Giesl an Berchtold, no. 83 vertraulich, Cetinje, 14 October 1912.

82 See, for example, the report by British nurses: 'during the first weeks the only bedding was in the form of mattresses, which were placed on the floor', in *The British Journal of Nursing* 51(1) (321) (26 July 1913), 1. Similarly, from the view of an American military doctor, Ford, *The Balkan Wars*, iv.

83 'The Treatment of the Sick and the Wounded in Constantinople', *The Lancet. A Journal of British and Foreign Medical and Chemical Science, Criticism, Literature and News* 180(4,660) (21 December 1912), 1,749; 'Constantinople', *The Lancet* 180(4,656) (23 November 1912), 1,470. The situation was considered to be better only for Greece, where, despite organizational problems, the wounded encountered better conditions: Dr Franz Goldhammer, 'Kriegsärztliche Erfahrungen aus dem griechisch-türkischen und griechisch-bulgarischen Krieg', in P[aul] v. Bruns (ed.), *Kriegschirurgische Erfahrungen aus den Balkankriegen 1912/13* (Tübingen: Laupp'sche Buchhandlung, 1914), 14–17.

84 Muhtar Paşa, *Meine Führung im Balkankriege*, 133 (quotation). On the situation in San Stefano, see Baring, *Letters from the Near East*, 162–87. On the number of casualties, OeStA, HHStA P.A. XII 440. Evidenzbureau des k.u.k. Generalstabes, Tagesbericht, 4 December 1912: T. no. 1612, 4 December 1912: Tschataldscha Linie.

85 On the impact on the Bulgarian army, cf. Christian Promitzer, 'Combating Cholera during the Balkan Wars: The Case of Bulgaria', in Pettifer and Buchanan, *War in the Balkans*, 76–101. I thank Christian Promitzer for making the manuscript of this article available to me before publication. Cf. the first-hand description from the Chataldzha front in Khr. Nedialkov, *Chataldzha: Spomeni i vpechatlenija na uchasnik* [Chataldzha: Memories and Impressions of a Participant] (Sofia: Pechatnitsa na Armeiiskiia Voenen-izdatelskii fond, 1924), 27–29, and also 'Niakolko dumi za cholerata v Bulgarska voiska prez voinata' [Some Words about the Cholera in the Bulgarian Army during the War], *Letopis na Lekarskija Săjuz v Bălgariia*

8–10 (1913), 501–9, which mentions 60,000 cholera casualties among the Bulgarian, Greek, Serbian and Turkish armies and population.
86 Their number can hardly be calculated precisely, but it certainly exceeded several hundred. Konstantin Trošev, in his work on Czech doctors, counts 242 sanitary missions in Bulgaria alone, with 224 medical doctors and more than 300 nurses. Russian missions were the most numerous, followed by missions from the Austrian part of the monarchy and from Bohemia; cf. Trošev, Češkí lěkaři, 135–37. Slightly different figures, based on the Bulgarian Red Cross, are in Georgiev and Trifonov, *Istoriia na Bŭlgarite*, 95–100; cf. also the reports of Red Cross missions in *Bulletin International de la Croix-Rouge* 44(173) (1913), 56–60; ibid. 44(174) (1913), 138–45; ibid. 44(175) (1913), 217–20. In Serbia, more than 300 medical experts, among them 120 doctors, most of them from Russia, were present during the wars: Ilija Petrović, 'Foreign Medical Help in Serbian Liberation Wars until 1918', *Archive of Oncology* 18(4) (2010), 143–48; Ana Stojić, 'Pomoć Belgijskog Crvenog Krsta Kraljevini Srbiji tokom Balkanskih Ratova' [The Assistance of the Belgian Red Cross to the Kingdom of Serbia during the Balkan Wars], *Miscellanea* 32 (2011), 529–42. As a first systematic analysis of Austrian assistance, see also Indira Duraković, 'Experimentierfeld Balkan: Ärzte am Schauplatz der Balkankriege 1912/13', *Südost-Forschungen* 68 (2009), 298–327.
87 Claire Stobart, *War and Women: From Experience in the Balkans and Elsewhere* (London: Bell & Sons, 1913).
88 Breitner, *Kriegstagebuch*, 158, 163; Ladislaus von Fényes, *Tagebuch eines Mannes vom Roten Kreuz: Erlebnisse aus dem Balkankrieg* (Berlin: Verlag von Karl Siegesmund, 1913), 8; Alexander Fraenkel, 'Einige allgemeine Bemerkungen zur modernen Kriegschirurgie', in Bruns, *Kriegschirurgische Erfahrungen*, 1–13, here 1–3. See also Anton Dilger and Arthur W. Meyer, 'Kriegschirurgische Erfahrungen aus den beiden Balkankriegen 1912/13', *Deutsche Zeitschrift für Chirurgie* 127(3–4) (1914), 225–379, here 265; Antonín Wiesner, *Moderní válka po stránce lékaře* [The Modern War from the Perspective of the Doctor] (Prague: Vlastním nákladem J. Otto, 1913), 4. Members of an American mission, who left the Serbian-Bulgarian theatre of war after only a few days, were obviously, as the Serbs and the American consul-general complained, 'more interested in their studies' than in providing help: quoted by Ignjatović, 'Srpsko ratno hirurško iskustvo, IV. deo', 225. On the medical interests of Austrian doctors, see also Heinz Flamm, 'Das Österreichische Rote Kreuz und österreichische Bakteriologen in den Balkankriegen 1912/13 – Zentennium des ersten Einsatzes der Bakteriologie auf Kriegsschauplätzen', *Wiener Medizinische Wochenschrift* 162(7–8) (2012), 132–47.
89 Alfred Exner, *Kriegschirurgie in den Balkankriegen* (Stuttgart: Enke, 1915), 7.
90 Anton Waldmann, *Arzt und Soldat, Berlin 1936: Festschrift zum 60. Geburtstag des Heeres-Sanitätsinspekteurs im Reichskriegsministerium Generaloberstabsarzt Prof. Dr. Anton Waldmann* (Berlin, 1938).
91 Clyde Sinclair Ford, *Gunshot Roentgenograms: A Collection of Roentgenograms Taken in Constantinople during the Turco-Balkan War, 1912–1913, Illustrating Some Gunshot Wounds in the Turkish Army* (War Department, Office of the

Surgeon General, Bulletin 9, October 1915) (Washington, DC: Government Printing Office, 1916).

92 Josef Hamburger, 'Der Sanitätsdienst im Balkankriege', *Der Militärarzt* 48(7) (25 April 1914), 129–40, here 137, 140.

93 'Der Balkankrieg hat keine eingreifende Aenderung in den Anschauungen der Kriegschirurgie gebracht, er hatte aber für letztere eine große Bedeutung als Schule für praktische Tätigkeit': *Klinisch-Therapeutische Wochenschrift* 20(10) (10 March 1913), 310; Tintner, 'Kriegschirurgische Erfahrungen', 50. Fritz Tintner appreciated the Balkan Wars as a testing ground not only because 'the new weapons enriched our knowledge', but also because 'the unpleasant effect of insufficient medical care produced such ugly consequences'.

94 Fred Fox, *The Balkan Peninsula* (London: Black, 1915), 143.

95 Cf., for example, the information given by the Austrian Red Cross Mission: 'Aus den ärztlichen Gesellschaften Österreichs: Erfahrungen aus dem Balkankriege', *Klinisch-Therapeutische Wochenschrift* 20(8) (24 February 1913), 245. See also Stobart, *War and Women*, 11–15; and the description of the Bulgarian field hospitals near the Čorlu front line by the Russian war correspondent N.P. Mamontov, *S bolgarskimi voiskami*, 165. He mentions dying soldiers lying on the floor.

96 Ivan G. Popov, *Spomeni ot bălgarsko-turskata voina prez 1912–1913* [Memories from the Bulgarian-Turkish War] (Sofia: Pechat. Gutenberg, 1914), 110.

97 Cf. the memories of the nurse Catharina Sturzenegger, *Serbisches Rotes Kreuz*, 61–63; Josef Ballner, 'Kriegschirurgische Erfahrungen aus dem Bulgarisch-Türkischen Kriege', *Der Militärarzt* 47(10) (24 May 1913), 145.

98 Bertold Reder, 'Der Krankenzug der Österreichischen Gesellschaft vom Roten Kreuze auf dem bulgarisch-serbischen Kriegsschauplatz', *Der Militärarzt* 48(2) (7 February 1914), 33–45, here 41. Cf. also the inspection report by the delegate of the International Red Cross, Dr Marval, *Bulletin International de la Croix-Rouge* 44(174) (April 1913), 145–63.

99 Dilger and Meyer, 'Kriegschirurgische Erfahrungen', 370; von Fényes, *Tagebuch eines Mannes vom Roten Kreuz*, 81; Noel Buxton, *The Wounded* (World Peace Foundation Pamphlet Series 3[2]) (February 1913), 4; Central-Comitee der Deutschen Vereine vom Roten Kreuz (ed.), *Beiträge zur Kriegsheilkunde aus den Hilfsunternehmungen der Deutschen Vereine vom Roten Kreuz während des Italienisch-türkischen Feldzug 1912 und des Balkankrieges 1912/13* (Berlin: Springer, 1914), 157–58. Among the wounded Bulgarian soldiers, 27 per cent came to a hospital only after a trip of up to five days on an oxcart and another two to three days by train: Hamburger, 'Der Sanitätsdienst im Balkankriege', 133. See also OeStA, HHStA P.A. XII 441. Liasse XLV/3: Balkankrieg, Evidenzbureau des k.u.k. Generalstabes: Tagesbericht, 7 February 1913: Bulgarien. Eindrücke von der bulgarischen Armee im Feldzuge 1912.

100 'The British Red Cross in the Balkan War', *The Lancet* 182(4,961) (26 July 1913), 235.

101 *Verhandlungen der Deutschen Gesellschaft für Chirurgie*, 214. See also Otto Polák, *Dojmy lékaře z Balkánské války* [Impressions of a Doctor from the Balkan Wars] (Prague: Vlastním nákladem J. Otto, 1913), 18.
102 Béla K. Király, 'East Central European Society and the Warfare in the Era of the Balkan Wars', in Király and Djordjević, *East Central European Society and the Balkan Wars*, 11.
103 Orlando Figes, *The Crimean War: A History* (New York: Metropolitan Books, 2012).
104 Cf. the sometimes differing figures in Ratković-Kostić, 'Srpska vojska u XIX. veku', 42; for 1885, see Jovanović, *Vlada Milana Obrenovića*, 254; Borislav Ratković, 'Mobilizacija srpske i turske vojske za prvi balkanski rat oktobra 1912 godine' [The Mobilization of the Serbian and the Turkish Army for the First Balkan War in October 1912], *Vojnoistorijski glasnik* 36(1) (1985), 200–202.
105 For Bulgaria, cf. the official figures in Ministerstvo na Voinata (ed.), *Voinata mezhdu Bălgariia i Turtsiia 1912–1913 god* [The War between Turkey and Bulgaria 1912–1913], Vol. I: *Podgotovka na voinata* [The Preparation for the War] (Sofia: Ministerstvo na Voinata, 1937), 566; Radko Dimitriev, *Treta armiia v Balkanskata voina 1912 godina* [The Third Army during the Balkan War 1912] (Sofia: Armeiski Voenno-izdatelski fond, 1922).
106 For Greece, see Helen Gardikas-Katsiadakis, 'The Balkan Wars 1912–13: Their Effect on the Everyday Life of Civilians', in Council of Europe, *Crossroads of European Histories*, 89–100, here 90.
107 Reder, 'Der Krankenzug der Österreichischen Gesellschaft vom Roten Kreuze', 38.
108 Oberst M. Gärtner, 'Über die Verwendung der Feldartillerie im Balkankriege 1912/13', *Streffleur's Militärische Zeitschrift* 55(7) (1914), 1,038; Oskar Hanasiewicz, 'Militärärztliche und militärische Eindrücke aus dem Balkankrieg 1912/13', *Streffleur's Militärische Zeitschrift* 55(7) (1914), 1,096.
109 Popov, *Spomeni*, 51–55; Nedialkov, *Chataldzha*, 33.
110 Kutschbach, *Die Serben im Balkankrieg*, 60, 137–39.
111 Ludwig Schliep, *Im Julifeldzug 1913 auf dem Balkan* (Berlin: Paetel, 1914), 65–66.
112 OeStA, HHStA P.A. XII 390. Liasse XLV/3: Balkankrieg: Generalkonsul Ritter von Zambaur an Berchtold, no. 27 geheim, Skutari, 10 March 1913: Fortgesetztes Bombardement der Stadt Skutari und dessen Folgen.
113 Colin Ross, *Im Balkankrieg* (Munich: Martin Mörikes Verlag, 1913), 91. Cf., similarly, Emanuel Škatula, *Válka na Balkáně* [The Balkan War] (Prague: Práva Lidu, 1913), 422.
114 German General Staff, *Kriegsgeschichtliche Einzelschriften, Heft 50: Der Balkankrieg 1912/13, Erstes Heft*, 151–52.
115 Exner, *Kriegschirurgie in den Balkankriegen*, 44, also 23.
116 Général Herr, *Sur le théâtre de la guerre des Balkans: Mon journal des routes (17. novembre–15. décembre 1912)* (Paris/Nancy: Berger-Levrault, 1913), 27; Rohde, *Unsere Gefechtsvorschriften*, 23; Dilger and Meyer, 'Kriegschirurgische Erfahrungen', 354, 364.
117 'Dnevnik na voinika Raicho Maidovski po vremen na voinata să Sărbiia' [The Diary of the Soldier Raicho Maidovski in the Time of the War with

Serbia], in Georgiev and Trifonov, *Istoriia na Bŭlgarite*, 202–4. Cf. also the diary of the Bulgarian orthodox priest Ivan Dochev, who had volunteered during the war, '*Saga za Balkanskata voina: Dnevnik na Sveshtenik Ivan Dochev*' [The Story of the Balkan War: The Diary of the Priest Ivan Dochev] (Sofia: Iztok-zapad, 2012), 55. Referring to reports from the Bulgarian military psychologist Spiridon Kazandzhiev, historian Snežana Dimitrova describes similar experiences: Snežana Dimitrova, 'Of Other Balkan Wars: Affective Worlds of Modern and Traditional (The Bulgarian Example)', *Perceptions. Journal of International Affairs* XVIII(2) (2013), 29–54, here 32. Cf. a similar description from the Greek war theatre in T.S. Hutchison, *An American Soldier under the Greek Flag at Bezanie* (Nashville, TN: Greek-American Publ. Comp., 1913), 165.

118 OeStA, HHStA P.A. XII 391. Von Herzfeld an Berchtold, no. 17/res. Adrianople, 17 April 1913: 2. Teil des Berichts über die Belagerung Adrianopels. Cf. the experiences of an Ottoman officer in 'Im Nachtangriff von Adrianopel', *Reichspost*, 14 November 1912.

119 Popov, *Spomeni*, 105–7.

120 'Die schwierige Lage der bulgarischen Armee', *Neue Freie Presse*, 24 November 1912.

121 Based on a report by General von der Goltz, who had been in charge of the reform of the Ottoman army: Politisches Archiv des Auswärtigen Amtes (PA AA), R 14 223 Akten betr. den Balkankrieg, Bd. 8: Kaiserl. Dt. Botschaft Pera, 7 November 1912, Privatbrief Frh. von Wangenheim.

122 Kutschbach, *Die Serben im Balkankrieg*, 130.

123 Azmanov, *Moiata epokha*, 86. Cf. also a similar report in OeStA, HHStA P.A. XII 441. Liasse XLV/3: Balkankrieg, Evidenzbureau des k.u.k. Generalstabes, Tagesbericht, 7 February 1913: Bulgarien. Eindrücke von der bulgarischen Armee im Feldzuge 1912; and Howell, *The Campaign in Thrace*, 157.

124 Ross, *Im Balkankrieg*, 79.

125 Stobart, *War and Women*, 80; Herbert F. Baldwin, *A War Photographer on Thrace: An Account of Personal Experiences during the Turco-Bulgarian War 1912* (London: T.F. Unwin, 1912), 150.

126 Škatula, *Válka na Balkáně*, 448. Similarly, the Hungarian medical assistant Ladislaus von Fényes spoke about a 'Freudenfest der Verheerung und Vernichtung' (a celebration of devastation and destruction): von Fényes, *Tagebuch eines Mannes vom Roten Kreuz*, 116.

127 Roger Chickering, 'Militärgeschichte als Totalgeschichte im Zeitalter des totalen Krieges', in Thomas Kühne and Benjamin Ziemann (eds), *Was ist Militärgeschichte?* (Paderborn: Schöningh, 2000), 301–14, here 307.

128 Richard C. Hall, *The Balkan Wars 1912–1913: Prelude to the First World War* (London/New York: Routledge, 2000), 131–32.

129 'Der Krieg machte sich nicht nur bis ins letzte Haus fühlbar, sondern er war geradezu der Alleinherrscher, dem das ganze Getriebe des Volks- und Staatslebens widerspruchslos diente.' Reder, 'Der Krankenzug der Österreichischen Gesellschaft vom Roten Kreuze', 33.

130 For Bulgaria, cf. *Fremdenblatt*, 11 October 1912; for Montenegro, OeStA, HHStA P.A. XII 385. Liasse XLV/3: Balkankrieg, k.u.k. Militärattaché in

Cetinje. Res. no. 110. Mobilisierung in Montenegro. Cetinje, 6 October 1912.
131 With the exception of Greece, this obviously did not reach very significant numbers. Austrian diplomats in the United States did not confirm the high figures of repatriates mentioned in the press. For Greece, they estimated that the number might have reached 6,000 to 7,000 persons, for the rest of the Balkan states no more than 2,000: OeStA, HHStA P.A. XII 387. Liasse XLV/3: Balkankrieg, Frh. v. Zwiedineck an Berchtold, no. XCIX-M, Washington, 5 December 1912, streng vertraulich; ibid., Abschrift eines Schreibens des k.u.k. Konsuls Kirchknopf an den k.u.k. Geschäftsträger, New York, 19 October 1912; ibid., Abschrift eines Schreibens des k.u.k. Generalkonsuls von Nuber an den k.u.k. Geschäftsträger, New York, 24 October 1912; ibid., Beilage ad Bericht ddo. Washington, 5 December 1912, no. XCIX-M. Bericht aus Chicago, 6 October 1912, no. 276, reservat; ibid., no. 288, res. Chicago, 29 October 1912.
132 OeStA, HHStA P.A. XII 385. Vizekonsul Fillunger an Berchtold, no. 73 geheim, Odessa, 12 October 1912.
133 Mehmet Hacısalihoğlu, 'Inclusion and Exclusion: Conscription in the Ottoman Empire', *Journal of Modern European History* 5 (2007), 264–86; Erik Jan Zürcher, 'The Ottoman Conscription System 1844–1914', *International Review of Social History* 43(3) (1998), 437–49; Fikret Adanır, 'Christliche Rekruten unter dem Halbmond: Zum Problem der Militärdienstpflicht für Nichtmuslime im spätosmanischen Reich', in Gerhard Grimm (ed.), *Von der Pruth-Ebene bis zum Gipfel des Ida: Festschrift zum 70. Geburtstag von Emanuel Turczynski* (Munich: Südosteuropa-Gesellschaft, 1989), 153–64.
134 Cf. in this sense also the memoirs of the Ottoman head of staff Mahmud Muhtar Paşa, *Meine Führung im Balkankriege*, 164. Neither did foreign analysts hold the Christian soldiers in any sense responsible for the bad performance of the Ottoman army during the war. Cf. OeStA, HHStA P.A. XII 441. Liasse XLV/3: Balkankrieg, Tagesbericht, 28 May 1913: Evb. NO 2000/28: Über die Ursachen der türkischen Niederlagen.
135 The Red Crescent, which had been formed in 1867 and was formally recognized in 1877, had previously promoted the idea of a nursing school for women; however, it was created only in the aftermath of the wars. See Zuhal Özaydın, 'Upper Social Strata Women and Nursing in Turkey', *Nursing History Review* 14 (2006), 161–74, here 163–64.
136 *Srpkinje u službi otadžbini i narodu za vreme Balkanskih ratova 1912 i 1913 g. kao i za vreme Svetskog rata od 1914–1920* [The Female Serb Serving the Fatherland and the People during the Balkan Wars 1912/13] (Belgrade: Jugoslovenska ženska sekcija Fidaka, 1933), 26. 'Narodna odbrana', the irredentist organization involved in political and paramilitary activities, before the outbreak of the war also urged Serbian women not only to fulfil their duties as nurses, but also to join the *Sokol* with its semi-military gymnastic activities and the rifle clubs: *Narodna odbrana* [People's Defence] (Belgrade: Nova štamparija Davidović, 1911), 25.
137 Eyal Ginio, 'Mobilizing the Ottoman Nation during the Balkan Wars (1912–1913): Awakening from the Ottoman Dream', *War in History* 12(2) (2005), 156–77, here 156.

138 Roger Chickering, 'Total War: The Use and Abuse of a Concept', in Manfred F. Boemke and Roger Chickering (eds), *Anticipating Total War: The German and American Experience, 1871–1914* (Cambridge: Cambridge University Press, 1999), 13–26; Stig Förster, 'Das Zeitalter des totalen Krieges, 1861–1945', *Mittelweg* 36(6) (1999), 12–29.

139 Stanoje Stanojević, *Srpsko-turski rat 1912 godine* [The Serbian-Turkish War] (Belgrade: Kon, 1928), 206. Similarly, Dušan Z. Putniković, *Ratni memoari. Knjiga prva: Rat sa Turcima 1912 god* [War Memories. First Book: The War with the Turks 1912] (Niš: Štamparija Sveti Car Konstantin, 1938), 5–6.

140 Cf. Ioannis Zelepos, *Die Ethnisierung griechischer Identität 1870–1912: Staat und private Akteure vor dem Hintergrund der 'Megali Idea'* (Munich: Oldenbourg, 2002). On textbooks and nationalism, cf. Christina Koulouri, *Dimensions idéologiques de l'historicité en Grèce (1834–1914): Les manuels scolaires d'histoire et de géographie* (Frankfurt/M.: Peter Lang, 1991).

141 Cf. Czar Ferdinand's order of the day to the army, no. 15, 6 September 1912, in Kosta Nikolov, *Treta otdelna Armiia v bălgaro-turskata voina prez 1912–1913 godini,* chast I: *Lozengradska operaciia* [The Third Army during the Bulgarian-Turkish War 1912–1913, Part I: The Lozengrad Operation] (Sofia: Voenen zhurnal, 1914), 152.

142 OeStA, HHStA P.A. XII 385. Liasse XLV/3: Balkankrieg, von Braun an Berchtold, no. 46, Athens, 26 October 1912: Manifestation der Allianz.

143 *Srpske Novine* 1229 (6 October 1912), 1.

144 Y. Doğan Çetinkaya, '"Revenge! Revenge! Revenge!" "Awakening a Nation" through Propaganda in the Ottoman Empire during the Balkan Wars (1912–1913)', in Hans-Lukas Kieser, Kerem Öktem and Maurus Reinkowski (eds), *World War I and the End of the Ottomans: From the Balkan Wars to the Armenian Genocide* (London/New York: Taurus, 2015), 77–102; Y. Doğan Çetinkaya, 'Illustrated Atrocity: The Stigmatisation of Non-Muslims through Images in the Ottoman Empire during the Balkan Wars', *Journal of Modern European History* 12(4) (2014), 460–78.

145 Muhtar Paşa, *Meine Führung im Balkankriege*, 120–21.

146 Jovan Cvijić, 'Balkanski rat i Srbija' [The Balkan War and Serbia], *Srpski Kniževni Glasnik* 29(9) (1912), 651–64; Aleksandar Belić, 'Srbija i stara Srbija' [Serbia and Old Serbia], *Ilustrovana ratna kronika* 2 (25 October [7 November] 1912), 2.

147 Editorial, *Ilustrovana ratna kronika* 1 (18 [31] October 1912), 1.

148 Cvijić, 'Balkanski rat i Srbija', 664.

149 Cf., in particular, Vladan Djordjević, *Die Albanesen und die Großmächte* (Leipzig: Hirzel, 1913). For similar tendencies among the Serbian public discourse at this time, see Holm Sundhaussen, 'Serbische Volksgeschichte: Historiker und Ethnologen im Kampf um Volk und Raum vom Ende des 19. bis zum Ende des 20. Jahrhunderts', in Manfred Hettling (ed.), *Volksgeschichten im Europa der Zwischenkriegszeit* (Göttingen: Vandenhoeck & Ruprecht, 2003), 301–25; Predrag J. Marković, *Ethnic Stereotypes: Ubiquitous, Local or Migrating Phenomena? The Serbian-Albanian Case* (Bonn: Michael-Zikic-Stiftung, 2003), 55–60. Differing from Sundhaussen in his argument, Marković emphasizes that even at that time more ambivalent pictures of the Albanians were present within the Serbian discourse.

150 As quoted in *Ilustrovana ratna kronika* 1 (18 [31] October 1912), 8.
151 Keith Brown, '"Wiping Out the Bulgarian Race": Hatred, Duty and National Self-Fashioning in the Second Balkan War', in Omer Bartov and Eric Weitz (eds), *Shatterzone of Empires: Coexistence and Violence in the German, Habsburg, Russian and Ottoman Borderlands* (Bloomington, IN: Indiana University Press, 2013), 298–317; this semi-racist perception was already evident during the late nineteenth century in the context of the Macedonian question. Cf. Adamantios Skordos, 'Das panslawische Feindbild im Griechenland des 19. und 20. Jahrhunderts', *Südost-Forschungen* 71 (2012), 76–105, here 91–94.
152 George W. Gawrych, 'The Culture and Politics of Violence in Turkish Society, 1903–1914', *Middle Eastern Studies* 22(3) (1986), 307–30; Elçin Kürsat-Ahlers, 'Die Brutalisierung von Gesellschaft und Kriegsführung im Osmanischen Reich während der Balkankriege (1903–1914)', in Andreas Gestrich (ed.), *Gewalt im Krieg: Ausübung, Erfahrung und Verweigerung von Gewalt in Kriegen des 20. Jahrhunderts* (Münster: Lit Verlag, 1996), 50–74. For children's literature, see Cüneyd Okay, 'The Impact of Balkan Wars on Children's Poetry in the Ottoman Empire', *Études balkaniques* 42(1) (2006), 89–99.
153 'România mandatară a civilizației Europene' [Romania's Mission for the European Civilization], *Gazeta ilustrată* 2 (6 July 1913), 1.
154 Cf., as one of the many examples, Putniković, *Ratni memoari*, 6, describing the feeling of 'revenge' when entering Kosovo in 1912.
155 Carl Schmitt, 'Totaler Feind, totaler Krieg, totaler Staat', in Carl Schmitt, *Positionen und Begriffe* (Berlin: Duncker & Humblot, 1994 [1937]), 268–273.
156 On poetry during the Balkan Wars, cf. Evelina Kelbecheva, 'Voina i tvorchestvo' [War and Creativity], *Godishnik na Sofiiskiia universitet Sv. Kliment Okhridski; Centăr po kulturoznanie* 80/81 (1987/88), 101–74, here 101–13. In a rather affirmative and uncritical way, see also Strahil Popov, 'Balkanskata voina i bălgarskata literatura' [The Balkan Wars and Bulgarian Literature], *Literaturna misăl* 27(7) (1983), 84–104.
157 Isidora Sekulić, 'Nekim našim omladincima' [To Some of Our Youngsters], *Slovenski jug*, 31(9) (1912), 242.
158 *Ilustrovana ratna kronika* 1 (18 October 1912), 1.
159 Stéphane Audoin-Rouzeau and Annette Becker, *14–18: Understanding the Great War* (New York: Hill and Wang, 2002), 116.
160 Rumjana Koneva, *Goliamata sreshta na bălgarskiia narod: Kulturata i predizvikatelstva na voinite 1912–1918 g.* [The 'Big Meeting' of the Bulgarian People: Culture and the Challenge of the Wars 1912–1918] (Sofia: Akad. Izdat. Prof. Marin Drinov, 1995); Kelbecheva, 'Voina i tvorchestvo', 101–74; Evelina Kelbecheva, 'Between Apology and Denial: Bulgarian Culture during World War I', in Ariel Roshwald and Richard Stites (eds), *European Culture in the Great War* (Cambridge: Cambridge University Press, 1999), 215–42.
161 Mihajlo Vojvodić, 'Naučnici Srbije i prvi balkanski rat' [Scientists from Serbia and the First Balkan War], in SANU, *Prvi Balkanski rat*, 33–51.

162 Cf. Ljubinka Trgovčević, *Naučnici Srbije i stvaranje Jugoslavije* [Scientists from Serbia and the Creation of Yugoslavia] (Belgrade: Narodna knjiga, 1986).
163 Cf., for the role of the Bulgarian Orthodox Church, Svetozăr Eldărov, *Pravoslavieto na voina: Bălgarska pravoslavna cărkva i voinite na Bălgariia 1878–1945* [Orthodoxy and War: The Bulgarian Orthodox Church and the War in Bulgaria] (Sofia: Voenno izdat., 2004), 163–69.
164 Cf. Ivan Ilchev, *Rodinata mi – prava ili ne! Vănshnopoliticheska propaganda na balkanskite stran 1821–1923* [My Homeland – Right or Wrong! Foreign Policy Propaganda in the Balkan Countries 1821–1923] (Sofia: Universitetsko izdat. Sv. Kliment Okhridski, 1996), 432–39.
165 Cf. the detailed rules and instructions for journalists in Bulgaria in René Puaux, *De Sofia à Tchataldja* (Paris: Perrin, 1913), 74–81. For the practice of applying these rules, cf. the Bulgarian historian Nikola Milev, who served in the censorship department during the war: Nikola Milev, *Pod stenite na Odrin* [At the Walls of Edirne] (Tărnovo: ASTA, 1993), 13. For Greece, cf. OeStA, HHStA P.A. XII 385. Liasse XLV/3: Balkankrieg, Frh. von Braun an Seine Excellenz Leopold Grafen von Berchtold, no. 41, F. vertraulich. Athens, 12 October 1912. For Serbia, ibid., von Ugron an Berchtold no. 112, Belgrad, 19 October 1912: Proklamation des Krieges in Serbien.
166 Cf., for Montenegro, OeStA, HHStA P.A. XII 412. Liasse XLV/5 Balkankrieg: Frh. von Giesl an Berchtold: Frage der Entsendung des k.u.k. Militär-Attachés in das montenegrinische Hauptquartier bei Beginn der Operationen, no. 78-B vertraulich, Cetinje, 6 October 1912. For Serbia and Greece, ibid., Stephan von Ugron an Berchtold, no. 264 Res.: Nichtzulassung fremder Militärattachés auf dem Kriegsschauplatz, Belgrad, 19 October 1912; ibid., K.u k. Kriegsministerium no. 3536, Vienna, 24 July 1913. For Bulgaria, ibid., Graf Tarnowski Telegram no. 250, Sofia, 20 October 1912. Only after many futile attempts did military attachés in the Ottoman Empire finally get access to the front lines; cf. ibid., Telegram Markgraf Pallavicini, Pera, 19 October 1912, no. 493; ibid., Telegram no. 529, 30 October: Akkreditierte Attachés sind nach mehreren Aufschüben mittlerweile auf Kriegsschauplatz aufgebrochen.
167 Fox, *The Balkan Peninsula*, 98. Fox concludes that 'the Balkan War probably will close the book of the war correspondent' (p. 107). Similarly, see von Mach, *Briefe aus dem Balkankrieg*, 74–76; Ross, *Im Balkankrieg*, 106–10.
168 Ute Daniel, 'Der Krim-Krieg 1853–1856 und die Entstehungskontexte moderner Kriegsberichterstattung', in Ute Daniel (ed.), *Augenzeugen: Kriegsberichterstattung vom 18. bis 21. Jahrhundert* (Göttingen: Vandenhoeck und Ruprecht, 2006), 40–67.
169 Reginald Rankin, *The Inner History of the Balkan War* (London: Constable and Comp, 1914), 61.
170 On the *Ilustrovana kronika rata*, cf. Milan Miljković, 'War Poetry and the Visual Culture of War: The Case of the Illustrated War Chronicle (Belgrade)', *Zeitschrift für Balkanologie* 52(2) (2016), 201–16, here 215.
171 Cf., on the regional and international coverage of the wars in film, Petar Kardjilov, 'The First Balkan War and the Cinematographer Chronicle Documentaries Filmed at the Balkan Fronts', *Études balkaniques* XLVIII(3)

(2013), 122–49; Dobrinka Parusheva, 'Svetlina vărchu voinata: Vizualno predstavjane na voinata v bălgarskata iliustrovana presa, kraja na XIX. i nachaloto na XX. vek' [Svetlina about the War: Visual Representation of the War in the Bulgarian Illustrated Press], *Bălgarska etnologiia* 3 (2014), 275–98, here 290, 295; Karl Kaser, 'Vizualizatsija na Balkanite: Balkanskite voini, Părvata Svetovna Voina i vizualnata modernizatsiia' [The Visualization of the Balkans: The Balkan Wars, the First World War and the Visual Modernization], *Bălgarska etnologiia* 3 (2014), 332–51.

172   Cf., for Serbia, Jaša Tomić, *Rat na Kosovu i Staroj Srbiji 1912 godine* [The War in Kosovo and Old Serbia in the Year 1912] (Novi Sad: dr-a Svetozara Miletića, 1913 [reprinted 1999]), 54–59; Mišić, *Moje uspomene*, 271. For Bulgaria, cf., among many others, the leading politician Simeon Radev, *Ot triumf do tragediia* [From Triumph to Tragedy] (Sofia: Strelets, 2003), 11. For a military source, cf. Nikolov, *Treta otdelna Armiia*, 21, who mentions an 'unexpected enthusiasm' among the recruited soldiers.

173   See the examples from the press in Weber, *Die Balkankriege*, 48.

174   On Fényes, cf. Gábor Demeter, 'The Balkan Wars 1912–1913 in the Hungarian Press, Military Literature and Personal Memoirs', unpublished manuscript.

175   Von Fényes, *Tagebuch eines Mannes vom Roten Kreuz*, 46; Major Felix Wagner, 'Meine Eindrücke vom thrazischen Kriegsschauplatz und von der türkischen Armee im Zweiten Balkankrieg', *Streffleur's Militärische Zeitschrift* 55(2) (1914), 258.

176   The term refers to the alleged overall euphoria in Germany regarding the war when fighting started in August 1914. The assumption of this 'August experience', long taken for granted in the research literature, has now been convincingly questioned by several authors. Cf., for France, Jean-Jacques Becker, *Comment les français sont entrés dans la guerre* (Paris: Presses de la Fondation Nationale des Sciences Politiques, 1977); for Germany, cf., among others, the study of local reactions to the war by Benjamin Ziemann, *Front und Heimat: Ländliche Kriegserfahrungen im südlichen Bayern 1914–1923* (Essen: Klartext, 1997).

177   Lancelot L. Farrar, Jr., 'Aggression Versus Apathy: The Limits of Nationalism during the Balkan Wars 1912–1913', *East European Quarterly* 37(3) (2003), 257–80.

178   Hochwaechter, *Mit den Türken in der Front*, 3.

179   Cf. the Austrian reports from Trapezunt, Damaskus and Adana, OeStA, HHStA P.A. XII 385. Liasse XLV/3: Balkankrieg, v. Moricz an Berchtold, no. 4648, Trapezunt, 13 October 1912; ibid., Ranzi an Berchtold, no. 55/res. Damaskus, 14 October 1912; ibid., 386, K.u.K. Vice-Consulat d'Autriche-Hongrie J. no. 223, Adana, 24 October 1912: Vertraulicher Bericht; ibid., P.A. XII 411. Liasse XLV/V: Balkankrieg; Generalkonsul von Moricz berichtet über das Meeting für den Krieg, Z 39, Trapezunt, 7 October 1912; ibid., Generalkonsul von Moricz, berichtet über die Stimmung, Z 42, Trapezunt, 16 October 1912; ibid., Consul Dr Ranzi: Eindruck der türkischen Niederlagen auf die hiesige Bevölkerung, no. 65/res. Damascus, 15 November 1912.

180 While the reports from Üsküb/Skopje and Janina found an 'indisputable pro-war mood' (unleugbare kriegsfreudige Stimmung), particularly among the Albanian population and the younger Turkish officers, diplomats from Monastir/Bitola reported that even among the Muslim population hardly any spontaneous or more profound enthusiasm was perceivable ('Aber selbst unter den Mohamedanern kann von einem spontanen und tiefgreifenden Enthusiasmus nicht gesprochen werden'): OeStA, HHStA P.A. XII 385. Heimroth an Berchtold, no. 114, Üsküb, 8 October 1912; ibid., 385, Halla an Berchtold, no. 121, Monastir, 13 October 1912, vertraulich: Die Mobilisierung; ibid., P.A. XXXVIII Konsulate 384. Janina 1911–1917, Bilinski an Berchtold, Eindruck der Mobilisierungsnachricht, no. 79 vertraulich, Janina, 7 October 1912.

181 'Die feurigen Reden, die einige Studenten hielten, um die Menge zu Schivio-Rufen zu begeistern, fanden keinen Widerhall. Trotzdem bemerkte man nie Unwilligkeit über den Krieg. Es war in den letzten Jahren tüchtig gearbeitet worden, der Armee im besonderen hatte man große Sorgfalt gewidmet.' Adolf Vischer, *An der serbischen Front: Erlebnisse eines Arztes auf dem serbisch-türkischen Kriegsschauplatz 1912* (Basel: Spittler, 1913), 19.

182 OeStA, HHStA P.A. XII 385. Liasse XLV/3: Balkankrieg, k.u.k. Militärattaché in Belgrad, Res. no. 197, 6 October 1912: Die Stimmung in Belgrad; ibid., von Ugron an Berchtold, no. 10g.B., Belgrad, 15 October 1912; ibid., k.u.k. Militärattaché in Belgrad Res. no. 232: Die Stimmung in Belgrad und die Stellung der Armee im Lande: 'daß von einer kriegerischen Stimmung oder von einer besonderen Begeisterung in der Bevölkerung nicht gesprochen werden kann'; ibid., Stephan von Ugron an Berchtold, no. 113.B., Belgrad, 20 October 1912, Vorlage zweier Notizen des Gerenten des k.u.k. Vize-Konsulates in Nisch. Similarly, see the report by the German Embassy: PA AA, R 14 218 Akten betr. den Balkan-Krieg 1912/13, Bd. 3: Kaiserl. Dt. Gesandtschaft für Serbien no. 62 an S.E. Reichskanzler Bethmann-Hollweg, 4 December 1912.

183 PA AA, R 14 218 Akten betr. den Balkan-Krieg 1912/13, Bd. 1: Kaiserl. Dt. Ges. für Serbien no. 69 an S.E. Reichskanzler Bethmann-Hollweg, 20 December 1912; ibid., R 14 220 Bd. 5, 16 October 1912.

184 OeStA, HHStA P.A. XII 438. Liasse XLV/15: Balkankrieg, Gerent Ledinegg an Seine Excellenz Leopold Grafen von Berchtold, no. 12, Antivari, 22 June 1913: Militärisches-Teilweise Mobilisierung. Already in late November 1912, the Austrian military attaché from Cetinje reported that while enthusiasm for the war among the population had not disappeared, it was obvious that it had waned considerably. He even reported on deserting soldiers. Cf. ibid. 386. K.u.k. Militärattaché in Cetinje, no. 237 Res. Politische Situation in Montenegro, Cetinje, 26 November 1912; similarly, ibid., 387, k.k. Bezirkshauptmannschaft Res. 1594: Montenegro, Krieg mit der Türkei, Cattaro, 5 December 1912.

185 'Dokumentalen razkaz za balkanskata voina', 254. For Sofia, cf. also OeStA, HHStA P.A. XII 385. Liasse XLV/3: Tarnowski an Berchtold, no. 77 A-B, Sofia, 12 October 1912, speaking of 'calm determination' rather than 'noisy euphoria'. Similar also is the report in the *Neue Freie Presse*,

8 November 1912 ('Der Tag der Mobilisierung in Bulgarien'), which saw 'no noise, no joy, but determination'.
186 Gardikas-Katsiadakis, 'The Balkan Wars 1912-1913', 90.
187 Nikola Ivanov, *Balkanskata voina 1912/13* [The Balkan Wars 1912/13], Vol. II (Sofia: Pečatn. na Armeiskiia voenno-izd. fond, 1924), 113. On rumours about mutinies during the spring of 1913, see also G.K. Abadzhiev, *Deistviia na 1. Brigada ot 5.p. Dunavska diviziia v Voinite prez 1912–1913 god* [The Military Engagement of the 5th Danube Division during the Wars of 1912–1913] (Sofia: Pechatnitsa na Armeiiskia voenno-izdatelstvo fond, 1925), 58. Cf. also M. Veleva, 'Vojnishkite buntove prez 1913 g.' [Military Uprisings in 1913], *Istoricheski pregled* 14(1) (1958), 14–24; Richard C. Hall, '"The Enemy Is Behind Us": The Morale Crisis in the Bulgarian Army during the Summer of 1918', *War in History* 11(2) (2004), 209–19, here 210. On the deteriorating spirit among the soldiers, cf. also the diary of Nikola Dodov, who reports from censored letters by Bulgarian soldiers: Dodov, *Dnevnik*, 71, 87.
188 Cf. M. Arnaudova, 'Balkanskata voina v spomenite na Georgi Popaianov i Petko Chorbadzhiev (Rosen)' [The Balkan Wars in the Memory of Georgi Popaianov and Petko Chorbadzhiev (Rosen)], *Izvestiia na dărzhavnite archive* 47 (1984), 166–69, where one of the two witnesses, himself a volunteer, describes his depressed feelings when confronted with the many dead and dying soldiers both on the battlefield and in the field hospitals. Cf. also the diary of the Bulgarian priest Ivan Dochev, who had great patriotic passion at the beginning of the war and whose writing, while not losing its patriotic undertone, becomes more and more sober: *Saga za Balkanskata voina*, passim.
189 Čedomir Popov, *Istorija srpskog naroda* [History of the Serbian People], Vol. 6/1, *Od Berlinskog kongresa do ujedinjenja* [From the Congress of Berlin to Unification] (Belgrade: Srpska književna zadruga, 2000), 383, 401.
190 Ignjatović, 'Srpsko ratno hirurško iskustvo, IV. deo', 217; Ratković-Kostić, 'Srpska vojska u XIX. veku', 39. Cf. the slightly differing figures of 36,500 dead and 55,000 wounded in both wars in James M.B. Lyon, '"A Peasant Mob": The Serbian Army on the Eve of the Great War', *The Journal of Military History* 61(3) (1997), 481–503, here 484; for Bulgaria, see Hall, *The Balkan Wars*, 135; for Greece, see André Andréades et al., *Les effets économiques et sociaux de la guerre en Grèce* (Paris/New Haven, CT: Presses Univ. de France, 1928), 84. For the Ottoman army, Erickson calculated 50,000 killed in action, 75,000 casualties of diseases as well as 100,000 wounded; Erickson, *Defeat in Detail*, 329.
191 Hall, *The Balkan Wars*, 90.
192 Cf. the description by the Austrian medical doctor Hanasiewicz, who observed that in the streets one could find wounded and refugees everywhere, a sight that influenced the general mood in a negative way; Hanasiewicz, 'Militärärztliche und militärische Eindrücke', 1,096.
193 Cf. the Ottoman petitions against Greek and Bulgarian persecutions: OeStA, HHStA P.A. XII 411. Liasse XLV/V: Balkankrieg, Ambassade Impérial Ottomane, Note verbale no. 38150, 31 December 1912; ibid., 387, Pallavicini an Berchtold, no. 96, Constantinople, 26 December 1912:

Vorlage einer Pforten-Notiz: Bulgarische Greuel in Dedeagatsch und Cavalla; ibid., P.A. XII 438. Liasse XLV/15: Balkankrieg, Ambassade Impérial Ottomane: Note verbale no. 39306, 17 July 1913; ibid., Ambassade Impériale Ottomane, Note verbale no. 39431, Vienna, 20 August 1913; ibid., Ambassade Impériale Ottomane, Note verbale no. 39432, Vienna, 22 August 1913. For Bulgarian petitions concerning Serbian, Greek and Ottoman atrocities, see ibid., 438, Tarnowski an Berchtold, no. 47-C, Sofia, 14 August 1913: Notizen des bulg. Auswärtigen Amtes über griechische, serbische und türkische Grausamkeiten gegen Bulgaren; ibid., Tarnowski an Berchtold, no. 48 C, Sofia, 23 August 1913: Beilage; ibid., Légation Royale de Bulgarie: Note verbale no. 462, Vienna, 21 July 1913. Against the Serbs, ibid., Légation Royale de Bulgarie, Note verbale no. 429, Vienna, 21 July 1913. From the Serbian side against Bulgaria, ibid., Königl. Serbische Gesandtschaft an das Kaiserliche und Königliche Ministerium des Aeusseren, Vienna, 8/21 July 1913: Promemoria. For Greek protests against Bulgaria, see, for example, ibid., Frh. von Mittag an von Berchtold, no. 66, Sofia, 12 October 1913: Enquete-Resultate über die Vorgänge in Doxate.

194 On the Ottoman side, cf., among others, Comité de publication des atrocités balcaniques, *Les atrocités des coalisés Balkaniques no. 1* (Constantinople, 1913). For a semi-official Ottoman publication, cf. Jean Ruby, *La Guerre d'Orient et les Atrocités des États Balkaniques: Rapport et documents* ([no place], 1912). Several documentations were exchanged between the Bulgarian and the Greek sides during the Second Balkan War: Comité de publication des atrocités balcaniques, *Atrocités bulgares en Macédoine* (Athens, 1913); idem, *Les cruautés bulgares 1912–1913* (Athens, 1914); idem, *The Crimes of Bulgaria in Greece* (Washington, DC, 1914); Prof. Dr L. Miletitch, *Atrocités Grecques en Macédoine pendant la Guerre Greco-Bulgare* (Sofia, 1913). And as a response to the Greek accusations, *Réponse a la brochure des professeurs des universités d'Athènes 'Atrocités Bulgare en Macédoine' par les professeurs de l'université de Sophia* (Sofia, 1913). Bulgarian Women's Associations also took part in this media war against their Greek counterparts: OeStA, HHStA P.A. XII 438. Liasse XLV/15: Balkankrieg: Les voleurs crient 'au voleur'. Réponse des femmes bulgares à la prostestation des femmes greques contre les atrocités bulgares. Sofia, 24 November 1913.

195 Cf., for example, OeStA, HHStA P.A. XII 438. Telegramm no. 1306, Adrianople, 7 September 1913 signed by inhabitants of local Muslim villages from Western Thrace; ibid., 386, Bilinski an Seine Excellenz Leopold Grafen von Berchtold, no. 91, Janina, 23 November 1912: Griechische Greueltaten an der mohamedanischen und wallachischen Bevölkerung; ibid., 388, Kral an Berchtold, no. 5, 8 January 1913: Untaten bulgarischer und griechischer Banden im Sandžak Drama, reporting a petition of the local population about atrocities; ibid., 392, Mensdorff an Berchtold, no. 50-D, London, 23 May 1913: Eingabe der albanesischen Delegierten über von Griechen begangene Grausamkeiten. From Greek communities against Bulgarian atrocities, see ibid., P.A. XXXVIII Konsulate 374: Adrianopel 1906–1917, M. von Nettovich an Berchtold: Intervention griechischer Bewohner wegen der von den Bulgaren

begangenen Greueltaten, no. 79, Adrianople, 30 October 1913; ibid., von Herzfeld an Berchtold: Unterdrückung der griechischen Bevölkerung, Z 32./P., Adrianople, 16 April 1914.
196 Not by chance, his war reports, forgotten and ignored for decades, were reprinted during the Yugoslav wars of the 1990s: Leo Trotzki, *Die Balkankriege 1912/13* (Essen: Arbeiterpresse-Verlag, 1996 [1926]). On Trotsky as a war correspondent, cf. also Maria Todorova, 'War and Memory: Trotsky's War Correspondence from the Balkan Wars', *Perceptions. Journal of International Affairs* XVIII(2) (2013), 5–28.
197 Von Mach, *Briefe aus dem Balkankrieg*, 72–76. Suspicious for his obviously often fabricated information in particular is Hermenegild Wagner, war correspondent for the Vienna based *Reichspost*. Cf. the English edition of his wartime memories: Hermenegild Wagner, *With the Victorious Bulgarians* (New York/Boston, MA: Houghton Mifflin Co., 1913). For a careful discussion of the correspondents' information on atrocities, cf. Weber, *Die Balkankriege*, 25–35, 44.
198 Cf. Carl Pauli, *Kriegsgreuel. Erlebnisse im türkisch-bulgarischen Krieg 1912: Nach den Berichten von Mitkämpfern und Augenzeugen bearbeitet* (Minden: Wilhelm Köhler o. J., [1913]); Leo Freundlich, *Albaniens Golgotha: Anklageakten gegen die Vernichter des Albanervolks* (Vienna: J. Roller, 1913), included also in the recently edited enlarged correspondence: Leo Freundlich, *Die Albanische Korrespondenz: Agenturmeldungen aus Krisenzeiten Juni 1913–August 1914*, ed. Robert Elsie (Munich: Oldenbourg, 2012). See also Carlo Villavicenzo, *Im belagerten Scutari: Nach Aufzeichnungen der Skutariner Jesuiten* (Vienna: Verlag d. Kongregationszeitschr., 1913).
199 Carnegie Endowment for International Peace, *Report of the International Commission to Inquire into the Causes and Conduct of the Balkan Wars* (Washington, DC: The Endowment, 1914). For the background of the commission, see Nadine Akhund, 'The Two Carnegie Reports: From the Balkan Expedition of 1913 to the Albanian Trip of 1921', *Balkanologie* 14(1–2) (2012), 1–17, http://balkanologie.revues.org/index2365.html (accessed 1 April 2014).
200 Cf., for example, PA AA, R 14 222, Dt. Botschaft Pera an Reichskanzler Bethmann-Hollweg, 24 October 1912; OeStA, HHStA P.A. XII 388. Prochaska an Berchtold, no. 5, Prizren, 30 January 1913: Die Kämpfe in Luma, claiming that due to the situation there is hardly any chance of getting unbiased information.
201 OeStA, HHStA P.A. XII 388. Graf Mensdorff an Berchtold no. 11 G, London, 31 January 1913: Interpellation im englischen Unterhause über Grausamkeiten am Balkan; ibid., 389, Graf Mensdorff an Berchtold, no. 16 F, London, 15 February 1913; ibid., 390, Mensdorff an Berchtold, no. 21, London, 3 March 1913: Massacres von Albanesen durch serbische Truppen.
202 The Austrian Foreign Ministry, for example, suggested to its ministers that news about Serbian atrocities should be made public, but without giving the impression that they were based on Austrian sources: OeStA, HHStA P.A. XII. 386. Liasse XLV/3: Balkankrieg 386, Für den Einlauf, Vienna, 19 November 1912.

203 The Austrian consul in Macedonia, Heimroth, for example, time and again sent his own assistants in the field to check the news on atrocities as closely as possible before reporting to Vienna: OeStA, HHStA P.A. XII. 386. Telegramm an von Ugron no. 2703, Belgrad, 15 November 1912, or ibid., 389, Heimroth an Berchtold, no. 26, Uesküb, 9 February 1913: Gausamkeiten der Serben gegen Albaner. Hesitating to confirm Serbian atrocities, see, for example, ibid., 388, Ledinegg an Berchtold, vertraulich, Antivari, 10 January 1913. For similar reluctant British diplomats, see ibid., 390, Mensdorff an Berchtold, no. 21, London, 3 March 1913: Massacres von Albanesen durch serbische Truppen. The French consulate in August 1912 sent its own mission to prove Greek accusations of Bulgarian atrocities, coming to the conclusion that without any doubt cruelties were committed by the regular army, but on a much lesser scale than claimed: ibid., 438, Telegramm Baron Braun, no. 463, Athens, 3 August 1912. The French correspondent Henry Barby, generally sympathetic to the Serbian cause, is biased when he rejects Austrian reports on violence by the Serbian army as unfounded 'alleged cruelties' ('prétendues atrocités'); cf. Henry Barby, *La Guerre des Balkans: Les victoires serbes* (Paris: Bernard Grasset, 1913), 255.

204 OeStA, HHStA 390 Ugron an Berchtold, no. 67 A-C, vertraulich, Belgrad, 27 March 1913: Mitteilungen des italienischen Militärattachés über die serbischen Greueltaten. With regard to Bulgarian accusations against the Greek army, see ibid., 438, Kral an Berchtold, no. 150, Salonich, 9 August 1913: Eingabe des bulgarisch-katholischen Bischofs für Mazedonien an einige Grossmächte; ibid., P.A. XXXVIII Konsulate 374: Adrianopel 1906–1917, von Herzfeld an Berchtold: Ansiedelung mohamedanischer Flüchtlinge und Lage der griechischen Bevölkerung, Z 31./P., Adrianople, 8 April 1914.

205 Cf., for example, the report by the consulate officer in Kirkilisse on the Bulgarian occupation of the district, OeStA, HHStA. P.A. XII Türkei 389, Pallacivini an Berchtold, no. 7 F, Constantinople, 6 February 1913: Die Bulgaren in Kirkilisse and of the Austrian Vicekonsul in Serres; ibid., 438, Kral an Berchtold, no. 114, Salonich, 30 June 1913: Vorlage eines Berichts des k.u.k. Vizekonsuls in Serres.

206 The reliability of a long report by the Italian bishop Miedia about Serbian violence against the Albanian and Muslim population in Üsküb/ Skopje, for example, was discussed in detail by the Austrian consulate, who concluded it to be well founded at least in the general picture it conveyed: OeStA, HHStA., P.A. XII Türkei 389, Dr von Heimroth an Seine Excellenz Leopold Grafen von Berchtold, no. 26, Uesküb, 9 February 1913: Grausamkeiten der Serben gegen Albaner; cf. also the report by a 'nationally minded' Bulgarian priest on Bulgarian (!) violence, ibid., 387, Kral an Berchtold, no. 209, Salonich, 17 December 1912: Die bulgarischen Greuel im Inneren; reports by railway servants, ibid., 388, Kral an Berchtod, no. 7, Salonich, 7 January 1913.

207 Cf., for example, the *Daily Chronicle* of 12 November 1912 with regard to Serbian violence against Albanians; similarly, with regard to Serbian politics against the Muslim population in Macedonia, see OeStA, HHStA

P.A. XII 386. Türkei Liasse XLV/3: Balkankrieg, von Ugron an Berchtold, no. 136, E Belgrad, 15 November 1912: Nachrichten aus Üsküb; and with regard to the Bulgarian politics, ibid., Kral an Berchtold, no. 187, Salonich, 23 November 1912: Greueltaten der Bulgaren auf dem flachen Lande Mazedoniens.

208 Theodora Dragostinova recently stressed for the Bulgarian-Greek the continuity of ethnic homogenization. The process started before the Balkan Wars, accelerated during the war and was 'completed' after its end. Theodora Dragostinova, 'Continuity vs. Radical Break: National Homogenization in the Greek-Bulgarian Borderlands before and after the Balkan Wars', *Journal of Genocide Research* 18(4) (2016), 405–26.

209 Usually complaints about attacks on Muslim villages, besides other acts of violence, include the general information that 'women and young girls were violated'. OeStA, HHStA P.A. XII 390, von Päzel an Berchtold, no. 14, Prizren, 9 March 1913: Aeusserung zu einigen, in einem Memorandum des Prizrener katholischen Erzbischofs angeführten Greueltaten; ibid., von Heimroth an von Ugron in Belgrad, no. 22/po. Uesküb, 18 March 1913: Protest des franz. Gesandten wg. serbischer Übergriffe im Kaza Gilan Anfang März; ibid.: k.u.k. Militärattaché in Cetinje, 17 March 1913, Z. 1324: Grausamkeiten montenegrinischer Truppen; ibid., 391, Generalkonsul Kral an Berchthold, no. 71, Salonich, 21 April 1913: Die Zwangskonversionen der türkischen Landbevölkerung durch die Bulgaren: Bericht aus Cavalla; ibid., 389, Heimroth an Berchtold, no. 26 streng vertr., Uesküb, 9 February 1913: Grausamkeiten der Serben gegen Albaner; ibid., 413, S.M.S. Kais. u. König. Maria Theresia. Res. no. 410. Missionsbericht für die Zeit vom 10 bis 12 November 1912, Salonich, 13 November 1912 on the Bulgarian occupation of Salonika; OeStA, HHStA P.A. XII 206. Berichte 1912 VII–XII, 1913 I–IX: Markgraf Pallavicini an Berchtold: Beschwerde des ökumenischen Patriarchates über Ausschreitungen der bulgarischen Okkupationstruppen gegen die griechisch-orthodoxe Bevölkerung, no. 34, Jeniköy, 19 June 1913; ibid., P.A. XXXXVIII Konsulate 416. Saloniki 1913–1915: Generalkonsul Kral an Berchtold, Prekäre Lage der Land- und Stadtbevölkerung im Inneren Mazedoniens, Zl. 104, Salonich, 23 June 1913 on sexual violence by the Bulgarian army in Serres; ibid., P.A. XXXVIII Konsulate 397. Monastir 1912–1914, 1916: Vizekonsul Zitkovszky an Berchtold: Serbische Greuel, no. 142, 13 December 1913; for a British account, cf. also Cpt. Boyle's detailed report on his trip to Thracian villages shortly after the war had ended, in which he wrote about rape, though this sounds stereotypical and the results hard to verify: The National Archive, Royal Navy (TNA, RN): ADM 116/1193, Cpt. Boyle to Sir F. Elliot, Athens, 5 August 1913.

210 The many reports on mutilation, for example, were often told in semantic stereotypes of the traditional 'Türkengreuel' ('Turkish atrocities'), but nevertheless were confirmed from time to time by foreign medical doctors, who were confronted with injuries obviously resulting from acts of mutilation. Cf. OeStA, HHStA P.A. XII. 386. Tarnowski an Berchtold, no. 84 A–E, Sofia, 5 November 1912: Zum Kriege.

211 Stefan Sotiris Papaioannou, *Balkan Wars between the Lines: Violence and Civilians in Macedonia 1912–1918*, Ph.D. dissertation (Maryland: University of Maryland, 2012), 122–39.
212 Referring to a 'highly reliable' Bulgarian priest, the Austrian consul-general in Saloniki reported 'an intimate cooperation' between the regular army and the 'bands' in Bulgarian-occupied Macedonia in early 1913, thereby making practically all official orders to restrict the activities of the bands irrelevant. OeStA, HHStA 389, Kral an Berchtold, no. 30, Salonica, 5 February 1913: Atrocitäten und Plünderungen der bulgarischen Banden während des Krieges.
213 PA AA, R 14 276, Bericht des österreichischen Generalkonsuls in Üsküb, 24 October 1913; similar reports in ibid., R 14 221, Akten betr. den Balkankrieg, Bd. 4: Dt. Residentur Cetinje, 20 October 1912; ibid., R 14 222, Akten betr. die Balkan-Kriege 1912/13, Bd. 7: Kaiserl.-Dt. Konsulat Saloniki, no. 3209, 25 October 1912.
214 'If isolated cases of crimes have occurred', as the Serbian government wrote in response to an intervention by the British government, 'the offenders have been punished … in the same manner as all offences committed by the members of comitadji bands which could not be controlled by the military authorities'. OeStA, HHStA P.A. XII. 389. Liasse XLV/3: Balkankrieg 389, Mensdorff an Berchtold, no. 19, London, 28 February 1913: Beilage Memorandum des Foreign Office. Similarly, for the Bulgarian position, Radev, *Ot triumf do tragediia*, 67; see also Bulgarian Foreign Minister Stanchoff in a conversation with the Austrian consul-general in Saloniki, OeStA, HHStA P.A. XII 387. Liasse XLV/3: Balkankrieg 387, Kral an Berchtold, no. 197, Salonich, 5 December 1912: Gespräch mit Minister Stanchoff. The Greek government rejected all complaints about acts of violence against the civilian population, explaining the few it could not deny as pure 'revenge' for the many 'Turkish atrocities': ibid., 388: Telegramm Baron Braun, no. 1275, Athens, 7 January 1913.
215 OeStA, HHStA P.A. XII 386. Kral an Berchtold, no. 188, vertraulich, Salonica, 22 November 1912: Die Ereignisse von Serres; ibid., 390, Legationssekretär Bilinski an Seine Excellenz Leopold Grafen von Berchtold, no. 24, Janina, 27 March 1913: Situation in Janina; ibid., 414 P.A. XII. Türkei Liasse XLV/5: Balkankrieg, Kral an Berchtold Zl 213/ vertraulich: Die Zustände in Cavalla.
216 OeStA, HHStA P.A. XII 386. Politischer Gegenstand no. 126, Üsküb, 18 November 1912. Similarly, from the Macedonian theatre of war, the Austrian consul in Saloniki, Kral, reported with respect to the Bulgarian army that despite some orders forbidding arbitrary violence against civilians, owing to the 'intimate cooperation' between the regular army and the irregular forces, the army had in no way tried to stop the activities of the bands: ibid., Kral an Berchtold, no. 30, Salonica, 5 February 1913: Atrocitäten und Plünderungen der bulgarischen Banden während des Krieges. A French fact-finding commission came to the conclusion that 'Bulgarian' atrocities against the Greek population, however exaggerated they may have been in local reports, had been organized 'in a systematic

way' by the army: ibid., 438 P.A. XII. Türkei Liasse XLV/15: Balkankrieg, Telegramm Baron Braun, no. 463, Athens, 3 August 1912.
217 OeStA, HHStA. P.A. XII 390. Heimroth an von Ugron, no. 12/pa, Üsküb, 18 March 1913.
218 Cf., for example, Andrija Jovičević, *Dnevnik iz balkanskih ratova* [Diary from the Balkan Wars] (Belgrade: Službeni list SRJ, 1996), 125; Azmanov, *Moiata epokha*, 95; Dodov, *Dnevnik*, 32; Stefan Khristov Kamburov, *Edin mnogo dălg păt: Dnevnik na Stoian Khristov Kamburov* [A Very Long Way: The Diary of Stoian Khristov Kamburov] (Sofia: Pres izdatelstvo, 2003), 17, who writes about paramilitary volunteers (*opălchentsi*) burning down Muslim houses and 'taking away what they could carry' of what had been left behind by the fleeing Turkish population; similarly, see Nikolov, *Treta otdelna Armiia*, 129.
219 Papaioannou, *Balkan Wars between the Lines*, 128–32.
220 OeStA, HHStA P.A. XII 385. Konsul Halla an von Berchtold, no. 130 vertraulich, Monastir, 30 October 1912: Die Verteidigung Monastirs; ibid., 386, Generalkonsul Kral an von Berchtold, no. 189, Salonich, 26 November 1912: Bericht der k.u.k. Consularagentie in Cavalla vom 8.d.M. Zl: 343 über die Ereignisse in Drama und Cavalla.
221 Jörg Baberowski, 'Einleitung: Ermöglichungsräume exzessiver Gewalt', in Jörg Baberowski and Gabriele Metzler (eds). *Gewalträume: Soziale Ordnungen im Ausnahmezustand*, Frankfurt/M. 2012, 7–27.
222 Cf. the fighting around Ioannina in November 1912, about which Austrian observers reported that 'andartes and the village population' committed atrocities against the local Muslim and Wallachian population. OeStA, HHStA P.A. XII 385. Bilinski an Berchtold, no. 89, Janina, 17 November 1912: Zur Situation. Here it is reported that paramilitaries *and* the 'local population committed awful crimes against soldiers and the unarmed Muslim population'. See also the report by the German major in the Ottoman army Günter to the German Foreign Office in PA AA, R 14 225 Akten betr. den Balkan-Krieg, Bd. 10: 22/23 October 1912. On violence committed by Greek andartes, cf. also the diary by French consul Guy Chantepleure (pseudonym of Jeanne-Caroline Violet-Dussap), who was in the city during the siege: Guy Chantepleure, *La ville assiégée: Janina Octobre 1912–Mars 1913* (Paris: Calmann-Lévy, 1913), 230.
223 Kamburov, for example, describes in his diary how local Bulgarian peasants burned the Ottoman *tefter* (register) after their village had been 'liberated' by Bulgarian forces, thus preventing any claim on property by the fleeing Turkish population. Kamburov, *Edin mnogo dălg păt*, 23. Reports about the local Serbian population from Mitrovica distributing the land of their Muslim neighbours among themselves can be found in OeStA, HHStA P.A. XII 391. v. Uron an Berchtold, no. 82 a-B, Belgrad, 15 April 1913: Militärische und politische Berichte aus Nisch und Mitrovitza, Beilage.
224 Cf. examples from the following reports: PA AA, R 14 222, Kaisl.-Dt. Konsulat Saloniki, 25 October 1912; ibid., Kaisl. Gesandtschaft Sofia, no. 70, Abschrift eines Berichts des öster. Konsuls Herzfeld in Adrianopel.

225 Cf., for example, the report on the city of Monastir in OeStA, HHStA P.A. XII 389. Atrocitäten und Plünderungen der bulgarischen Banden während des Krieges; similarly, for Monastir and Üsküb, ibid., 386, Halla an Berchtold, no. 137, Monastir, 25 November 1912: Die Auslieferung Monastirs an die Serben; ibid., 386, Politischer Bericht Dr Heimroth, no. 125, Üsküb, 18 November 1912; ibid., 388, Halla an Berchtold, no. 6, vertraulich Monastir, 17 January 1913: Verwüstung der mohamedanischen Distrikte des Vilajets Monastir. Under the pretext of collecting weapons, as reported from the Greek and Bulgarian conquest of Salonica, soldiers 'being guided by local vagabonds' entered the houses in the city's Turkish and Jewish quarter, plundering whatever they could find. Ibid., Kral an Berchtold, no. 183, Salonica, 17 November 1912: Die Ausschreitungen der bulgarischen und griechischen Truppen. The Austrian consul in Adrianople reported his own observations that after the Bulgarian conquest of the city, 'the mob' together with soldiers and *komitadži* had plundered the houses of beds, other furniture and 'even a piano'. Ibid., 391, Tarnowski an Berchtold, no. 27, E, Sofia, 14 April 1913; Beilage Dr Max von Herzfeld, no. 1/re Adrianople, 9 April 1913: Inzidenzfall nach der Einnahme der Stadt. For the city of Kavalla, see the report based on first-hand observations after the Bulgarians had left the city, by British Navy Cpt. Boyle, TNA, RN: ADM 116/1193, Cpt. Boyle to Sir F. Elliot, Athens, 5 August 1913 [3751], confidential.

226 PA AA, R 14 230, Akten betr. den Balkan-Krieg Bd. 15: Bericht des österreichischen Konsuls in Janina, 11 March 1913. See the more detailed original report on the conquest of Janina, in OeStA, HHStA P.A. XII 390. Liasse XLV/3: Balkankrieg, Bilinski an Berchtold, no. 12, Janina, 11 March 1913: Fall der Festung Janina. His colleague Halla from Monastir/Bitola spoke in a similar way about 'an unbound Christian population' when Greek soldiers had entered the city of Korca. Ibid., 388, Halla an Berchtold, no. 1, Monastir, 4 January 1913: Der Einzug der Griechen in Korca.

227 OeStA, HHStA P.A. XII, 389. Heimroth an Berchtold, no. 26, streng vertraulich, Uesküb, 9 February 1913.

228 Von Fényes, *Tagebuch eines Mannes vom Roten Kreuz*, 102.

229 Kamburov, *Edin mnogo dălg păt*, 19. A very similar description can also be found in the diary of Petăr Zhechev Kurdomanov: Stanka Georgieva, *Voinishki dnevnik na Petăr Zhechev Kurdomanov za Balkanskata voina* [The War Diary of Petăr Zhechev Kurdomanov on the Balkan Wars] (Sofia: RITT, 2001), 81. Based on 'neutral' eyewitnesses, whom he assumed to be reliable, the Austrian consulate officer Bilinski reported similar cases from the Greek conquest of Ioanina. OeStA, HHStA P.A. XII 390. Liasse XLV/3: Balkankrieg, Legationssekretär Bilinski an Berchtold, no. 24, Janina, 27 March 1913: Situation in Janina.

230 PA AA, R 14 220 Akten betr. den Balkan-Krieg 1912/13, Bd. 5: Telegramm no. 49 aus Cetinje an AA, 19 October 1912; OeStA, HHStA P.A. XII 386. Liasse XLV/3: Balkankrieg, k.u.k. Militärattaché in Belgrad Res. no. 283: Einfluß der Sicherheitsverhältnisse in den neu besetzten Gebieten bei einem Kriege mit der Monarchie; based on the information of a Swiss railway engineer in Üsküb, ibid., 386, Stephan von Ugron an Berchtold,

no. 136 E, Belgrad, 15 November 1912: Nachrichten aus Üsküb; ibid., 387, Kral an Berchhold, no. 203, Salonich, 9 December 1912: Die Greuel von Strumitza; ibid., P.A. XII 438. Liasse XLV/15: Balkankrieg, Graf Tarnowski an Berchthold, no. 48 D, Sofia, 17 August 1913: Massacrierung bulgarischer Kriegsgefangener; on the alleged killing of prisoners by Serbian soldiers in Prizren, ibid., P.A. XXXVIII Konsulate 405, Prizren 1912–1914: Telegramm no. 236, 6 April 1914, 5.20 Uhr. Austrian Prince Windisch-Graetz, who witnessed the war as part of a Bulgarian unit, also speaks about the killing of prisoners during the campaign at Dedeagach. See, based on Windisch-Graetz's personal notes, Alfred von Dietl, *Taktische Schilderungen aus den Balkankriegen 1912/13*, Vol. I (Vienna: Seidel, 1914), 29.

231 The Bulgarian side, for example, claimed to have taken 20,000 prisoners after the battle of Kirkilisse. OeStA, HHStA P.A. XII 385. Liasse XLV/3: Balkankriege, Telegramm Graf Tarnowski, no. 5019, Sofia, 24 October 1912. After the Greek conquest of Saloniki, up to 25,000 prisoners of war were reported. Ibid., 386, Freiherr von Braun an Berchtold, no. 52, Athens, 10 November 1912: Zur Besetzung Saloniki's durch die griechische Armee. On the increasing number of prisoners of war, cf. also the reports by the International Red Cross, *Bulletin International de la Croix Rouge* 173 (1913), 56–60.

232 On interventions by the Ottoman government against Bulgaria, cf. PA AA, Kaiserliche Deutsche Botschaft in Konstantinopel, betr. Balkankrieg, Spec. 202 VII 8a, Bd. 84: Sublime Porte, Ministère des Affaires Étrangères no. 34 032, 26 June 1913; OeStA, HHStA P.A. XII. Türkei Liasse XLV/21 Balkankrieg, Ambasssade Impériale Ottomane: Note verbale. Au Ministère Impérial et Royal des Affaires Étrangères no. 3938 3, 7 August 1913 ('… que les bulgares poussent leur sauvagerie jusqu'à massacrer les prisonniere de guerre Ottomans se trouvant en Bulgarie'); ibid., 392, Graf Tarnowski, Sofia, 12 April 1913: Telegramm in Chriffren; and against Greece, ibid., 386, Kral an Berchtold, no. 186, Salonica, 23 November 1912: Nichteinhaltung der Uebergabebedingungen durch die Griechen in Salonich; against Serbia, ibid., 411, Ambassade Impériale Ottomane no. 37857: Note verbale, Vienna, 19 November 1912. On Bulgarian complaints against Greece, cf. ibid., P.A. XV Bulgarien 75: Berichte, Weisungen, Varia 1913, Telegramm 658 Baron Mittag, Sofia, 5 November 1913; for Greek accusations against Bulgaria, see ibid., P.A. XII 438. Frh. von Braun an Berchtold, no. 28, Athens, 20 June 1913: Behandlung griechischer Kriegsgefangener seitens Bulgarien.

233 OeStA, HHStA P.A. XII 391. Dr Max von Herzfeld an Berchthold, no. 17/ res. Adrianople, 17 April 1913: 2. Teil des Berichts über die Belagerung Adrianopels. This issue was confirmed even by the Bulgarian general Vazov, who however explained the situation by the general shortage of food in the city and blamed cholera for most of the prisoner deaths. The situation improved over time, but did not reach 'international standards', as the Austrian consul noticed. Ibid., 392, Graf Tarnowski no. 29-D, Sofia, 22 April 1913: Unterbreitet Bericht no. 14, Res.ddo. 19 April 1913 über Lage türkischer Kriegsgefangener in Adrianopel. On the situation in the camp in Niš, cf. ibid., 411, Stephan von Ugron an Berchtold: Beilage

zu Bericht no. 125, 3 November 1912. Based on the information of his consulate officer from Kirkilisse, the Austrian ambassador to the Ottoman Empire, Pallavicini, reported that Ottoman prisoners were treated with 'une façon inhumaine'. Ibid., 389, Pallavicini an Berchtold, no. 7 F, Constantinople, 6 February 1913: Die Bulgaren in Kirkkilisse. Similarly, see British diplomatic reports on Turkish prisoners of war at Corfu and in Salonica: TNA, RN: ADM 116/1192, Report on Affairs at Corfu, 13 April 1913; ibid., 116/11990: Turco-Balkan War 3, Report on Affairs in Salonika, 24 November 1913. On the miserable food supply of prisoners in Montenegro, see OeStA, HHStA P.A. XII 385. Giesl an Berchtold, no. 89, vertr., Cetinje, 28 October 1912: Unterredung mit König Nikola. The Carnegie Commission also reported on hunger among the prisoners in Greek-controlled Macedonia. Ibid., 438, Prinz Emil Fürstenberg an Berchthold no. 41 D, Athens, 6 September 1913: Die Carnegie-Mission in Griechenland.

234 OeStA, HHStA P.A. XII 385. Légation Royale de Bulgarie, no. 445, 26 July 1913: Note verbale, in which the Bulgarian Foreign Ministry rejected the Ottoman accusation that the Bulgarian army had killed more than 3,000 prisoners of war at the camp of Stara Zagora alone.

235 Complaints about the mistreatment of prisoners of war were sometimes obviously instrumentalized to exercise diplomatic pressure in view of the open questions concerning the postwar settlement. Cf., for example, the Ottoman note on the killing of Turkish prisoners of war by Bulgarian forces, OeStA, HHStA P.A. XII. Türkei Liasse XLV/21 Balkankrieg: Ambassade Impériale Ottomane: Note verbale. Au Ministère Impérial et Royal des Affaires Étrangères no. 39383, 7 August 1913; ibid. Note verbale no. 39410, 12 August 1913.

236 PA AA, Kaiserl.-Dt. Botschaft in Konstaninopel für 1912/13, Betr. Balkan-Krieg Spec. 202 VII 8 a, Bd. 73, Kaiserl.-Dt. Gesandtschaft Belgrad no. 89, 23 November 1912 on Ottoman complaints against Serbia; ibid., Bd. 84, Kais. Dt. Ges. Athen, J. no. 1723, 29 July 1913; ibid. Kaiserl.-Dt. Gesandtschaft Sofia, J. no. 1749, 23 August 1913; ibid., Bd. 73, Kaiserl. Dt. Ges. Athen, no. 1058, 22 November 1912. On a generally fair treatment, see also 'Die Berichte englischer Kriegskorrespondenten', *Neues Wiener Tageblatt*, 26 October 1912; 'Die ersten türkischen Gefangenen im bulgarischen Hauptquartier', *Neue Freie Presse*, 24 October 1912.

237 Cf. Central-Comitee der Deutschen Vereine vom Roten Kreuz, *Beiträge zur Kriegsheilkunde aus den Hilfsunternehmungen der Deutschen Vereine vom Roten Kreuz*, 674, 681, 717, 705–53.

238 *Bulletin International de la Croix Rouge* 175 (1913), 200–206.

239 Papaioannou, *Balkan Wars between the Lines*, 306.

240 Herfried Münkler, *Gewalt und Ordnung: Das Bild des Krieges im politischen Denken* (Frankfurt/M.: Fischer Taschenbuch-Verlag, 1992), 111.

241 Adam Roberts, 'Land Warfare: From Hague to Nuremberg', in Michael Howard et al. (eds), *The Laws of War: Constraints of Warfare in the Western World* (New Haven, CT: Yale University Press, 1994), 116–39, here 117.

242 John Horne and Alan Kramer, *Deutsche Kriegsgreuel 1914: Die unumstrittene Wahrheit* (Hamburg: Hamburger Edition, 2004); Alan

Kramer, '"Greueltaten": Zum Problem der deutschen Kriegsverbrechen in Belgien und Frankreich', in Gerhard Hirschfeld, Gerd Krumeich and Irina Renz (eds), *'Keiner fühlt sich hier mehr als Mensch...': Erlebnis und Wirkung des Ersten Weltkriegs* (Frankfurt/M.: Fischer Taschenbuch-Verlag, 1996), 104–39.
243 Joanne Bourke, *An Intimate History of Killing* (London: Granta, 1999), 26–30.
244 Isabel Hull, 'Prisoners in Colonial Warfare: The Imperial German Example', in Sybille Scheipers (ed.), *Prisoners in War* (Oxford: Oxford University Press, 2010), 157–72.
245 Alan Kramer, 'Prisoners in the First World War', in Scheipers, *Prisoners in War*, 75–90.
246 Hans Mommsen, 'Anfänge des ethnic cleansing und der Umsiedelungspolitik im Ersten Weltkrieg', in Eduard Mühle (ed.), *Mentalitäten – Nationen – Spannungsfelder: Studien zu Mittel- und Osteuropa im 19. und 20. Jahrhundert, Festschrift für Hans Lemberg* (Marburg: Verlag Herder-Institut, 2001), 147–62, here 147.
247 Abazi, 'Between Facts and Interpretations', 218.
248 Koselleck coined the term 'Sattelzeit' in Reinhart Koselleck, 'Einleitung', in Otto Brunner, Werner Conze and Reinhart Koselleck (eds), *Geschichtliche Grundbegriffe: Historisches Lexikon zur politisch-sozialen Sprache in Deutschland*, vol. 1 (Stuttgart 1972), XIII–XXIII.
249 Howell, *The Campaign in Thrace*, 141.
250 Audoin-Rouzeau and Becker, *14–18: Understanding the Great War*, 59.

Bibliography

Abadzhiev, G.K. *Deistviia na 1. Brigada ot 5.p. Dunavska diviziia v Voinite prez 1912–1913 god*. [The Military Engagement of the 5th Danube Division during the Wars of 1912–1913]. Sofia: Pechatnitsa na Armeiiskia voenno-izdatelstvo fond, 1925.
Abazi, Enika. 'Between Facts and Interpretations: Three Images of the Balkan Wars of 1912–13', in James Pettifer and Tom Buchanan (eds), *War in the Balkans: Conflict and Diplomacy before World War I* (London: Tauris, 2016), 203–25.
Adanır, Fikret. 'Christliche Rekruten unter dem Halbmond: Zum Problem der Militärdienstpflicht für Nichtmuslime im spätosmanischen Reich', in Gerhard Grimm (ed.), *Von der Pruth-Ebene bis zum Gipfel des Ida: Festschrift zum 70. Geburtstag von Emanuel Turczynski* (Munich: Südosteuropa-Gesellschaft, 1989), 153–64.
Akhund, Nadine. 'The Two Carnegie Reports: From the Balkan Expedition of 1913 to the Albanian Trip of 1921'. *Balkanologie* 14(1–2) (2012), 1–17, http://balkanologie.revues.org/index2365.html (accessed 1 April 2014).
Andréades, André, et al. *Les effets économiques et sociaux de la guerre en Grèce*. Paris/New Haven, CT: Presses Univ. de France, 1928.

Antić, Čedomir. 'Crisis and Armament: Economic Relations between Great Britain and Serbia 1910–1912'. *Balcanica* 36 (2005), 151–63.
Arnaudov, Michail. *Istoriia na Sofiiskiia univerzitet Sv. Kliment Okhridski prez părvoto mu polustoletie 1888–1938* [History of the University of Sofia St. Kliment of Ohrid during Its First 50 Years 1888–1939]. Sofia: Prodvorna pechatnitsa, 1939.
Arnaudova, M. 'Balkanskata voina v spomenite na Georgi Popaianov i Petko Chorbadzhiev (Rosen)' [The Balkan Wars in the Memory of Georgi Popaianov and Petko Chorbadzhiev (Rosen)]. *Izvestiia na dărzhavnite archive* 47 (1984), 159–80.
Audoin-Rouzeau, Stéphane, and Annette Becker. *14–18: Understanding the Great War*. New York: Hill and Wang, 2002.
Azmanov, Dimităr. *Moiata epokha 1878–1918* [My Era 1878–1918]. Sofia: Izdat. na Ministerstvoto na Otbranata Sv. Georgi Pobedonosets, 1995.
Baberowski, Jörg. 'Einleitung: Ermöglichungsräume exzessiver Gewalt', in Jörg Baberowski and Gabriele Metzler (eds), *Gewalträume: Soziale Ordnungen im Ausnahmezustand*. Frankfurt/M: Campus Verlag, 2012, 7–27.
Baldwin, Herbert F. *A War Photographer on Thrace: An Account of Personal Experiences during the Turco-Bulgarian War 1912*. London: T.F. Unwin, 1912.
Ballner, Josef. 'Kriegschirurgische Erfahrungen aus dem Bulgarisch-Türkischen Kriege'. *Der Militärarzt* 47(10) (24 May 1913), 145–46.
Barby, Henry. *La Guerre des Balkans: Les victoires serbes*. Paris: Bernard Grasset, 1913.
Baring, Maurice. *Letters from the Near East 1909 and 1912*. London: Smith, Elder and Co., 1913.
Becker, Jean-Jacques. *Comment les français sont entrés dans la guerre*. Paris: Presses de la Fondation Nationale des Sciences Politiques, 1977.
Belić, Aleksandar. 'Srbija i stara Srbija' [Serbia and Old Serbia]. *Ilustrovana ratna kronika* 2 (25 October [7 November] 1912), 2.
Beyrau, Dietrich. 'Einführende Bemerkungen', in Bruno Thoß and Hans-Erich Volkmann (eds), *Erster Weltkrieg – Zweiter Weltkrieg: Ein Vergleich* (Paderborn: Schöningh, 2002), 729–734.
Beyrau, Dietrich, et al. (eds). *Formen des Krieges: Von der Antike bis zur Gegenwart*. Paderborn: Schöningh, 2007.
Biondich, Mark. *The Balkans: Revolutions, Wars and Political Violence since 1878*. Oxford: Oxford University Press, 2011.
——. 'The Balkan Wars: Violence and Nation-Building in the Balkans 1912–13'. *Journal of Genocide Research* 18(2) (2016), 389–404.
Boeckh, Katrin. *Von den Balkankriegen zum Ersten Weltkrieg: Kleinstaatenpolitik und ethnische Selbstbestimmung auf dem Balkan*. Munich: Oldenbourg, 1996.
Bourke, Joanne. *An Intimate History of Killing*. London: Granta, 1999.
Breitner, Burghard [Bruno Sturm]. *Kriegstagebuch: Balkankrieg 1913*. Vienna/Leipzig: Braumüller, 1913.
Brown, Keith. '"Wiping Out the Bulgarian Race": Hatred, Duty and National Self-Fashioning in the Second Balkan War', in Omer Bartov and Eric Weitz (eds), *Shatterzone of Empires: Coexistence and Violence in the German, Habsburg, Russian and Ottoman Borderlands* (Bloomington, IN: Indiana University Press, 2013), 298–317.

Bruns, P[aul] v. (ed.). *Kriegschirurgische Erfahrungen aus den Balkankriegen 1912/13*. Tübingen: Laupp'sche Buchhandlung, 1914.
Buxton, Noel. *The Wounded*. World Peace Foundation Pamphlet Series 3(2) (February 1913).
——. *With the Bulgarian Staff*. New York: The Macmillan Comp., 1913.
Carnegie Endowment for International Peace. *Report of the International Commission to Inquire into the Causes and Conduct of the Balkan Wars*. Washington, DC: The Endowment, 1914.
Central-Comitee der Deutschen Vereine vom Roten Kreuz (ed.). *Beiträge zur Kriegsheilkunde aus den Hilfsunternehmungen der Deutschen Vereine vom Roten Kreuz während des Italienisch-türkischen Feldzug 1912 und des Balkankrieges 1912/13*. Berlin: Springer, 1914.
Çetinkaya, Y. Doğan. '"Revenge! Revenge! Revenge!" "Awakening a Nation" through Propaganda in the Ottoman Empire during the Balkan Wars (1912–1913)', in Hans-Lukas Kieser, Kerem Öktem and Maurus Reinkowski (eds), *World War I and the End of the Ottomans: From the Balkan Wars to the Armenian Genocide* (London/New York: Taurus, 2015), 77–102.
——. 'Illustrated Atrocity: The Stigmatisation of Non-Muslims through Images in the Ottoman Empire during the Balkan Wars'. *Journal of Modern European History* 12(4) (2014), 460–78.
Chantepleure, Guy. *La ville assiégée: Janina Octobre 1912–Mars 1913*. Paris: Calmann-Lévy, 1913.
Chickering, Roger. 'Total War: The Use and Abuse of a Concept', in Manfred F. Boemke and Roger Chickering (eds), *Anticipating Total War: The German and American Experience, 1871–1914* (Cambridge: Cambridge University Press, 1999), 13–26.
——. 'Militärgeschichte als Totalgeschichte im Zeitalter des totalen Krieges', in Thomas Kühne and Benjamin Ziemann (eds), *Was ist Militärgeschichte?* (Paderborn: Schöningh, 2000), 301–14.
Comité de publication des atrocités balcaniques. *Atrocités bulgares en Macédoine*. Athens, 1913.
——. *Les atrocités des coalisés Balkaniques no. 1*. Constantinople, 1913.
——. *Les cruautés bulgares 1912–1913*. Athens, 1914.
——. *The Crimes of Bulgaria in Greece*. Washington, DC, 1914.
Cvijić, Jovan. 'Balkanski rat i Srbija' [The Balkan War and Serbia]. *Srpski Knižcvni Glasnik* 29(9) (1912), 651–64.
Daniel, Ute. 'Der Krim-Krieg 1853–1856 und die Entstehungskontexte moderner Kriegsberichterstattung', in Ute Daniel (ed.), *Augenzeugen: Kriegsberichterstattung vom 18. bis 21. Jahrhundert* (Göttingen: Vandenhoeck und Ruprecht, 2006), 40–67.
Demeter, Gábor. 'The Balkan Wars 1912–1913 in the Hungarian Press, Military Literature and Personal Memoirs', manuscript, http://www.academia.edu/1887496/The_Balkan_Wars_1912-1913_in_the_Hungarian_Press_Military_Literature_and_Personal_Memoirs (accessed 1 April 2014).
Denda, Dalibor. 'Tajni raport putnika Damjana Vlajića 1907 godine o naoružanju i opremi srpske vojske' [The Secret Report of the Traveller Damjan Vlajich in 1907 about the Armament and Gear of the Serbian Army]. *Vojnoistorijski glasnik* 46(2) (2008), 213–30.

———. *Automobili u srpskoj vojsci 1908–1918* [Automobiles in the Serbian Army]. Belgrade: Institut za strategijska istraživanja, 2008.
Desbriere, Colonel breveté. *Aperçu sur la Campagne de Thrace*. Paris: Librairie Chapelot, 1913.
Despot, Igor. *The Balkan Wars in the Eyes of the Warring Parties: Perceptions and Interpretations*. Bloomington, IN: iUniverse, Inc., 2012.
Dietl, Alfred von. *Taktische Schilderungen aus den Balkankriegen 1912/13*. Vol. I. Vienna: Seidel, 1914.
Dilger, Anton, and Arthur W. Meyer. 'Kriegschirurgische Erfahrungen aus den beiden Balkankriegen 1912/13'. *Deutsche Zeitschrift für Chirurgie* 127(3–4) (1914), 225–379.
Dimitriev, Radko. *Treta armiia v Balkanskata voina 1912 godina* [The Third Army during the Balkan War 1912]. Sofia: Armeiski Voenno-izdatelski fond, 1922.
Dimitrova, Snežana. 'Of Other Balkan Wars: Affective Worlds of Modern and Traditional (The Bulgarian Example)'. *Perceptions: Journal of International Affairs* XVIII(2) (2013), 29–54.
Diner, Dan. *Das Jahrhundert verstehen: Eine universalhistorische Deutung*. Frankfurt/M.: Fischer Taschenbuchverlag, 2000.
Djordjević, Vladan. *Die Albanesen und die Großmächte*. Leipzig: Hirzel, 1913.
Djurdjeva, Mile. 'Narodna vojska u Srbiji 1861–1889' [The National Army in Serbia 1861–1889]. *Vojnoistorijski glasnik* 10(4) (1959), 78–93.
'Dnevnik na voinika Raicho Maidovski po vremen na voinata să Sărbiia' [The Diary of the Soldier Raicho Maidovski in the Time of the War with Serbia], in V. Georgiev and S. Trifonov (eds), *Istoriia na Bălgarite 1878–1912 v dokumenti* [History of Bulgaria 1878–1912 in Documents], Vol. II, *1912–1918* (Sofia: Prosveta, 1996), 202–4.
Dodov, Nikola. *Dnevnik na Balkanskata voina*. Sofia: Voenno izdat., 2006.
'Dokumentalen razkaz za Balkanskata voina: Iz nepublikovanata kniga na Petăr Stoilov' [Documentary Narrative on the Balkan War: From the Unpublished Book of Petăr Stoilov]. *Istorichesko bădeshte* 1–2 (2003), 252–78.
Dragostinova, Theodora. 'Continuity vs. Radical Break: National Homogenization in the Greek-Bulgarian Borderlands before and after the Balkan Wars'. *Journal of Genocide Research* 18(4) (2016), 405–26.
Duraković, Indira. 'Experimentierfeld Balkan: Ärzte am Schauplatz der Balkankriege 1912/13'. *Südost-Forschungen* 68 (2009), 298–327.
Eldărov, Svetozăr. *Pravoslavieto na voina: Bălgarska pravoslavna cărkva i voinite na Bălgariia 1878–1945* [Orthodoxy and War: The Bulgarian Orthodox Church and the War in Bulgaria]. Sofia: Voenno izdat., 2004.
Erickson, Edward J. (ed.). *Defeat in Detail: The Ottoman Army in the Balkans 1912–13*. Westport, CT: Praeger, 2003.
Exner, Alfred. *Kriegschirurgie in den Balkankriegen*. Stuttgart: Enke, 1915.
Farrar, Lancelot L. Jr. 'Aggression Versus Apathy: The Limits of Nationalism during the Balkan Wars 1912–1913'. *East European Quarterly* 37(3) (2003), 257–80.
Fényes, Ladislaus von. *Tagebuch eines Mannes vom Roten Kreuz: Erlebnisse aus dem Balkankrieg*. Berlin: Verlag von Karl Siegesmund, 1913.
Ferguson, Niall. *The War of the World: Twentieth-Century Conflict and the Descent of the West*. London: Penguin Books, 2007.

Figes, Orlando. *The Crimean War: A History*. New York: Metropolitan Books, 2012.
Flamm, Heinz. 'Das Österreichische Rote Kreuz und österreichische Bakteriologen in den Balkankriegen 1912/13 – Zentennium des ersten Einsatzes der Bakteriologie auf Kriegsschauplätzen'. *Wiener Medizinische Wochenschrift* 162(7–8) (2012), 132–47.
Ford, Clyde Sinclair. *The Balkan Wars: Being a Series of Lectures Delivered at the Army Service Schools*. Washington, DC: Press of the Army Service Schools, 1915.
———. *Gunshot Roentgenograms: A Collection of Roentgenograms Taken in Constantinople during the Turco-Balkan War, 1912–1913, Illustrating Some Gunshot Wounds in the Turkish Army* (War Department, Office of the Surgeon General, Bulletin 9, October 1915). Washington, DC: Government Printing Office, 1916.
Förster, Stig. 'Das Zeitalter des totalen Krieges, 1861–1945'. *Mittelweg* 36(6) (1999), 12–29.
Fox, Fred. *The Balkan Peninsula*. London: Black, 1915.
Fraenkel, Alexander. 'Einige allgemeine Bemerkungen zur modernen Kriegschirurgie', in P[aul] v. Bruns (ed.), *Kriegschirurgische Erfahrungen aus den Balkankriegen 1912/13* (Tübingen: Laupp'sche Buchhandlung, 1914), 1–13.
Freundlich, Leo. *Albaniens Golgotha: Anklageakten gegen die Vernichter des Albanervolks*. Vienna: J. Roller, 1913.
———. *Die Albanische Korrespondenz: Agenturmeldungen aus Krisenzeiten Juni 1913–August 1914*, ed. Robert Elsie. Munich: Oldenbourg, 2012.
Gardikas-Katsiadakis, Helen. 'The Balkan Wars 1912–13: Their Effect on the Everyday Life of Civilians', in Council of Europe (ed.), *Crossroads of European Histories: Multiple Outlooks on Five Key Moments in the History of Europe* (Strasbourg: Council of Europe Publ., 2006), 89–100.
Gärtner, M. Oberst. 'Über die Verwendung der Feldartillerie im Balkankriege 1912/13'. *Streffleur's Militärische Zeitschrift* 55(7) (1914), 1,038.
Gavrilović, Vera. 'Žene lekari u Prvom Balkanskom ratu' [Women Doctors in the First Balkan War], in SANU (ed.), *Prvi Balkanski rat: Okrugli sto povodom 75. godišnjice 1912–1987* [The First Balkan War: Round Table on the Occasion of the 75th Anniversary 1912–1987] (Belgrade: SANU, 1991), 97–104.
Gawrych, George W. 'The Culture and Politics of Violence in Turkish Society, 1903–1914'. *Middle Eastern Studies* 22(3) (1986), 307–30.
Georgiev, Velichko, and Staiko Trifonov (eds). *Istoriia na Bŭlgarite 1878–1912 v dokumenti* [History of Bulgaria 1878–1912 in Documents], Vol. II, *1912–1918*. Sofia: Prosveta, 1996.
Georgieva, Stanka. *Voinishki dnevnik na Petăr Zhechev Kurdomanov za Balkanskata voina* [The War Diary of Petăr Zhechev Kurdomanov on the Balkan Wars]. Sofia: RITT, 2001.
German General Staff. *Kriegsgeschichtliche Einzelschriften, hg. vom Großen Generalstabe. Kriegsgeschichtliche Abteilung I: Heft 50: Der Balkankrieg 1912/13, Erstes Heft, Die Ereignisse auf dem thrazischen Kriegsschauplatz bis zum Waffenstillstand*. Berlin, 1914.
Ginio, Eyal. 'Mobilizing the Ottoman Nation during the Balkan Wars (1912–1913): Awakening from the Ottoman Dream'. *War in History* 12(2) (2005), 156–77.

Gjordjewitj [Djordjević], Vladan. *Die Entwicklung der öffentlichen Gesundheitspflege im serbischen Königreich vom XII. Jahrhundert bis 1883*. Berlin: Pasch, 1883.

Goldhammer, Franz. 'Kriegsärztliche Erfahrungen aus dem griechisch-türkischen und griechisch-bulgarischen Krieg', in P[aul] v. Bruns (ed.), *Kriegschirurgische Erfahrungen aus den Balkankriegen 1912/13* (Tübingen: Laupp'sche Buchhandlung, 1914), 14–17.

Hacısalihoğlu, Mehmet. 'Inclusion and Exclusion: Conscription in the Ottoman Empire'. *Journal of Modern European History* 5 (2007), 264–86.

Hall, Richard C. *The Balkan Wars 1912–1913: Prelude to the First World War*. London/New York: Routledge, 2000.

———. '"The Enemy Is Behind Us": The Morale Crisis in the Bulgarian Army during the Summer of 1918'. *War in History* 11(2) (2004), 209–19.

———. 'The Next War: The Influence of the Russo-Japanese War on Southeastern Europe and the Balkan Wars of 1912–1913'. *Journal of Slavic Military Studies* 17(3) (2004), 563–77.

Hamburger, Josef. 'Der Sanitätsdienst im Balkankriege'. *Der Militärarzt* 48(7) (25 April 1914), 129–40.

Hanasiewicz, Oskar. 'Militärärztliche und militärische Eindrücke aus dem Balkankrieg 1912/13'. *Streffleur's Militärische Zeitschrift* 55(7) (1914), 1,096.

Herr, Général. *Sur le théâtre de la guerre des Balkans: Mon journal des routes (17. novembre–15. décembre 1912)*. Paris/Nancy: Berger-Levrault, 1913.

Hochwaechter, Günter von. *Mit den Türken in der Front im Stabe Mahmud Muchtar Pashas – Mein Kriegstagebuch über die Kämpfe bei Kirk Kilisse, Lüle Burgas und Cataldza*. Berlin: Mittler, 1913.

Horne, John, and Alan Kramer. *Deutsche Kriegsgreuel 1914: Die unumstrittene Wahrheit*. Hamburg: Hamburger Edition, 2004.

Howard, Michael. *War in European History*. Oxford: Oxford University Press, 1976.

Howell, Major P. *The Campaign in Thrace: Six Lectures*. London: H. Rees, 1913.

Hull, Isabel. 'Prisoners in Colonial Warfare: The Imperial German Example', in Sybille Scheipers (ed.), *Prisoners in War* (Oxford: Oxford University Press, 2010), 157–72.

Hutchison, T.S. *An American Soldier under the Greek Flag at Bezanie*. Nashville, TN: Greek-American Publ. Comp., 1913.

Ignjatović, Mile. 'Srpsko ratno hirurško iskustvo, I. deo: Ratna hirurgija u vreme srpsko-turskih ratova' [Serbian Military Surgery I: Military Surgery during the Serbian-Turkish Wars]. *Vojnosanitetski pregled* 60(5) (2003), 631–40.

———. 'Srpsko ratno hirurško iskustvo, II. deo: Ratna hirurgija u Srbiji u vreme Srpsko-bugarskog rata' [Serbian Military Surgery II: Military Surgery during the Serbian-Bulgarian War]. *Vojnosanitetski pregled* 60(6) (2003), 757–62.

———. 'Srpsko ratno hirurško iskustvo, IV. deo: Ratna hirurgija u Srbiji u vreme balkanskih ratova' [Serbian Military Surgery IV: Military Surgery during the Balkan Wars]. *Vojnosanitetski pregled* 61(2) (2004), 217–29.

Ilchev, Ivan. *Rodinata mi – prava ili ne! Vănshnopoliticheska propaganda na balkanskite stran 1821–1923* [My Homeland – Right or Wrong! Foreign Policy Propaganda in the Balkan Countries 1821–1923]. Sofia: Universitetsko izdat. Sv. Kliment Okhridski, 1996.

――. 'The Balkan Wars in Recent Bulgarian Historiography and Textbooks', in Council of Europe (ed.), *Crossroads of European Histories: Multiple Outlooks on Five Key Moments in the History of Europe* (Strasbourg: Council of Europe Publ., 2006), 111–18.
Immanuel, Friedrich. *Der Balkankrieg 1912: Vol. 4.* Berlin: Mittler, 1913.
Ivanov, Nikola. *Balkanskata voina 1912/13* [The Balkan Wars 1912/13]. Vol. II. Sofia: Pečatn. na Armeiskiia voenno-izd. fond, 1924.
――. *Spomeni 1861–1918* [Memoirs 1861–1918]. Vol. II. Sofia: Izdat. na Ministerstvoto na Otbranata Sv. Georgi Pobedonosets, 1997.
James, Lionel. *With the Conquered Turk: The Story of a Latter-Day Adventurer.* Boston, MA: Small, Mayard and Comp., 1913.
Jovanović, Slobodan. *Vlada Milana Obrenovića* [The Reign of Milan Obrenovich] (Sabrana dela, 5). Belgrade: BIGZ, 1990.
――. *Vlada Aleksandra Obrenovića* [The Reign of Alexander Obrenovich] (Sabrana dela, 7). Belgrade: BIGZ, 1990.
Jovanović-Batut, Milan. *Medicinski fakultet srpskog univerziteta* [The Medical Faculty of the Serbian University]. Belgrade, 1899.
Jović, Pavle. 'Vojni lekari – prvi državni pitomci za studije medicine u inostranstvu' [Medical Doctors – The First State Sponsored Students for Medicine Abroad]. *Vojnosanitetski pregled* 59(2) (2002), 215–16.
Jovičević, Andrija. *Dnevnik iz balkanskih ratova* [Diary from the Balkan Wars]. Belgrade: Službeni list SRJ, 1996.
Kamburov, Stefan Khristov. *Edin mnogo dălg păt: Dnevnik na Stoian Khristov Kamburov* [A Very Long Way: The Diary of Stoian Khristov Kamburov]. Sofia: Pres izdatelstvo, 2003.
Kardjilov, Petar. 'The First Balkan War and the Cinematographer Chronicle Documentaries Filmed at the Balkan Fronts'. *Études balkaniques* XLVIII(3) (2013), 122–49.
Kaser, Karl. 'Vizualizatsiia na Balkanite: Balkanskite voini, Părvata Svetovna Voina i vizualnata modernizatsiia' [The Visualization of the Balkans: The Balkan Wars, the First World War and the Visual Modernization]. *Bălgarska etnologiia* 3 (2014), 332–51.
Keegan, John. *Die Kultur des Krieges.* Reinbek: Rowohlt, 1995.
Keisinger, Florian. *Unzivilisierte Kriege im zivilisierten Europa? Die Balkankriege und die öffentliche Meinung in Deutschland, England und Irland 1876–1913.* Paderborn: Schöningh, 2008.
Kelbecheva, Evelina. 'Voina i tvorchestvo' [War and Creativity]. *Godishnik na Sofiiskiia universitet Sv. Kliment Okhridski; Centăr po kulturoznanie* 80/81 (1987/88), 101–74.
――. 'Between Apology and Denial: Bulgarian Culture during World War I', in Ariel Roshwald and Richard Stites (eds), *European Culture in the Great War* (Cambridge: Cambridge University Press, 1999), 215–42.
Király, Béla K. 'East Central European Society and the Warfare in the Era of the Balkan Wars', in Béla K. Király and Dimitrije Djordjević (eds), *East Central European Society and the Balkan Wars* (War and Society in East Central Europe, XVIII) (New York: Columbia University Press, 1987), 3–13.
Knorr, Emil. *Entwicklung und Gestaltung des Heeres-Sanitätswesens der europäischen Staaten.* Hannover: Helwig, 1880.

Kolarov, Vasil. *Pobedi i porazheniia: Dnevnik* [Victories and Defeats: Diary]. Sofia: Christo Botev, 2001.

Kolev, Jordan. *Bălgarskata inteligentsiia 1878–1912* [The Bulgarian Intelligentsia 1878–1912]. Sofia: Univ. Izdat. Sv. Kl. Okhridski, 1992.

Koliopulos, John. *Brigands with a Cause*. Oxford: Clarendon Press, 1987.

Koneva, Rumjana. *Goliamata sreshta na bŭlgarskiia narod: Kulturata i predizvikatelstva na voinite 1912–1918 g.* [The 'Big Meeting' of the Bulgarian People: Culture and the Challenge of the Wars 1912–1918]. Sofia: Akad. Izdat. Prof. Marin Drinov, 1995.

Koulouri, Christina. *Dimensions idéologiques de l'historicité en Grèce (1834–1914): Les manuels scolaires d'histoire et de géographie*. Frankfurt/M.: Peter Lang, 1991.

Kramer, Alan. '"Greueltaten": Zum Problem der deutschen Kriegsverbrechen in Belgien und Frankreich', in Gerhard Hirschfeld, Gerd Krumeich and Irina Renz (eds), *'Keiner fühlt sich hier mehr als Mensch...': Erlebnis und Wirkung des Ersten Weltkriegs* (Frankfurt/M.: Fischer Taschenbuch-Verlag, 1996), 104–39.

———. 'Prisoners in the First World War', in Sybille Scheipers (ed.), *Prisoners in War* (Oxford: Oxford University Press, 2010), 75–90.

Kürsat-Ahlers, Elçin. 'Die Brutalisierung von Gesellschaft und Kriegsführung im Osmanischen Reich während der Balkankriege (1903–1914)', in Andreas Gestrich (ed.), *Gewalt im Krieg: Ausübung, Erfahrung und Verweigerung von Gewalt in Kriegen des 20. Jahrhunderts* (Münster: Lit Verlag, 1996), 50–74.

Kutschbach, Albin. *Die Serben im Balkankrieg*. Stuttgart: Franckh, 1913.

Lyon, James M.B. '"A Peasant Mob": The Serbian Army on the Eve of the Great War'. *The Journal of Military History* 61(3) (1997), 481–503.

Mach, Richard von. *Briefe aus dem Balkankrieg 1912–1913*. Berlin: Eisenschmidt, 1913.

Mamontov, N.P. *S bolgarskimi voiskami ot Balkan' do Chataldzhi: Zapiski voennago korrespondenta* [With the Bulgarian Armies from the Balkan to Chataldzha: Notes of a War Correspondent]. Moscow: Tovar. Tipogr. A. I. Mamontova, 1913.

Marin, Georgi. 'Prinosăt na bălgarskata aviaciia văv voennoto delo prez balkanskata voina 1912–1913' [The Contribution of Bulgarian Aviation to Military Activities during the Balkan Wars 1912–1913], in Bălgarsko Istorichesko Druzhestvo (ed). *Bălgariia 1300: Institutsiia i dărzhavnata traditsiia* [Bulgaria 1300: Institutions and State Traditions]. Vol. III (Sofia: Bălgarsko Istorichesko Druzhestvo, 1983), 649–57.

Marković, Predrag J. *Ethnic Stereotypes: Ubiquitous, Local or Migrating Phenomena? The Serbian-Albanian Case*. Bonn: Michael-Zikic-Stiftung, 2003.

Matharel, Camille Louis de. *Balkanskata voina prez pogled na edin frantsuzin* [The Balkan Wars as Viewed by a Frenchman]. Sofia: Voenno izdatelstvo, 1977.

Mazower, Mark. *Dark Continent: Europe's Twentieth Century*. New York: Vintage Books, 1998.

McKenzie, David. 'Officer Conspirators and Nationalism in Serbia 1901–1914', in Stephen Fischer-Galațați and Béla K. Király (eds), *Essays on War and Society in East Central Europe, 1740–1920* (Boulder, CO: Social Science Monographs, 1987), 117–150.

Meyer, Heinrich. *Der Balkankrieg 1912/13 und seine Lehren*. Munich: Meyer, 1913.

Meyer, Julius, Oberstleutnant. *CVIII. Neujahrsblatt der Feuerwerker-Gesellschaft (Artillerie-Kollegium) in Zürich auf das Jahr 1913: Aus den Balkan-Kriegen*. Zurich: Kommissionsverlag Beer und Co., 1913.

Michail, Eugene. 'Western Attitudes to War in the Balkans and the Shifting Meanings of Violence, 1912–1991'. *Journal of Contemporary History* 47(2) (2012), 219–39.

Michalopoulos, Dimitris. 'The Evolution of the Greek Army (1828–1868)', in Béla K. Király (ed.), *The Crucial Decade: East Central European Society and National Defense, 1859–1870* (New York: Columbia University Press, 1984), 317–30.

Mijalkovski, Milan. 'Četničke (gerilske) jedinice Kraljevine Srbije – borci protiv terora turskog okupatora' [Chetnik (Guerrilla) Units in the Kingdom of Serbia – Fighters against the Terror of the Turkish Occupational Forces]. *Zbornik radova Instituta za savremenu istoriju* 9 (2007), 59–81.

Mijatovič, Ivan. 'Šesdeset godina Vojnotechničkog glasnika: Ishodište vojnotehničke misli u vojnoj štampi Kneževine/Kraljevine Srbije' [Sixty Years of the Military-Technical Journal: The Starting Point of Military-Technical Thinking in the Army Press of the Principality/Kingdom of Serbia]. *Vojnotehnički glasnik* 60(2) (2012), 7–25.

Miletitch, L. *Atrocités Grecques en Macédoine pendant la Guerre Greco-Bulgare*. Sofia, 1913.

Milev, Nikola. *Pod stenite na Odrin* [At the Walls of Edirne]. Tărnovo: ASTA, 1993.

Miličević, Milić. 'Vitalni činioci razvoja srpske vojske tokom XIX. veka' [Vital Factors of the Development of the Serbian Army during the Nineteenth Century]. *Vojnoistorijski glasnik* 41(1–2) (1993), 46–55.

——. 'Socijalno poreklo oficirskog kadra školovanog u Srbiji od 1850 do 1901 godine' [The Social Background of the Officer Cadre Educated in Serbia from 1850 to 1901]. *Godišnjak za društvenu istoriju* 2(2) (1995), 194–201.

——. *Reforma vojske Srbije 1897–1900* [The Reform of the Serbian Army 1897–1900]. Belgrade: Vojnoizdavački Zavod, 2002.

Miljković, Milan. 'War Poetry and the Visual Culture of War: The Case of the Illustrated War Chronicle (Belgrade)'. *Zeitschrift für Balkanologie* 52(2) (2016), 201–16.

Ministerstvo na Voinata (ed.). *Voinata mezhdu Bălgariia i Turtsiia 1912–1913 god* [The War between Turkey and Bulgaria 1912–1913], Vol. I: *Podgotovka na voinata* [The Preparation for the War]. Sofia: Ministerstvo na Voinata, 1937.

Mišić, Živojin. *Strategija* [Strategy]. Belgrade: Vojnoizdavački i novinski centar, 1907 [reprint 1993].

——. *Moje uspomene* [My Memories]. Belgrade: BIGZ, 1978.

Mommsen, Hans. 'Anfänge des ethnic cleansing und der Umsiedelungspolitik im Ersten Weltkrieg', in Eduard Mühle (ed.), *Mentalitäten – Nationen – Spannungsfelder: Studien zu Mittel- und Osteuropa im 19. und 20. Jahrhundert, Festschrift für Hans Lemberg* (Marburg: Verlag Herder-Institut, 2001), 147–62.

Müller, Rolf-Dieter. *Militärgeschichte*. Cologne/Vienna/Weimar: Böhlau, 2009.

Münkler, Herfried. *Gewalt und Ordnung: Das Bild des Krieges im politischen Denken*. Frankfurt/M.: Fischer Taschenbuch-Verlag, 1992.

Narodna odbrana [People's Defence]. Belgrade: Nova štamparija Davidović, 1911.

Nedialkov, Dimităr. *Văzdushnata mosht na Carstvo Bălgariia*. Chast I [The Airpower of the Bulgarian Kingdom, Part I]. Sofia: Fark OOD, 2001.

Nedialkov, Khr. *Chataldzha: Spomeni i vpečatlenija na učasnik* [Chataldzha: Memories and Impressions of a Participant]. Sofia: Pechatnitsa na Armeiiskiia Voenen-izdatelskii fond, 1924.

'Niakolko dumi za cholerata v Bulgarska voiska prez voinata' [Some Words about the Cholera in the Bulgarian Army during the War], *Letopis na Lekarskija Săjuz v Bălgariia* 8–10 (1913), 501–9.

Nikolov, Kosta. *Treta otdelna Armiia v bălgaro-turskata voina prez 1912–1913 godini*, chast I: *Lozengradska operaciia* [The Third Army during the Bulgarian-Turkish War, Part I: The Lozengrad Operation]. Sofia: Voenen zhurnal, 1914.

Okay, Cüneyd. 'The Impact of Balkan Wars on Children's Poetry in the Ottoman Empire'. *Études balkaniques* 42(1) (2006), 89–99.

Özaydın, Zuhal. 'Upper Social Strata Women and Nursing in Turkey'. *Nursing History Review* 14 (2006), 161–74.

Papaioannou, Stefan Sotiris. *Balkan Wars between the Lines: Violence and Civilians in Macedonia 1912–1918*. Ph.D. dissertation. Maryland: University of Maryland, 2012.

Parusheva, Dobrinka. '*Svetlina* vărchu voinata: Vizualno predstavjane na voinata v bălgarskata iliustrovana presa, kraja na XIX. i nachaloto na XX. Vek' [*Svetlina* about the War: Visual Representation of the War in the Bulgarian Illustrated Press]. *Bălgarska etnologiia* 3 (2014), 275–98.

Paşa, Mahmud Muhtar. *Meine Führung im Balkankriege 1912*. Berlin: Mittler, 1913.

Pauli, Carl. *Kriegsgreuel. Erlebnisse im türkisch-bulgarischen Krieg 1912: Nach den Berichten von Mitkämpfern und Augenzeugen bearbeitet*. Minden: Wilhelm Köhler o. J., [1913].

Petrović, Ilija. 'Foreign Medical Help in Serbian Liberation Wars until 1918'. *Archive of Oncology* 18(4) (2010), 143–48.

Polák, Otto. *Dojmy lékaře z Balkánské války* [Impressions of a Doctor from the Balkan Wars]. Prague: Vlastním nákladem J. Otto, 1913.

Popov, Čedomir. *Istorija srpskog naroda* [History of the Serbian People], Vol. 6/1, *Od Berlinskog kongresa do ujedinjenja* [From the Congress of Berlin to Unification]. Belgrade: Srpska književna zadruga, 2000.

Popov, Ivan. *Spomeni ot bălgarsko-turskata voina prez 1912–1913* [Memories from the Bulgarian-Turkish War]. Sofia: Pechat. Gutenberg, 1914.

Popov, Strahil. 'Balkanskata voina i bălgarskata literatura' [The Balkan Wars and Bulgarian Literature]. *Literaturna misăl* 27(7) (1983), 84–104.

Promitzer, Christian. 'Combating Cholera during the Balkan Wars: The Case of Bulgaria', in James Pettifer and Tom Buchanan (eds), *War in the Balkans: Conflict and Diplomacy before World War I* (London: Tauris, 2016), 76–101.

Pršić, Miloje. 'Stvaranje i razvoj vojnog školstva u Srbiji od 1830 do 1919 godine' [The Creation and the Development of Military Schools in Serbia between 1830 and 1919]. *Vojno Delo* 50(2) (1998), 115–47.

Puaux, René. *De Sofia à Tchataldja*. Paris: Perrin, 1913.

Putniković, Dušan Z. *Ratni memoari. Knjiga prva: Rat sa Turcima 1912 god.* [War Memories. First Book: The War with the Turks 1912]. Niš: Štamparija Sveti Car Konstantin, 1938.

Radev, Simeon. *Ot triumf do tragediia* [From Triumph to Tragedy]. Sofia: Strelets, 2003.

Rakočević, Novica. 'The Organization and the Character of the Montenegrin Army in the First Balkan War', in Béla K. Király and Dimitrije Djordjević (eds), *East Central European Society and the Balkan Wars* (War and Society in East Central Europe, XVIII) (New York: Columbia University Press, 1987), 112–25.

Rankin, Reginald. *The Inner History of the Balkan War*. London: Constable and Comp, 1914.

Ratković, Borislav. 'Mobilizacija srpske i turske vojske za prvi balkanski rat oktobra 1912 godine' [The Mobilization of the Serbian and the Turkish Army for the First Balkan War in October 1912]. *Vojnoistorijski glasnik* 36(1) (1985), 200–202.

———. 'Mobilization of the Serbian Army for the First Balkan War', in Béla K. Király and Dimitrije Djordjević (eds), *East Central European Society and the Balkan Wars* (War and Society in East Central Europe, XVIII) (New York: Columbia University Press, 1987), 146–57.

Ratković-Kostić, Slavica. 'Srpska vojska u XIX. veku' [The Serbian Army in the Nineteenth Century]. *Vojnoistorijski glasnik* 41(1–2) (1993), 25–45.

———. 'Generalštab srpske vojske 1876–1903' [The General Staff of the Serbian Army 1876–1903]. *Vojnoistorijski glasnik* 41(1–2) (2003), 11–32.

———. 'Usvojavanje savremenih sistema naoružanja u srpskoj vojsci krajem XIX veka' [The Adoption of the Modern System of Armament in the Serbian Army at the End of the Nineteenth Century]. *Vojnoistorijski glasnik* 43(1–2) (2005), 11–43.

———. *Evropeizacija srpske vojske 1878–1903* [The Europeanization of the Serbian Army 1878–1903]. Belgrade: Vojnoistorijski institut, 2007.

———. 'Razvoj doctrine u vojsci Kraljevine Srbije 1882–1903' [The Development of the Military Doctrine in the Kingdom of Serbia]. *Vojnoistoriski glasnik* 45(1–2) (2007), 65–82.

Reder, Bertold. 'Der Krankenzug der Österreichischen Gesellschaft vom Roten Kreuze auf dem bulgarisch-serbischen Kriegsschauplatz'. *Der Militärarzt* 48(2) (7 February 1914), 33–45.

Reichmann, Jan Christoph. *'Tapfere Askers' und 'Feige Araber': der osmanische Verbündete aus der Sicht deutscher Soldaten im Orient 1914–1918'*. Ph.D. dissertation. Münster: University of Münster, 2009.

Réponse à la brochure des professeurs des universités d'Athènes 'Atrocités Bulgare en Macédoine' par les professeurs de l'université de Sophia. Sofia, 1913.

Riabinin, A.A. *Balkanskaia voina* [The Balkan War]. St. Petersburg, 1913.

Roberts, Adam. 'Land Warfare: From Hague to Nuremberg', in Michael Howard et al. (eds), *The Laws of War: Constraints of Warfare in the Western World* (New Haven, CT: Yale University Press, 1994), 116–39.

Rohde, Hans. *Unsere Gefechtsvorschriften und der Balkankrieg*. Berlin: Eisenschmidt, 1915.

Ross, Colin. *Im Balkankrieg*. Munich: Martin Mörikes Verlag, 1913.

Ruby, Jean. *La Guerre d'Orient et les Atrocités des États Balkaniques: Rapport et documents*. [No place], 1912.

Saga za Balkanskata voina: Dnevnik na Sveshtenik Ivan Dochev [The Story of the Balkan War: The Diary of the Priest Ivan Dochev]. Sofia: Iztok-zapad, 2012.

Schliep, Ludwig. *Im Julifeldzug 1913 auf dem Balkan*. Berlin: Paetel, 1914.
Sekulić, Isidora. 'Nekim našim omladincima' [To Some of Our Youngsters]. *Slovenski jug* 31(9) (1912), 242.
Škatula, Emanuel. *Válka na Balkáně* [The Balkan War]. Prague: Práva Lidu, 1913.
Skordos, Adamantios. 'Das panslawische Feindbild im Griechenland des 19. und 20. Jahrhunderts'. *Südost-Forschungen* 71 (2012), 76–105.
Srpkinje u službi otadžbini i narodu za vreme Balkanskih ratova 1912 i 1913 g. kao i za vreme Svetskog rata od 1914–1920 [The Female Serb Serving the Fatherland and the People during the Balkan Wars 1912/13]. Belgrade: Jugoslovenska ženska sekcija Fidaka, 1933.
Stanojević, Stanoje. *Srpsko-turski rat 1912 godine* [The Serbian-Turkish War]. Belgrade: Kon, 1928.
Stanojević, Vladimir. *Istorija srpskog vojnog saniteta* [History of Serbian Military Medicine]. Belgrade: Vojnoizdavački i novinski centar, 1992.
Stefanović, Svetlana. *Nation und Geschlecht: Frauen in Serbien von der Mitte des 19. Jahrhunderts bis zum Zweiten Weltkrieg*. Ph.D. dissertation. Leipzig: University of Leipzig, 2011.
Stobart, Claire. *War and Women: From Experience in the Balkans and Elsewhere*. London: Bell & Sons, 1913.
Stojić, Ana. 'Pomoć Belgijskog Crvenog Krsta Kraljevini Srbiji tokom Balkanskih Ratova' [The Assistance of the Belgian Red Cross to the Kingdom of Serbia during the Balkan Wars]. *Miscellanea* 32 (2011), 529–42.
Stojičević, Aleksandar. *Istorija naših ratova za oslobodjenje i ujedinjenje* [The History of Our Wars of Liberation and Unification]. Belgrade: Štamparija Gl. Saveza Srpskih Zemljorad Zadruga, 1936.
Sturzenegger, Catherina. *Serbisches Rotes Kreuz und internationale Liebestätigkeit während der Balkankriege 1912/13*. Zurich: Orell Füssli, 1914.
Sundhaussen, Holm. 'Serbische Volksgeschichte: Historiker und Ethnologen im Kampf um Volk und Raum vom Ende des 19. bis zum Ende des 20. Jahrhunderts', in Manfred Hettling (ed.), *Volksgeschichten im Europa der Zwischenkriegszeit* (Göttingen: Vandenhoeck & Ruprecht, 2003), 301–25.
Tangeberg, Johannes. 'Semi-Barbarians, Courageous Patriots, Orientalists: Swedish Views of the Balkan Wars in 1912/13'. *Godišnjak za društvenu istoriju* 11(1) (2004), 55–71.
Timofeev, Alexey. 'Serbskie chetniki nakanune i v chode Balkanskih voin: social'nyi fenomen, natsional'naia traditsiia i voennaia taktika' [The Serbian Chetniks before and during the Balkan Wars: Social Phenomenon, National Tradition and Military Tactic], in Rita Grishina (ed.), *Modernizatsiia vs. voina: Chelovek na Balkanach nakanune i vo vremia Balkanskych voin (1912–1913)* [Modernization vs. War: Man in the Balkans before and during the Balkan Wars in 1912–1913] (Moscow: Institut slavianovedeniia Rossiiskoi akademii nauk, 2012), 102–22.
Tintner, Fritz. 'Kriegschirurgische Erfahrungen im Bulgarisch-Türkischen Feldzug'. *Der Militärarzt* 47(4) (1 March 1913), 54.
Todorova, Maria. *Imagining the Balkans*. Oxford/New York: Oxford University Press, 1997.
———. 'War and Memory: Trotsky's War Correspondence from the Balkan Wars'. *Perceptions. Journal of International Affairs* XVIII(2) (2013), 5–28.

Tomić, Jaša. *Rat na Kosovu i Staroj Srbiji 1912 godine* [The War in Kosovo and Old Serbia in the Year 1912]. Novi Sad: dr-a Svetozara Miletića, 1913 [reprinted 1999].
Trgovčević, Ljubinka. *Naučnici Srbije i stvaranje Jugoslavije* [Scientists from Serbia and the Creation of Yugoslavia]. Belgrade: Narodna knjiga, 1986.
Trošev, Konstantin. *Češkí lěkaři v Bulharsku v době Balkánských válek (1912–1913)* [Czech Doctors in Bulgaria during the Balkan Wars 1912–1913]. Varna: Slavena, 2003 [Prague: Univerzita Karlowa, 1984].
Trotzki, Leo. *Die Balkankriege 1912/13*. Essen: Arbeiterpresse-Verlag, 1996 [1926].
Unger, Michael. *Die bayerischen Militärbeziehungen zur Türkei vor und im Ersten Weltkrieg*. Frankfurt/M.: Peter Lang, 2003.
Veleva, M. 'Vojnishkite buntove prez 1913 g.' [Military Uprisings in 1913]. *Istoricheski pregled* 14(1) (1958), 14–24.
Veremis, Thanos. 'The Officer Corps in Greece 1912–1936'. *Byzantine and Modern Greek Studies* 2(1) (1976), 113–33.
Verhandlungen der Deutschen Gesellschaft für Chirurgie: 42. Congress, abgehalten zu Berlin, 26.–28. März 1913 (Berlin, 1913).
Villavicenzo, Carlo. *Im belagerten Scutari: Nach Aufzeichnungen der Skutariner Jesuiten*. Vienna: Verlag d. Kongregationszeitschr., 1913.
Vischer, Adolf. *An der serbischen Front: Erlebnisse eines Arztes auf dem serbisch-türkischen Kriegsschauplatz 1912*. Basel: Spittler, 1913.
Voinata – takava, kakvato beshe: Bălgariia v Părvata Balkanska Voina 1912–1913 g. [The War as it Really Was: Bulgaria during the First Balkan War 1912–1913]. Sofia: Univ. Izd. Sv. Kliment Okhridski, 2012.
Vojvodić, Mihajlo. 'Naučnici Srbije i prvi balkanski rat' [Scientists from Serbia and the First Balkan War], in SANU (ed.), *Prvi Balkanski rat. Okrugli sto povodom 75. godišnjice 1912–1987* [The First Balkan War: Round Table on the Occasion of Its 75th Anniversary, 1912–1987] (Belgrade: SANU, 1991), 33–51.
Vuksanović-Anić, Draga. *Stvaranje moderne srpske vojske* [The Formation of the Modern Serbian Army]. Belgrade: Srpska književna zadruga, 1993.
Wagner, Hermenegild. *With the Victorious Bulgarians*. New York/Boston, MA: Houghton Mifflin Co., 1913.
Wagner, Major Felix. 'Meine Eindrücke vom thrazischen Kriegsschauplatz und von der türkischen Armee im Zweiten Balkankrieg'. *Streffleur's Militärische Zeitschrift* 55(2) (1914), 258.
Waldmann, Anton. *Arzt und Soldat, Berlin 1936: Festschrift zum 60. Geburtstag des Heeres-Sanitätsinspekteurs im Reichskriegsministerium Generaloberstabsarzt Prof. Dr. Anton Waldmann*. Berlin, 1938.
Wallach, Jehuda. *Anatomie einer Militärhilfe: Die preußisch-deutschen Militärmissionen in der Türkei 1835–1919*. Düsseldorf: Droste, 1976.
Wawro, Geoffrey. *Warfare and Society in Europe 1792–1914*. London/New York: Routledge, 2000.
Weber, Antje. *Die Balkankriege 1912–1913 und das Ende der 'Türkei in Europa'*. Ph.D. dissertation. Tübingen: University of Tübingen, 2012.
Wiesner, Antonín. *Moderní válka po stránce lékaře* [The Modern War from the Perspective of the Doctor]. Prague: Vlastním nákladem J. Otto, 1913.

Yilmazer, Bülent. 'Ottoman Aviation, Prelude to Military Use of Aircraft', in Edward J. Erickson (ed.), *Defeat in Detail: The Ottoman Army in the Balkans 1912–13* (Westport, CT: Praeger, 2003), Appendix A, 347–70.

Zelepos, Ioannis. *Die Ethnisierung griechischer Identität 1870–1912: Staat und private Akteure vor dem Hintergrund der 'Megali Idea'*. Munich: Oldenbourg, 2002.

Ziemann, Benjamin. *Front und Heimat: Ländliche Kriegserfahrungen im südlichen Bayern 1914–1923*. Essen: Klartext, 1997.

Životić, Aleksandar. 'Srpski gerilski odredi na prostoru stare Srbije 1911–1912' [Serbian Guerrilla Units in Old Serbia 1911–1912], *Zbornik radova Instituta za savremenu istoriju* 9 (2007), 119–36.

Zürcher, Erik Jan. 'The Ottoman Conscription System 1844–1914'. *International Review of Social History* 43(3) (1998), 437–49.

Part II
Beyond the Balkans: Diplomatic and Geopolitical Aspects

 2

Ottoman Diplomacy on the Origins of the Balkan Wars
Gül Tokay

This chapter reassesses the origins of the Balkan Wars through the correspondence of Ottoman diplomatic envoys. The emphasis, however, is on how Ottoman officialdom interpreted the importance of regional issues such as the Cretan case and the Albanian issue in conjunction with the Macedonian question leading to the first Balkan War. So far, in Turkish historiography, the Balkan Wars have mostly been treated as another Turco-Bulgarian conflict, with the view that Bulgarian ambitions over Macedonia were the force behind the formation of the Balkan League and the commencement of war. On the other hand, issues such as the escalation of Serbo-Albanian tensions, the Albanian question and the Cretan case have been treated, with very few exceptions, as separate issues when examining the causes of the Balkan Wars. However, recent research in the Ottoman archives reveals that these latter issues may not have been the sole causes of the wars but rather were the factors that gave the decisive impetus to the formation of the Balkan alliance.

The background to the developments dates back to the 1878 Treaty of Berlin, signed at the end of the Russo-Turkish war. In Berlin, with the efforts of the European powers, a new status quo was adopted in the Balkans, which was to remain intact for thirty-five years. But the Young Turk Revolution of July 1908, followed by the October crisis (namely Bulgaria's declaration of independence), Austria-Hungary's annexation of Bosnia and Herzegovina, and the Cretans' demand for unification with Greece seriously challenged the settlement of the Berlin Treaty. More importantly, it showed that the Balkan states were no longer satisfied with the Berlin settlement and that any cooperation between the great powers was now an extremely remote possibility, circumstances that made war – a regional war, at least – all but inevitable.

Thus, the escalation of Austro-Serbian tensions after the appointment of Leopold von Berchtold as the Austro-Hungarian foreign minister in February 1912 and the Italian occupation of the Dodecanese islands in the Aegean Sea in May 1912 provided the final push in forming alliances among the Balkan states.

Within this framework, the present chapter, with the assistance of primary Ottoman documents and some European sources, reassesses the origins of the Balkan Wars and partially fills an existing gap in the historiography not only of the Balkan Wars but of the late Ottoman Empire as well. Ottoman documents provided the main research sources for this chapter, and there is the possibility that these sources do not always reflect the full picture, but were restricted by the Ottoman perspective. However, with new sources and reasoning, this chapter undoubtedly brings a different perspective to the question and opens areas for future research.

The Formation of Alliances, 1909–12

As Alexander Mavroyeni, the Ottoman ambassador in Vienna (1911–12), argued on the eve of the Balkan Wars, it was the changes in the 'Constantinople regime' in the aftermath of the Young Turk Revolution of 1908,[1] on the one hand, and the Ottomans' unwillingness to implement reforms for their Christian subjects, on the other, that ultimately caused the formation of the alliances leading to the war.[2] When the new regime began implementing stricter policies through their centralization efforts and the control mechanisms introduced on the Macedonian lands by 1909, Christian communities, as well as Muslim Albanians, lost many privileges they had previously enjoyed. There was a resultant increase in insurgent activities, contributing to the already existing turmoil.[3] However, more recent research indicates that it was, firstly, Austrian support for the Albanians under Austrian Foreign Minister Leopold von Berchtold, at the expense of Serbian and Montenegrin ambitions, and, secondly, Ottoman hesitance in solving the Cretan issue after the Italian occupation of the Dodecanese in May 1912, that finally compelled the formation of the Balkan alliances.[4]

The crises of Bulgarian independence, which brought the two states to the brink of war, ended with the treaty of April 1909, but this did not result in the expected peace in the Macedonian provinces. The Bulgarians subsequently stepped up their insurgent activities in Macedonia via the various wings of the Bulgarian movement.[5] In conjunction with developments after the October crisis of 1908, many Bulgarian officials

– especially King Ferdinand himself – favoured Bulgarian unification with the Macedonian provinces, namely Salonica, Monastir and Kosovo, and were thus waiting for an opportune moment for intervention. The Bulgarian foreign minister, Stefan Paprikov (1908–10), on the other hand, noted that the Macedonian question was the crucial regional problem regardless of the situation, and could not be decided without the more or less direct participation of the other Balkan states. In the meantime, Premier Ivan Geshov (1911–13) believed he would be able to achieve Macedonian unification by allying with Serbia against the Ottoman Empire.[6] Despite the fact that Macedonian unification was one of the new state's ultimate foreign policy goals, a more comparative research approach indicates that granting autonomous status would probably have delayed the formation of alliances and even prevented the war.[7] Ivan Geshov in particular was worried that a premature declaration of war would have negative consequences, and his views coincided with such prominent Ottoman statesmen of the period as Kamil and Izzet Paşas.

In the immediate aftermath of the annexation crises, Serbian–Ottoman relations were generally peaceful. There was also a short period of discussions on a possible agreement on mutual cooperation between the two states, but this was removed from the agenda after British interference, with Foreign Secretary Sir Edward Grey at the helm. The Serbian government could not risk losing British friendship and had to abandon the idea. The situation soon deteriorated, and the Serbs grew increasingly restless over the Albanians' outrageous behaviour and attacks in the Rumelian provinces, voicing their discontent with the local authorities' favouritism towards the Albanians, especially in the *vilayet* [province] of Kosovo.[8] Moreover, various propaganda organs and Macedonian emigrants fostered anti-Ottoman public opinion in the Serbian mainland; it was revealed that Serbs, especially in Ipek and Prishtina, where local circumstances were dire enough for them to seek assistance, were regularly coming under attack from the Albanians with the full knowledge of the Ottoman authorities.[9]

Already in early 1911, Fuad Hikmed Bey, the Ottoman minister (1910–12), wrote from Belgrade about an official entente – brought about by the Young Turks' aggressive policies in Macedonia – including Serbia, Montenegro, Greece and Bulgaria.[10] Furthermore, the future of the Sanjak of Novi Pazar was uncertain for the Serbs, who were convinced that the Austrian withdrawal from the Sanjak in 1909 was merely a temporary political measure.

Austrian expansionist designs in the peninsula, especially in Kosovo and the Sanjak after the Austrian annexation crises, and the escalation of Albanian insurgent activities and a series of Albanian uprisings (undoubtedly supported by the Austrians), forced the Serbs to ultimately sign an agreement with the Bulgarians, despite the existing differences between the two states. For the Albanians, however, the rigid policies of the Young Turks deprived them of the privileges they had previously enjoyed, leading to an increase in their activities in the provinces and to demands for independence, or, at the very least, autonomy.

The Albanians were already dissatisfied with the fact that the Treaty of Berlin excluded them from the Macedonian reforms, while promising, through Article 23, to improve the conditions of Christian subjects. With the implementation of the Macedonian reforms at the turn of the century, there was constant tension between the Muslim Albanians and the reformers, including the *Eshraf* (Muslim gentry, local notables) and the *Ulema* (respected Muslim scholars, mainly in religious affairs and law), notably in Monastir and Kosovo. Furthermore, discontent was voiced in the region about the existence of European supervision, as well as the strict measures introduced by Hilmi Paşa, the inspector general. Under these circumstances, a series of local uprisings by Albanians protesting the situation took place, and more and more Muslim insurrectionary bands were formed, contributing to the existing turmoil in the provinces.[11] After the 1908 revolution, despite the European reformers being given unlimited leave and being sent home, it was now the Young Turks' stricter policies that further deprived many local Albanians of their privileged status. Many local Albanian notables and leaders found that their interests competed and clashed with those of the Young Turk regime, further contributing to the unrest fomenting in the region.[12]

Despite the officials' denials, the Albanians had already secured the support of the Austrians and the Italians. With the support of many Italian officials, numerous Italian cities witnessed pro-Albanian demonstrations, demanding either autonomy or independence.[13] The Montenegrins also sent emissaries to Albania to rouse the local population, providing food and shelter to the insurgents, despite warnings by Russian officials.[14] There is evidence among Ottoman sources that the Montenegrins encouraged certain prominent Albanian revolutionary leaders – such as Isa Boletini – to revolt in Ipek. Despite being a loyal Ottoman, Boletini's interests clashed with the measures implemented by the Young Turks.[15] Besides, Albanians abroad hoped to receive official assistance for their demands and support to pressure the Ottoman administration for reforms, which they had been promised but had not yet materialized.[16]

Once the Italians and Austrians began to cooperate in regional affairs, the creation of an Albanian state acquired greater importance, as it would act as a buffer zone against Serbian and Montenegrin designs in the Adriatic. Since the late nineteenth century, both the Italians and the Austrians had insisted that the equilibrium in the Adriatic was not to be challenged by a third party, consequently raising the Albanian question to an international platform. But local factors and a power shift among local Albanian leaders produced by the Young Turk regime's new control mechanisms were probably the main reasons for the escalation in the Albanian movement and their demand for autonomy.[17]

The other important ongoing conflict that played a role in finalizing the Balkan alliances – especially the Greco-Bulgarian alliance in May 1912 – was the Cretan issue.[18] After a series of uprisings in the second half of the nineteenth century, the European powers assumed joint control over Crete in 1898, with the Sultan retaining his sovereign rights over the island.[19] Although Christians were a distinct majority on the island, Greeks did not have any power. There were rumours that the Russians secretly supported Greek aspirations to the island, whereas Austria-Hungary and Germany did not want to get involved. However, all the European powers wished to preserve and maintain the status quo for as long as possible and tried to prevent Greece's annexation of Crete, despite their sympathies lying with the island's Christians. They were aware that an annexation would negatively impact both the other Aegean islands under Ottoman control, inhabited mostly by Greeks, and the aspirations of the Balkan states.[20] The British in particular were worried that a change in the status quo, which would possibly have consequences in the other Aegean islands, would upset the equilibrium in the eastern Mediterranean.

When the Cretans demanded unification with Greece in 1908 following the October crisis, the Ottomans implemented an economic boycott to pressure the Cretans to give up their demands. The operation lasted until the island's unification with Greece in 1913, harming both governments.[21] Ottoman sources reveal that after 1908, Cretan revolutionary bands contributed to the existing turmoil more than the Greeks. Over the years, with the internationalization of the island's question, the nomination of a Greek high commissioner and the stationing of a local Greek *Militia* [soldiery] led to the island's gradual Hellenization. Under these circumstances, Ottoman rule over the island could be considered nominal at best. As many experienced Turkish and Greek statesmen stated on the eve of the Balkan Wars, uncertainty over the island was one of the main reasons for the Greek–Bulgarian alliance.[22]

The Road to War, March–October 1912

Although the Balkan states attempted to establish alliances among themselves starting in 1910, it was the events of spring 1912 that finalized the alliances. This *rapprochement* coincided with the appointment of Berchtold as Austro-Hungarian foreign minister following the death of Alois Lexa von Aehrental (1906–12) and the Italian occupation of the Dodecanese islands in the Aegean in May 1912. Although traditional Austro-Hungarian policy supported the status quo in the Balkans, Berchtold made no secret of his support for an Albanian state at the expense of Serbian and Montenegrin ambitions.[23] Furthermore, uncertainties about the future of the Aegean islands after the Italian occupation accelerated the finalization of the Greco-Bulgarian alliance. It also provoked Greek irredentism in Ottoman-held islands and encouraged the Cretans to once again demand unification with Greece.[24]

The Serbo-Bulgarian treaty was signed in March 1912; the Balkan alliance was more or less finalized by May 1912 with the signing of the Bulgarian–Greek treaty. During the Bulgarian–Serbian negotiations, there was a short impasse regarding the Struga Valley, but the problem was overcome after the Bulgarians yielded the territory to Serbia. A Serbo-Montenegrin alliance was finalized only in the first half of October.[25] The Ottoman documents reveal that the Montenegrins needed Serbo-Bulgarian assistance against any possible Ottoman attack. Under these circumstances, it was only on the eve of the war that agreements were reached with the Montenegrins, while the Romanians, due to their friendly relations with Vienna, opted to steer clear of any formal alliances.[26]

The Sublime Porte viewed the conflicting interests of the Bulgarians and Serbians in Macedonia as a guarantee of the status quo in Southeastern Europe.[27] Moreover, Ottoman envoys in the Balkan capitals dismissed any chance of a Greco-Bulgarian accord, as the Bulgarian king thought little of the Greeks' military capacity and because of the schism that divided the Bulgarian Exarchate and the Ecumenical Patriarchate. It was the Greeks' naval superiority and, more importantly, as Greek Prime Minister Eleftherios Venizelos (first premiership, 1910–15) stated on a number of occasions, the Cretan question that was the primary cause of the Greco-Bulgarian alliance. If the Ottoman Empire had permitted Greece's annexation of Crete, the Bulgarian–Greek alliance may never have materialized, and war may have never started or at least would have been delayed.[28]

The formation of alliances did not cause major anxieties in Ottoman or European circles, in which it was simply considered a defensive measure in response to developments in the peninsula.²⁹ The Ottoman minister in Sofia, Naby Bey, was misled by the Bulgarian premier Ivan Geshov, who assured him that the Bulgarian manoeuvres were mainly to maintain the status quo against Austrian aggression.³⁰ The Bulgarian–Serbian agreement may have been defensive in nature towards Austria-Hungary, but from Constantinople's vantage point it was construed as offensive towards Turkey.³¹ Only the French prime minister Raymond Poincaré (1912–13 as prime minister; 1913–20 as president) was concerned that a Balkan war had now become inevitable. Russian foreign minister Sergei Sazonov, on the other hand, having been cautious of Austria-Hungary since the 1908 crisis, was convinced that a future war in the peninsula depended on Berchtold's designs there.³²

While the Ottoman Empire did not show much anxiety about the formation of alliances, recent research in the Ottoman foreign ministerial archives reveals that once news about the alliance between the Balkan states reached the Ottoman capital, which coincided with the Italian occupation of the Dodecanese, the Ottomans initiated bilateral peace talks with Italy.³³ Furthermore, just before he was forced to resign as foreign minister in June 1912, Assim Bey asked the great powers to use their influence in the Balkan capitals to prevent the advent of war.³⁴ Assim Bey served in Sofia as Ottoman minister before being appointed as the foreign minister in 1911; he was therefore able to closely observe developments in the region over the years. In his correspondence with other officials, he expressed concern at the situation's deterioration and the ever-increasing possibility of war. Furthermore, certain sceptical Ottoman officials – Kamil Paşa in particular – argued that the government's reluctance to solve the Cretan issue had played a significant role in the Greek–Bulgarian treaty's finalization and that Macedonian autonomy may have prevented the Bulgarian alliance with the Serbs.³⁵

In July 1912, the cabinet of Said Paşa (grand vizier, 1911–12), backed by the Committee of Union and Progress (more commonly known as the Young Turks), resigned and a new ministry was formed under Gazi Ahmed Mukhtar Paşa, whose priority was to end the Albanian uprisings and war with the Italians.³⁶ Ottoman officials, however, were uncomfortable with the Italian occupation of the Dodecanese and were convinced that it would have a serious impact on Turco-Greek relations.³⁷ In the meantime, despite denials from Greek officials, news from the Ottoman islands about a significant increase in Greek irredentism soon reached the Ottoman Foreign Ministry. Ottoman envoys, especially the Ottoman ambassador in Athens, repeatedly warned their ministry of Greek 'intrigues'.³⁸

In the meantime, the situation in Crete grew increasingly unstable and difficult for the island's remaining Muslims. With the departure of Ottoman troops, many Muslims chose to emigrate, and the issue became progressively problematic for the Ottoman diplomacy to handle on the international level.[39] More importantly, however, the danger for the remaining Muslims in Crete persisted, and the Ottoman Ministry therefore asked the great powers – especially the British – for assistance in safeguarding the status quo and protecting the island's Muslims. But over the summer, with the boycott still in force, there were rumours that an annexation would take place in October, after the formation of the Balkan alliance.[40]

During the summer of 1912, the Albanian uprisings and Austro-Hungarian support for the creation of an autonomous Albania also caused anxiety.[41] While the Ottomans offered concessions to the Albanians in the *vilayets* of Kosovo, Scutari, Monastir and Janina, reforms in the rest of the Christian communities did not progress. The circumstances escalated existing tensions in the Macedonian provinces and intensified preparations for a possible war in the Balkans, especially among the Serbs.[42]

While Austria-Hungary supported the Albanian reforms, and buttressed Albanian national sentiment by pressuring for the opening of Albanian schools and institutions, it also encouraged the Albanians towards insurrection. Italy, on the other hand, allowed agitators within its own borders, permitting the presence of certain revolutionary Albanians and gaining support among Italo-Albanians.[43] Italian Foreign Minister Antonino di San Giuliano, however, denied rumours of any official Italian involvement in stirring up unrest among the largely Catholic Malisore tribes of northern Albania.[44] The available sources reveal that, with the Austrians' and Italians' encouragement of peaceful or revolutionary methods, more and more Albanian committees started to meet in various European capitals demanding independence or at least autonomy.

Throughout the period, Austria-Hungary cooperated with the rest of the powers over the Macedonian issue. Nevertheless, Berchtold also maintained that he could intervene to prevent Serbian and Montenegrin expansion in Kosovo and the Sanjak if and when the time came. In the meantime, he developed close working relations with the Ottoman ambassador in Vienna, Mavroyeni Bey, while the long-serving Austrian ambassador in Constantinople, Johann von Pallavicini, also exercised some influence in the Ottoman capital.[45] This close relationship between the Austrians and Ottomans influenced Ottoman decision-making, especially in terms of support for the Albanian concessions of August

1912. Yet at the same time, this same relationship contributed to the deterioration of Turco-Serbian relations in the summer of 1912.⁴⁶ By early autumn, Serbian circles began to see war as the only option.

For Italy, the Albanian question and the creation of an Albanian state were not minor issues. As di San Giuliano stated on more than one occasion, preventing disruption of the Adriatic's equilibrium was essential, but under the prevailing circumstances, the priority was to end the Turco-Italian war and confront the larger issue at a more opportune moment.⁴⁷ In August, after the Internal Macedonian Revolutionary Organization (IMRO, the Macedonian wing of the Bulgarian movement) instigated what came to be known as the Kochana incident, in which the Ottomans killed many Bulgarians, the Macedonian tensions reached their peak.⁴⁸ After the Kochana massacre, war seemed inevitable. For many Bulgarians, it represented the final push. It was only the Bulgarian prime minister Geshov who still hoped the Ottoman government would yield to political concessions to Macedonia and save the situation. He worried that a premature declaration of war would be far more disturbing. Geshov still considered an autonomy of sorts an option and attempted to reach a solution that would satisfy all the nationalities involved, thus avoiding war.⁴⁹ But a multitude of voices within Bulgarian official circles – including King Ferdinand – clamoured for war as the only option.

In the meantime, Ottoman official circles and Ottoman envoys abroad held that only the establishment of autonomous administrations would satisfy the Bulgarian–Macedonian committees.⁵⁰ But Ahmed Mukhtar Paşa's government was deaf to such claims, believing that the government's internally initiated reforms and an end to the Italian war would ease the situation.⁵¹ Undoubtedly, Mukhtar Paşa was an experienced soldier, but he lacked the political vision to lead the state under the circumstances. He thought the empire's problems would lessen once the military reforms were completed.

By late summer, it was not local developments but the differences between the great powers over the affairs in the peninsula that proved to be detrimental to attempts to solve the crisis in the Balkans via diplomatic means alone. While Austria-Hungary was in favour of maintaining the status quo for its future ambitions in Kosovo and Novi Pazar, the Russians favoured an expansion of Slavic territories in the peninsula and a separation – under Russian influence – of Europe from the Ottoman Empire.⁵² Over the late summer, Sazonov embarked on a European tour, mainly to establish an official opinion regarding developments in the Balkans. However, it soon dawned on him that cooperation between the powers was all but unachievable and that diplomatic circles had started to see war in the peninsula as a tangible alternative.[53] Under these circumstances, it would not be wrong to argue that the European powers began to accept the prospect of a localized war in the Balkans as a realistic alternative. They could not progress with reforms that would ease the existing turmoil in the Macedonian provinces or convince the Ottomans to take further steps to improve the conditions of their Christian subjects.[54]

By September, news reached Gabriel Effendi, the Ottoman foreign minister (1912–13), that the German cabinet considered war to be inevitable and was inviting the powers to consult with each other to find ways to localize the conflict and avoid further complications.[55] Around the same time, in a friendly conversation with Tevfik Paşa, the Ottoman ambassador in London (1909–14), Sazonov stated that efforts should concentrate on attempting to postpone the war in the Balkans, as it seemed the Ottomans could neither relent nor win it.[56] Now Ottoman circles began to seriously consider the possibility of war breaking out between the Empire and the Balkan states. Although many believed that the Bulgarians were behind the formation of the Balkan League and thus the commencement of war, Geshov, observing a warlike situation, decided to deliver a final ultimatum to the Ottomans and tried to come up with a scheme that would satisfy all nationalities involved. Geshov ultimately wanted Bulgaria's unification with the Macedonian provinces, but he thought the Bulgarian army was not ready to declare war on the Ottoman Empire; he also did not fully trust the alliance with Serbia. On the other hand, the rest of the Bulgarian officials were impatient and wanted to declare war on the Ottomans. The Bulgarian government's opinion was split more than anything else.

The proposals – based on Article 23 of the Berlin Treaty – were not radical. But they were too little too late, and by early October, in the midst of these discussions, Gabriel Effendi reported to Ottoman embassies on simultaneous general mobilizations in the Balkan states. He believed that the Montenegrins had aggressive designs, which he thought to be spontaneous rather than a coordinated action.[57] Peace was signed with Italy on 15 October, and the following day Turkey broke off diplomatic relations with the Balkan states. On 17 October, the Ottomans declared war against the Balkan allies. Soon after the war commenced, Ahmed Mukhtar resigned and the pro-British Kamil became the grand vizier.

From the Declaration of War to the London Conferences: October–December 1912

Under these circumstances, the great powers had to consent to war in the hope that it would remain localized. They thus declared their neutrality. Furthermore, the great powers jointly stated that they would not permit any changes to the territorial status of the Balkan states, nor would they allow any interventions into the sovereign rights of the Sultan. Lastly, the powers decided to put further pressure on the Ottoman Empire to implement the reforms based on Article 23 of the Berlin Treaty.[58]

However, aside from these official declarations, the powers were not completely against the idea of a partition of the Ottoman territories in Southeastern Europe based on the principle of nationality.[59] Despite enjoying cordial relations with the Porte, Berchtold stated that it was the Ottoman government that was responsible for the maltreatment of the different nationalities in European Turkey, and went on to say that, under the prevailing circumstances, a middle way had to be found to satisfy them all.[60] Furthermore, the Berlin Treaty signatories – namely the great powers – knew that the Balkans 'belonged' to the Balkan people, and it was the signatories' divergent interests and insistence on the status quo that hindered the people of the peninsula from fulfilling the demographic, geographic and nationalistic demands that had been voiced since 1878.[61]

By the time the Ottomans declared war, they had already prepared for the military option; offensive campaigns on the western and Thracian fronts were duly launched, despite the poor conditions of their armed forces. By early November, Gabriel Effendi had already informed the Ottoman envoys abroad that the Ottoman armies had been defeated and that the status quo was now likely to be modified in favour of the Balkan states.[62] Furthermore, by December 1912, Greek naval forces had occupied most of the Ottoman-held Aegean islands.[63] Despite the great powers' declaration of support for the status quo, Russian Foreign Minister Sazonov warned the Ottoman ambassador in St. Petersburg, Turkhan Paşa (1908–14), that only Ottoman arms could safeguard the Empire's territorial integrity. With the outbreak of war, Ottoman diplomats, especially those with experience, such as Rifaat Paşa in Paris, knew that the great powers' decision to maintain the status quo would only stand in the case of an Ottoman victory, an approach that was hardly unfamiliar to experienced Ottoman statesmen like Kamil Paşa who believed that only military gains and losses during the war shaped diplomacy.[64]

The ceasefire talks, which commenced on 20 November, were formally initiated on 25 November; on 3 December, an armistice was signed between the Ottoman Empire and the Balkan allies, with the exception of Greece, who wanted the war to drag on in an attempt to claim Janina. The allies demanded that the Ottomans surrender all European territories including the province of Adrianople and agreed to convene a conference in London ten days later.

Two conferences opened on 16–17 December in London. The St. James Conference was convened between the Balkan allies and the Ottoman Empire. The Ambassadors' Conference was staged for the signatories of the Berlin Treaty, under the presidency of Sir Edward Grey, the British foreign secretary, who had earlier suggested that the ambassadors of the great powers in London should meet to consult with the Balkan allies and discuss issues of mutual interest, including the question of Albania, the question of the Aegean islands and the question of a Serbian outlet to the Adriatic.[65] On the way to the conference, Ottoman negotiators were informed that the Porte was ready to negotiate on all questions, including Albania and Crete, and was willing to yield all territories west of Adrianople to the allies on the condition that Adrianople and the islands would remain under Ottoman rule.[66] Despite being one of the main factors in the formation of the Greco-Bulgarian alliance, there was little debate about the Cretan issue. During the conferences' early stages, the Ottomans rescinded their claims to the island; in 1913, Crete was unified with Greece. The Ottomans hoped to use Crete as a bargaining chip vis-à-vis the rest of the Aegean islands, a strategy that ultimately ended in disappointment.[67]

The Albanian issue, on the other hand, was one of the key issues of the ambassadorial conference. Throughout the event, Austria-Hungary and Italy's core issue was their support for Albanian independence.[68] The problem of balancing the Balkan allies' territorial aspirations with the creation of an Albanian state had represented their main problem.[69] The Austrians and Italians were particularly worried that the new state's borders would be drawn in favour of pan-Slavism and pan-Hellenism.[70] However, they did have the support of the Germans, who followed a passive policy throughout the Balkan crisis and acted in concordance with their Austrian allies.

With tension escalating between Russia and Austria-Hungary, the Ottomans were convinced that the Russians were playing a dangerous game. After a conversation with the former Russian foreign minister Aleksandr Izvol'skii in Paris, Ottoman Ambassador Rifaat sent a report stating that Russia was trying to prevent the establishment of Albania under the aegis of Austria-Hungary, while also pushing the Ottomans to keep it as an autonomous province, knowing the Albanians had not been loyal for a long time. According to Rifaat, this policy was mainly pursued to maintain regional instability, which would, in the long run, benefit the Serbs. Nevertheless, the policy also ran the risk of courting hazardous consequences in the future, leading to a major conflict involving the great powers as well.[71]

In the meantime, the primary concern of the British, especially Foreign Secretary Edward Grey, was to prevent any of the great powers from acquiring a naval base in the Aegean, which would disturb the eastern Mediterranean's status quo. The British in particular had substantial interests in the region and especially in Egypt. Maintaining the existing power balance and preventing change in favour of another great power was of the utmost importance for Grey.[72] While the British wanted the Italians to withdraw from the Dodecanese, they did not want the islands to be placed under Greek rule.[73] Italian interests in the Mediterranean also remained, despite the resolution of the Libyan issue at the end of the Turco-Italian war. Greek ambitions in the Aegean similarly clashed with Italian aspirations in the eastern Mediterranean. Conversely, Italy was deeply concerned by Greek activities in Epirus and southern Albania.[74] Under the circumstances, the Italian occupation of the Dodecanese became a bargaining tool over the course of the Balkan Wars and during the debates on the establishment of the new Albanian state's borders – an issue that persisted well after the Balkan Wars.[75] At a very early stage, with the transfer of the Albanian question to the ambassadorial conference, the Ottomans' role in the issue became merely symbolic. They did not wield any influence at the Ambassadors' Conference in London.

Concluding Remarks

With the Berlin Treaty of 1878, the European powers adopted a status quo in the Balkans that lasted for thirty-five years. Although they 'forgot' – as it was written in the dispatches – that the Balkans belonged to the Balkan people, their irresolvable divergent interests contributed to turmoil in the area. But for the same reason, as long as circumstances permitted, the great powers upheld the status quo in the peninsula.[76]

After the Balkan Wars ended, Berchtold openly stated that the only way war could have been prevented would have been to pressure Serbia and Montenegro to give up their designs in Sanjak and Kosovo and to withdraw their claims for an outlet in the Adriatic.[77] For the Ottomans, the only way they could have avoided or delayed war would have been by granting autonomy to Macedonia and by ceding Crete to Greece. Soon after the war commenced, Ottoman diplomats knew that only an Ottoman victory would maintain the status quo. Given the regional developments discussed in this study, politics on the eve of the war could not be *passivum*, a non-warlike situation, as Ottoman correspondence put it. All of the great powers hoped to avoid a European war, but when war in the Balkans became inevitable, they implemented a policy of non-intervention, hoping to localize the conflict. This was more or less the picture on the eve of the Great War, in the view of Hariciye, the Ottoman Foreign Ministry.

Gül Tokay is Visiting Professor at the School of Communication, Arts and Social Sciences at Richmond University, London. Her recent publications include 'Ottoman Diplomacy, the Balkan Wars and the Great Powers', in Dominik Geppert et al. (eds), *The Wars before the War: Conflict and International Politics before the Outbreak of the First World War* (Cambridge University Press, 2015) and 'Austro-Ottoman Relations and the Origins of World War One, 1912–14', *Perceptions. Journal of International Affairs* 22(2–3) (2015). She co-edited, with Sinan Kuneralp and others, the pluri-volume edition of *Ottoman Diplomatic Documents* (Isis Press, 2011–16).

Notes

1. The Ottoman foreign ministerial documents mostly refer to 'Constantinople'. I use the original place names stated in the documents throughout, rather than their contemporary names.
2. BBA (Prime Ministerial Archives – Başbakanlık Arşivi, Istanbul), HRSYS (Ottoman Foreign Ministerial Archives, Political Section) 1957/1, Mavroyeni to Gabriel, Vienna, 13 October 1912. For a bibliographic study on the Balkan Wars, see Hakan Bacanli, 'A Bibliography of the Balkan Wars', *Journal of Turkish World Studies* 12(2) (2012), 265–307.
3. Sinan Kuneralp and Gül Tokay (eds), *Ottoman Documents on the Origins of World War One*, Vol. VII: *The Balkan Wars 1912–1913* (Istanbul: Isis, 2012); Gül Tokay, 'The Origins of the Balkan Wars: A Reinterpretation', in Hakan Yavuz and Isa Blumi (eds), *War and Nationalism: The Balkan Wars, 1912–1913 and Their Sociopolitical Implications* (Salt Lake City, UT: Utah University Press, 2013), 182–87.
4. Sinan Kuneralp (ed.), *Ottoman Documents on the Origins of World War One*, Vol. III: *The Final Stage of the Cretan Issue, 1899–1913* (Istanbul: Isis, 2009), 584–86; Sinan Kuneralp (ed.), *Ottoman Documents on the Origins of World*

War One, Vol. VI: *The Aegean Islands Issue, 1912–1914* (Istanbul: Isis, 2012), 11; Tokay, 'The Origins of the Balkan Wars', 183–84.

5   Sinan Kuneralp and Gül Tokay (eds), *Ottoman Documents on the Origins of World War One*, Vol. IV: *The Macedonian Issue, 1879–1912*, Part 2, *1905–1912* (Istanbul: Isis, 2011). For an interesting assessment of the Young Turks' Macedonian policy, see Mehmet Hacısalihoğlu, 'The Young Turk Policy in Macedonia', in Yavuz and Blumi, *War and Nationalism*, 100–31.

6   Richard C. Hall, *The Balkan Wars: Prelude to the First World War* (London/New York: Routledge, 2000), 9–12. For the Bulgarian prime minister's views on unification, see Ivan E. Gueshoff [Geshov], *L'Alliance Balkanique* (Paris: Hachette, 1915); Elena Statelova, *The Rough Road to Statecraft: The Life of Bulgaria's Ivan E. Gueshoff*, trans. Matt Brown (Sofia: Academic Press, 1994).

7   Hikmet Bayur, *Sadrazam Kamil Paşa, Siyasi Hayatı* [The Political Life of Grand Vezier Kamil Paşa] (Ankara: Sanat Basımevi, 1954), 319; Richard C. Hall, 'Bulgaria and the Origins of the Balkan Wars', in Yavuz and Blumi, *War and Nationalism*, 85–99.

8   TNA (The National Archives, London), FO (Foreign Office documents) 195/2453, Bax-Ironside to Grey, Sofia, 4 January 1913; Tokay, 'The Origins of the Balkan Wars', 182–83; Isa Blumi, 'Impacts of the Balkan Wars: The Uncharted Paths from Empire to Nation', in Yavuz and Blumi, *War and Nationalism*, 528–57.

9   BBA, HRSYS 119/29, Fuad Hikmed to Assim, Belgrade, 20 March 1912.

10 Kuneralp and Tokay, *Ottoman Documents on the Origins of World War One*, Vol. IV, Fuad Hikmed to Rifaat, Belgrade, 19 February 1911, 447–48.

11 Gül Tokay, 'A Reassessment of the Macedonian Question, 1878–1908', in Hakan Yavuz and Peter Sluglett (eds), *War and Diplomacy: The Russo-Turkish War of 1877–1978 and the Treaty of Berlin* (Salt Lake City, UT: Utah University Press, 2011), 261–64.

12 Blumi, 'Impacts of the Balkan Wars', 528–40.

13 BBA, HRSYS 119/27, Mavroyeni to Assim, Vienna, 24 February 1912.

14 BBA, HRSYS 147/65, Sadreddin to Rifaat, Cettinge, 10 July 1911.

15 Blumi, 'Impacts of the Balkan Wars', 534–41.

16 BBA, HRSYS 147/2, Reshid to Rifaat, Vienna, 24 February 1911.

17 For an interesting reassessment of Berchtold after the Balkan Wars, see BBA, HRSYS 171/60, Mavroyeni to Said Halim, Vienna, 22 November 1913; Peter Bartl, *Albanische Muslime zur Zeit der Unabhängigkeitsbewegung, 1878–1912* (Wiesbaden: Harrassowitz, 1968), 180–83; Isa Blumi, *Reinstating the Late Ottoman Empire: Alternative Balkan Modernities, 1800–1912* (New York: Palgrave Macmillan, 2011).

18 Kuneralp, *Ottoman Documents on the Origins of World War One*, Vol. III.

19 There were series of uprisings against the Ottoman administration by Cretan Christians demanding similar rights to the island's Muslims and calling for the establishment of a confessional system, which later gave way to demands to unify with Greece.

20 Kuneralp, *Ottoman Documents on the Origins of World War One*, Vol. III, 12–14.

21 Ibid., Ghalib Kemaly to Rifaat, Athens, 11 August 1911, 507–8.

22 Ibid., Ghalib Kemaly to Assim, Athens, 6 January 1912, 548–49.
23 BBA, HRSYS 171/34, Mavroyeni to Gabriel Effendi, 27 September 1912; BBA, HRSYS 1096/82, Mavroyeni to Gabriel Effendi, Vienna, 28 September 1912; Tokay, 'The Origins of the Balkan Wars', 187–89; Tamara Scheer, 'A Micro-Historical Experience in the Late Ottoman Balkans: The Case of Austria-Hungary in Sanjak of Novi Pazar, 1879–1908', in Yavuz and Blumi, *War and Nationalism*, 197–229.
24 Kuneralp, *Ottoman Documents on the Origins of World War One*, Vol. VI.
25 Cf. Katrin Boeckh, *Von den Balkankriegen zum Ersten Weltkrieg: Kleinstaatenpolitik und ethnische Selbstbestimmung auf dem Balkan* (Munich: R. Oldenbourg Verlag, 1996), 28–29.
26 BBA, HRSYS 345/2, Tevfik to Gabriel, London, 10 August 1912.
27 Gueshoff [Geshov], *L'Alliance Balkanique*, 15–63; Tokay, 'The Origins of the Balkan Wars', 184–87.
28 Bilal Şimşir, *Ege Sorunu, Belgeler, 1912–1913* [The Aegean Question, Documents, 1912–1913], Vol. 1, 2nd ed. (Ankara: Turkish Historical Foundation, 1989); TNA, FO 424/242, Elliot to Grey, Athens, 14 February 1913, 520–21.
29 BBA, HRSYS 343/1, Mukhtar to Gabriel, Athens, 21 August 1912.
30 BBA, HRSYS 342/8, 'Bordereau du dossier, Entente Serbo-Bulgarie', Tevfik to Assim, London, 11 June 1912; Rifaat to Assim, Paris, 14 June 1912.
31 TNA, FO 195/2453, Bax-Ironside to Grey, Sofia, 6 January 1913.
32 Tokay, 'The Origins of the Balkan Wars', 187–88; for a personal account by Sazonov, see Sergei Sazonov, *Fateful Years, 1909–1916: The Reminiscences of Sergei Sazonov* (New York: Ishi Printing, 2008 [first published 1928]), 64–66.
33 Sinan Kuneralp (ed.), *Ottoman Diplomatic Documents on the Origins of World War One: The Turco-Italian War, 1911–12* (Istanbul: Isis, 2011), 12; Francesco Caccamo, 'The Balkan Wars in the Italian Perspective', in Yavuz and Blumi, *War and Nationalism*, 230–49. For an earlier study on the subject, see Timothy Childs, *Italo-Turkish Diplomacy and the War over Libya, 1911–1912* (Leiden: Brill, 1990).
34 Kuneralp and Tokay, *Ottoman Documents on the Origins of World War One*, Vol. VII, 11–13.
35 Bayur, *Sadrazam Kamil Paşa*, 313–24.
36 BBA, HRSYS 151/93, Aristarchi to Gabriel, Den Haag, 10 August 1912; Kuneralp and Tokay, *Ottoman Documents on the Origins of World War One*, Vol. VII, 12–13.
37 Kuneralp, *Ottoman Diplomatic Documents on the Origins of World War One: The Turco–Italian War*, 12.
38 Ibid., 11.
39 BBA, HRSYS 518/2, Tevfik to Assim, London, 29 June 1912; Kuneralp, *Ottoman Documents on the Origins of World War One*, Vol. III, 592–93.
40 Kuneralp, *Ottoman Documents on the Origins of World War One*, Vol. III, Gabriel to the Envoys, Hariciye, 14 October 1912, 597.
41 BBA, HRSYS 151/44, Mavroyeni to Assim, Vienna, 28 June 1912.
42 BBA, HRSYS 171/34, Mavroyeni to Gabriel Effendi, Vienna, 27 September 1912. In fact, Albanians' reforms were nothing radical and covered areas

such as use of their own language, amnesty and a return of arms. The discussion only touched on the question of autonomy.

43 For Austrian support of the Albanian instructed schools, see BBA, HRSYS 119/32, Mavroyeni to Assim, Vienna, 27 April 1912. Furthermore, news reached the Ottoman Foreign Ministry that the Austrians and the Italians were provoking Albanians towards insurrection: BBA, HRSYS 150/30, Mavreyoni to Assim, Vienna, 27 January 1912; BBA, HRSYS 151/44, Mavroyeni to Assim, 28 June 1912.
44 Caccamo, 'The Balkan Wars in the Italian Perspective', 234.
45 Sinan Kuneralp (ed.), *Studies on Ottoman Diplomatic History III, Dépêches d'Alexandre Mavroyeni Bey, Ambassadeur de Turquie à Vienne au ministre Ottoman des affaires étrangères, Decembre 1911–Octobre 1912* (Istanbul: Isis, 1989); Tokay, 'The Origins of the Balkan Wars', 186–87.
46 TNA, FO 881/10224, Vaughan to Grey, Bucharest, 29 September 1912; BBA, HRSYS 171/53, Naby to Said Halim, Rome, 29 October 1913; Sinan Kuneralp and Gül Tokay (eds), *Ottoman Diplomatic Documents on the Origins of World War One: The Albanian Issue* (Istanbul: Isis, forthcoming).
47 BBA, HRSYS 171/60, Huseyin Hilmi to Said Halim, Vienna, 19 November 1913; Caccamo, 'The Balkan Wars in the Italian Perspective', 234.
48 TNA, FO 881/10224, Granville to Grey, Sofia, 20 August 1912; Hall, 'Bulgaria and the Origins of the Balkan Wars', 96–97.
49 Hall, 'Bulgaria and the Origins of the Balkan Wars', 97.
50 Kuneralp and Tokay, *Ottoman Documents on the Origins of World War One*, Vol. IV, Mavroyeni to Gabriel, Vienna, 24 July 1912, 478–79.
51 BBA, HRSYS 151/93, Aristarchi to Gabriel, Den Haag, 10 August 1912; Tokay, 'The Origins of the Balkan Wars', 189–90.
52 TNA, FO 881/10224, Buchanan to Grey, St. Petersburg, 30 August 1912; BBA, HRSYS 1957/1, Turkhan to Gabriel, St. Petersburg, 30 September 1912.
53 Sazonov, *Fateful Years*, 43–76.
54 Ibid.
55 For the correspondence of Ottoman envoys on the coming of the war, see Kuneralp and Tokay, *Ottoman Documents on the Origins of World War One*, Vol. VII, 74–100.
56 Ibid., Tevfik to Gabriel, London, 21 September 1912, 86–87; on the mobilizations, see ibid., 98–108.
57 Hrant Bey Noradounghian, *Vers la guerre balkanique et vers la première guerre mondiale* (Istanbul: La Turquie Moderne, 1950); Hrant Bey Noradounghian, *Les Balkans et la Russie à la vielle de la première guerre mondiale: Mémoires d'un diplomate Ottoman*, 2nd ed. (Istanbul: Isis, 2010).
58 BBA, HRSYS 1957/1, Mavroyeni to Gabriel, Vienna, 8 October 1912.
59 BBA, HRSYS 1096/82, Mavroyeni to Gabriel, Vienna, 25 September 1912.
60 BBA, HRSYS 1096/82, Mavroyeni to Gabriel, Vienna, 28 September 1912.
61 Caccamo, 'The Balkan Wars in the Italian Perspective', 232–33, 242–44.
62 Noradounghian, *Vers la guerre balkanique*; Noradounghian, *Les Balkans et la Russie*.
63 Kuneralp, *Ottoman Documents on the Origins of World War One*, Vol. VI, Rifaat to Gabriel, Paris, 30 November 1912, 41.

64 Bayur, *Sadrazam Kamil Paşa*, 362. For the discussions leading to a ceasefire, see Kuneralp and Tokay, *Ottoman Documents on the Origins of World War One*, Vol. VII, 188–260.
65 For the details, see Ernst Christian Helmreich, *The Diplomacy of the Balkan Wars 1912–1913* (Cambridge, MA: Harvard University Press, 1938), 249–80; Necdet Hayta, *Balkan Savaşlarının Diplomatik Boyutu ve Londra Büyükelçiler Konferansı, 17 Aralık 1912–11 Augustos 1913* [The Diplomacy of the Balkan Wars and London Ambassadors' Conference, 17 December 1912–11 August 1913] (Ankara: Ankara Araştırma Merkezi, 2008); Kuneralp and Tokay, *Ottoman Documents on the Origins of World War One*, Vol. VII, 313–434; Gül Tokay, 'Ottoman Diplomacy, the Balkan Wars, and the Great Powers', in Dominik Geppert, William Mulligan and Andreas Rose (eds), *The Wars before the War* (Cambridge: Cambridge University Press, 2015), 58–75.
66 Kuneralp and Tokay, *Ottoman Documents on the Origins of World War One*, Vol. VII, 340–50; Bayur, *Sadrazam Kamil Paşa*, 370–78.
67 Kuneralp and Tokay, *Ottoman Documents on the Origins of World War One*, Vol. VII, Reshid to Gabriel, London, 7 January 1913; Gabriel to Ambassadors, Constantinople, 8 January 1913, 374–76.
68 Caccamo, 'The Balkan Wars in the Italian Perspective', 232–33, 242–44.
69 Ibid., 237.
70 BBA, HRSYS 119, Naby to Gabriel, Rome, 16 December 1912.
71 Kuneralp and Tokay, *Ottoman Diplomatic Documents on the Origins of World War One: The Albanian Issue*, Rifaat to Said Halim, Paris, 25 March 1913.
72 Şimşir, *Ege Sorunu*, 161–68; TNA, FO 421/282, Murray to Grey, Admiralty, 29 June 1912, 201–5.
73 TNA, FO 424/235, Grey to Bertie, FO, 15 November 1912; Kuneralp and Tokay, *Ottoman Documents on the Origins of World War One*, Vol. VII, Naby to Gabriel, Rome, 12 December 1912, 302–6.
74 Caccamo, 'The Balkan Wars in the Italian Perspective', 239–40.
75 Ibid.
76 BBA, HRSYS 171/60, Mavroyeni to Said Halim, Vienna, 22 November 1913; Kuneralp and Tokay, *Ottoman Diplomatic Documents on the Origins of World War One: The Albanian Issue*, Naby to Said Halim, Rome, 24 February 1913.
77 BBA, HRSYS 1866/6, Huseyin Hilmi to Said Halim, Vienna, 19 September 1913.

Bibliography

Bacanli, Hakan. 'A Bibliography of the Balkan Wars'. *Journal of Turkish World Studies* 12(2) (2012), 265–307.

Bartl, Peter. *Albanische Muslime zur Zeit der Unabhängigkeitsbewegung, 1878–1912*. Wiesbaden: Harrassowitz, 1968.

Bayur, Hikmet. *Sadrazam Kamil Paşa, Siyasi Hayatı* [The Political Life of Grand Vezier Kamil Paşa]. Ankara: Sanat Basımevi, 1954.

Blumi, Isa. *Reinstating the Late Ottoman Empire: Alternative Balkan Modernities, 1800–1912*. New York: Palgrave Macmillan, 2011.

——. 'Impacts of the Balkan Wars: The Uncharted Paths from Empire to Nation', in Hakan Yavuz and Isa Blumi (eds), *War and Nationalism: The Balkan Wars, 1912–1913 and Their Sociopolitical Implications* (Salt Lake City, UT: Utah University Press, 2013), 528–57.

Boeckh, Katrin. *Von den Balkankriegen zum Ersten Weltkrieg: Kleinstaatenpolitik und ethnische Selbstbestimmung auf dem Balkan*. Munich: R. Oldenbourg Verlag, 1996.

Caccamo, Francesco. 'The Balkan Wars in the Italian Perspective', in Hakan Yavuz and Isa Blumi (eds), *War and Nationalism: The Balkan Wars, 1912–1913 and Their Sociopolitical Implications* (Salt Lake City, UT: Utah University Press, 2013), 230–49.

Childs, Timothy. *Italo-Turkish Diplomacy and the War over Libya, 1911–1912*. Leiden: Brill, 1990.

Gueshoff [Geshov], Ivan E. *L'Alliance Balkanique*. Paris: Hachette, 1915.

Hacısalihoğlu, Mehmet. 'The Young Turk Policy in Macedonia', in Hakan Yavuz and Isa Blumi (eds), *War and Nationalism: The Balkan Wars, 1912–1913 and Their Sociopolitical Implications* (Salt Lake City, UT: Utah University Press, 2013), 100–31.

Hall, Richard C. *The Balkan Wars: Prelude to the First World War*. London/New York: Routledge, 2000.

——. 'Bulgaria and the Origins of the Balkan Wars', in Hakan Yavuz and Isa Blumi (eds), *War and Nationalism: The Balkan Wars, 1912–1913 and Their Sociopolitical Implications* (Salt Lake City, UT: Utah University Press, 2013), 85–99.

Hayta, Necdet. *Balkan Savaşlarının Diplomatik Boyutu ve Londra Büyükelçiler Konferansı, 17 Aralık 1912–11 Augustos 1913* [The Diplomacy of the Balkan Wars and London Ambassadors' Conference, 17 December 1912–11 August 1913]. Ankara: Ankara Araştırma Merkezi, 2008.

Helmreich, Ernst Christian. *The Diplomacy of the Balkan Wars 1912–1913*. Cambridge, MA: Harvard University Press, 1938.

Kuneralp, Sinan (ed.). *Studies on Ottoman Diplomatic History III, Dépêches d'Alexandre Mavroyeni Bey, Ambassadeur de Turquie à Vienne au ministre Ottoman des affaires étrangères, Decembre 1911–Octobre 1912*. Istanbul: Isis, 1989.

——. *Ottoman Documents on the Origins of World War One*, Vol. III: *The Final Stage of the Cretan Issue, 1899–1913*. Istanbul: Isis, 2009.

——. *Ottoman Diplomatic Documents on the Origins of World War One: The Turco-Italian War, 1911–12*. Istanbul: Isis, 2011.

——. *Ottoman Documents on the Origins of World War One*, Vol. VI: *The Aegean Islands Issue, 1912–1914*. Istanbul: Isis, 2012.

Kuneralp, Sinan, and Gül Tokay (eds). *Ottoman Documents on the Origins of World War One*, Vol. IV: *The Macedonian Issue, 1879–1912, Part 2, 1905–1912*. Istanbul: Isis, 2011.

——. *Ottoman Documents on the Origins of World War One*, Vol. VII: *The Balkan Wars 1912–1913*. Istanbul: Isis, 2012.

——. *Ottoman Diplomatic Documents on the Origins of World War One: The Albanian Issue*. Istanbul: Isis, forthcoming.

Noradounghian, Hrant Bey. *Vers la guerre balkanique et vers la première guerre mondiale*. Istanbul: La Turquie Moderne, 1950.

———. *Les Balkans et la Russie à la vielle de la première guerre mondiale: Mémoires d'un diplomate Ottoman*. 2nd ed. Istanbul: Isis, 2010.

Sazonov, Sergei. *Fateful Years, 1909–1916: The Reminiscences of Sergei Sazonov*. New York: Ishi Printing, 2008 [first published 1928].

Scheer, Tamara. 'A Micro-Historical Experience in the Late Ottoman Balkans: The Case of Austria-Hungary in Sanjak of Novi Pazar, 1879–1908', in Hakan Yavuz and Isa Blumi (eds), *War and Nationalism: The Balkan Wars, 1912–1913 and Their Sociopolitical Implications* (Salt Lake City, UT: Utah University Press, 2013), 197–229.

Şimşir, Bilal. *Ege Sorunu, Belgeler, 1912–1913* [The Aegean Question, Documents, 1912–1913]. Vol. 1. 2nd ed. Ankara: Turkish Historical Foundation, 1989.

Statelova, Elena. *The Rough Road to Statecraft: The Life of Bulgaria's Ivan E. Gueshoff*. Trans. Matt Brown. Sofia: Academic Press, 1994.

Tokay, Gül. 'A Reassessment of the Macedonian Question, 1878–1908', in Hakan Yavuz and Peter Sluglett (eds), *War and Diplomacy: The Russo-Turkish War of 1877–1978 and the Treaty of Berlin* (Salt Lake City, UT: Utah University Press, 2011), 253–72.

———. 'The Origins of the Balkan Wars: A Reinterpretation', in Hakan Yavuz and Isa Blumi (eds), *War and Nationalism: The Balkan Wars, 1912–1913 and Their Sociopolitical Implications* (Salt Lake City, UT: Utah University Press, 2013), 176–196.

———. 'Ottoman Diplomacy, the Balkan Wars, and the Great Powers', in Dominik Geppert, William Mulligan and Andreas Rose (eds), *The Wars before the War* (Cambridge: Cambridge University Press, 2015), 58–75.

 3

Austria-Hungary, Germany and the Balkan Wars
A Diplomatic Struggle for Peace, Influence and Supremacy
Alma Hannig

'Of all Balkan problems the South-Slavic or, rather, the Serbian question is the one of greatest importance for the monarchy. It is closely aligned to our vital interests, its resolution in terms of Greater Serbia would be suitable to call our conditions of existence into question.'[1] These were the words of the Austro-Hungarian foreign minister, Count Leopold von Berchtold (1863–1942), appealing to Germany on the occasion of an intensive 'diplomatic fight'[2] between the two allies in the summer of 1913. After the severe defeat suffered by Bulgaria in the Second Balkan War, and only a few days before the Bucharest peace treaty, the Viennese Foreign Ministry (Ballhausplatz) tried to explain to the Germans the political difficulties resulting from the Balkan Wars. Berchtold criticized Berlin's lack of interest and understanding of the 'permanent and unbridgeable' Austro-Serbian antagonism with regard to Serbia's aspirations for Austrian territories.[3] Although the Dual Monarchy did not have aggressive intentions towards Serbia, Berchtold refused Germany's advice to cooperate with Belgrade, treating it as proof of Berlin's 'misjudgement of the fundamental clash of interests'.[4] Another clash of interests formed a greater problem for the Ballhausplatz, emerging during the Balkan Wars and intensifying under the new German state secretary for foreign affairs, Gottlieb von Jagow (1863–1935), who refused to accept the leading role of Austria-Hungary regarding the Balkans and ignored Vienna's vital interests in the region.

As the only European great power without colonial ambitions, the Habsburg Monarchy had a strong interest in fostering its economic and political involvement in the Balkans.[5] Its main concern was to preserve a hegemonic position and the status quo. While Austrian foreign policy was entirely concentrated on Southeastern Europe, Germany was interested in this region only for two reasons. First, Germany was about to increase its trade relations with the Balkan states, and, second, it tried to prevent conflict between Austria-Hungary and Russia, as Russia's focus on the Balkans intensified following its defeat in the Russo-Japanese war of 1905. Compared to other regions, Germany's economic involvement in Southeastern Europe (mainly arms exports and loan politics) was minimal and could not compete with that of France and Russia.[6] For this reason, the Balkans never became a relevant factor for decision-making in Berlin.[7]

The Balkan Wars and their consequences became an important turning point for the central powers, changing their position within the system of European great powers. The purpose of this chapter is to analyse the diplomatic perceptions of the Balkan Wars in Berlin and Vienna, including their plans and actions during the crisis in 1912/13. Furthermore, I want to show how and why a 'diplomatic fight' over the appropriate policy in the Balkans broke out between the two allies, and what consequences the crisis had for the future cooperation and reputation of the alliance. Although domestic policy complicated the foreign policy in both countries, it must be omitted from the scope of this chapter.[8]

When the Italo-Turkish war over Libya began in 1911, Germany and Austria-Hungary adopted different positions. The latter was concerned about Italy's expansion, the weakening of the Ottoman Empire and the impact of the war on the national movements in the Balkans. While Germany did not share these concerns, it faced a dilemma: it cooperated with the Ottoman Empire in economic and military affairs, but was also allied to Italy. Eventually, the Germans chose to support Italy. Berlin was not interested in the national movements of the Balkan peoples and underestimated their relevance for a multinational state such as Austria-Hungary. Consequently, Germany failed to inform Vienna about the existence of the Bulgaro-Serb alliance and later the Balkan League in 1912.[9]

In a diplomatic note addressed to all European great powers in the late summer of 1912, the new Austro-Hungarian foreign minister, Count Leopold von Berchtold, who had been appointed in February, announced Vienna's interest in preserving the peace and status quo in the region and requested support.[10] The German secretary for foreign affairs, Alfred von Kiderlen-Wächter (1852–1912), was annoyed with Berchtold's address and warned the German chancellor, Theobald von Bethmann Hollweg (1856–1921), against Germany playing the 'Austrian satellite in the Orient'.[11]

The Central Powers and the First Balkan War

At the beginning of the First Balkan War in October 1912, when the Balkan League attacked the Ottoman Empire, all European great powers exercised a policy of 'wait and see', mainly expecting the Ottoman Empire to resist the attack. The central powers declared their interest in the integrity of the Ottoman Empire, but refused any military involvement.[12] In contrast to their Austrian partner, neither Bethmann Hollweg nor Kiderlen-Wächter put forward any specific political programme for the Balkans.[13] The principal aims of German foreign policy were to preserve the peace in Europe and to stabilize its position within the system of European powers. Both of these goals were to be achieved by an improvement of Anglo-German relations.[14] Given this policy, the rapid defeat of the Ottoman Empire surprised the political leaders in Berlin, especially because the Ottomans were trained by German instructors and supplied with German weapons. However, Germany agreed to accept the territorial changes, as all great powers did – except for the Habsburg Monarchy. German public opinion, as well as all of Western Europe, admired the South Slavs' military action. Even Emperor Wilhelm II was enthusiastic about the bravery and the success of the Balkan states, calling them 'the seventh great power'.[15] He also regarded Serbia's claim to access to the Adriatic Sea as justified and as being without negative effects for Austrian interests.[16] For Austria-Hungary, however, Serbian access to the Adriatic Sea was a serious problem, as it feared that Russia would use it as a naval base. The Dual Monarchy was forced to reconsider its Balkan policy, as the Serbian territorial expansion made the monarchy vulnerable to becoming the next target for a Serbian attack. A group of leading diplomats at the Ballhausplatz discussed future policies and defined the vital interests of Austria-Hungary in Southeastern Europe as maintenance of the status quo in the Balkans and prevention of any other state settling on the eastern coast of the Adriatic Sea.[17] In order to achieve this, an Albanian state was to be created, which would be defended by military action if necessary. Austria-Hungary expected the Balkan states to consolidate their economic relations with Vienna and to accept Salonica as a free commercial port.[18] While waiving its own claims for territorial expansion, the Dual Monarchy demanded territorial compensation for its ally Romania in the case of an expansion of Bulgaria.[19] The situation changed in November 1912, when Serbian forces arrived at the Adriatic coast and Russia carried out a trial mobilization near the northeastern border of Austria, which led to concerns in Vienna that sudden cavalry raids could disrupt the vital Austrian rail links in Galicia.[20] Austria-Hungary's response was to reinforce its troops in Galicia and Bosnia. While France and Great Britain heightened their military readiness, Germany officially supported the Dual Monarchy, but kept its military activity at a low level.[21] As the conflict threatened to escalate, Berchtold discussed the measures 'in case of the ... no longer ruled out eventuality of a winter war' with the common minister of finance, the prime ministers of Austria and Hungary, as well as the leaders of the military, the chief of general staff and the common war minister.[22] The political leaders of both central powers tried to hold back their respective militaries, which were pleading for war.[23]

Nevertheless, for the first time, the heir to the throne in Austria-Hungary, Archduke Franz Ferdinand (1863–1914), supported military action.[24] In preparation for a war against Serbia, the archduke planned to inform the monarchs and chiefs of general staff of Germany, Romania and Russia, hoping to gain support from his allies and to prevent the Tsar from entering the war. Franz Ferdinand's envoys, two well-known 'hawks', the former military attaché in Russia, Prince Gottfried zu Hohenlohe (1867–1932), and the former chief of general staff, Franz Conrad von Hötzendorf (1852–1925), were to be sent to Saint Petersburg and Bucharest respectively. The archduke himself went to Berlin, accompanied by his chief of general staff, Blasius Schemua (1856–1920). The meetings in Germany and Romania went well, as both Franz Ferdinand and Conrad received the expected assurance of military support.[25]

However, neither Bethmann Hollweg nor Kiderlen-Wächter, who had pleaded for a conference of great powers to put an end to the Balkan conflicts, were informed. Kiderlen, the German state secretary for foreign affairs, stopped the initiative when he dissuaded Berchtold from sending Hohenlohe to Russia and, in an article published in the semi-official *Norddeutsche Allgemeine Zeitung*, warned every great power against precipitous steps and acting alone.[26] Bethmann Hollweg tried to reduce the negative consequences of Kiderlen's actions for Austro-German relations when he declared in the Reichstag that, should Austria-Hungary be attacked by 'a third party, and their existence thereby threatened, then we, true to our alliance obligations, would have to step resolutely to the side of our ally'.[27] This was a 'double strategy':[28] while Kiderlen-Wächter determined the limits and refused to support Austria's belligerent policy, Bethmann Hollweg helped to diminish Viennese dissatisfaction over Kiderlen's article and at the same time signalled to the Triple Entente Germany's solidarity with the Habsburg Monarchy.

A declaration by the British government followed, in which it stated that in case of a general war, caused by German support for Austria-Hungary and involving France, Great Britain would not be able to remain neutral.[29] The German emperor panicked and, on 8 December 1912, called a crisis conference with his military leaders Alfred von Tirpitz, Helmuth von Moltke and Admiral Georg Alexander Müller, in order to discuss the eventuality of a general war. Ever since the 1960s, this conversation has been the subject of considerable controversy among historians dealing with the question of whether or not this so-called War Council (*Kriegsrat*) did decide to prepare and start a general war in Europe.[30] While Moltke clearly opted for a preventative war 'the sooner, the better', Tirpitz pleaded for a further delay (at least for eighteen months).[31] No concrete decision was made, and again the chancellor and the foreign secretary were neither notified nor consulted. Much later, they were told that the government should make the German public aware that Germany might enter a European war in support of Austria-Hungary's Balkan policies. Some historians have argued that the 'War Council' revealed the leading position of the German emperor in the decision-making process and set the course for war preparations. Others have considered it as being a response to an international crisis without any serious consequences. In the end, the conference did not lead to an official press campaign, nor was it the starting point for systematic German war preparations. It did, however, accelerate the preliminary draft of a new armaments bill already under way, which was similar to the army laws adopted by all the continental powers as a result of the First Balkan War.[32]

Finally, as Britain and Germany had no genuine interests in the Balkans but shared the common aim of preserving peace, they cooperated to organize an ambassadors' conference for the great powers.[33] For Bethmann Hollweg, this was a welcome opportunity to approach his target of an Anglo-German *détente*. In his instructions for the German ambassador in London, Prince Lichnowsky (1860–1928), the chancellor formulated that Germany and Great Britain should influence the belligerent parties in order to keep the peace among the great powers. Furthermore, Anglo-German cooperation in this question would offer 'a good basis for the improvement of our general political relations with England'.[34]

Meanwhile in Austria-Hungary, Archduke Franz Ferdinand still argued in favour of a war and, in December 1912, appointed two 'hawks', Conrad von Hötzendorf and Alexander von Krobatin, as chief of general staff and minister of war, respectively. However, Berchtold accepted the proposal for a conference in London. Although the Triple Alliance was renewed, Berchtold was successful in advising the Emperor Franz Joseph to opt for a peaceful solution.[35] The entire incident demonstrates, on the one hand, that Germany did not have aggressive plans and actually preserved the peace, as Kiderlen-Wächter recorded in a letter to his sister.[36] On the other hand, it shows that Austro-Hungarian war plans could not work without definite support from Germany. Moreover, this was the only occasion before July 1914 in which Vienna made plans for a war against Serbia.

When the Ambassadors' Conference in London began in December 1912, the great powers were willing to accept some territorial changes in the Balkans due to the military successes of the Balkan League. Berchtold, though, required a declaration that the new borders would be definitive and irreversible, in order to prevent any future expansion of Serbia. Without any plans for an enlargement of Austria-Hungary, he required compensation for Romania and the creation of an autonomous Albania.[37] The first conversations went well, but the discussion of the future Albanian frontiers required concessions from Vienna and Saint Petersburg.[38] Concerned with the 'belligerent mood'[39] in Austria-Hungary, Berlin warned Vienna not to risk war with Russia, which would lead to a war between the alliances and expose Germany to French and British attacks.[40] Bethmann Hollweg's plan to use the Anglo-German cooperation regarding the Balkans 'as a starting point for future good relations' seemed to work, as he stated in January 1913 that 'it was worth more than any Naval Agreement or political understanding'.[41] At the same time, he had to remind his austrophobic ambassador in London, Prince Lichnowsky, to support Austria-Hungary, for any weakening of the Austro-Hungarian partner would imply a weakening of Germany itself.[42]

The disarmament agreement between Russia and Austria-Hungary put an end to the greatest risk of a continental escalation in March 1913. Bethmann Hollweg and the British foreign secretary, Sir Edward Grey, continued to pressure Russia and Austria for a peaceful solution of the question of the Albanian borders.[43] Both the German chancellor and British foreign secretary were satisfied with the improvement of Anglo-German relations and showed mutual recognition for their respective peace efforts.[44] Even the British and German press promoted an Anglo-German *détente*.[45] Despite the successes during the negotiations, Austria-Hungary was disappointed about what happened in London: Germany and Italy supported Vienna only insufficiently, and the resolutions adopted by the great powers were respected neither by Serbia nor by Montenegro. Only the threat of Austrian military action forced the Montenegrin troops to withdraw from the Albanian city of

Shkoder/Skutari in May 1913.⁴⁶ A few months later, the same happened with Serbia, when Serbian troops occupied territories that had been awarded to Albania.⁴⁷ Besides the enormous costs for the mobilization of the army, the main consequence for Austria-Hungary of the Ambassadors' Conference was that Berchtold doubted the efficacy of the conference's diplomacy as the great powers showed indifference. The ruling circles in Vienna realized the limits of 'armed diplomacy'.⁴⁸ Berlin was convinced that the British played the key role in resolving the Skutari crisis and was disappointed when Foreign Secretary Grey returned to the Entente at the culmination of the crisis, fearing that Britain would be isolated from France and Russia.⁴⁹

A 'Diplomatic Fight' between Germany and Austria-Hungary

After the sudden death of Kiderlen-Wächter, who was an experienced diplomat and an expert on Southeastern Europe, the German policy on the Balkans changed, complicating the relations between Austria-Hungary and Germany. The new state secretary for foreign affairs, Gottlieb von Jagow, was the former German ambassador to Rome and a committed Social Darwinist who believed in a forthcoming war between the 'Slavs and Teutons', as did almost all leading political and military circles in Berlin.⁵⁰ This thinking was dominated by the idea of the Russian or Slav peril and the assumption that the central powers were gradually weakening in comparison to Russia.⁵¹ The worries and fears in Germany of Russia and Slavdom intensified massively during the Balkan Wars because of the rapid expansion of all Balkan states and Russia's trial mobilization in December 1912. While his Bulgarophile predecessor had supported Austrian plans for a *rapprochement* with Sofia, Jagow instead suggested cooperation with the non-Slavic Balkan states (Romania and Greece) in order to 'contain the Slav wave on the Balkans'.⁵² Astonishingly, the new state secretary refused to cooperate with Bulgaria, but simultaneously recommended a *rapprochement* with Serbia.⁵³ Jagow apparently did not notice or care about the contradictions in his views: he declared the 'Slav peril' as the greatest danger for the future of the central powers, although a large part of the Austro-Hungarian peoples were Slavs, and wanted to contain 'the Slav wave' in cooperation with one of the most aggressive Slavic countries of that time. Above all, this policy showed Jagow's total lack of understanding regarding Austria-Hungary's vital interests, which were threatened by Belgrade. Emperor Wilhelm II and Chancellor Bethmann Hollweg shared his views and tried to add the Ottoman Empire to Romania and Greece in the fight against the 'Panslavic danger'.[54]

While German foreign policy before the Great War was generally characterized by disparity and conflicts over responsibilities among the leading personalities of the empire, it became remarkably congruent in the summer of 1913.[55] At the same time, different conceptions of a Balkan policy existed in Austria-Hungary: the Foreign Ministry pleaded for closer cooperation with Bulgaria, the strongest and most successful country in the First Balkan War, in order to build a protective wall against Serbia.[56] Archduke Franz Ferdinand, however, supported the German foreign policy and refused Bulgaria as a partner. Similar to Emperor Wilhelm II and the political leaders in Berlin, the Austro-Hungarian heir to the throne mistrusted Bulgaria, including King Ferdinand, who was viewed as unreliable and dependent on Russia and France.[57] The military leaders in Vienna, for their part, mostly argued for a war against Serbia.

When the Second Balkan War started and Austria-Hungary's ally Romania joined Serbia in the fight against Bulgaria, Vienna faced a dilemma. On the one hand, Austria felt obliged to support Romania's claims, but on the other hand it needed Bulgaria to check Serbia. Although Franz Ferdinand, and even Conrad von Hötzendorf, refused an intervention for the benefit of Bulgaria, Berchtold actually considered it in order to prevent further Serbian expansion.[58] Germany strictly rejected an intervention and contributed to the preservation of the European peace, but this time without the knowledge of Great Britain.[59] Berchtold's attempt to manoeuvre between Sofia and Bucharest failed, and in the end both sides were dismayed at not receiving more support from the Dual Monarchy.[60]

The Peace of Bucharest, signed in August 1913, marked the end of the Second Balkan War and demonstrated notable disagreements between Germany and Austria-Hungary. Wary of the alliance between Serbia and Romania as well as of their enormous expansions at the expense of Bulgaria, the Habsburg Monarchy demanded a modification of the peace settlement in favour of Bulgaria. Berlin was content with the success of Romania and Greece and refused a revision of the settlement.[61] Although he was not supposed to act without prior consultation with the chancellor, Wilhelm II congratulated and decorated the King of Romania in a published telegram upon the conclusion of peace in Bucharest.[62] Here, the emperor's family ties to Romania and Greece (King Carol I was a Hohenzollern and one of the emperor's sisters was married to the Greek monarch), as well as the military success in the Second Balkan War, were decisive. As Austria-Hungary could not object, it submitted, and at that moment the failure of its foreign policy became evident: Romania was alienated, Bulgaria was disappointed and Serbia had doubled in size, while Russian influence in the region had increased. Vienna felt 'betrayed and sold out'[63] by Berlin, and it seemed as if Germany had taken over Austria-Hungary's Balkan policy. In the following months, the Ballhausplatz formulated several memoranda and sent special envoys to Berlin, trying to persuade the ally of the accuracy of Vienna's Balkan policy.[64] One of these documents was Berchtold's decree of 1 August 1913, cited at the beginning of this chapter, in which he developed the Austro-Hungarian conception for the Balkans in compliance with the changed situation after the Balkan Wars. Although Berchtold did not wish for a war against Serbia, he was convinced that it would eventually happen, due to Russian and Serbian aggression. In order to prevent it or at least to create the best possible conditions for war, a 'configuration [of] natural allies' should be formed. This implied an alliance with Sofia. Berchtold listed every counterargument against the German Balkan policy: first he argued that Bulgaria's relations with Russia had deteriorated because of Russia's lack of support for Bulgaria during the Balkan Wars.[65] Secondly, he put Romania's loyalty into question because of its cooperation with Serbia. Finally, Berchtold explained that an alliance with Greece would not be an adequate substitute for one with Bulgaria, for Vienna would have no chance of winning a war against Russia, Serbia and Bulgaria.

The Ballhausplatz repeatedly communicated the necessity to adopt a common approach and to act jointly with Germany.[66] The Hungarian prime minister, István Tisza (1861–1918), who was highly respected in Berlin, also underlined the enormous importance of 'intimate cooperation' between the central powers.[67] He supported and sometimes even initiated Berchtold's foreign policy.[68] Acknowledging Germany's Balkan plans, he insisted on integrating Bulgaria into a common alliance. Being aware of Germany's fear of Russia, Tisza used Berlin's metaphor of the 'encirclement' on the Dual Monarchy and underlined the dangers for Germany should the Austro-Hungarian military forces be bound by Russian, Serbian and eventually Romanian troops.[69] The only way out of this 'iron ring'[70] would be an alliance with Bulgaria, flanked by Romanian, Greek and Turkish benevolence. The paradigm used by Berchtold and Tisza recurred in all relevant diplomatic writings and conversations between Berlin and Vienna – yet without any visible effect on German foreign policy, which was characterized by several misinterpretations.[71] The German government underestimated the depth of the relations between Romania and Russia, as well as those between Russia and Greece. It assumed that Serbia had been weakened so much by the two Balkan Wars that Austria-Hungary did not have to fear Belgrade in the near future. Germany also misinterpreted the position of Russia, assuming that its influence had diminished in the Balkans, as Saint Petersburg had not been able to prevent the Balkan League from falling apart. And finally, Berlin misjudged the intensity of Russo-British relations and continued to believe that an Anglo-German *détente* was possible.

German conduct during the next crisis in the Balkans in October 1913 provoked the opposite perception in London. When the Serbian army and Greek irregular formations occupied Albanian territories, Berlin asked Great Britain for help in exerting diplomatic pressure in Belgrade and Athens. Before London could react, Austria had presented an ultimatum to Belgrade and an Austro-Italian *démarche* to Athens. British impressions of Germany's unreliability and its incapability of controlling its junior partners intensified, as everyone assumed that Germany had had knowledge of the diplomatic steps of its allies before it asked for British assistance.[72] At the same time, suspicion rose in Vienna that Austria's interests were being sacrificed by Germany for the sake of strengthening the Anglo-German *détente*.[73]

In the last months before the outbreak of the Great War, the leading circles of the central powers focused on the reliability of Romania. The austrophobic atmosphere in the country, the conflicts over the Romanian minority in Hungary, and Bucharest's alliance with Austria's 'deadly enemy'[74] Serbia made the Ballhausplatz question the value of the alliance.[75] The archduke was the only one among the Austrian ruling elites who trusted the loyalty and authority of the King of Romania, and therefore refused to cooperate with Bulgaria.[76] The uncertainty of what would happen after King Carol's death was of particular concern. Austrian attempts to improve and clarify relations between Vienna and Bucharest by sending an intimate friend of Franz Ferdinand, Count Ottokar Czernin (1872–1932), as an envoy to Romania, failed.[77] The Austrian chief of staff had serious doubts about Romania's reliability and demanded the fortification of the Hungaro-Romanian frontier in Transylvania.[78] Berlin, still not accepting Bulgaria as an alternative to Romania, criticized Berchtold for putting pressure on King Carol by asking him to make the Austro-Romanian alliance public.[79] After the Russian royal visit to Romania in June 1914, the probability of Romanian loyalty towards the Triple Alliance sank. This was one of the main topics of conversation during the last meeting between Wilhelm II and Franz Ferdinand in Konopiště, Bohemia on 12 and 13 June 1914. One day later, Foreign Minister Berchtold came to Konopiště too, discussing the same subject with the heir to the throne. After his return to Vienna, Berchtold directed one of the Ballhausplatz officials, Franz von Matscheko, to draw up a memorandum on the future Balkan policy, focusing on Romania's unreliability.[80]

The addressee of the memorandum was Germany, which was to be provoked by the perceived Russian and French aggressiveness and their subversive activities against the Triple Alliance in the Balkans.[81] In order to find out whether Romania had changed its foreign policy, it was to be asked to publicly declare its alliance with the central powers. Should Romania refuse to do so, then Bulgaria had to be won for the alliance and the Hungarian frontiers with Romania had to be fortified.[82] The memorandum ended by requesting that Berlin adopt the Austro-Hungarian plans. As the memorandum was finalized on 24 June 1914, only four days before the assassination of Franz Ferdinand, it never reached its recipient in this form. Revised and complemented by aggressive statements against Serbia, it was delivered by the Austro-Hungarian diplomat, Count Alexander Hoyos (1876–1937), to Berlin on 5 July 1914. At this moment, the aims of the Habsburg foreign policy had changed from a peaceful solution – the forming of an anti-Serbian coalition – to a war that would improve the position of the Dual Monarchy.

In the last months and weeks before the war, the German government was increasingly concerned with the deteriorating position of the German Empire within the European system of powers, caused especially by the tensions with Russia regarding the military mission of Lieutenant General Liman von Sanders (1855–1929) in Constantinople, and the stagnation of the Anglo-German *détente*. Progressively, the peaceful and anglophile politics of Bethmann Hollweg and Jagow seemed to be doomed to failure.[83] Consequently, when, in July 1914, Vienna demanded support from Berlin in the case of a war against Russia, Germany quickly decided in favour of its alliance partner.

Conclusion

In summary, the Balkan Wars had a completely different significance for Germany and Austria-Hungary and they caused a souring of relations between the two allies. The position of the two central European states within the concert of great powers was different and this difference increased during and after the Balkan Wars. Germany's economic and military strength was highly respected and presumably feared by all European states. The Dual Monarchy, on the contrary, was perceived as the next 'sick man of Europe' after the Ottoman Empire. During the Balkan Wars, Austria-Hungary's position deteriorated even more, as the expansion of Romania and Serbia increasingly became hegemonic in Southeastern Europe, and Russia increased its political influence. While Austria-Hungary felt threatened by the enlargement of Serbia and the general strengthening of the national movements in the Balkans, Berlin treated the conflicts as an opportunity to demonstrate its disinterest in the region and its general peacefulness.[84] This demonstration was primarily directed towards Great Britain, with the aim of improving Anglo-German relations.

Vienna and Berlin did have one thing in common – the fear of pan-Slavism. However, they feared it for different reasons: while national and chauvinistic movements threatened the stability and integrity of the Austro-Hungarian state, Germany was afraid of Russian power and strength, especially in combination with its system of satellite states in the Balkans. Due to their distinct state structures, their ideas about how to come to terms with pan-Slavism also differed. For Austria-Hungary, where almost half of the population were Slavs, it was essential to have at least one Slavic country as a partner. For Germany, it seemed more reasonable to build an anti-Slavic coalition in the Balkans with Romania, Greece and possibly the Ottoman Empire. The only Slavic state with which Berlin was willing to cooperate was Serbia, which in turn was unacceptable for the Dual Monarchy, as it perceived the Serbian government as irreconcilable towards Vienna. Even though Germany never managed to win over Greece or the Ottoman Empire for an alliance, or to improve the relations with Romania, it stuck to its plan, which was based on several misjudgements regarding the Balkan states and Russia. The Ballhausplatz's main priority of forging an alliance with Bulgaria, which in retrospect seems the most reasonable consideration, was rejected by Berlin. Isolating Serbia and blocking Russian influence in the Balkans would have reduced the general risk of war and strengthened the position of the Dual Monarchy in Southeastern Europe. Two features were characteristic of the Austro-Hungarian foreign policy during this period: an enormous dependence on Germany and the disunity among the leading circles in Vienna regarding the Balkan policy. The latter finally caused Berlin to take over the political leadership on the matter.

Any assessment of Austro-Hungarian foreign policy during the Balkan Wars must be negative. Vienna missed its main political target of keeping the peace and status quo in the Balkans during the First Balkan War. At first glance, the Austro-Hungarian policy appeared to be partially successful, as two of her demands were fulfilled – Serbia was not granted access to the Adriatic, and Albania was founded. However, both demands were only reached after long negotiations and under the threat of violence. The lack of support from its allies and the lack of interest and commitment of the other great powers at the Ambassadors' Conference in London shattered the credibility of the Concert of Europe in the eyes of the decision-makers in the Habsburg Monarchy.

The only real war scare that was provoked by Austria-Hungary before the Great War was initiated by the heir to the throne, often referred to as the 'Prince of Peace'.[85] His intentions were not to destroy the Serbian state or to annex territories, but to demonstrate the power of Austria-Hungary as well as to secure its prestige and the Habsburg hegemony in the Balkans. This was however defused by Kiderlen-Wächter. On several occasions during the Balkan Wars, Berlin exercised a policy of moderation and appeasement in favour of peace-keeping. When Austria-Hungary realized that Germany would not support a military solution, it concentrated all its activity on the formation of a new Balkan League, under its leadership and directed against Serbia, convincing Germany of the necessity to support the League. None of the political concepts of the Ballhausplatz for the Balkans since the Treaty of Bucharest included aggressive plans for a war against Serbia or any war aims at all.[86] There was nothing in these documents that would support the thesis that Vienna was looking for a pretext to start a war against Serbia.[87] Rational political calculations, not pacifism, were decisive for Berchtold's peaceful plans: Austria-Hungary's insecurity regarding the loyalties of its allies; the doubtfulness of the integrity of the state and military in case of a war against a Slavic country; the danger of a revolution; the high financial costs; and the unpredictable reaction of the other great powers were all grave arguments against war. Territorial expansion was not desirable for domestic reasons. In fact, there was nothing to achieve in a war that could not be achieved peacefully. Austria-Hungary's military development, inherent military weakness and comparatively low military investments were also good arguments to avoid a war.[88] If many documents still refer to a possible war, however, mostly assuming that Serbia or Russia would start it, it was by no means a paradox, for no (great) power refused war as an instrument of policy at that time. However, Austria-Hungary was not yearning for war. Vienna's main problem in finding a peaceful solution was Berlin, which was permanently opposed to an alliance with Bulgaria for ideological and dynastic reasons.[89]

Austria-Hungary's integrity and position as a great power, as well as the stability of the Triple Alliance, were important for Germany, but it never understood or respected the needs of the Dual Monarchy.[90] The obsession of leading circles in Berlin with a forthcoming war between 'Slavs and Teutons' often impeded rational political considerations.

Germany's 'dual strategy' of restraining Austria-Hungary from involvement in the conflict and simultaneously signalling support to the Triple Entente helped to preserve the peace. In the long term, however, this policy failed: for months, German policymakers had oscillated between moments of support for Austria-Hungary and declarations of extreme political caution. Vienna never felt certain of its allies' support, which resulted in distrust and disillusion; eventually, this destabilized the alliance and undermined Austria-Hungary's position among the European system of states.[91]

The main target of German foreign policy before the Great War was also not reached: Anglo-German cooperation in the Balkans did not lead to a general improvement of their bilateral relations. German hopes for British neutrality and the weakening of British ties to France and Russia turned out to be illusionary. The only success of Anglo-German cooperation – the avoidance of a war between the great powers in 1912 and 1913 – turned out to be fatal in July 1914, when the other great powers believed that Great Britain and Germany would once again restrain their allies and prevent a European war.[92]

To conclude, there is an urgent need for more research on the significance of the change of the *dramatis personae* in Vienna and Berlin. What role did Bethmann Hollweg's complete inexperience in foreign policy play when he became German chancellor? What role did Berchtold's inexperience in the Viennese headquarters or in the Balkans play? His personality and his methods of work completely differed from those of his powerful predecessor, Alois Lexa von Aehrenthal, who was admired by most of his subordinates. In Germany, the death of Kiderlen-Wächter meant that one of the most influential personalities and the best expert on Southeastern Europe in Berlin was replaced by Gottlieb von Jagow, who had gained his diplomatic experience in Luxemburg and Italy. Above all, Jagow was obsessed with the idea of the forthcoming war between 'the Slavs and Teutons', which was highly problematic with regard to the Habsburg Monarchy. Other important changes in personnel concerned positions such as the chiefs of political sections in Vienna (who were the most important political advisers of the minister), the Austro-Hungarian ambassadors in Russia, Serbia, Montenegro and Romania as well as the German ambassadors in England, Italy and the Ottoman Empire. An analysis of these changes, the different attitudes and perceptions of the aforementioned diplomats, as well as their impact on the shaping of the Austro-Hungarian and German policies would provide new, important insights regarding the role of the central powers during and after the Balkan Wars.

Alma Hannig teaches Modern European History at Bonn University and works as a museum and exhibition curator in Vienna. She is the author of *Franz Ferdinand: Die Biografie* (Amalthea, 2013) and co-editor of *Die Familie Hohenlohe im 19. und 20. Jahrhundert: Eine europäische Dynastie im 19. und 20. Jahrhundert* (Böhlau, 2013). Her most recent publications include articles and chapters in journals and edited collections: 'Archduke Franz Ferdinand: An Uncharming Prince?' in Frank Lorenz Müller/Heidi Mehrkens (eds), *Royal Heirs and the Uses of Soft Power in Nineteenth-Century Europe* (Palgrave, 2016), 139–160, '"A Leap into the Dark": Germany and the July Crisis' in Jean-Paul Bled/Jean-Pierre Deschodt (eds), *La crise de Juillet 1914 et l´Europe* (SPM, 2016) 93–104, and 'The Land of Contrasts and Contradiction: Perceptions of Romania among the Austro-Hungarian Diplomats on the Eve of the Great War' in Claudiu-Lucian Topor/Daniel Cain/Alexandru Istrate (eds), *Through the Diplomats´ Eyes: Romanian Social Life in the Late 19th and Early 20th Century*, (Parthenon, 2016) 73–95.

Notes

1 Decree to Berlin, 1 August 1913, *Österreich-Ungarns Außenpolitik von der bosnischen Krise 1908 bis zum Kriegsausbruch 1914: Diplomatische Aktenstücke des österreichisch-ungarischen Ministeriums des Äussern* (hereafter ÖUA), vol. VII (Vienna/Leipzig: Österreichischer Bundesverlag für Unterricht, Wissenschaft und Kunst, 1930), no. 8157, pp. 1–7, here 1–2.
2 Karl Schwendemann, 'Grundzüge der Balkanpolitik Österreich-Ungarns von 1908–1914', *Berliner Monatshefte* 8 (1930), 203–26, here 216.
3 ÖUA, vol. VII, no. 8157, p. 3.
4 Ibid.
5 The best of the classic accounts are still Francis Roy Bridge, *From Sadowa to Sarajevo: The Foreign Policy of Austria-Hungary, 1866–1914* (London: Routledge & Kegan Paul, 1972); and Samuel R. Williamson, *Austria-Hungary and the Origins of the First World War* (New York: Macmillan, 1991).
6 Dörte Löding, *Deutschlands und Österreich-Ungarns Balkanpolitik von 1912–1914 unter besonderer Berücksichtigung ihrer Wirtschaftsinteressen*, unpublished Ph.D. dissertation (Hamburg: University of Hamburg, 1969), 28, 31; Stefan Kestler, *Betrachtungen zur kaiserlich-deutschen Rußlandpolitik: ihre Bedeutung für die Herausbildung des deutsch-russischen Antagonismus zwischen Reichsgründung und Ausbruch des Ersten Weltkrieges (1871–1914)* (Hamburg: Dr. Kovac, 2002), 466, 469. Ironically, Germany realized its economic and commercial prospects mainly at the cost of Austria-Hungary.
7 Richard J. Crampton, *The Hollow Detente: Anglo-German Relations in the Balkans, 1911–1914* (London: G. Prior, 1979), 27. See also Konrad Canis, *Der Weg in den Abgrund: Deutsche Außenpolitik 1902–1914* (Paderborn: Schöningh, 2011), 482.

8. Wolfgang J. Mommsen, 'Domestic Factors in German Foreign Policy before 1914', *Central European History* 6 (1973), 3–43, here 35–37; Jürgen Angelow, *Kalkül und Prestige: Der Zweibund am Vorabend des Ersten Weltkrieges* (Cologne/Weimar/Vienna: Böhlau, 2000); Fritz Klein, 'Politische und wirtschaftliche Interessen in der Balkanpolitik Deutschlands und Österreich-Ungarns 1912', in Fritz Klein (ed.), *Neue Studien zum Imperialismus vor 1914* (Berlin: Akademie Verlag, 1980), 109–34.
9. Holger Afflerbach, *Der Dreibund: Europäische Großmacht- und Allianzpolitik vor dem Ersten Weltkrieg* (Vienna/Cologne/Weimar: Böhlau, 2002), 692–708.
10. ÖUA, vol. IV, no. 3687, pp. 339–40: Telegram, 13 August 1912. See also ÖUA, vol. IV, no. 3633, p. 285; and ibid., no. 3744, p. 388.
11. Kiderlen to Bethmann Hollweg, 2 September 1912, in *Die Große Politik der europäischen Kabinette 1871–1914: Sammlung der diplomatischen Akten des Auswärtigen Amtes* (hereafter GP), vol. 33 (Berlin: Deutsche Verlagsgesellschaft für Politik und Geschichte, 1927), no. 12135, p. 93. See also Ernst Jäckh (ed.), *Kiderlen-Wächter, der Staatsmann und Mensch*, Vol. II (Berlin/Leipzig: DVA, 1924), 187–89.
12. For the Balkan Wars, see Richard C. Hall, *The Balkan Wars 1912–1913: Prelude to the First World War* (London/New York: Routledge, 2000); Katrin Boeckh, *Von den Balkankriegen zum Ersten Weltkrieg: Kleinstaatenpolitik und ethnische Selbstbestimmung auf dem Balkan* (Munich: R. Oldenbourg, 1996). For the central powers, see Herbert Michaelis, *Die deutsche Politik während der Balkankriege 1912/13*, unpublished Ph.D. dissertation (Waldenburg, 1929), 21; Alma Hannig, 'Die Balkanpolitik Österreich-Ungarns vor 1914', in Jürgen Angelow (ed.), *Der Erste Weltkrieg auf dem Balkan: Perspektiven der Forschung* (Berlin: be.bra, 2011), 35–56.
13. Eberhard v. Vietsch, *Bethmann Hollweg: Staatsmann zwischen Macht und Ethos* (Boppard/Rh.: Harald Boldt, 1969), 151.
14. Klaus Hildebrand, *Das vergangene Reich: Deutsche Außenpolitik von Bismarck bis Hitler* (Munich: R. Oldenbourg, 2008), 249–55, 277–87.
15. Eugene Michail, 'Western Attitudes to War in the Balkans and the Shifting Meanings of Violence, 1912–1991', *Journal of Contemporary History* 47(2) (2012), 219–39, here 223. The opposite happened during the Second Balkan War: see ibid., 225–27; Florian Keisinger, *Unzivilisierte Kriege im zivilisierten Europa? Die Balkankriege und die öffentliche Meinung in Deutschland, England und Irland 1876–1913* (Paderborn: Schöningh, 2008), 102–3, 121, 179. For the attitude of Wilhelm II, see GP, vol. 33, no. 12320, 12277, 12297.
16. Michaelis, *Die deutsche Politik während der Balkankriege*, 52. See also GP, vol. 33, no. 12339, 12349, 12481.
17. ÖUA, vol. IV, no. 4118, pp. 659–61; ibid., no. 4128, pp. 668–70; ibid., no. 4140, p. 676; and ibid., no. 4170, pp. 698–702, here 698–99. Austro-Hungarian diplomats were still hoping that the situation in the Balkans could be reversed by a conference of the great powers, at which they expected British and German support. Konrad Canis, *Die bedrängte Großmacht: Österreich-Ungarn und das europäische Mächtesystem. 1866/67–1914*, (Paderborn: Schöningh, 2016), 399–401.
18. Franz-Josef Kos, *Die politischen und wirtschaftlichen Interessen Österreich-Ungarns und Deutschlands in Südosteuropa 1912/1913: Die Adriahafen-, die*

Saloniki- und die Kavallafrage (Vienna/Cologne/Weimar: Böhlau, 1996), 15–48.
19 The idea was to demonstrate the importance of the alliance and at the same time to maintain the rivalries between the Balkan states: ÖUA, vol. IV, no. 4140, p. 676 and ibid., no. 4170, pp. 698–702.
20 Günther Kronenbitter, *'Krieg im Frieden!' Die Führung der k.u.k. Armee und die Großmachtpolitik Österreich-Ungarns 1906–1914* (Munich: R. Oldenbourg, 2003), 394.
21 David Stevenson, 'Militarization and Diplomacy in Europe before 1914', *International Security* 22(1) (1997), 125–61, here 142–45.
22 Moravský zemský archive (hereafter MZA) Brno, K. 140, Berchtold Papers: Berchtold Memoirs, 3 November 1912.
23 Political Archive of Foreign Office, Berlin (hereafter PA AA), Pourtalès Private Papers: Kiderlen-Wächter to Pourtalès, 19 November 1912.
24 Alma Hannig, *Franz Ferdinand: Die Biographie* (Vienna: Amalthea, 2013), 176–84.
25 Telegrams, 22 November 1912, in ÖUA, vol. IV, no. 4559, p. 971; ibid., no. 4571, p. 979; and ibid., no. 4719, p. 1082. See also Private Papers Sophie Hohenberg, Schlossarchiv Artstetten, K 668: Franz Ferdinand to His Wife Sophie, 21 November 1912: 'Everything goes brilliantly. I am very happy'; 22 November 1912: 'I feel gorgeous, I am very happy that everything went very well'.
26 Private Archive Fischer-Colbrie, Vienna: Gottfried Hohenlohe Private Papers, Hohenlohe Diary, 20 and 21 November 1912; *Norddeutsche Allgemeine Zeitung*, 25 November 1912. See also Geheimes Staatsarchiv Preußischer Kulturbesitz, Berlin, VI.HA; Jäckh, *Kiderlen-Wächter*, 191; Kiderlen to Johanna, 19 November 1912, Cleinow Private Papers, 110.
27 GP, vol. 33, pp. 445–46.
28 Jost Dülffer, Martin Kröger and Rolf-Harald Wippich, *Vermiedene Kriege: Deeskalation von Konflikten der Großmächte zwischen Krimkrieg und Erstem Weltkrieg 1865–1914* (Munich: R. Oldenbourg, 1997), 652. For counterarguments, see Canis, *Der Weg in den Abgrund*, 487.
29 GP, vol. 39, pp. 119–21.
30 Christopher Clark, *Wilhelm II: Die Herrschaft des letzten deutschen Kaisers* (Munich: DVA, 2008), 195–97; John C.G. Röhl, *Wilhelm II: Der Weg in den Abgrund 1900–1941*, 2nd ed. (Munich: C.H. Beck, 2009), 963–66; Fritz Fischer, *Krieg der Illusionen: Die deutsche Politik von 1911 bis 1914*, 2nd ed. (Düsseldorf: Droste, 1978), 231–34.
31 Documentation on the 'War Council' is printed in John C.G. Röhl, 'An der Schwelle zum Weltkrieg: eine Dokumentation über den "Kriegsrat" vom 8. Dezember 1912', *Militärgeschichtliche Mitteilungen* 21(1) (1977), 77–134.
32 Stevenson, 'Militarization and Diplomacy', 159.
33 Richard J. Crampton, 'The Balkans as a Factor in German Foreign Policy, 1912–1914', *Slavonic and East European Review* 55(3) (1977), 370–90, here 372; Crampton, *The Hollow Detente*, 27.
34 GP, vol. 34.1, no. 12592, p. 103: Bethmann Hollweg to Emperor Wilhelm II, 31 December 1912.

35 Hugo Hantsch, *Leopold Graf Berchtold: Grandseigneur und Staatsmann*, Vol. I (Graz/Vienna/Cologne: Styria, 1963), 362–64. Unsure whether his approach would be accepted by Franz Joseph, Berchtold had all political documents evacuated from the Austro-Hungarian embassy in Saint Petersburg, which was a typical precautionary measure in the case of a war: Haus-, Hof- und Staatsarchiv Wien, PA I 493, Liasse XLV: Balkan-Konflagration 1912–1913 (no. 1–14).

36 Ralph Forsbach, *Alfred von Kiderlen-Wächter (1852–1912): Ein Diplomatenleben im Kaiserreich*, Vol. II (Göttingen: Vandenhoeck & Ruprecht, 1997), 745. See also the report of the Belgian envoy to Berlin: Beyens to Davignon, 30 November 1912, in Auswärtiges Amt (ed.), *Belgische Aktenstücke 1905–1914: Berichte der belgischen Vertreter in Berlin, London und Paris an den Minister des Äußeren in Brüssel* (Berlin: Mittler, 1914), 112–14, here 113.

37 ÖUA, vol. V, no. 4924, 4925, pp. 126–31.

38 Robert R. Kritt, *Die Londoner Botschafterkonferenz 1912–1913*, unpublished Ph.D. dissertation (Vienna: University of Vienna, 1960), 204–5. See also Dülffer, Kröger and Wippich, *Vermiedene Kriege*, 654; and Canis, *Der Weg in den Abgrund*, 488–90.

39 PA AA, Pourtalès Private Papers: Jagow to Pourtalès, 2 February 1913; Lerchenfeld to Hertling, 2 February 1913, in Ernst Deuerlein (ed.), *Briefwechsel Hertling-Lerchenfeld 1912–1917: Dienstliche Privatkorrespondenz zwischen dem bayerischen Ministerpräsidenten Georg Graf von Hertling und dem bayerischen Gesandten in Berlin Hugo Graf von und zu Lerchenfeld*, Vol. I (Boppard/Rh.: H. Boldt, 1973), 221.

40 GP, vol. 34.1, no. 12818, p. 347: Bethmann Hollweg to Berchtold, 10 February 1913. Moltke and Wilhelm II argued in a similar way: see Moltke to Conrad, in Conrad von Hötzendorf, *Aus meiner Dienstzeit 1906–1918*, Vol. III (Vienna: Rikola, 1922), 144–46; Wilhelm II to Franz Ferdinand, 26 February 1913, in Robert A. Kann, *Erzherzog Franz Ferdinand Studien* (Munich: R. Oldenbourg, 1976), 76–78.

41 G. P. Gooch and Harold Temperley, *British Documents on the Origins of the War, 1898–1914* (London: His Majesty's Stationery Office, 1926–1938), Vol. IX, Part II, no. 500, cited in Crampton, 'The Balkans as a Factor', 377.

42 GP, vol. 34.1, no. 12763, pp. 281–82: Bethmann Hollweg to Lichnowsky, 30 January 1913. See also Lerchenfeld to Hertling, 2 February 1913, in Deuerlein, *Briefwechsel Hertling-Lerchenfeld*, Vol. I, 221.

43 Dülffer, Kröger and Wippich, *Vermiedene Kriege*, 654. For a rather negative interpretation of British and German efforts, see Canis, *Der Weg in den Abgrund*, 488–90. For more on the disarmament agreement, see Kronenbitter, 'Krieg im Frieden!', 413; and Alma Hannig, 'Prinz Gottfried zu Hohenlohe-Schillingsfürst (1867–1932): Ein Liebling der Kaiserhöfe', in Alma Hannig and Martina Winkelhofer (eds), *Die Familie Hohenlohe: Eine europäische Dynastie im 19. und 20. Jahrhundert* (Cologne/Vienna/Weimar: Böhlau, 2013), 229–70, here 239–42.

44 Sir Edward Grey of Fallodon, *Twenty-five Years: 1892–1916*, Vol. I (New York: Stokes, 1925), 247–48, 265, 268–69; GP, vol. 34.2, no. 12982, p. 516: Jagow to Tschirschky, 17 March 1913.

45 Dominik Geppert, *Pressekriege: Öffentlichkeit und Diplomatie in den deutsch-britischen Beziehungen (1896–1912)* (Munich: R. Oldenbourg, 2007), 414–18; Keisinger, *Unzivilisierte Kriege*, 181.
46 The great powers assigned Skutari to the new Albanian state on 22 March 1913: see Boeckh, *Von den Balkankriegen zum Ersten Weltkrieg*, 46.
47 Williamson, *Austria-Hungary and the Origins*, 151–54.
48 David Stevenson, *Armaments and the Coming of War: Europe, 1904–1914* (Oxford: Clarendon Press, 1996), 275.
49 GP, vol. 34.2, no. 13207, pp. 737–38: Jagow to Lichnowsky, 26 April 1913; Christel Gade, *Gleichgewichtspolitik oder Bündnispflege? Maximen britischer Außenpolitik (1909–1914)* (Göttingen/Zürich: Vandenhoek & Ruprecht, 1997), 180–83.
50 Gottlieb von Jagow, *Ursachen und Ausbruch des Weltkrieges* (Berlin: Reimar Hobbing, 1919), 193.
51 Patrick Bormann, 'Furcht und Angst als Faktoren deutscher Weltpolitik 1897–1914', in Patrick Bormann, Thomas Freiberger and Judith Michel (eds), *Angst in den internationalen Beziehungen* (Göttingen: V+R unipress, 2010), 71–90, here 75.
52 ÖUA, vol. V, no. 6275, pp. 1039–41, here 1039: Jagow to Berchtold, 23 March 1913. See the same argumentation of the German chancellor: GP, vol. 34.2, no. 13108, p. 641: Bethmann Hollweg to Treutler, 8 April 1913.
53 GP, vol. 34.2, no. 12965, p. 492: Jagow to Tschirschky, 14 March 1913; ibid., no. 13012, pp. 548–51: Jagow to Berchtold, 23 March 1913; ibid., no. 13292, pp. 825–27: Jagow, Record, 11 May 1913.
54 Wolfgang J. Mommsen, 'Kaiser Wilhelm II and German Politics', *Journal of Contemporary History* 25 (1990), 289–316, here 304; GP, vol. 39, no. 15716, p. 337: Treutler to Jagow, 24 March 1914. See also ÖUA, vol. VI, no. 7566, p. 778. Still the best analysis of Bethmann Hollweg's views is Konrad H. Jarausch, *The Enigmatic Chancellor: Bethmann Hollweg and the Hubris of Imperial Germany* (New Haven, CT/London: Yale University Press, 1973).
55 Alexander König, *Wie mächtig war der Kaiser? Kaiser Wilhelm II. zwischen Königsmechanismus und Polykratie von 1908 bis 1914* (Stuttgart: Steiner, 2009), 272–75; Dieter Hoffmann, *Der Sprung ins Dunkle: Oder wie der I. Weltkrieg entfesselt wurde* (Leipzig: Militzke, 2010), 137.
56 ÖUA, vol. VI, no. 7566, pp. 776–78, here 777: Berchtold to Szögyény, 1 July 1913; Hannig, 'Die Balkanpolitik Österreich-Ungarns vor 1914', 48–50. See also ÖUA, vol. V, no. 5903, pp. 796–97; and ibid., no. 6126, p. 939.
57 MZA Brno, K. 133, Berchtold Papers: Franz Ferdinand to Berchtold, 16 January 1913; ÖUA, vol. V, no. 6127, p. 941; ibid., no. 6275, p. 1040; ÖUA, vol. VI, no. 6862, p. 318; ibid., no. 7566, p. 777; and GP, vol. 34.2, no. 13012, pp. 549–50.
58 MZA Brno, K. 133, Berchtold Papers: Franz Ferdinand to Berchtold, 4 July 1913 and 24 July 1913; ibid., Conrad to Berchtold, 2 July 1913 and 12 July 1913. See also Horst Brettner-Messler, *Die Balkanpolitik Conrad v. Hötzendorfs (Dezember 1912 bis Oktober 1913)*, unpublished Ph.D. dissertation (Vienna: University of Vienna, 1966), 82–85.
59 ÖUA, vol. VI, no. 7748, p. 883: San Giuliano to Mérey.

60 Ibid., no. 6833, pp. 298–99; ibid., no. 6903, p. 358; ibid., no. 7152, p. 521; and ibid., no. 7399, pp. 664–65.
61 Williamson, *Austria-Hungary and the Origins*, 148–49; Ludwig Bittner, 'Die Verantwortlichkeit Österreich-Ungarns für den Ausbruch des Weltkrieges', in Josef Nadler and Heinrich Srbik (eds), *Österreich: Erbe und Sendung im deutschen Raum*, 3rd ed. (Salzburg/Leipzig: Pustet, 1936), 185–206, here 195.
62 GP, vol. 35, no. 13732, no. 13733, no. 13734 and no. 13741, pp. 359–67. For the role of the German emperor according to the constitution, see Mommsen, 'Kaiser Wilhelm II and German Politics', 292.
63 GP, vol. 35, no. 13750, p. 379: Tschirschky to Jagow, 13 August 1913.
64 GP, vol. 39, no. 15803, pp. 458–60: Tschirschky to Jagow, 29 November 1913; ibid., no. 15822, pp. 500–502: Waldthausen to Bethmann Hollweg, 17 April 1914; and ibid., no. 15829, pp. 513–15: Waldthausen to Bethmann Hollweg, 5 May 1914.
65 ÖUA, vol. VII, no. 8157, p. 4.
66 Ibid., pp. 1–7. See also ibid., no. 8708, pp. 353–58; ibid., no. 9482, pp. 974–99; and ÖUA, vol. VIII, no. 9918, pp. 186–95.
67 ÖUA, vol. VII, no. 8474, pp. 198–201, here 200–201.
68 Ibid., no. 9482, pp. 974–99.
69 Ibid., p. 976; ibid., no. 8474, p. 200; ÖUA, vol. VIII, no. 9902, p. 174; and ibid., no. 8474, pp. 198–201.
70 ÖUA, vol. VII, no. 9482, p. 977.
71 Ibid., no. 8708, pp. 353–58; ibid., no. 9032, pp. 588–94; ÖUA, vol. VIII, no. 9674, pp. 42–43; ibid., no. 9739, pp. 80–81.
72 FO, Carnock 800/370: Cartwright to Nicolson, private, 27 September 1913, cited in Crampton, 'The Balkans as a Factor', 384.
73 This impression already existed during the Ambassadors' Conference. See GP, vol. 34.2, no. 12982, p. 517: Jagow to Tschirschky, 17 March 1913.
74 ÖUA, vol. VII, no. 8708, p. 355.
75 Ibid., no. 8699, pp. 346–47, and no. 9032, pp. 588–94.
76 MZA Brno, K. 133, Berchtold Papers: Franz Ferdinand to Berchtold, 16 January 1913, 6 July 1913, 8 August 1913, 12 October 1913 and 10 April 1914.
77 ÖUA, vol. VII, no. 9032, pp. 588–94.
78 Hötzendorf, *Aus meiner Dienstzeit*, Vol. III, 647, 757.
79 ÖUA, vol. VIII, no. 9639, p. 14, and no. 9739, p. 80.
80 Ibid., no. 9918, pp. 186–95, here 193.
81 Ibid., no. 9918, pp. 187–89.
82 Ibid., pp. 194–95.
83 Gade, *Gleichgewichtspolitik oder Bündnispflege*, 193. See also Christopher Clark, *The Sleepwalkers: How Europe Went to War in 1914* (London: Penguin Books, 2012), 340–49.
84 Alma Hannig, 'Angst und die Balkanpolitik Österreich-Ungarns vor dem Ersten Weltkrieg', in Bormann, Freiberger and Michel, *Angst in den internationalen Beziehungen*, 93–113, here 96–99, 103–4.
85 Kann, *Erzherzog Franz Ferdinand Studien*, 21, 85; Rudolf Kiszling, *Erzherzog Franz Ferdinand von Österreich-Este: Leben, Pläne und Wirken am Schicksalsweg der Donaumonarchie* (Graz/Cologne: Böhlau, 1953), 99.

86 Bridge, *From Sadowa to Sarajevo*, 368.
87 For the thesis that Austria was looking for a pretext for war, see Lothar Höbelt, *Franz Joseph I. Der Kaiser und sein Reich: Eine politische Geschichte* (Vienna/Cologne/Weimar: Böhlau, 2009), 144; Jürgen Angelow, 'Der "Kriegsfall Serbien" als Willenstherapie: Operative Planung, politische Mentalitäten und Visionen vor und zu Beginn des Ersten Weltkrieges', *Militärgeschichtliche Zeitschrift* 61 (2002), 315–36, here 319. For the opposite view, see Paul W. Schroeder, '"Stealing Horses to Great Applause": Austria-Hungary's Decision in 1914 in Systemic Perspective', in Holger Afflerbach and David Stevenson (eds), *An Improbable War: The Outbreak of World War I and European Political Culture before 1914* (Oxford: Berghahn Books, 2007), 17–42, here 18–23; Ales Skrivan, *Schwierige Partner: Deutschland und Österreich-Ungarn in der europäischen Politik der Jahre 1906–1914* (Hamburg: Dölling und Galitz, 1999), 257.
88 For a comparison of the great powers' military capacities, see Clark, *The Sleepwalkers*, 217.
89 Berchtold and Hoyos regarded the German rejection of an alliance with Bulgaria as one of the crucial points to explain why the peaceful, alternative Balkan policy failed: Private Archive of Count Hardegg, Vienna, Berchtold Private Papers: Berchtold to Hoyos, 29 August 1927, and Hoyos' response, 31 August 1927.
90 Günther Kronenbitter, 'Bundesgenossen? Zur militärpolitischen Kooperation zwischen Berlin und Wien 1912 bis 1914', in Walther L. Bernecker and Volker Dotterweich (eds), *Deutschland in den internationalen Beziehungen des 19. und 20. Jahrhunderts* (Munich: Ernst Vögel, 1996), 143–68, here 160.
91 GP, vol. 39, no. 15804, p. 461: Flotow to Bethmann Hollweg, 29 November 1913. See also Skrivan, *Schwierige Partner*, 372; Canis, *Der Weg in den Abgrund*, 515.
92 Paul M. Kennedy, *The Rise of the Anglo-German Antagonism 1860–1914* (London: Allen & Unwin, 1980), 456; Crampton, *The Hollow Detente*, 171–72. See also GP, vol. 36,1, no. 13781.

Bibliography

Afflerbach, Holger. *Der Dreibund: Europäische Großmacht- und Allianzpolitik vor dem Ersten Weltkrieg*. Vienna/Cologne/Weimar: Böhlau, 2002.

Angelow, Jürgen. *Kalkül und Prestige: Der Zweibund am Vorabend des Ersten Weltkrieges*. Cologne/Weimar/Vienna: Böhlau, 2000.

———. 'Der "Kriegsfall Serbien" als Willenstherapie: Operative Planung, politische Mentalitäten und Visionen vor und zu Beginn des Ersten Weltkrieges'. *Militärgeschichtliche Zeitschrift* 61 (2002), 315–36.

Auswärtiges Amt (ed.). *Belgische Aktenstücke 1905–1914: Berichte der belgischen Vertreter in Berlin, London und Paris an den Minister des Äußeren in Brüssel*. Berlin: Mittler, 1914.

Bittner, Ludwig. 'Die Verantwortlichkeit Österreich-Ungarns für den Ausbruch des Weltkrieges', in Josef Nadler and Heinrich Srbik (eds), *Österreich: Erbe und Sendung im deutschen Raum*. 3rd ed. (Salzburg/Leipzig: Pustet, 1936), 185–206.

Boeckh, Katrin. *Von den Balkankriegen zum Ersten Weltkrieg: Kleinstaatenpolitik und ethnische Selbstbestimmung auf dem Balkan*. Munich: R. Oldenbourg, 1996.

Bormann, Patrick. 'Furcht und Angst als Faktoren deutscher Weltpolitik 1897–1914', in Patrick Bormann, Thomas Freiberger and Judith Michel (eds), *Angst in den internationalen Beziehungen* (Göttingen: V+R unipress, 2010), 71–90.

Brettner-Messler, Horst. *Die Balkanpolitik Conrad v. Hötzendorfs (Dezember 1912 bis Oktober 1913)*. Unpublished Ph.D. dissertation. Vienna: University of Vienna, 1966.

Bridge, Francis Roy. *From Sadowa to Sarajevo: The Foreign Policy of Austria-Hungary, 1866–1914*. London: Routledge & Kegan Paul, 1972.

Canis, Konrad. *Der Weg in den Abgrund: Deutsche Außenpolitik 1902–1914*. Paderborn: Schöningh, 2011.

——. *Die bedrängte Großmacht: Österreich-Ungarn und das europäische Mächtesystem. 1866/67–1914*. Paderborn: Schöningh, 2016.

Clark, Christopher. *Wilhelm II: Die Herrschaft des letzten deutschen Kaisers*. Munich: DVA, 2008.

——. *The Sleepwalkers: How Europe Went to War in 1914*. London: Penguin Books, 2012.

Crampton, Richard J. 'The Balkans as a Factor in German Foreign Policy, 1912–1914'. *Slavonic and East European Review* 55(3) (1977), 370–90.

——. *The Hollow Detente: Anglo-German Relations in the Balkans, 1911–1914*. London: G. Prior, 1979.

Deuerlein, Ernst (ed.). *Briefwechsel Hertling-Lerchenfeld 1912–1917: Dienstliche Privatkorrespondenz zwischen dem bayerischen Ministerpräsidenten Georg Graf von Hertling und dem bayerischen Gesandten in Berlin Hugo Graf von und zu Lerchenfeld*. Vol. I. Boppard/Rh.: H. Boldt, 1973.

Dülffer, Jost, Martin Kröger and Rolf-Harald Wippich. *Vermiedene Kriege: Deeskalation von Konflikten der Großmächte zwischen Krimkrieg und Erstem Weltkrieg 1865–1914*. Munich: R. Oldenbourg, 1997.

Fischer, Fritz. *Krieg der Illusionen: Die deutsche Politik von 1911 bis 1914*. 2nd ed. Düsseldorf: Droste, 1978.

Forsbach, Ralph. *Alfred von Kiderlen-Wächter (1852–1912): Ein Diplomatenleben im Kaiserreich*. Vol. II. Göttingen: Vandenhoeck & Ruprecht, 1997.

Gade, Christel. *Gleichgewichtspolitik oder Bündnispflege? Maximen britischer Außenpolitik (1909–1914)*. Göttingen/Zürich: Vandenhoek & Ruprecht, 1997.

Geppert, Dominik. *Pressekriege: Öffentlichkeit und Diplomatie in den deutsch-britischen Beziehungen (1896–1912)*. Munich: R. Oldenbourg, 2007.

Grey, Edward Sir of Fallodon. *Twenty-five Years: 1892–1916*. Vol. I. New York: Stokes, 1925.

Hall, Richard C. *The Balkan Wars 1912–1913: Prelude to the First World War*. London/New York: Routledge, 2000.

Hannig, Alma. 'Angst und die Balkanpolitik Österreich-Ungarns vor dem Ersten Weltkrieg', in Patrick Bormann, Thomas Freiberger and Judith Michel (eds), *Angst in den internationalen Beziehungen* (Göttingen: V+R unipress, 2010), 93–113.

——. 'Die Balkanpolitik Österreich-Ungarns vor 1914', in Jürgen Angelow (ed.), *Der Erste Weltkrieg auf dem Balkan: Perspektiven der Forschung* (Berlin: be.bra, 2011), 35–56.

——. *Franz Ferdinand: Die Biographie.* Vienna: Amalthea, 2013.

——. 'Prinz Gottfried zu Hohenlohe-Schillingsfürst (1867–1932): Ein Liebling der Kaiserhöfe', in Alma Hannig and Martina Winkelhofer (eds), *Die Familie Hohenlohe: Eine europäische Dynastie im 19. und 20. Jahrhundert* (Cologne/Vienna/Weimar: Böhlau, 2013), 229–70.

Hantsch, Hugo. *Leopold Graf Berchtold: Grandseigneur und Staatsmann.* Vol. I. Graz/Vienna/Cologne: Styria, 1963.

Hildebrand, Klaus. *Das vergangene Reich: Deutsche Außenpolitik von Bismarck bis Hitler.* Munich: R. Oldenbourg, 2008.

Höbelt, Lothar. *Franz Joseph I. Der Kaiser und sein Reich: Eine politische Geschichte.* Vienna/Cologne/Weimar: Böhlau, 2009.

Hoffmann, Dieter. *Der Sprung ins Dunkle: Oder wie der I. Weltkrieg entfesselt wurde.* Leipzig: Militzke, 2010.

Hötzendorf, Conrad von. *Aus meiner Dienstzeit 1906–1918.* Vol. III. Vienna: Rikola, 1922.

Jäckh, Ernst (ed.). *Kiderlen-Wächter, der Staatsmann und Mensch.* Vol. II. Berlin/Leipzig: DVA, 1924.

Jagow, Gottlieb von. *Ursachen und Ausbruch des Weltkrieges.* Berlin: Reimar Hobbing, 1919.

Jarausch, Konrad H. *The Enigmatic Chancellor: Bethmann Hollweg and the Hubris of Imperial Germany.* New Haven, CT/London: Yale University Press, 1973.

Kann, Robert A. *Erzherzog Franz Ferdinand Studien.* Munich: R. Oldenbourg, 1976.

Keisinger, Florian. *Unzivilisierte Kriege im zivilisierten Europa? Die Balkankriege und die öffentliche Meinung in Deutschland, England und Irland 1876–1913.* Paderborn: Schöningh, 2008.

Kennedy, Paul M. *The Rise of the Anglo-German Antagonism 1860–1914.* London: Allen & Unwin, 1980.

Kestler, Stefan. *Betrachtungen zur kaiserlich-deutschen Rußlandpolitik: ihre Bedeutung für die Herausbildung des deutsch-russischen Antagonismus zwischen Reichsgründung und Ausbruch des Ersten Weltkrieges (1871–1914).* Hamburg: Dr. Kovac, 2002.

Kiszling, Rudolf. *Erzherzog Franz Ferdinand von Österreich-Este: Leben, Pläne und Wirken am Schicksalsweg der Donaumonarchie.* Graz/Cologne: Böhlau, 1953.

Klein, Fritz. 'Politische und wirtschaftliche Interessen in der Balkanpolitik Deutschlands und Österreich-Ungarns 1912', in Fritz Klein (ed.), *Neue Studien zum Imperialismus vor 1914* (Berlin: Akademie Verlag, 1980), 109–34.

König, Alexander. *Wie mächtig war der Kaiser? Kaiser Wilhelm II. zwischen Königsmechanismus und Polykratie von 1908 bis 1914.* Stuttgart: Steiner, 2009.

Kos, Franz-Josef. *Die politischen und wirtschaftlichen Interessen Österreich-Ungarns und Deutschlands in Südosteuropa 1912/1913: Die Adriahafen-, die Saloniki- und die Kavallafrage.* Vienna/Cologne/Weimar: Böhlau, 1996.

Kritt, Robert R. *Die Londoner Botschafterkonferenz 1912–1913*. Unpublished Ph.D. dissertation. Vienna: University of Vienna, 1960.

Kronenbitter, Günther. 'Bundesgenossen? Zur militärpolitischen Kooperation zwischen Berlin und Wien 1912 bis 1914', in Walther L. Bernecker and Volker Dotterweich (eds), *Deutschland in den internationalen Beziehungen des 19. und 20. Jahrhunderts* (Munich: Ernst Vögel, 1996), 143–68.

——. *'Krieg im Frieden!' Die Führung der k.u.k. Armee und die Großmachtpolitik Österreich-Ungarns 1906–1914*. Munich: R. Oldenbourg, 2003.

Löding, Dörte. *Deutschlands und Österreich-Ungarns Balkanpolitik von 1912–1914 unter besonderer Berücksichtigung ihrer Wirtschaftsinteressen*. Unpublished Ph.D. dissertation. Hamburg: University of Hamburg, 1969.

Michail, Eugene. 'Western Attitudes to War in the Balkans and the Shifting Meanings of Violence, 1912–1991'. *Journal of Contemporary History* 47(2) (2012), 219–39.

Michaelis, Herbert. *Die deutsche Politik während der Balkankriege 1912/13*. Unpublished Ph.D. dissertation. Waldenburg, 1929.

Mommsen, Wolfgang J. 'Domestic Factors in German Foreign Policy before 1914'. *Central European History* 6 (1973), 3–43.

——. 'Kaiser Wilhelm II and German Politics'. *Journal of Contemporary History* 25 (1990), 289–316.

Röhl, John C.G. 'An der Schwelle zum Weltkrieg: eine Dokumentation über den "Kriegsrat" vom 8. Dezember 1912'. *Militärgeschichtliche Mitteilungen* 21(1) (1977), 77–134.

——. *Wilhelm II: Der Weg in den Abgrund 1900–1941*. 2nd ed. Munich: C.H. Beck, 2009.

Schroeder, Paul W. '"Stealing Horses to Great Applause": Austria-Hungary's Decision in 1914 in Systemic Perspective', in Holger Afflerbach and David Stevenson (eds), *An Improbable War: The Outbreak of World War I and European Political Culture before 1914* (Oxford: Berghahn Books, 2007), 17–42.

Schwendemann, Karl. 'Grundzüge der Balkanpolitik Österreich-Ungarns von 1908–1914'. *Berliner Monatshefte* 8 (1930), 203–26.

Skrivan, Ales. *Schwierige Partner: Deutschland und Österreich-Ungarn in der europäischen Politik der Jahre 1906–1914*. Hamburg: Dölling und Galitz, 1999.

Stevenson, David. *Armaments and the Coming of War: Europe, 1904–1914*. Oxford: Clarendon Press, 1996.

——. 'Militarization and Diplomacy in Europe before 1914'. *International Security* 22(1) (1997): 125–61.

Vietsch, Eberhard v. *Bethmann Hollweg: Staatsmann zwischen Macht und Ethos*. Boppard/Rh.: Harald Boldt, 1969.

Williamson, Samuel R. *Austria-Hungary and the Origins of the First World War*. New York: Macmillan, 1991.

 4

Not Just a Prelude
The First Balkan War Crisis as the Catalyst of Final European War Preparations
Michael Hesselholt Clemmesen

This is *not* about the First Balkan War. The purpose of this chapter is to describe some of the immediate and derived effects the war had on the armed services of European states far from the war zone. What is presented here is the summary of an extended research into the Danish defence preparations from 1909 to 1914, in which the final investigation focuses on the roots of the formerly unexplained acceleration that took place from two years to a year before the Great War. The 1911 Agadir Crisis had been too short to generate the difficult political decisions necessary to implement the Danish 1909 defence laws.

What happened from October 1912 was driven by the perception – nourished by the press as well as diplomatic and intelligence sources – that there was a real risk that the Balkan Crisis would escalate into a great power war. Thereafter Danish territorial waters were likely to be used by either Germany or Great Britain, involved through their commitments to Austria-Hungary and the French–Russian alliance. To establish the link of effects from the distant war to the Danish defence preparations, it is necessary to investigate and describe the influence of the crisis on war preparations in Germany and Great Britain. This had not previously been done in relation to the British reactions. The crisis reactions by Denmark's neighbouring neutral power, Sweden, was examined to compare perceptions and decisions in Stockholm with those in Copenhagen. The narrative here outlines research results published in 2012.[1]

The unexpected and dramatic events early in the war in the Balkans moved the response of the European great powers from mild concern to provoking military build-up and potential conflict between

Austria-Hungary and Russia. As a consequence, combat readiness in armies and navies of both the remaining great powers and the faraway small neutrals was increased. However, the rise in combat readiness was not the most important effect. The crisis prompted a concentration, acceleration and revision in the character of the national professional military and naval planning, as well as the diplomatic preparations for war. It directly triggered preparations of a fundamentally new and urgent character. After the Balkan Crisis, a great power war was no longer just a possibility; indeed, the chief generals and admirals – then key policymakers – now considered major war inevitable and fast approaching. They acted accordingly from late autumn 1912 onwards.

The First Balkan War had an important and direct catalytic influence on what happened in August 1914. In a way, it played a role comparable to that of the Spanish Civil War and of the Sudetenland Crisis before the Second World War. It acted as a test ground for new weapons and tactics, as would the Spanish Civil War later. Aircraft were used extensively and a Greek submarine was deployed. The dramatic early Bulgarian results seemed to demonstrate that quick manoeuvre victories were still realistic. As the Sudetenland Crisis would do later, the Balkan Crisis accelerated and focused war preparations as the armed service leaders understood that a great power war could be imminent. In the title of his important concise book, Richard Hall called the Balkan Wars a prelude to the Great War.[2] This chapter describes how it was far more than a mere prelude.

It must be underlined that the great power reactions were not a response to the start of the general Balkan War in mid October. The conflict was widely thought to bring *only* a humanitarian crisis, as the Ottoman Empire was expected to brutally pacify the region after her eventual victory. The cause of the international crisis was the operational Ottoman defeat that brought the risks in early November of a Bulgarian capture of Constantinople. The erring diplomatic expectations as well as the collapse of the regional balance of power in Southeastern Europe immediately led to interacting crisis reactions among the great powers. In Germany and Great Britain, as well as in neutral Sweden and small Denmark, the responses were far more comprehensive and serious than in the summer of 1911 during the Agadir Crisis.

When Serbian control of part of the Albanian coast became a reality a couple of weeks later, the Balkan Crisis came very close to causing a great power war via Austrian intervention and Russian response, and the after-effects of that view from the brink of war undermined traditional, bureaucratic and political constraints normally limiting preparations for offensive or defensive warfare.

October 1912

After the Balkan League mobilization, Montenegro declared war on the Ottoman Empire on 8 October followed by Bulgaria, Greece and Serbia on 17 October. As the Turco-Italian war ended on 18 October, the great powers hoped that the conflict could be kept a regional one. On 21–23 October, the initial Ottoman defeats followed the Bulgarian breakthrough of the main Ottoman defence lines in Thrace from 28 October to 3 November.

On 30 September, Rear-Admiral Albert Hopman from Alfred von Tirpitz's *Reichsmarineamt* took note of the mobilization of the Balkan states' armies in his diary entry. He thought that it might have been instigated by the British foreign secretary, Sir Edward Grey, as a plot to split Italy from her partners in the Triple Alliance. He expected a Russian–Austrian confrontation. The next day, he noted crisis reactions of the German stock exchange and intelligence that Russia 'test mobilized' a significant number of army corps. In mid October, Hopman wrote that Great Britain seemed to approach Germany and Austria-Hungary in a common attempt to manage the crisis.

At the same time, just before the week-old conflict between the Ottoman Empire and small Montenegro became a general war on the peninsula, the Danish diplomats in Berlin reported that the German government saw the outbreak as inevitable in spite of formal expressions of optimism. German diplomats admitted that there was a risk of Austrian intervention and of Russian reaction if Bulgaria and Serbia acquired significant territorial gains.

A couple of days later, the newly arrived Danish envoy reported, from his first conversation with the foreign secretary Alfred von Kiderlen-Wächter, that the German diplomat hoped for an inconclusive outcome of the fighting. It would give the great powers the chance thereafter to dictate the relations between the combatants. He also underlined that the end of the Turco-Italian war increased the chances of avoiding a spread of the war to involve the great powers. On 19 October, Hopman noted that Kaiser Wilhelm II analysed the coming conflict in a neutral way, seeing the Balkan War just as the 'returning flood' of the Christians after the Turkish Muslim wave. He thought that the Balkan states were likely to do well. One could not be certain that Russia was behind the war.

During the following days, Hopman wrote about the Balkan states' advances, and on the last day of the month he noted that all the great powers had now accepted the altered situation in the Balkans and that they were united in the effort to keep peace. On 1 November, the

Bulgarian threat against Constantinople led the French and the British to dispatch ships to the conflict zone in the eastern Mediterranean, and the next day the Kaiser decided to send German ships to join them.[3]

The British move at the outset of the crisis, which brought a critical German reaction, had been developed in early 1912. One of the first initiatives of the Admiralty War Staff, established just after New Year to conduct formal Admiralty war planning, had been to create a system whereby full manning of so-called nucleus manned vessels could be carried out in a way that 'should not create apprehension in diplomatic circles'. In order to achieve this image of normality, supplementary manning exercises were to take place at least twice a year and be conducted at irregular periods. As a result, the '… most important of the precautionary measures to be taken in anticipation of possible war would thus be frequently tested'.[4]

Otherwise, the year 1912 was used to consider, exercise and analyse the new operational strategy for meeting the German fleet in the North Sea, after the option of a close blockade of the German bases in the Heligoland Bight had been abandoned during the winter. Throughout the previous months, the young First Lord of the Admiralty (the naval secretary) Winston Churchill had tried in vain to convince the rest of the cabinet that a naval agreement could and should be made with France that allowed the Royal Navy to withdraw its modern battleships from the Mediterranean so that they could strengthen the Home Fleets in the North Sea.[5]

The Danish envoy in London was new in the post, similar to his colleague in Berlin. Most of the senior Danish diplomats had been rotated to a new post in September 1912. The envoy in London rotated from Vienna. He reported from his first contacts in the Foreign Office in early October that they were uncertain about what would happen. During the envoy's audience with the king one week later, King George V saw the situation as 'serious and dangerous'. Other senior diplomats in town doubted that the great powers would be able to act in unity, even if it would mean an immense defeat of diplomacy if they failed to do so. On 1 November, the envoy underlined the risk that resulted from the fact that few had foreseen the Ottoman defeat. There was the possibility that a victorious state would feel free to take an initiative that would threaten the general peace.[6] Thus, for the two great powers considered here, the first threatening and then open regional war brought diplomatic concerns, but no significant rise in military or naval readiness. No steps were necessary because both had operational naval forces, and some of these were in the Mediterranean on the way to the conflict zone.

For the Nordic neutrals, the situation was fundamentally different. Their armed forces were merely training-mobilization structures, and in order to develop even a basic defence capability, they had to take extraordinary steps to show determination, to enhance the warning capability and to create operational army formations and naval units. Therefore, it is natural that the first reactions to the Balkan War took place here. Where the great powers had fully manned navy units and army formations, the Nordic neutrals totally depended on calling-up of trained reservists. The steps taken now in fact defined what was to be repeated in July and August of 1914.

Even if Sweden had separated from Norway in 1905, both the national elite and the European powers considered her a medium-sized modern state with a significant military potential. Even if the armed services leaders as well as King Gustav V, his family and the rest of the national conservative elite agreed with the now ruling liberals and their social democrat supporters that the country should avoid ties to the great powers and endeavour to remain neutral in their wars, serious differences in outlook and expectations did exist among the various groupings.[7] The liberals under Prime Minister Karl Staaff combined the intention to defend neutrality in all directions with a natural sympathy for the western democracies and with a determination to gain full government control of the armed forces.

The Swedish conservative elites were guided by a determination to safeguard the king's formal supreme command of the forces. Critical of parliamentary democracy, they admired the autocratically ruled Germany and considered national defence a royal prerogative. After the liberal government had taken over in November 1911, it had tried to gain control over how the armed forces should be organized, the symbolic issue being whether the navy would obtain modern fast mini-dreadnought type vessels. The elites saw Russia as the hereditary and predatory enemy of their country, and they considered it unlikely that the Russian armed forces would accept Swedish neutrality after Russia had regained strength after the 1904–5 defeat and revolutionary mayhem.

After a successful conservative public campaign in support of the navy, the liberals had gracefully conceded defeat in relation to this issue in May 1912, but otherwise the government continued work to develop an affordable neutrality defence structure. September had been used for a demanding mobilizations exercise where trained conscript reservists had been called up to man the fortress district on the northern Swedish border with Russian-ruled Finland.[8]

On 4 October, two days after the Swedish authorities had received information from its Constantinople envoy about the risks of war, they decided to accelerate the planned mobilization and defence preparations on the large southeastern island of Gotland. These preparations could be considered directed against both Russia and Germany. On 12 October, the envoy to Vienna reported that both the Russians and the Austrians seemed aware that 'it was risky to play with matches'. However, nine days later, the envoy to Berlin underlined that no decision-makers dared to predict what would happen.

On 15 October, the Swedish government asked the Naval Staff to present proposals for steps to establish a neutrality guard. Two days later the chief of staff suggested that a combined squadron with a couple of armoured ships, a cruiser, some torpedo boats and submarines as well as patrol craft should form at the southern base of Karlskrona, ready to be dispatched to the west coast. At the same time, mines and other defence material for the key areas on that coast were to be made ready for deployment. Älvsborg Fortress was to be readied and supported by a permanent minefield. Another squadron – meant for the Sound and smaller than the first – was to be formed in Stockholm. In the ships of the main Coastal Fleet, the serving conscripts of class 1911 were to extend their service beyond their planned release in mid December until the next annual class was trained and ready to take over.

These proposals were based on the analyses in two memoranda by the Naval and General Staffs, written during the previous couple of months within the framework of the government's work with the future defence organization. The first was signed on 25 October. It covered Sweden's strategic position in a European war. The second, signed on 31 October, covered the threat of a blockade of the Swedish fleet by analysing recent historical cases.[9]

Where Sweden was a confident medium state, the recklessness and defeat of the 1864 Second Schleswig War had taught Denmark the necessity of adjusting its expectations and behaviour to living in the shadow of the German Empire. As Sweden, Denmark was neutral, but Danish foreign policy and its defence profile had to pay special attention to the needs and wishes of Germany, to counterbalance the popular hostility towards the massive neighbour which was nourished by the political conflict over North Schleswig. Berlin would have to be convinced that Denmark would never join her enemies and that it would use her limited armed forces against any attempt at using its territory for operations against Germany.

In 1912, Sweden still had immature political-military relations that hampered the development of a defence structure. In Denmark, the liberal government was in the slow process of implementing the defence laws from autumn 1909. And in 1911, during the Agadir Crisis, Klaus Berntsen, prime and defence minister, had broken the independence and the will of the army generals with the support of King Frederik VIII. Crown Prince Christian had supported the generals and shared their defeat and thus learned to respect Berntsen; and he remembered the lessons after he acceded to the throne as Christian X in the spring of 1912.

Another difference between Sweden and Denmark was that all leading Swedish politicians would fight – and go on fighting – if attacked. In Denmark, after the liberals took over in 1901, the issue was how long one would be obliged to fight. Only the small group of right-wing conservatives agreed with the regular officers that national honour demanded Denmark continue fighting for as long as possible. However, even the army leadership only prepared for a two-month siege of the Copenhagen Fortress.

The defence laws would end the focus of defence of the Copenhagen Fortress against both land and sea attack. Instead, an improved ability to defend the capital against naval bombardment and coup landing as well as with the creation of an improved field army made up of most of the first-line units would be put in place. The latter would conduct a forward defence of the main island, Zealand.

More than half of the infantry garrisons of Jutland-Funen were to be moved to western and southern Zealand to form a new division, tasked with forward defence of the eastern coast of the Great Belt, the strait that would be used by a British fleet entering the Baltic to attack Germany. Some of the modern torpedo boats and submarines now being built for the navy would use a new protected base in the shallow waters bordering the Great Belt to counter belligerent use of Danish territorial waters as a logistic base (logically the British as the Germans had their main Baltic base nearby).

As already indicated, Copenhagen followed the crisis closely and then did what little it could to discreetly improve readiness. During the Agadir Crisis one year earlier, the General Staff had established a permanently manned duty officer post that would receive information about developing crises from both intelligence and diplomatic sources. If necessary, he could alert the key personnel of the army, navy and government. All were living in close proximity to each other.

The first reaction to the Balkan Crisis was the king's note on 23 October ordering the War Office to be restrictive when issuing foreign travel permits to officers. The next, more important step was taken on 25 October when the Danish navy established a permanent intelligence station in the Copenhagen navy base. During the previous years, the service had developed its central radio station and supplemented the cable-based reporting network with wireless telegraphy stations on lightships as well as naval vessels and civilian state ships planned to be used by the navy after mobilization. The new intelligence station could not only supplement the General Staff duty officer by giving information about foreign presence in Danish waters, but it could also give tactical warning of a potential coup landing or bombardment force approaching Copenhagen, and act as a central operations centre for control of the naval units.

On 28 October, the defence minister issued his permanent directive for cooperation and command relations between the different commanders and staffs during defence preparations and after mobilization. The draft directive had been debated throughout all of 1912. Now it would come into force on 1 November, four days later.[10]

November–December 1912 (Germany and Great Britain)

The final part of the first main fighting period of the war occurred with the Greek capture of Salonica on 9 November, the successful Ottoman defence of Constantinople in the First Battle of Çatalca on 17–18 November and the Serbian capture of Durrës on the Adriatic coast on 29 November, one day after the Albanians had declared independence in Vlorë. From 3 December, a two-month armistice followed between the Ottoman Empire and Bulgaria, Serbia and Montenegro.

On 3 November 1912, Berlin received information that the British Royal Navy had mobilized. The crews of three destroyer flotillas had been assembled. The 'exercises' to hide the completion of the nucleus manned crew units, which had been decided in late winter, had not yet had the time to establish a routine that could fool the diplomats. After the British support of France during the Agadir Crisis one year earlier, the Germans were suspicious and angered by the loss of face. The Kaiser ordered that the German navy be aware of the British action. Hopman linked the British action to the crisis, but was uncertain of its meaning. The British denial the following day of naval mobilization was received with little credibility in Berlin, and on 14 November Hopman noted that Tirpitz remained 'nervous'. However, during the following days Berlin registered several positive statements from London that indicated that Britain did not seek war.[11]

On 15 November, Serbian troops reached the Adriatic coast, and on the same day Danish intelligence noted German army logistical preparations for war. From 17 to 20 November, Kaiser Wilhelm visited the anti-British naval officers in Kiel, which may have inspired him to his hard-line attitude upon his return to Berlin on 21 November, as he foresaw a war for national survival between Germany and the France–Russia–Britain combination. The next day he granted guarantees of German support to the visiting Austrian chief of General Staff, and on 23 November he held consultations with the chancellor and leaders of the army and the navy about the possibilities of further expansion of their forces. Tirpitz informed the Kaiser that the focus should be on readying the existing units. Additional major ships could not be operational until 1916. On the same day, Hopman noted intelligence of large Russian forces concentrating on the Austrian border, of Austrian mobilization of several army corps against Russia, of French troop deployment towards the Belgian border, as well as of British–Belgian consultations about a landing of British forces. The German General Staff was now pessimistic.

On 24 November, Tirpitz clarified that precautionary measures had to be taken. When the chancellor stated that neither France nor Britain wanted war, Kaiser Wilhelm had considered the statement 'childish'. There was agreement between the Kaiser and his leaders that the focus had to be placed on early force improvements. The chancellor promised Helmuth von Moltke, the chief of staff, that he could present a new army plan by spring, 'if that was not too late'.

The next morning the situation was still tense, and in addition there was news that France had tried to attract Romania to the Entente. A decision was taken to accelerate completion of the battleships and cruisers, to concentrate the older battleships in the reserve squadron and to move the remaining units in the Baltic to the relative safety of Kiel. The bases of Kiel and Wilhelmshaven would be directed to initiate discreet mobilization measures.

With these decisions taken, Tirpitz still did not think that the British wanted war, and remained hopeful even after Berlin received an agent report from Britain in the early afternoon that made clear that all the nucleus manned units of the Royal Navy – the Second Fleet – were now fully manned. On that day, the navy plan for a war against Britain in the North Sea was presented to Kaiser Wilhelm for approval, and to follow up on the previous day's promise, the chancellor asked Moltke to outline a plan for reinforcing the army to a level that would ensure victory in a future war. During November, Kaiser Wilhelm deliberated on the navy plan for war against a combination of France and Russia. Both that plan and the plan for a North Sea war against Britain were approved by the Kaiser on 3 December.[12]

Three weeks into November, both the Albanian coast and Constantinople elements of the crisis were clear, with the former requiring direct German support to Austria-Hungary, bringing risks of war with the Entente. Therefore, Germany concentrated the main part of its navy in the North Sea to reduce vulnerability. The British focus at the beginning of November had been in the eastern Mediterranean, but by mid month, the intensity of the crisis and the risk of war apparently inspired the fast completion of the first ever modern Royal Navy operational 'War Plan'. However, earlier that month the crisis had led to progress in the French–British consultations on naval cooperation. On 8 November, agreement had been reached on how to work together in the English Channel and the essential work to develop common code books was progressing, as were the politically far more complex talks about division of responsibilities in the Mediterranean.

The draft War Plan for the Home Fleets was sent by the Admiralty War Staff to the commander-in-chief, Admiral Sir George Callaghan, for comments on 25 November, on the same day that the German fleet concentrated in Wilhelmshaven and when Kaiser Wilhelm was presented with the German draft plan. It is most likely that both developments were nourished directly by the crisis rather than influenced by concrete intelligence about the other side. The operational idea of the British plan was new, reflecting the failure of an alternative concept during the annual naval manoeuvres in the late summer and the resulting agreement between the Staff and the admiral that the latter needed to have more authority delegated. Rather than just stating the tasks and forces available, the plan guided Callaghan in displaying the Admiralty's thoughts about the challenges and priorities.[13]

German suspicion was triggered by the Royal Navy destroyer flotilla mobilization of early November; nevertheless, the relations between the two countries did not fuel the escalation of the crisis. This changed rather dramatically during the first week of December. The German chancellor Bethmann Hollweg's speech to the Reichstag on 2 December, with its unconditional support for Austria-Hungary, may have been considered both welcome and moderate in Germany and Austria-Hungary. However, it had to be read differently by British officials. The next day, the British government had Lord Haldane, the Lord Chancellor, contact the German ambassador for consultations. Haldane was probably chosen because of his leadership in the failed naval disarmament mission to Germany earlier that year, and he made clear to the ambassador that Great Britain would intervene in a continental war to prevent a French defeat.

The ambassador immediately sent a report about the conversation. The Kaiser only read the report on the morning of 8 December upon returning from one of his extended hunting excursions. Even though the British position had remained the same since 1905 and been repeated during the 1911 Agadir Crisis, it made Kaiser Wilhelm furious. He considered Haldane's statement a 'hidden threat and a declaration of the decision to fight', and he called his leading army and naval officers for a meeting, later labelled a 'War Council', to discuss whether or not a war should be accepted right away. The civilian government was not invited. Moltke indicated that the army was ready. However, Tirpitz needed time, until mid 1914, for the completion of the Kiel Canal enlargement and the Heligoland base, the German Bight coastal defences and to increase the number and quality of the U-boats. And the Grand Admiral pointed out that Moltke was incorrect in considering the army ready. He knew from the previous meetings during the crisis that the army needed to be expanded by training a larger portion of the conscripts.

The meeting thereafter continued with the Kaiser's decision and directives for war preparations to take place in the following months. Planning against Britain was to be given priority. The navy had to focus on the construction of U-boats that could attack the British transports to the continent. During the meeting, it was also agreed that German public opinion would have to be prepared for a possible conflict, and the armed services were to develop joint operational plans for war against Britain. On the same day, Germany and Austria-Hungary agreed to participate in the London Ambassadors' Conference that was to create a framework for great power management of the Balkan War Crisis. Participation was a logical consequence of the decision to postpone war, if possible.

Even if the German leaders wanted to avoid an immediate war, they could not be certain that they would succeed, and monitored by foreign intelligence and diplomats, they maintained and developed their force readiness level throughout the rest of the year. The army accelerated its recruit training and it prepared and guarded the railways. December became the first culmination of the crisis.[14] The Ambassador's Conference had by now started, yet the Royal Navy's planning continued through December, with the most important element being the formal issuing of the War Plan on 16 December. The Plan was mildly adjusted on the basis of the comments from Admiral Callaghan. It was complemented by the more traditional 'War Order' to the commander-in-chief. During the next weeks, the Plan and the Order were followed by orders to the subordinate fleets and squadrons as well as the independent flag officers.[15] During December, the Admiralty was finally confronted with the fact that it did not have the necessary expertise to plan the deployment to and support of the British Expeditionary Force in France. It therefore asked experienced civilian management – two shipowners – to develop a plan. Their report was ready by April 1913.[16]

November–December 1912 (the Small Neutrals)

Swedish diplomats and intelligence monitored the development of the crisis, and on 15 November the government decided to authorize conscript service time extension for the coast and border guard soldiers. Such an extension had previously only been authorized for the navy, but it would be a necessary precondition for maintaining a neutrality guard in a great power war.

On 19 November, the Swedish naval minister asked for increased defence readiness along the west coast in the Gothenburg region. The Kattegat coast was considered suitable for naval bases controlling both the Skagerrak and northern exits of the Danish Straits, and thus interesting to both the German and the British navies. Following the German decision on the morning of 25 November to dispatch the High Seas Fleet units in the Baltic to Wilhelmshaven, they exercised in the Kattegat. The appearance of the German navy off the western coast on 25 November highlighted the risk that one of the great power navies would use the deep fiords of the coast as bases against the opponent, and this triggered a quick decision by the government. On that day, the government decided to activate the Älvsborg Fortress which guarded the access to Gothenburg and to prepare its batteries and a minefield.

On the following day, the naval minister proposed not only to form two squadrons for Gothenburg and the Sound that had been suggested by the chief of the Naval Staff in October, but also to activate the main Coastal Fleet and base it at Karlskrona. On 27 November, the government decided to act, and a couple of days later the two squadrons were on their way, and the main fleet was in place for its 'winter manoeuvres'. The west coast squadron – the Gothenburg Detachment – was instructed to respond to any violations of Swedish neutrality and territory, in cooperation with the regional army commander.

It is likely that the early and robust reaction was catalysed by the domestic political situation in Sweden. The liberal government needed to prove its determination to the highly critical royal family and conservative opposition. The government did so in a way that underlined its will to guard and defend the country's neutrality in all directions, not only against the main threat that inspired the opposition: a Russian invasion over the land border in the north. It is no coincidence that the Swedish intelligence effort during the crisis focused on Russia. It was controlled by the conservative diplomats and senior officers. On the arrival of the two squadrons detached to the west coast and the Sound in early December, the regional coastal watch organization was activated to support them.[17]

In Denmark, the government was careful not to take any action that might be noticed in Germany and could be read as a hostile measure. However, during the obvious rise in international tension in November, Prime Minister Berntsen saw the need for a confidential discussion between the members of government and the armed services leaders. Even if he considered war to be an unlikely folly, his consorts, including the generals, considered it proper to have a discussion on the status of intelligence and defence readiness, the procedures for calling up the neutrality guard or full mobilization, as well as the force to build-up to the levels authorized by the Danish 1909 defence laws. The meetings took place on 9 and 16 November within the framework of the Danish National Defence Council, a group acknowledged but never formally established. Beyond the mutual exchange of information, the main result of the meetings was an understanding that it would be sensible to spend more effort and money on foreign intelligence.

Such meetings were never repeated, probably because they offered a forum for the service leaders, particularly for the generals, to present the defects and shortcomings in a way that was difficult to control and contain, especially since it was generally believed that information would always be leaked to the press and thereafter be noticed abroad. Until that moment, planning for an early, limited mobilization of a standing neutrality guard had focused on creating a defence of Copenhagen against a coup landing and on guarding the railways on Zealand to be used during mobilization. However, in December, it was decided to have a similar call-up for part of the army in Jutland to maintain a force for guarding the border zone and harbours that might be used in British landing operations, chiefly the new large export and fishery port of Esbjerg close to the border. Thus, the Danish reaction was limited to political-military consultation and coordination. The Swedish steps to increase defence readiness in late November were seen as most unfortunate, as they made it very difficult to explain to the public why Denmark did nothing.[18]

To states that combined the intention to remain neutral with a responsibility for littoral waters of potential strategic importance to the navies of likely involved great powers, the specific character of common Declarations of Neutrality could become a key to the chances of avoiding or managing violations of the territorial waters. During the Crimean War, Denmark and the Dual Monarchy of Sweden-Norway had coordinated their declarations. Since 1909, Denmark and Sweden had negotiated to develop similar common declarations where the harmony would reinforce the message of determination to the belligerents in a future conflict between a Baltic Sea littoral power and an outside naval power. Both Sweden and Denmark needed to restrict access to their fortified naval base areas and both had to avoid their territorial waters being used by a belligerent. As a special requirement, Denmark had to define the rules for belligerent vessels' passage of the international Danish Straits. The rules were to be consistent with the Hague Convention rules for neutral rights and obligations. However, they were also to support the chosen Danish defence position, by forbidding belligerent (British) use of the territorial waters at the same time as there was to be general free access waters, considered essential for German use of Kattegat as a forward defence area. The development was not easy, as the Swedes seemed to think that they could dictate the result, and as the Danish Foreign Ministry proved unable to comprehend the strategic implications of conceding to Swedish pressure. Progress achieved during the late summer of the 1911 Agadir Crisis was insufficient, and the Swedes only showed flexibility from 10 October, after the Balkan War had started. The final progress took place after 16 November, when the Danish navy's arguments were accepted by its government. It thereafter guided the agreement reached in early December and signed by representatives of the two states – and Norway – on 21 December. The common Declaration of Neutrality remained valid during the Great War and was only supplemented during that war by Swedish and Norwegian limitations on belligerent submarines using their waters. The common declaration led to rumours that the three states considered entering into a defensive alliance.[19]

January–May 1913 (Germany and Great Britain)

The hostilities in the Balkans were resumed on 3 February 1913. The Turks' counterattack in Thrace from 20 to 23 February was contained by the Bulgarians, who thereafter finally captured the fortress town of Adrianople (Edirne) by assault on 11 March. Fighting ended when the garrison of Shkodër (Shkodra, Scutari) in Albania had to surrender to the Montenegrins on 23 April. After great power military pressure was applied on Serbia and Montenegro to avert an

Italian–Austrian intervention in Albania, the war was formally ended in London on 30 May.

During the winter of 1913, the Danish General Staff reported intelligence on constant development of German armed force readiness. Admiral Hopman noted on 15 January that a decision was taken to acquire a naval aviation force of ten airships and forty-eight airplanes. Later that month, the navy had developed a concept for the use of these forces: the airplanes were to be used against the Royal Navy's blockading units in the German Bight and the zeppelins deployed for reconnaissance operations and bombardment in the North Sea and Danish waters.

In the War Council (*Kriegsrat*) on 8 December, the Kaiser had directed the army and the navy to create a joint plan for a war against Britain. One of the results has survived only as a Danish intelligence translation of an outline plan from mid February for the transport of a large invasion force early in a British–German war, according to principles agreed on 22 December. The operation would be supported by the future airship fleet, so it was probably not seen as likely to be carried out in the immediate future. Considering how the two armed services typically altogether lacked the will and ability to coordinate their operations, the outline plan should probably be seen as window-dressing to satisfy the Kaiser. Even so, Danish intelligence reported that practical landing experiments were conducted in the following months.

However, the two services did take the order to be ready seriously. Planning and preparations continued in spite of the period of relaxation of tension between Germany and Britain from early February 1913. During the spring, the navy and the army reached an agreement on how an *Admiralstab* element was to be integrated into the mobile Imperial Headquarters, allowing the naval officers to use the General Staff library to reduce the necessity for motor transport.[20]

During the winter, the British Admiralty War Staff continued developing War Orders for the subordinate and independent flag officers. For most of January, the tension remained high, but at the end of the month the tension had abated enough for Churchill to feel free to start searching for advice mirroring his own views, a project that would culminate in the purging of resilient and independent-minded officers in April–July 1914, to gain full control of the navy.

As previously mentioned, the crisis had nourished the coordination of the French and the Royal Navies. Finally, in April, agreement was reached in the politically sensitive area of cooperation in the Mediterranean. Thereafter, the Admiralty War Staff moved quickly to issue a War Plan covering a war against Germany, in which Britain was allied with France.

After having removed the staff officers that he considered insufficiently aggressive, Churchill succeeded in adjusting the language of some policy sentences in the War Plan and the War Orders just prior to the war. Although he did not manage to change the strategy towards more offensive operations, the texts that guided the Royal Navy during the first two years of the war were now completed.[21]

January–May 1913 (the Small Neutrals)

Probably in mid January, Stockholm received intelligence from St. Petersburg that the Russians would raid the Swedish navy, in an attempt to paralyse it in the run-up to war. The information confirmed the basic threat perceptions of the professional navy – and army – leadership. In mid January, the intelligence report triggered a request from the navy chief of staff to adjust the deployment of the Coastal Fleet to reduce the vulnerability to such a Russian operation. By late January, the commander of the Coastal Fleet reinforced the request, which led to a conflict with the government, who insisted on maintaining neutrality in all directions.

On 1 February, the government decided to reject the redeployment request, and on 24 February it decided to demobilize the Swedish Coastal Fleet. Thereafter, only the Gothenburg Detachment was maintained. On 8 February, the Coastal Fleet commander used his experience from the winter exercises to underline the need for large seaworthy armoured ships. This implied criticism of government policy and may have added to the government's determination to demobilize the fleet. The reduction of readiness to a mere symbolic level is also likely to have mirrored the awareness in Stockholm that the tensions between Britain and Germany had been significantly reduced by late February.[22]

During the winter, the public reaction to the crisis had become extremely awkward for the Danish government. Leaked information about the unaddressed equipment needs of the armed forces, but especially about the serious weakness of the 'North Front' of the Copenhagen Fortress, led to a defence collection campaign, where public statements underlined that the population saw Germany as the most likely enemy. Personally convinced that a great power war could be averted, Prime Minister Berntsen regarded the entire campaign as a plot to undermine the political support he sought for a democratic reform of the constitution.[23]

During the previous two and a half years, the prime minister had successfully blocked the domestically highly controversial move of army units and their garrisons from Jutland-Funen to west and south Zealand. In mid January, critical intelligence was used by the army leadership to force the government to order the repositioning. The move to the new garrisons took place in spring. Thereby, the final and critical element of the army's defence strategy, which had developed over twenty years, fell into place. Even before the units moved, their officers were put to work doing detailed reconnaissance for the new coastal and infrastructure guard missions that would occupy them from August 1914.[24] At the same time, the designated Danish commanding admiral finally accepted the 'Operation Plan' outline of the small Naval Staff, even if it limited his full freedom and flexibility to use his units as he saw fit in an unforeseeable future.[25]

In late spring, when the international crisis had ended the need for Danish defence invisibility, the War Office director succeeded in convincing the sceptical Klaus Berntsen that the planned large-scale mobilization exercise, required by the text of the Army Act of 1909, could take place in September. It was the first such exercise ever, and the experience of planning and directing the activity unfolded into an effective, full-scale dress rehearsal for the partial mobilization that took place without friction in early August the next year.

The Danish Ministry of Foreign Affairs had constantly and effectively resisted any cooperation with the General Staff Intelligence Section. Supported by the decisions during the November 1912 crisis 'Defence Council' meetings, the leader of the Intelligence Section set out on a recruiting trip, robustly convincing or coercing honorary consuls and other Danes in Norway, Sweden, Britain and Germany that they were obliged to report to him.[26]

Final Note

The Balkan War Crisis, and thus its implications for what happened in the late summer of 1914, has slipped below the horizon of the Anglo-Saxon and other Western histories of the pre-Great War period. A very good reason for this is that the crisis was deliberately made invisible in Winston Churchill's influential 1923 narrative *The World Crisis*, describing the prewar years.[27]

Churchill had good personal and political reasons for ignoring the crisis in his book. The critical events took place before he gained decisive influence over the Admiralty. The War Plan issued when the crisis intensified in late November 1912 by the new Admiralty War Staff was consolidated and refined in close cooperation with the Home Fleets' commander-in-chief, Sir George Callaghan, during the crisis and the following year. The plan was felt to be humiliating by the ambitious young First Lord of the Admiralty, as it ignored his perception of threat of the risk of an early German coup landing on the British coast. It flouted his political needs and deep-felt impatience as it did not give the navy a clear, aggressive and visible role early in the short war that he anticipated. By delegating operational responsibility to Callaghan, it also ignored his immature but constant wish to control and command directly. There was no need to advertise even years later that he used the final months of the crisis, and the year thereafter, to undermine the planning and the influence of the War Staff that he had been appointed as First Lord during the Agadir Crisis to create.[28]

Beyond the increased readiness seen in all four states during the crisis, the international tension triggered and inspired different types of new war preparations. In Germany, it was the post-*Kriegsrat* activities that focused both army and navy war preparations as well as force developments on what could be achieved in months rather than several years. Moreover, some symbolic and some very practical joint army–navy planning was achieved. In Britain, the main results were the development of the naval War Plans and War Orders, including the agreement with France. In Sweden, the new element in the war preparations was the development and the testing of a naval and a coastal neutrality guard. In Denmark, the focus was thereafter placed on all types of defence preparations that could be achieved discreetly, on the collection of money that made it possible to close equipment and fortification gaps, on the achievement of the delayed and politically very difficult redeployment of the army to match the defence strategy, and finally on the post-crisis mobilization exercise.

Michael Hesselholt Clemmesen is a retired Danish Army Brigadier General and Senior Research Fellow (em.) at the Institute for Military History and War Studies of the Danish Defence College. He is the Editor-in-Chief of *Fra Krig og Fred: Dansk Militærhistorisk Kommissions Tidsskrift* and author of several books and articles on the 1907–14 strategic history, the most relevant here being *Det lille land før den store krig: De danske farvande, stormagtsstrategier, efterretninger og forsvarsforberedelser omkring kriserne 1911–13* (Syddansk Universitetsforlag, 2012).

Notes

1 Michael H. Clemmesen, *Det lille land før den store krig: De danske farvande, stormagtsstrategier, efterretninger og forsvarsforberedelser om kriserne 1911–13* [The Small Country before the Great War: Danish Waters, Great Power Strategies, Intelligence and Defence Preparations during the Crises 1911–1913] (Odense: Syddansk Universitetsforlag, 2012). Most of the remaining notes here will refer to the key literature and sources used for writing the monograph.
2 Richard C. Hall, *The Balkan Wars 1912–1913: Prelude to the First World War* (London: Routledge, 2000).
3 The reactions in Berlin have to a significant degree been drawn from Michael Epkenhans (ed.), *Das ereignisreiche Leben eines 'Wilhelminers': Tagebücher, Briefe, Aufzeichnungen 1901 bis 1920 von Albert Hopman* (Munich: Oldenbourg Wissenschaftsverlag, 2004), 247–53. For contemporary Danish knowledge of the views of Berlin, see Rigsarkivet (RA) [Danish State Archives]: Marinestaben, Emneordnede sager, Pk. 35–35a: Depeche no. LV, 'Balkankrisen', Berlin, 13 October 1912; Depeche no. LIV, 'Balkan. Italo-tyrkiske Forhandlinger'; Depeche no. LVI, 'Balkankrisen', Berlin, 14 December 1912; Depeche no. LVII, 'Balkankrisen og den tyrkisk–italienske Krig', Berlin, 18 October 1912; Depeche no. LVIII, 'Grev Moltkes første Besøg hos Herr v. Kiderlen–Waechter', Berlin, 19 October 1912.
4 The National Archives of United Kingdom (TNA), ADM 116/3096, Confidential from Chief of War Staff of 23 February 1912, 'Second Fleet. Amendment of W. List. Periodic Test Mobilisations'.
5 See Paul G. Halpern, *The Mediterranean Naval Situation 1908–1914* (Cambridge, MA: Harvard University Press, 1971), 13–93.
6 For the Danish knowledge of early British views of the crisis, see RA, Marinestaben, Emneordnede sager, Pk. 35–35a: Depeche no. XXVII, London, 6 October 1912; Depeche no. XXVIII, 'Balkankrisen', London, 9 October 1912; Depeche no. XXIX, London, 10 October 1912; Depeche no. XXX, 'Balkankrigen', London, 11 October 1912; Depeche no. XXXI, 'Balkankrigen', London, 12 October 1912; Depeche no. XXXII, 'Balkankrigen', London, 16 October 1912; Udenrigsministeriet, Depecher, London, 1909–1912, Pk. 249: Depeche no. XXXIII, London, 28 October 1912; Depeche no. XXXIV, 'Balkankrigen', London, 1 November 1912; Clemmesen, *The Royal Navy's Strategy Discourse Up to the Great War.*
7 For a general outline of Sweden during the crisis, see Erik Norberg, 'Balkankriget och Sveriges försvar' [The Balkan War and the Defence of Sweden], in Wilhelm M. Calgren et al. (eds), *Utrikespolitik och Historia: Studier tillägnade Wilhelm M. Carlgren den 6 maj 1987* [Foreign Policy and History: Studies Conferred on Wilhelm M. Carlgren on 6 May 1987] (Stockholm: Militärhistoriska förlaget, 1987), 199–218.
8 One of the general analyses of the Swedish defence policies of the period is Kent Zetterberg, *Militärer och Politiker: En studie i militär professionnalisering, innovationsspridning och internationellt inflytande på de svenska försvarsberedningar 1911–1914* [Soldiers and Politicians: A Study of the Influence of Military Professionalization, Spreading Innovation

and International Influence on Swedish Defence Reports, 1911–1914] (Stockholm: Militärhistoriska Förlaget, 1988).
9 Based mainly on the following files from the Swedish General Staff and Naval Staff: Krigsarkivet (KrA) [Swedish War Archives]: Generalstaben. Utrikesavdelningen. Serie E.I.f. Inkomna meddelanden av depescher. Volym no. 1. 1912–1914. Utrikes Departementet. Meddelande af depescher no. 52. Konstantinopel, 2 October 1912; Berlin, 21 October 1912; Marinstaben. Exp. Serie B I. Koncept. Mob.- och stst. Avd. 1912. Volym no. 14: C.S.D. no. 101 H of 17 October 1912 including 'P.M. angående beredskapsåtgärder som anses böra vidtages vid marinen med anledning af det nuvarande politiska läget'. Hemlig 118 H/1912 'Kungl. Maj:t har i nåder befall' with 'Bestämmelser angående intagandet af försvarsberedskap vid Älvsborgs fästning för neutralitetsskydd'; Chefen för Marinstaben rettet til Chefen för Sjöforsvarsdepartementet no. 140 H of 26 November 1912 to Statsrådet; Marinstaben. Exp. Serie B II. Koncept. Kommunikationsavd. 1912. Volym no. 17: (Chefen för Sjöförsvarsdepartementet) Hemlig. Koncept of 25 October 1912 til Chefen för landtförsvarsdepartementet; attached: Koncept no. 104. Hemlig. Försvarsberedningarna. Hvilke farer äro i händelse af ett krig i Europa att vänta för Sveriges neutralitet? Hvilke tillkomna arméen och hvilka marinen vid afvärjandet af sådana faror; (Chefen för Sjöförsvarsdepartementet) Hemlig. no. 110 H of 31 October 1912 to Chefen för landtförsvarsdepartementet; attached: Försvarsberedningarne. Hvilke slutsatser äro af erfarenheter från senaste krig att hämta angående faran för en blockad af svenska kusten, och hvilka hufvudsakliga åtgärder kunna i händelse af ett krig från svensk sida vidtagas för at bryta en sådan blockad.
10 The description is comprised from Clemmesen, *Det lille land*, 69–132, 154–225, 267–81, as no other work exists.
11 Epkenhans, *Das ereignisreiche Leben eines 'Wilhelminers'*, 253–58.
12 For the reactions in Berlin, see Epkenhans, *Das ereignisreiche Leben eines 'Wilhelminers'*, 258–68; Bundesarchiv, Militärarchiv (BAMA) [German Military Achives], RM5/898/6, Ganz Geheim! Von Hand zu Hand! O-Sache! Zum Immediatvortrag A. 3037 IV, Berlin, 25 November 1912, 'Operationsbefehl für den Nordseekriegsschauplatz'; and Von Hand zu Hand! O-Sache! Zum Immediatvortrag A. 3037 Infolge von A. 854 IV/12, Berlin, 25 November 1912, 'Entwurf zum Operationsbefehl für den Krieg gegen England'; Michael Epkenhans, *Die wilhelminische Flottenrüstung 1908–1914: Weltmachtstreben, industrieller Fortschritt, soziale Integration* (Munich: Oldenbourg Wissenschaftsverlag, 1991), 319n35, 325–26; Jörg-Uwe Fischer, *Admiral des Kaisers: Georg Alexander von Müller als Chef des Marinekabinetts Wilhelms II.* (Frankfurt/M.: Verlag Peter Lang, 1991), 127–28; Ivo Nikolai Lambi, *The Navy and German Power Politics 1862–1914* (Boston, MA: Harper Collins Publishers, 1984), 397–405.
13 Halpern, *The Mediterranean Naval Situation*, 93–114; TNA, ADM 116/3412, War Plans and War Orders. Home Fleets and Detached Squadrons, November 1912 to December 1913, pp. 7–26, Admiralty. Secret & Personal N-0020/12 of 25 November 1912 to Admiral Sir George A. Callaghan, GCVO, KCB, H.M.S. NEPTUNE; FO 371/1360, pp. 646–48, 'Movement of

German Warships. Reports Inconveniences Caused to Danish Traffic by Passage of German Fleet through Great Belt', no. 97, 27 November 1911.

14 Primarily: Epkenhans, *Die wilhelminische Flottenrüstung*, 327–36, and idem, *Das ereignisreiche Leben eines 'Wilhelminers'*, 268–77, 286–90. However, for the 'War Council', see also John C.G. Röhl, *Kaiser, Hof und Staat: Wilhelm II. und die deutsche Politik* (Munich: C.H. Beck Verlag, 1995), 175–202; Fischer, *Admiral des Kaisers*, 128–31; Paul M. Kennedy, 'The Development of German Naval Operations Plans against England, 1896–1914' [1974], reprinted in Andrew Lambert (ed.), *Naval History 1850–Present*, Vol. I (Aldershot: Ashgate, 2007), 295–324, here 316–17; Terence Zuber, *The Real German War Plan 1904–1914* (Stroud: The History Press, 2011), 116–20.

15 TNA, ADM 116/3412, War Plans and War Orders. Home Fleets and Detached Squadrons. November 1912 to December 1913: List of Contents, p. 1; pp. 27–45, 'War Plans M 0020/12'; pp. 47–145, 'Secret. War Orders. The Commander-in-Chief, Home Fleets, 16 December 1912', 'War Plans. Issue to Home Ports', 19 December 1912, 'War Orders – Admiral of Patrols', 9 January 1913, 'War Plans. Issue to Commodore (T)', 9 January 1913, 'War Orders – 4th Cruiser Squadron', 10 January 1913, 'Memorandum – Defence of Home Ports', 11 February 1913, 'Memorandum of Commander in Chief Home Fleets on Disposition of Cruiser Squadrons and Flotillas', 12 February 1913, 'Draft Orders for 2nd and 3rd Cruiser Squadrons and First Fleet Flotillas – Receipt and Return of', 12 February 1918.

16 Stephen Cobb, *Preparing for Blockade: Naval Contingency for Economic Warfare* (London: Ashgate, 2013), 187–88.

17 For the Swedish crisis decisions, see KrA, Marinstaben Exp. Serie E I. Ink. Handlingar. Mob.- och stat. avd. 1912. Volym no. 16: Kungl. Sjöförsvarsdepartementets Kommando-Expedition no. 75 H, 76 H and 77 H of 25 November 1912 til Chefen för Marinstaben; Marinstaben. Exp. Serie B II. Koncept. Kommunikationsavd. 1912. Volym no. 17: Chefen för Sjöforsvarsdepartementet no. 125 H of 26 November 1912; Chef. Sjöf. Dep. no. 149 H of 26 November 1912 (with three attached instructions dated 28 November 1912); Generalstabens arkiv. Chefsexp. Hemlige handl. Serie: E. Inkomna handlingar. I. Huvudserie. 1912: Gustaf etc. Hemlig of 15 November 1912 to Arméförvaltningen. Gustaf etc. Hemlig of 15 November 1912 til Arméförvaltningens artilleri-, fortifikations- och intendentsdepartement; Marinstaben. Exp. Serie B II. Koncept. Kommunikationsavd. 1913. Volym no. 18: (Chefen för Marinstaben) of 27 August 1913 'I skrifvelse N:r 135 H den 30 Nov. 1912 ...'. For British monitoring of the Swedish naval preparations, see TNA, FO 371/1478, pp. 21ff. no. 52. Consular. Stockholm, 2 December 1912. 'Swedish Coast Squadron. Vessels Engaged in Winter Manoeuvres'.

18 The key files for the Danish discussion during these weeks are: RA, T. V. Gardes Privatarkiv, Pk. 2. Dagbøger, 9, 11, 12 and 13 November 1912; Krigsministeriet, 5. Kontor. Pk. A 159. Forsvarsrådets oprettelse and Pk. A 160. Forsvarsrådets møder; Direktør generalmajor N.B. Ulrichs referatprotokol 1910–1918, notater 9 November, 15 November and 19 December 1912; Generalstabens Operationssektion. Indkomne. Sager 1912–13 Pk. 3. 2 GK FTR M. 473 of 27 November 1912 about the 'Enlarged

Peace force' in Jutland-Funen; 2 GK FTR M.552 of 31 December 1912 to 'Den designerede Overgeneral' about 'Formering af en Sikringsstyrke i 2. Generalkommandodistrikt'. Generalstabens Operations-sektion. Kopibog. Design OGN svarer positivt ved FTR O.Nr. 129 of 4 December 1912.

19 Clemmesen, *Det lille land*, 336–45.

20 Epkenhans, *Das ereignisreiche Leben eines 'Wilhelminers'*, 290–322; BAMA, RM/5/1614, Ganz Geheim! Von Hand zu Hand! O-Sache. Zu A. 293 IV, Berlin, 23 January 1913. Verwendung der Luftwaffe im Kriege gegen England-Frankreich; RM/2/1816/F1/I, Der Staatssekretär des Reichs–Marine–Amts B. no. A. IVa. 594, Berlin, 22 February 1913 and RM/2/1816/F1/7, Der Staatssekretär des Reichs-Marine-Amts no. M. 1229, Berlin, 23 April 1913 to Chef des Marinekabinetts 'Auf das Schreiben vom 27. März 1913'. For the Danish intelligence results, see mainly RA, Marinestaben, A. Emneordnede sager (1904–1932), Pk. 34: Efterretningssager m.m. Generalstabens Efterretningssektion: Strængt Fortroligt 'Afskrift af Bemærkninger fra Chefen for den tyske Marines Admiralstab til den tyske Marineminister angaaende Samvirken mellem Hær og Flåde ved de forberedende Arbejder vedrørende Indskibning af et eventuelt Ekspeditionskorps', but also other reports from the same intelligence file collection.

21 TNA, ADM 116/3412, War Plans and War Orders. Home Fleets and Detached Squadrons. November 1912 to December 1913, pp. 243–302, 419–34: e.g. Secret. 'War Orders No 2 for the Commander-in-Chief Home Fleets', draft of 18–19 April 1913; M–0032/13, Admiralty. Secret and Personal to Admiral George A. Callaghan, GCVO, KCB; 'Co-operation of English and French Fleets', collection of 25 September 1913 of directives from the summer of 1913; Clemmesen, *The Royal Navy's Strategy Discourse*.

22 For the key files relating to the threat perception and political reactions, see KrA, Chefen för Kustflottan. Högste Befälhavaran över 1912–1913 Års Kustflotta. Serie F. Utgående och inkomna skrivelser 1912–1913. Volym no. 1. no. 29 H of 16 January 1913 til Konungen; no. 36 H of 27 January 1913 til Konungen; no. 53 H of 24 February 1913 to Konungen; Marinstaben. Exp. Serie B II. Kommunikationsavd. 1913. Volym no. 18. (Chefen för Sjöförsvarsdepartementet) no. 8 H of 16 January 1913 to Telegrafstyrelsen; Chefen för Marinstaben no. 10 H of 17 January 1913; (Chefen för Marinstaben). 'Koncept Hemlig. Fartygsmaterielens förläggning under fredstid; Wilhelm Dyrssens arkiv. Volym 14. Notat: På hvad sätt skall konungen och krigsministren erhålla biträde ved kommandomåls handläggande ...'; Marinstaben. Exp. Serie I. Ink. handlingar mob- og stat. avd. 1913. Volym no. 18. Kungl. Sjöförsvarsdepartementets Kommando-Expedition no. 16 H of 8 February 1913 til Chefen för Marinstaben; Kungl. Sjöförsvarsdepartementets Kommando-Expedition. no. 23 H of 24 February 1912 til Chefen för Marinstaben; Chefen för Göteborgavdelingen (via Sjöförsvars Departementets Kommando-Expedition no. 57 H) of 28 February 1913 til Konungen.

23 Klaus Berntsen, *Erindringer fra Rigsdags- og Ministeraar* [Memories from the Rigsdag and the Ministry] (Copenhagen: V. Pio, 1925), 224–30; Peter Munch, *Erindringer 1909–1914: Indenrigsminister og Forsvarsminister* [Memories 1909–1914: Ministry of Interior and Defence] (Copenhagen:

Nyt Nordisk Forlag, 1960), 120; Bilag XIII: Skrivelser mellem Komiteen for den frivillige Forsvarsindsamling og Forsvarsministeren, *Beretning afgiven af Kommissionen Til Undersøgelse og Overvejelse af Hærens og Flaadens fremtidige Ordning* [Report from the Commission Tasked with Investigation and Consideration of the Future Organization of the Army and the Navy] (Copenhagen: Rigsdagen, 1922); Kongehuset, Christian X (CHRX) [Royal Archives, Christian X]: Bemærkninger P 6. 'Eremitage Værket': Notater 23 December and 30 December 1913 with 2 January and 4 January 1913; Bemærkninger P 6, Bilag. Notat fra 13 January 1913.

24 Det Kongelige Bibliotek (KB) (Danish Royal Library), Ny Kgl. Samling 5082, 4o August Tuxens Brevsamling. II. Breve fra fremmede. 4. Fra J.V. Gørtz. Læg 1913–1915. Brev af 16–20 January 1913; RA, Direktør generalmajor N.B. Ulrichs referatprotokol 1910–1918, notater 1 January to 25 January 1913; Partiet Venstre. Rigsdagsgruppen: Udvalgsprotokol 1910–1931 m.m. Pk. IV 1–10. Bind no. 7. Venstre 1912–1914. Protokol 11 January, 15 January and 17 January 1913; Krigsministeriet. 5. Kontor. Kopibog, fortrolige skrivelser, 22 October 1912–20 February 1913, 125–29. Krigsministeriet. Fortroligt. M 89 of 17 January 1913 til 1. Generalkommando. Krigsministeriet. Fortroligt. M 90 of 17 January 1913 til 2. Generalkommando. Krigsministeriet. Fortroligt. M 91 of 17 January 1913 til Generaldirektøren for Statsbanerne.

25 RA, T. V. Gardes privatarkiv. Pk. 2. Dagbøger. Notater 2 January, 9 January, 27 January and 16 April 1913; Marinestaben, Emneordnede sager, Pk. 24. Alarmeringssager m.m. Læg: Manuskript til Operationsplanens II Del. (Koncept). Fortroligt. Manuskript til Operationsplan.

26 RA, Direktør generalmajor N.B. Ulrichs referatprotokol 1910–1918, notater 16 May 1913, and the only description of the exercise based on the ministry file in Clemmesen, *Det lille land*, 457–62.

27 Winston S. Churchill, *The World Crisis 1911–1914* (London: Thornton Butterworth, 1923).

28 The prewar role of Winston Churchill has been analysed in Clemmesen, *Det lille land*, 257–67, 433–48. The research for the book forms the main basis for this chapter. The analysis of the development is, in most fields, in line with that of Shawn T. Grimes, *Strategy and War Planning in the British Navy, 1887–1918* (Melton: Boydell Press, 2012), 176–89; Clemmesen, *The Royal Navy's Strategy Discourse*.

Bibliography

Berntsen, Klaus. *Erindringer fra Rigsdags- og Ministeraar* [Memories from the Rigsdag and the Ministry]. Copenhagen: V. Pio, 1925.

Churchill, Winston S. *The World Crisis 1911–1914*. London: Thornton Butterworth, 1923.

Clemmesen, Michael H. *Det lille land før den store krig: De danske farvande, stormagtsstrategier, efterretninger og forsvarsforberedelser om kriserne 1911–13* [The Small Country before the Great War: Danish Waters, Great Power

Strategies, Intelligence and Defence Preparations during the Crises 1911–1913]. Odense: Syddansk Universitetsforlag, 2012.

———. *The Royal Navy's Strategy Discourse Up to the Great War – In Outline*, http://www.clemmesen.org/articles/Royal_Navy_Strategy_Discourse.pdf (accessed 15 May 2013).

Cobb, Stephen. *Preparing for Blockade: Naval Contingency for Economic Warfare*. London: Ashgate, 2013.

Epkenhans, Michael. *Die wilhelminische Flottenrüstung 1908–1914: Weltmachtstreben, industrieller Fortschritt, soziale Integration*. Munich: Oldenbourg Wissenschaftsverlag, 1991.

——— (ed.). *Das ereignisreiche Leben eines 'Wilhelminers': Tagebücher, Briefe, Aufzeichnungen 1901 bis 1920 von Albert Hopman*. Munich: Oldenbourg Wissenschaftsverlag, 2004.

Fischer, Jörg-Uwe. *Admiral des Kaisers: Georg Alexander von Müller als Chef des Marinekabinetts Wilhelms II*. Frankfurt/M.: Verlag Peter Lang, 1991.

Grimes, Shawn T. *Strategy and War Planning in the British Navy, 1887–1918*. Melton: Boydell Press, 2012.

Hall, Richard C. *The Balkan Wars 1912–1913: Prelude to the First World War*. London: Routledge, 2000.

Halpern, Paul G. *The Mediterranean Naval Situation 1908–1914*. Cambridge, MA: Harvard University Press, 1971.

Kennedy, Paul M. 'The Development of German Naval Operations Plans against England, 1896–1914' [1974]. Reprinted in Andrew Lambert (ed.), *Naval History 1850–Present*. Vol. I (Aldershot: Ashgate, 2007), 295–324.

Lambi, Ivo Nikolai. *The Navy and German Power Politics 1862–1914*. Boston, MA: Harper Collins Publishers, 1984.

Munch, Peter. *Erindringer 1909–1914: Indenrigsminister og Forsvarsminister* [Memories 1909–1914: Ministry of Interior and Defence]. Copenhagen: Nyt Nordisk Forlag, 1960.

Norberg, Erik. 'Balkankriget och Sveriges försvar' [The Balkan War and the Defence of Sweden], in Wilhelm M. Calgren et al. (eds), *Utrikespolitik och Historia: Studier tillägnade Wilhelm M. Carlgren den 6 maj 1987* [Foreign Policy and History: Studies Conferred on Wilhelm M. Carlgren on 6 May 1987] (Stockholm: Militärhistoriska förlaget, 1987), 199–218.

Röhl, John C.G. *Kaiser, Hof und Staat: Wilhelm II. und die deutsche Politik*. Munich: C.H. Beck Verlag, 1995.

Zetterberg, Kent. *Militärer och Politiker: En studie i military professionnalisering, innovationsspridning och internationellt inflytande på de svenska försvarsberedningar 1911–1914* [Soldiers and Politicians: A Study of the Influence of Professionalization, Spreading Innovation and International Influence on Swedish Defence Reports, 1911–1914]. Stockholm: Militärhistoriska Förlaget, 1988.

Zuber, Terence. *The Real German War Plan 1904–1914*. Stroud: The History Press, 2011.

Part III
Armies, Soldiers, Irregulars

 5

THE OTTOMAN MOBILIZATION IN THE BALKAN WAR
Failure and Reorganization
Mehmet Beşikçi

Any analysis of the Ottoman experience of the Balkan War from the new military history perspective has to start by placing the war in a proper context. The Balkan War of 1912–13[1] should be situated at the intersection of two interconnected processes in military history. The first phase had a local character and was somewhat unique to late Ottoman history: the Ottoman Balkan War was not an isolated event. It was a part of a longer war series, which has been called 'the ten-year war period'. From the start of the Ottoman-Italian war in Libya in 1911 to the end of the Turkish National Struggle in 1922,[2] Ottoman-Turkish forces had been almost uninterruptedly engaged in military conflict.[3] If the unconventional Ottoman military actions and counterinsurgency operations, such as those in Yemen and Albania from the end of the nineteenth century through the 1910s, are included in the picture, then the time span and intensity of this process become extended even further.

The second process was global: the nature of warfare had been changing since the mid nineteenth century.[4] Warfare was becoming what military historians have described as 'total war'.[5] The concept of total war, or the totalization of warfare, refers to a process in which mobilization for war became much more intensive and extensive, requiring belligerent states to mobilize all of their resources for the war effort. This transformation, which made warfare much more catastrophic, resulted from a combination of factors. These included:

> industrialized mass society, nationalism, chauvinism, and racism, the participation of the masses in politics, mass armies equipped and provisioned with modern weapons, industrialized economies that

provided the means for large-scale destruction, and the erosion of distinctions between soldiers and civilians.[6]

The American Civil War (1861–65) and the German Wars of Unification (1864–71) are regarded as the first major examples of such total warfare.[7] The Russo-Japanese war of 1904–5 was another precursor to catastrophic conflicts in the age of world wars,[8] prior to the Balkan War of 1912–13. The industrial, bureaucratic and military infrastructure of a particular country would determine how intensely that country would experience the transformation to such warfare and how well it would be able to match the demands thereof. However, while this process produced unique conditions in different countries, certain macro-level changes were common and unfolded in similar fashions in different contexts, including the Ottoman Empire.[9] For example, in the age of total wars, the conventional demarcation line between the battlefront and the home front faded away; the two became closely intertwined. In this sense, the entire society of belligerent countries was required to contribute to the war effort, such as by providing permanent military labour, mainly through conscription, to be utilized efficiently by the armies.

This chapter argues that in this two-pronged process, the ability to permanently and effectively mobilize manpower is a crucial determinant of the military performance of a belligerent country at war. Among the many challenges that the Ottoman armed forces faced during the Balkan War, perhaps the most prominent was that of ensuring effective mobilization of manpower. Based on statistics, official documentation, general histories of the war and ego documents (memoirs and diaries) of Ottoman soldiers, this chapter aims to show that the major reason for the Ottoman defeat in the Balkan War was its failure to ensure effective mobilization. This study also tries to shed light on how this failure was discussed in the Ottoman official circles and the public sphere just after the defeat through printed texts. These discussions constituted the basis for a major overhaul of the Ottoman military in late 1913 and early 1914. The modernization resulted in improved mobilization capacities, completed in time for the First World War. The mobilization discourse additionally became more nationalistic.

The Issue of Effective Mobilization

During the Balkan War of 1912–13, effective mobilization of manpower generally meant two things. First, the Ottoman military had to enlist enough men for a multi-front war in a sustainable and timely manner.

Second, the Ottoman military had to utilize the recruited manpower efficiently, that is, train them for modern warfare and deploy them methodically and swiftly onto the battlefield. Both of these aspects required an infrastructural capacity and good military planning, which were exactly what the Ottomans lacked. The Ottoman state could neither muster enough troops nor was it able to use the mobilized manpower in an efficient way.

The available statistical figures testify almost perfectly to the failure of Ottoman mobilization. According to an official estimate, the general population of the Ottoman Empire on the eve of the Balkan War was around twenty-six million.[10] Out of this population, the total number of men eligible for active military service (namely, men between the ages of twenty and twenty-five) was 1,080,000. Together with the reserves (men between the ages of twenty-six and forty), this number would reach four million. The number of army personnel during peacetime was 280,000 and it was planned that 450,000 men would be added during wartime.[11] However, these generous estimates on paper never materialized in practice.

The Ottoman campaign plan for the Balkan War anticipated two major theatres of war, one in the east and one in the west.[12] The eastern front covered Eastern Thrace, where combat would mainly be against the Bulgarian army. The western front covered the Macedonian region, where the Ottoman forces would engage with the rest of the Balkan Alliance, namely with the Montenegrin, Greek and Serbian armies. Instead of using the existing army structure, the Ottoman military decided to form two new field armies out of various available units. These two armies, which were geographically isolated, were deployed into the two main theatres of the war, as the Eastern Army (Şark Ordusu) based in Eastern Thrace and the Western Army (Garb Ordusu) based in Macedonia.[13] The mobilization of manpower for the Balkan War was based on this campaign plan.[14] The Ottoman military expected that in order to become fully mobilized, the Eastern Army would need 478,848 men and the Western Army 333,815 men, adding up to 812,663 men (see Table 5.1).[15]

Table 5.1. Amount of manpower planned to be mobilized for the Ottoman armies before the Balkan War

Army/Theatre of War	Number of Men Needed
Western Army (Garb Ordusu)	333,815
Eastern Army (Şark Ordusu)	478,848
Total	812,663

When the war started, however, this was far from the reality. The numbers of men actually mobilized during the early phases of the war, for both armies, remained far below the targeted levels. The total number of men enlisted for the Eastern Army, which started fighting on 22 October 1912, was only about 115,000 on 21 October. The situation was no better for the Western Army. On 19 October 1912, the number of men mobilized amounted to around 175,000 (see Table 5.2).[16] The total number of both armies (290,000) only came to around 35 per cent of the total number planned for mobilization (812,663). Various Ottoman unit commanders testified, in their diaries and memoirs published after the war, that the numbers of mobilized men for their units were considerably lower than the numbers planned at the beginning of the war; similarly, their quality of training and performance was generally below expected levels.[17]

A simple comparison of the basic demographical statistics of the Ottoman Empire to those of the other Balkan powers sheds more light on the seriousness of the failure in Ottoman mobilization. Table 5.3 shows that although the Ottoman Empire was demographically much larger, its capacity was significantly lower than that of the Balkan Alliance states, with respect to the ratio of mobilized men to the general population.[18]

What were the reasons for this incapacity? Why was the Ottoman state so far below the targeted number of men in the mobilization plan? Why was it comparatively less prepared than its adversaries? The reasons can be categorized under three main headings.

The first of these reasons was the state's poor infrastructural power. At the time of the Balkan War, the Ottoman state suffered serious deficiencies in the functioning of its conscription system. An effective operation of this system required a reliable census to determine where the potential manpower could be found. Such a demographic mechanism

Table 5.2. Manpower actually mobilized for the Ottoman armies in the Balkan War (at the start of the war)

Army/Theatre of War	Number of Men
Western Army (Garb Ordusu)	175,000
Eastern Army (Şark Ordusu)	115,000
Total	290,000*

*Note that this is the total number of men mobilized in the initial phase of the war. New recruitments occurred in the course of the war and, therefore, the cumulative total number of men mobilized throughout the war must have been higher. However, no data are available on this in the sources.

Table 5.3. Comparison of manpower mobilization figures: Ottomans and Balkan Alliance

	Ottoman Armies	Balkan Alliance Armies			
	Ottoman Empire	Bulgaria	Serbia	Greece	Montenegro
Population (1912)	26,000,000	4,300,000	3,000,000	2,666,000	250,000
Theatres of War					
Eastern Theatre	115,000	200,000	–	–	–
Western Theatre	175,000	33,000	130,000	80,000	31,000
Total	290,000	233,000	130,000	80,000	31,000
Percentage of population mobilized	1.11%	5.41%	4.33%	3.00%	12.4%

required an expansion and reorganization in state bureaucracy, which would include an efficient recruitment organization, economic power to supply provisions to conscripts, as well as security forces and efficient sanctions to combat draft evasion and desertion.[19] Modern conscription required the state to permeate deeper into its provincial regions, to be able to utilize the existing manpower pool efficiently. In the Ottoman Empire, this was to be carried out by recruiting offices to be established in each local district. These recruiting offices were supposed to collect and keep demographic records of their localities, and enforce military service law. The beginning of Ottoman conscription goes back to the reign of Mahmud II (r. 1808–39).[20] Conscription was also one of the main agenda points of the Reorganization Edict (*Tanzimat*) of 1839, which ushered in major administrative reforms towards the creation of a centralized bureaucracy, an efficient fiscal system and a powerful army.[21] Thus, an appropriate bureaucratic organization was not absent in the Ottoman Empire at the time of the Balkan War. However, there were still huge gaps in the system,[22] as it was not geographically standardized and implementation was impeded by the lack of infrastructure in the rural provinces.[23] This was particularly the case in the economically underdeveloped tribal Kurdish-populated parts of Southeastern Anatolia and certain regions of the Ottoman Middle East, where a nomadic lifestyle was still dominant. Here, it was near impossible to implement the conscription system. Consequently, the pool from which a large-scale manpower mobilization was to be drawn was considerably reduced. As a way of compensating for this deficiency, the Ottoman state resorted to enlisting manpower in a tribal form. The state encouraged tribal leaders to join the Ottoman armed forces by forming 'volunteer' units out of their local populations, under their own leadership, in return for certain political and material gains. One of the best examples of this practice was the *Hamidiye* Cavalry Regiments, which were established by Abdülhamid II (r. 1876–1909), and continued in different forms throughout the Balkan War. This was an irregular militia composed of select Kurdish tribes.[24] However, even implementing such alternative practices was impossible in some regions, where the state not only lacked control but also did not have close connections with local leaders, such as in Yemen. Such regions were left completely out of the recruitment system. Resorting to the recruitment of volunteers on a more general level in all regions was another form of balancing the ill-functioning conscription system during the Balkan War. Nevertheless, both the number and the military capabilities of the volunteers were not at a satisfactory level and did not make any decisive impact on the Ottoman performance during the war.[25]

The second main reason for the failed mobilization during the Balkan War involved the Ottoman military service legislation. At the time of the Balkan War, the Ottoman state still used the military service law that had been issued in 1886.[26] Although there was an attempt to update it in 1909, this law was outdated and did not meet the current conditions of wartime. The chief problem was the existence of a long list of exemptions. Some segments of society were exempt from military service on religious, bureaucratic, geographic or ethnic grounds. The 1909 regulations, which tried to limit these exemptions, aimed to enlarge the manpower pool for the armed forces and to use conscription as an instrument for integrating the different religious and ethnic communities of the Ottoman Empire after the 1908 revolution. For example, as will be discussed in more detail below, Ottoman non-Muslims began to be enlisted in the army systematically.[27] But certain exemptions still remained. Due to financial constraints of the state, the exemption fee (*bedel*) could not be abolished entirely. The state could not relinquish this financial resource. The exemption fee practice, namely paying the state a certain amount of money instead of doing military service, continued to be applied mainly to non-Muslim Ottomans, but well-off Muslim Ottomans could also be eligible for it under certain conditions.[28] Moreover, draft evasion increased, especially among the Muslim population after the 1909 regulations, as the exemption status of many Muslim groups was restricted. For instance, *medrese* students who failed to pass their exams in time were no longer exempted and thus included in the draft. This revision was unpopular as many people had made use of this exemption to evade military service, including illiterate peasants.[29] Furthermore, acts of resistance emerged in regions that were previously excluded from the recruitment system, particularly among the men drafted from the Laz and the Kurds in Anatolia and the Arabs in Arab provinces.[30] Consequently, the actual manpower pool available for mobilization was considerably smaller than the general population of the country suggested.

The third reason was related to the underdeveloped transport network. In modern warfare, transporting the recruited troops to the war zone on time was as important as recruitment itself. The available railway structure in the Ottoman Empire was insufficient to ensure complete mobilization within the scheduled time period. Where available, it was single-track and very slow.[31] Problems caused by the poor transportation system were often underlined in the first-hand accounts of Ottoman commanders and other contemporary observers.[32] It was noted, for example, that approximately half of the Anatolian units never reached their destinations.[33] Additionally, the Greek navy, of which the armoured cruiser *Averof* was the most prominent element, prevented the Ottomans from using the sea lanes effectively. As a result, the geographical vastness of the Ottoman Empire became a disadvantage in comparison to the Balkan Alliance powers. Subsequently, many Ottoman military units mobilized too slowly and incompletely. 'The end result in both theatres was the launching of premature offensives without the full forces necessary to ensure victory.'[34]

Besides these main reasons, there were also secondary yet significant factors that contributed to the failure of Ottoman mobilization, both quantitatively and qualitatively. When the Balkan War started, some sections of the Ottoman armed forces were still engaged in counterinsurgency operations in various regions. For example, a reinforced divisional group under the command of Chief of the General Staff Ahmed İzzet Pasha (1864–1937) was situated in Yemen to suppress a rebellion. Similarly, several regiments were still in Macedonia, while others guarded the Aegean Sea harbours and islands against possible Italian (and later Greek) amphibious attacks.[35] Many first-hand testimonies underlined the over-involvement in counterinsurgency operations by the Ottoman armed forces, contributing to substantial delays and hamstringing of the mobilization efforts.[36]

Another important factor was the Ottoman government's decision in the summer of 1912 to demobilize more than 70,000 reserve troops who had been called up for duty in 1908.[37] The precise reason for this much-questioned act is unclear. Reasons most cited include the plain reluctance of these troops to remain under arms, having already served for three years and the majority originating from the Ottoman Balkan territories; the fear of a possible rebellion among the reluctant troops; the inability of Ottoman authorities to foresee an imminent war in the Balkans; and pressure from the great powers (such as Britain) on the Ottoman state.[38] In any case, since the Balkan War broke out only a few months later, this decision further diminished the already insufficient quantitative capacity of the Ottoman forces.

Thus far, the emphasis has been placed on the failure to recruit enough troops. As discussed above, an effective mobilization of troops was impeded by problems encountered in recruitment; however, even a relatively small army can be used efficiently. Due to the prominent problem of an incompetent reserve system, the Ottoman mobilization failed to capitalize here too.

The Ottoman reserve system (*redif teşkilatı*) that was in use during the Balkan War was, to a large extent, out of date, as it belonged to a nineteenth-century Ottoman reality. It was designed during the 1830s as a local militia force – a quasi 'provincial army' mainly to provide domestic security.[39] The initial aim of this reserve was to establish an effective armed force in the provinces where the regular army was unable to sustain control, where conscription was dysfunctional, and where the central government's monopoly of power did not reach.[40] The Ottoman state attempted to integrate this reserve system, which had been a *de facto* separate entity at the beginning, into the conscription system of the military service law of 1846. By this law, the enlisted men were subject to a seven-year reserve service after completing a five-year active military service; these reserves would be called up for one month of military training each year at their local reserve centre. Each Ottoman sub-province (*sancak*) was to have its own local reserve division. These divisions could thus be used for ensuring domestic security in their localities, on the one hand, or mobilized to the battlefield in wartime to support the regular forces, on the other hand.[41]

However, despite the attempts to modernize the reserve system and integrate it into the regular army, its heavy provincial character remained. This is in part due to its organization as individual provincial reserves, as well as the state's insistence on maintaining them as domestic security forces in the provinces. According to the military service law of 1886, which made some slight modifications to the reserve system, those who completed their three-year active military service were subsequently subject to seventeen years in the reserve units. The reserve units would gather at least twice a year for training and would have their own officers and weapons. In reality, however, the training was never held regularly and many reserve units either had very old rifles or had no weapons whatsoever. Moreover, although some reserve units had some experience in enforcing domestic security, many did not have any combat experience at all. Despite such deficiencies, the Ottoman military decided to mobilize the reserve units, not as auxiliary forces but as main combat forces.[42]

On the eve of the Balkan War, the Ottoman reserve system was only a little different from its structure in the mid nineteenth century. There were six reserve inspectorates (*redif müfettişliği*) in the empire, the centres of which were located in Istanbul, Salonica, Erzincan, Baghdad, Damascus and İzmir. Attached to these inspectorates were fifty-four reserve divisions based in the provinces, each taking the name of the province or sub-province in which it was located.[43] According to the 1910 reorganization regulations of the Ottoman military,[44] the wartime army would total 540,000 reserve troops at the moment of a general mobilization. This number amounted to just under half of the entire wartime army personnel.[45] Despite its largely outdated nature, the Ottoman military still considered the reserve system a very significant element of its military strength in the early twentieth century.

Although accurate statistics concerning the reserves are not available, various first-hand accounts consistently point out that the number of mobilized reserves was quite low and many reserve divisions were only able to recruit about half of the targeted numbers.[46] The reserves were still intended to constitute a significant element of the army structure and many Ottoman commanders were sceptical of the impact the reserves would make. Based on his observations in previous battles, Abdullah Pasha (1846–1937), commander of the Eastern Army, for example did not expect any military efficiency from the reserves.[47] Hamit Ercan, a contemporary observer who joined as a petty officer and served as a training officer in a reserve unit during the Balkan War, stated that the reserves were poorly trained and lacked discipline.[48] Similarly, Rahmi Apak, who served in the Çanakkale reserve division as an *aide-de-camp* while he was still a cadet in the War College, remarked that one of the main reasons for defeat was the insistence on using the poorly trained and low-skilled reserves 'who constituted almost more than half of the Turkish army' as combat forces.[49] This was also emphasized by an Ottoman Armenian journalist, Aram Andonyan, as a major reason contributing to the defeat.[50] A German officer serving in the Ottoman Western Army, Major Gustav von Hochwächter, noted in his diaries that there were even 'blind and lame' draftees among the reserves. Many of these reserves received their military training a long time ago, when they used muzzle loading rifles, and were inexperienced in using new rifles.[51]

Another important problem in the reserve system was the lack of officers to command the reserve units, the shortage of schooled officers being a general problem in the Ottoman army. The total number of officers expected at the time of mobilization was 30,653; however, the number of officers by the end of 1911 was only 16,121.[52] This left the Ottoman army with a remarkable gap of 14,532 officers. To reconcile this deficiency, a serious problem since the military modernization of the nineteenth century, the Ottoman military formed a system of reserve officers (*ihtiyat zâbitleri*) from 1891 onwards. Higher education graduates, eligible for compulsory military service, were placed as low- and middle-ranking officers in the armed forces during their service.[53] While this system became quite well established by the time of the Balkan War, it was still far from satisfying the shortages of officers in the entire armed forces. Moreover, the available reserve officers were mostly used in regular army units. Therefore, the reserve units' need for officers continued to be met almost entirely by an older and more widespread practice of appointing unschooled rankers (*alaylı* officers).[54] Yet another problematic aspect in this respect was that the few schooled officers who were appointed to fill key positions in the reserve units were those who had been away from combat units for many years and worked mostly in administrative or educational posts, lacking combat experience.[55]

A serious lack of endurance in the Ottoman armed forces was prevalent from the earliest moments of the war. Lack of endurance appeared to be most widespread during retreats, at which the Ottoman forces turned out to be the least prepared and the most ineffective. Mahmud Muhtar Pasha (1867–1935), commander of the Third Corps and the Second Army in the eastern theatre, for example described how the Ottoman troops easily lost their unit cohesion and deserted at the retreat from the Battle of Kırkkilise to Çatalca, at the beginning of the war. According to him, 'since an organized retreat was an ability bestowed only on well-trained and well-organized armies, the Ottoman army's retreat quickly turned into a desertion'.[56] A similar view was shared by Abdullah Pasha, who depicted the Ottoman catastrophic retreat as 'a bitter trial' (*acı bir imtihan*).[57]

While it can be argued that desertions constituted a general problem in the Ottoman army during the Balkan War, it is not surprising that most cases of desertion seem to have occurred among the reserve troops. Mahmud Muhtar consistently criticized the high frequency of desertions in the reserve units and considered it a major factor undermining the Ottoman war performance.[58] Widespread desertions among the reserves were also emphasized as a major problem by various low- and middle-ranking officers who served in the Ottoman army during the war.[59] Despite strict measures to prevent desertions, such as executing captured deserters on the spot or firing at those leaving their posts during battle,[60] high numbers of desertions continued to bog down the Ottoman armed forces until the end of the war.

Non-Muslims in the Ottoman Army

With an amendment made to the military service law in 1909, non-Muslim Ottomans began to be enlisted in the armed forces systematically for the first time.[61] In the previous periods, except for their occasional enlistment in specific military fields such as in the navy or medical corps,[62] Ottoman non-Muslims had been excluded from military service in return for an exemption fee. The exemption fee practice remained after 1909, but its extent was restricted. When the Young Turks came to power after the 1908 revolution, conscription started to be regarded as a means of integrating the dissolving empire.[63] The aim was both pragmatic and political: the inclusion of non-Muslims in the compulsory military system would not only enlarge the available manpower for the armed forces, but it would also serve as cement for the Ottoman citizenry.

With the onset of the Balkan mobilization, the Ottoman military was optimistic about non-Muslim enlistment, as one-quarter of the wartime army personnel was expected to constitute non-Muslim recruits.[64] This estimate turned out to be over-optimistic. Nevertheless, a notable number of non-Muslims joined the Ottoman army, not only from among the Christian and Jewish populations in the Ottoman Balkan region, but also from among the Anatolian non-Muslims (together with Kurdish and Arab reserve forces) at various stages of the war.[65] However, the performance of the recruited non-Muslims was generally disappointing for Ottoman military authorities.

The Ottoman army was not well prepared to become a multi-religious and multiethnic army; it required a substantial reorganization within the army structure to absorb the incoming non-Muslim soldiers. A number of the Ottoman commanders themselves were not convinced that employing non-Muslims in combat units would increase the army's effectiveness. For example, Ali İhsan Sâbis, a major during the Balkan War and author of a well-known treatise evaluating the reasons for the defeat, argued that the recruitment of non-Muslims created a problem of morale in terms of using Islamic propaganda as a mobilizing discourse. In his view, it was difficult to make use of an Islamic holy war discourse to encourage enlisted men to fight effectively in an army of people from different religions.⁶⁶ In fact, Ottoman authorities were highly suspicious of the numerous Bulgarian, Greek and Serbian potential recruits who resided in the Ottoman Empire fighting against their co-nationals.⁶⁷

On the other hand, Ottoman non-Muslims were not particularly enthusiastic about military service, bordering on general reluctance.⁶⁸ The reluctance and low morale among the Ottoman non-Muslim recruits caught the attention of foreign observers, such as Leon Trotsky, who visited the war zone as a war correspondent.⁶⁹ As Fikret Adanır's recent work reveals, cases of draft evasion and desertion among Ottoman non-Muslims were quite common.⁷⁰ Moreover, there is evidence that there were some non-Muslims, especially among the Bulgarians, Greeks and Serbs residing in the Ottoman territory, who volunteered for the armies or the militias of the Balkan states.⁷¹ As a contemporary observer noted, when the Ottomans were defeated and had to surrender Edirne to the Bulgarians, some non-Muslims in the city, especially Armenians, cheered on the Bulgarian soldiers.⁷²

Fikret Adanır further argues that low morale and desertions among Ottoman non-Muslims contributed to their consideration as 'unreliable' by the rising Turkish nationalists, many of whom held them responsible for the defeat. This approach to non-Muslims would become the prevailing opinion both in the official circles and in the public sphere hit by the traumatic defeat. However, while a general reluctance among non-Muslims towards military service was evident, the accusation that they were responsible ignored the multiple factors that actually brought about the defeat. First of all, desertions constituted a general problem during the Balkan War, involving almost all elements of Ottoman society, including Muslim Turks. Various high-ranking commanders, such as Mahmud Muhtar Pasha and Abdullah Pasha, disapproved of the low morale and desertions among the reserve units, mostly from Anatolia; they did not specifically blame non-Muslims. Secondly, Ottoman non-Muslims did not constitute a homogeneous entity. There is evidence that, whereas desertions were more common among the non-Muslim recruits from the Ottoman Balkan territory,⁷³ most Anatolian non-Muslims proved to be most resolute in their duties until the end of the war.⁷⁴

Post-Defeat Discussions and Attempts at Reorganization

The Balkan defeat was a real trauma for Ottoman-Turkish society. Hafız Hakkı Pasha's (1879–1915) choice of title for his short treatise on the defeat, 'The Debacle' (*Bozgun*), accurately represented the general mood in the Ottoman public sphere after the defeat.[75] Besides the treatise, the Ottoman public sphere engaged in extensive discussion on the reasons for the defeat directly after the war as well. Not only military authorities but also many former army officers, journalists, authors and even ordinary readers of newspapers and periodical journals participated in this debate. This merits attention in the sense that no other military event in Turkish history, including the Republican era, has ever been discussed and analysed in such an open fashion. Some literary genres, particularly war memoirs, exploded after the Balkan defeat.[76]

Some of the most recurrent themes that were underlined as self-criticism in this post-defeat discussion included catastrophic mobilization of manpower; incompetent command structures, especially the inefficiency of unschooled rankers; and lack of morale, not only in the army but also in society in general. There was almost a common consensus in official and public circles that it was imperative to bring 'a new spirit and enthusiasm' to the army.[77] Such recurrent themes in this literature constituted the basis of the reorganization that took place in the Ottoman military soon after the Balkan defeat. The Ottoman conscription system in general and the mobilization scheme in particular underwent a major overhaul.

Reforming the army was a primary point of agenda for the Committee of Union and Progress (CUP) government, which had established single-party rule by a coup on 23 January 1913.[78] To launch an extensive reorganization, the Regulation for the General Organization of the Military was issued on 14 February 1913.[79] This process was significantly expedited when Enver Pasha (1881–1922), the leading CUP leader in military affairs, became the minister of war on 3 January 1914.[80] An important foreign contribution was included, after the Ottoman state signed an agreement with the German military on 14 December 1913. The German Military Mission, under the leadership of Liman von Sanders (1855–1929), came to the Ottoman Empire to help reform various aspects of the military, including the conscription system.[81]

The main goal of the post-Balkan defeat reform process was to create an efficient army structure that could be rapidly and effectively mobilized in wartime. Some major changes in the Ottoman conscription system constituted an important part of these attempts. Firstly, the outdated and much criticized reserve system, which had made almost no positive contribution to the war effort, was abolished. In its place, an individual-based reserve system was designed and put into practice. In this new system, reserve units were to be integrated with the regular army in a functional way by expertise, rather than being used as separate combat units. In this way, although the result was hardly perfect and certain problems remained, the mobilization of reserves during the First World War became comparatively much more effective.[82]

Secondly, a new law for military service was issued on 12 May 1914.[83] The main purpose of preparing a new law was to minimize the exemptions in order to expand the available manpower pool for military service. As mentioned above, the 1909 regulations made an attempt in this direction, but they were not systematic or standardized due to ambiguities in legislation and deficiencies in practice. A revision of the military service law was necessary as the manpower pool of the Ottoman Empire was considerably reshaped after the Balkan War. Approximately 340,000 casualties[84] fell, which reduced the size of the army significantly, and new arrangements in the conscription system were needed for the immigration of around 400,000 Muslim refugees from the lost territories in the Balkans into the empire.[85] The new law sought to absorb this huge population into military service in an efficient way, but also provided them with a reasonable period of leave to facilitate their adaptation to their new homes. This period of leave was set to six years in peacetime, but would be reduced to three months in wartime.

Thirdly, in connection to the new legislation, the system of recruiting offices that implemented the draft at a local level was reorganized and extended. In order to increase the efficiency of conscription, the old system, which considered the entire empire as a single unit, was abandoned. Instead, the Ottoman Empire was divided into twelve new conscription divisions on the basis of corps zones. Each conscription division came under the supervision of the particular corps command in that zone. Districts were established as the smallest administrative units, where recruiting offices were established. By 1914, there was a total of 362 recruiting offices across the empire.[86]

It should be noted that the post-Balkan defeat reforms, with regard to the conscription system, maintained the political – but also pragmatic – vision of the 1909 revisions, namely to extend the military service obligation to all segments of society, including the non-Muslim Ottomans. Hence, non-Muslims continued to be drafted into the Ottoman armed forces more extensively compared to previous periods. However, as mentioned above, within the atmosphere of rising Turkish nationalism after the Balkan defeat, suspicion regarding the reliability of non-Muslims increased. Whereas Ottoman authorities never thought of excluding non-Muslims from conscription, they deemed it necessary to take extra measures to keep them under control after they were drafted into the army.[87] As a result, it became a widespread practice in the Ottoman army to employ the non-Muslim enlisted men in unarmed services, especially with the start of the First World War. The Labour Battalions were formed for this purpose, fulfilling the double function of performing practical menial work as well as keeping the enlisted non-Muslims under close supervision. By this mechanism, the authorities thought that any possibility of an armed rebellion (or any other problem of disobedience) could be prevented. This type of battalion had been initially formed during the Balkan War under the name of Service Battalions (*Hizmet Taburları*).[88] The Labour Battalions were used extensively during the First World War.[89]

Concluding Remarks

What sort of changes did the post-Balkan defeat reorganization bring about in the Ottoman system of mobilization in general? It can be argued that these changes increased the Ottoman military's efficiency significantly. This is true especially in comparison to the Ottoman performance during the First World War. Table 5.4 shows the ratios of the total numbers mobilized during the First World War of some major European powers in relation to their general populations.[90]

As is seen in this table, the mobilization capacity of the Ottoman Empire was not at the top, but it had improved compared to the same ratio at the beginning of the Balkan War (slightly more than 1 per cent; see Table 5.3). This does not imply, however, that the Ottoman

Table 5.4. Comparison of manpower mobilization throughout the First World War

Country	Population	Number of Men Mobilized	Percentage
Ottoman Empire	22,000,000	2,900,000	13.1
Germany	66,853,000	13,250,000	19.8
Austria-Hungary	51,390,000	7,800,000	15.1
France	39,600,000	8,410,000	21.2
Italy	35,845,000	5,615,000	15.6
Russia (–1917)	160,700,000	13,700,000	8.5

mobilization system had overcome its major setbacks entirely. Certain problems remained to a large extent throughout the First World War. For example, the Ottoman state continued to be largely unable to implement its conscription system in the tribal and nomadic-populated regions of Eastern Anatolia and the Ottoman Middle East; the underdeveloped infrastructure in transportation and logistics seriously delayed the mobilization process; high numbers of desertions significantly undermined the Ottoman war performance; and Ottoman conscription became more discriminatory towards non-Muslims. But it is evident that thanks to the reforms after the Balkan defeat, the endurance and efficiency level of the Ottoman armed forces remarkably increased during the First World War.[91]

Mehmet Beşikçi is a lecturer in late Ottoman and modern Turkish history at Yildiz Technical University in Istanbul. His area of specialty is late Ottoman wars and society, on which he has authored various articles and books, both in English and Turkish, including *The Ottoman Mobilization of Manpower in the First World War: Between Voluntarism and Resistance* (Brill, 2012).

Notes

1 The Balkan War is sometimes also mentioned in the plural as the Balkan Wars, since it was actually a two-phase war. The first phase started on 8 October 1912, in which the Ottoman Empire fought against a coalition consisting of Greece, Bulgaria, Serbia and Montenegro. The main battles took place in the first phase of the war and the Ottoman forces suffered a heavy defeat; the first phase ended on 10 June 1913 with the signing of the Treaty of London. The second phase was a conflict between Bulgaria and other Balkan states, which presented the Ottomans with an opportunity to regain Edirne in July 1913. In referring to the war, I prefer to use the singular form as the Balkan War, because this usage significantly implies that the two phases actually constituted an integrated event. Moreover, the original Ottoman usage was also singular (*Balkan Harbi*). On the general history of the Ottoman Balkan War, see *Türk Silahlı Kuvvetleri Tarihi: Balkan Harbi (1912–1913)* [History of the Turkish Armed Forces: The Balkan War (1912–1913)] (Ankara: Genelkurmay Basımevi, 1979); *Balkan Harbi (1912–1913)*, Vol. 1: *Harbin Sebepleri, Askeri Hazırlıklar ve Osmanlı Devletinin Harbe Girişi* [The Balkan War, 1912–1913: The Origins of the War, Military Preparations and the Ottoman State's Entry in the War] (Ankara: Genelkurmay Basımevi, 1970); Aram Andonyan, *Balkan Savaşı* [The Balkan War], 2nd ed., trans. Zaven Biberyan (Istanbul: Aras Yayıncılık, 1999); Edward J. Erickson, *Defeat in Detail: The Ottoman Army in the Balkans, 1912–1913* (Westport, CT:

Praeger, 2003); Richard C. Hall, *The Balkan Wars: Prelude to the First World War* (London: Routledge, 2000).
2   This period includes the Ottoman-Italian war in Libya of 1911–12, the Balkan War of 1912–13, the First World War of 1914–18 and the Turkish National Struggle (the Turkish War of Independence) of 1919–22.
3   The term 'the Ten-Year War' (*On Yıllık Harp*) has become almost common in Ottoman/Turkish history. It was first used by authors who themselves participated in these wars or witnessed this period. See, for example, Fahrettin Altay, *10 Yıl Savaş (1912–1922) ve Sonrası: Görüp Geçirdiklerim* [The Ten-Year War and Afterwards: What I Lived Through] (Istanbul: İnsel Yayınları, 1970); İzzettin Çalışlar, *On Yıllık Savaşın Günlüğü: Balkan, Birinci Dünya ve İstiklal Savaşları* [The Diary of the Ten-Year War: The Balkan, First World and Independence Wars], ed. İsmet Görgülü and İzzeddin Çalışlar (Istanbul: Yapı Kredi Yayınları, 1997).
4   See Jeremy Black, *War in the Nineteenth Century* (Cambridge: Polity Press, 2009).
5   On the concept of 'total war', see Roger Chickering, 'Total War: The Use and Abuse of a Concept', in Manfred F. Boemeke, Roger Chickering and Stig Förster (eds), *Anticipating Total War: The German and American Experiences, 1871–1914* (Cambridge: Cambridge University Press, 1999), 13–28.
6   Stig Förster, 'Introduction', in Roger Chickering and Stig Förster (eds), *Great War, Total War: Combat and Mobilization on the Western Front, 1914–1918* (Cambridge: Cambridge University Press, 2000), 1–18, here 4.
7   See, for example, Stig Förster and Jörg Nagler (eds), *On the Road to Total War: The American Civil War and the German Wars of Unification, 1861–1871* (Cambridge: Cambridge University Press, 1997). David Bell places the beginning of this process of totalization as early as the Napoleonic Wars. See David A. Bell, *The First Total War: Napoleon's Europe and the Birth of Warfare As We Know It* (New York: Mariner Books, 2007).
8   See, for example, David Wolff et al. (eds), *The Russo-Japanese War in Global Perspective* (Leiden: Brill, 2007).
9   For a discussion of total war in the Ottoman context, see Mehmet Beşikçi, 'Topyekûn Savaş Kavramı ve Son Dönem Osmanlı Harp Tarihi' [The Concept of Total War and Late Ottoman Military History], *Toplumsal Tarih*, 198 (2010), 62–69.
10 There is no single accurate number for the total population of the Ottoman Empire at the threshold of the Balkan War. While there seems to be a consensus on the number of twenty-six million, some sources give it as twenty-four million. For the population figures, see Hall, *The Balkan Wars*, 18; Fevzi Çakmak, *Garbî Rumeli'nin Sûret-i Ziyaı ve Balkan Harbinde Garp Cephesi* [The Loss of Western Rumelia and the Western Front in the Balkan War], 2nd ed., ed. Ahmet Tetik (Istanbul: İş Bankası Kültür Yayınları, 2012), 13; *Balkan Harbi (1912–1913)*, Vol. 1, 74.
11 *Balkan Harbi (1912–1913)*, Vol. 1, 74.
12 For a compact and critical analysis of the Ottoman campaign plan in the Balkan War, which was ill-prepared in various aspects, see F.A.K. Yasamee, 'Ottoman War Planning and the Balkan Campaign of October–December

1912', in Eugenia Kermeli and Oktay Özel (eds), *The Ottoman Empire: Myths, Realities and 'Black Holes'* (Istanbul: The Isis Press, 2006), 347–66.
13 Mesut Uyar and Edward J. Erickson, *A Military History of the Ottomans from Osman to Atatürk* (Santa Barbara, CA: Praeger, 2009), 226.
14 See Serkan Er, *Osmanlı Ordusunda Seferberlik Planı: Balkan Harbi Örneği* [The Mobilization Planning in the Ottoman Army: The Case of the Balkan War], MA Thesis Istanbul, (The Turkish War Academy Strategic Research Institute, 2012).
15 *Balkan Harbi (1912–1913)*, Vol. 1, 132–33; Er, *Osmanlı Ordusunda*, 68, 77.
16 Çakmak, *Garbî Rumeli'nin Sûret-i Ziyaı*, 95; Kemal Soyupak and Hüseyin Kabasakal, 'The Turkish Army in the First Balkan War', in Béla K. Király and Dimitrije Djordjevic (eds), *East Central European Society and the Balkan Wars* (New York: Columbia University Press, 1987), 158–62, here 159.
17 Among many such examples, see Tahsin Yıldırım and İbrahim Öztürkçü (eds), *1328 Balkan Harbi'nde Şark Ordusu Kumandanı Abdullah Paşa'nın Balkan Harbi Hâtırâtı* [The Memoirs of Abdullah Pasha, the Commander of the Eastern Army in the Balkan War of 1912] (Istanbul: DBY, 2012), 149; Sema Demirtaş (ed.), *Zeki Paşa'nın Balkan Savaşı Hatıratı* [Zeki Pasha's Memoirs of the Balkan War] (Istanbul: Alfa, 2012), 11–12; Kâzım Karabekir, *Edirne Hatıraları* [Edirne Memoirs], ed. Ziver Öktem (Istanbul: Yapı Kredi Yayınları, 2009), 28–29; Çalışlar, *On Yıllık Savaşın Günlüğü*, 32.
18 For the population figures, see Hall, *The Balkan Wars*, 18; Çakmak, *Garbî Rumeli'nin Sûret-i Ziyaı*, 13; *Balkan Harbi (1912–1913)*, Vol. 1, 74 and Necdet Hayta and T. Seçkin Birbudak, *Balkan Savaşları'nda Edirne* [Edirne during the Balkan Wars] (Ankara: Genelkurmay Basımevi, 2010), 20–21. See also Carnegie Endowment for International Peace, *Report of the International Commission to Inquire into the Causes and Conduct of the Balkan Wars* (Washington, DC: The Endowment, 1914), 418.
19 Jan Lucassen and Erik J. Zürcher, 'Introduction: Conscription and Resistance. The Historical Context', in Erik J. Zürcher (ed.), *Arming the State: Military Conscription in the Middle East and Central Asia* (London: I.B. Tauris, 1999), 10.
20 Gültekin Yıldız, *Neferin Adı Yok: Zorunlu Askerliğe Geçiş Sürecinde Osmanlı Devleti'nde Siyaset, Ordu ve Toplum (1826–1839)* [The Private Has No Name: Politics, Army and Society in the Ottoman Empire during the Transition to Compulsory Military Service, 1826–1839] (Istanbul: Kitabevi Yayınevi, 2009).
21 Tobias Heinzelmann, *Cihaddan Vatan Savunmasına: Osmanlı İmparatorluğu'nda Genel Askerlik Yükümlülüğü, 1826–1856* [From the Holy War to the Defence of the Fatherland: Compulsory Military Service in the Ottoman Empire, 1826–1856], trans. Türkis Noyan (Istanbul: Kitap, 2009); Veysel Şimşek, *Ottoman Military Recruitment and the Recruit, 1826–1853* (Ankara: The Institute of Economics and Social Sciences of Bilkent University, 2005), http://www.thesis.bilkent.edu.tr/0002992.pdf (accessed 18 February 2014).
22 For a more detailed account of Ottoman conscription from its beginning through the First World War, with special emphasis on later periods, see Mehmet Beşikçi, 'Mobilizing Military Labor in the Age of Total War:

Ottoman Conscription before and during the Great War', in Erik J. Zürcher (ed.), *Fighting for a Living: A Comparative History of Military Labour, 1500–2000* (Amsterdam: Amsterdam University Press, 2014), 535–68.

23 See Mehmet Hacısalihoğlu, 'Borders, Maps, and Censuses: The Politicization of Geography and Statistics in the Multi-ethnic Ottoman Empire', in Jörn Leonhard and Ulrike von Hirschhausen (eds), *Comparing Empires: Encounters and Transfers in the Long Nineteenth Century* (Göttingen: Vandenhoeck & Ruprecht, 2011), 171–210.

24 See Janet Klein, *The Margins of Empire: Kurdish Militias in the Ottoman Tribal Zone* (Stanford, CA: Stanford University Press, 2011). See also Martin van Bruinessen, *Agha, Shaikh and State: The Social and Political Structures of Kurdistan* (London: Zed Books, 1992).

25 On Ottoman volunteers during the Balkan War, see Mehmet Özdemir, 'Balkan Harbi'nde Gönüllüler ve Gönüllü Askeri Birlikler' [Volunteers and Voluntary Military Units in the Balkan War], *Askeri Tarih Araştırmaları Dergisi* 3(5) (2005), 71–102.

26 For the text of the law, see *Düstûr* [Code of Laws], Series I, Vol. 5, 656–94.

27 Ufuk Gülsoy, *Osmanlı Gayrimüslimlerinin Askerlik Serüveni* [The Conscription Adventure of Ottoman Non-Muslims] (Istanbul: Simurg, 2000), 127–40.

28 It can be said that compulsory military service in the Ottoman Empire was always the duty of the lower classes. For a summary explanation of the exemption fee, see H. Bowen, 'Badal', in P. Bearman, Th. Bianquis, C.E. Bosworth, E. van Donzel, W.P. Heinrichs (eds), *Encyclopedia of Islam, Vol. 1*. Second ed. Consulted online on 1 August 2017, http://dx.doi.org/10.1163/1573-3912_islam_SIM_0988, 855.

29 On the issue of conscripting Ottoman *medrese* students, see Amit Bein, 'Politics, Military Conscription, and Religious Education in the Late Ottoman Empire', *International Journal of Middle East Studies* 38(2) (2006), 283–301.

30 Stanford J. Shaw, *The Ottoman Empire in World War I*, Vol. 1 (Ankara: Türk Tarih Kurumu Basımevi, 2006), 166–70.

31 *Balkan Harbi (1912–1913)*, Vol. 1, 73.

32 See, for example, Beliğ Uzdil, *Balkan Savaşı'nda Mürettep 1nci Kolordu'nun Harekâtı* [The Operations of the First Mixed Corps in the Balkan War], ed. Ahmet Tetik and Şeyda Büyükcan (Ankara: Genelkurmay Basımevi, 2006), 50; Ömer Zeki Çobanoğlu, *Balkan Savaşı ve Doğu Ordusu'nn Bozgunu* [The Balkan War and the Debacle of the Eastern Army], ed. Hülya Toker (Istanbul: Alfa, 2012), 207–8.

33 Uyar and Erickson, *Military History of the Ottomans*, 227.

34 Erickson, *Defeat in Detail*, 335.

35 Uyar and Erickson, *Military History of the Ottomans*, 225–26.

36 See, for example, A. [Ali İhsan Sâbis], *Balkan Savaşı'nda Neden Bozguna Uğradık?* [Why Were We Defeated in the Balkan War?], ed. Hülya Toker (Istanbul: Alfa, 2012), 24–25, 65; Demirtaş, *Zeki Paşa'nın Balkan Savaşı Hatıratı*, 13.

37 *Balkan Harbi (1912–1913)* [The Balkan War, 1912–1913], abridged ed. (Ankara: Genelkurmay Basımevi, 1979), 16–17.

38 See Suat Zeyrek, *Birinci Balkan Savaşı Yenilgisinin İç ve Dış Sebepleri* [The Domestic and International Reasons for the Defeat in the First Phase of the Balkan War], Ph.D. dissertation (Istanbul: Istanbul University, 2012), 182–88.
39 Musa Çadırcı, *Tanzimat Sürecinde Türkiye: Askerlik* [Turkey in the Reorganization Era: Military Service] (Ankara: İmge, 2008), 27–63.
40 Yıldız, *Neferin Adı Yok*, 248–60.
41 Cahide Bolat, *Redif Askeri Teşkilatı (1834–1876)* [The Military Reserve Organization, 1834–1876], Ph.D. dissertation (Ankara: Ankara University, 2000), 75–76.
42 For a detailed account of the failure of the Ottoman reserve system in the Balkan War, see Mehmet Beşikçi, 'Balkan Harbi'nde Osmanlı Seferberliği ve Redif Teşkilatının İflası' [Ottoman Mobilization in the Balkan War and the Bankruptcy of the Reserve System], *Türkiye Günlüğü* 110 (2012), 27–43.
43 *Balkan Harbi (1912–1913)*, Vol. 1, 102–4.
44 Uyar and Erickson, *Military History of the Ottomans*, 220–23.
45 *Balkan Harbi (1912–1913)*, Vol. 1, 101, 104.
46 A. [Ali İhsan Sâbis], *Balkan Harbi'nde Askerî Mağlubiyetlerimizin Esbâbı: Neden Münhezim Olduk?* [The Reasons for Our Military Failure in the Balkan War: Why Were We Defeated?], Vol. 2 (Istanbul: Kitabhâne-i İslam ve Askerî, 1913), 5–6.
47 Yıldırım and Öztürkçü, *Abdullah Paşa'nın Balkan Harbi Hâtırâtı*, 96.
48 Levent Alpat, Ahmet Mehmetefendioğlu and Ozan Arslan (eds), *Bir Osmanlı Askerinin Anıları: Balkan Savaşı'ndan Kurtuluş'a, Hamit Ercan* [Memoirs of an Ottoman Soldier: Hamit Ercan from the Balkan War to the War of Independence] (İzmir: Şenocak, 2010), 31–36.
49 Rahmi Apak, *Yetmişlik Bir Subayın Hatıraları* [Memoirs of a Seventy-Year-Old Army Officer] (Ankara: Türk Tarih Kurumu Basımevi, 1988), 91.
50 Andonyan, *Balkan Savaşı*, 469.
51 Gustav von Hochwaechter, *Balkan Savaşı Günlüğü: 'Türklerle Cephede'* [Diaries of the Balkan War: In the Battlefield with the Turks], 2nd ed., trans. Sumru Toydemir, (Istanbul: İş Bankası Kültür Yayınları, 2009), 62.
52 *Balkan Harbi (1912–1913)*, Vol. 1, 134.
53 On the evolution of the system of reserve officers in the late Ottoman Empire, see Mehmet Beşikçi, "İhtiyat Zâbiti'nden 'Yedek Subay'a: Osmanlı'dan Cumhuriyet'e Bir Zorunlu Askerlik Kategorisi Olarak Yedek Subaylık ve Yedek Subaylar, 1891–1930' [The System of Reserve Officers as a Category of Compulsory Military Service from the Ottoman Empire through the Turkish Republic], *Tarih ve Toplum: Yeni Yaklaşımlar* 13 (2011), 45–89.
54 Ahmet Bedevî Kuran, *Harbiye Mektebi'nde Hürriyet Mücadelesi* [Struggle for Liberation in the War College] (Istanbul: İş Bankası Kültür Yayınları, 2009), 15.
55 Uyar and Erickson, *Military History of the Ottomans*, 232.
56 Mahmud Muhtar, *Balkan Harbi: Üçüncü Kolordu'nun ve İkinci Doğu Ordusunun Muharebeleri* [The Balkan War: The Battles of the Third Corps and the Second Western Army], ed. A. Basad Kocaoğlu (Istanbul: İlgi Kültür Sanat, 2012), 124. See also pp. 32, 38, 94.

57 Yıldırım and Öztürkçü, *Abdullah Paşa'nın Balkan Harbi Hâtırâtı*, 278.
58 Muhtar, *Balkan Harbi*, 26, 29, 38, 42, 104, 106, 129, 164, 170.
59 See, for example, Ratip Kazancıgil, *Hafız Rakım Ertür'ün Anılarından Balkan Savaşı'nda Edirne Savunması Günleri* [The Defence of Edirne in the Balkan War according to Hafız Rakım Ertür's Memoirs] (Kırklareli: Sermet Matbaası, 1986), 18; Nurettin Peker, *Tüfek Omza: Balkan Savaşı'ndan Kurtuluş Savaşı'na Ateş Hattında Bir Ömür* [Port Arms! A Life on the Line of Fire from the Balkan War through the War of Independence], ed. Orhan Peker and Hilal Akkartal (Istanbul: Doğan Kitap, 2009), 67; Çobanoğlu, *Balkan Savaşı ve Doğu Ordusu'nn Bozgunu*, 242.
60 Yıldırım and Öztürkçü, *Abdullah Paşa'nın Balkan Harbi Hâtırâtı*, 310; Muhtar, *Balkan Harbi*, 34; Demirtaş, *Zeki Paşa'nın Balkan Savaşı Hatıratı*, 80; Ömer Seyfettin, *Balkan Harbi Hatıraları* [Memoirs of the Balkan War], ed. Tahsin Yıldırım (Istanbul: DBY, 2011), 139; İlyas Çavuş, 'Bir Çavuşun Balkan Harbi Anıları, I' [Memoirs of a Sergeant in the Balkan War], ed. Ahmet Hazerfen, *Tarih ve Toplum* 21 (1985), 152.
61 For the text of the law, see *Düstûr*, Series II, Vol. I, 420.
62 Heinzelmann, *Cihaddan Vatan Savunmasına*, 206.
63 See Mehmet Hacısalihoğlu, 'Inclusion and Exclusion: Conscription in the Ottoman Empire', *Journal of Modern European History* 5(2) (2007), 264–86.
64 Çakmak, *Garbî Rumeli'nin Sûret-i Ziyaı*, 25, 85; Sait Pertev Demirhan, *Balkan Savaşı'nda Büyük Genel Karargâh* [The Great General Headquarters during the Balkan War], ed. Sema Demirtaş (Istanbul: Alfa, 2012), 11.
65 Zeyrek, *Birinci Balkan Savaşı Yenilgisi*, 256.
66 A. [Ali İhsan Sâbis], *Balkan Savaşı'nda Neden Bozguna Uğradık?*, 68–69.
67 Hall, *The Balkan Wars*, 18. See also Taha Akyol, *Rumeli'ye Elveda: 100. Yılında Balkan Bozgunu* [Farewell to Rumeli: The Balkan Defeat in Its 100th Anniversary], 2nd ed. (Istanbul: Doğan Kitap, 2013), 215–47.
68 Gülsoy, *Osmanlı Gayrimüslimlerinin Askerlik Serüveni*, 165–66.
69 Leon Trotsky (Lev Troçki), *Balkan Savaşları* [The Balkan War], trans. Tansel Güney (Istanbul: Arba Yayınları, 1995), 190, 232–33.
70 Fikret Adanır, 'Non-Muslims in the Ottoman Army and the Ottoman Defeat in the Balkan War of 1912–1913', in Ronald G. Suny, Fatma M. Göçek and Norman M. Naimark (eds), *A Question of Genocide: Armenians and Turks at the End of the Ottoman Empire* (Oxford/New York: Oxford University Press, 2011), 113–25.
71 Uyar and Erickson, *Military History of the Ottomans*, 234.
72 Eyüp Durukan, *Günlüklerde Bir Ömür* I: *Balkan Harbi'nde Edirne Kuşatması (1911–1913)* [A Life in Diaries I: The Siege of Edirne in the Balkan War], ed. Murat Uluğtekin (Istanbul: İş Bankası Kültür Yayınları, 2013), 458–59.
73 For some specific examples of desertion cases, see Karabekir, *Edirne Hatıraları*, 54, 76.
74 Gülsoy, *Osmanlı Gayrimüslimlerinin Askerlik Serüveni*, 167.
75 Hafız Hakkı, *Bozgun* [The Debacle] (Istanbul: Matbaa-ı Hayriye ve Şürekası, 1914).
76 For a compact analysis of this literature, some of which has already been cited in this chapter, see Mesut Uyar, 'Osmanlı Askerî Rönesansı: Balkan

Bozgunu İle Yüzleşmek' [The Ottoman Military Renaissance: Facing the Balkan Debacle], *Türkiye Günlüğü* 110 (2012), 65–74.

77 *Türk Silahlı Kuvvetleri Tarihi*, Vol. 3, Part 6: *1908–1920* [History of the Turkish Armed Forces] (Ankara: Genelkurmay Basımevi, 1971), 192.

78 M. Naim Turfan, *Rise of the Young Turks: Politics, the Military and Ottoman Collapse* (London: I.B. Tauris, 2000), 205–13.

79 For the complete text of the regulation, see *Osmanlı Ordu Teşkilatı* [The Ottoman Army Organization] (Ankara: Milli Savunma Bakanlığı, 1999), 147–61.

80 Enver remained at this post through the end of the war, until 14 October 1918.

81 *Birinci Dünya Harbinde Türk Harbi*. Vol. I: *Osmanlı İmparatorluğu'nun Siyasi ve Askeri Hazırlıkları ve Harbe Girişi* [The Turkish War in the First World War. Vol. 1: Political and Military Preparations of the Ottoman State and Its Entry in the War] (Ankara: Genelkurmay Basımevi, 1970), 179–80.

82 Shaw, *The Ottoman Empire*, 116. For a comprehensive analysis of Ottoman mobilization in the First World War, see Mehmet Beşikçi, *The Ottoman Mobilization of Manpower in the First World War: Between Voluntarism and Resistance* (Leiden: Brill, 2012).

83 For the text of the law, see *Düstûr*, Series II, Vol. 6, 662–704.

84 Erickson estimates that the number of total Ottoman casualties during the Balkan War was about 340,000, of which 50,000 were killed in action, 75,000 died of disease, 100,000 were wounded, and 115,000 were prisoners of war. See Erickson, *Defeat in Detail*, 329.

85 Justin MacCarthy, *Death and Exile: The Ethnic Cleansing of Ottoman Muslims, 1821–1922* (Princeton, NJ: The Darwin Press, 1995), 161. See also Ahmet Halaçoğlu, *Balkan Harbi Esnasında Rumeli'den Türk Göçleri, 1912–1913* [Turkish Migrations from Rumeli during the Balkan War] (Ankara: Türk Tarih Kurumu Yayınları, 1995).

86 *Türk Silahlı Kuvvetleri Tarihi*, Vol. 3, Part 6, 210 and appendix 8.

87 Çakmak, *Garbî Rumeli'nin Sûret-i Ziyaı*, 25.

88 For examples of disarming 'unreliable' non-Muslim conscripts to employ them in menial jobs during the Balkan War, see Karabekir, *Edirne Hatıraları*, 77–78.

89 See Beşikçi, *Ottoman Mobilization of Manpower*, 129–39; Zekeriya Özdemir, *I. Dünya Savaşı'nda Amele Taburları* [The Labour Battalions in the First World War] (Ankara: Gazi Üniversitesi, 1994); Erik J. Zürcher, 'Ottoman Labour Battalions in World War I', in Hans-Lukas Kieser and Dominik J. Schaller (eds), *The Armenian Genocide and the Shoah* (Zürich: Chronos, 2002), 187–96; Cengiz Mutlu, *Birinci Dünya Savaşı'nda Amele Taburları* (Istanbul: IQ Kültür Sanat Yayıncılık, 2007).

90 Beşikçi, *Ottoman Mobilization of Manpower*, 115.

91 See Edward J. Erickson, *Ordered to Die: A History of the Ottoman Army in the First World War* (Westport, CT: Greenwood Press, 2001); idem, *Ottoman Army Effectiveness in World War I: A Comparative Study* (London: Routledge, 2007).

Bibliography

A. [Ali İhsan Sâbis]. *Balkan Harbi'nde Askerî Mağlubiyetlerimizin Esbâbı: Neden Münhezim Olduk?* [The Reasons for Our Military Failure in the Balkan War: Why Were We Defeated?]. Vol. 2. Istanbul: Kitabhâne-i İslam ve Askerî, 1913.
——. *Balkan Savaşı'nda Neden Bozguna Uğradık?* [Why Were We Defeated in the Balkan War?]. Ed. Hülya Toker. Istanbul: Alfa, 2012.
Adanır, Fikret. 'Non-Muslims in the Ottoman Army and the Ottoman Defeat in the Balkan War of 1912–1913', in Ronald G. Suny, Fatma M. Göçek and Norman M. Naimark (eds), *A Question of Genocide: Armenians and Turks at the End of the Ottoman Empire* (Oxford/New York: Oxford University Press, 2011), 113–25.
Akyol, Taha. *Rumeli'ye Elveda: 100. Yılında Balkan Bozgunu* [Farewell to Rumeli: The Balkan Defeat in Its 100th Anniversary]. 2nd ed. Istanbul: Doğan Kitap, 2013.
Alpat, Levent, Ahmet Mehmetefendioğlu and Ozan Arslan (eds). *Bir Osmanlı Askerinin Anıları: Balkan Savaşı'ndan Kurtuluş'a, Hamit Ercan* [Memoirs of an Ottoman Soldier: Hamit Ercan from the Balkan War to the War of Independence]. İzmir: Şenocak, 2010.
Altay, Fahrettin. *10 Yıl Savaş (1912–1922) ve Sonrası: Görüp Geçirdiklerim* [The Ten-Year War and Afterwards: What I Lived Through]. Istanbul: İnsel Yayınları, 1970.
Andonyan, Aram. *Balkan Savaşı* [The Balkan War]. 2nd ed. Trans. Zaven Biberyan. Istanbul: Aras Yayıncılık, 1999.
Apak, Rahmi. *Yetmişlik Bir Subayın Hatıraları* [Memoirs of a Seventy-Year-Old Army Officer]. Ankara: Türk Tarih Kurumu Basımevi, 1988.
Balkan Harbi (1912–1913) [The Balkan War, 1912–1913]. Abridged ed. Ankara: Genelkurmay Basımevi, 1979.
Balkan Harbi (1912–1913). Vol. 1: *Harbin Sebepleri, Askeri Hazırlıklar ve Osmanlı Devletinin Harbe Girişi* [The Balkan War, 1912–1913: The Origins of the War, Military Preparations and the Ottoman State's Entry in the War]. Ankara: Genelkurmay Basımevi, 1970.
Bein, Amit. 'Politics, Military Conscription, and Religious Education in the Late Ottoman Empire'. *International Journal of Middle East Studies* 38(2) (2006), 283–301.
Bell, David A. *The First Total War: Napoleon's Europe and the Birth of Warfare As We Know It.* New York: Mariner Books, 2007.
Beşikçi, Mehmet. 'Topyekûn Savaş Kavramı ve Son Dönem Osmanlı Harp Tarihi' [The Concept of Total War and Late Ottoman Military History]. *Toplumsal Tarih* 198 (2010), 62–69.
——. "İhtiyat Zâbiti'nden 'Yedek Subay'a: Osmanlı'dan Cumhuriyet'e Bir Zorunlu Askerlik Kategorisi Olarak Yedek Subaylık ve Yedek Subaylar, 1891–1930' [The System of Reserve Officers as a Category of Compulsory Military Service from the Ottoman Empire through the Turkish Republic]. *Tarih ve Toplum: Yeni Yaklaşımlar* 13 (2011), 45–89.

———. 'Balkan Harbi'nde Osmanlı Seferberliği ve Redif Teşkilatının İflası' [Ottoman Mobilization in the Balkan War and the Bankruptcy of the Reserve System]. *Türkiye Günlüğü* 110 (2012), 27–43.

———. *The Ottoman Mobilization of Manpower in the First World War: Between Voluntarism and Resistance*. Leiden: Brill, 2012.

———. 'Mobilizing Military Labor in the Age of Total War: Ottoman Conscription before and during the Great War', in Erik J. Zürcher (ed.), *Fighting for a Living: A Comparative History of Military Labour, 1500–2000* (Amsterdam: Amsterdam University Press, 2014), 535–68.

Birinci Dünya Harbinde Türk Harbi. Vol. I: *Osmanlı İmparatorluğu'nun Siyasi ve Askeri Hazırlıkları ve Harbe Girişi* [The Turkish War in the First World War. Vol. 1: Political and Military Preparations of the Ottoman State and Its Entry in the War]. Ankara: Genelkurmay Basımevi, 1970.

Black, Jeremy. *War in the Nineteenth Century*. Cambridge: Polity Press, 2009.

Bolat, Cahide. *Redif Askeri Teşkilatı (1834–1876)* [The Military Reserve Organization, 1834–1876]. Ph.D. dissertation. Ankara: Ankara University, 2000.

Bowen, H. 'Badal', in P. Bearman, Th. Bianquis, C.E. Bosworth, E. van Donzel, W.P. Heinrichs (eds), *Encyclopedia of Islam, Vol. 1*. Second ed. Consulted online on 1 August 2017, http://dx.doi.org/10.1163/1573-3912_islam_SIM_0988

Bruinessen, Martin van. *Agha, Shaikh and State: The Social and Political Structures of Kurdistan*. London: Zed Books, 1992.

Çadırcı, Musa. *Tanzimat Sürecinde Türkiye: Askerlik* [Turkey in the Reorganization Era: Military Service]. Ankara: İmge, 2008.

Çakmak, Fevzi. *Garbî Rumeli'nin Sûret-i Ziyaı ve Balkan Harbinde Garp Cephesi* [The Loss of Western Rumelia and the Western Front in the Balkan War]. 2nd ed. Ed. Ahmet Tetik. Istanbul: İş Bankası Kültür Yayınları, 2012.

Çalışlar, İzzettin. *On Yıllık Savaşın Günlüğü: Balkan, Birinci Dünya ve İstiklal Savaşları* [The Diary of the Ten-Year War: The Balkan, First World and Independence Wars]. Ed. İsmet Görgülü and İzzeddin Çalışlar. Istanbul: Yapı Kredi Yayınları, 1997.

Carnegie Endowment for International Peace. *Report of the International Commission to Inquire into the Causes and Conduct of the Balkan Wars*. Washington, DC: The Endowment, 1914.

Çavuş, İlyas. 'Bir Çavuşun Balkan Harbi Anıları, I' [Memoirs of a Sergeant in the Balkan War]. Ed. Ahmet Hazerfen. *Tarih ve Toplum* 21 (1985), 152.

Chickering, Roger. 'Total War: The Use and Abuse of a Concept', in Manfred F. Boemeke, Roger Chickering and Stig Förster (eds), *Anticipating Total War: The German and American Experiences, 1871–1914* (Cambridge: Cambridge University Press, 1999), 13–28.

Çobanoğlu, Ömer Zeki. *Balkan Savaşı ve Doğu Ordusu'nn Bozgunu* [The Balkan War and the Debacle of the Eastern Army]. Ed. Hülya Toker. Istanbul: Alfa, 2012.

Demirhan, Sait Pertev. *Balkan Savaşı'nda Büyük Genel Karargâh* [The Great General Headquarters during the Balkan War]. Ed. Sema Demirtaş. Istanbul: Alfa, 2012.

Demirtaş, Sema (ed.). *Zeki Paşa'nın Balkan Savaşı Hatıratı* [Zeki Pasha's Memoirs of the Balkan War]. Istanbul: Alfa, 2012.

Durukan, Eyüp. *Günlüklerde Bir Ömür I: Balkan Harbi'nde Edirne Kuşatması (1911–1913)* [A Life in Diaries I: The Siege of Edirne in the Balkan War]. Ed. Murat Uluğtekin. Istanbul: İş Bankası Kültür Yayınları, 2013.

Er, Serkan. *Osmanlı Ordusunda Seferberlik Planı: Balkan Harbi Örneği* [The Mobilization Planning in the Ottoman Army: The Case of the Balkan War]. MA thesis. Istanbul, The Turkish War Academy Strategic Research Institute, 2012.

Erickson, Edward J. *Ordered to Die: A History of the Ottoman Army in the First World War*. Westport, CT: Greenwood Press, 2001.

———. *Defeat in Detail: The Ottoman Army in the Balkans, 1912–1913*. Westport, CT: Praeger, 2003.

———. *Ottoman Army Effectiveness in World War I: A Comparative Study*. London: Routledge, 2007.

Förster, Stig, and Jörg Nagler (eds). *On the Road to Total War: The American Civil War and the German Wars of Unification, 1861–1871*. Cambridge: Cambridge University Press, 1997.

———. 'Introduction', in Roger Chickering and Stig Förster (eds), *Great War, Total War: Combat and Mobilization on the Western Front, 1914–1918* (Cambridge: Cambridge University Press, 2000), 1–18.

Gülsoy, Ufuk. *Osmanlı Gayrimüslimlerinin Askerlik Serüveni* [The Conscription Adventure of Ottoman Non-Muslims]. Istanbul: Simurg, 2000.

Hacısalihoğlu, Mehmet. 'Inclusion and Exclusion: Conscription in the Ottoman Empire'. *Journal of Modern European History* 5(2) (2007), 264–86.

———. 'Borders, Maps, and Censuses: The Politicization of Geography and Statistics in the Multi-ethnic Ottoman Empire', in Jörn Leonhard and Ulrike von Hirschhausen (eds), *Comparing Empires: Encounters and Transfers in the Long Nineteenth Century* (Göttingen: Vandenhoeck & Ruprecht, 2011), 171–210.

Hakkı, Hafız. *Bozgun* [The Debacle]. Istanbul: Matbaa-ı Hayriye ve Şürekası, 1914.

Halaçoğlu, Ahmet. *Balkan Harbi Esnasında Rumeli'den Türk Göçleri, 1912–1913* [Turkish Migrations from Rumeli during the Balkan War]. Ankara: Türk Tarih Kurumu Yayınları, 1995.

Hall, Richard C. *The Balkan Wars: Prelude to the First World War*. London: Routledge, 2000.

Hayta, Necdet and T. Seçkin Birbudak. *Balkan Savaşları'nda Edirne* [Edirne during the Balkan Wars]. Ankara: Genelkurmay Basımevi, 2010.

Heinzelmann, Tobias. *Cihaddan Vatan Savunmasına: Osmanlı İmparatorluğu'nda Genel Askerlik Yükümlülüğü, 1826–1856* [From the Holy War to the Defence of the Fatherland: Compulsory Military Service in the Ottoman Empire, 1826–1856]. Trans. Türkis Noyan. Istanbul: Kitap, 2009.

Hochwaechter, Gustav von. *Balkan Savaşı Günlüğü: 'Türklerle Cephede'* [Diaries of the Balkan War: In the Battlefield with the Turks]. 2nd ed. Trans. Sumru Toydemir. Istanbul: İş Bankası Kültür Yayınları, 2009.

Karabekir, Kâzım. *Edirne Hatıraları* [Edirne Memoirs]. Ed. Ziver Öktem. Istanbul: Yapı Kredi Yayınları, 2009.

Kazancıgil, Ratip. *Hafız Rakım Ertür'ün Anılarından Balkan Savaşı'nda Edirne Savunması Günleri* [The Defence of Edirne in the Balkan War According to Hafız Rakım Ertür's Memoirs]. Kırklareli: Sermet Matbaası, 1986.

Klein, Janet. *The Margins of Empire: Kurdish Militias in the Ottoman Tribal Zone*. Stanford, CA: Stanford University Press, 2011.

Kuran, Ahmet Bedevî. *Harbiye Mektebi'nde Hürriyet Mücadelesi* [Struggle for Liberation in the War College]. Istanbul: İş Bankası Kültür Yayınları, 2009.

Lucassen, Jan, and Erik J. Zürcher. 'Introduction: Conscription and Resistance. The Historical Context', in Erik J. Zürcher (ed.), *Arming the State: Military Conscription in the Middle East and Central Asia* (London: I.B. Tauris, 1999), 1–20.

MacCarthy, Justin. *Death and Exile: The Ethnic Cleansing of Ottoman Muslims, 1821–1922*. Princeton, NJ: The Darwin Press, 1995.

Muhtar, Mahmud. *Balkan Harbi: Üçüncü Kolordu'nun ve İkinci Doğu Ordusunun Muharebeleri* [The Balkan War: The Battles of the Third Corps and the Second Western Army]. Ed. A. Basad Kocaoğlu. Istanbul: İlgi Kültür Sanat, 2012.

Mutlu, Cengiz. *Birinci Dünya Savaşı'nda Amele Taburları*. Istanbul: IQ Kültür Sanat Yayıncılık, 2007.

Osmanlı Ordu Teşkilatı [The Ottoman Army Organization]. Ankara: Milli Savunma Bakanlığı, 1999.

Özdemir, Mehmet. 'Balkan Harbi'nde Gönüllüler ve Gönüllü Askeri Birlikler' [Volunteers and Voluntary Military Units in the Balkan War]. *Askeri Tarih Araştırmaları Dergisi* 3(5) (2005), 71–102.

Özdemir, Zekeriya. *I. Dünya Savaşı'nda Amele Taburları* [The Labour Battalions in the First World War]. Ankara: Gazi Üniversitesi, 1994.

Peker, Nurettin. *Tüfek Omza: Balkan Savaşı'ndan Kurtuluş Savaşı'na Ateş Hattında Bir Ömür* [Port Arms! A Life on the Line of Fire from the Balkan War through the War of Independence]. Ed. Orhan Peker and Hilal Akkartal. Istanbul: Doğan Kitap, 2009.

Seyfettin, Ömer. *Balkan Harbi Hatıraları* [Memoirs of the Balkan War]. Ed. Tahsin Yıldırım. Istanbul: DBY, 2011.

Shaw, Stanford J. *The Ottoman Empire in World War I*. Vol. I. Ankara: Türk Tarih Kurumu Basımevi, 2006.

Şimşek, Veysel. *Ottoman Military Recruitment and the Recruit, 1826–1853*. Ankara: The Institute of Economics and Social Sciences of Bilkent University, 2005. http://www.thesis.bilkent.edu.tr/0002992.pdf (accessed 18 February 2014).

Soyupak, Kemal, and Hüseyin Kabasakal. 'The Turkish Army in the First Balkan War', in Béla K. Király and Dimitrije Djordjevic (eds), *East Central European Society and the Balkan Wars* (New York: Columbia University Press, 1987), 158–62.

Trotsky, Leon (Lev Troçki). *Balkan Savaşları* [The Balkan War]. Trans. Tansel Güney. Istanbul: Arba Yayınları, 1995.

Turfan, M. Naim. *Rise of the Young Turks: Politics, the Military and Ottoman Collapse*. London: I.B. Tauris, 2000.

Türk Silahlı Kuvvetleri Tarihi. Vol. 3, Part 6: *1908–1920* [History of the Turkish Armed Forces]. Ankara: Genelkurmay Basımevi, 1971.

Türk Silahlı Kuvvetleri Tarihi: Balkan Harbi (1912–1913) [History of the Turkish Armed Forces: The Balkan War (1912–1913)]. Ankara: Genelkurmay Basımevi, 1979.

Uyar, Mesut. 'Osmanlı Askerî Rönesansı: Balkan Bozgunu İle Yüzleşmek' [The Ottoman Military Renaissance: Facing the Balkan Debacle]. *Türkiye Günlüğü* 110 (2012), 65–74.

Uyar, Mesut, and Edward J. Erickson. *A Military History of the Ottomans from Osman to Atatürk*. Santa Barbara, CA: Praeger, 2009.

Uzdil, Beliğ. *Balkan Savaşı'nda Mürettep 1nci Kolordu'nun Harekâtı* [The Operations of the First Mixed Corps in the Balkan War]. Ed. Ahmet Tetik and Şeyda Büyükcan. Ankara: Genelkurmay Basımevi, 2006.

Wolff, David et al. (eds). *The Russo-Japanese War in Global Perspective*. Leiden: Brill, 2007.

Yasamee, F.A.K. 'Ottoman War Planning and the Balkan Campaign of October–December 1912', in Eugenia Kermeli and Oktay Özel (eds), *The Ottoman Empire: Myths, Realities and 'Black Holes'* (Istanbul: The Isis Press, 2006), 347–66.

Yıldırım, Tahsin, and İbrahim Öztürkçü (eds). *1328 Balkan Harbi'nde Şark Ordusu Kumandanı Abdullah Paşa'nın Balkan Harbi Hâtırâtı* [The Memoirs of Abdullah Pasha, the Commander of the Eastern Army in the Balkan War of 1912]. Istanbul: DBY, 2012.

Yıldız, Gültekin. *Neferin Adı Yok: Zorunlu Askerliğe Geçiş Sürecinde Osmanlı Devleti'nde Siyaset, Ordu ve Toplum (1826–1839)* [The Private Has No Name: Politics, Army and Society in the Ottoman Empire during the Transition to Compulsory Military Service, 1826–1839]. Istanbul: Kitabevi Yayınevi, 2009.

Zeyrek, Suat. *Birinci Balkan Savaşı Yenilgisinin İç ve Dış Sebepleri* [The Domestic and International Reasons for the Defeat in the First Phase of the Balkan War]. Ph.D. dissertation. Istanbul: Istanbul University, 2012.

Zürcher, Erik J. 'Ottoman Labour Battalions in World War I', in Hans-Lukas Kieser and Dominik J. Schaller (eds), *The Armenian Genocide and the Shoah* (Zürich: Chronos, 2002), 187–96.

 6

The Thracian Theatre of War 1912
Richard C. Hall

The Balkan Wars of 1912–13 were the first important European conflict of the twentieth century. They initiated fighting that would become widespread throughout Europe two years later. In the First Balkan War, a loose coalition of Balkan states – Bulgaria, Greece, Montenegro and Serbia – confronted the Ottoman Empire. The most important theatre in this complex clash between Orthodox Christian nationalism and proto-Turkish nationalism was Thrace, the Ottoman province (*vilayet*) located in the southeastern-most part of the European continent.[1]

After gaining national autonomy from the Ottoman Empire in 1878 as a result of the Russo-Ottoman war, the new Bulgarian principality was in a difficult strategic position. The new state's primary foreign policy objective was located in Macedonia, southwest of Bulgaria and still under Ottoman rule. Both Greece and Serbia contested Bulgarian claims to Macedonia. The chief threat to Bulgarian security, however, came from Bulgaria's former Ottoman rulers, whose demographic, economic and political centre at Constantinople lay southeast of Bulgaria. Bulgarian military planners, therefore, had to contend with a political *desideratum* in Macedonia, on Bulgaria's southwestern frontier, and a military threat from Thrace, on Bulgaria's southeastern frontier.

Geography dictated that Thrace would be the decisive theatre in the war between the Balkan allies and the Ottoman Empire in the autumn of 1912. Only about one hundred miles separated the Bulgarian frontier from the Ottoman capital Constantinople. The slightly rolling terrain lacked natural obstacles to impede the manoeuvre of the Bulgarian and Ottoman armies. Important Ottoman fortifications guarded the northeastern Thracian flank at Kırkkilise/Lozengrad and the most important Thracian city Adrianople (Edirne, Odrin). The final Ottoman defensive line at Chataldzha (Çatalca) stretched from the Black Sea to the Sea of Marmara about twenty-five miles from Constantinople.

A Bulgarian success in Thrace could bring the war to the door of the ancient imperial city. An Ottoman victory in Thrace would open the way for an invasion of the Bulgarian heartland.

Plans

Bulgaria's geography presented its military with a strategic difficulty. The main Bulgarian political goal lay to the west in Macedonia. The chief military threat to Bulgaria was to the east in Thrace. The Bulgarian General Staff understood that Macedonia must be conquered in Thrace. The Bulgarians also appreciated that in a prolonged conflict the Ottoman command could shift significant forces from its Asian territories to Thrace. These could overwhelm the Bulgarians by weight of numbers. Nevertheless, this process would require time. The Bulgarian General Staff calculated that the Ottomans would not completely concentrate a 200,000–250,000-man army in Thrace until three weeks into the war.[2] Therefore, the Bulgarians had to achieve a decisive result as quickly as possible.

At the beginning of the twentieth century, the Bulgarian General Staff developed a strategic plan, which envisioned a defensive posture in the west to prevent an Ottoman attack on Sofia from Macedonia and a rapid offensive into Thrace.[3] This plan underwent several modifications in the years before the outbreak of the First Balkan War. In the final version, General Ivan Fichev (1860–1931), the Italian-trained chief of staff, located the Bulgarian forces near the Thracian frontier. These included the Bulgarian First Army with 79,370 men commanded by General Vasil Kutinchev (1859–1941); the Second Army with 122,748 men commanded by General Nikola Ivanov (1861–1940); and the Third Army of 94,884 men led by the colourful General Radko Dimitriev (1859–1918).[4] In addition, the Bulgarians deployed a small cavalry division attached to the First Army. These troops constituted more than 60 per cent of the total Bulgarian forces.[5] According to Fichev's plan, the Bulgarian Second Army would advance to the Ottoman fortress at Adrianople, while the Bulgarian First Army would mass between Adrianople and the fortress of Kırkkilise/Lozengrad, and the Bulgarian Third Army would form northeast of the First Army behind the Bulgarian cavalry division.

The Bulgarian strategic plan then envisioned the Second Army screening the strong fortress of Adrianople. The First Army would advance forward while the Third Army swept from behind the cavalry and moved around the Ottoman right flank, overwhelming the obsolete fortifications at Kırkkilise/Lozengrad and joining the First Army to force a decisive battle around Lüleburgaz (Liuleburgas).⁶ At this point, the Bulgarian government contemplated asking for Russian diplomatic intervention to stop the war and to compel the Ottomans to accept an autonomous (pro-Bulgarian) regime in Macedonia.⁷ This would prevent the Ottomans from employing their superior numbers.

The Bulgarian plan was bold. The area between Adrianople and Kırkkilise/Lozengrad was open, undulating downland, inviting an attack. East of Kırkkilise/Lozengrad, however, where the Third Army would make its turn, lay the slopes of a rugged ridge the Bulgarians called the Strandzha Planina. The Bulgarian General Staff made a thorough study of this region in 1911, and the Bulgarians doubted that the Ottomans would anticipate a move there.⁸ The plan depended on the speed and precision with which the First and Third Armies could coordinate their movements. The Bulgarians took care to conceal their real intentions. On the eve of the outbreak of the war, the deputy commander in chief of the Bulgarian army, Mihail Savov (1857–1928), indicated to foreign journalists that the main goal of the campaign was the Ottoman fortress at Adrianople.⁹ This was a sophisticated plan that required considerable skill for the coordination of the movements of the three armies.

Geography also presented the Ottoman command with a strategic quandary. Constantinople was proximate to the Bulgarian border and therefore vulnerable to a Bulgarian attack. The Ottoman territories of Albania, Kosovo and Macedonia in the western Balkan peninsula were also surrounded by four hostile Balkan states, but connected to Thrace only by a thin strip of Aegean littoral.¹⁰ Because of communication and logistical difficulties, compounded by the Greek navy's control of the Aegean Sea, Ottoman forces were unlikely to mount a strong conventional defence in these western territories. These factors indicated that, for the Ottomans, the decisive battle for the western Ottoman territories would be in Thrace.

The Ottoman General Staff anticipated that the Bulgarians would take the initiative in Thrace, advancing in two lines, with a main thrust towards Kırkkilise/Lozengrad and a secondary movement towards Dimotika in southwestern Thrace.¹¹ The Ottomans also thought that the Bulgarians would enjoy initial numerical superiority, which would wane as the Ottomans transferred reinforcements from Anatolia. The Ottomans wanted to divide the oncoming Bulgarians against the fortress of Adrianople. They would then undertake a decisive counterattack, which would encircle and annihilate the weaker of the two Bulgarian forces. This plan was formulated in 1910 by the then

Ottoman chief of general staff Ferik Ahmed Izzet Paşa (1864–1937) and was based upon German military thinking.[12] The instrument of Ottoman power in Thrace was the Eastern (Thracian) Army, which at the time of mobilization would consist of three regular corps, three provisional corps (*redif*), a cavalry division, and the fortress troops in Adrianople and Kırkkilise/Lozengrad under the overall command of Ferik Abdullah Paşa (1846–1937).[13]

The number of Ottoman troops available at the beginning of the war remains elusive. The commander of the Ottoman Third Corps, General Mahmud Muhtar Paşa (1867–1935), later wrote that the Eastern Army had 150,000 men.[14] An English observer remarked that the Ottoman forces appeared to be in a position of strength.[15] Nevertheless, due to incompetence and poor transportation infrastructure, many of the troops assigned to the Eastern Army were not in place at the beginning of the war.[16] The quality of the provisional units varied considerably in terms of equipment, motivation and training. Undoubtedly, the Ottomans failed to efficiently mobilize their forces. In any event, at the beginning of the war the Bulgarians apparently outnumbered their Ottoman opponents. But the Ottoman command evinced confidence in its preparations. Huseyin Nazim Paşa (1848–1913), the Ottoman chief of staff, in saying goodbye to some officers, said encouragingly: 'Farewell my comrades, do not forget to take with you your full-dress uniforms, because you will need them for the grand entry into Sofia two months from now'.[17] This was overly optimistic.

Kırkkilise/Lozengrad

The war between Bulgaria and the Ottoman Empire began on 17 October.[18] The expectations of the Bulgarians were evident in the diary entry of Col. Petŭr Tantilov (1861–1937), an artillery officer in the Bulgarian Third Army: 'War! At last the national desire is fulfilled. We must triumph! We must take revenge, we must unify Greater Bulgaria'.[19] The Bulgarians immediately executed their plan; their armies began advancing from their set positions. They quickly broke through the Ottoman border forces. The Ottomans were slower to act. Only on 21 October, before the full concentration of its forces, did the Ottoman command order the implementation of its offensive plan. The initial Ottoman attacks encountered not the anticipated three Bulgarian divisions, but the bulk of the Bulgarian army. The Ottomans had seriously underestimated the number of Bulgarians they would face. They had thought most of the Bulgarian army would attack into

Macedonia, the main goal of Bulgarian policy.[20] While the Ottoman offensive met the advancing units of the Bulgarian First Army, the Bulgarian Second Army moved towards Adrianople on 22 October to block any attempt by the fortress troops to assist the Ottoman offence.

During the evening of 22 October, the Bulgarian Third Army, amidst heavy rain, launched an infantry assault supported by artillery on the antiquated fortifications of Kırkkilise/Lozengrad, shouting the Bulgarian war cry *na nozh* [with the knife] as they advanced.[21] The Ottoman troops responded by yelling *Allah, Allah*. They were unable to withstand the Bulgarians. At the same time, elements of the First Army easily contained an Ottoman sortie from Adrianople. The Ottomans abandoned Kırkkilise/Lozengrad on 23 October in a panic. They even abandoned airplanes and sanitation supplies.[22] The commander of the Ottoman Third Corps, General Muhtar Paşa, later wrote of this disaster:

> Military history gives no other such example of a similar rout beginning without cause. Without fighting the Bulgarians had achieved a great victory. Without having been pressured by the enemy, beaten only by the bad weather and the conditions of the roads, the Turks fled as if they had suffered an irreparable disaster, and lost one-third of their war materials.[23]

General Muhtar Paşa was not entirely correct. Fighting did occur at Kırkkilise/Lozengrad. The Bulgarians sustained 1,279 casualties at Kırkkilise/Lozengrad, mostly in the Third Army.[24] The fortifications themselves played little role in the events. The Ottomans suffered about 1,500 killed and wounded and lost 2,000–3,000 prisoners.[25] The surprise flanking operation had succeeded beyond the Bulgarians' expectations. They congratulated themselves that their success was due to the 'good form and skilful fulfilment of the strategic plan'.[26] The Bulgarian success was based upon the speed of their deployment as well as the Ottoman command's underestimation of the number of Bulgarians invading Thrace and the failure of the Ottoman right wing to deal with the oncoming Bulgarian Third Army.[27] Muhtar Paşa himself noted that

> the causes of our defeat are to be found in our bad military organization and in the poor discipline of our reservists. The main cause, however, was the rain, which continued for a week and completely destroyed the morale of our army, rendering the roads impassable for three days to our supply trains and artillery.[28]

In the aftermath of their defeat, the Ottomans retreated in disorder to the southeast. Before this battle, the Bulgarian government intended to appeal to the great powers to intervene in the war. This way the government hoped to avoid defeat and to obtain its goals in Macedonia through a European congress. After the victory, however, there was little inclination in the military to pursue intervention. Tsar Ferdinand telegraphed the Bulgarian government, 'Bulgaria has decided to wage war until the end'.[29]

Lüleburgaz-Pınarhisar/Liuleburgas-Bunar Hisar

The victory at Kırkkilise/Lozengrad persuaded the Bulgarian General Staff to introduce a modification to Fichev's plan. On 29 October, it ordered the Bulgarian Second Army to besiege Adrianople.[30] The commander of the Bulgarian Second Army, General Nikola Ivanov, wanted to rush and seize Adrianople at the beginning of the war.[31] Fichev strongly opposed an immediate attack on Adrianople, asserting that such an attack would require both the First and Second Armies to surround Adrianople and the Third Army to cover it.[32] He committed most of the Bulgarian army's heavy artillery to the besieging forces, thus depriving the onrushing First and Third Armies of heavy artillery support.[33] In practical terms, however, this meant that the heaviest pieces did not have to travel long distances. At this point, the Bulgarians were uncertain of whether Russia would permit them to retain Adrianople.

At the same time, in order to have sufficient forces to impose a total siege, the Bulgarians called upon their Serbian allies for assistance. The Serbs complied. By this time, they had overcome most Ottoman resistance in Macedonia and Kosovo. The Second Serbian Army, commanded by General Stepa Stepanović (1856–1929), arrived by 12 November to tighten the ring around Adrianople. This enabled the Bulgarians to transfer the Third Balkan Division and two brigades from the Ninth Pleven Division to the forces slowly advancing towards Constantinople.

After the Kırkkilise/Lozengrad victory, the friction of war began to affect the Bulgarians. Instead of pursuing the fleeing Ottomans, they rested for three days, and the Bulgarian cavalry lost contact with the enemy. General Muhtar Paşa later wrote that had the Bulgarians attempted a pursuit, the Ottoman situation would have been 'truly critical'.[34] As a result of Bulgarian inactivity, the Ottomans brought reinforcements from Constantinople and established a defensive position running along a long ridge between the villages of Lüleburgaz and Pınarhisar. A small stream in front of the ridge, the Karagaç Dere, presented a natural obstacle in front of the Ottoman positions.

When the Bulgarian armies did resume their advance to engage the enemy in the anticipated decisive battle, the Third Army, urged forward by its charismatic commander General Radko Dimitriev, separated from the First Army. On 29 October, the Bulgarian Third Army attacked the Ottoman positions in front of Lüleburgaz and Pınarhisar.[35] General Dimitriev had wanted to initiate the attack even earlier. He insisted that the enemy was in 'tremendous disorganization'.[36] Generals Savov and Fichev, however, restrained him because of concerns that the Ottoman forces outnumbered him.[37] Fichev, the cautious chief of staff, wanted to delay the attack until the First Army was closer to the battle zone. But General Dimitriev persuaded Tsar Ferdinand and General Savov to sanction the attack.[38] The Bulgarian command's caution was sensible because of the strength of the Ottoman positions and the Bulgarian logistical system's precarious condition.

Abdullah Paşa, the Ottoman commander, intended to hold the line in his left and centre and to sweep around the Bulgarians' left flank with his right.[39] This proved difficult, and the battle along the Ottoman positions lasted for four cold, rainy days. A German officer serving in the Ottoman army later wrote: 'It rained as heavily as it possibly could'.[40] When the Bulgarian First Army – delayed because of the miserable weather and bad roads – reached the battle zone's southern end later the same day, it came under the command of Dimitriev, the general already on the field. After three days of particularly hard fighting, including attacks and counterattacks on both sides, the Bulgarians prevailed. An English correspondent who observed how fresh troops from the Ottoman Third Corps failed to advance later wrote that

> even the heroic efforts of Mahmoud's [Muhtar's] previously unbeaten infantry could not drive back the enemy, who fought with unparalleled determination and ferocity, absolutely throwing away their lives in the Japanese manner whenever a point had to be taken or won.[41]

On 31 October, the Ottoman left flank collapsed as the Bulgarian First Army crossed the Ergene River to envelop Ottoman positions. At the same time, the Bulgarian Third Army fought its way around the Ottoman right flank. General Dimitriev ordered, 'Have at them energetically. If you can't advance, then rally and embolden yourselves at all cost. Above all move forward'.[42] At this point the centre disintegrated. The result was the same as at Kırkkilise/Lozengrad. On 2 November, the Ottomans panicked, retreating in disorder. Muhtar Paşa commented that 'once more we have witnessed the sadness of a new debacle analogous to that of Kırkkilise. It is difficult to explain the reasons'.[43] In fact, the reasons are straightforward. Besides the attacking Bulgarians' above-mentioned attitude of self-sacrifice, effective artillery fire was also crucial to their success. The previously mentioned English observer noted that for every battery the Turks seemed to have in action, the Bulgarians were able to produce half a dozen, and whereas the Turkish fire was desultory and ill directed, the Bulgarian shells burst in a never ceasing storm on the Turkish positions with a maximum of effect. In fact, the enemy seemed to have so little respect for the Turkish batteries that they seldom directed their fire against them, but concentrated it on the infantry, who suffered enormous losses, and became sadly demoralized.[44]

The Ottomans may have missed an opportunity to turn the Bulgarian right flank around Lüleburgaz by attacking southeasterly from the Adrianople fortress,[45] which could have caught the Bulgarians unprepared. Unlike at Kırkkilise/Lozengrad, the Ottomans failed to stir from Adrianople.

The battle was costly for both sides. The Bulgarians suffered 20,162 casualties, including 2,536 dead, with the majority in the more heavily engaged Third Army.[46] The Ottomans lost at least 22,000 men, including 3,000 prisoners of war, and much artillery and other military equipment.[47] This was the bloodiest battle of the entire Balkan cycle of conflict in 1912–13, and it was the largest battle in Europe between the Franco-German war and the First World War in terms of numbers involved and casualties suffered.

The Bulgarians had succeeded in sweeping around the Ottoman right flank and forcing a decisive battle at Lüleburgaz.[48] The Ottomans suffered a second disastrous defeat a little over a week later. The victories at Kırkkilise/Lozengrad and Lüleburgaz-Pınarhisar profoundly changed Bulgarian policy. The Russians now agreed that Bulgaria could have Adrianople. The government's plan to seek Russian intervention to stop the war on favourable terms was abandoned.[49] Now the Bulgarian Tsar and the army were determined to pursue a military resolution to the war.

Chataldzha (Çatalca)

After their defeat at Lüleburgaz-Pınarhisar, the Ottomans retreated towards their final lines of defence before Constantinople at Chataldzha/Çatalca. The Bulgarians were too exhausted to pursue them. Had they done so, even just with their cavalry division, they might have inflicted further damage on the demoralized remnants of the Ottoman Eastern Army – or even gained a decisive victory in the war.

The Bulgarian army resumed its advance on 6 November. The Bulgarians knew little about the Chataldzha/Çatalca fortifications; they had not anticipated that their forces would come this far. Their best information dated from 1906 when an enterprising staff officer had made an unauthorized inspection of the Chataldzha/Çatalca works.[50] The Chataldzha/Çatalca line stretched about thirty miles from the Black Sea to the Sea of Marmara. Of this length, about half was manmade fortifications constructed in 1877–78 and renovated several times. There were trenches, machine gun positions and light artillery. Heavy artillery was situated to the rear, while the rest of the position consisted of natural obstacles, such as swamps, lakes and sea arms.[51]

The issue now pitted Bulgarian enthusiasm against Ottoman tenacity. On 8 November, the Ottoman government made a formal request for an armistice to the Balkan allies through Mikhail Giers (1856–1932), the Russian minister in Constantinople.[52] Bulgarian Tsar Ferdinand (1861–1948) received the request on 12 November. This coincided with the original Bulgarian plan. Had the Bulgarians responded positively to this request, they would have been in a good position to negotiate positive peace terms. Tsar Ferdinand, however, was determined to enter Constantinople triumphantly. On 14 November, Ferdinand ordered an attack on the Chataldzha/Çatalca lines. At the same time, he met with Generals Fichev and Savov. Both officers expressed reservations about undertaking an attack on these lines.[53] Savov, nevertheless, agreed to go to Chataldzha/Çatalca himself to discuss the attack with the commanders of the First and Third Armies before making a final recommendation. By this time, a new complication had emerged: cholera broke out in the Bulgarian army, causing significant losses. During the period from 17 November to 3 December at Chataldzha/Çatalca, 29,719 Bulgarian soldiers contracted cholera, of whom 4,615 died.[54] Approximately one out of six Bulgarian soldiers fell ill. Cholera afflicted the Ottoman forces as well, but they were close to their main medical resources in Constantinople. At the time of the attack, the Ottomans outnumbered the Bulgarians 190,000 to 176,081.[55] Obviously the Bulgarians had to attack under difficult circumstances. At his meeting with the commander in place, General Dimitriev, Savov ruminated: 'What should we do? We shall try, God willing. That way the Tsar, the Bulgarian nation and also you and I will have clean consciences before our posterity that we did everything humanly possible'. Dimitriev responded: 'Yes, history and posterity for the past 1,000 years cannot forgive Krum and Simeon for failing to attack and take Constantinople when they came here. Doubtless we would not be forgiven either'.[56] This exchange between the two Bulgarian generals reflected the nationalist ideology that motivated them and many of their subordinates.

General Dimitriev drew up the plan of attack. He proposed a general attack all along the Ottoman positions by both Bulgarian armies, with the First in the south and the Third in the north, supported by artillery during the entire attack.⁵⁷ There was no effort at tactical subtlety. Instead, after an artillery barrage, the Bulgarians intended to order their infantry to charge and seize the enemy's fortified positions. These were First World War tactics on the eve of the First World War.

In the meantime, the Ottomans transferred reinforcements from Anatolia and strengthened their positions at Chataldzha/Çatalca. Their forces were arrayed in three corps, with the First Corps in the north, the Second in the middle of the positions and the Third in the south. The Bulgarian attack began at 05.00h on 17 November. After some initial success, the Bulgarians found themselves pinned down all along the lines by Ottoman artillery fire. Fire from Ottoman warships in the Black Sea and the Sea of Marmara effectively supplemented the Ottoman artillery.⁵⁸ The Bulgarians lacked the means to counter the Ottoman naval fire. Most of the Bulgarian heavy artillery remained at Adrianople. One English observer from the Ottoman side commented that the Bulgarian attacks were 'the most futile and wasteful thing he had ever seen in his life'.⁵⁹ The Bulgarian effort continued into the next day. Nevertheless, the Bulgarians were unable to maintain a sustained presence in the Ottoman positions. After a bayonet attack, one Bulgarian battalion did succeed in surprising and occupying an Ottoman fortified position in the northern sector. The Bulgarians might have turned the entire line from this position. The Ottomans, however, discovered and soon ejected them by a sustained artillery barrage followed by a determined counterattack on the morning of the 18th. At about 14.00h on 18 November, Dimitriev ordered the attacks discontinued. The Bulgarians lost 1,482 killed, 9,120 wounded and 1,401 missing.⁶⁰ Ottoman casualties were probably fewer than 5,000 in total.⁶¹ Both Fichev and Savov attributed the Bulgarian attack's failure to the lack of modern tactical knowledge in the Bulgarian officer corps.⁶² Their ineffective artillery support posed another problem. While they enjoyed a slight superiority in the numbers of artillery pieces, their weapons were lighter than those of the Ottomans and lacked the range to provide cover for the attack and to counter the Ottoman artillery.⁶³ Also, the Ottoman artillery fire proved to be a formidable obstacle to the Bulgarian attack.⁶⁴ Both sides then settled into their trench positions.

The defeat at Chataldzha/Çatalca left the Bulgarian army in a perilous situation. On 22 November, General Dimitriev reported the combined strength of the Bulgarian First and Third Armies as 85,597 soldiers ready for battle.⁶⁵ The Bulgarian troops were benumbed by exhaustion, starved by an inadequate logistical system and plagued by cholera. Their offensive potential was finished, at least for the time being. No further Bulgarian operations at Chataldzha/Çatalca were possible. Savov at this point was prepared to accept peace at any price.[66] He telegraphed the government, 'It is necessary to do everything possible to secure an armistice'.[67] The Bulgarians were now ready to proceed with the armistice process,[68] which was confirmed on 3 December. Both sides remained in place until the renewal of fighting on 3 February 1913.

Conclusion

The Thracian campaign was the most important action of the First Balkan War. This was the only theatre that had the possibility to impart a decisive result to the war. The Thracian campaign consisted of three major engagements. The Bulgarians triumphed at Kırkkilise/Lozengrad and at Lüleburgaz-Pınarhisar and forced the Ottomans to retreat. Their successes were due to the sophistication of their strategic plan and the crudeness of their tactics, as well as the Ottoman forces' disorganization. In both instances, they failed to press their advantage to pursue the defeated Ottomans. Had they done so after either of these battles, they might have achieved a decisive victory. Similarly, an armistice after Lüleburgaz-Pınarhisar would have left the Bulgarian army largely intact and rested. The Bulgarian command and government could have anticipated a resolution of the conflict on very favourable terms.

But after two disastrous defeats, the Ottomans rallied to save Constantinople at Chataldzha/Çatalca. There they took advantage of shortened lines of communication and logistics and were able to capitalize on their superior numbers. At the end of the Thracian campaign, both sides were exhausted and for the time being were incapable of further military operations.

In the end, none of the battles were decisive. Minor engagements also occurred around Adrianople after it came under siege, and in southwestern Thrace. An armistice was signed on 3 December at Chataldzha/Çatalca, but subsequent negotiations in London failed to achieve a settlement. The war resumed on 30 January 1913. Many aspects of the pending wider conflict – the First World War – emerged during the Thracian campaign. The Bulgarians attempted a wide turning manoeuvre, not unlike the German *Schlieffen Plan*, with their armies. Both sides incurred heavy casualties due to the extensive use of artillery and machine guns. Neither the Bulgarian nor the Ottoman cavalry played an important role in the Thracian campaign. The Bulgarian cavalry, in fact, was extraordinarily inactive. The failure of the Bulgarian infantry attack against the entrenched Ottoman positions supported by effective artillery foreshadowed the futile allied offensive tactics employed on the western front in the First World War. The Bulgarians and Ottomans stalemated in trench warfare outside of Chataldzha/Çatalca. Disease played an important role in enervating both armies. One interesting aspect of the campaign was the appearance of the Ottoman navy, whose intervention in the Chataldzha/Çatalca battle represents rare cooperation between land and naval forces in a single engagement. Perhaps the most important aspect of the Thracian battles was the Ottoman military revival. After two devastating defeats, the Ottoman army rallied to save Constantinople. In doing so, it began a process that would culminate in victory at Gallipoli three years later.

Richard C. Hall is Professor of History Emeritus at Georgia Southwestern State University in Americus, Georgia. He is a veteran of the United States Army. He is the author of *Bulgaria's Road to the First World War* (East European Monographs, 1996), *The Balkan Wars 1912–1913: Prelude to the First World War* (Routledge, 2000), *Consumed by War: European Conflict in the 20th Century* (University Press of Kentucky, 2009), *Balkan Breakthrough: The Battle of Dobro Pole 1918* (Indiana University Press, 2010) and *The Modern Balkans: A History* (Reaktion Books, 2011).

Notes

1 This article is a revision of chapter 2 of my book, *The Balkan Wars 1912–1913: Prelude to the First World War* (London: Routledge, 2000).
2 Ministerstvo na Voinata, Shtab na Armiiata-voenno-istoricheska komisiya (ed.), *Voinata mezhdu Bŭlgariia i Turtsiia 1912–1913 god* [The War between Bulgaria and Turkey 1912–1913], Vol. I–VII (Sofia: Dŭrzhavna pechatnitsa, 1933–37), here Vol. II, 41. Hereafter referred to as *Voinata*.
3 Ibid., Vol. I, 363–71.
4 The figures for the First and Third Armies are from ibid., Vol. II, 657–58. The figure for the Second Army is from ibid., Vol. I, 566.
5 Alexander Vachkov, *The Balkan War 1912–1913* (Sofia: Angela, 2005), 94.
6 Ivan Fichev, *Balkanskata voina 1912–1913* [The Balkan War 1912–1913] (Sofia: Dŭrzhavna pechatnitsa, 1940), 89–91; Radko Dimitriev, *Treta armiia v Balkanskata voina 1912 godina* [The Third Army in the Balkan War 1912–1913] (Sofia: Armeiski voenno-izdatelski fond, 1922), 51.
7 Richard C. Hall, *Bulgaria's Road to the First World War* (Boulder, CO: East European Monographs, 1996), 104–7.
8 S. Toshev, *Pobedeni bez da budem biti* [Lost Victories] (Sofia: Armeiski voenno-izdatelski fond, 1924), 246–47.
9 Henry Dugard (Louis Thomas), *Histoire de la guerre contre les Turcs 1912–1913* (Paris: Les Marches de L'Est, 1913), 71. The titular commander in chief

of the Bulgarian forces was Tsar Ferdinand, who was not noted for his military demeanour or expertise.

10 These territories included the vilayets of Işkodra (Scutari), Kosovo, Manastir (Bitola, Monastir), Sēlanik (Salonika, Solun) and Yanya (Ioánnina, Janina).
11 Edward Erickson, *Defeat in Detail: The Ottoman Army in the Balkans, 1912–1913* (Westport, CT: Praeger, 2003), 78.
12 Ibid.
13 Ibid., 83.
14 Moukhtar Pacha [Muhtar Paşa], *Mon commandement au cours de la campagne de Balkans* (Paris: Berger-Levrault, 1913), 2.
15 Lionel James, *With the Conquered Turk: The Story of a Latter-Day Adventurer* (Boston, MA: Small, Maynard, 1913), 53–54.
16 Igor Despot, *The Balkan Wars in the Eyes of the Warring Parties: Perceptions and Interpretations* (Bloomington, IN: iUniverse, 2012), 82.
17 Ellis Ashmead-Bartlett, *With the Turks in Thrace* (New York: George H. Doran, 1913), 78.
18 Bulgaria used the Julian calendar until 14 April 1916. All dates, however, are given according to the Gregorian calendar (new style). Montenegro, the smallest Balkan ally, initiated hostilities on 8 October.
19 Georgi Markov, *Bŭlgariya v Balkanskiia sŭyuz sreshtu Osmanskata imperiia 1912–1913* [Bulgaria and the Balkan Alliance against the Ottoman Empire 1912–1913] (Sofia: Nauka i izkustvo, 1989), 43.
20 Erickson, *Defeat in Detail*, 85–86.
21 A British staff officer noted: 'Like the Japanese the Bulgarians have made a fetish of the bayonet'. Major P. Howell, *The Campaign in Thrace* (London: Hugh Rees Ltd., 1913), 156–57.
22 Despot, *The Balkan Wars*, 84.
23 Moukhtar Pacha, *Mon commandement au cours*, 43.
24 *Voinata*, Vol. II, 285, 313.
25 Bernard Paul Louis Boucabeille, *La guerre Turco-Balkanique, 1912–1913* (Paris: Librairie Chapelot, 1913), 155.
26 *Voinata*, Vol. II, 574.
27 Erickson, *Defeat in Detail*, 99–100.
28 National Archives, Washington, DC, War College Division, General Correspondence 1902–1920, RG 165–7277–213, p. 2. Lieutenant Sherman Miles, 'Captured Turkish Dispatch', 11 January 1913.
29 Markov, *Bŭlgariia v Balkanskiia sŭiuz*, 49–50.
30 *Voinata*, Vol. V [first part], 275–76.
31 Nikola Ivanov, *Spomeni* [Memoirs] (Sofia: Sv. Georgi Pobedonosets, 1996), 21.
32 Fichev, *Balkanskata voina 1912–1913*, 178.
33 Dimitŭr Azmanov, *Bŭlgarski visshi voenachalnitsi prez Balkanskata i Pŭrvata svetovna voina* [Bulgarian High Commanders in the Balkan and the First World War] (Sofia: Voenno izdatelstvo, 2000), 86.
34 Moukhtar Pacha, *Mon commandement au cours*, 49.
35 Kiril Kosev, *Podvigŭt* [The Valiant Deed] (Sofia: Voennoizdatelstvo, 1983), 67–88.

36 Markov, *Bŭlgariia v Balkanskiia sŭiuz*, 58.
37 *Voinata*, Vol. III, 9; Fichev, *Balkanskata voina 1912–1913*, 130–31.
38 *Voinata*, Vol. III, 74.
39 James, *With the Conquered Turk*, 166–67; Ashmead-Bartlett, *With the Turks*, 155.
40 Gustav von Hochwaechter, *Mit den Türken an der Front: Im Stabe Mahmud Muchtar Paschas* (Berlin: Ernst Siegfried Mittler und Sohn, 1913), 63.
41 Ashmead-Bartlett, *With the Turks*, 155. Along the same lines, see also Friedrich Immanuel, *Der Balkankrieg 1912–1913*, Vol. II (Berlin: Ernst Siegfried Mittler und Sohn, 1913–14), 4. Here Mahmoud refers to Moukhtar Pacha.
42 Markov, *Bŭlgariia v Balkanskiia sŭiuz*, 67.
43 Moukhtar Pacha, *Mon commandement au cours*, 134.
44 Ashmead-Bartlett, *With the Turks*, 145.
45 Howell, *The Campaign in Thrace*, 119.
46 *Voinata*, Vol. III, 525, 618–20.
47 Moukhtar Pacha, *Mon commandement au cours*, 138; Dimitriev, *Treta armiia v Balkanskata voina 1912 godina*, 296. The usually reliable Immanuel wrote of 'extraordinarily high' Turkish battlefield losses and gives the figure of 25,000; Immanuel, *Der Balkankrieg 1912–1913*, Vol. II, 37.
48 A good tactical criticism of the Bulgarian plan at Lüleburgaz is found in Howell, *The Campaign in Thrace*, 131–32. A corresponding analysis of Turkish mistakes is given in Hochwaechter, *Mit den Türken an der Front*, 66–67.
49 Hall, *Bulgaria's Road to the First World War*, 107–8.
50 *Voinata*, Vol. IV, 173.
51 For a description of the positions, see James, *With the Conquered Turk*, 318; Boucabeille, *La guerre Turco-Balkanique*, 178.
52 Narodno Sŭbranie (ed.), *Doklad na parlamentarnata izpitalna komisiia* [Report of the Parliamentary Investigation Commission] (Sofia: Dŭrzhavna pechatnitsa, 1918–19), 261–62, no. 3; Otto Hoetzsch (ed.), *Die internationalen Beziehungen im Zeitalter des Imperialismus: Dokumente aus den Archiven der zarischen und der provisorischen Regierungen*, 3rd ser. IV, Vol. I (Berlin: Steiniger, 1942), 231.
53 Fichev, *Balkanskata voina 1912–1913*, 200.
54 *Voinata*, Vol. IV, 625. Cholera first appeared among the retreating Ottoman troops. The casualties amounted to roughly one-sixth of the total Bulgarian force. See Noel Buxton, *With the Bulgarian Staff* (New York: Macmillan, 1913), 155–56; Moukhtar Pacha, *Mon commandement au cours*, 151–52.
55 *Voinata*, Vol. IV, 608.
56 Dimitriev, *Treta armiia v Balkanskata voina 1912 godina*, 317–18. Khan Krum (c. 803–814) and Tsar Simeon (893–927) were medieval Bulgarian rulers who attempted to take Constantinople.
57 Fichev, *Balkanskata voina 1912–1913*, 213–14.
58 Erickson, *Defeat in Detail*, 133.
59 James, *With the Conquered Turk*, 343.
60 *Voinata*, Vol. IV, 138, 608.
61 Erickson, *Defeat in Detail*, 135.

62 *Prilozhenie kŭm tom pŭrvi ot dokladna parlamentarnata izpitalna komisiia* [Supplement to the First Volume of the Parliamentary Investigation Commission] (Sofia: Dŭrzhavna pechatnitsa, 1918–19 [Savov]), 274; Fichev, *Balkanskata voina 1912–1913*, 221.
63 See, for example, *Voinata*, Vol. IV, 241; James, *With the Conquered Turk*, 347.
64 *Voinata*, Vol. IV, 397–98, 405.
65 Ibid., Vol. IV, 466. This figure did not include specialists such as engineers, railway men, etc.
66 Stoian Danev, 'Primirieto v Chataldzha na 20 noemvrii 1912' [The Armistice at Chataldzha 20 November 1912], *Rodina* III(2) (1940), 94–106, here 96.
67 Markov, *Bŭlgariia v Balkanskiia sŭiuz*, 149.
68 Hall, *Bulgaria's Road to the First World War*, 119.

Bibliography

Ashmead-Bartlett, Ellis. *With the Turks in Thrace*. New York: George H. Doran, 1913.
Azmanov, Dimitŭr. *Bŭlgarski visshi voenachalnitsi prez Balkanskata i Pŭrvata svetovna voina* [Bulgarian High Commanders in the Balkan and the First World War]. Sofia: Voenno izdatelstvo, 2000.
Boucabeille, Bernard Paul Louis. *La guerre Turco-Balkanique, 1912–1913*. Paris: Librairie Chapelot, 1913.
Buxton, Noel. *With the Bulgarian Staff*. New York: Macmillan, 1913.
Danev, Stoian. 'Primirieto v Chataldzha na 20 noemvrii 1912' [The Armistice at Chataldzha 20 November 1912]. *Rodina* III(2) (1940), 94–106.
Despot, Igor. *The Balkan Wars in the Eyes of the Warring Parties: Perceptions and Interpretations*. Bloomington, IN: iUniverse, 2012.
Dimitriev, Radko. *Treta armiia v Balkanskata voina 1912 godina* [The Third Army in the Balkan War 1912–1913]. Sofia: Armeiski voenno-izdatelski fond, 1922.
Dugard, Henry (Louis Thomas). *Histoire de la guerre contre les Turcs 1912–1913*. Paris: Les Marches de L'Est, 1913.
Erickson, Edward. *Defeat in Detail: The Ottoman Army in the Balkans, 1912–1913*. Westport, CT: Praeger, 2003.
Fichev, Ivan. *Balkanskata voina 1912–1913* [The Balkan War 1912–1913]. Sofia: Dŭrzhavna pechatnitsa, 1940.
Hall, Richard C. *Bulgaria's Road to the First World War*. Boulder, CO: East European Monographs, 1996.
———. *The Balkan Wars 1912–1913: Prelude to the First World War*. London: Routledge, 2000.
Hochwaechter, Gustav von. *Mit den Türken an der Front: Im Stabe Mahmud Muchtar Paschas*. Berlin: Ernst Siegfried Mittler und Sohn, 1913.
Hoetzsch, Otto (ed.). *Die internationalen Beziehungen im Zeitalter des Imperialismus: Dokumente aus den Archiven der zarischen und der provisorischen Regierungen*. 3rd ser. IV, Vol. I. Berlin: Steiniger, 1942.
Howell, P. Major. *The Campaign in Thrace*. London: Hugh Rees Ltd, 1913.

Immanuel, Friedrich. *Der Balkankrieg 1912–1913*. Vol. II. Berlin: Ernst Siegfried Mittler und Sohn, 1913–14.
Ivanov, Nikola. *Spomeni* [Memoirs]. Sofia: Sv. Georgi Pobedonosets, 1996.
James, Lionel. *With the Conquered Turk: The Story of a Latter-Day Adventurer*. Boston, MA: Small, Maynard, 1913.
Kosev, Kiril. *Podvigŭt* [The Valiant Deed]. Sofia: Voennoizdatelstvo, 1983.
Markov, Georgi. *Bŭlgariia v Balkanskiia sŭyuz sreshtu Osmanskata imperiia 1912–1913* [Bulgaria and the Balkan Alliance against the Ottoman Empire 1912–1913]. Sofia: Nauka i izkustvo, 1989.
Ministerstvo na Voinata, Shtab na Armiiata-voenno-istoricheska komisiia (ed.). *Voinata mezhdu Bŭlgariia i Turtsiia 1912–1913 god* [The War between Bulgaria and Turkey 1912–1913]. Vol. I–VII. Sofia: Dŭrzhavna pechatnitsa, 1933–37.
Moukhtar Pacha [Muhtar Paşa]. *Mon commandement au cours de la campagne de Balkans*. Paris: Berger-Levrault, 1913.
Narodno Sŭbranie (ed.). *Doklad na parlamentarnata izpitalna komisiia* [Report of the Parliamentary Investigation Commission]. Sofia: Dŭrzhavna pechatnitsa, 1918–1919.
Prilozhenie kŭm tom pŭrvi ot dokladna parlamentarnata izpitalna komisiia [Supplement to the First Volume of the Parliamentary Investigation Commission]. Sofia: Dŭrzhavna pechatnitsa, 1918–19 (Savov).
Toshev, S. *Pobedeni bez da budem biti* [Lost Victories]. Sofia: Armeiski voenno-izdatelski fond, 1924.
Vachkov, Alexander. *The Balkan War 1912–1913*. Sofia: Angela, 2005.

 7

Morale, Ideology and the Barbarization of Warfare among Greek Soldiers
Spyridon Tsoutsoumpis

Rebecca West noted in her classic travel book *Black Lamb and Grey Falcon*, first published in 1941, 'violence was indeed all I knew of the Balkans'.[1] West was not alone in this observation. Maria Todorova has commented that, for much of the twentieth century, violence was 'the leitmotiv of the Balkans'.[2] This perception of the region was far from novel; however, it became embedded in popular and academic narratives only during the Balkan Wars, a conflict that progressively came to exemplify all that was peculiar to the peninsula: mindless, atavistic violence, lust for power and political philistinism. Several weeks after the outbreak of the First Balkan War, the British liberal magazine *The Nation* argued characteristically that the war proved that 'none of the Balkan peoples have yet fully emerged from the state of savagery to which Turkish rule had condemned them'.[3] Almost a century later, the tone had hardly changed. An article in *Time* magazine, aptly titled 'The Balkan Wars: 100 Years Later, a History of Violence', reminded its readers of Winston Churchill's witticism, 'The Balkans ... generate more history than they can locally consume',[4] and argued that the Balkan Wars were unlike any other conflict waged in Europe and must be understood as a sectarian conflict analogous to those waged in the more remote areas of the Middle East and Africa.

This imagery shaped the representation of the protagonists of the war: the combat soldiers. If the British Tommies were 'lions led by donkeys', the Balkan soldiers were at best childlike peasants,[5] ignorant of the issues that were at stake during the war, and at worst semi-primitive rustics driven to frenzy by jingoist leaders. Accordingly, the violence of the war and the tenacity of the soldiers were attributed to the region's premodern culture. These views were summarized by George Kennan in his introduction to the 1993 re-edition of the Carnegie Report: 'the strongest motivating factor involved in the Balkan wars was ... aggressive nationalism. But that nationalism, as it manifested itself on the field of battle, drew on deeper traits of character inherited, presumably, from a distant tribal past'.[6] The permeability of such views, coupled with the powerful political connotations involved in studying the period and a probable fear that a discussion of the combatants' attitudes would be detrimental to national narratives of the war, has led historians to steer clear of any discussion of the soldiers' experiences and to focus their attention instead on strategy and politics. As a result, the face of battle in the Balkan Wars remains, for the most part, obscure. Very little is known about how soldiers experienced the war and combat, and how they tried to deal with the exertions of campaigning, the fear of death and the act of killing. At the same time, even though historians have studied extensively the various forms that violence took and its political connotations, we still know very little about how soldiers were induced to commit violence against civilians and how they rationalized such actions.

The present chapter addresses this shortcoming in the existing historiography by focusing on the experiences of Greek combat soldiers and officers. The chapter turns to a source that has been largely neglected by historians – the personal testimonies of soldiers, including memoirs, diaries and letters. The first memoirs and histories of the war appeared immediately after the peace agreement of 1913. The majority of these accounts were written by middle-class men and were published in Athens. The short distance between the war and the publication of these memoirs kept them largely free of the problems of memory and hindsight that affect this type of literature. Nevertheless, these sources were not entirely free of problems, as audience expectations and political concerns led many memoirists to downplay the more disagreeable aspects of their experience. The public's fascination with the wars abated during the Great War. It reached its nadir after the Asia Minor debacle of 1922. In the following decades, the Balkan Wars remained largely *terra incognita*.

The break-up of Yugoslavia and the rise of Balkan nationalisms during the 1990s reinvigorated interest in the conflict and resulted in the publication of several scholarly studies and personal testimonies, including two invaluable edited collections of diaries and letters, Lydia Triha's *Imerologia kai Grammata apo to Metopo* and Petros Papapolyviou's *Ipodouloi Eleftherotai Adelfon Alitroton*. The first volume contains testimonies of privates and officers from 'Old Greece'[7] deposited in the

Hellenic Literary and Historical Archive (ELIA) in Athens, while the second volume is a compilation of the testimonies of Greek Cypriot volunteers.[8] Despite their immediacy, such sources are not entirely unproblematic; letters are often composed with a particular audience in mind – parents, spouses, siblings. This leads the writers to conform to their readers' expectations and thus to consciously omit events that they might find inappropriate.[9] Diaries are free of such concerns; however, the proximity to the events often hindered the soldiers' ability to reflect on and reconstruct coherent narratives of their experiences in their diaries.[10] Despite these problems, such sources provide invaluable insights into the experience of the soldiers when they discuss taboo issues – looting, rape, the killing of prisoners – that memoirists avoided.

A careful reading of these accounts can facilitate a more nuanced understanding of the experiences of the men who fought in the war, the ways in which they understood the war and the factors that sustained them through hardship and led them to risk their lives and ultimately to break the foremost social taboo, against killing. Nationalist ideology provided an important impetus; however, the war challenged the ideological and cultural preconceptions of the soldiers. Hardship, the anonymity of modern warfare and the tenacious resistance of the non-Greek populations came as a shock to a soldiery that was expecting a swift war of liberation. As enthusiasm receded, soldiers sought new ways to address the strain of warfare; religion, ideas of honour and primary group ties came to play an increasingly important role in that respect. At the same time, the nature of the operations led to a mounting brutalization of the soldiers. War was increasingly narrated in explicitly racialized terms that characterized the enemy combatants and population as the absolute 'other'. Such views served to facilitate the widespread atrocities that were committed.

'The Honourable Struggle for Our Nation's Great Ideal': The Role and Nuances of Ideology

Nationalist ideology played an important role in the motivation of the Greek soldier. To understand its importance and effect, one must first understand the social, cultural and political values of the society in which the soldiers were born and which asked them to sacrifice their lives in its defence. The importance of nationalism cannot be overemphasized in any discussion of early twentieth-century Greece. Indeed, until the Asia Minor debacle of 1922, the energies and aspirations of politicians and civilians alike were focused on the realization of the Greek national credo, the *Megali Idea* [Great Idea], which advocated the union of all formerly Hellenic lands in a Greater Greek kingdom.

The content of the *Megali Idea* is particularly elusive. For the greater part of the nineteenth century, the *Megali Idea* had strong religious overtones. Greek territorial expansion was associated with the triumph of the Orthodox East against both Islam and the degenerate and heretical West, while Russia was seen as the foremost ally that would facilitate the triumph of Hellenism.[11] Several political thinkers rejected expansionist nationalism, however, and instead claimed that the natural superiority of Greek culture would eventually bring the other Balkan nationalities to the cause of Hellenism and even Hellenize the Ottoman Empire from within.[12]

Nevertheless, the defeat of 1897 in the Greco-Ottoman War and the rise of rival Balkan nationalisms led to important realignments. The *Megali Idea* became more secular, while policymakers and intellectuals looked increasingly for inspiration to British and French imperialism. The Greeks viewed themselves as an imperial nation whose mission in the Balkan peninsula differed little from those of France and Britain in East Asia and North Africa, bringing order, culture and Christianity to populations that were seen as backward, savage and, despite their European origins, essentially Asiatic. Evidence of these views could be seen in the unanimous support for the British war effort during the Second Boer War (1899–1902).[13] Students from the University of Athens held vigils for the British war dead, while the university's rector hailed them as martyrs fallen for the triumph of civilization in the 'Dark Continent'.[14]

Irredentist ideas were fused with Social Darwinist arguments to produce an ideology that, according to Mark Mazower, 'verged on a sort of political messianism'.[15] Intellectuals such as Ion Dragoumis (1878–1920), the doyen of Greek nationalists, and Neoklis Kazazis (1849–1936), the rector of Athens University and founder of the irredentist society *Ellinismos*, gave to the *Megali Idea* an almost millenarian tinge. Kazazis and Dragoumis lauded warfare as a way to regenerate the nation's racial stock and cure the evils of feminism and socialism. Kazazis embraced a Social Darwinian view of warfare. In a series of influential lectures, published under the title *Ten Homilies to the Greek Youth*, he noted that the war was the only way of stemming the process of national degeneration and the eventual submission of Greece to the hardier Slavic races. War, according to Kazazis, 'determines ... the rise and the decline of nations'; it is 'the single most important factor in the evolution of humankind ... through war nations attain the spiritual and physical virility that can lead them to progress and prosperity'.[16]

Kazazis called on the youth to imitate the ancient Greeks and Romans, who viewed death on the field of battle as 'the most sacred act', arguing that war can be won only 'through will, the determination to die, to sacrifice oneself'.[17]

These ideas were reflected in the wartime rhetoric. Upon the announcement of hostilities, the minister of foreign affairs declared to an enthusiastic parliament that the war was a 'crusade of the Orthodox states of the Haemus peninsula'. The Balkan nations thus brought the fight to the 'Asiatic conquerors' who once 'threatened Europe, reaching the gates of Vienna'. Yet this was not solely a religious venture; it was also 'a crusade for progress, civilization and freedom'.[18] Premier Eleftherios Venizelos (1864–1936) similarly declared the war 'a struggle for civilization'.[19] In October 1912, 120,000 men crossed the Greco-Turkish border in order to realize the dream of a Greater Greece.[20]

These ideas had an important influence on the conduct of the war, for they shaped the way Greek officers and soldiers understood the war's aims, and perceived and treated their opponents. Kostadinos Hristofidis, a law student who interrupted his studies to volunteer, wrote, in a letter to his family: 'nationality and not religion is what divides one race from the other in this world, and national fanaticism is much stronger than religious fanaticism'.[21] Hristofidis was not irreligious; several members of his family were clerics, and he noted repeatedly in his correspondence that his faith helped him to endure some of the worse aspects of the war.[22] However, his letters also reveal the waning influence of religion in the way Greek soldiers perceived the war and the growing impact of radical nationalism and Social Darwinian views. Hristofidis admitted that war and killing contradicted the teachings of the Church. However, he considered war intrinsic to humankind: 'national egotism and the instinct of self-preservation, these two great forces that are responsible ... for moving one race against the other, will never cease to exist'.[23] For men like Hristofidis, the war was a struggle between Hellenic civilization, which was described in classical and Western terms, and Asiatic barbarism, represented by both the Ottoman Turks and the Bulgarians. Alexandros Poulopoulos, an infantry private and Leeds University graduate, noted in his diary that his commanding officer, Captain Aristotelis Kouvelis, said to the men in his platoon: 'our duty is to fight in defence of civilization, and those who claim that our enemies are no different from us are wrong, for in the present case we wage a war for civilization'.[24]

These ideas resonated even with men who had little liking for or inclination towards army life, such as Anastasios Stratigopoulos, an Athenian middle-class writer with liberal views. Stratigopoulos noted in his memoir that his first feeling upon enlisting was one of 'exasperation ... because I was being deprived of my independence'.[25] Stratigopoulos disliked the army and ridiculed the jingoist rhetoric of the regular officers, whose pro-German ideas he disparaged. Stratigopoulos, like many other middle-class Greeks, was an ardent Anglophile and a Germanophobe who saw militarism as a threat to European civilization; he was also highly interested in Ottoman culture and architecture. However, he did not doubt the necessity or the justness of the war. Stratigopoulos viewed the Balkan Wars as a cause of humanity and civilization: 'I bore arms to defend the rights of humanity', he noted, and 'this eased the moral burden that had been troubling me since I joined the army'.[26] This view was reinforced by the fact that the war was taking place in an area that had profound classical associations. Stratigopoulos fought in the Aegean campaign that resulted in the liberation of the eastern Aegean islands. He noted how he wept when he first caught sight of Lesvos and realized he would take part in the liberation of 'a land of greatness immemorial, the land of Sappho, of Alcaeus, of Arion, of Terpandros, of Pittakos'.[27]

Stratigopoulos's references to classical Greece were far from uncommon. Middle-class officers and rank-and-file soldiers alike alluded in their diaries and letters to the classical associations of the liberated territories. Pella in Macedonia and Dodona in Epirus became stopovers for educated soldiers and officers. Philipos Dragoumis noted poetically in his diary of the Epirus campaign: 'a few miles after Theriakisi, the ravine ends. There is the village of Alpohori and next to it Ancient Dodona. I wonder what the oak leaves presage as they overhear the echoes of this war we modern Greeks wage'.[28] Some men spent their free time inspecting classical ruins and undertaking their own amateur field excavations. Captain Konstadinos Vasos noted proudly in his diary: 'I discovered ... a life-size ancient statue depicting a young rider as well as some scattered columns and vessels'.[29] Soldiers who fought on the Macedonian front were obsessed with locating the birthplace of Alexander the Great and discovering parallels between the modern inhabitants and their ancestors.[30] These associations reinforced the Greek territorial claims, as well as the view of the war as a clash between East and West, civilization and barbarity.[31]

These men saw themselves not only as liberators of their oppressed brethren but also as nation builders who were initiating a new era for Hellenism, in which the war was only the first step. Dragoumis noted in his diary: 'our highest ideal ... is the creation of a new civilization here in the east'.[32] Cultural progress was going to be accompanied by material progress that would render Greece a major regional power. In his memoir, published a few months after the end of the war, Lieutenant Miltiadis Lidorikis, a lawyer and politician in civilian life, described Macedonia as the 'New Promised Land', which had been laid to waste by Turkish mismanagement and the slovenly attitudes of the Greek Macedonians, who were 'ignorant and accustomed to bending their heads'. The restoration of Macedonia to its former glory was going to be achieved through the settlement of Greeks from Greece proper, who would teach and supervise the locals.[33]

These ideas provided powerful motivation for the soldiers. It is telling that enlistment far exceeded the goal of 120,000 men set by the Ministry of War. Volunteers from abroad and Greece were actually turned away by the army authorities. A nineteen-year-old law student wrote in a letter to his father after enlisting:

> You shouldn't be angry with me for enlisting, because what else did I learn in the school you sent me to but to love our fatherland ... and if we who are young ... and can better understand our duty to the fatherland do not join the honourable struggle for the realization of our nation's great ideal, who then will fight?[34]

Ideology was not only important in the enlistment process but also helped men to rationalize loss, killing and hardship as necessary means to a higher end. Artillery officer Nikolaos Petimezas noted in his diary of the Epirus campaign that 'it is a pity that human beings lose their lives in this way. Yet, these monsters must leave ... our beautiful fatherland'.[35] Hristodoulos Sozos, the mayor of Lemesos, who volunteered and served as a private soldier, wrote to his family:

> I am a soldier and therefore I have to suffer all kinds of hardship. I lack sleep ... I am cold; I do all the chores soldiers have to do and risk my life at the front line. This is war ... God is on our side, because He knows that we are in the service of an idea. It is really strange ... how all of us withstand the hunger, the marches and the lack of sleep. However, the power of the idea and the love of our fatherland warm our hearts.[36]

Nevertheless, as the war progressed there was a change in what the ideology entailed. In the first weeks of the war, the armed forces and the individual soldiers kept a reserved stance. In a series of proclamations addressed to the non-Greek population, the military authorities presented the war as a civilizing mission that would be beneficial for citizens, regardless of their creed. An army proclamation stated that the 'overthrow of the Turkish authorities in the occupied territories will bring freedom, progress and civilization to all the inhabitants of Macedonia ... all the Macedonians, irrespective of language and religion, will enjoy the same rights under Greek rule'.[37] Soldiers who were caught looting or maltreating civilians were severely punished. On one occasion, Prince Constantine (1868–1923) attacked a group of looters with his whip and encouraged officers to treat looters with the utmost strictness.[38]

These attitudes were not dictated solely by a sense of military propriety but also by the need to demonstrate Greece's capacity for carrying out its civilizing mission. For the Greeks, the Balkan peninsula was, as William Miller noted, a 'Hellenic Peninsula'.[39] The influence of Hellenism might have receded after centuries of Ottoman rule, but it remained *terra nostra*. The task of Greece was to redeem the peninsula's inhabitants, whatever their religious and linguistic affiliation, from their current state of savagery and remould them as citizens of a Greater Greece. Ethnographic, historical and linguistic arguments were used to support these views. Greek academics and political thinkers argued that the Albanians were not a separate nationality, as their alleged ancestors, the Pelasgians, were racially related to the ancient Greeks. The only possible course for the Albanians was absorption into a Greater Greece and eventual assimilation. Slavic peasants were similarly presented as pure Greeks who had lost their language as a result of Ottoman oppression and negligence but had remained steadfastly Greek, nevertheless.[40]

Such views exercised a powerful influence on the way soldiers regarded these populations. The poem by Antonios Malliaros, a Cretan volunteer who fought in both wars, encapsulates these views. Malliaros described the Muslim Albanians as 'barbarians' who 'trudged like goats from one rock to the other' in their mountain homeland and spoke a strange and barbaric language. Yet the Albanians were redeemable, as Malliaros noted, they were 'our brothers',[41] whom the Turks forced to renounce their language and faith, but 'the time has come to be redeemed / they will find again their language and their faith'.[42]

Many soldiers influenced by these views were puzzled by the hostility of these populations to the Greek army.[43] Giorgios Paraskevopoulos, a captain in the 12th Infantry Regiment, was surprised by the presence of Albanian soldiers and irregulars in the Ottoman army. When he came upon a group of Turkish officers after the battle of Giannitsa, he asked 'if any of them was Albanian', and when a young lieutenant answered positively, Paraskevopoulos berated him for fighting on the wrong side: '"how can you fight alongside them", I asked him, "your position is right here with us"'.[44] Soldiers in western Macedonia were equally surprised by the hostile mood of Slavic peasants. 'They are savage and inhospitable', noted an infantry soldier, 'they see the Greek soldiers as no different from the Turks'.[45]

'This Is a War of Extermination': The Combat Experience and the Barbarization of Warfare

The idea of the civilizing mission was also accompanied by an intense sense of cultural superiority. The assimilationist policies of the Greeks paid no heed to the national aspirations and cultures of the non-Greek inhabitants of the new lands, whom they viewed as intrinsically inferior. This opinion was reinforced by the army's encounters with the new lands and their inhabitants. Turkish towns and their inhabitants were seen as prime examples of the East–West antithesis. The towns were depicted as chaotic, dirty and lacking the rational planning of modern European towns. Lieutenant P. Hatzihristos noted, upon entering the liberated city of Elassona: 'we finally reached the town. This is a proper Turkish town, with its mosques … its cobbled streets, its narrow, dirty roads. Every single thing is Turkish'.[46] Major Leonidas Paraskevopoulos similarly noted, upon entering Ioannina: 'the town is absolutely disgusting, as is every other Turkish town'.[47]

Religion was also used to highlight the differences. Islam was viewed as backward and barbaric.[48] In the collective imagination of the Greek soldiers, Muslim clerics played a role similar to that attributed to Catholic priests by the German army of 1914.[49] German Protestant soldiers saw the Catholic priests as unscrupulous extremists who incited the citizenry of Belgium to acts of fanatical hatred against the German army.[50] Muslim 'hodjas', a generic term for Muslim clerics, were similarly regarded as fanatics who swayed the ignorant mass of peasants to resist and encouraged them to brutalize captured Greek soldiers. A Greek army doctor noted: 'the villages near Kozani resisted tenaciously … that was what their naïve hodjas ordained. These pitiable servants of Islam should have followed the lead of the brave Turkish army that took to its heels'.[51] Mosques were thought to be dens of conspiracy where clerics hid arms and planned insurrections, while minarets, like church towers in the First World War, were understood to be hiding spots for snipers. Stories about clerics who led peasants to revolt or sniped at soldiers abounded. The most famous story was that of the two Muslim clerics of the town of Elassona who tried to stall the advance of a Greek unit by barricading themselves in the minaret and shooting wildly at the mass of soldiers. According to another version, they were targeting Crown Prince Constantine.[52] Such stories were, for the most part, inaccurate and were disavowed by the army authorities, who were afraid that they might lead to atrocities, but to no avail. Greek soldiers brutalized and in some cases shot Muslim clerics for instigating resistance in western Macedonia. The soldiers also plundered and set fire to mosques across Macedonia and Epirus.[53]

Most of the testimonies argue that patriotism played little role in Muslim resistance, pointing out that instead villagers were persuaded to resist by the fanatical clerics' promises of sexual gratification and culinary pleasures in 'the Muslim Elysian Fields', as infantry private Isidoros Fragiskos ironically noted in his memoir. These representations served to rob the Muslim villagers' resistance of any patriotic or noble motives in the eyes of the Greeks. To them, the opposition was instead the product of superstition, stupidity and bigoted fanaticism regarding the forces of progress represented by the Greek army.[54]

Perceptions of Turkish savagery were further coloured by the actions of the peasantry. As the Greek army marched into Macedonia, Christian turned against Muslim, and vice versa, and old hatreds rose to the surface, resulting in appalling levels of interpersonal violence and the widespread settling of scores. These events had a profound effect on the mentality of Greek soldiers, as they seemed to validate the worst popular stereotypes about Turkish barbarity. Dragoumis noted in his diary that a group of Turkish prisoners 'looked more like beasts than humans'.[55] Such views were common among rank-and-file soldiers, who destroyed mosques, attacked Muslim civilians and humiliated them publicly by making them step on their fezzes.[56] Ioannis Pigasios, a Greek Cypriot doctor who was a volunteer in the Greek army, was reprimanded by a soldier for showing interest in a group of Turkish prisoners. The soldier told Pigasios that several doctors had been killed by prisoners, before he unleashed a tirade against a group of Turkish prisoners, exclaiming that they 'were beasts and not human beings. What's the chance of a Turk being a decent human being?'[57] Pigasios's views progressively came to reflect those of his fellow fighters. In a later entry, he noted that '[the Turks] are despicable and savage beings'.[58]

The perceived duplicitousness and lack of humanity of the Turks was further confirmed by the ruses allegedly used by enemy soldiers. Diaries and letters abound with stories of enemy soldiers calling out in Greek to isolated soldiers, pretending to be wounded comrades or officers who had lost their way. Stories about soldiers who feigned surrender, only to murder their would-be captors, were also quite common.[59] Such stories were transferred *mutatis mutandis* to the Second Balkan War, with the Bulgarians taking the part of the Turks. Determining the truthfulness of such stories is a challenge. Some of the wildest rumours, concerning, for example, the poisoning of wells, the killing of Greek doctors and medics by prisoners and later the practices of Bulgarian soldiers trained to extract prisoners' eyes with special tools, were patently false.[60]

Mutilation and torture did take place, but on a much smaller scale than suggested. Few authors actually met victims of such practices, while references to such instances are largely absent from the exceptionally well-documented official history of the war.[61]

Nevertheless, rumour, myth and hearsay were not enough to trigger barbarous acts against enemy soldiers and civilians. The barbarization of warfare was a slow, gradual process that was shaped as much by ideology, myth and rumour as by the everyday experience of the men. The 'horrible Turk' and his capacity for savagery were staples of prewar popular culture, and such views were augmented by the memory of the 1897 defeat. 'We are weak and timid', noted a reserve infantry officer, 'they are strong and powerful … and this sense of weakness … deprives us of our courage and masculinity'.[62] These representations had a direct impact on the soldiers' attitudes. In the first weeks of the war, most soldiers were in a constant state of agitation. The terrible physical exertion of campaigning, the lack of appropriate clothing, greatcoats and boots in many units and the suffering from hunger and disease exacerbated the fear and excitability of the soldiers.[63] Stratis Ktenaveas noted in his memoir that 'the men were in such a state of mind that … a single rumour was enough to cause panic'.[64] Soldiers on guard duty shot at each other and at friendly patrols, and sometimes entire units disintegrated upon hearing a few shots being fired or getting rumours of an enemy advance.[65] The nature of warfare and modern weaponry played an equally important role in the creation and spreading of rumours. The horrific effects of shrapnel that pulverized faces and destroyed limbs touched deep anxieties about masculinity and contributed to widespread fears about mutilation.[66] The encounter of the soldiers with the corpses of fallen soldiers that had been unearthed and mauled by the elements and beasts gave further credence to such rumours.[67]

The combination of physical exertion, anxiety and fear led to a progressive numbing of sensibility among the soldiers, who fell prey to the wildest rumours and vented their frustration by brutalizing civilians and prisoners.[68] Many soldiers even broke the foremost taboo against scavenging corpses. 'Man becomes a beast during war', noted Petimezas, who was shocked by these acts: 'many [corpses] are left completely naked'.[69] Rumour, myth, ideology and everyday experience therefore resulted in the creation of a new, brutalized mindset. Ktenaveas noted in his memoir: 'the continuous marches … the combat and the constant clashes have led the men a long way from their civilian beliefs. The life they led until recently was now forgotten'.[70]

Two weeks after the initiation of hostilities, Lieutenant Ioannis Tsigaridis wrote to his father:

> This war is sacred and noble ... but it is also destructive. We have prevented the men from looting thus far with great difficulty, but often we are not able to stop them at all .... Here in Servia ... the soldiers ... broke into the Turkish houses, which they looted thoroughly, setting fire to some of them.[71]

The events described by Tsigaridis were not isolated incidents. Indeed, the brutalization of the soldiers had started in some cases to impair discipline and threaten the cohesion of some units. Captain Dimitrios Daras, an officer in the 8th Evzone (Highland) Regiment, wrote to his family two months after the Serbia incident that 'several units have become uncontrollable and they have almost disintegrated, God help us if this war goes on'.[72] The barbarization of warfare was not limited to looting. Alarmed by the setbacks faced by the Ottoman army, Muslim villagers took up arms against the advancing Greek army. The Greeks met with particularly fierce resistance in the Kailaria area of western Macedonia and in southern Albania.[73] Guerrillas harried patrols and supply lines and attacked Greek villages. In many cases, isolated Greek soldiers were lynched by Muslim villagers who took their arms and clothes and left their corpses exposed as a warning.[74]

Irregular warfare waged by Ottoman army deserters, peasants and enemy irregulars blurred the lines not only between combatant and civilian, but also between legitimate and illegitimate forms of violence. As a result, soldiers progressively saw civilians as legitimate targets and used increasingly violent methods to pacify the countryside. Rumours and narratives of civilian atrocities, particularly mutilation, played an important role in further brutalizing the men. The association of these practices with the enemy civilians gave an almost apocalyptic tone to the war, leading soldiers to perceive the conflict as a Manichean struggle between good and evil. An officer who took part in the campaign noted that after encountering the mutilated bodies of their comrades, 'the men ... decided to turn this area into Sodom and Gomorrah'.[75] The military authorities also endorsed progressively harsher measures against civilians. Irregulars were shot on the spot without a trial. The killing of prisoners, which was initially rare, became customary. By the time the Greek army had reached Albania, where it again met resistance, such practices had become the norm.[76] An infantry officer noted in December 1912: 'today I fully understood the savagery of the war. Women and children were crying. The villagers were being mowed down like sparrows. The houses were all alight from one end to the other. Hideous, hideous'.[77]

These experiences created a continuum of violence, reshaping the war from a liberal imperialist venture into a ruthless struggle for civilization. Such views reached hysterical proportions during the Second Balkan War, which was progressively seen to be a racial struggle against an enemy that was perceived as less than human. Soldiers referred to the Bulgarians as bears – *arkoudiaraioi* – and attributed to the Bulgarian soldiers and peasants almost superhuman capacities of endurance and a perverse taste for cruelty. Many educated soldiers attributed the barbarity of Bulgarians to their alleged Asiatic origins. They described them as a degenerate 'mongrel' race, part Slavic, part Asiatic, and derided them as Tatars and descendants of Krum, the Turkic chieftain who led the Bulgarian tribes against the Byzantine Empire in the ninth century.[78] These men saw the conflict as a Darwinian struggle for survival, 'a struggle of extermination that will judge which race will survive in Macedonia and which race will perish'.[79]

The understanding of the war as a fight for civilization served to undermine the accepted rules of warfare, leading to an ever greater acceleration of atrocities, because the enemy was not simply a rival military force but represented the entire enemy culture and civilian population identified as the absolute 'other'.[80] Tsigaridis wrote to his father: 'the fanaticism and savagery of both sides is unheard of. We destroy all that is Bulgarian and they destroy anything that is Greek'.[81] Such attitudes were further exacerbated by the fear of irregulars. The experience in Epirus and western Macedonia had created a precedent.[82] Greek soldiers and officers were haunted by the spectre of Bulgarian irregulars, whose capacity for cruelty and martial abilities had rendered them infamous in prewar literature.[83] Memoirs of the Macedonian struggle[84] and propagandist tracts described the Bulgarian guerrillas as savages who gouged out prisoners' eyes and mutilated their faces and limbs. According to one author, the savagery of the 'kaffirs of Africa pales' in comparison with Bulgarian barbarity.[85] The army took ruthless punitive measures. Armed civilians were shot on the spot, while communities that harboured insurgents were bombed and put to the torch. Soldiers were encouraged to take no prisoners. A Cypriot volunteer noted in his diary: 'our officers do not want prisoners; the major orders us to kill them all; he constantly tells us to kill the bears'.[86]

The brutalization of the soldiers reached extraordinary proportions as, hardened by hunger, adverse weather conditions and months of fighting, many descended into outright criminal activities. Soldiers roamed the countryside and held entire villages hostage in return for payment of ransom. Rape, theft and individual robbery were also common despite the efforts of the military authorities to curtail them.[87] The brutalization of the men led to a breakdown in discipline. An artillery officer noted that 'the terrifying escalation of passion, the brutalization of the soldiers from the continuous combat and the commanding voice of the instinct of self-preservation had set aside reason, mercy and even discipline'.[88]

'We Are Mere Numbers': The Changing Face of Morale

These experiences had a profound effect on soldiers' perceptions and morale. Most Greeks imagined that the war would be a swift, adventurous affair. These expectations were shaped by the educational system, jingoist literature and the press, which presented the war as a romantic affair where the lone hero or a small group of comrades faced their opponents in chivalrous face-to-face combat.[89] The protracted period of relative peace in the area and in the rest of Europe also contributed to the shaping of such expectations. Greece was not unique in this respect. The extension of public education and the creation of citizen armies exposed a growing number of Europeans to militaristic ideas. The press, popular culture and the educational system promoted an idealized image of the war as a noble, chivalric adventure, a notion that was adopted with enthusiasm by a great part of the British, German and French publics.[90] These representations exercised a powerful influence, even over men who were opposed to the war, like P. Hatzihristos, a middle-class professional with social democratic views, who noted on the eve of the war:

> War ... despite all the horrors ... has an almost mystical power, a mysterious attraction that draws you in. It inflames a strange feeling that makes you want to taste the excitement of combat, the hardship and the suffering of campaign life. Now, you will be able to see and feel and live all the things you read about as a child, all the stories you heard and you fantasized about and maybe, if you are lucky enough, you will come back alive and share your own tales ... with an admiring audience.[91]

Such romantic expectations were soon challenged. The Balkan Wars 'marked a new quality of warfare'[92] that was characterized by the rising significance of artillery fire and the gradual waning of close-quarter combat. A contemporary medical report noted that 'infantry fire is diminishing in seriousness, artillery fire is increasing. The wounds made by shrapnel were always severe; bones were pulverized, tissues torn, thorax and cranium crushed'.[93] Soldiers quickly discovered that victory was not determined by pluck and bayonet but rather by the artillery, the new king of the battlefield, and by the machine guns that were used with lethal skill by all belligerents and demonstrated to the men the limitations of individual heroism in the face of superior firepower. The effects of modern weaponry on the bodies of men were shocking even to seasoned professional soldiers like Paraskevopoulos, who wrote: 'it was horrible when we reached the enemy positions ... amputated legs, scattered brains, corpses lying, horrible. No matter how much I write I simply cannot describe it ... horror'.[94]

These experiences undermined heroic imaginings of war and martial masculinity. Often soldiers found it impossible to convey the realities of combat. Paraskevopoulos wrote to his wife: 'you have to be here to understand what this really is. Reading a letter is simply not enough ... one cannot understand what this is ... unless one takes part in it'.[95] An infantry soldier noted similarly in his diary after the battle of Kilkis: 'it is impossible to describe what happened'.[96] The sense of alienation and awe found in many testimonies is reminiscent of soldier writing of the Great War.[97] Combat was seen as a supernatural phenomenon that had spiralled out of control and attained its own independent existence, devouring everything that stood in its way. Men were particularly shocked by the effects of shelling; one soldier described shelling as 'something supernatural, the wrath of God, you feel that you have suddenly diminished, that you can't do anything to defend yourself'.[98] In some accounts, battle attains an unreal, almost dreamlike quality akin to that of a film, where one is a spectator unable to act or to influence the course of events. A chaplain in the Fifth Division described the shelling during the Battle of Kilkis as something 'out of a motion picture'.[99] Combat, according to the same author, had a similarly unreal quality: 'I felt like a sleepwalker, as if I was drugged or drunk ... there was no fear, no emotion, only drunkenness, and a state of unconsciousness'.[100]

Many men were further disappointed both by the brutality of counter-partisan warfare – Petimezas noted in his diary: 'the war in Epirus has become a disgusting bandit hunt that teaches us nothing and is beyond any tactical rules'[101] – and by the realities of army life that valued obedience and order more highly than individual initiative and personal bravery. Skandalakis noted in his memoir:

> Those who went to the war expecting to experience a superior way of life were bitterly disappointed ... contemporary warfare has nothing appealing about it ... the rigid spirit of discipline crushes the combatant's soul, dissolves all sense of individuality into the collective and subjugates initiative to the rules ... [The soldier] ... is a machine and not a human being.[102]

Skandalakis further wrote that the sense of accomplishment the soldiers derived from combat and hand-to-hand fighting had been diminished, because combat was waged from afar against an enemy who 'battles, moves and manoeuvres invisibly'.[103] Evangelos Hatzioannou, a Greek Cypriot volunteer, noted similarly: 'we don't belong to ourselves anymore ... we have lost our personality ... we are mere numbers who move and act according to the commands of our superior officer'.[104]

The only appeal of war, according to Skandalakis, was the 'lust for danger' and the 'hellish sound of the modern war machines'.[105] Indeed, for some soldiers, combat was a place that provided an unusual sense of excitement and aesthetic pleasure. Infantry soldier Emannouil Sofoulis noted in his diary:

> The sound coming out of thousands of Mannlichers and Mausers, the terrible noise of the machine guns, the hellish roar of the shells ... the wails of the wounded ... make these moments frantic .... Mars really reigns on the battlefield. These crucial moments offer much pleasure: they are truly magical.[106]

However, for most men the excitement of combat quickly paled, giving way to a more cynical and even callous attitude towards death and combat. Sadness or shock over the loss of a comrade was transformed into 'a sense of satisfaction that they had escaped harm'.[107] War, according to Paraskevopoulos, liberated men from the conventions of civilian life but also made soldiers prone to asocial behaviour. 'War makes us beasts', wrote Paraskevopoulos to his wife, 'it deprives us of all these things that make us human'.[108] A few weeks later, Paraskevopoulos wrote: 'The road is crammed with the bodies of beasts and ... soldiers. But we have become accustomed to this spectacle ... you sit down to eat something and right next to you or opposite you there is a dead body, *s'il n'etait rien* [sic]'.[109]

Contact with the peasantry of the liberated territories also damped down the soldiers' fervour. The Greek soldiers expected to be greeted as liberators. The army was well received in the majority of the Macedonian and Epirote towns; however, the situation in the rural areas was much different. Some communities, especially in Epirus, greeted the soldiers with enthusiasm and even took up arms to assist the army,[110] but the majority of the peasants tended to be much more restrained. Nationalist ideas had made limited inroads in the rural areas of northern Greece, where peasants still identified with clan, village and Church rather than with the nation-state.[111] The foremost concern of the peasants was to save their property and family from the ravages of war. Many peasants acted in an opportunistic way, helping all belligerents who crossed their path and taking advantage of their presence when possible, but desisting from taking either side. These attitudes infuriated the soldiers, who saw anything less than wholehearted support as tantamount to treason. Hristos Soulis described the peasants in the plain of Ioannina as 'lice ... whose sole purpose was to take the skin off the backs of the soldiers'.[112] A similar situation in eastern Macedonia led the soldiers 'to curse demons and gods for risking their lives for these people who are Greeks only in name ... and see us as if we were an occupying force'.[113] Soldiers regarded such attitudes as evidence of a lack of national feeling and as ungratefulness among the peasants, whose image was recast from that of the unredeemed brother to the ungrateful *tourkosporos* (Turkish seed or Turk-lover).

These experiences, combined with the intense deprivation that the soldiers confronted throughout the war, posed a profound challenge to their morale and understanding of the war. Cases of self-mutilation to obtain removal from combat to safety behind the lines were rare in the early days but became increasingly common. During the Epirus campaign, there were cases of men refusing to obey orders, retiring from the front or even threatening their officers.[114]

Nevertheless, in spite of such challenges, morale did not collapse. Furthermore, despite the initial shock of combat, notions of heroic masculinity were not dismissed by the soldiers, who came to espouse a more subtle heroic ideal founded upon endurance and upon the ability to suffer and withstand hardship rather than to be proficient in killing. Heroism, Paraskevopoulos thus argued, was not proved on the battlefield as civilians might think, as this was 'an elementary duty',[115] but in the capacity to withstand hardship, dirt, hunger and boredom.[116] Therefore, as everyday experience led to the gradual erosion of the ideological premises that led soldiers to enlist and fight, other factors emerged that enabled them to meet the psychological and physical challenges of combat and campaigning. The notion of martyrdom, religion and primary group ties became increasingly important. The replacement of archetypal masculine attributes such as élan and aggressiveness by traits such as endurance and stoicism enabled the soldiers to come to terms with the reality of mechanized warfare and to reinvent ideas of martial heroism. At the same time, primary group ties and religion enabled men to instil a new meaning into the war and to counter their feelings of alienation, fear and despondency.

Captain Nikolaos Petimezas argued, in a series of articles published in 1914 under the pseudonym Lavras, that the resilience of Greek soldiers was due to primary group ties. According to Petimezas, shared experiences of combat and hardship gradually led to the creation of close-knit communities of men who were bound by common suffering and the burden of an experience that could not be conveyed to outsiders.[117] The nature of operations also bolstered primary group affiliations. The ruggedness of the terrain meant that most actions were fought at the platoon or company level. Inevitably this led men to identify even more with their group of comrades.[118] Many soldiers described the relations within the primary group in evocative terms that presented the group as a surrogate family. Stratigopoulos characteristically noted that among the men in his platoon, he felt he was 'a member of a family'.[119]

However, the primary group ties were often more complicated than this. Often, highly egotistical behaviour coexisted with unalloyed kindness. Thieving was endemic, and time and again famished soldiers fought over provisions and loot. Some men did not hesitate to leave their wounded comrades unattended despite their pleas for help or to expose them to danger in order to maintain their own safety during combat.[120] These incidents were not the rule, but they demonstrate the limitations of primary group ties in the face of hardship, for the desire to save one's own life and satisfy one's most basic urges for food, water and warmth often overcame any inhibitions. An infantry private noted in his memoir of the Macedonian front that campaign life is the 'perfect model' of Hobbes's *status naturalis*, because each man was, first and foremost, interested in pursuing his own personal needs.[121] Recent studies on the First World War also noted that hardship could lead both to the formation of intense personal relations and to highly egotistical behaviour, especially when soldiers came from different social backgrounds.[122]

Ideas of honour were very important in this respect because they served to delineate and reinforce 'proper' conduct in the primary groups. Honour was at the centre of the Greek male's moral and social universe. It was conditioned on displays of masculine prowess and exemplified in the bearing and usage of firearms and the ability to redress slights and protect individual and familial reputation with physical force. The failure to adhere to these ideals could result in a loss of individual and familial status.[123] Despite the profound challenges and the receding importance of heroic masculinity, ideas of honour retained their importance and were used to induce soldiers to fight and to conform to group expectations. Andreas Zografos, a Cretan university student, noted in his memoir of the Epirus campaign that what kept him and his fellow comrades fighting in the face of mounting hardship was *egoismos*, a word that can be roughly translated as 'honour' or 'self-regard'. Despite his tiredness, he wrote, he kept going for fear of losing face in front of his comrades.[124]

Ideas of honour were associated with duty, particularly among upper-class men. Major Ippokratis Papavasileiou described in a letter the case of a young upper-class lieutenant who refused to be attached to the divisional headquarters: 'Zarifis came to implore me with tears in his eyes to let him stay in his regiment ... because his honour wouldn't allow him to leave his platoon before he had seen combat and he was afraid that his fellow officers would think ill of him'.[125] However, honour was important in inducing men not only to fight, but also to act in the way that was expected within the group. Men who acted against the primary group interests could be brutally humiliated by their peers. Ditties and jibes were often used to expose the misconduct of comrades and shame them into conformity. Unrepentant offenders were isolated by the rest of the group, who refused to talk to them or recognize their presence. Theft was also used and, in the more extreme cases, beatings.[126] At the same time, the local character of most groups forced men to conform, for news about improper conduct could reach their home communities, resulting in a loss of face both for them and for their families. Therefore, the fear of being shamed in their home communities and within their group of comrades played a major role in policing and enforcing 'proper attitudes'.[127]

Primary group ties helped the soldiers to deal with loneliness, material destitution and health problems. Yet these affiliations could not help them to face the fear of death and their sense of powerlessness in the face of mechanized warfare. Thus, soldiers turned to religion, luck and superstition in order to come to terms with these aspects of the war. The Orthodox Church, in the form of chaplains, had an official presence in the army. Chaplains had a variety of roles; they acted as propagandists and ministered to the spiritual needs of the men, preaching sermons before combat, administering the sacrament, soothing the injured and often shaming stragglers and shirkers. Chaplains reminded the men of their task, to sacrifice their lives as Christian soldiers, and underlined the religious aspect of the war. They presented the soldier as a martyr, an ascetic in arms who not only faced death on the battlefield but also had constantly to fend off the temptations associated with army life: theft, unlawful killing, drunkenness and illicit sex.[128] Such imagery was also employed by the military authorities. After the Greek victory in Ioannina, Major Labros Sinaniotis, the commander of the 1st Independent Cretan Regiment, praised his men for 'their exemplary fortitude' and 'defiance of danger'[129] and declared the soldiers who had been killed during the four-month-long operations 'to be martyrs ... whose sacrifice equates to that of Christ'.[130]

These representations gave a positive meaning to death in combat by presenting the fallen soldiers as martyrs whose sacrifice facilitated the rebirth of the nation.[131] However, the extent to which such ideas were adopted by soldiers must be assessed with caution. Associations between combat and martyrdom permeated the personal testimonies of middle-class soldiers. Ktenaveas described his fallen comrades as 'martyrs for the faith who had found the sleep of the just'.[132] Petimezas noted in his diary after a particularly fierce engagement on the Epirus front that 'the men of the 7th and 8th Regiments underwent martyrdom'.[133] These associations were even more explicit in a letter from Lieutenant Ioannis Tsigaridis to his family:

> My beloved family, I beg you with all my heart to leave all your sorrows behind. My duty to the fatherland is sanctified and holy, and if this small sacrifice that you offer through me to our fatherland saddens you, then you forsake your duty to our fatherland ... implore God to grant me victory in the war or a glorious death in the field of battle.[134]

The situation was more complex among the rank and file. The available evidence suggests that religious observance heightened during the war, while the experience of combat induced many men to rediscover their faith.[135] The beliefs of the soldiers combined official church practices with popular rituals. Many soldiers developed a mystical view of the war and their task. Hristofidis described the battlefield as a uniquely spiritual *topos* that brought the human and the divine closer. In a letter, he described a vision he had of a saint who intervened to save him. It seems that such experiences were common among soldiers, especially those of peasant origins.[136] Furthermore, burials, wakes and services held in the memory of fallen comrades also served to underline the relation between death in combat and martyrdom. An infantry private noted in his diary that during a church service, 'we all broke into tears ... we wept for our brothers ... whom we lost ... in the line of duty'.[137]

The effect of such ideas on the conduct and perception of soldiers is more difficult to determine. Alexander Watson and Patrick Porter attributed both the remarkable endurance of the British army and the escalation of violence on the Western Front to sacrificial ideology.[138] However, for the Greeks, sacrificial ideals and religion were not so important in prompting men to kill, but rather in helping them to accept and rationalize loss and the prospect of death. These ideas led men to see the war as a God-ordained trial which they could neither avert nor resist but had to accept with stoicism and resignation. Such ideas led to the emergence of a preponderantly fatalistic attitude among soldiers, who considered that their actions had little effect and that death and injury, victory and defeat, lay in the hands of God. This outlook eased the moral burden of killing and helped men to deal with hardship and the loss of comrades.

Such attitudes are very much in evidence in the personal testimonies of men. The chaplain of the 5th Infantry Division noted in his memoir that many soldiers declined to take cover because, as they confided to him, 'they are firing here, they are firing there ... a bullet is a matter of chance. If it is destined to find one it will find him'.[139] This attitude of stoic resignation was noted by an infantry officer in the same division. As soldiers were ordered to advance, 'most men crossed themselves. An *evzone* shouted: "let the will of God and His All Holy Mother be done". "Amen" was the response of many soldiers'.[140] Giorgos Kastelanos, an infantry volunteer from Cyprus, wrote to his mother, who had advised him to keep out of danger: 'you write to me that I must take care of myself ... if a bullet is destined to eat you it will eat you no matter where you are. A man who goes to war in order to fight with honour ... must not fear death. The bullet has eaten thousands like us'.[141]

However, fatalism did not result in complete passivity. On the contrary, it served to bolster both traditional religiosity and folk rituals, as many soldiers considered that the observant practice of such rituals could enhance their chances of survival. Men crossed themselves and joined in group prayers before and during combat. During barrages, soldiers found solace in prayer, reciting the Salutations or the Jesus prayer:

> As we lay there ... we heard the sound of incoming shells ... nobody moved ... you only heard men beseeching the All Holy Mother of God and the Saints, a man next to me held a little cross in his hands which he kissed while he called 'Jesus, Jesus', incessantly.[142]

Prayer was not the only propitiatory means provided by religion. Many men wore amulets, such as small icons, crucifixes or fragments of the Holy Cross, under their vests. Soldiers wrote to their families asking for amulets and crucifixes. Many soldiers also wrote home asking their families to pray for them, to beseech a specific saint or to order a liturgy to be performed on an important day. Peasant soldiers also transferred many of their beliefs and rituals to the battlefield. Dreams, rituals, weather events and gestures provided the soldiers with clues to the outcome of military engagements.[143] These practices restored a sense of control to soldiers' everyday lives and helped them to deal with the anxiety of army life. Furthermore, as the war continued, religion came to play an important role in the reconceptualization of identities. As ideas of hyper-masculinity gave way to subtler understandings of the soldier as a martyr and sufferer, religious imagery – the cavalcade, Christ's suffering or the martyrdom of saints – was used by the soldiers to validate and provide meaning to their experience of the war.

Conclusion

Historians have presented the soldiers of the Balkan Wars as driven by a primitive, almost tribal nationalism that dictated both the men's resilience and the extreme violence of the war. However, as this chapter shows, neither the experience of the soldiers nor the violence they perpetrated can be attributed to Balkan parochialism. Recent studies on the Great War have shown that violence against prisoners and civilians and destruction of cultural symbols and places of worship were committed by all belligerent parties. As Alan Kramer noted, 'cultural destruction was not merely an incidental phenomenon in the Great War, but intrinsic to it'.[144] The reasons behind this extreme violence are numerous. The shift from a limited war fought between professional armies over dynastic issues to a war fought between citizen-soldiers over ideological issues led to growing polarization, which often resulted in the demonization of the national 'other', as the enemy was no longer the enemy's military but its entire culture. This development was exemplified in the stereotypes of the subhuman Slav and the barbarous Turk that were invoked by the Greeks to facilitate and justify violence. Similar stereotypes proliferated among all belligerent parties during the Great War and reached their height of development during the Second World War.

However, these ideas, which ultimately originated in an elite composed of intellectuals, politicians and artists, were mostly addressed to a middle-class audience. Accordingly, their impact on the rank and file must be carefully assessed. The association between ideology and morale has been fiercely debated by historians, particularly First World War scholars, who often have vehemently opposed the idea that soldiers might have been motivated by ideology. However, more recent research has suggested that educational expansion, popular culture and wartime propaganda did lead soldiers to adopt such ideas. Alexander Watson and Patrick Porter's study of sacrificial ideology shows that such ideas were widespread, albeit in a somewhat simplistic and crude form, among British and German servicemen of all classes and played an important role in the maintenance of morale and the shaping of the way men viewed the war.[145] The influence and power of ideology among Greek soldiers was far from negligible. The notion that Greece had a special destiny and a mission to civilize the East, the conviction that Greek civilization was superior to that of its barbaric rivals and a deeply held belief that the sacrifices of their fallen comrades should not be in vain inspired the Greek soldiers, and helped them to face adversity, fear and the prospect of death.

Moreover, ideas that anthropologists and social historians have previously associated with the Balkans, such as the cult of masculinity and an association between manliness and killing, are largely absent from the testimonies of soldiers. References to joyous killing similar to those described by Joanna Bourke in her *Intimate History of Killing* are also very rare.[146] Paul Fussell argued that irony is the foremost characteristic of Great War writing. Its equivalent among the Greeks is reticence.[147] Soldiers avoid describing themselves either as predators or as victims; instead, the image of the war is dominated by a figure of the soldier as a stoic who endures hardship and danger patiently and gracefully.

Religion played an important role both in the construction of these images and in the everyday lives of soldiers. The tradition of Orthodox Christianity, with its stress on self-denial and submission to the will of God, coloured the way men viewed this conflict. Soldiers saw the war as a necessary, almost God-ordained trial that they had to endure and accept with fortitude and patience. The root of this transformation must be sought in the nature of the war itself. The discrepancy between heroic expectation and the realities of the battlefield challenged traditional views of masculinity and heroism and led men to embrace a more subtle heroic ideal.

The importance of ideology was not limited to helping soldiers endure the tribulations of combat and life at the front. Ideology also contributed to the growing barbarization of warfare. Historians have seen violence as a tool of ethnic engineering, while they have attributed the ferocity of all belligerent parties to manipulation of the Balkan 'tradition' of violence.[148] These views are questionable because they fail both to differentiate among the experiences of different men and to recognize the importance of ideology and everyday experience. This oversimplification leads them to reproduce, unwittingly, a worn-out stereotype of culpable and fanatical Balkan warriors. However, as this chapter has shown, the causes of violent atrocities were more complex. Ben Shepherd argues in his masterful studies of the Wehrmacht in the Balkans and on the Eastern Front that the patterns and ferocity of violence are determined as much by conditions on the ground as by ideology. Alan Kramer and John Horne, similarly, underline the importance of the ground experience – deprivation, rumours, lack of experience, hardship and rapid movement – in the perpetration of atrocities in Belgium and northern France.[149] Violence during the Balkan Wars had comparable roots. It is certain that the impetus for violence existed, for Greek irredentism was characterized by deep racialist undertones that were initially contained by military discipline and a desire to gain the allegiance of the liberated populations. However, what ultimately prompted violence were the nature and conditions of warfare. Soldiers were for the most part inexperienced, raw recruits who were reared in an idealized war culture. The extreme hardship they underwent and the disparity between the conditions of the front and the idealized preconceptions of war led to a progressive numbing of the soldiers' sensitivities and contributed to the radicalization of ideology. Indeed, what makes the Balkan Wars stand out not only among previous conflicts in the peninsula but also among previous European wars is their modernity, in terms of both ideology and the means of destruction employed.

Spyridon Tsoutsoumpis holds a Ph.D. in Military History from the University of Manchester and is currently employed as a Research Fellow at the School for Advanced Studies in Sofia. He has written extensively on the military history of the Balkans, the Greek resistance organizations and the cultures of paramilitarism in Southeastern Europe during the long nineteenth century. He recently published his first academic monograph titled *A History of the Greek Resistance in the Second World War: The People's Armies* (Manchester University Press 2016). He is currently working on a new social history of the Greek Civil War.

Notes

1. Rebecca West, *Black Lamb and Grey Falcon* (New York: Penguin Books, 1967), 21.
2. Maria Todorova, 'The Balkans: From Discovery to Invention', *Slavic Review* 53(2) (1994), 453–82, here 475.
3. 'Public Opinion and the Balkan Peace', *The Nation* 13 (1913), 700.
4. Ishaan Tharoor, 'The Balkan Wars: 100 Years Later, a History of Violence', *Time* magazine, 8 October 2012, http://world.time.com/2012/10/08/the-balkan-wars-100-years-later-a-history-of-violence/ (accessed 10 March 2013).
5. Thomas Christopher Birdwood, *Old Europe's Suicide, or, The Building of a Pyramid of Errors, an Account of Certain Events in Europe during the Period 1912–1919* (London: Allen Lane, 1920), 31.
6. George F. Kennan, 'Introduction. The Balkan Crises: 1913 and 1993', in *The Other Balkan Wars: A 1913 Carnegie Endowment Inquiry in Retrospect with a New Introduction and Reflections on the Present Conflict by George F. Kennan* (Washington, DC: Carnegie Endowment for International Peace, 1993), 3–16, here 11.

7 'Old Greece' was a byword for the pre-1912 kingdom.
8 Petros Papapolyviou (ed.), *Ipodouloi Eleftherotes Adelfon Alitroton, Epistoles, Polemika Imerologia kai Antapokriseis Kiprion Ethelodon apo tin Ipeiro kai tin Makedonia 1912–1913* [Enslaved Liberators of Unredeemed Brothers, Letters, War Diaries and Correspondence of Cypriot Volunteers from Epirus and Macedonia 1912–1913] (Nicosia: Kentro Epistimonikon Erevnon, 1999); Lydia Triha (ed.), *Imerologia kai Grammata apo to Metopo* [Diaries and Letters from the Front] (Athens: ELIA, 1993).
9 Catherine Merridale, 'Culture, Ideology and Combat in the Red Army, 1939–45', *Journal of Contemporary History* 41(2) (2006), 305–24, here 312.
10 Michael Roper, *The Secret Battle: Emotional Survival in the Great War* (Manchester: Manchester University Press, 2009), 22–23.
11 John Nicolopoulos, 'From Agathangelos to the Megale Idea: Russia and the Emergence of Modern Greek Nationalism', *Balkan Studies* 26(1) (1985), 41–56, here 41.
12 Douglas Dakin, 'The Greek Unification and the Italian Risorgimento Compared', *Balkan Studies* 10(1) (1969), 1–10, here 10.
13 William Miller, *Greek Life in Town and Country* (London: George Newnes, 1905), 46.
14 Spyros Adrachas et al. (eds), *Panepistimio: Ideologia kai Paideia, Istoriki Diastasi kai Prooptikes* [University: Ideology and Education, Historical Aspect and Perspectives] (Athens: IAEA, 1989), 287.
15 Mark Mazower, 'The Messiah and the Bourgeoisie: Venizelos and Politics in Greece, 1909–1922', *Historical Journal* 35(9) (1992), 885–905, here 895.
16 Neoklis Kazazis, *Deka Logoi pros tin Elliniki Neotita* [Ten Homilies to the Greek Youth] (Athens: Peris, 1900), 231.
17 Ibid., 238.
18 Georgios Tsokopoulos, *Istoria Ellinitourkikou polemou 1912–1913* [A History of the Greco-Turkish War in 1912–1913], Vol. I (New York: Atlantis, 1914), 107.
19 Ibid., 108.
20 Walter Harrington Crawfurd Price, *The Balkan Cockpit: The Political and Military Story of the Balkan Wars in Macedonia* (London: Laurie, 1914), 57.
21 Papapolyviou, *Ipodouloi Eleftherotes*, 433.
22 Ibid., 435.
23 Ibid., 433.
24 Triha, *Imerologia kai Grammata apo to Metopo*, 40.
25 Anastasios Stratigopoulos, *Eis Lesvon: Ekstrateia, Efialtai kai Oneira* [In Lesvos: Campaign, Nightmares and Dreams] (Kalamai, 1914), 45.
26 Ibid., 101.
27 Ibid., 28.
28 Filippos Dragoumis, *Imerologio Ekstrateias* [Campaign Diary] (Athens: Dodoni, 2006), 254.
29 Triha, *Imerologia kai Grammata apo to Metopo*, 192.
30 Nikos Zorogiannidis, *Imerologio Maxon kai Polemikon Epixeiriseon* [Diary of Battles and Military Operations] (Thessaloniki: IMXA, 1986), 33; Dionisios Livieratos, *Ores Maxis, Imerologio 23 Fevrouariou–Oktovriou 1913* [Hours of

Combat, Diary 23 February–October 1913] (Athens: Elliniki Evroekdotiki, 1992), 32–33.
31 For the association between archaeology and nationalism, see Yannis Hamilakis and Eleana Yalouri, 'Sacralising the Past, Cults of Archaeology in Modern Greece', *Archaeological Dialogues* 6(2) (1999), 115–35.
32 Dragoumis, *Imerologio Ekstrateias*, 150.
33 Miltiadis Lidorikis, *Polemikes Ediposeis Evzonou* [War Impressions of an Evzone] (Athens: Fexis, 1914), 35.
34 Papapolyviou, *Ipodouloi Eleftherotai*, 392–93.
35 Nikolaos Petimezas, *Imerologion Ekstrateias, 1912–1913* [Campaign Diary, 1912–1913] (Athens: Pankalavritini Enosi, 1981),128.
36 Papapolyviou, *Ipodouloi Eleftherotai*, 308.
37 *Ebros*, 15 October 1912.
38 Spiros Melas, *Oi Polemoi 1912–1913* [The Wars 1912–1913] (Athens: Biris, 1958), 113.
39 Miller, *Greek Life in Town and Country*, 139.
40 Hristina Koulouri, *Istoria kai Geografia sta Ellinika Sxoleia (1834–1914)* [History and Geography in Greek Schools (1834–1914)] (Athens: EIE, 1988), 130.
41 Antonios Malliaros, *Poiima Peri tis Draseos tou A Anexartitou Tagmatos Kriton* [Poem on the Activities of the First Independent Cretan Battalion] (Athens: Zaharioudakis, 1914), 43.
42 Ibid., 44.
43 Giorgos Paraskevopoulos, *Eikones apo ton Proto Polemo* [Scenes from the First War] (Athens: Typois Avgis, 1914), 55, 63.
44 Ibid., 57.
45 Isidoros Fragiskos, *Polemikon Imerologio Oplitou tis V Merarxias kata ton Ellino-Tourkikon Polemo* [War Diary of a Soldier in the V Division during the Greco-Turkish War] (Alexandreia: Typois Proodou, 1914), 47.
46 P.G. Hatzihristos, *Anamniseis Ekstrateias 1912* [Memories of the Campaign 1912] (Katerini: Mati, 2006), 82.
47 Leonidas Paraskevopoulos, *Valkanikoi Polemoi, 1912–1913, Epistoles Pros tin Sizigo tou Koula* [Balkan Wars, 1912–1913, Letters to His Wife Koula] (Athens: Kastaniotis, 1998), 188.
48 Papapolyviou, *Ipodouloi Eleftherotai*, 225–26.
49 John Horne and Alan Kramer, *German Atrocities: A History of Denial* (New Haven, CT: Yale University Press, 2001), 103–6.
50 John Horne and Alan Kramer, 'German "Atrocities" and Franco-German Opinion, 1914: The Evidence of German Soldiers' Diaries', *The Journal of Modern History* 66(1) (1994), 1–33, here 25.
51 Papapolyviou, *Ipodouloi Eleftherotai*, 225.
52 Xenophon Stratigos, *O Ellinotourkikos Polemos tou 1912* [The Greco-Turkish War of 1912] (Athens: Elliniki, 1932), 48.
53 Fragiskos, *Polemikon Imerologio Oplitou*, 92–93; Triha, *Imerologia kai Grammata apo to Metopo*, 75.
54 Fragiskos, *Polemikon Imerologio Oplitou*, 44. The literature on the connection between representations of the 'other' and atrocity is extensive. Omer Bartov argued in his classic, *Hitler's Army: Soldiers, Nazis, and War in the*

Third Reich (New York: Oxford University Press, 1991), that anti-Semitic and anti-Slavic ideas radicalized the conduct of the Wehrmacht on the Eastern Front, leading to widespread atrocities. Craig Cameron also argued in his study of the First Marine Division in the Pacific, *American Samurai: Myth and Imagination in the Conduct of Battle in the First Marine Division 1941–1951* (Cambridge: Cambridge University Press, 2002), that racist representations of the Asian 'other' were responsible for the barbarization of warfare in the Pacific. A similar argument was made by John Dower in his pivotal *War without Mercy: Race and Power in the Pacific War* (New York: Pantheon Books, 1986). More recent studies have taken a more nuanced approach. Ben Shepherd and Waitman W. Beorn argued that the patterns of violence and the effectiveness of such stereotypes depended on a series of factors, including leadership, institutional culture and ground conditions: Ben Shepherd, 'The Clean Wehrmacht, the War of Extermination, and Beyond', *The Historical Journal* 52(2) (2009), 455–73; Waitman W. Beorn, 'Calculus of Complicity: The Wehrmacht, the Anti-Partisan War, and the Final Solution in White Russia, 1941–42', *Central European History* 44 (2011), 308–37.
55 Dragoumis, *Imerologio Ekstrateias*, 90.
56 Ibid., 108.
57 Papapolyviou, *Ipodouloi Eleftherotai*, 219.
58 Ibid., 220.
59 Paraskevopoulos, *Valkanikoi Polemoi*, 80–81; Triha, *Imerologia kai Grammata apo to Metopo*, 205.
60 *Ebros*, 10 October 1912 and 14 November 1912.
61 *O Ellinikos Stratos kata tous Valkanikous Polemous tou 1912–1913, Tomos A Epixeiriseis en Makedonia kata ton Tourkon* [The Greek Army during the Balkan Wars of 1912–1913, Volume One Operations against the Turks in Macedonia] (Athens: Ethniko Tipografeio, 1939).
62 Hatzihristos, *Anamniseis Ekstrateias 1912*, 33.
63 Triha, *Imerologia kai Grammata apo to Metopo*, 59; Albert Henry Trapman, *The Greeks Triumphant* (London: Forster Groom, 1915), 57.
64 Stratis Ktenaveas, *Makedoniki Estrateia* [The Macedonian Campaign] (Athens: Fexis, 1914), 30.
65 Zorogiannidis, *Imerologio Maxon*, 30–31; Dragoumis, *Imerologio Ekstrateias*, 50.
66 Joanna Bourke, *Dismembering the Male: Men's Bodies, Britain and the Great War* (London: Reaktion Books, 1996).
67 'Surgery in the Balkans War', *The British Medical Journal* 1(2,725) (1913), 623–24; Lidorikis, *Polemikes Ediposeis*, 31.
68 Georgios Kosmas, *Ellinikoi Polemoi, Valkanikoi, Ellinoitalikos, Simmoritopolemos* [Greek Wars, the Balkan Wars, Greco-Italian, the Bandit War] (Athens: Ellinikon Fos, 1967), 412.
69 Petimezas, *Imerologion Ekstrateias, 1912–1913*, 120.
70 Ktenaveas, *Makedoniki Estrateia*, 143.
71 Papapolyviou, *Ipodouloi Eleftherotai*, 349.
72 Triha, *Imerologia kai Grammata apo to Metopo*, 233–34.
73 Nikolaos G. Artis, *Eikones ek ton Polemon mas* [Scenes from Our Wars] (Athens: Sakelarios, 1930), 200.

74 Triha, *Imerologia kai Grammata apo to Metopo*, 61.
75 P. Panagakou, *Simvolin eis tin Istorian tis Dekaetias 1912–1922* [Contribution to the History of the 1912–1922 Decade] (Athens: n.p., 1961), 80.
76 Triha, *Imerologia kai Grammata apo to Metopo*, 66.
77 Ibid., 64.
78 Livieratos, *Ores Maxis*, 61; Dragoumis, *Imerologio Ekstrateias*, 348–49.
79 Emmanouil Voiklis, *Polemikes Selides* [Scenes from the War] (Samos: Giokarinis, 1913), 7.
80 For a general treatment of this issue, see Wolfgang Höpken, 'Performing Violence: Soldiers, Paramilitaries and Civilians in the Twentieth-Century Balkan Wars', in Alf Lüdtke and Bernd Weisbrod (eds), *No Man's Land of Violence: Extreme Wars in the Twentieth Century* (Göttingen: Wallstein Verlag, 2006), 211–50, here 222.
81 Papapolyviou, *Ipodouloi Eleftherotai*, 361.
82 Triha, *Imerologia kai Grammata apo to Metopo*, 212.
83 Dionisios Koutsoukalis, *Zografies apo tin Makedonia, Morihovo 1905* [Paintings from Macedonia, Morihovo 1905] (Peiraias: Typois Annageniseos, 1908).
84 The Macedonian struggle was a guerrilla struggle fought between Bulgarian and Greek irregulars in Macedonia between 1904 and 1908; see Douglas Dakin, *The Greek Struggle in Macedonia: 1897–1913* (Thessaloniki: Institute for Balkan Studies, 1966).
85 Koutsoukalis, *Zografies*, 106.
86 Emannouil Emannouil, *Imeroliogio I Polemikes Selides* [Diary or Pages from the War] (Thessaloniki: Germanos, 1996), 96.
87 Liubomir Miletitch, *Atrocités Grecques en Macédoine, pendant la Guerre Gréco-Bulgare* (Sofia: Imprimière de l'Etat, 1913), 157–62; Livieratos, *Ores Maxis*, 61, 76–77.
88 I.N. Skandalakis, *Polemos, Ediposeis Polemistou apo ton EllinoVoulgarikon Polemon tou 1913* [War, A Combatant's Impressions of the Greco-Bulgarian War of 1913] (Thessaloniki: Sofoklis Papanestoras, 1913), 174.
89 Hristina Koulouri, *Athlitismos kai Opseis tis Astikis koinonikotitas, Gymnastika kai Athlitika Somateia 1870–1922* [Athleticism and Aspects of Bourgeois Sociability: Gymnastic and Athletic Associations 1870–1922] (Athens: EIE, 1997), 69–73; Adrachas et al. (eds), *Panepistimio*, 277–88.
90 Omer Bartov, 'Reality and the Heroic Image in War', *History and Memory* 1(2) (1989), 99–122.
91 Hatzihristos, *Anamniseis Ekstrateias 1912*, 62.
92 Höpken, 'Performing Violence', 291.
93 'Surgery in the Balkans War', *The British Medical Journal* 1(2,725) (1913), 624.
94 Paraskevopoulos, *Valkanikoi Polemoi*, 44.
95 Ibid., 123.
96 Pindaros-Dimitrios Androulis, *To Imerologio enos stratioti* [A Soldier's Diary] (Athens: n.p., 1971), 61.
97 Modris Eksteins, *The Rites of Spring, the Great War and the Birth of the Modern Age* (New York: Houghton Mifflin, 2003).
98 Voiklis, *Polemikes Selides*, 9.

99 D. Kallimahos, *Apo to Stratopedo, I Epopoiia tou EllinoVoulgarikou Polemou* [From the Camp, the Epic of the Greco-Bulgarian War] (Cairo, 1914), 47.
100 Ibid., 65.
101 Petimezas, *Imerologion Ekstrateias, 1912–1913*, 36.
102 Skandalakis, *Polemos*, 140.
103 Ibid., 141.
104 Papapolyviou, *Ipodouloi Eleftherotai*, 397.
105 Skandalakis, *Polemos*, 141.
106 Voiklis, *Polemikes Selides*, 67.
107 Skandalakis, *Polemos*, 150.
108 Paraskevopoulos, *Valkanikoi Polemoi*, 126.
109 Ibid., 204.
110 Alexandrou Livadeos, *Oi Prodromoi tis Apeleftheroseos ton Ioanninon* [The Heralds of the Liberation of Ioannina] (Athens: n.p., 1984).
111 Basil G. Gounaris, 'Social Cleavages and National "Awakening" in Ottoman Macedonia', *East European Quarterly* 29(4) (1995), 409–27; Spyros Ploumidis, 'Nuances of Irredentism: The Epirote Society of Athens (1906–1912)', *The Historical Review/La Revue Historique* 8 (2011), 149–70.
112 Hristos Soulis, *Polemikes Selides* [Pages from the War] (Ioannina: Sindesmos apofoiton Zosimaias Sxolis, 2006), 202.
113 Livieratos, *Ores Maxis*, 38–39, 45.
114 *O Ellinikos Stratos kata tous Valkanikous Agones tou 1912–1913* [The Greek Army during the Balkan Struggle of 1912–1913], Vol. B, *Epixeiseis en Epiro* [Operations in Epirus] (Athens: Ethniko Tipografeio, 1932), 244–45, 301, 310.
115 Paraskevopoulos, *Valkanikoi Polemoi*, 105.
116 Ibid., 106.
117 Lavras, 'Oi Poliorkitai' [The Besiegers], *Estia*, 20 April 1914, 3 May 1914, 2–3.
118 Stratigos, *O Ellinotourkikos Polemos tou 1912*.
119 Stratigopoulos, *Eis Lesvon*, 109.
120 Artis, *Eikones ek ton Polemon mas*, 16; Dragoumis, *Imerologio Ekstrateias*, 46; Voiklis, *Polemikes Selides*, 38.
121 I. Farmakidou, *I Ipohorisi tou Sorovits* [The Sorovits Retreat] (Athens: Fexis, 1914), 25.
122 Benjamin Ziemann, *War Experiences in Rural Germany: 1914–1923* (Oxford/New York: Berg, 2007), 114.
123 John K. Campbell, *Honour, Family and Patronage: A Study of Institutions and Moral Values in a Greek Mountain Community* (Oxford/New York: Oxford University Press, 1973).
124 Andreas Zografos, *Ipirotiki Ekstrateia* [The Campaign in Epirus] (Heraklion: Nea Efimerida, 1914), 23; for *egoismos*, see Michael Herzfeld, *The Poetics of Manhood, Contest and Identity in a Cretan Mountain Village* (Princeton, NJ: Princeton University Press, 1985).
125 Triha, *Imerologia kai Grammata apo to Metopo*, 274.
126 Ktenaveas, *Makedoniki Estrateia*, 78; D.D. Kabanis, *Anamniseis tou Polemou kai tis Eirinis* [Memories of War and Peace] (Athens: Gnosi, 1983), 52–53.

127 Theodoros Pagalos, *Ta Apomnimonefmata mou: 1897–1947* [My Memoirs 1897–1947] (Athens: Aetos, 1959), 233; Ioannis Karavitis, *O Valkanotourkikos Polemos* [The Greco-Turkish War] (Athens: Petsivas, 2001), 200.
128 Kostadinos Kallinikos, *O Xristianismos kai o Polemos* [Christianity and War] (Manchester: Norbury Nantzio and Co., 1919), 80–85; Polikarpos Zahos, *Polemikai Selidai* [Pages from the War], Vol. II (Athens: Augi, 1915), 9, 22–23; K. Timotheos, *Poimadikoi Logoi, Patriotikia Kirigmata, Ithikoi Xaraktires, Epistolai kai Egiklioi* [Pastoral Speeches, Patriotic Sermons, Letters and Encyclicals] (Athens: Leonis, 1914), 58–75.
129 *Kritikon Iroon, pros Aionia Timin kai Anamnisin ton Iroikos Pesodon kai Trafmatisthedon Kriton kata tous dio Nikiforous Polemikous Agones Enadion ton Tourkon kai ton Voulgaron 1912–1913* [Cretan Monument for the Eternal Honour and Memory of the Heroically Fallen and Wounded Cretans during the Victorious War against the Turks and the Bulgarians] (Chania: Anexartitos, 1913), 23.
130 Ibid., 24.
131 Alan Kramer, *Dynamic of Destruction: Culture and Mass Killing in the First World War* (Oxford: Oxford University Press, 2007), 166, 177.
132 Ktenaveas, *Makedoniki Estrateia*, 111.
133 Petimezas, *Imerologion Ekstrateias, 1912–1913*, 148.
134 Papapolyviou, *Ipodouloi Eleftherotes*, 343.
135 Petimezas, *Imerologion Ekstrateias, 1912–1913*, 117.
136 Papapolyviou, *Ipodouloi Eleftherotes*, 434–35.
137 Ibid., 393.
138 Alexander Watson and Patrick Porter, 'Bereaved and Aggrieved: Combat Motivation and the Ideology of Sacrifice in the First World War', *Historical Research* 83(219) (2010), 146–63.
139 Kallimahos, *Apo to Stratopedo*, 50.
140 Lidorikis, *Polemikes Ediposeis*, 18.
141 Papapolyviou, *Ipodouloi Eleftherotai*, 111.
142 Voiklis, *Polemikes Selides*, 19.
143 Hatzihristos, *Anamniseis Ekstrateias 1912*, 66; Stratigopoulos, *Eis Lesvon*, 11; Triha, *Imerologia kai Grammata apo to Metopo*, 222, 233.
144 Kramer, *Dynamic of Destruction*, 159.
145 Watson and Porter, 'Bereaved and Aggrieved', 146–47.
146 Joanna Bourke, *An Intimate History of Killing: Face-to-Face Killing in Twentieth-Century Warfare* (London: Basic Books, 1999).
147 Paul Fussell, *The Great War and Modern Memory* (Oxford/New York: Oxford University Press, 2000), 29–37.
148 Tasos Kostopoulos, *Polemos kai Ethnokatharsi, I Xehasmeni plevra mias dekaetous ethnikis exormisis* [War and Ethnic Cleansing: The Forgotten Side of a Ten-Year National Mission] (Athens: Vivliorama, 2007).
149 Ben Shepherd, *War in the Wild East: The German Army and Soviet Partisans* (Cambridge, MA: Harvard University Press, 2004); Ben Shepherd, *Terror in the Balkans: German Armies and Partisan Warfare* (Cambridge, MA: Harvard University Press, 2012); Horne and Kramer, 'German "Atrocities" and Franco-German Opinion'.

Bibliography

Adrachas, Spyros et al. (eds). *Panepistimio: Ideologia kai Paideia, Istoriki Diastasi kai Prooptikes* [University: Ideology and Education, Historical Aspect and Perspectives]. Athens: IAEA, 1989.

Androulis, Pindaros-Dimitrios. *To Imerologio enos stratioti* [A Soldier's Diary]. Athens: n.p., 1971.

Artis, Nikolaos G. *Eikones ek ton Polemon mas* [Scenes from Our Wars]. Athens: Sakelarios, 1930.

Bartov, Omer. 'Reality and the Heroic Image in War'. *History and Memory* 1(2) (1989), 99–122.

———. *Hitler's Army: Soldiers, Nazis, and War in the Third Reich*. New York: Oxford University Press, 1991.

Beorn, Waitman W. 'Calculus of Complicity: The Wehrmacht, the Anti-Partisan War, and the Final Solution in White Russia, 1941–42'. *Central European History* 44 (2011), 308–37.

Birdwood, Thomas Christopher. *Old Europe's Suicide, or, The Building of a Pyramid of Errors, an Account of Certain Events in Europe during the Period 1912–1919*. London: Allen Lane, 1920.

Bourke, Joanna. *Dismembering the Male: Men's Bodies, Britain and the Great War*. London: Reaktion Books, 1996.

———. *An Intimate History of Killing: Face-to-Face Killing in Twentieth-Century Warfare*. London: Basic Books, 1999.

Cameron, Craig. *American Samurai: Myth and Imagination in the Conduct of Battle in the First Marine Division 1941–1951*. Cambridge: Cambridge University Press, 2002.

Campbell, John K. *Honour, Family and Patronage: A Study of Institutions and Moral Values in a Greek Mountain Community*. Oxford/New York: Oxford University Press, 1973.

Dakin, Douglas. *The Greek Struggle in Macedonia: 1897–1913*. Thessaloniki: Institute for Balkan Studies, 1966.

———. 'The Greek Unification and the Italian Risorgimento Compared'. *Balkan Studies* 10(1) (1969), 1–10.

Dower, John. *War without Mercy: Race and Power in the Pacific War*. New York: Pantheon Books, 1986.

Dragoumis, Filippos. *Imerologio Ekstrateias* [Campaign Diary]. Athens: Dodoni, 2006.

Eksteins, Modris. *The Rites of Spring, the Great War and the Birth of the Modern Age*. New York: Houghton Mifflin, 2003.

Emannouil, Emannouil. *Imeroliogio I Polemikes Selides* [Diary or Pages from the War]. Thessaloniki: Germanos, 1996.

Farmakidou, I. *I Ipohorisi tou Sorovits* [The Sorovits Retreat]. Athens: Fexis, 1914.

Fragiskos, Isidoros. *Polemikon Imerologio Oplitou tis V Merarxias kata ton Ellino-Tourkikon Polemo* [War Diary of a Soldier in the V Division during the Greco-Turkish War]. Alexandreia: Typois Proodou, 1914.

Fussell, Paul. *The Great War and Modern Memory*. Oxford/New York: Oxford University Press, 2000.

Gounaris, Basil G. 'Social Cleavages and National "Awakening" in Ottoman Macedonia'. *East European Quarterly* 29(4) (1995), 409–27.
Hamilakis, Yannis, and Eleana Yalouri. 'Sacralising the Past, Cults of Archaeology in Modern Greece'. *Archaeological Dialogues* 6(2) (1999), 115–35.
Hatzihristos, P.G. *Anamniseis Ekstrateias 1912* [Memories of the Campaign 1912]. Katerini: Mati, 2006.
Herzfeld, Michael. *The Poetics of Manhood, Contest and Identity in a Cretan Mountain Village*. Princeton, NJ: Princeton University Press, 1985.
Höpken, Wolfgang. 'Performing Violence: Soldiers, Paramilitaries and Civilians in the Twentieth-Century Balkan Wars', in Alf Lüdtke and Bernd Weisbrod (eds), *No Man's Land of Violence: Extreme Wars in the Twentieth Century* (Göttingen: Wallstein Verlag, 2006), 211–50.
Horne, John, and Alan Kramer. 'German "Atrocities" and Franco-German Opinion, 1914: The Evidence of German Soldiers' Diaries'. *The Journal of Modern History* 66(1) (1994), 1–33.
———. *German Atrocities: A History of Denial*. New Haven, CT: Yale University Press, 2001.
Kabanis, D.D. *Anamniseis tou Polemou kai tis Eirinis* [Memories of War and Peace]. Athens: Gnosi, 1983.
Kallimahos, D. *Apo to Stratopedo, I Epopoiia tou EllinoVoulgarikou Polemou* [From the Camp, the Epic of the Greco-Bulgarian War]. Cairo, 1914.
Kallinikos, Kostadinos. *O Xristianismos kai o Polemos* [Christianity and War]. Manchester: Norbury Nantzio and Co., 1919.
Karavitis, Ioannis. *O Valkanotourkikos Polemos* [The Greco-Turkish War]. Athens: Petsivas, 2001.
Kazazis, Neoklis. *Deka Logoi pros tin Elliniki Neotita* [Ten Homilies to the Greek Youth] Athens: Peris, 1900.
Kennan, George F. 'Introduction. The Balkan Crises: 1913 and 1993', in *The Other Balkan Wars: A 1913 Carnegie Endowment Inquiry in Retrospect with a New Introduction and Reflections on the Present Conflict by George F. Kennan* (Washington, DC: Carnegie Endowment for International Peace, 1993), 3–16.
Kosmas, Georgios. *Ellinikoi Polemoi, Valkanikoi, Ellinoitalikos, Simmoritopolemos* [Greek Wars, the Balkan Wars, Greco-Italian, the Bandit War]. Athens: Ellinikon Fos, 1967.
Kostopoulos, Tasos. *Polemos kai Ethnokatharsi, I Xehasmeni plevra mias dekaetous ethnikis exormisis* [War and Ethnic Cleansing: The Forgotten Side of a Ten-Year National Mission]. Athens: Vivliorama, 2007.
Koulouri, Hristina. *Istoria kai Geografia sta Ellinika Sxoleia (1834–1914)* [History and Geography in Greek Schools (1834–1914)]. Athens: EIE, 1988.
———. *Athlitismos kai Opseis tis Astikis koinonikotitas, Gymnastika kai Athlitika Somateia 1870–1922* [Athleticism and Aspects of Bourgeois Sociability: Gymnastic and Athletic Associations 1870–1922]. Athens: EIE, 1997.
Koutsoukalis, Dionisios. *Zografies apo tin Makedonia, Morihovo 1905* [Paintings from Macedonia, Morihovo 1905]. Peiraias: Typois Annageniseos, 1908.
Kramer, Alan. *Dynamic of Destruction: Culture and Mass Killing in the First World War*. Oxford: Oxford University Press, 2007.
Kritikon Iroon, pros Aionia Timin kai Anamnisin ton Iroikos Pesodon kai Trafmatisthedon Kriton kata tous dio Nikiforous Polemikous Agones Enadion

ton Tourkon kai ton Voulgaron 1912–1913 [Cretan Monument for the Eternal Honour and Memory of the Heroically Fallen and Wounded Cretans during the Victorious War against the Turks and the Bulgarians]. Chania: Anexartitos, 1913.

Ktenaveas, Stratis. *Makedoniki Estrateia* [The Macedonian Campaign]. Athens: Fexis, 1914.

Lavras. 'Oi Poliorkitai' [The Besiegers]. *Estia*, 20 April 1914, 3 May 1914.

Lidorikis, Miltiadis. *Polemikes Ediposeis Evzonou* [War Impressions of an Evzone]. Athens: Fexis, 1914.

Livadeos, Alexandrou. *Oi Prodromoi tis Apeleftheroseos ton Ioanninon* [The Heralds of the Liberation of Ioannina]. Athens: n.p., 1984.

Livieratos, Dionisios. *Ores Maxis, Imerologio 23 Fevrouariou–Oktovriou 1913* [Hours of Combat, Diary 23 February–October 1913]. Athens: Elliniki Evroekdotiki, 1992.

Malliaros, Antonios. *Poiima Peri tis Draseos tou A Anexartitou Tagmatos Kriton* [Poem on the Activities of the First Independent Cretan Battalion]. Athens: Zaharioudakis, 1914.

Mazower, Mark. 'The Messiah and the Bourgeoisie: Venizelos and Politics in Greece, 1909–1922'. *Historical Journal* 35(9) (1992), 885–905.

Melas, Spiros. *Oi Polemoi 1912–1913* [The Wars 1912–1913]. Athens: Biris, 1958.

Merridale, Catherine. 'Culture, Ideology and Combat in the Red Army, 1939–45'. *Journal of Contemporary History* 41(2) (2006), 305–24.

Miletitch, Liubomir. *Atrocités Grecques en Macédoine, pendant la Guerre Gréco-Bulgare*. Sofia: Imprimière de l'Etat, 1913.

Miller, William. *Greek Life in Town and Country*. London: George Newnes, 1905.

Nicolopoulos, John. 'From Agathangelos to the Megale Idea: Russia and the Emergence of Modern Greek Nationalism'. *Balkan Studies* 26(1) (1985), 41–56.

O Ellinikos Stratos kata tous Valkanikous Agones tou 1912–1913 [The Greek Army during the Balkan Struggle of 1912–1913]. Vol. B, *Epixeiseis en Epiro* [Operations in Epirus]. Athens: Ethniko Tipografeio, 1932.

O Ellinikos Stratos kata tous Valkanikous Polemous tou 1912–1913, Tomos A Epixeiriseis en Makedonia kata ton Tourkon [The Greek Army during the Balkan Wars of 1912–1913, Volume One Operations against the Turks in Macedonia]. Athens: Ethniko Tipografeio, 1939.

Pagalos, Theodoros. *Ta Apomnimonefmata mou: 1897–1947* [My Memoirs 1897–1947]. Athens: Aetos, 1959.

Panagakou, P. *Simvolin eis tin Istorian tis Dekaetias 1912–1922* [Contribution to the History of the 1912–1922 Decade]. Athens: n.p., 1961.

Papapolyviou, Petros (ed.). *Ipodouloi Eleftherotes Adelfon Alitroton, Epistoles, Polemika Imerologia kai Antapokriseis Kiprion Ethelodon apo tin Ipeiro kai tin Makedonia 1912–1913* [Enslaved Liberators of Unredeemed Brothers, Letters, War Diaries and Correspondence of Cypriot Volunteers from Epirus and Macedonia 1912–1913]. Nicosia: Kentro Epistimonikon Erevnon, 1999.

Paraskevopoulos, Giorgos. *Eikones apo ton Proto Polemo* [Scenes from the First War]. Athens: Typois Avgis, 1914.

Paraskevopoulos, Leonidas. *Valkanikoi Polemoi, 1912–1913, Epistoles Pros tin Sizigo tou Koula* [Balkan Wars, 1912–1913, Letters to His Wife Koula]. Athens: Kastaniotis, 1998.

Petimezas, Nikolaos. *Imerologion Ekstrateias, 1912–1913* [Campaign Diary, 1912–1913]. Athens: Pankalavritini Enosi, 1981.
Ploumidis, Spyros. 'Nuances of Irredentism: The Epirote Society of Athens (1906–1912)'. *The Historical Review/La Revue Historique* 8 (2011), 149–70.
Price, Walter Harrington Crawfurd. *The Balkan Cockpit: The Political and Military Story of the Balkan Wars in Macedonia*. London: Laurie, 1914.
Roper, Michael. *The Secret Battle: Emotional Survival in the Great War*. Manchester: Manchester University Press, 2009.
Shepherd, Ben. *War in the Wild East: The German Army and Soviet Partisans*. Cambridge, MA: Harvard University Press, 2004.
———. 'The Clean Wehrmacht, the War of Extermination, and Beyond'. *The Historical Journal* 52(2) (2009), 455–73.
———. *Terror in the Balkans: German Armies and Partisan Warfare*. Cambridge, MA: Harvard University Press, 2012.
Skandalakis, I.N. *Polemos, Ediposeis Polemistou apo ton EllinoVoulgarikon Polemon tou 1913*. [War, A Combatant's Impressions of the Greco-Bulgarian War of 1913]. Thessaloniki: Sofoklis Papanestoras, 1913.
Soulis, Hristos. *Polemikes Selides* [Pages from the War]. Ioannina: Sindesmos apofoiton Zosimaias Sxolis, 2006.
Stratigopoulos, Anastasios. *Eis Lesvon: Ekstrateia, Efialtai kai Oneira* [In Lesvos: Campaign, Nightmares and Dreams]. Kalamai, 1914.
Stratigos, Xenophon. *O Ellinotourkikos Polemos tou 1912* [The Greco-Turkish War of 1912]. Athens: Elliniki, 1932.
Timotheos, K. *Poimadikoi Logoi, Patriotikia Kirigmata, Ithikoi Xaraktires, Epistolai kai Egiklioi* [Pastoral Speeches, Patriotic Sermons, Letters and Encyclicals]. Athens: Leonis, 1914.
Todorova, Maria. 'The Balkans: From Discovery to Invention'. *Slavic Review* 53(2) (1994), 453–82.
Trapman, Albert Henry. *The Greeks Triumphant*. London: Forster Groom, 1915.
Triha, Lydia (ed.). *Imerologia kai Grammata apo to Metopo* [Diaries and Letters from the Front]. Athens: ELIA, 1993.
Tsokopoulos, Georgios. *Istoria Ellinitourkikou polemou 1912–1913* [A History of the Greco-Turkish War in 1912–1913]. Vol. I. New York: Atlantis, 1914.
Voiklis, Emmanouil. *Polemikes Selides* [Scenes from the War]. Samos: Giokarinis, 1913.
Watson, Alexander, and Patrick Porter. 'Bereaved and Aggrieved: Combat Motivation and the Ideology of Sacrifice in the First World War'. *Historical Research* 83(219) (2010), 146–63.
West, Rebecca. *Black Lamb and Grey Falcon*. New York: Penguin Books, 1967.
Zahos, Polikarpos. *Polemikai Selidai* [Pages from the War]. Vol. II. Athens: Augi, 1915.
Ziemann, Benjamin. *War Experiences in Rural Germany: 1914–1923*. Oxford/New York: Berg, 2007.
Zografos, Andreas. *Ipirotiki Ekstrateia* [The Campaign in Epirus]. Heraklion: Nea Efimerida, 1914.
Zorogiannidis, Nikos. *Imerologio Maxon kai Polemikon Epixeiriseon* [Diary of Battles and Military Operations]. Thessaloniki: IMXA, 1986.

 8

A Forgotten Lesson
The Romanian Army between the Campaign in Bulgaria (1913) and the Tutrakan Debacle (1916)
Claudiu-Lucian Topor

Only three years elapsed between the 1913 military campaign in Bulgaria and the battle at Tutrakan in 1916. Rivalries could not be erased or lessons understood in this short amount of time. A reading of the chronicles (with their missing parts) that describe the two events can easily be misleading. The actual connection between the two is not immediately apparent. For both events, the documents of the time discuss the rivalry between Romanians and Bulgarians. In 1913, the Romanians were victorious based on the background of the Balkan War; 1917 brought the Bulgarians their revenge, this time in the context of the First World War. The issue is not the dispute's continuity, but rather the final *denouement*. Without underestimating the effects of the Bulgarians' success, we are left wondering what happened to the Romanian army. How was it possible for Romania, at one point seen as the arbiter of Balkan disputes, to dive unprepared into the Great War and to succumb to its enemies? It is only fitting to attempt a lucid analysis of the two events just mentioned. The consequences of the 1913 Bulgarian campaign have been subject only to superficial research. The aftermath of the Romanian victory in the Second Balkan War created a state of exaltation and of ultimate confidence in the army's potential. The event was presented in a pathos-filled manner. The consequences of the defeat at Tutrakan were at some point made the subject of evaluations, but unfortunately of exaggeratedly denigrating and pessimistic ones. Its causes were revealed in a court-like setting: accused and guilty parties all round. In both situations, historical truth was skilfully veiled. This study recognizes the need for a lucid reflection that compares the unfolding of both conflicts. This comparison takes into account the military strength, training, weaponry and logistics, medical services, discipline and the army's moral conduct. Ultimately, the research aims to shed light on the manner in which the Romanian political decision-makers and military authorities used the experience of past wars to plan and develop strategies for the future.

Crossing the Danube: Military Operations (1913)

The 1913 Bulgarian campaign was not a moment of glorious bravery for the Romanian soldiers. As a result of the Second and Fourth Bulgarian Armies' attack in Macedonia on the night of the 29 to 30 June 1913, the war of the former Balkan allies had already begun when the most important events unfolded. The Romanian army did not come up against significant resistance from the Bulgarian troops,[1] as their main focus lay in fighting Serbia and Greece.[2] The psychological impact was very important, as Bulgaria, who faced three unleashed enemies, had to capitulate. The Romanian army crossing the Danube was decisive for the fate of the war, as Bulgaria, at the time of the Romanian invasion, had stabilized the Greek and Serbian fronts and mounted a counteroffensive.[3] Romania mobilized five army corps, each comprising two active divisions and one reserve division. The event was a genuine display of force. By the evening of 25 June, a total of 930,000 Romanian citizens arrived at the regimental headquarters, of which 460,000 soldiers were retained, a number that was far too high given the Bulgarian army's limited capacity to respond.[4]

The mobilization was surprisingly enthusiastic and swift. The popularity of the decision was also due to the fact that Romania, after thirty-six years of peace and prosperity, was eager to embark on a new military adventure. Spirits were high in Bucharest. There was a general ebullience. Café patrons would spontaneously break out into patriotic song, and the region on the Danube banks – the existence of which had been largely ignored by the general population only a few months before – suddenly became the most Romanian place in all Romania, and the Bulgarians Romania's all-time enemy.[5]

The surprise mobilization had the expected effect. The Bulgarian military authorities believed the Romanian army would require at least twelve days to group. It was thought that in this interval Bulgaria would settle its accounts with Serbia or Greece, before Romania was able to intervene with maximum effectiveness. These calculations were no match for the reality. The Romanian army mobilized in just eight days (22–30 June). Once the troops were assembled, the army marched into Bulgarian territory to stop hostilities, acquire new territories beyond the border and force the Balkan states to make peace.[6] The attack against Bulgaria was intended to be a rapid offensive in the Sofia-Kyustendil direction, occupying the strategic Silistra-Tutrakan-Balchik line.[7] The five army corps concentrated in Dobruja, backed up by a division of reservists, marched in two columns towards Balchik-Tutrakan, first occupying the city of Dobrich (Tenth Division). The crossing of the Danube was assisted by pontoon bridges assembled at Turnu-Măgurele and Corabia, the latter built in record time (only seven hours). On Bulgarian territory, where Romanian troops were met with only minimal resistance,[8] they were deployed in Orhanie (First Corps, its mission being to defend the hill at Araba-Konak), Lukovit (Second Corps), Zumakov (Third Corps) and Etropole (Fourth Corps). The First Cavalry Division (Berkovitsa) and the First Reserve Division (Vratsa) flanked this array of troops. The Second Reserve Division and the Thirty-third Reservists' Brigade were still available in Pleven, where they were defending Prince Ferdinand's headquarters. Success was complete. Only eighteen days after mobilization, the Romanian army arrived within twenty-five kilometres of Sofia and within ten kilometres of Philippopolis.[9]

Defending the Homeland: The Battle at Tutrakan (1916)

Unlike the Bulgarian campaign, the battle at Tutrakan was the Romanian army's baptism of fire in the First World War. Just as mobilization took place with enthusiasm, the populace of Bucharest was experiencing a moment of elation. The prime minister, Ion I.C. Brătianu (1864–1927), succeeded in convincing everyone that, as a result of his cunning diplomacy, Romania had postponed its participation in the war until the last stage of hostilities. Therefore, the 1916 intervention, like the one in 1913, appeared as a show of force rather than a full-scale war. The Bulgarians were supposed to stand still; the Germans to be busy with the resistance on the Western Front; and the Austrians, exhausted, to be crushed between the Brusilov offensive from the north and Sarrail's offensive from the south. The war would be a strategic walk in the park, like the 1913 campaign in Bulgaria. Specialists estimated that, after three weeks, the Romanian troops would arrive in Budapest. Some were even talking about Vienna and Berlin.[10] Only three days after war was declared, in the sweltering summer of 1916, a cabinet member reassured General Ion Culcer that the autumn would bring a general peace in Europe. 'I was very flattered', remembered the former commander of the First Army, 'when I heard that we would be the ones changing the balance in the current war and therefore we would be able to dictate at the ensuing peace conference'.[11]

The clash with reality was unforgiving. Tutrakan was a military episode that engendered significant sacrifices, deaths, casualties and troops missing in action.[12] It was a real Romanian Verdun. The strategic advantage belonged to Bulgaria from the very beginning, as it had concentrated significant forces on its border with Romania, in Southern Dobruja. General Stefan Toshev led its Third Army. German units, Austrian batteries and Turkish reserves, equipped with modern weapons in plentiful supply, supported an impressive deployment of Bulgarian forces (sixty-two infantry battalions, fifty-five artillery batteries, twenty-three cavalry squadrons, three engineer battalions and one mine-launching battalion).[13] Here were people with different educations, customs and mentalities, fighting side by side, Orthodox Christians and Muslims, Catholics, Protestants, Jews and atheists. The Balkan miner stood next to the Viennese factory worker, the illiterate peasant from Anatolia next to the bourgeois from the Rhine. All of them came under the command of Marshal August von Mackensen, who had previously defeated the Serbs. He was well known for his decisive strikes and for his commitment to total war.[14] On the other side stood Tutrakan, a monstrosity, a bridgehead without the bridge, as Marshal Alexandru Averescu (1859–1938) called it with fierce irony.[15]

The Romanian army's organization was defensive. There were two lines of defence, fifteen centres consisting of buried, low-visibility redoubts, artillery shelters and barbed wire networks enabling them to hold out heroically to the last man. General Constantin Teodorescu was in command of the bridgehead. He was supposed to resist as the leader of the Seventeenth Division, on a border route that was favourable to an attack from the Bulgarian side.[16] Together with Silistra and Pazardjik, Tutrakan formed the triangle of the Romanian defence on the right bank of the Danube. The Bulgarian offensive had to be repelled, so that the Russian divisions, led by Zaionchikovski,[17] could counterattack decisively. But the Romanian troops deployed on the Danube were not the best trained. Nor were their commanders among the most skilled. The Romanian army had concentrated its main forces in the Carpathian passes, the border that had been the starting point for its offensive into Transylvania on 15 August. It was not Bulgaria that appeared as the most significant enemy, but Austria-Hungary instead.

Similar to the case of the 1913 campaign, the clash's immediate effect seemed predominantly psychological. The defeat demoralized the troops, and the commanders acted hastily.[18] The population panicked and began seeking refuge. With heavy hearts, the Romanians living in the villages located on the former border had to leave their homes. Their hard-earned livelihoods had to be abandoned to the hands of the enemy.[19] Depression seemed even deeper in Bucharest. When the news of Tutrakan's fall came, panic set in. Fears that the Bulgarians would cross the Danube and invade Bucharest in just a few hours beset the well-off bourgeoisie.[20] Many in the upper classes, fearing for their lives and their wealth, fled the country, taking with them silverware, jewellery and even carpets.[21] In order to stop any defeatist rumours from spreading, the government closed down Capşa's café. Again, the 1913 campaign was brought back to public attention. Its memory was still alive in the souls of Romanians, and people spoke about it continuously. 'It was a bad example for us', lawyer Vasile Th. Cancicov concedes, going on to explain the reason: 'To take the Quadrilateral [i.e. Southern Dobruja] without discharging a single rifle was a discouragement for those who would have liked to obtain the Ardeal [Transylvania] without any losses. Reality has given us a wake-up call. The war we have entered is terrible and will be bloody'.[22]

From Victory to Failure: A Comparative Approach

The search was on for those responsible for the debacle. Tutrakan fell less than a week after Romania had entered the war. The Romanian army had lost the strategic initiative. Before the Romanian troops could reach the Magyar steppe and Budapest, the German, Austro-Hungarian, Bulgarian and Turkish troops had reached the Wallachian Plain and Bucharest. The Bucharest military 'genius' had disparaged an opponent that had impressive war training, as well as the equipment and front-line experience that the Romanian army lacked.[23] A thorny new issue tore the consciousness of the embittered population: was the Romanian army prepared for the 1916 campaign? Official histories show the authorities' remarkable efforts to train and equip the army in the event of war. However, the war found Romania on its way to maturity, not yet having reached it.[24] While much had been done in the three years since the Bulgarian campaign, the odds appeared to be against Romania: from the drafting of the operation plan (the now-famous 'Z hypothesis', a campaign plan that deployed 75 per cent of the armed forces in the Carpathians, moving towards the north and northwest, and 25 per cent of the forces on the Danube, moving south), to the orders placed for weapons, the training of troops and the staffing of divisions. The proof consists in the remarkable number of accounts, notes, records and front-line memoirs that show, across the board, serious dysfunctions. General Radu R. Rosetti, mobilized at the Central Headquarters, talked about the lack of any preliminary research concerning the hypothesis of the war with Austria-Hungary and Germany before 1914. His barbs, aimed at Averescu, exonerated Brătianu and General Dumitru Iliescu, his chief advisor.[25] What about Alexandru Averescu? What did the marshal have to say, the most popular character in the army and the author of the famous manoeuvre at Flămânda?[26] First of all, he criticized the mobilization's timing: 'We did not decide to do this when Bulgaria was lacking weapons and ammunition, when Turkey was exhausted, when Serbia was on its feet; what were we waiting for?'[27] Then, in a pitiful attempt to idealize the army of 1913, he invoked the detrimental changes that had happened during the years of neutrality, when the army's combative value was diluted by the increase in the number of divisions consisting of untrained, poorly armed soldiers:

> It took us just two years of useless hesitations to allow an army that had proven excellently operational in 1913 to be shattered and forced to return to the organization of 1914 after three months of skirmishes. This was thanks to the good judgement of the French officers at the Central Headquarters, who realized immediately our power of recovery and the technical and tactical value of the remaining troops, who were able to regroup in Moldavia after the retreat from the river Argeș![28]

But was the Romanian army ready for war in the campaign waged in Bulgaria? General Constantin N. Hârjeu (1856–1928), minister of war at the time, considered the Romanian army ready for combat by comparing its level of preparedness to that of the Balkan belligerents' armies. It could operate successfully provided that it was not necessary to mobilize all the effectives, or provided that the operation was followed immediately by combat action.[29] Hence, its combat capacity needed much improvement. It can easily be noted that many of the shortcomings that became obvious during the 1913 campaign also resurfaced in the 1916 war: first the weaponry, then deficiencies in the supply and medical services, as well as acts of indiscipline. The logistics and administration personnel did not have adequate supplies to maintain the subsistence service in Bulgaria. The field kitchens (using Marmite cans) could only feed 224,000 troops. The regimental trains for the forty reserve battalions did not have enough supply carriages. Each mobile pantry was accompanied by a field kitchen, but supplied only forty-five thousand rations, an insufficient number for army corps with a larger number of troops.[30] It is not surprising, then, that the soldiers received 'a meal which was hastily put together', often 'water mixed with mud'[31] and a quarter of a kilogram of (usually mouldy) bread each day,[32] because the regiment 'did not have the required supplies'.[33] Each man had to take care of himself. In the tragic retreat during the 1916 war, troops suffered from cold and hunger, although they should not have lacked food. As Alexandru Lascarov-Moldovanu, an eyewitness to the event, recounts, unarmed, straggling soldiers with confused looks, tattered and muddied coats and torn boots would walk into people's yards and, out of breath, ask for food and shelter. Glancing apprehensively around, they would say: 'We've been marching for a week …We're cold … Give us something to eat…'.[34] Moreover, it is common knowledge that in the 1913 campaign the auxiliary services crossed the Danube very late, and that troops were forced to pass through cholera-contaminated regions after exhausting marches.[35] Despite the fact that the most elementary supplies were missing (serum, bandages, quinine),[36] doctors did their duty. The men received medical help as far as possible, though fear of contamination also caused typical egotistical reactions, resulting, in some cases, in the medical personnel's exaggerated self-protection.[37]

Indeed, the cholera epidemic caused a significant number of casualties. In Orhanie, thirty to forty dead bodies were given a common burial each day. The picture of the hospital in this Bulgarian town remained a sombre one in the memory of the eyewitnesses. While some rooms echoed with the laments of those tormented by the disease, others were filled with the sounds of shuffling feet of those who had been cured, while in another pavilion people were dying. Those who had just passed away were immediately taken to the lime pits, where simple earth mounds reminded the living that underneath them lay the final resting place of Romanian soldiers.[38]

Some of these mistakes were perpetuated in the 1916 campaigns. Doctor Constantin Angelescu, who had been tasked with the organization of the army medical service before the war, found many gaps in the planning for the mobilization of the medical service from the first day. The strategists in the Ministry offices had planned the rushed offensive into Transylvania immediately after the declaration of war, without bearing in mind that military regulations stipulated that medical services must be mobilized on the fourth day of general mobilization. They effectively left the troops without any medical support. The border crossing was met with stronger resistance than expected, and there were already a number of casualties, meaning that the only *in situ* field medical formations were unable to pick up all the wounded soldiers and provide them with the required assistance.[39] The wounded at Tutrakan suffered the same fate. On the morning of 24 August, convoys started to arrive in Bucharest. Here they found all the hospitals unprepared, as they were not slated to be operational until three weeks later.[40] Bearing in mind the ravages of the 1913 cholera epidemic, strong measures were planned to prevent a similar occurrence. Some of them materialized: the soldiers were vaccinated against cholera and typhoid fever, and over 700,000 doses of antitetanus serum were purchased.[41] Nevertheless, there were no delousing stations and no quarantine centres or barracks.

The army's weapons and equipment become irrelevant in a comparative analysis. The 1913 campaign did not use vast quantities of ammunition, whereas in the 1916 battles the absence of ammunition was acutely felt. In the years of neutrality, the efforts to purchase modern weapons and replenish ammunition reserves intensified. In the absence of a national industry, however, the only option was to import all the supplies. But where should they be bought? And, more importantly, how? Germany and Austria-Hungary, the main arms manufacturers until 1914, had drastically limited their deliveries to Romania, due to political uncertainty. A neutral country is not supposed to prepare for war. But if it does make preparations, who knows when it will forsake its neutrality and, more importantly, whose side it will join? The remaining option was the other group of forces, that is, the Entente powers. All eyes were on France, but the needs of Romania's Latin sibling were too great at that moment. It had to bear the brunt of the war effort, fighting against the Germans' remarkable firepower. France needed every machine gun, every projectile. There was no question of sending any to Romania. Despite the difficulties, the Ministry of War placed several orders with renowned manufacturers. Colonel Vasile Rudeanu, director superior of weaponry, was sent repeatedly on missions abroad to contract war supplies.[42] When he returned from his 1915 visit to Austria-Hungary, Switzerland, Italy and France, he presented the Ministry with a detailed report. This report showed, *inter alia*, that he had managed to secure contracts for the supply of twenty million calibre 6.5 mm full metal jacket bullets, from the Manfred Weiss factory in Budapest; two armoured vehicles equipped with machine guns, but without ammunition, from the French Société Anonyme des Etablissements Delaunay-Belleville; three automobile trucks from the Adolph Saurer factory in Arbon, together with spare parts; and fifty thousand pairs of boots from the Endicott factory in New York, as well as lead, brass and sodium nitrate from various American exporters. All the supplies were supposed to arrive in the country on the Thessaloniki–Niš–Prakhovo–Turnu Severin railway route.[43] However, after Serbia's capitulation, this route could not be used. As the Bosphorus and Dardanelles Straits were in the hands of the Central

Powers, the only hypothetical supply route remained the one passing through the remote Russian ports of Archangelsk and Vladivostok, which was inoperative in the cold season. Numerous war supplies, ammunition and weapons remained stranded in warehouses or on the Russian railroads. Others arrived damaged, or could not be used due to the lack of instructions accompanying them. This explains why, apart from a lack of experience, the Romanian army lacked sufficient modern means of warfare – machine guns, means of communications, aeroplanes – in the 1916 clashes.[44]

Finally, we come to the subject of the troops' conduct. The 1913 campaign was not devoid of indiscipline.[45] A lot of hostility from the age of the Balkan Wars remains. During the neutrality years, little was done to eradicate hatred and to integrate the Bulgarian population of the Quadrilateral. The neighbours from across the Danube were viewed with distrust.[46]

The behaviour of the Romanian authorities was not favourable to the harmonization of social relations, although this was not an extension of the soldiers' behaviour. A few memories about the actions of the troops were recorded, tarnishing the honour of the Romanian army. Although the locals were instructed not to profiteer from their produce (0.40 lei for a kilogram of beef, 1.20 lei for a goose, 0.005 lei for a kilogram of hay, 0.0005 lei for a kilogram of straw),[47] many abuses occurred. In Vratsa, a military apparel warehouse was robbed, after serving as a quarantine hospital for Bulgarians suffering from cholera. In Orhanie, the commanders distributed clothes that used to belong to cholera patients to the soldiers.[48] Romanian officers would steal saddles from military warehouses, and sewing machines and mirrors from people's homes.[49] Cattle were requisitioned without payment. So was fodder, flour, tobacco and horses for transport. Such offences became so numerous that it was necessary to reintroduce corporal punishment.[50] Many army corps committed irregularities resulting in unlawful profits, but at the same time many precious possessions were destroyed. In the Petrohan Pass, the highest point of the Sofia-Vidin route, the residence of the last Battenberg prince (who used it mostly for overnight stays when he returned from hunting) was vandalized; in the same place, the meteorological station was set on fire and destroyed, together with the instruments and the scientists' observation notes.[51]

The revenge taken by the Bulgarian soldiers a few years later exceeded the imagination. Propaganda had taught them that the Romanians had attacked Bulgaria treacherously in 1913, while the men south of the Danube were busy fighting on other front lines and could not defend the elderly, women or children. The moment had been long in the making, and when the opportunity for revenge presented itself, the cruelty had no limits. Many records of the time are available, some of them written in excessively violent language. Out of this savagery, the account of a simple soldier appears especially surreal:

> I, soldier Neculai I. Urde of the 74th Regiment, 19th company, hereby declare that while I was fighting as a rifleman ... I was in Tutrakan when the earth was crumbling on top of our soldiers in the trenches from the blows of the enemy's shells. The enemy ambushed our soldiers and stabbed them with bayonets, lifting them up and putting them down again, gouging the eyes of some, cutting off the ears or noses of others; I escaped by running, I retreated to the left, but in a few minutes I was hit in the leg and I retreated further to Tutrakan. This was on the evening of 24th August.[52]

Ordinary Romanians quickly took to heart the rumours of massacres and atrocities; an unprecedented Bulgarophobe current formed instantly. Even women reacted aggressively. The private diary of Arabella Yarka, the heir of an aristocratic family and a fixture of Bucharest high society, reads:

> Tutrakan has fallen and we are very worried. Twelve thousand Romanian prisoners! They say that Bulgarian women gouge the eyes of our wounded using forks, and that they pour boiling water from the windows on passing Romanian soldiers. A cursed nation! But we'll crush them, we'll defeat them yet! Woe to them when that day comes![53]

The war diary of Yvonne Blondel, daughter of Camille Blondel (1854–1935), France's former minister in Bucharest, reads as follows:

> Every day we see that the Bulgarians have remained the savages they have always been, lacking any scruples. They are not part of the civilized world and have no place in Europe. Their instincts remain those of bloodthirsty brutes, a fitting imitator of their current allies and masters.[54]

After the 1913 campaigns, such descriptions cultivated the growing Romanian–Bulgarian rivalry. Many ethnic Bulgarians enlisted in the Romanian army deserted the ranks.[55] The Romanians did not keep their heads either; strongly affected, the troops were ordered to commit atrocious acts against the Bulgarian population across the Danube in this failed replica of the Flămânda manoeuvre. They hastened to comply, killing women, the elderly and children.[56]

Lessons of the War

Few lessons were learned in Romania after the army's 1913 campaign. The governments and politicians assimilated the least. Blinded by a victory obtained in a war of attrition, they neglected the army's needs. Under the shelter of a fragile peace (the Bucharest Peace Treaty of 10 August 1913), Romanian diplomacy did nothing to consolidate its political gains. The crisis of July 1914 caught Romania unprepared for war and incoherent in its decision-making. The temporary solution of neutrality and – two years later – the intervention in the war were both consequences of external pressures and severe social turmoil. The main consequence of the Balkan Wars was the change in Romania's external alliances. Austria-Hungary turned from ally into enemy. For the army, this was not good news. Before 1914, nobody had seriously considered the hypothesis of an offensive across the Carpathians. The probability of a war with Russia oriented all military training, the location of fortifications and operational plans. Suddenly, everything had to change under the limit of discretion required by the imperatives of neutrality.

The war against Austria-Hungary was nothing like the triumphal campaign of 1913. It was a war between coalitions. Bulgaria was part of a strong military alliance, together with Germany, Austria-Hungary and the Ottoman Empire. Romania had joined the Entente powers, but only Russia was committed to providing Romania with military support. The military cooperation between Romania and Russia did not work, however. The troops led by General Zaionchikovski arrived too late in Dobruja and were unable to avoid defeat. The disaster at Tutrakan left a vivid impression, because the lessons of the 1913 campaign had not been learned. The army appeared as unprepared as ever. It was evident that Romanian politicians had learnt nothing from the lessons of the past.

Claudiu-Lucian Topor is Assistant Professor in the Modern History Department of the University 'Alexandru Ioan Cuza' in Iași. He is the author of *Germania și neutralitatea României (1914/1916): Studii istorice* [Germany and the Neutrality of Romania, 1914–1916: Historical Studies] (Editura Universitatii Alexandru Ioan Cuza, 2017) and the editor of several academic collections, including *The 'Unknown War' from Eastern Europe: Romania between Allies and Enemies (1916–1918)* (Editura Universitatii Alexandru Ioan Cuza, 2016, co-edited with Alexander Rubel) and *Through the Diplomats' Eyes: Romanian Social Life in the Late 19th and Early 20th Century* (Editura Universitatii Alexandru Ioan Cuza, 2016, co-edited with Daniel Cain and Alexandru Istrate).

Notes

1. Some historians even talk about a 'military stroll' in Southern Dobruja. See Katrin Boeckh, *Von den Balkankriegen zum Ersten Weltkrieg: Kleinstaatenpolitik und ethnische Selbstbestimmung auf dem Balkan* (Munich: Oldenbourg Verlag, 1996), 59.
2. In mid June, Bulgaria had 600,000 men mobilized. Most of the troops marched towards Macedonia and took up positions against the Serb and Greek forces. The First Army was deployed in the Vidin-Berkovitsa region, the Third Army in the Kyustendil-Radomir area, and the Fourth Army occupied the Rodosto-Štip-Kočani triangle. The Second Army troops were stationed in the eastern part of Thrace, but part of them were transferred to the Macedonian front. Just one incomplete division was left on the border between Romania and Turkey.
3. Richard C. Hall, *The Balkan Wars 1912–1913: Prelude to the First World War* (London: Routledge, 2002), 118.
4. Mareşal Alexandru Averescu, *Notiţe zilnice din război* [Daily Notes about the War], Vol. I, *1914–1916 (Neutralitatea)* [1914–1916 (Neutrality)] (Bucharest: Editura Militară, 1992), 83.
5. Zoe Cămărăşescu, *Amintiri. Frumuseţe, graţie, armonie, nobleţe: Adică tot ce am pierdut!* [Memories. Beauty, Grace, Harmony, Nobility: That's to Say, Everything I Have Lost!] (Bucharest: Casa Editorială Ponte, 2011), 320.
6. Corvin M. Petrescu, *Istoricul campaniei militare din anul 1913* [The History of Military Campaign in the Year 1913] (Bucharest: Tipografia Jockey-Club, 1914), 21, 40.
7. Colonel George G. Garoescu, *Războaiele balcanice, 1912–1913 şi campania română din Bulgaria* [The Balkan Wars, 1912–1913 and the Romanian Campaign in Bulgaria] (Sfântu Gheorghe: Tipografia Centrului de Instrucţie al Infanteriei, 1935), 128. See also Arhivele Naţionale ale Romaniei (The Romanian National Archives), Bucharest, fund Casa Regală (Royal House), folder 2/1913, 1–2: *Memoriul privitor la îndrumarea operaţiunilor armatei române în cazul că ar interveni în conflictul serbo-bulgar, 17 iunie 1913* [Memorandum about the Romanian Army Operations: Guidance for Involvement in the Serbo-Bulgarian Conflict, 17 June 1913].
8. The only significant act of valour in the entire campaign was the capture of a Bulgarian brigade in Ferdinandovo.
9. Alain de Penennrun, *40 jours de guerre dans les Balkans: La campagne serbo-bulgare en juillet 1913* (Paris: Librairie Chapelot, 1914), 203–7.
10. Constantin Argetoianu, *Pentru cei de mâine: Amintiri din vremea celor de ieri* [For Those Alive Tomorrow: Memories of the Time of Those Who Lived through Yesterday], Vol. III, Part V *(1916–1917)* (Bucharest: Editura Humanitas, 1992), 15, 18.
11. Generalul I. Culcer, *Note şi cugetări asupra campaniei din 1916: În special asupra operaţiunilor Armatei I-a* [Notes and Thoughts on the 1916 Campaign: Especially on the Operations of the First Army] (Iaşi: Tipografia ziarului Tribuna, 1918), 11.
12. The most detailed description of the battle in Tutrakan can be found in a monograph written by Colonel Constantin Zagorit between 1918 and 1923

(Constantin Zagorit, *Turtucaia: Descriere amănunțită a pregătirii de războiu a cetății și a luptelor care s-au întâmplat acolo după povestirile ostașilor care au luat parte la aceste lupte. Comoară de învățăminte pentru ofițerii de toate treptele.Greșeli și scăderi ale unui început de războiu dar care nu trebuie să se mai întâmple și fapte de vitejie neîntâlnite în istoria militară a omenirii, și care trebuie să servească drept pildă ostașilor în viitor.* Cu un atlas anexat, Institutul de Arte Grafice 'Concurența', Ploești, 1939). Unlike common history and military writings based on official documents, Zagorit's imposing monograph draws on the numerous private communications of officers and soldiers who actually fought the battle. As the archives of the units that fought the battle of Tutrakan have been lost, Colonel Zagorit's documentary is one of the most precious sources still available.

13 Constantin Kirițescu, *Istoria războiului pentru întregirea României 1916–1919* [The History of the War for Romanian Reunification, 1916–1919], Vol. I (Bucharest: Editura Științifică și Enciclopedică, 1989), 314.

14 Theo Schwarzmüller, *Zwischen Kaiser und Führer. Generalfeldmarschall August von Mackensen: Eine politische Biographie* (Paderborn: Ferdinand Schöningh Verlag, 1995), 137.

15 Mareșalul Alexandru Averescu, *Răspunderile* [Responsibilities] (Bucharest: Editura Albatros, 1999), 66.

16 Generalul G.A. Dabija, *Armata română în răsboiul mondial (1916–1918)* [The Romanian Army in the World War (1916–1918)], Vol. I (Bucharest: Editura I.G. Hertz, 1928), 179–82.

17 General Andrei Medardovitovich Zaionchikovski, commander of the Russian 47th Army Corps, consisting of two Russian divisions and a Serb one, with a strength of around thirty thousand men. Later on, he was commander of the Eastern Operative Group and then of the Dobruja Army (consisting of large bodies of Romanian and Russian army). He was replaced, due to his failures, by General Vladimir Vladimirovich Zakharov. The Dobruja Army was then called the Danube Army.

18 General de Divizie N. Mihaiescu, *Amintiri și învățăminte din războiul de întregire a neamului 1916–1919* [Memories and Lessons from the War for Reunifications, 1916–1919] (Bucharest: Tipografia ziarul Universul, 1936), 17–18.

19 General R. Scărișoreanu, *Fragmente din războiul 1916–1918: Istorisiri documentate* [Fragments of the War 1916–1918: Documented Stories] (Bucharest: Tiparul Cavaleriei, 1934), 63.

20 Constantin Bacalbașa, *Bucureștii de altădată* [Once Upon a Time in Bucharest], Vol. IV *(1910–1914)* (Bucharest: Albatros, 2007), 274.

21 Sabina Cantacuzino, *Din viața familiei I.C. Brătianu: Războiul 1914–1919* [From I.C. Bratianu's Family Life: The 1914–1919 War] (Bucharest: Editura Universul, 1937), 12.

22 Vasile Th. Cancicov, *Impresiuni și păreri personale din timpul războiului României: Jurnal zilnic 13 August 1916–31 decembrie 1918. Cu o scrisoare introductivă de Take Ionescu* [Impressions and Personal Opinions during Romania's War: Daily Diary 13 August 1916–31 December 1918, With an Introductory Letter by Take Ionescu], Vol. I (Bucharest: Atelierele Societății Universul, 1921), 43.

23 Dorin Dobrincu, 'O catastrofă uitată: Campania armatei române din 1916' [A Forgotten Disaster: The 1916 Campaign of the Romanian Army], *Xenopoliana* 11(3–4) (2003), 143–57, here 152.
24 General Scarlat Panaitescu, *Rolul României în războiul mondial* [The Role of Romania in the World War] (Bucharest: Imprimeriile Independența, 1919), 12–13.
25 General Radu R. Rosetti, *Mărturisiri (1914–1919)* [Confessions (1914–1919)] (Bucharest: Editura Modelism, 1997), 71.
26 After the defeat at Tutrakan, the chiefs of staff changed the Romanian army's strategic priorities. The Council of War held in Periș (2–15 September 1916) adopted unclear decisions. It ordered the organization of a great offensive south of the Danube, but also the continuation of the offensive in Transylvania, which was impossible from a strategic point of view, due to the low number of available troops. General Alexandru Averescu devised an ingenious plan of operations, which included a frontal attack by the Dobruja Army simultaneously deployed with a broad flanking manoeuvre across the Danube that was set up in the Oltenița-Giurgiu sector, next to the village of Flămânda. After two weeks, during which the available forces were assembled, reconnoitres were made, access roads were built, telephone and telegraph connections were established, material for building a pontoon bridge was collected and supplies were brought in. Combat action began on 18 September and went on until 1 October 1916. Due to heavy rain and the arrival of the Austrian monitors belonging to the Danube flotilla in the area of the river crossing, the manoeuvre was suspended and subsequently cancelled. For details, see Petre Out et al. (eds), *100 de mari bătălii din istoria României* [100 Great Battles in Romanian History] (Bucharest: Orizonturi Publishing, 2009), 282–88.
27 Averescu, *Notițe zilnice*, 83.
28 Ibid.
29 General C.N. Herjeu, *Studii și critice militare: Din învățămintele răsboaielor din 1913 și 1916–1918* [Military Studies and Criticisms: From the Lessons of the Wars of 1913 and 1916–1918] (Bucharest: Editura Librăriei Stănciulescu, 1921), 139.
30 Petrescu, *Istoricul campaniei*, 112.
31 Dimitrie Dimiu, *Amintirile unui rezervist: note și impresii din campania anului 1913* [Memories of a Reservist: Notes and Impressions of the 1913 Campaign] (Bucharest: Editura Minerva, 1914), 88.
32 Lev Troțki [Leon Trotsky], *România și războiul balcanic* [Romania and the Balkan War] (Iași: Editura Polirom, 1998), 72–73.
33 C. Paul and A. Marcu, *Campania în Bulgaria* [Campaign in Bulgaria] (Bucharest: Editura Institutului de Arte Grafice Flacăra, 1913), 68.
34 Alexandru Lascarov-Moldovanu, *Cohortele morții* [Cohorts of Death] (Bucharest: Cartea Românească, 1930), 55–56.
35 Averescu, *Notițe zilnice*, 83.
36 Nicolae Iorga, *Acțiunea militară a României: În Bulgaria cu ostașii noștrii* [Romania's Military Action: In Bulgaria with Our Soldiers] (Vălenii de Munte: Tipografia Societății Neamul Românesc, 1913), 179.

37 General I. Atanasiu, *Avântul țării: campania din 1913 în Bulgaria* [Forward with the Country: The 1913 Campaign in Bulgaria] (Cluj: Institutul de Arte Grafice Ardealul, 1925), 4.
38 Dimiu, *Amintirile unui rezervist*, 82.
39 Argetoianu, *Pentru cei de mâine*, 20.
40 Alexandru Marghiloman, *Note politice 1897–1924* [Political Notes, 1897–1924] (Bucharest: Editura de Arte Grafice Eminescu, 1927), 171.
41 Vasile Bianu, *Însemnări din războiul României Mari* [Notes from the War for Greater Romania], Vol. I (Cluj: Institutul de Arte Grafice Ardealul, 1925), 57.
42 Ministerul Apărării Naționale, Serviciul Istoric din cadrul Marelui Stat Major, *România în războiul mondial 1916–1919* [Romania during the World War, 1916–1919], Vol. I (Bucharest: Imprimeria Națională, 1934), 44–50.
43 Arhivele Naționale ale României, București (ANR), *Fond Președinția Consiliului de Miniștri* [Fund of the Presidency of Cabinet Council], folder 22/1915, file 289–90.
44 D.D. Patrașcanu, *Vinovații 1916–1918* [The Guilty Ones, 1916–1918] (Bucharest: Editura Lumina, 1918), 103.
45 See *The Other Balkan Wars: A 1913 Carnegie Endowment Inquiry in Retrospect, with a New Introduction and Reflections on the Present Conflict by George F. Kennan*, reprint (Washington, DC: Brookings Institutions Publications, 1993); Generaloberst Helmuth von Moltke, *Erinnerungen. Briefe, Dokumente 1877–1916: Ein Bild vom Kriegsausbruch, erster Kriegsführung und Persönlichkeit des ersten militärischen Führers des Krieges* (Stuttgart: Der Kommende Tag A-G Verlag, 1922), 374.
46 G.C. Dragu, *Răsboiul nostru: Credința în dreptate, Câteva articole de ziare apărute între 1913–1919* [Our War: Faith in Justice, Several Newspaper Articles Published 1913–1919] (Bucharest: M. Eminescu Graphic Arts Institute Press, 1919), 16.
47 Dimiu, *Amintirile unui rezervist*, 60–61.
48 Troțki, *România și războiul balcanic*, 73.
49 Ibid., 76.
50 Atanasiu, *Avântul țării*, 39.
51 *The Other Balkan Wars: A 1913 Carnegie Endowment Inquiry in Retrospect*, 232.
52 Gheorghe I. Brătianu, *File rupte din cartea războiului* [Pages Torn from the Book of War] (Bucharest: Editura Scripta, 2006), 27.
53 Arabella Yarka, *De pe o zi pe alta: Carnet intim 1913–1918* [From One Day to Another: Intimate Scrapbook, 1913–1918] (Bucharest: Editura Compania, 2010), 96.
54 Yvonne Blondel, *Jurnal de război 1916–1917: Frontul de sud al României* [War Diary 1916–1917: Romania's Southern Front] (Bucharest: Institutul Cultural Român, 2005), 62.
55 Scărișoreanu, *Fragmente din războiul*, 27.
56 Ștefănescu Galați, *1916–1918: Amintiri din războiu* [1916–1918: Memories of the War] (Iași: Viața Românească, 1921), 77.

Bibliography

Argetoianu, Constantin. *Pentru cei de mâine: Amintiri din vremea celor de ieri* [For Those Alive Tomorrow: Memories of the Time of Those Who Lived through Yesterday]. Vol. III, Part V *(1916–1917)*. Bucharest: Editura Humanitas, 1992.
Atanasiu, I., General. *Avântul țării: campania din 1913 în Bulgaria* [Forward with the Country: The 1913 Campaign in Bulgaria]. Cluj: Institutul de Arte Grafice Ardealul, 1925.
Averescu, Mareșal Alexandru. *Notițe zilnice din război* [Daily Notes about the War]. Vol. I, *1914–1916 (Neutralitatea)* [1914–1916 (Neutrality)]. Bucharest: Editura Militară, 1992.
——. *Răspunderile* [Responsibilities]. Bucharest: Editura Albatros, 1999.
Bacalbașa, Constantin. *Bucureștii de altădată* [Once Upon a Time in Bucharest]. Vol. IV *(1910–1914)*. Bucharest: Albatros, 2007.
Bianu, Vasile. *Însemnări din războiul României Mari* [Notes from the War for Greater Romania]. Vol. I. Cluj: Institutul de Arte Grafice Ardealul, 1925.
Blondel, Yvonne. *Jurnal de război 1916–1917: Frontul de sud al României* [War Diary 1916–1917: Romania's Southern Front]. Bucharest: Institutul Cultural Român, 2005.
Boeckh, Katrin. *Von den Balkankriegen zum Ersten Weltkrieg: Kleinstaatenpolitik und ethnische Selbstbestimmung auf dem Balkan.* Munich: Oldenbourg Verlag, 1996.
Brătianu, Gheorghe I. *File rupte din cartea războiului* [Pages Torn from the Book of War]. Bucharest: Editura Scripta, 2006.
Cămărășescu, Zoe. *Amintiri. Frumusețe, grație, armonie, noblețe: Adică tot ce am pierdut!* [Memories. Beauty, Grace, Harmony, Nobility: That's to Say, Everything I Have Lost!]. Bucharest: Casa Editorială Ponte, 2011.
Cancicov, Vasile Th. *Impresiuni și păreri personale din timpul războiului României: Jurnal zilnic 13 August 1916–31 decembrie 1918. Cu o scrisoare introductivă de Take Ionescu* [Impressions and Personal Opinions during Romania's War: Daily Diary 13 August 1916–31 December 1918, With an Introductory Letter by Take Ionescu]. Vol. I. Bucharest: Atelierele Societății Universul, 1921.
Cantacuzino, Sabina. *Din viața familiei I.C. Brătianu: Războiul 1914–1919* [From I.C. Bratianu's Family Life: The 1914–1919 War]. Bucharest: Editura Universul, 1937.
Culcer, I. Generalul. *Note și cugetări asupra campaniei din 1916: În special asupra operațiunilor Armatei I-a* [Notes and Thoughts on the 1916 Campaign: Especially on the Operations of the First Army]. Iași: Tipografia ziarului Tribuna, 1918.
Dabija, G.A., Generalul. *Armata română în răsboiul mondial (1916–1918)* [The Romanian Army in the World War (1916–1918)]. Vol. I. Bucharest: Editura I.G. Hertz, 1928.
Dimiu, Dimitrie. *Amintirile unui rezervist: note și impresii din campania anului 1913* [Memories of a Reservist: Notes and Impressions of the 1913 Campaign]. Bucharest: Editura Minerva, 1914.
Dobrincu, Dorin. 'O catastrofă uitată: Campania armatei române din 1916' [A Forgotten Disaster: The 1916 Campaign of the Romanian Army]. *Xenopoliana* 11(3–4) (2003), 143–57.

Dragu, G.C. *Războiul nostru: Credința în dreptate, Câteva articole de ziare apărute între 1913–1919* [Our War: Faith in Justice, Several Newspaper Articles Published 1913–1919]. Bucharest: M. Eminescu Graphic Arts Institute Press, 1919.

Galați, Ștefănescu. *1916–1918: Amintiri din războiu* [1916–1918: Memories of the War]. Iași: Viața Românească, 1921.

Garoescu, George G., Colonel. *Războaiele balcanice, 1912–1913 și campania română din Bulgaria* [The Balkan Wars, 1912–1913 and the Romanian Campaign in Bulgaria]. Sfântu Gheorghe: Tipografia Centrului de Instrucție al Infanteriei, 1935.

Hall, Richard C. *The Balkan Wars 1912–1913: Prelude to the First World War*. London: Routledge, 2002.

Herjeu, C.N., General. *Studii și critice militare: Din învățămintele răsboaielor din 1913 și 1916–1918* [Military Studies and Criticisms: From the Lessons of the Wars of 1913 and 1916–1918]. Bucharest: Editura Librăriei Stănciulescu, 1921.

Iorga, Nicolae. *Acțiunea militară a României: În Bulgaria cu ostașii noștrii* [Romania's Military Action: In Bulgaria with Our Soldiers]. Vălenii de Munte: Tipografia Societății Neamul Românesc, 1913.

Kirițescu, Constantin. *Istoria războiului pentru întregirea României 1916–1919* [The History of the War for Romanian Reunification, 1916–1919]. Vol. I. Bucharest: Editura Științifică și Enciclopedică, 1989.

Lascarov-Moldovanu, Alexandru. *Cohortele morții* [Cohorts of Death]. Bucharest: Cartea Românească, 1930.

Marghiloman, Alexandru. *Note politice 1897–1924* [Political Notes, 1897–1924]. Bucharest: Editura de Arte Grafice Eminescu, 1927.

Mihaiescu, N., General. *Amintiri și învățăminte din războiul de întregire a neamului 1916–1919* [Memories and Lessons from the War for Reunifications, 1916–1919]. Bucharest: Tipografia ziarul Universul, 1936.

Ministerul Apărării Naționale, Serviciul Istoric din cadrul Marelui Stat Major. *România în războiul mondial 1916–1919* [Romania during the World War, 1916–1919]. Vol. I. Bucharest: Imprimeria Națională, 1934.

Moltke, Helmuth von, Generaloberst. *Erinnerungen. Briefe, Dokumente 1877–1916: Ein Bild vom Kriegsausbruch, erster Kriegsführung und Persönlichkeit des ersten militärischen Führers des Krieges*. Stuttgart: Der Kommende Tag A-G Verlag, 1922.

The Other Balkan Wars: A 1913 Carnegie Endowment Inquiry in Retrospect, with a New Introduction and Reflections on the Present Conflict by George F. Kennan. Reprint. Washington, DC: Brookings Institutions Publications, 1993.

Out, Petre et al. (eds). *100 de mari bătălii din istoria României* [100 Great Battles in Romanian History]. Bucharest: Orizonturi Publishing, 2009.

Panaitescu, Scarlat, General. *Rolul României în războiul mondial* [The Role of Romania in the World War]. Bucharest: Imprimeriile Independența, 1919.

Patrașcanu, D.D. *Vinovații 1916–1918* [The Guilty Ones, 1916–1918]. Bucharest: Editura Lumina, 1918.

Paul, C., and A. Marcu. *Campania în Bulgaria* [Campaign in Bulgaria]. Bucharest: Editura Institutului de Arte Grafice Flacăra, 1913.

Penennrun, Alain de. *40 jours de guerre dans les Balkans: La campagne serbo-bulgare en juillet 1913*. Paris: Librairie Chapelot, 1914.

Petrescu, Corvin M. *Istoricul campaniei militare din anul 1913* [The History of Military Campaign in the Year 1913]. Bucharest: Tipografia Jockey-Club, 1914.

Rosetti, Radu R., General. *Mărturisiri (1914–1919)* [Confessions (1914–1919)]. Bucharest: Editura Modelism, 1997.

Scărişoreanu, R., General. *Fragmente din războiul 1916–1918: Istorisiri documentate* [Fragments of the War 1916–1918: Documented Stories]. Bucharest: Tiparul Cavaleriei, 1934.

Schwarzmüller, Theo. *Zwischen Kaiser und Führer. Generalfeldmarschall August von Mackensen: Eine politische Biographie*. Paderborn: Ferdinand Schöningh Verlag, 1995.

Troţki, Lev [Leon Trotsky]. *România şi războiul balcanic* [Romania and the Balkan War]. Iaşi: Editura Polirom, 1998.

Yarka, Arabella. *De pe o zi pe alta: Carnet intim 1913–1918* [From One Day to Another: Intimate Scrapbook, 1913–1918]. Bucharest: Editura Compania, 2010.

SERBIAN CHETNIKS
Traditions of Irregular Warfare

Alexey Timofeev

This chapter describes the origins of guerrilla warfare, waged by the Serbian irregulars (chetniks) during the Balkan Wars, and their methods and aims. The purpose is to show the chetniks' composite character, as a mixture of traditional and contemporary influences in military tactics. The relevance of this topic lies in the fact that the mixture of old myths and new – almost experimental – ideas is typical for the role of the Balkans as a kind of full-scale 'laboratory' for the world powers and their global policy, even in the present day. The traditions of *haiduchia* (from the word *hajduk*, *hajduci* or *haiduci* in the plural) are still significant in the social and cultural environment of the Balkans. The historical sources for this article have been selected in an attempt to tell the story of irregular warfare from a chetnik's perspective. Due to the peculiarity of the theme, most of the sources used for this article are memoirs and recollections.

Haiduchia: The General Development of the Chetnik Movement as a Social Phenomenon

For a very long period of time, the Slavic peoples of the Balkan peninsula were under non-Christian control and did not have their own states. Throughout the five centuries of Ottoman domination, these members of the European family of nations lost elements of their previously widespread social and public institutions, to the extent that these were modified and acquired specific new features and forms.[1] Simultaneously, new, typically 'Balkan' social and cultural phenomena emerged. One of those phenomena was haiduchia, which was typical for the mountainous and remote regions of the Western and Central Balkans. This practice entailed leaving the world of law and obedience to the authorities and escaping to the mountains in search of freedom and independence.[2]

Within centuries, traditions and ideas of behaviour of haiduchia participants developed in Serbian society. These traditions and ideas were depicted by the Serbian people in a complex interlacing of epic poetry, common law, specific ethnographic features and national Orthodoxy. For example, St. George's Day, celebrated on 6 May, became *haiduk meeting day* as the barren mountains once again acquire a lavish green veil. Similarly, St. Dimitri's Day on 8 November was considered *haiduk parting*, when the advancing cold forced haiduchia participants to leave the mountains to spend the winter in secret shelters provided by reliable people. These collaborators delivered provisions to the shelters, supplied the haiduks with information, and in return received a portion of loot. Robbery was one of the main occupations of the participants of haiduchia. Nevertheless, there still were definite rules and restrictions. On the one hand, there were those protecting the poor, as only assaults on traders and tax collectors were considered 'honest'; on the other hand, there were those limiting murders, which were only allowed as revenge for treachery or as 'self-defence', be it during an attack by authorities or in cases of resistance by the victim. Besides robberies, the haiduks also engaged in kidnapping for ransom. Sometimes participants of haiduchia united in a group, called a četa (*cheta*, hence *chetnik* – a member of a *cheta*), at the head of which there was a chieftain, the so-called *vojvoda* or *harambasha* in Turkish.[3] During Ottoman domination, haiduchia represented an analogy of real insurgent activity in miniature, one way of expressing resistance against the alien domination, which was superior in strength:

> Though at the beginning of the 19th century similar manifestations of resistance usually led not to reducing but to increasing the extent of oppression, they acted as stimulators for raising the national spirit, that became evident from the glorification of insurgent leaders and groups in South Slavic national epic poetry. They helped the people to save the hope for possible release from a foreign yoke. Certainly, the armed actions of some persons or small groups sometimes turned into or bordered on gangsterism. But if gangsterism was turned against the foreign oppressor, it was considered as heroism.[4]

However, with the emergence of independent nation-states in the Balkans, haiduchia became an expression of a civilizational backlog and of an underdeveloped agrarian society. Yet it also reflected a conflict between the state and peasants, including resistance of the country population to the new and primitive bureaucracy, which made the people perceive haiduchia in a simplistic romanticized way and to celebrate its representatives as courageous and free 'mountain tsars'.[5] The Serbian writer Svetolik Ranković (1863–99) described this dual representation of haiduchia participants in his novel, precisely entitled *The Mountain Tsar*, published in 1897.[6] By the middle of the nineteenth century, the haiduchia phenomenon on Serbian territory had degenerated into gangsterism. The authorities of the restructured Kingdom of Serbia managed to eliminate it almost completely, although some incidents still occurred in the most remote mountainous regions of the country.[7]

Retreating into the mountains of the Serbian kingdom, haiduchia did not disappear from the hearts of the Serbian population and co-nationals outside of the kingdom. It remained in the people's memory in the form of individual interventions in the *sanctum sanctorum* of any state – the use of violence to solve internal and external conflicts.[8] However, the Serbian state, initially formed as the result of a popular uprising in 1815, for a long time was compelled to delegate part of its law enforcement duties to its citizens. Thus, up to the beginning of the 1880s, the Serbian army literally remained the people's army. Attempts to eradicate such practices by confiscating military weapons from the population led to the *Timok Rebellion* of 1883. This rebellion was not only a consequence of political opposition but also the result of the reluctance of the broad Serbian masses to follow the way of the accelerated modernization of the state.[9] Contemporaries, such as Georg Rosen, the German consul-general in Belgrade (1867–75), noticed a certain echo of haiduchia in the national mentality, not only among the Serbians but also among other South Slavic peoples of the Balkans still living under Ottoman rule.[10]

The use of violence as a solution to foreign policy tasks became one of the basic political principles in the Balkans by the end of the nineteenth century. Haiduchia turned out to be an asymmetric answer to the violent behaviour of the great powers, who were cutting the Balkan map at their own discretion.[11] The traditional tendency to use violence to solve 'unsolvable problems' (à la haiduk) was not only typical for the rural population. The gloss of education added persuasiveness, cogency and consistency to the representatives of the national *intelligentsia*, who were unable to find any other way to solve the existing problems. According to the words of the most well-known Serbian scientist in the field of humanities, Jovan Cvijić (1865–1927):

> … the Serbian national problem needs to be solved by violence. Both small Serbian states should, first of all, prepare for it by military and educative means in the most active way, support the national energy in

the Serbian people on the occupied territories and use the first more or less suitable circumstances to solve the Serbian question.[12]

The former head of Serbian military intelligence, Dragutin Dimitrijević-Apis (1876–1917), speaking about the organization of the secret Serbian revolutionary society Unity or Death in his final speech at the Salonika trial, described even more specifically the role of the highly educated segment of society in turning haiduchia into the tool of solution for the international problems:

> Back in 1904, I was included into a committee for activities in Old Serbia and Macedonia ... forming that committee we asked for suggestions from our most known people and the most competent professionals in these questions. One of them, a highly respected and world-renowned professor of our university, condescended to us and with the most convincing proofs convinced us that only a rifle, a grenade and a dagger could rescue Serbians in Old Serbia and Macedonia from inevitable death, implying that the last moment of existence of Serbians had come.[13]

The aspiration to apply an 'asymmetric answer' and 'insubordinate violence' in order to achieve definite foreign policy purposes was typical for other Balkan states as well. They drew 'inspiration' from actions of the Ottoman Porte, which used its *bashi-bazouks*,[14] irregular units of Albanians and Muslim Slavs, to suppress rebels and to render pressure upon disobedient Christians. Moreover, the use of violence was promoted by the situation that had developed in the Balkans during the last quarter of the nineteenth century. Vast Christian-inhabited territories in the European part of the Ottoman Empire were still under the control of Constantinople, the largest of those territories being Macedonia. In those regions, the Ottoman Empire actively pursued strategies of reducing the number of the local Christian population, encouraging evictions and limiting the rights of Christians, and resorting to the help of local Muslims. At the same time, after the Berlin Congress of 1878, the leading European states came to certain arrangements and aspired to a status quo policy.

There were several unsuccessful attempts at a direct military confrontation between the armies of the newly formed Christian states and the army of the declining Porte, such as the Serbian-Ottoman War of 1876 and the Greco-Ottoman War of 1897. In direct contrast, there was a rather successful Bulgarian policy of supporting the promotion of teachers and priests, and at the same time relying on the rifles and daggers of the komits; in the last decade of the nineteenth century, such a policy was conducted in Macedonia (the *vilayet* of Salonica and parts of the *vilayet* of Manastir/Bitola), the areas of Old Serbia (the *vilayet* of Kosovo) and Thrace (the *vilayet* of Adrianople/Edirne/Odrin). The

Bulgarian komits served as an important factor in strengthening the role of the Bulgarian Exarchate Church and the Bulgarian schools. After 1903, Serbia and Greece began to follow the Bulgarian example, and the Serbian chetniks and Greek andarts acted similarly to the Bulgarian komits.[15] As a result of the activity of the Bulgarian, Serbian and Greek revolutionary committees, Macedonia turned into 'a huge boiling copper' in which, for the first time, the world faced such phenomena as 'terrorism' and 'international police forces'. Russians who visited the European part of the Ottoman Empire brought home such expressions as 'Macedonian bomb' (*makedonka*) and 'Macedonian shooting'. The character of these Balkan innovations in military science is rather indicative. Macedonian bombs were primitive hand grenades – cast spheres filled with home-made explosives consisting of a combination of Berthollet salt and sugar, hermetically sealed with wax. These 'komit apples' were equipped with fuses and, before throwing such a bomb, the chetniks lighted the fuse with the help of hand-rolled cigarettes stuffed with strong and fragrant Macedonian tobacco. Macedonian bombs had weak killing power, an unpredictable radius of destruction, and were rather a tool of terror and intimidation, operating in a very limited range. 'Macedonian shooting' referred to another terrorist-type activity, involving the shooting of two short firearms simultaneously, one in each hand. This increased the firepower of the shooter, while essentially reducing his accuracy. This Macedonian trend also effected psychological harm more than physical losses, given that it could affect the enemy only in close combat.[16]

Chetnik Organization and Paramilitary Tactics

The participation of the Serbian chetniks in the Balkan Wars was a very important stage of the development of haiduchia. For the South Slav peoples – more exactly, for speakers of the Shtokavian dialect of the Serbo-Croatian language – hostilities with an 'asymmetric' character were not a novelty. The particular position of their homeland in the mountainous border zone of the Austro-Hungarian Empire and the Ottoman Empire in the seventeenth and eighteenth centuries promoted the development not only of such a phenomenon as haiduchia, but also of special skills and combat tactics. These special skills and tactics were unusual during an era when military operations were conducted in a way resembling today's military parade formations. The skills of the South Slavic peoples were actively used by the neighbouring empires in the formation of light infantry and cavalry units. According to Walter

Laqueur, the well-known Western historian of irregular warfare tactics, up to the middle of the eighteenth century the European military discourse had not known much about the tactics of operations in small military units:[17]

> Specific works on partisan warfare only began to appear in the mid-eighteenth century and they drew their main inspiration from the activities of the small, light, highly mobile (and semiprivate) units which were employed in the Austrian army since the 17th century. These units, composed of Pandurs and Croats, had amassed considerable combat experience in the areas bordering Turkey. Later on, albeit on a smaller scale, such detachments became part of the French army.[18]

However, the development of the idea of a guerrilla war in Serbia itself was much more stimulated by the activities of another military formation – the Serbian Freikorps (Free Corps), formed on the territories of the Austro-Hungarian Empire. These units were composed of ethnic Serbs – volunteers to put obstacles in the way of Ottoman bandits, small individual formations and couriers; additionally, they were used for raids deep into the territory controlled by the Ottomans.[19] A considerable part of the operations during the First Serbian Uprising (1804–13) can be considered unorganized guerrilla warfare (*Kleinkrieg*). After the establishment of the independent Serbian principality in 1817, the idea of using guerrilla operations more systematically did not arise immediately in the Serbian army. On the contrary, at first the formation of a regular army took place, which was not completed until the reign of King Milan Obrenović (1854–1901). Still, the word *chetnik* was first defined by scholar Vuk Karadžić in his Serbian language dictionary in 1818.[20] The first book written by a Serbian author about guerrilla warfare was published in Russia and in the Russian language; however, it drew little attention from the author's compatriots,[21] as at that time in Serbia translations of foreign authors enjoyed much greater popularity.[22] The first independent work that eventually labelled the terminology of organized *chetnik war* was published only in 1868.[23] It is necessary to note that these works appeared as a reflection of contemporary events, namely the Serbian revolt in Austria-Hungary in 1848 and the planned all-Slav rebellion in the Ottoman Empire in 1867. The Serbian army attempted to use chetnik units for the first time during the Eastern Crisis of 1875–78, under the command of Miloš Milojević (1840–97) and Nićifor Dučić (1832–1900).[24] The experience of the Bosnia-Herzegovina uprising of 1875–78 strongly affected Serbian chetnik operations at the beginning of the twentieth century in Macedonia and Old Serbia.[25] During this period, the *modus vivendi* of chetnik organizations in the adjacent territory in peacetime was formed. It was formally established as a non-governmental movement that did not have the official approval of parliament or the government, but existed with the consent of the state. The chetnik organization was supported by active government officials and officers, who backed it both financially and with arms from the state arsenals. A similar model of action was typical both for Bulgarian ('Macedonian') komits and Greek andarts. From 1903, the chetniks were directed by the Serbian revolutionary organization, composed of an association of individuals, including prominent servicemen and politicians. From 1906, the chetniks were supported by the secret 'supreme board' at the Consular Department of the Serbian Ministry of Foreign Affairs. From 1908 to 1909, the activity of the chetas was suspended, but the new mass organization 'National Defence' became interested in chetnik personnel. Consequently, in 1911 the Serbian chetnik activities were renewed under the direct influence of enthusiasts from the organization Unity or Death, closely connected with the Serbian military intelligence service. As a result, the command over the Serbian chetniks passed to the participants of the small organization Union or Death, in which officers dominated, operating from behind the facade of their membership in the mainly civil mass organization 'National Defence', but sometimes acting openly, as military intelligence officers of the Serbian General Staff.[26] Similar informality was typical for actions of the Serbian military elite as a whole. For instance, the retired general of the Russian army, Evgenii Martinov, recollected his observations of the Balkan War period:

> There were very few personnel in the staff of the Supreme Command. For example, only two officers worked in the Operational Department ... It is impossible not to notice the specifically close relations between officers of various departments who carried out almost all the tasks by direct contacts, without any excessive bureaucratic correspondence.[27]

This close interlacing of the military machinery, secret societies and private initiative became especially evident in the activities of the chetnik organizations at the beginning of the twentieth century. During this time, opaque preparations were carried out with chetniks of Serbian origins by several officers of the military intelligence, using army equipment. The actual training for the chetnik movement was conducted in 1903–12.[28] The preparations were organized for inhabitants of the Ottoman Empire as well as for nationally minded Serbian youths from Austria-Hungary. According to the memoirs of one of the members of the organization Union or Death, Major Aca Blagojević, during the annexation crisis of 1908, several students, among them Bogdan Žeraić, Vladimir Gaćinović and Dragitun Kokanović, were brought from the Viennese and Zagreb universities to Vranje, the centre of the Serbian chetnik activities directed at Macedonia and Old Serbia. In his memoirs, Blagojević wrote: 'During 4 months in Vranje, I trained these students for work in the villages of Bosnia and Croatia with the aim to prepare the people for an uprising against Austria'.[29] Another description of such a training course dates back to 1912, when a group of youths arrived without passports in Belgrade via the Austrian town of Zemun at the end of June. For six weeks, the youths were trained in mountain camps in southern Serbia. Under field conditions, the students received training in the theory and practice of guerrilla actions; they were taught how to survive in the wild, how to shoot, how to make home-made and how to use factory-made grenades; and they practised the use of explosives for diversions on bridges and railway lines. More accelerated training courses were organized in the urban areas, where manuals on mine warfare and tactics of chetnik operations were studied.[30] Upon completion of training, some participants became active chetnik volunteers. For example, a group of students from Bosnia (including Gavrilo Princip) arrived in Prokuplje on 25 September 1912, and at the beginning of October the best students were admitted to the chetnik unit under the command of the chetnik *vojvoda*[31] Vojislav Tankosić, a major in the Serbian military intelligence and one of the leaders of Union or Death.[32]

Chetniks and the Balkan Wars

The Austrian authorities knew about the chetnik activities and were rightly concerned about them. Nevertheless, in 1912 it was not yet the Austro-Hungarian Empire's but the Ottoman Empire's time to be concerned.[33] The official Serbian authorities, and most of the educated society, still found a considerable difference between these two empires, and so the outbreak of full-scale chetnik operations was prevented on Austro-Hungarian territory. The administrator of Serbian policy, Prime Minister Nikola Pašić (1845–1926), convinced zealous military officials that it was 'not the same thing to use terrorist methods in the Ottoman Empire and in Austro-Hungary'. Five years after the Balkan Wars, in 1917, he still argued that:

> ... it was necessary to operate so in Turkey, as there Bulgarians, Greeks and Turks had similar organizations, therefore we also needed it. But Europe knew about it. We had informed Europe that in Turkey we could be protected only by the weapon, and Europe knew it and condemned Turkey to great suffering. It couldn't have been permitted in Austria. It

is an old state. It has a thousand-year-old dynasty. Europe would not have tolerated it, and we would look very nasty in the eyes of Europe in that case, as even now we are attributed with different plots and assassinations.[34]

However, in his memoirs Vasilije Trbić[35] notes that certain Serbian preparatory activities in relation to Austria-Hungary still took place. In the spring of 1912, Trbić arrived from Veles in Belgrade, where he was informed by the successor to the throne about negotiations with Bulgaria, about plans to divide up Macedonia, and about a joint plan of the Balkan countries to drive the Turks out of the Balkans. The Serbian military circles were concerned that the Austro-Hungarian Empire would come to the aid of the Ottoman Empire. The day after his arrival, Trbić had a conversation with Major Milan Vasić, the secretary of 'National Defence' and a member of Union or Death. Vasić drew Trbić's attention to the necessity of reconnoitring 'the situation at the Erdut-Bogojevo Bridge over the Danube in order to find out the possibility of disabling it in case of emergency'. Trbić, a native of Eastern Slavonia, immediately thought of his relative Jovan, who was a switchman on this strategically significant bridge over the Danube, deep in Austro-Hungarian territory. With a false Ottoman passport, Trbić left for Austria to visit Jovan and to carefully examine the bridge. Trbić convinced Jovan that in case of the 'need for the Serbian people', he should help by destroying the bridge by remote detonation, by laying an anti-train mine or a mine with a clockwork mechanism. For the execution of this plan, Trbić promised to send 'the master' with 'the gift'; he then left for Belgrade and from there returned to Macedonia.[36]

By the end of August 1912, Trbić was replaced by Milan Djokić as chief of the Mountain Staff. Djokić was a second lieutenant in the Serbian army who, before training in Serbia, had been a sergeant in the Serbian cheta operating in Macedonia up to 1908. The new chief of the Mountain Staff accepted command over the chetas[37] and proceeded with the reconnaissance of auxiliary roads, secret tracks and mountain passes. Trbić then left for Belgrade again, where from the middle of August until the middle of September he worked together with two majors of the Serbian General Staff, Milan Milovanović and Milan Milovanović-Pilac, on specifying maps of Macedonia for combat operations. At approximately seven o'clock on the evening of 2 October, the successor to the throne, Aleksandar, visited the office of the General Staff and talked to Trbić personally, as he had also done before. The next day, the officers of the Serbian General Staff asked Trbić to leave for Macedonia again. Consequently, on that same evening Trbić took the train to Skopje without a passport, but with money and a revolver.

Prewar Chetnik Activities

On 3 October 1912, the last Serbian train wanting to cross the border into the Ottoman Empire was stopped by the Ottomans, after which the border was closed due to the oncoming war. Trbić, among other suspicious people, was captured by the Ottoman police, but managed to escape and was able to return to his home in Teovo in the Azot mountain area to the southwest of Veles at the Babuna Mountain, with a pro-Serbian Orthodox Slavic population. Through his relatives, Trbić notified several fellows from the village cheta, who waited for him with weapons and supplies at the appointed place in the mountains. On the evening of 4 October 1912, the chetnik unit, consisting of six chetniks and the vojvoda Trbić, started their fight against the Turks for the final liberation of their native land – the main task for which they had been preparing.

The next day, these actions commenced with the expulsion of the Ottoman tax inspector and two Ottoman police officers from the village of Orahov Do. Trbić let them know through his messengers that any lingering of Ottoman officials in the Christian villages would end 'in tears for them'. On the same day, the authoritative vojvoda, who had departed into the mountains, was joined by new chetniks; by nightfall, the cheta was composed of fifteen people. One day later, Trbić's group increased to thirty people. The vojvoda contacted the commander of the Mountain Staff, Djokić, and informed him about the latest news from Belgrade. The list of priority tasks for chetniks included: the violation of the Ottoman communications network in the enemy's rear; the prevention of the recruitment and mobilization of transport units and carriers for the Ottoman troops; and the spreading of chaos and disorganization in the enemy's rear regions.

On 6 October 1912, six Ottoman police officers who arrived on the scene to mobilize carts, horses, carriers and reservists became the first victims of the new cheta. When the police officers arrived at the village of Mokreni, they decided to begin with a cup of coffee in a café, where they were suddenly attacked by twelve of Trbić's chetniks. Four peasants present in the café joined the attack without wasting any words. As the police officers were being tied up, Trbić came into the room and stated that, in general, he 'knew all those people as being not bad people ... But there was no time for sentiments'.[38] Using the butts of their rifles, the chetniks drove the police officers out of the village and hanged them in the next grove. The officers' rifles were given to the peasants from the village of Mokreni who had joined the cheta.

The chief of the police station in the village of Soglje found out about the loss of his men and summoned half of the Ottoman cavalry from Veles. The cavalry arrived the next day, 7 October, to conduct the investigation in Mokreni. The remaining peasants in the village fled in panic; moreover, the chetniks had also disappeared. *Askers*, Ottoman soldiers, seized the local priest, Father Damian, shot him and left the village. The police officers did not appear in the village; the returning peasants removed the hanged officers from the tree and buried them at the edge of the wood, awaiting further developments.

On the same day, the Ottoman authorities sent one more expedition to Azot, consisting of 250 bashi-bazouks, who proceeded in plundering Trbić's homestead in the village of Teovo, killing his young son and his brother and abducting his young daughter, his wife and her relatives, taking them to Veles as hostages. Trbić was with his cheta at the time in the region of Prilep, where he was engaged in further activation of rural chetas. He only learned about the sad news a few days later, but did not leave his cheta. Trbić did send a message to the elder of the nearest village to Teovo, the large Albanian Muslim village of Soglje, asking him to intercede in Veles for his family's release. If they were not released, Trbić promised that he would burn Soglje immediately, with all its inhabitants. In his memoirs, Trbić wrote: 'I had not any more time to help my family. The same evening my family was released'.[39]

By that time there were already about one hundred chetniks in Trbić's cheta, and further instructions from Belgrade were expected by pigeon post. Additional weapons were obtained from Djokić, the commander of the Mountain Staff. Djokić's chetniks controlled the region of Poreče, and Trbić decided to return with his cheta to Azot in order to continue actions against the communication lines of the Ottoman army. The chetniks managed to interrupt the cable line between Veles and Prilep in fifty places and crushed the transport that had accumulated on the Veles–Prilep road around Crnička Reka. Some security guards accompanying the wagons ran away, and the chetniks allowed the remaining peasants working as carriers to unharness their oxen and leave. The Ottoman military transport was then set on fire. Advancing on the success, Trbić decided to continue to put psychological pressure upon the enemy and to retaliate for the plundering of his house. The vojvoda learned that the appointed commander of the local militia, a rich merchant from Prilep named Adem-Aga, had bought wealthy estates in local villages for each of his five adult sons, and held around two thousand sheep on the slopes of the Babuna Mountain. Trbić advised Adem-Aga and his subordinates not to leave the Prilep suburbs or to attack Serbian villages, in order not to risk the property and the lives of his sons. After that, neither the police nor military servicemen appeared again in the Serbian mountain villages of Azot, and the chief of the police station and his remaining policemen left the village of Soglje. The village elder of Soglje asked Trbić for protection and defence of the village. The vojvoda promised not to disturb the village under the condition of assistance in getting in contact with the city of Veles, which, due to the circumstances, the Orthodox peasants of Azot were not allowed to enter. Thus, Trbić re-established contact with his network of informants in Veles, which was chosen by the Turks as the location to gather their forces that were headed for Macedonia. Thinking ahead, and supported by local peasants, Trbić began to prepare the approach for the Serbian army to Veles.

Chetniks at War

The first shots of the Balkan War sounded on 9 October 1912 on the Montenegrin-Ottoman border.[40] The chetniks' mobilization, which began as early as 28 September in Vranje, allowed for the formation of several combat groups, composed of volunteers from Serbia, Montenegro and Austria-Hungary. These groups were under the command of the headquarters, which received orders from the chief of the Supreme Command of the Serbian army, Radomir Putnik (1847–1917). The major of the Serbian border guards, Alimpij Marijanović, was engaged in the mobilization, organization and coordination of the chetas. Orders to the chetnik commanders were given by the respective army commanders of the territories in which they were stationed. Confidential orders were conveyed by Major Vasić, who was appointed chief of the Intelligence Department of the Supreme Command of the chetnik organization and personally arrived at the front. On Macedonian territory, there were two Mountain Staffs. One of them was responsible for the region of Skopska Crna Gora–Kriva Palanka; the other – the Transvardar Staff – was responsible for the region of Azot–Poreče.[41] Under the command of experienced Serbian vojvodas, several combat groups were formed, which had to fulfil their tasks in an area of regular Serbian army action.

The Serbian war plan was as follows: the First Serbian Army would advance along the valley of the South Morava in the direction of Kumanovo and Skopje; the Second Serbian Army was based in the region of Kyustendil and Dupnitsa in Bulgaria; the Third Serbian Army was based in the Kursumlija territory towards Kosovo; lastly, the Ibar detachment was to head in the direction of the Sandzak of

Novopazar (Novi Pazar). The chetniks were expected to support the regular army in various ways. The group of vojvoda Vuk (V. Popović), together with local chetas, which Trbić had been sent to form, had to provide support for the First Serbian Army. Such support actions were not planned for the Second Serbian Army. The Ibar detachment had to execute its actions only with the forces of several chetas, while the main concentration of chetnik forces was designated to the operations of the Third Serbian Army, where four chetnik groups were active, namely those of Lab, Gniljane, Lisice and Lukovo. The group of Lab was headed by Major Tankosić, who had gathered 505 chetniks under his command. Having attacked an Ottoman border post, these chetniks became the first Serbian soldiers to engage in combat operations. However, this attack was not authorized by the Supreme Command, and to a certain degree this move was motivated by Tankosić's desire to prevent the possibility of peace talks with the Ottoman Empire and instead to proceed in a war of liberation of the Serbian lands.[42] During further operations, the chetniks were used as the vanguard of the advancing armies, emaciating the enemy's line of defence and securing ground for the main Serbian forces.[43]

From 23 to 24 October, Serbian guns could be heard roaring in Kumanovo, fired by chetniks hiding on the slopes of the Babuna Mountain. Within two days, units of the broken and defeated Ottoman army started to move from Veles to Prilep. Chetniks headed by Trbić took up positions on the mountain pass by Babuna, having left their native villages under the control of inhabitants of Soglje. The people from Soglje tried their best to distract the retreating Ottoman troops from the Orthodox villages, foreseeing the possibility of chetnik retaliation. Finally, on the evening of 1 November 1912, Trbić's chetniks joined the advance division of the Serbian army – the cheta headed by Popović. On 3 November, Trbić's cheta, together with the 4th battalion of the 16th regiment of the 17th Moravian division of the Serbian army, attempted to seize the Mukos pass on the Babuna Mountain. The 17th Moravian division soon approached and replaced the chetniks, allowing them to disengage and instead manoeuvre to enter Prilep on 5 November 1912, 'on the back' of the retreating Ottoman army.

Individual soldiers from the shattered Ottoman army still passed through the streets of Prilep while the Serbian armies were just a three-hour march from the city. In the meantime, Trbić's chetniks occupied the Community City Council of Prilep, where the city's representatives had gathered. Because the Serbian regular army was approaching very quickly, leaving its supply convoys far behind, the chetniks ordered the city inhabitants to prepare the necessary supplies for the Serbian army.

When the Serbian troops entered Prilep, Popović's chetniks carried out tasks of protection and investigation. The chetniks arrested and shot some of the most outstanding opponents of the Serbian army.

Colonel Pavle Jurišić-Šturm, commander of the Drina division, sent Trbić's cheta to search for provisions for the army, to provide the necessary supplies according to requisition obligations, and to seal up the Ottoman state warehouses in the neighbouring villages. In addition, vojvoda Trbić plundered the estates of Adem-Aga, the chieftain of the bashi-bazouks, who had attacked the vojvoda's house earlier. Trbić gave the cattle, the main property of the bashi-bazouks, to the Serbian army. When Major Vasić arrived in the Prilep region, a new important task was set before Trbić's chetniks.

It is worth mentioning that the cases described below were not the only acts of 'extrajudicial punishment' that chetnik vojvodas carried out by order from above (in these cases by order of M. Vasić). For example, I. Trifunović describes another case, which occurred at the beginning of September 1912, when, a month before the beginning of the First Balkan War, vojvoda Vuk Popović received a letter from M. Vasić in which the latter informed his 'Dear V.' that, 'if the war begins', the police inspector Abdoul H. 'shouldn't live to witness it'. This 'demand of National Defence' was swiftly executed, and inspector Abdoul H. as well as several of his colleagues were shot during an ambush.[44]

Major Vasić announced to Trbić that the Serbian cavalry regiment, who were lodging in the villages of Desovo and Brailovo for the night, had been deceptively surrounded and killed. Vasić demanded Trbić 'to grab Arnauts from Desovo and Brailovo; to shoot all men, to burn villages, and then to bring reliable Serbs who have merits before our organization and lodge them there at the place of the Albanian villages'.[45] In the village of Desovo, Trbić and thirty of his chetniks grabbed and shot all local Albanian men (111 in total) and burned the community, leaving the local women and children homeless. In Brailovo, where Albanians had settled some decades ago and expelled almost all local Orthodox inhabitants, Trbić acted 'more mildly'. He found out who had participated in the attack on the Serbian cavalry, shot those sixty-six Albanians, but did not burn the village. One Orthodox Slavic family still lived in the village, among twenty Albanian families. As Trbić wrote later:

> I realized that it was my mistake to burn Desovo. The Turks acted in such a way in 1903, during the Macedonian revolt, when they burned Christian Orthodox villages in the Bitola Vilayet and I didn't want to become similar to the Turks in this way.[46]

Furthermore, Trbić's chetniks were engaged in patrolling villages and establishing a local administration in the region of Prilep and Veles.

After the start of the Second Balkan War, on 30 June 1913, Trbić received a personal telegram from the supreme commander of the Serbian army, Radomir Putnik, with the order to mobilize chetniks on the right bank of the Vardar, to create a Vardar group and to drive off the enemy in the area from Gracki to Gevgelija at the head of this group. With the exception of Popović's combat group, which carried out a special task in another sector of the front, all Serbian chetas were subordinated to Trbić. His group already consisted of two hundred men and was now joined by the glorified chetas of Jovan and Jovan Dolgać. Trbić's unit of chetniks was ordered to liquidate the groups of Bulgarian komits that had penetrated into the territories occupied by the Serbian army, and afterwards to prevent new incursions of komits, without engaging in combat with units of the regular Bulgarian army – unless there was a special order. After the retreat of the Bulgarian army, Trbić's chetniks were also engaged in the search and elimination of the secret service network left behind by the receding enemy. In carrying out this task, Trbić faced another problem, creating many difficulties for the local population: after the beginning of the military operations, the commander of the Serbian garrison at the Demir Kapija railway station organized a group of local Turks under the command of several former Serbian chetnik volunteers from the advance elements of the Serbian army. That group proclaimed itself adherent to 'the Serbian chetniks', but became notorious for looting shops in the centre of Gevgelija with the motivation that 'All the same, Bulgarians would get it!' Trbić's chetniks disarmed the impostors. The Turks among them were whipped and released to their residence, whereas the Serbian accomplices, who also received whippings, were tied up and sent to the Supreme Command of the Serbian army. The stolen property was returned to the citizens of Gevgelija. Trbić's men participated in the disclosure and the elimination of several more acts of brigandage and violence by local Muslims, who tried to plunder local villages where the Bulgarian Exarchate Church worked.

After the signing of the Treaty of Bucharest in 1913, peace still did not come to Macedonia. Trbić named the events of 1913 the Third Balkan War, or the war with Albania. During that 'war', the chetniks subordinated to Trbić continued to carry out functions similar to those of the 'Field Gendarmerie for the maintenance of rudimentary administration in the liberated regions ... for a pacification of the local population that sometimes led to terrorist actions against civilians'.[47]

Conclusion

To sum up, it should be noted that the use of Serbian chetniks in the triune role of 'saboteurs-scouts-gendarmerie' is convergently similar to the use of komits in the Bulgarian and andarts in the Greek armies.[48] In their activities, extremely backward and extremely advanced tendencies in military science and organization are fancifully intertwined. On the one hand, this was a multipurpose and improvised phenomenon, leaning on spontaneous 'haiduk habits' of the local population. On the other hand, a novelty undoubtedly consisted in the ideas concerning the asymmetric conduction of combat operations; the deployment of subversive groups behind the front line prior to full-scale operations; the spreading of propaganda among the local population; and the formation of combat insurgent groups in the rear of the enemy. As a result, any violent action by the enemy only kindled the fire of rebellion. Despite some features of barefaced violence and cruelty – on the verge of war crimes, sometimes almost going beyond that verge – in these actions, it was possible to notice the signs of a new kind of warfare, which van Creveld called 'non-trinitarian or non-Clausewitzian'.[49] The Serbian military, as well as their Bulgarian colleagues, continued to supplement their traditional practice of haiduchia and the chetnik movement with active publishing work, acquainting chetniks and komits with the world's latest developments in military equipment in the field of guerrilla actions.[50] It is necessary to recognize that during the Balkan Wars groups of chetniks and komits acted much more successfully than the groups of guerrilla-hunters formed in Russia during World War I, despite the long traditions of guerrilla war development there.[51] Even the *makedonka*, a seemingly primitive improvisation, used by Bulgarian komits and Serbian chetniks alike at the end of the nineteenth and at the beginning of the twentieth century, produced by the Serbian military industry in Kragujevac since 1904 (sealed in a specially cast case piece of low-brisant explosive supplied with Bickford fuse with the pressed-out detonator inside the grenade), was a rather up-to-date weapon in the early twentieth century. In the Russo-Japanese War (1904–5), the Russian and Japanese soldiers used shell sleeves and lead tubes filled with dynamite as manual grenades, and the Japanese even used bamboo trunks and jam jars with pyroxylin. It was only after the Russo-Japanese War that the large European armies started to revive the forgotten weapon of the grenadiers.[52] Not without reason, two years after the end of the Balkan Wars, the Serbian military received recognition from contemporaries as they managed to make a breakthrough in conducting special operations. In 1916 in

Macedonia and Serbia, the Serbian chetniks for the first time in military history landed planes to the rear of the enemy for the organization and carrying out of diversions and revolts.[53]

Alexey Timofeev is Senior Research Associate at the Institute of the Modern History of Serbia in Belgrade and Associate Professor in the Department of Modern History at Belgrade University. His scholarly interests focus on conflicts in Southeastern and Eastern Europe in the twentieth century. Between 1999 and 2017, he published six monographs, five editions of sources, as well as fifty-nine articles and reports. Between 2010 and 2017, he (co-)organized several exhibitions on the Holocaust and on war crimes in the Balkans in the twentieth century. He recently published *Splintered Wind: Russians and the Second World War in Yugoslavia* (Publishing House of Modest Kolerov, 2014).

Notes

1 The influence of the insurgency traditions and the role of the military factor in the development of the Serbian state were significant. Mihail Belov, 'Serbskaia povstancheskaia gosudarstvennost i ee ideologicheskoe obosnovanie' [Insurgent Serbian Statehood and Its Ideological Justification], in V.K. Volkov (ed.), *Dvesti let novoi serbskoi gosudarstvennosti* [Two Hundred Years of the Modern Serbian State] (St. Petersburg: Aleteia, 2005), 39–53; Iaroslav Vishniakov, *Voennyi faktor i gosudarstvennoe razvitie Serbii nachala 20 veka* [The Military Factor and State Development of Serbia in the Early 20th Century] (Moscow: MGIMO/U, 2012).

2 A phenomenon of convergent similarity arose in other nations of the Balkan peninsula as well (Turkish 'Kırcaali' and Albanian 'kachaki'). Partial similarity, like the idea of escaping from authorities to become 'free people', can be typologically found in other historical periods as well – from Robin Hood to Stenka Razin (1630–71). Nevertheless, the specific phenomenon of hayduchiya represented characteristic typological features for the social history of the Balkan peninsula for six centuries.

3 Dušan Popović, *O hajducima. Deo 1–2* [About Hayduchiya. Part 1–2] (Belgrade: Narodna štamparija, 1930–31); Vid Vuletić Vukasović, *Poslednji hajduci u Lici i drugim nekim našim krajevima* [The Last Hayduks in Lika and Some Other Parts of Our Country] (Belgrade: Sv. Sava štamparija, 1923); Miodrag Stojanović, *Hajduci i klefti u narodnom pesništvu* [Hayduks and Klefts in Folk Poetry] (Belgrade: Srpska akademija nauka i umetnosti, 1984).

4 Jozo Tomasevich, *The Chetniks* (Stanford, CA: Stanford University Press, 1975), 115.

5 Andrej Mitrović, *Ustaničke borbe u Srbiji 1916–1918* [Rebellious Fighting in Serbia 1916–1918] (Belgrade: Srpska književna zadruga, 1987).
6 Svetolik Ranković, *Gorski car* [The Mountain Tsar] (Belgrade: Srpska književna zadruga, 1897).
7 Radoš Ljušić, 'Hajdučija u užičkom kraju u vreme vladavine kneza Miloša i kneza Mihaila' [Hayduchiya in Uzice Region during the Reign of Prince Miloš and Prince Michael], *Užički zbornik* 14 (1985), 73–100; Vojislav Marjanović, *Ivan Babejić – poslednji gorski car Homolja: hajdučija u Homolju i Zviždu* [Ivan Babejić – the Last Mountain King of Homolje: Hayduchiya in Homolje and Zvižd] (Kučevo: Magnat, 2000); Milisav Djenić, *Zločini u ime pravde: zlatiborska hajdučija* [Crimes in the Name of Justice: The Hayduchiya of Zlatibor] (Čajetina: Kulturno-sportski centar, 2005); Milić Antonijević, *Hajduci Homolja: monografija o homoljskoj hajdučiji* [Hayduks of Homolje: Monograph on the Hayduchiya of Homolje] (Petrovac na Mlavi: Stojadinović, 2006); Olivera Milosavljević, 'Hajdučija u Užičkom okrugu u vreme druge vladavine kneza Miloša' [The Hayduchiya in the District Užice during the Second Reign of Prince Miloš], *Istorijska baština* 19 (2010), 17–25; Olivera Milosavljević, 'Hajdučija u Čačanskom okrugu sredinom 19. Veka' [Hayduchiya in Čačak District in the Middle of the 19th Century], *Zbornik radova Narodnog muzeja* 39 (2009), 117–48.
8 Andrei Shemiakin, 'Narod i vlast' v nezavisimoi Serbii' [People and Power in Independent Serbia], in V.K. Volkov (ed.), *Dvesti let novoi serbskoj gosudarstvennosti* [Two Hundred Years of the Modern Serbian State] (St. Petersburg: Aleteia, 2005), 177–92; Latinka Perović, *Između anarhije i autokratije/Srpsko društvo na prelazima vekova (XIX–XXI)* [Between Anarchy and Autocracy/Serbian Society at the Turn of the Centuries (19th–21st Century)] (Belgrade: Helsinški odbor za ljudska prava u Srbiji, 2006).
9 At the same time, this refusal of accelerated modernization played a considerable role in the genesis and ideology of the most powerful political movement of independent Serbia – the Serbian radicals. See, for more details, Andrei Shemiakin, *Ideologiia Nikoly Pashicha: Formirovanie i evolutsiia (1868–1891)* [The Ideology of Nikola Pašić: The Formation and Evolution (1868–1891)] (Moscow: Indrik, 1998).
10 Georg Rosen, *Die Balkan-Heiduken: Ein Beitrag zur inneren Geschichte des Slawentums. (Nachdruck von 1876 mit einem Vorwort von Boian Valtchev)* (Berlin: OEZ, 2009). Some authors trace the influence of the epic tradition of haiduks on the mentality and daily behaviour of the population of the Western Balkans to the present time; see Ivo Žanjić, *Prevarena povijest: Guslarska estrada, kult hajduka i rat u Hrvatskoj i Bosni i Hercegovini, 1990–1995. godine* [Cheated Story: Guslar Estrada, Hayduk Cult and War in Croatia and Bosnia and Herzegovina from 1990 to 1995] (Zagreb: Durieux, 1998).
11 This answer was the only outlet from the classical style of behaviour put forth by the 'big' states in relation to the 'small' one, which in the 1960s was accurately summed up by movie director Stanley Kubrick (1928–99): 'The great nations have always acted like gangsters, and the small nations like prostitutes' (*The Guardian*, 5 June 1963).

12 Jovan Cvijić, *Aneksija Bosne i Hercegovine i srpski problem* [The Annexation of Bosnia and Herzegovina and the Serbian Problem] (Belgrade: Državna štamparija kraljevine Srbije, 1908).
13 Borivoje Nešković, *Istina o Solunskom procesu* [The Truth about the Saloniki Trial] (Belgrade: Narodna knjiga, 1953), 277–278.
14 Bashi-bazouks (Turk. *başıbozuk*) were irregular soldiers of the Ottoman army, recruited from among local Muslim poor and particularly known for being brutal and undisciplined. See Rhoads Murphey, *Ottoman Warfare, 1500–1700* (London: UCL Press, 1999).
15 Douglas Dakin, *The Greek Struggle in Macedonia, 1897–1913* (Thessaloniki: Institute for Balkan Studies, 1993); Aleksei Timofeev, *Krest, kinzhal i kniga: Staraia Serbiia v politike Belgrada. 1878–1912* [Cross, Dagger, and Book: Old Serbia in the Policy of Belgrade. 1878–1912] (St. Petersburg: Aleteia, 2007).
16 Vasiljie Trbić, *Memoari* [Memoirs], 2 Vols. (Belgrade: Cultura, 1996); Stevan Simić, *Srpska revolucionarna organizacija: Komitsko četovanje u Staroj Srbiji i Makedoniji 1903–1912* [The Serbian Revolutionary Organization: The Chetnik Movement in Old Serbia and Macedonia 1903–1912] (Belgrade: Cultura, 1998); Stanislav Krakov, *Plamen četništva* [The Flame of the Chetnik Movement] (Belgrade: Hipnos, 1990).
17 There was virtually no need to have special units for harassing the enemy until the eighteenth century, when the magazine supply system appeared, i.e. the rear zone in the modern understanding of this term.
18 Walter Laqueur, *Guerrilla Warfare: A Historical & Critical Study* (New Brunswick, NJ: Transaction Publishers, 1997), 101.
19 Vladimir Belić, *Ratovi srpskog naroda u 19 veku (1788–1918)* [Wars of the Serbian People in the 19th Century (1788–1918)] (Belgrade: Izdavačko i knjižarsko preduzeće G. Kon a. d, 1937).
20 The deployment of a cheta in the mountains and in fighting interactions with the enemy was called četovanije (chetovanije), the analogue of a raid, but unlike the latter, the mission was carried out not on a specified route but in an area of constant activity. The special 'Mountain Staff' was organized to coordinate the activity of chetas in a certain area and to keep contact with the central organization.
21 This book was written by the russified Serb Ivan Vuić, who in his youth had become a prototype of Lermontov's *Fatalist*. He became a major-general in the Russian service, as well as a professor of strategy, tactics and military history at the Nicholas General Staff Academy; see Ivan Vuić, *Malaia voina, sostavil dlia rukovodstva v Imperatorskoi voennoi akademi Gvardeiskago Generalnago Shtaba polkovnik Vuić* [The Small War, the Manual Compiled for the Imperial Guard Military Academy of the General Staff] (St. Petersburg: Tipografiia E. Praca, 1850).
22 Matija Ban, *Pravila o četničkoj vojni, Protolmačio iz poljskoga sa nekim promenama, izmetcim i dodatcima Matija Ban* [Chetnik War Rules, Translated from Polish with Some Changes and Additions] (Belgrade: Knigopečatanie Kneževine srpske, 1848); *Načela četovanja napisao Don Santijago Paskual i Rubijo biv. oficir u štabu đen. Mine, s nemačkog preveo Dragašević oficir i profesor* [Principles of Chetnik Actions, Compiled by Don Santiago Pascual y Rubio – Former Officer at the Headquarters of Gen. Mine, Translated

from German by Dragašević, Officer and Professor] (Belgrade: Državna pečatnica, 1868).
23 Ljubomir Ivanović, Četovanje ili četničko ratovanje [Chetovaniye or Chetnik Warfare] (Belgrade: Državna pečatnica, 1868).
24 Jovan Hadži-Vasiljević, *Spomenica Društva sv. Save 1886–1936* [Memorial of the Society of St. Sava 1886–1936] (Belgrade: Društvo Sv. Save, 1936); National Library of Serbia, Collection of J. Hadži-Vasiljević, Military Papers of M.S. Milojević, Letters 1–331 (1876–1889); Dušan Martinović, *Portreti* [The Portraits], Vol. 2 (Cetinje: Centralna narodna biblioteka SR Crne Gore, 1987).
25 Vladimir Dedijer, *Sarajevo 1914* (Belgrade: Prosveta, 1966).
26 Biljana Vučetić, 'Srpska revolucionarna organizacija u Osmanskom carstvu na početku XX. veka' [The Serbian Revolutionary Organization in the Ottoman Empire at the Beginning of the 20th Century], *Istorijski časopis* 53(1) (2006), 359–74; Predrag Pejić, Četnički pokret u kraljevini Srbiji 1903–1918 [The Chetnik Movement in the Kingdom of Serbia 1903–1918] (Kragujevac: Novi pogledi, 2007); Timofeev, *Krest, kinzhal i kniga*, 140–48.
27 Evgenii Martinov, *Srbi u ratu sa carem Ferdinandom* [Serbs in the War against Tsar Ferdinand] (Belgrade: Knjižarnica Gece Kona, 1913), 80.
28 Čedomir Popović, 'Četnička škola u Prokuplju' [The School of Chetniks in Prokuplje], *Nova Evropa* 9(10–11) (1927), 323–27; Timofeev, *Krest, kinzhal i kniga*, 140–62.
29 Dedijer, *Sarajevo 1914*, 903.
30 Vojislav Bogićević (ed.), *Sarajevskij atentat, Pisma i saopštenja* [The Assassination in Sarajevo, Letters and Reports] (Sarajevo: Svjetlost, 1965).
31 A Slavic term that originally denoted the principal commander of a military force.
32 Dedijer, *Sarajevo 1914*, 318.
33 Ibid., 694.
34 Milan Živanović, *Pukovnik Apis: Solunski proces hiljadu devetsto sedamnaeste* [Colonel Apis: The Salonica Trial in 1917] (Belgrade: Cultura, 1955), 568.
35 Vasilije Trbić, a citizen of Austria-Hungary, without a military rank, graduated in 1902–3 from the theological school in Karyes (Mount Athos). From then he was engaged in the organization of the Serbian chetnik movement in Macedonia. In 1912, Trbić became the commander of the Mountain Staff in Macedonia at the age of thirty-one. He spent fifteen years in Macedonia, acquired an abundance of friendly relations and learned the local languages. With the money he received from Serbia (and by means of informal support from the chetnik organization), Trbić managed to raise a family and purchase a large-scale farm.
36 Trbić, *Memoari*, Vol. I, 280–84.
37 In fact, at that time it was an organizational network, because the majority of chetniks (from the so-called rural groups of chetniks) stayed home, hiding their weapons and waiting for a signal.
38 Trbić, *Memoari*, Vol. II, 7.
39 Ibid., 8.
40 The starting of military operations by Montenegro, earlier than by the other allies, aimed at distracting part of the Ottoman forces operating

against Serbia. Therefore on 4 October border skirmishes between the Montenegro and Ottoman armies commenced. Cf. Nikolai Pastuchov (ed.), *Balkanskaia voina: 1912–1913 gg.* [The Balkan War: 1912–1913] (Moscow: Tovarishchestvo izdatel'skogo dela, 1914).

41 Petar Stojanov, *Makedoniia vo vremeto na balkanskite i prvata svetska vojna (1912–1918)* [Macedonia at the Time of the Balkan Wars and the First World War (1912–1918)] (Skopje: Institut za natsionalna istoriia, 1969); Pejić, *Četnički pokret u kraljevini Srbiji 1903–1918*, 122–24; Vladimir Ilić, 'Učešće srpskih komita u Kumanovskoj operaciji 1912. godine' [The Participation of the Serbian Komits in the Kumanovo Operation in 1912], *Vojnoistorijski glasnik* 43(1–3) (1992), 179–217, here 214–16.

42 Živojin Mišić, *Moje uspomene* [My Memories] (Belgrade: Cultura, 1969). However, this was not the first border collision. On 4 October, the Albanians had attacked the Serbian border post in the area of Merdar: see Borislava Lilić, *Memoari srpskih ratnika (1912–1918)* [Memories of Serbian Warriors (1912–1918)] (Belgrade: Institut za savremenu istoriju, 2004).

43 Ilija Trifunović, *Trnovitim stazama* [The Thorny Passes] (Belgrade: Štamparija Glavnog saveza srpskih zemljoradničich zadruga, 1933).

44 Ibid., 40.

45 Ibid.

46 Trbić, *Memoari*, Vol. II, 17–19.

47 Tomasevich, *The Chetniks*, 117; Nikolai Shevalie (Nikolai Gasfeild), *Pravda o voine na Balkanakh: Zapiski voennogo korrespondenta* [The Truth about the War in the Balkans: Notes of a War Correspondent] (St. Petersburg: Tipolitografiia Iakor', 1913), 69–70; Ivan Taburno, *O serbskikh bitvakh (vpechatleniia ochevidtsa voiny serbov s turkami 1912 g.)* [About Serbian Battles (An Eyewitness's Impressions of the Serb War with the Turks in 1912)] (St. Petersburg: Novoe vremia, 1913), 63.

48 Dakin, *The Greek Struggle in Macedonia*, 447–50; Todor Petrov, 'Deistviiata na partizanskite cheti v tila na protivnika' [The Actions of Chetnik Groups behind the Enemy Lines], *Natsionalno-osvoboditelnoto dvizhenie na makedonskite i trakiiskite bŭlgari 1878–1944*, Vol. 3 (Sofia: Akademichno izdatelstvo Marin Drinov, 1997), 274–82.

49 That is, without a clear separation of the three components (the population, the army and the state) as in classical wars according to Clausewitz. See Martin van Creveld, *The Transformation of War* (New York: Free Press, 1991).

50 It was, for example, used in the chetnik training manual *Chetnik*, translated and compiled by M. Đorđević on the basis of books of the English hero of the Anglo-Boer wars, General Robert Baden-Powell: Robert Baden-Powell, *Reconnaissance and Scouting* (London: Gayle & Polden, 1884); idem, *Aids to Scouting for NCOs and Men* (London: Gayle & Polden, 1899); idem, *Scouting for Boys* (London: Windsor House, Bream's Buildings, E.C.: Horace Cox, 1908). See also works of the Prussian expert on the history of guerrilla and special operations, Wilhelm Balk, translated by Zh. Mishich: Wilhelm [Viljem] Balk, *Taktika. Nauka o boju: Noćne borbe, Borbe oko šuma i mesta. Borbe oko tesnaca. Borbe oko rečnih tokova. Planinski rat. Četničko ratovanje i etapna služba* [Tactics. The Science of Combat: The Night Battle, the Battle in a Forest and in a Village. The Battles around the Gorge. The Battles

near Rivers. The Mountain War. Chetnik Warfare and Service] (Belgrade: Balcan, 1912); and a synthesis of the Russian theory of partisan warfare by the Bulgarian military theorist T. Panov: Teodor Panov, *Partizanski nabegi* [The Partisan Raids] (Sofia: Voeni Zhurnal, 1911).

51 Petr Vershigora, *Voennoe tvorchestvo narodnykh mass* [Combat Creativity of the Masses] (Moscow: Voenizdat, 1961); Vladimir Kvachkov, *Spetsnats Rossii* [Russian Special Forces] (Moscow: Russkaia panorama, 2007).

52 Boris Pribylov and Evgeni Kravchenko, *Ruchnie i ruzheinye granaty* [Hand and Rifle Grenades] (Moscow: Arctika, 2008); Anastasios Liáskos and Basileios Nikóltsios, *Ta ópla tou makedonikoú agóna (1904–1908)* [The Weapons of the Macedonian Struggle (1904–1908)] (Thessaloniki: Image & Word, 2008).

53 'Praktika maloi voiny v okkupirovannoi Serbii', in M. Rybakov (ed.), *Praktika maloi voiny v okkupirovannoi Serbii* [The Small War Practice in the Occupied Serbia] (Moscow: VA RKKA, 1936), 1–21; Arthur Ehrhardt, *Der Kleinkrieg: Geschichtliche Erfahrungen und künftige Möglichkeiten* (Potsdam: Voggenreiter, 1934), 64–78.

Bibliography

Antonijević, Milić. *Hajduci Homolja: monografija o homoljskoj hajdučiji* [Haiduks of Homolje: Monograph on the Haiduchia of Homolje]. Petrovac na Mlavi: Stojadinović, 2006.

Baden-Powell, Robert. *Reconnaissance and Scouting*. London: Gayle & Polden, 1884.

———. *Aids to Scouting for NCOs and Men*. London: Gayle & Polden, 1899.

———. *Scouting for Boys*. London: Windsor House, Bream's Buildings, E.C.: Horace Cox, 1908.

Balk, Wilhelm [Viljem Balk]. *Taktika. Nauka o boju: Noćne borbe, Borbe oko šuma i mesta. Borbe oko tesnaca. Borbe oko rečnih tokova. Planinski rat. Četničko ratovanje i etapna služba* [Tactics. The Science of Combat: The Night Battle, the Battle in a Forest and in a Village. The Battles around the Gorge. The Battles near Rivers. The Mountain War. Chetnik Warfare and Service]. Trans. Zh. Mishich. Belgrade: Balcan, 1912.

Ban, Matija. *Pravila o četničkoj vojni, Protolmačio iz poljskoga sa nekim promenama, izmetcim i dodatcima Matija Ban* [Chetnik War Rules, Translated from Polish with Some Changes and Additions]. Belgrade: Knigopečatanie Kneževine srpske, 1848.

Belić, Vladimir. *Ratovi srpskog naroda u 19 veku (1788–1918)* [Wars of the Serbian People in the 19th Century (1788–1918)]. Belgrade: Izdavačko i knjižarsko preduzeće G. Kon a. d, 1937.

Belov, Mihail. 'Serbskaia povstancheskaia gosudarstvennost i ee ideologicheskoe obosnovanie' [Insurgent Serbian Statehood and Its Ideological Justification]. In V.K. Volkov (ed.), *Dvesti let novoi serbskoi gosudarstvennosti* [Two Hundred Years of the Modern Serbian State] (St. Petersburg: Aleteia, 2005), 39–53.

Bogićević, Vojislav (ed.). *Sarajevskij atentat, Pisma i saopštenja* [The Assassination in Sarajevo, Letters and Reports]. Sarajevo: Svjetlost, 1965.
Creveld, Martin van. *The Transformation of War*. New York: Free Press, 1991.
Cvijić, Jovan. *Aneksija Bosne i Hercegovine i srpski problem* [The Annexation of Bosnia and Herzegovina and the Serbian Problem]. Belgrade: Državna štamparija kraljevine Srbije, 1908.
Dakin, Douglas. *The Greek Struggle in Macedonia, 1897–1913*. Thessaloniki: Institute for Balkan Studies, 1993.
Dedijer, Vladimir. *Sarajevo 1914*. Belgrade: Prosveta, 1966.
Djenić, Milisav. *Zločini u ime pravde: zlatiborska hajdučija* [Crimes in the Name of Justice: The Haiduchia of Zlatibor]. Čajetina: Kulturno-sportski centar, 2005.
Ehrhardt, Arthur. *Der Kleinkrieg: Geschichtliche Erfahrungen und künftige Möglichkeiten*. Potsdam: Voggenreiter, 1934.
Hadži-Vasiljević, Jovan. *Spomenica Društva sv. Save 1886–1936* [Memorial of the Society of St. Sava 1886–1936]. Belgrade: Društvo Sv. Save, 1936.
Ilić, Vladimir. 'Učešće srpskih komita u Kumanovskoj operaciji 1912. Godine' [The Participation of the Serbian Komits in the Kumanovo Operation in 1912]. *Vojnoistorijski glasnik* 43(1–3) (1992), 179–217.
Ivanović, Ljubomir. *Četovanje ili četničko ratovanje* [Chetovaniye or Chetnik Warfare]. Belgrade: Državna pečatnica, 1868.
Krakov, Stanislav. *Plamen četništva* [The Flame of the Chetnik Movement]. Belgrade: Hipnos, 1990.
Kvachkov, Vladimir. *Spetsnats Rossii* [Russian Special Forces]. Moscow: Russkaia panorama, 2007.
Laqueur, Walter. *Guerrilla Warfare: A Historical & Critical Study*. New Brunswick, NJ: Transaction Publishers, 1997.
Liáskos, Anastasios, and Basileios Nikóltsios. *Ta ópla tou makedonikoú agóna (1904–1908)* [The Weapons of the Macedonian Struggle (1904–1908)]. Thessaloniki: Image & Word, 2008.
Lilić, Borislava. *Memoari srpskih ratnika (1912–1918)* [Memories of Serbian Warriors (1912–1918)]. Belgrade: Institut za savremenu istoriju, 2004.
Ljušić, Radoš. 'Hajdučija u užičkom kraju u vreme vladavine kneza Miloša i kneza Mihaila' [Haiduchia in Uzice Region during the Reign of Prince Miloš and Prince Michael]. *Užički zbornik* 14 (1985), 73–100.
Marjanović, Vojislav. *Ivan Babejić – poslednji gorski car Homolja: hajdučija u Homolju i Zviždu* [Ivan Babejić – The Last Mountain King of Homolje: Haiduchia in Homolje and Zvižd]. Kučevo: Magnat, 2000.
Martinov, Evgenii. *Srbi u ratu sa carem Ferdinandom* [Serbs in the War against Tsar Ferdinand]. Belgrade: Knjizarnica Gece Kona, 1913.
Martinović, Dušan. *Portreti* [The Portraits]. Vol. 2. Cetinje: Centralna narodna biblioteka SR Crne Gore, 1987.
Milosavljević, Olivera. 'Hajdučija u Čačanskom okrugu sredinom 19. Veka' [Haiduchia in Čačak District in the Middle of the 19th Century]. *Zbornik radova Narodnog muzeja* 39 (2009), 117–48.
———. 'Hajdučija u Užičkom okrugu u vreme druge vladavine kneza Miloša' [The Haiduchia in the District Užice during the Second Reign of Prince Miloš]. *Istorijska baština* 19 (2010), 17–25.
Mišić, Živojin. *Moje uspomene* [My Memories]. Belgrade: Cultura, 1969.

Mitrović, Andrej. *Ustaničke borbe u Srbiji 1916–1918* [Rebellious Fighting in Serbia 1916–1918]. Belgrade: Srpska književna zadruga, 1987.
Murphey, Rhoads. *Ottoman Warfare, 1500–1700*. London: UCL Press, 1999.
Načela četovanja napisao Don Santijago Paskual i Rubijo biv. oficir u štabu đen. Mine, s nemačkog preveo Dragašević oficir i profesor [Principles of Chetnik Actions, Compiled by Don Santiago Pascual y Rubio – Former Officer at the Headquarters of Gen. Mine, Translated from German by Dragašević, Officer and Professor]. Belgrade: Državna pečatnica, 1868.
Nešković, Borivoje. *Istina o Solunskom procesu* [The Truth about the Saloniki Trial]. Belgrade: Narodna knjiga, 1953.
Panov, Teodor. *Partizanski nabegi* [The Partisan Raids]. Sofia: Voeni Zhurnal, 1911.
Pastuchov, Nikolai (ed.). *Balkanskaia voina: 1912–1913 gg.* [The Balkan War: 1912–1913]. Moscow: Tovarishchestvo izdatel'skogo dela, 1914.
Pejić, Predrag. *Četnički pokret u kraljevini Srbiji 1903–1918* [The Chetnik Movement in the Kingdom of Serbia 1903–1918]. Kragujevac: Novi pogledi, 2007.
Perović, Latinka. *Između anarhije i autokratije/Srpsko društvo na prelazima vekova (XIX–XXI)* [Between Anarchy and Autocracy/Serbian Society at the Turn of the Centuries (19th–21st Century)]. Belgrade: Helsinški odbor za ljudska prava u Srbiji, 2006.
Petrov, Todor. 'Deistviiata na partizanskite cheti v tila na protivnika' [The Actions of Chetnik Groups behind the Enemy Lines], in Dobrin Michev (ed.), *Natsionalno-osvoboditelnoto dvizhenie na makedonskite i trakiiskite bŭlgari 1878–1944*. Vol. 3 (Sofia: Akademichno izdatelstvo Marin Drinov, 1997), 274–82.
Popović, Čedomir. 'Četnička škola u Prokuplju' [The School of Chetniks in Prokuplje]. *Nova Evropa* 9(10–11) (1927), 323–27.
Popović, Dušan. *O hajducima. Deo 1–2* [About Haiduchia. Part 1–2]. Belgrade: Narodna štamparija, 1930–31.
'Praktika maloi voiny v okkupirovannoi Serbii', in M. Rybakov (ed.), *Praktika maloi voiny v okkupirovannoi Serbii* [The Small War Practice in the Occupied Serbia] (Moscow: VA RKKA, 1936) 1–21.
Pribylov, Boris, and Evgeni Kravchenko. *Ruchnie i ruzheinye granaty* [Hand and Rifle Grenades]. Moscow: Arctika, 2008.
Ranković, Svetolik. *Gorski car* [The Mountain Tsar]. Belgrade: Srpska književna zadruga, 1897.
Rosen, Georg. *Die Balkan-Heiduken: Ein Beitrag zur inneren Geschichte des Slawentums. (Nachdruck von 1876 mit einem Vorwort von Boian Valtchev)*. Berlin: OEZ, 2009.
Shemiakin, Andrei. *Ideologiia Nikoly Pashicha: Formirovanie i evolutsiia (1868–1891)* [The Ideology of Nikola Pašić: The Formation and Evolution (1868–1891)]. Moscow: Indrik, 1998.
———. 'Narod i vlast' v nezavisimoi Serbii' [People and Power in Independent Serbia], in V.K. Volkov (ed.), *Dvesti let novoi serbskoi gosudarstvennosti* [Two Hundred Years of the Modern Serbian State] (St. Petersburg: Aleteia, 2005), 177–92.

Shevalie, Nikolai (Nikolai Gasfeild). *Pravda o voine na Balkanakh: Zapiski voennogo korrespondenta* [The Truth about the War in the Balkans: Notes of a War Correspondent]. St. Petersburg: Tipolitografiia Iakor', 1913.

Simić, Stevan. *Srpska revolucionarna organizacija: Komitsko četovanje u Staroj Srbiji i Makedoniji 1903–1912* [The Serbian Revolutionary Organization: The Chetnik Movement in Old Serbia and Macedonia 1903–1912]. Belgrade: Cultura, 1998.

Stojanov, Petar. *Makedoniia vo vremeto na balkanskite i prvata svetska voina (1912–1918)* [Macedonia at the Time of the Balkan Wars and the First World War (1912–1918)]. Skopje: Institut za natsionalna istoriia, 1969.

Stojanović, Miodrag. *Hajduci i klefti u narodnom pesništvu* [Hayduks and Klefts in Folk Poetry]. Belgrade: Srpska akademija nauka i umetnosti, 1984.

Taburno, Ivan. *O serbskikh bitvakh (vpechatleniia ochevidtsa voiny serbov s turkami 1912 g.)* [About Serbian Battles (An Eyewitness's Impressions of the Serb War with the Turks in 1912)]. St. Petersburg: Novoe vremia, 1913.

Timofeev, Aleksei. *Krest, kinzhal i kniga: Staraia Serbiia v politike Belgrada. 1878–1912* [Cross, Dagger, and Book: Old Serbia in the Policy of Belgrade. 1878–1912]. St. Petersburg: Aleteia, 2007.

Tomasevich, Jozo. *The Chetniks*. Stanford, CA: Stanford University Press, 1975.

Trbić, Vasiljie. *Memoari* [Memoirs]. 2 Vols. Belgrade: Cultura, 1996.

Trifunović, Ilija. *Trnovitim stazama* [The Thorny Passes]. Belgrade: Štamparija Glavnog saveza srpskih zemljoradničih zadruga, 1933.

Vershigora, Petr. *Voennoe tvorchestvo narodnykh mass* [Combat Creativity of the Masses]. Moscow: Voenizdat, 1961.

Vishniakov, Iaroslav. *Voennyi faktor i gosudarstvennoe razvitie Serbii nachala 20 veka* [The Military Factor and State Development of Serbia in the Early 20th Century)]. Moscow: MGIMO/U, 2012.

Vučetić, Biljana. 'Srpska revolucionarna organizacija u Osmanskom carstvu na početku 20 veka' [The Serbian Revolutionary Organization in the Ottoman Empire at the Beginning of the 20th Century]. *Istorijski časopis* 53(1) (2006), 359–74.

Vuić, Ivan. *Malaia voina, sostavil dlia rukovodstva v Imperatorskoi voennoi akademi Gvardeiskago Generalnago Shtaba polkovnik Vuić* [The Small War, the Manual Compiled for the Imperial Guard Military Academy of the General Staff]. St. Petersburg: Tipografiia E. Praca, 1850.

Vukasović, Vid Vuletić. *Poslednji hajduci u Lici i drugim nekim našim krajevima* [The Last Hayduks in Lika and Some Other Parts of Our Country]. Belgrade: Sv. Sava štamparija, 1923.

Žanjić, Ivo. *Prevarena povijest: Guslarska estrada, kult hajduka i rat u Hrvatskoj i Bosni i Hercegovini, 1990–1995. godine* [Cheated Story: Guslar Estrada, Hayduk Cult and War in Croatia and Bosnia and Herzegovina from 1990 to 1995]. Zagreb: Durieux, 1998.

Živanović, Milan. *Pukovnik Apis: Solunski proces hiljadu devetsto sedamnaeste* [Colonel Apis: The Salonica Trial in 1917]. Belgrade: Cultura, 1955.

Part IV
Civilians, Wounded, Invalids

10

THE FUTURE ENEMY'S SOLDIERS-TO-BE
Fear of War in Trieste, Austria-Hungary

Sabine Rutar

In March 1910, Karl Renner, who would head Austria's first postwar and post-imperial government in 1918, visited Trieste to deliver a lecture at the Circolo di studi sociali (Circle for Cultural Studies), the city's largest social democratic association. He spoke, in German, on 'The Modern Political Movement'. Renner saw a world war on the horizon, and he explained his apprehensions by a lesson drawn from history. As had been the case before the revolutionary year of 1848, he said, three decades had now passed since anything of real political significance had occurred. But things ripen unseen, and this time the hidden matters would not lead to a European revolution but rather to 'the enormous devastation of the world'.[1]

This chapter is about the fear of men who knew that they would be mobilized in the event of war, the anxieties of civilians who knew that they were 'soldiers-to-be'. Focusing on Austria-Hungary's cosmopolitan port city Trieste, located at the borders of the Balkans – read: South Slavia – the chapter provides a microhistorical close-up of a state of mind that pervaded the whole of Europe at the time, and the crisis-ridden Austro-Hungarian Empire in several idiosyncratic ways, of which Trieste represented one of the more complex cases.

As of yet, civilians have rarely been at the centre of scholarly attention when it comes to fear of war in the late imperial age. Jan Plamper explored the fear of soldiers *during* the First World War.[2] Others have examined fear as a motivating factor in international politics. Alma Hannig, for example, studied the role of fear between 1912 and 1914 in the decision-making of senior Austrian politicians with respect to the Balkans. She linked aspects of individual psychological dispositions to the apparently manifold anxieties that haunted Austro-Hungarian statesmen as they sought to carry out their policies.[3] Florian Keisinger showed that public opinion in many European countries had strongly associated the conflicts in Southeastern Europe with a more general sense of the danger of war for years prior to the outbreak of hostilities in October 1912.[4] It was during these years that the notion of the 'Balkan powder keg' gained decisive momentum, a stereotype that was forcefully reactivated during the Yugoslav wars of the 1990s.[5]

To be sure, Karl Renner's prediction of impending devastation was articulated in a specific political milieu and was thus also intended to reinforce the universal reproaches directed against the bourgeois-capitalist world by the international socialist movement.[6] But similar presentiments of a European, if not a global, conflagration can be found elsewhere; these were not limited to social democratically inclined individuals. In Trieste, with its large Slav population – mostly Slovenes, but also many Croats, Serbs and Czechs – the outbreak of war in the Balkans was perceived as happening in the city's 'backyard'. A substantial number of Trieste's workers, craftsmen, engineers and salesmen witnessed the intensified workings of Austria's arms industry – the building of warships – through their daily work in and around the city's shipyards and port.[7] The news about war being waged in the city's wider southeastern hinterland made already existing anxieties peak. A few years later, one of the most important areas of combat operations of the First World War, the Isonzo Front, would run through the city's northern hinterland and prove all anxieties justified.[8]

Everywhere in Europe, the socialists, 'in the decade prior to the First World War, distributed the most impressive and most elaborate propaganda for peace that Europe had known thus far'.[9] The members of the Second International had every reason to be concerned when they gathered in Basel in November 1912 to protest against the outbreak of war in the Balkans. A year earlier, Italy had attacked the Ottoman Empire, and the apparent weakness of the latter had encouraged the Balkan states to go forward with their attack in October 1912. When fighting between Italy and the Ottoman Empire had broken out, all the European great powers had exercised a policy of 'wait and see', mainly expecting the Ottomans to resist. The central powers had declared their interest in the integrity of the Ottoman Empire, but refused any military involvement. In the whole of Europe, the general atmosphere of mutual distrust continued to worsen, owing in part to the dangerous arms race, accompanied by nearly hysterical pro-armament propaganda.[10]

Yet despite the crises that shook the continent between 1911 and 1913, many Europeans remained confident that no major war would actually break out. Peace and stability were part of their life experience.

The 'matters ripening unseen' that Karl Renner had alluded to in 1910 in Trieste's Circolo di studi sociali seemed as if they had always been obvious to everyone only *after* the outbreak of the war in July 1914. Sönke Neitzel's suggestion seems appropriate to encompass the reactions to the war as proof of widespread agitated states of mind (*Kriegsaufregung*), which ranged from enthusiasm to deep anxieties and fear. In this chapter, this emotional agitation is made evident through an exemplary 'thick description' of the immediately preceding period. How did the war in the Balkans increase fears and anxieties?[11]

The Great War of 1914–18 has been described as the most important turning point in twentieth-century European history. The spreading forebodings of imminent apocalypse have been interpreted as a sign of the radical loss of value of knowledge and experience that had been transmitted from one generation to another. The result was individual as well as collective crises in the effort to make sense of the world.[12] Perhaps the best-known attempt to capture this 'lost world' and the crises it inflicted on those who witnessed it is the autobiography of Stefan Zweig, translated into English as *The World of Yesterday*.[13]

Austrian Trieste, in fact, was an emblem to this world that was about to become *of yesterday*. The city's ambivalent and competing identities were marked by an acute national conflict between Italians and Slovenes on the one hand, and a proud and striving cosmopolitan merchant self-image promoted by imperial politics on the other. Its geopolitical position made it more susceptible to the events in the Balkans than other places within the Austrian Empire, and beyond. In Trieste, the issue of war took on immediacy with the outbreak of fighting in the Balkans. To be sure, previous conflicts had been the subject of anti-militarist discourses that had little to do with whether Austria-Hungary was directly involved, as in the Bosnian annexation crisis of 1908, or not, as in the Italian-Ottoman war of 1911–12. The war in the Balkans ensued this anti-war rhetoric to take on a tone of acute alarm; it directly affected the city's social fabric. A substantial part of the city's population was Slovene, and thus a target of South Slav visionaries with an interest in state-building. The ways in which the city's already unstable social fabric was affected by the actual waging of war in its 'backyard' are at the centre of this chapter.

Fear and Aggression at the Borders of the Balkans

In 1912, Trieste was a booming merchant and industrial city, and the third largest city in Austria-Hungary. Only the capital cities, Vienna and Budapest, were larger; Trieste had overtaken even Prague. Since 1901, the government in Vienna had financed a huge infrastructural development programme, enlarging the port and thereby speeding up the industrialization process, which was in full swing at the outbreak of war in the Balkans. Since the second half of the nineteenth century, in particular, an enormous number of immigrants had come to live in the city. The living conditions of the newcomers were often precarious, despite the city's overall prosperity. In 1912, Trieste reported one of the highest rates of infant mortality in the Dual Monarchy.[14]

The irredentist movement, which was promoted in the Austrian Littoral and Tyrol largely by political actors in Italy, forcefully and aggressively sketched a plan to 'redeem' the iconic cities of Trieste and Trento and incorporate them into the Italian 'motherland'.[15] Yugoslavist ideas, on the other hand, circulated in various forms, but at the moment when war broke out in the Balkans, they rarely involved concrete plans for state-building. The 'trialist' solution was one variant of this Yugoslavism. The concept envisaged that the Dual Monarchy would be refashioned as a tripartite entity, a Triple Monarchy that would have a South Slav component, which was to include Trieste.[16] The city had the largest Slovene population, larger even than that of Ljubljana. Trieste's Slovene community of 57,000 made up about 25 per cent of the city's total population. It was a contested city, the site of an increasingly acute Italian–Slovene conflict.[17] Internationalist socialism had formed a small but firm political milieu during the first decade of the twentieth century, which, however, argued and worked rather helplessly in the face of the aggressive local conflicts inspired by nationalism.[18]

Italians

The mentioned large International Socialist Congress in Basel in November 1912 had been organized within a matter of weeks to protest against the outbreak of war in the Balkans. Reports from the congress were censored in the Habsburg press.[19] In Trieste, press coverage of the Basel gathering included the sarcastic comment in the Italian-language social democratic newspaper *Il Lavoratore* that the 'deeply ... Giolitti-inspired judgements and sentiments' of the municipal governors of Trieste were 'more Austrian than the Austrians', that they had staged 'a very vulgar joke and an utterly stupid bluff' with regard to public opinion, which they believed stood behind them. The municipal delegates advocated, the *Lavoratore* continued incredulously, the proclamation of a military state of emergency as part of their nationalist and anti-socialist agitation.[20] The report can only be understood in the context of the Italian aggression against the Ottoman Empire that had begun in September 1911. Generally, the European press had identified the Italian prime minister Giovanni Giolitti and his foreign minister Antonino di San Giuliano as the principal warmongers in this conflict, which it had perceived as threatening stability and peace overall.[21] Both of Italy's partners in the Triple Alliance, Germany and Austria-Hungary, deemed the Ottoman Empire to be an indispensable part of that stability. Italy's success in the Italo-Ottoman war, which ended in October 1912 with the territorial gains of Tripolitania, Cyrenaica and the Dodecanese, is generally perceived as the event that gave the Balkan states the final encouragement to attack the Ottoman Empire that same month.[22]

The Italian-Ottoman war was the first instance in which the Circolo di studi sociali, a non-political association under Austrian law, invited, with the permission of the local police, witnesses of the war from Italy. One was the war correspondent of the Italian Socialist Party newspaper L'Avanti! [Forward!], Michele Vaina. The other was Vincenzo Vacirca, a socialist from Sicily who had sought refuge in Austrian Trieste and Istria to evade prosecution by the Italian authorities.[23] All this information brings things full circle to make sense of the social democrats' charge that the Triestine Italian Liberal Nationals were 'Giolitti-inspired' with respect to the war in the Balkans: Giolitti and his followers had aggressively supported Italy's military adventure against the Ottomans and consequently would not hear of peace initiatives such as the socialist gathering in Basel. Their 'treason' was of a different kind than that which led the Austrian government to censor the Basel speeches.

That Austrian state policy and local politics did not work in tandem is demonstrated by yet another episode. In August 1913, the month that the Second Balkan War ended, the governor of Trieste, Konrad Hohenlohe-Schillingsfürst, issued a series of decrees dismissing Italian subjects from public employment in the city and making it more difficult for them to obtain Austrian citizenship. The decrees triggered a massive public outcry in Italy, where the measure was perceived as another step in a wider strategic plan to diminish the municipal power of the local Italian Liberal Nationals. In Italy, the decrees were seen and presented as a brutal and inhumane act that threw civil servants, who had done their duty flawlessly, into bankruptcy. This representation was fuelled by the fact that elections were imminent and any sign of leniency towards Austria needed to be avoided. In addition, the decrees were interpreted as yet another action advantageous to Trieste's Slav population and against the Italians. The enthusiastic welcome of Hohenlohe's decrees by the Slovenes in Trieste only added to this impression. The most significant feature of the public indignation, however, was its relationship to Italy's foreign policy. Cooperation with Austria-Hungary with regard to the Balkans was a heavily contested matter among the Italian public, who failed to see any real advantages for Italy in such a policy. All the more, Italians expected a more decent treatment of Italian subjects living in Austria-Hungary. In addition, Prime Minister Giolitti had systematically punished any public anti-Austrian manifestation for an entire decade, but here, for the first time, he failed to do so. A rather marginal event thus acquired a disproportionate impact and marked a turning point in Austrian–Italian relations. The Austrian Foreign Ministry, which was trying to maintain relations with Italy on a level of allied partners in the Triple Alliance, was not happy about the event, yet Hohenlohe, who was a close friend of Archduke Franz Ferdinand, would continue to act politically in ways that ran contrary to what Vienna would have wished.[24]

Slovenes

Slovenes in Trieste had their own perspective on the events in the Balkans, and anxiety was a fundamental sentiment for them, even beyond the fear of war. The fear of German and/or Italian aggressive nationalism led Slovenes to envision themselves as part of a future South Slav entity, vague and contested though the project remained well into the First World War. External observers like Robert William Seton-Watson (1879–1951), who in 1917–18 would serve the British Intelligence Bureau of the War Cabinet in the Enemy Propaganda Department and play a significant role in the founding of both Czechoslovakia and Yugoslavia, had excluded the Slovenes from trialist projects for geostrategic reasons. Precisely because of the German ambitions, he argued, any South Slav project that included the Slovenes would be doomed from the outset. Thus, the Slovenes saw themselves caught between the Scylla of German and Italian territorial expansionism and the Charybdis of *jugoslovenstvo*, which they perceived as Serb-, or Serb-Croat-dominated. In spite of, and also as a consequence of, the tendencies to overlook the Slovenes on the international scene, a Yugoslav solution seemed the lesser evil, and some thought so even if the price was to give up their own language for the Croatian language or to accept Serbian predominance. All this was to happen, to be sure, largely *within* an imagined restructured Austrian state.[25] In the Dual Monarchy, observers of the reactions of Slav peoples to the Balkan Wars focused on Bosnia, Dalmatia and Croatia, as well as the Czech and Slovak lands, where public demonstrations displayed support for the efforts of the Balkan League's Slavs in the war. The Slovenes were no exception to this. Yet, while a part of Slovene public opinion reacted enthusiastically and increasingly displayed Serbophile views, which by definition were seen as being anti-Austrian by the authorities, generally Slovene nationalist politicians continued to imagine Slovene nation-building solutions within the existing Austrian state framework.[26]

However, the Balkan Wars let emotions run high and sharpened the rhetoric concerning a future union of South Slavs. In February 1913, the Slovene social democratic newspaper *Zarja* [Dawn] demonstrated that it grasped the radical bizarreness of the situation in the Balkans. It attempted, but was unable, to organize a second conference of social democratic parties of the South Slav peoples:[27]

> With the situation in the Austro-Hungarian south as it is, all decisive factors in the Monarchy will have to fight, and the Yugoslav question is approaching an acute stage. In no way can things remain as they are now ... The executive committee wishes to suggest that our party take the initiative for a second Yugoslav conference, in order to hold discussions with the Croatian and Serbian comrades from the other half of the Monarchy and from Bosnia-Herzegovina about the work that will be necessary, and about a common approach to these issues.[28]

Shortly before the end of the First Balkan War, the paper voiced strong resentment against Austrian foreign policy:

> In reality our whole Balkan politics looks as if we forcefully wished to create only foes for ourselves there. From the beginning of the war, we have committed only stupidities in the Balkans. Of course, we committed stupidities earlier, too. Our trade policy towards Serbia was, from a purely Austrian viewpoint, always foolish. ... When the development of the Balkan War showed that we were getting a neighbour in the south that would count for something, it was time to clean up old sins and strive for some sympathy down there. It is insignificant whether Count Berchtold likes the Balkan peoples or not; even at home nobody asks for his love. But the sympathy of the Balkan peoples is indispensable for the Austrian economy, and the minister of foreign affairs has the damned obligation to respect the economic interests of his country.[29]

In the same vein, it declared that any broader engagement of the Habsburg Monarchy in favour of Albania, to deny the Serbs access to the Adriatic, would be folly:

> A big, middle-sized, or small Albania: what do we care, why should we care which one it will be; Shkodra, Prizren, Janina, what do we care for these towns, of which the majority of Austrians do not even know they exist in the world. Our boys and men are worth more than all these hamlets and all of Albania, which has not given the slightest proof of being

capable of existing. Neither will the victorious Balkan peoples accomplish all they yearn for; they will have to be content with narrower borders than they had imagined. Which gods have authorized us to establish a state precisely for the Albanians, a state that not even all of them request, and to spill the blood of our peoples for the Albanian borders? Who has authorized us, of all people, to further the Albanians with our military, if we do not even succeed in satisfying our own peoples?[30]

The socialist newspaper echoed the presentiments of a looming larger war with a sketch of the great powers' readiness to stop at nothing if it served their capitalist interests:

The diplomatic expression 'The Balkans for the Balkan peoples' means in straightforward language that is understood by normal people: put the non-Turkish Balkans under the supervision of the capitalist European great powers. The biggest contrast in Europe is the competition between German industry and trade and British industry and trade .... All jealousies between France and Germany, between Austria and Russia, are of secondary importance in comparison with the world competition between Britain and Germany.[31]

During these same weeks, on 12 April 1913, the Slovene writer Ivan Cankar (1876–1918) intervened in the debates surrounding war, peace and state-building projects. In a lecture that the social democratic cultural association Vzajemnost (Unity) organized in Ljubljana, Cankar spoke about 'Slovenes and Yugoslavs'. He criticized neo-Illyrist ideas and the readiness of certain Slovene politicians, intellectuals and cultural institutions to sacrifice the Slovene language and national individuality for the greater unity of the South Slavs:

Thank God there are not many of these Illyrians – one could almost count them on the fingers of one hand. ... It would be good to remember that in the Slav South there are not only Lozengrad and Kumanovo [sites of two victorious battles against the Ottomans in the First Balkan War], but there are also, so to say, and no offence, Maribor, Ljubljana, and Trieste. ... Under the Austrian stewards, in our prisons, in poverty, and fighting manifold plagues, we have raised our culture to such a high level that it is an ornament and a joy. It is an expression of a national strength that is the equal of the strength that prevailed at Lozengrad and Kumanovo.[32]

During the same lecture, Cankar became very emotional and called for a South Slav *Risorgimento*. His drastic words in the face of the attending Austrian police officer brought him a week in prison, despite his later withdrawal of his utterance: 'Let us leave Austria in its own shit. Let us be like Mazzini in Italy!'[33] This incident, however, remained a rare outburst even within the ranks of the Yugoslav Social Democratic Party (JSDS), the branch of the Austrian Social Democratic Party that gathered most of the Slovene socialists. One of the few other intellectuals among the Slovene social democrats, Albin Prepeluh, wrote in 1913 that 'the inflexibility of the real circumstances forces us to search for national liberation on this side rather than the other side of the political border'.[34]

When the former Balkan allies started fighting each other in the Second Balkan War over the territories they had just gained from the Ottoman Empire, among Trieste's Slovene social democrats the conflict was taken as proof that only a confederation of the Balkan states could bring a solution. Alas, apparently a great deal of blood-letting was needed first:

> A villain who defends this thrice-damned war unscrupulously makes allowances for its chauvinist provokers and even gets steamed up if somebody steps on his corns! That rabble of windbags in the name of some sort of Slavism. They will perhaps substitute their Slav *fungi* for thousands and thousands of killed brothers.[35]

Internationalism, Anti-Militarism and the Building of Warships

The confrontation between the nationalities and between the political camps in Trieste radicalized after the male members of the proletariat used their newly acquired voting rights to vote *en masse* for socialist candidates in the elections to the Viennese parliament (*Reichsrat*) in 1907. Paradoxically, it was precisely this very successful mobilization of the masses and the extension of political participatory rights that led to the subsequent stagnation of the socialist movement in the city. First, the electorate for the municipal diet continued to be based on census rights and was thus confined to the largest taxpayers. Second, despite the city's economic boom, the increasing and quite home-grown perception of a looming existential crisis was decisively nurtured by presentiments of war that went far beyond the local or even imperial Austrian contexts. Finally, the general instability of the urban social fabric contributed to a sociopolitical stand-off that was marked by hate speech and often by violently escalating nationalist confrontations.[36]

When it comes both to the experiences of soldiers and, as in the present chapter, men who anxiously see a war coming, urban dwellers – that is, industrial workers, craftsmen and salesmen – have rarely been a focus of research.[37] In 1914, about fifty thousand of them were mobilized in Trieste. In previous years, they had been in the civilian workforce, and many had worked in the armament industry, building warships. About fifteen thousand were smiths or belonged to iron-working occupational categories.[38] After 1911 at the latest, the resistance against the dominant capitalist bourgeoisie included a protest against the arms build-up, which in Trieste was visible to everyone, in the city's shipyards. In the words of a speaker at that year's May Day celebration:

> Let us not forget that while here the Italian, Slovene and German workers fraternize and hoist the red flag of the International, not far away, down there by the sea, … they are building new instruments for extermination that they will see given to brothers to kill brothers![39]

In mid September 1912, the Trieste social democrats inaugurated a new workers' home, in the midst of the working-class quarter San Giacomo. The attending police officer estimated 1,800 to 2,000 participants, among them socialist representatives from the Kingdom of Italy, several German social democrats from Vienna, and some representatives of the Tyrolian Italian social democrats, including the socialist delegate to the *Reichsrat*, Cesare Battisti (1875–1916). The Slovenes were strongly represented through the professional organizations that acted on behalf of the predominantly Slovene-speaking labour categories, that is the railway workers, the bricklayers and the bakers. The police officer's report contains the following observations:

> The representative of the Italian workers' party says that Italy would rather conquer the African coastal sands than elevate the level of education in its own country, which would be a much more urgent task, especially in southern Italy, where most people are illiterate. Dr. Puecher explains that behemoths of warships are being built, whose aim and purpose is unknown …. [With their new workers' home], the workers have built themselves a stronghold from which they wish education and civilized behaviour to spread.[40]

A few days before the huge Socialist Congress in Basel, the JSDS on 17 November 1912 organized one of the largest local anti-war gatherings in the new workers' home. The speakers were mostly Slovene social democrats, with Ivan Regent (1884–1967), party secretary and editor of the party newspaper *Zarja*, in the lead. Several Italian speakers are also documented. The resolution that was issued as a result of this gathering amounts to a local formal political expression of the internationally stated demands that the war be ended as soon as possible and that the Balkan peninsula be turned into a confederation of states.[41]

Anti-militarism had always been a part of the social democratic discourse. When war broke out in Trieste's 'backyard', the Balkans, in October 1912, presentiments of war or even world war intensified. Reports on the theatre of war were far from enthusiastic or heroic. The most frequent suggestion for a solution was precisely that of a Balkan confederation of states. Shortly before the outbreak of the First

Balkan War, the *Zarja* suggested that the Austrian workers ask the Austrian government to prevent an outbreak of war in the Balkans at all costs: 'Peace is our interest. The unhappy annexation of Bosnia has taught the Austrian people that it has no business in the Balkans. The whole Balkan region is not worth a bone of an Austrian soldier'.[42] Over the following days, the *Zarja* reported that the Bulgarian and Serbian socialists had also issued anti-war declarations, as had the executive group of the Austrian Social Democratic Party umbrella organization, with the signature also of the JSDS.[43]

When war did break out, the *Zarja* immediately denied any war enthusiasm and focused on the difficulties that it brought to the civilian population – scarcity, hunger, horror and anguish:

> Any war enthusiasm in Serbia has started to wane. The crops rot in the fields, as all the men went off to the military units. When the mobilization is finished, Belgrade will be without men. The Serbian merchants are very much afflicted; the people withdraw their savings from the banks; the value of money decreases; the railway and the city tramway have had to limit their operations. In the food service industry, employees are already scarce.[44]

The paper quoted a Slovene living in Sofia who testified to 'a heavy price rise in the Bulgarian capital'.[45] Some months later, a similar description from Sofia indicated that the situation had deteriorated: 'Now it is almost even worse than at the outbreak of war. There is hunger, cold and shortage'.[46]

The *Zarja* continued to publish accounts of the immediate impact of the war on the situation of the working poor. The newspaper turned its attention from the Balkan lands and cities to the more immediate surroundings, that is, the economic situation in the Slovene-inhabited lands. Dozens, if not hundreds, of Serbian workers had left their workplaces because they had been conscripted; trade connections had been cut as a result of the war, which had led to a work shortage. The paper even reported that workers were leaving for America owing to the lack of work.[47]

While such a focus on the social effects of the war on the poor was intended to function also as a corrective to any militarist narrative depicting war as something heroic, even necessary, the May Day speeches in Trieste in the years 1909 to 1913 illustrate well how anxieties increased in the face of war being waged 'down south'. When Austria had annexed Bosnia and Herzegovina in October 1908, Valentino Pittoni, the local leader of the Italian Social Democratic Party, had mentioned the danger of a general European war in his May Day speech of 1909: 'What are we to do if our fatherland is in danger?

Do we have a reason to identify with "fatherlands" …?'.⁴⁸ In 1912, Edmondo Puecher, like Karl Renner eighteen months earlier, foresaw a global conflagration: '… the possibility of a huge European conflict, of a general conflagration, reveals itself at every moment'.⁴⁹ One year later, on May Day 1913, the war in the Balkans was the central theme: '… never before have such threatening clouds covered the European sky'.⁵⁰ Pittoni gave a passionately anti-war speech, rhetorically conjured up the absolute necessity of anti-militarist propaganda, and sketched out the Balkan federation as a viable and long-lasting solution. He compared the proletariat to a giant in chains:

> While the giant rattles his chains and fixes his gaze on the May sun, confident that he sees the hour of redemption near, the gruesome and barbaric echo of the machinery of war has not yet waned, which, in the near Balkans, has exterminated hundreds of thousands of human lives! … The European governments will need other hundreds of thousands of strong and healthy young men, and further millions, for the defence of the capitalist society that they call 'fatherland'. … On this First of May, capitalism should look towards the bloody valleys of the Balkans and tremble at its works of death and destruction!⁵¹

The pleas to foster social democratic solidarity became entwined with anguished pleas for international peace-keeping:

> Never before was the orgy of nationalism so insane, so despicable. Never before was it so obvious that the nationalist chauvinists are vermin and the biggest enemies of the people. With deep regret, the socialists observe the bloody dance in the Balkans and its chaotic insanity. Yet this horrifying masquerade is but another proof that only socialism and democracy can accomplish the liberation of the peoples, can liberate them from these bloodsuckers and thugs and enable them to create a life according to their wishes and necessities.⁵²

The fear of war once more manifested itself forcefully at the very moment of the stipulation of peace among the Balkan belligerents:

> This is a farce, not a peace. This is a treaty that was stipulated under the pressure of the more powerful, invincible forces, and this is no peace that would provide for an arrangement according to the necessities of the Balkan peoples; this is no peace that is stipulated even with the intention that it be durable. In Bucharest they have divided territories. They have accomplished what the Balkan socialists warned against. Over the division of territories, the First Balkan War with Turkey broke out. Over the division of territories, the former allies slaughtered each other. Over such division, sooner or later, they will push the people to the slaughterhouse again.⁵³

Less than a year later, these presentiments would prove to have been grounded.

1914: Disillusionment, Biographic Ruptures

The outbreak of war following the July 1914 crisis saw the majority of social democrats in Germany and Austria supporting their respective governments. Only the socialists in Italy opposed the war, and remained neutral. To Trieste's socialists, this evolution of things brought about the final disillusionment, and this disenchantment was more than a political matter. It triggered profound biographic ruptures and personal crises. The restlessness that characterized party leader Valentino Pittoni's life after 1914 may serve as an example. The war and the official support of the Viennese government by the Austrian social democrats separated the Triestine Italian social democrats from their Austrian comrades, though many managed to maintain or re-establish their strong personal ties. To be sure, the Triestine Italian socialists did not become converts to irredentist ideas, even if their support of neutrality, the stance preferred by the Italian socialists in Italy, was interpreted in this way. They knew that the war meant the end of Trieste's important economic and political position; and they knew that their work of a lifetime was being destroyed.[54] At the beginning of 1915, Pittoni wrote to his brother Silvio that in this moment,

> ... in near isolation ... without the support of that powerful moral strength that is personal ambition ... after a life as a politician that has been paid for with the destruction of the individual, made of ... internal life ... it is the drunkenness of the struggle that sustains one, along with the deep conviction that one's cause is just ... [even if] one is persuaded that little or nothing has been accomplished.[55]

Pittoni exceeded the limits of his strength, and fell ill. Shortly before Italy's entry into the war on the side of the Entente, he wrote from the sanatorium in Ancarano/Ankaran, south of Trieste, to party leader Viktor Adler, who had invited him to participate in a gathering of the socialists of the central powers who were to issue a declaration for peace:

> I finally had to obey the instructions of my doctor, because I cannot take it anymore. The efforts and excitements of the last month have prevented any possibility of recovery from my illness, or more precisely, the various illnesses that have struck me ... I suffer from a corresponding nervous state of mind, which makes it impossible at the moment to think of any more radical therapy, because I lack mental tranquillity most of all ....[56]

After having been sent to the front for some months in June 1916, he resumed his parliamentary activities in 1917, when the Viennese *Reichstag* was reopened.[57] The State Archive in Trieste preserves an elaborate correspondence from 1916 between the military commanders, the Ministry of the Interior in Vienna and the governor of Trieste, Alfred Freiherr von Fries-Skene, discussing whether Pittoni was indispensable in his work of providing provisions for the city's population, substantially contributing to the maintenance of calm in the city, and thus to be exempted from military service, or if, in this way, he would fill the void that had been created by the removal of nationalist Italian newspapers and organizations with social democratic propaganda, which would backfire once the war was over.[58] Pittoni, until the very last, supported the idea of transforming the monarchy into a federation, in which Trieste would have a special status. In 1919, after the dissolution of the Habsburg Monarchy and the annexation of Trieste and Istria by Italy, Pittoni left Trieste and moved to Milan, where he led the local consumers' cooperative until 1925. The growing strength of fascism made him leave Milan again. He moved to Vienna, lived in modest economic circumstances, and headed the editorial office of the *Arbeiter-Zeitung* [Workers' Newspaper]. He supported Italian anti-fascist emigrants until his death in April 1933.[59]

Other socialists in Trieste failed more dramatically to accept the demise of the world they knew. Some reacted by developing a mental illness, like Michele Susmel, a typographer who for years had enthusiastically organized the activities of the mentioned cultural association Circolo di studi sociali. He committed suicide in 1924, two years after the fascist assumption of power.[60] Others reacted even more immediately with suicide, like Angelo Vivante, one of the few intellectuals in Trieste's socialist movement. He died on 1 July 1915, a few weeks after Italy had declared war on Austria-Hungary.[61] Additional research is needed to pursue the life trajectories of Slovene and German social democrats in Trieste. To be sure, their personal dilemmas of loyalty were of a different nature. Their fate was even more drastic: after the annexation of Trieste and Istria to Italy in 1918, and especially after the advent of fascism, Slovenes and Croats faced systematic political violence and left the region *en masse* for the newly founded Yugoslavia.[62]

Conclusion

How do the expectations inherent in political discourse and struggle on the one hand, and in life stories that included traumatic stress disorders upon the experience of violently losing one's life world (i.e. core contexts, convictions and meaning), on the other, 'speak' to one another?[63] Angelo Vivante, the lawyer and writer who chose to end his life rather than fight on either side in the war – the Austrian side or, by defection, the Italian side – may have written the most impressive, because radically anti-nationalist, analysis of the mental state of his native city Trieste at the moment of the outbreak of war in the Balkans. In 1912, he described in a nutshell the ambivalent role of the Slavs in the international power game:

> Today Austria still maintains its balancing function. … In a bizarre way, Austria is both a stimulus and a counter-stimulus for the German plans: it is useful … for resisting the Russian plans; but at the same time, because of the increasing influence of the Slavs in Austria, the centralized Austrian state is an obstacle to the creation of a Greater Germany 'from the Baltic Sea to the Adriatic'. Indeed, this centralism … will not last forever; actually, it may be its present dualist structure that will wear out first. … Pan-Slavism, that is, a monster state reaching from Moscow to Constantinople, has come to be seen as but an ugly utopia in the eyes of the South Slavs. Neo-Slavism, that is, the intellectual unity of all Slavs, is an attempt to renew pan-Slavism; yet it is nothing but its sentimental reflection, without any political substance. The southern Slavs in Austria, Hungary and the Balkans have become attracted to autonomist ideas in the course of their capitalist and intellectual evolution ….[64]

The microhistorical illustration in this chapter of what Andreas Helmedach, from the perspective of the Habsburg Monarchy, has called 'the history of the final failure of a political, social and cultural integration of large parts of East Central and Southeastern Europe, which had functioned over a long time',[65] echoes Benjamin Ziemann's interpretation of a radical devaluation of knowledge and experience,[66] as much as it empirically illustrates how the Zweigian 'world' became 'of yesterday', and what this meant to contemporaries. The Balkan Wars, the belligerent scenario in Trieste's 'backyard', brought existing anxieties about a larger war-to-be to a hitherto unseen peak. Word of the imminent end of the monarchy spread.[67]

One aspect is mirrored particularly well by the historical documentation preserved from Trieste's multiethnic and internationalist social democratic milieu: the inherent hybridity of identities and the multilayered quality of loyalties in this border zone, which, at least from the moment Italy and Austria-Hungary became belligerents on opposite sides in May 1915, was deeply saturated with experiences of violence, and would remain so for decades to come. The multiethnic social democratic milieu, which had still been a liveable option of cohabitation prior to the Great War, even though increasingly challenged by aggressive nationalist stances, re-emerged in radicalized and strongly nationalized forms in 1918, when Trieste was annexed by Italy. Scholars have investigated the challenges that 'incompatible' sets of loyalties posed to people, focusing on national identities. They have pointed out the broad existence of hybrid, fluid, even situative identities, which became deeply connected with experiences of violence and politicized quests to *choose* one identity over the other. It seems that this legacy of the destroyed 'world of yesterday' merits further attention – as much in the region at stake here as 'down south', in the Balkans.[68] The soldiers-to-be in Trieste feared mobilization and deployment to the front, not least because they sensed that they were to fight for a cause that had already been lost much earlier. They were afraid to see themselves torn between feelings of national and imperial loyalty. They feared becoming a part of the very game that would soon place this border region completely at the mercy of aggressive nationalism, when, a few years after the war's end, it became the spearhead of fascist power in Italy.

Sabine Rutar is Senior Researcher at the Leibniz Institute for East and Southeast European Studies in Regensburg. She is Editor-in-Chief of the quarterly *Südosteuropa. Journal of Politics and Society*; author of *Kultur – Nation – Milieu: Sozialdemokratie in Triest vor dem Ersten Weltkrieg* (Klartext, 2004); and editor of several academic collections, including *Violence in Late Socialist Public Spheres* (special issue of *European History Quarterly*, 2015) and *Beyond the Balkans: Towards an Inclusive History of Southeastern Europe* (Lit, 2014). Recently, she co-edited (with Katrin Boeckh) *The Balkan Wars from Contemporary Perception to Historic Memory* (Palgrave, 2017).

Notes

1 Conferenza Renner [Renner Lecture], *Il Lavoratore*, no. 2046, 5 March 1910. *Il Lavoratore* [The Worker] was the organ of the Italian Social Democratic Party in Trieste.
2 Jan Plamper, 'Fear: Soldiers and Emotion in Early Twentieth-Century Russian Military Psychology', *Slavic Review* 68(2) (2009), 259–83.
3 Alma Hannig, 'Angst und die Balkanpolitik Österreich-Ungarns vor dem Ersten Weltkrieg', in Patrick Bormann, Thomas Freiberger and Judith Michel (eds), *Angst in den internationalen Beziehungen* (Bonn: Bonn University Press, 2010), 93–113. Cf. also, with a focus on the Cold War, Bernd Greiner et al. (eds), *Angst im Kalten Krieg* (Hamburg: Hamburger Edition, 2009).

4 Florian Keisinger, *Unzivilisierte Kriege im zivilisierten Europa: Die Balkankriege und die öffentliche Meinung in Deutschland, England und Irland 1876–1913* (Paderborn: Schöningh, 2008).
5 Mark Biondich, 'Eastern Borderlands and Prospective Shatter Zones: Identity and Conflict in East Central and Southeastern Europe on the Eve of the First World War', in Jochen Böhler, Włodzimierz Borodziej and Joachim von Puttkamer (eds), *Legacies of Violence: Eastern Europe's First World War* (Europas Osten im 20. Jahrhundert, 3) (Berlin: De Gruyter, 2014), 25–50. Biondich identifies the Balkan Wars as the crucial event that 'played an important role in escalating norms of violence *in* the region and again focused the attention of the Great Powers *on* the region' (ibid., 42 [emphasis in the original]); cf. Raymond Detrez, 'Pre-national Identities in the Balkans', in Roumen Daskalov and Tchavdar Marinov (eds), *Entangled Histories of the Balkans*, Vol. 1: *National Ideologies and Language Policies* (Balkans Studies Library, 9) (Leiden: Brill, 2013), 13–65. Detrez states that the 'feeling of commonality and solidarity it [the Orthodox Christian or Romaic community] created was irreparably damaged during the Second Balkan War; what has remained of it is a masked unanimity vis-à-vis the real or imagined threat of Islam' (ibid., 63).
6 On the fervid discussions within the Second International about the imminent war and the preservation of peace, cf. Heiko Haumann and Laura Polexe, 'Debatten um Krieg und Frieden in der Zweiten Internationale', in Bernard Degen et al. (eds), *Gegen den Krieg: Der Basler Friedenskongress 1912 und seine Aktualität* (Basel: Christoph Merian, 2012), 133–40, here 133–36; Kevin J. Callahan, 'The International Socialist Peace Movement on the Eve of World War I Revisited: The Campaign of "War against War!" and the Basle International Socialist Congress in 1912', *Peace & Change* 29(2) (2004), 147–76. Callahan offers a list of all anti-war gatherings organized by the International Socialist Bureau (ibid., 160–63).
7 On the European arms race, see David Stevenson, *Armaments and the Coming of War: Europe 1904–1914* (Oxford: Clarendon Press, 1996); David G. Herrmann, *The Arming of Europe and the Making of the First World War* (Princeton, NJ: Princeton University Press, 1966); specifically on the Austro-Hungarian Empire, see Manfred Reinschedl, *Die Aufrüstung der Habsburgermonarchie von 1880 bis 1914 im internationalen Vergleich: Der Anteil Österreich-Ungarns am Wettrüsten vor dem Ersten Weltkrieg* (Beiträge zur Neueren Geschichte Österreichs, 16) (Frankfurt/M.: Peter Lang, 2001). In Austria, an enlargement of the number of yearly army recruitments had been debated and also carried out since 1903. Debate resumed and peaked again in the *Reichsrat*, the Viennese parliament, in the first half of 1912; cf. Rok Stergar, 'Fragen des Militärwesens in der slowenischen Politik 1867–1914', *Österreichische Osthefte* 46(3) (2004), 391–422.
8 In the Twelfth Battle of the Isonzo, also known as the Battle of Caporetto, from 24 October to 19 November 1917, the Italian army suffered its most traumatic defeat in the First World War. Caporetto is the Italian name of the town of Kobarid (Karfreit in German), today in Slovenia. The town features a prize-winning small museum dedicated to the Battles of the Isonzo; see the website of the Muzej 1. svetovne vojne Kobarid (Kobarid Museum of the

First World War), http://www.kobariski-muzej.si/ (accessed 21 February 2017). The museum inspired a recent, well-done overview of the history of the Isonzo Front: John Macdonald and Željko Cimprić, *Caporetto and the Isonzo Campaign: The Italian Front, 1915–1918* (Barnsley: Pen & Sword Military, 2011). For a comprehensive account from an Italian perspective, cf. Alberto Monticone, *La battaglia di Caporetto* [The Battle of Caporetto] (Udine: Gaspari editore, 1999). Slovenian research has recently focused on the everyday experiences of the Austrian subjects living in the region, most of whom were of Slovene ethnicity; cf. Vincenc Rajšp (ed.), *Soška fronta 1915–1917: Kultura spominjanja / Isonzofront 1915–1917: Die Kultur des Erinnerns* [The Isonzo Front, 1915–1917: The Culture of Remembrance] (Ljubljana: Založba ZRC, ZRC SAZU, 2010). For a general account from the perspective of the Habsburg Monarchy, cf. Manfred Rauchensteiner, *Der Erste Weltkrieg und das Ende der Habsburgermonarchie 1914–1918* (Vienna/Cologne/Weimar: Böhlau, 2013 [rev. ed. 1993]).

9 Cf. Bernard Degen, 'Die europaweite Ausstrahlung des Kongresses', in Degen et al., *Gegen den Krieg*, 141–50, here 142–49, 149. Cf. Jivka Damianova, 'La fédération contre l'alliance militaire: les socialistes balkaniques et les guerres balkaniques 1912–3', *Le Mouvement Social* 147 (1989), 69–85, for an assessment of the anti-war gatherings and other activities of the socialists in Sofia, Belgrade, Bucharest and Salonica before and, even more fervidly, after the hostilities had begun.

10 Cf. Richard C. Hall, *The Balkan Wars 1912–1913: Prelude to the First World War* (London/New York: Routledge, 2000); Katrin Boeckh, *Von den Balkankriegen zum Ersten Weltkrieg: Kleinstaatenpolitik und ethnische Selbstbestimmung auf dem Balkan* (Munich: Oldenbourg, 1996); Holger Afflerbach, *Der Dreibund: Europäische Großmacht- und Allianzpolitik vor dem Ersten Weltkrieg* (Vienna/Cologne/Weimar: Böhlau, 2002); Alma Hannig, 'Die Balkanpolitik Österreich-Ungarns vor 1914', in Jürgen Angelow (ed.), *Der Erste Weltkrieg auf dem Balkan: Perspektiven der Forschung* (Berlin: be.bra, 2011), 35–56.

11 Sönke Neitzel, *Blut und Eisen: Deutschland im Ersten Weltkrieg* (Zürich: Pendo Verlag, 2003), 40. Others also have convincingly deconstructed the myth of a general war euphoria when fighting started in August 1914. Cf., for Germany, the study of local reactions to the war by Benjamin Ziemann, *Front und Heimat: Ländliche Kriegserfahrungen im südlichen Bayern 1914–1923* (Essen: Klartext, 1997); for France, Jean-Jacques Becker, *Comment les français sont entrés dans la guerre* (Paris: Presses de la Fondation Nationale des Sciences Politiques, 1977).

12 Ziemann, *Front und Heimat*, 1.

13 Stefan Zweig, *Die Welt von gestern: Erinnerungen eines Europäers* (Berlin: Insel Verlag, 2013 [orig. 1942]).

14 Roberto Finzi and Giovanni Panjek (eds), *Storia economica e sociale di Trieste 1719–1918* [Economic and Social History of Trieste 1719–1918], Vol. 1, *La città dei gruppi* [The City of Groups] (Trieste: LINT, 2001); Roberto Finzi, Loredana Panariti and Giovanni Panjek (eds), *Storia economica e sociale di Trieste 1719–1918* [Economic and Social History of Trieste 1719–1918], Vol. 2, *La città dei traffici* [The City of Trade] (Trieste: LINT, 2003); Marina Cattaruzza, *La formazione del proletariato urbano: Immigrati, operai di mestiere,*

donne a Trieste dalla metà del secolo XIX alla prima guerra mondiale [The Formation of the Urban Proletariat: Immigrants, Workers, Women in Trieste from the Second Half of the 19th Century to the First World War] (Teoria e storia di classe, 13) (Turin: Musolini, 1979).

15 Marina Cattaruzza, *L'Italia e il confine orientale, 1866–2006* [Italy and Its Eastern Border] (Bologna: Il Mulino, 2007), 15–68; cf. the English translation *Italy and Its Eastern Border, 1866–2016* (New York: Routledge, 2017), which adds the last decade to the narration. For a political history of the Italian role in the international events anticipating the Balkan Wars, saturated with the belief that the Italian-inhabited Austrian lands were rightfully claimed by Italy, cf. Antonello Biagini, *L'Italia e le guerre balcaniche* [Italy and the Balkan Wars], 2nd ed. (Rome: Edizioni Nuova Cultura, 2012 [1st ed. 1990]).

16 Jože Prijevec, *'Trst je naš!' Boj Slovencev za morje (1848–1954)* ['Trieste Is Ours!' The Struggle of the Slovenes for the Sea] (Ljubljana: Nova revija, 2007), 40–59; cf. Carol Rogel, *The Slovenes and Yugoslavism, 1890–1914* (Boulder, CO: East European Quarterly, 1977).

17 Cf. Rolf Wörsdörfer, 'Habsburgisch-venezianisches Erbe und großer Krieg: Zweierlei nationale Einigung – Italien 1860, Südslawien 1918', in Rolf Wörsdörfer, *Krisenherd Adria 1915–1955: Konstruktion und Artikulation des Nationalen im italienisch-jugoslawischen Grenzraum* (Paderborn: Schöningh, 2004), 35–69.

18 Cf. Sabine Rutar, *Kultur – Nation – Milieu: Sozialdemokratie in Triest vor dem Ersten Weltkrieg* (Essen: Klartext, 2004); Marina Cattaruzza, *Socialismo adriatico: La socialdemocrazia di lingua italiana nei territori costieri della monarchia asburgica, 1888–1915* [Adriatic Socialism: Italian-Language Social Democracy in the Littoral Territories of the Habsburg Monarchy], 2nd ed. (Manduria: P. Lacaita, 2001).

19 The Austrian government banned the printing of the congress's manifest and the speeches by Edouard Anseele, Victor Adler, Hugo Haase, Jean Jaurès and Pieter Jelles Troelstra at the venue of the event, the Basel Cathedral. The reason stated was that they had called for high treason. Degen, 'Die europaweite Ausstrahlung des Kongresses', 145.

20 'Più austriaco dell'Austria' [More Austrian than the Austrians], *Il Lavoratore*, no. 2359, 4 December 1912.

21 Cf. the learned and balanced account by Hermann Wendel, 'Der türkisch-italienische Krieg', *Die neue Zeit: Wochenschrift der deutschen Sozialdemokratie* 30, 1(3) (20 October 1911), 65–72, who nevertheless referred to 'Giolitti's bandit prank' ('Banditenstreich Giolittis'), p. 69. Other social democratic papers used similar, if not even more drastic expressions; cf. 'Der Raubkrieg', *Lübecker Volksbote: Organ für die Interessen der werktätigen Bevölkerung* 18(230) (2 October 2011), 1: 'The classical land of *brigantaggio*, Italy, has just demonstrated that the tradition of banditry there has not yet died; to the contrary, it is very lively and of utmost efficiency'. For further quotes from the German press, cf. Afflerbach, *Der Dreibund*, 700. For a general assessment, cf. Timothy W. Childs, *Italo-Turkish Diplomacy and the War over Libya, 1911–1912* (Social, Economic, and Political Studies of the Middle East, 42) (Leiden: Brill, 1990).

22 It is interesting to note the nuances in tone in this commonly accepted assessment when it comes to different authors. Cf., e.g., the bestselling Christopher Clark, *The Sleepwalkers: How Europe Went to War in 1914* (London: Penguin, 2013), 42. Clark's formulation seems to echo contemporary stereotypes and almost consigns both Italy and the Balkan states to the status of rogue states: 'This unprovoked attack on one of the integral provinces of the Ottoman Empire triggered a cascade of opportunist attacks on Ottoman-controlled territory in the Balkans'. More matter-of-fact are Afflerbach, *Der Dreibund*, 687–708; and Alexander De Grand, *The Hunchback's Tailor: Giovanni Giolitti and Liberal Italy from the Challenge of Mass Politics to the Rise of Fascism, 1882–1922* (Westport, CT: Praeger, 2001), esp. Chapter 7, 'Domestic Reform and War'.
23 Archivio di Stato di Trieste, Direzione di Polizia, Atti Presidiali Riservati, b. 313: Atti del Circolo di studi sociali [Proceedings of the Circolo di studi sociali], 11 September, 16 September, 28 September 1912. The three lectures were titled 'How Italy Went to Tripoli', 'War Impressions' and 'Damages and Advantages of a Colonial War'. The police officer who was present took note of about 350 participants and did not see any reason to intervene. Cf. 'Conferenze Vacirca: L'Italia a Tripoli' [Vacirca Lectures: Italy in Tripoli], *Il Lavoratore*, no. 2253, 21 October 1911; 'Conferenze Vacirca: Il miraggio nazionalista (L'impresa di Tripoli)' [Vacirca Lectures: The Nationalist Illusion (The Tripoli Enterprise)], ibid., no. 2300, 13 April 1912; 'Le Conferenze Vaina al "Circolo di studi sociali"' [The Vaina Lectures at the 'Circolo di Studi Sociali'], ibid., no. 2349, 28 September 1912, and no. 2350, 2 October 1912.
24 Almost thirty thousand Italian subjects lived and worked in Trieste in 1913; as the decrees affected only about forty employees in public service and their families, the Italian reactions seem in fact exaggerated. Cf. Afflerbach, *Der Dreibund*, 794–97; De Grand, *The Hunchback's Tailor*, 175.
25 Vasilij Melik, *Slovenci v času Cankarjevega predavanja* [The Slovenes at the Time of Cankar's Lectures] (Maribor: Založba Obzorja, Izdaja Univerza v Mariboru in Zgodovinsko društvo Maribor, 1986), 203. Cf. Clark, *The Sleepwalkers*, 49, who describes the wish to *prevent* a tripartite Austrian Monarchy on the part of the conspirators from Serbia as one of the main motives for the assassination of Archduke Franz Ferdinand in Sarajevo in July 2014.
26 Rok Stergar, *Slovenci in vojska, 1867–1914: Slovenski odnos do vojaških vprašanj od uvedbe dualizma do začetka 1. svetovne vojne* [The Slovenes and the Military: The Slovene Attitude to Military Questions from the Introduction of Dualism to the Beginning of the First World War] (Ljubljana: Oddelek za Zgodovino Filozofske Fakultete, 2004), 227–33; Dušan Biber, 'Jugoslovanska ideja in slovensko narodno vprašanja v slovenski publicistiki med balkanskimi vojnami v letih 1912–1913' [The Yugoslav Idea and the Slovene National Question in the Slovene Media during the Balkan Wars in the Years 1912–1913], *Istorija XX veka* [History of the 20th Century] 1 (1959), 285–324. On the public echoes of the wars in Croatia, see Igor Despot, *Balkanski ratovi 1912.–1913. i njihov odjek u Hrvatskoj* [The Balkan Wars and Their Echoes in Croatia] (Zagreb: Nova Plejada, 2013).

27 The first such gathering of South Slav socialists took place in Ljubljana in November 1909 in reaction to the Austrian annexation of Bosnia-Herzegovina; cf. Franc Rozman, 'Ob sedemdesetletnici Tivolske resolucije' [70 Years since the Tivoli Resolution], *Kronika. Časopis za slovensko krajevno zgodovino* [Chronicle. Journal for Slovene Regional History] 27 (1979), 180–84. Generally, on the initiatives of socialists in Southeastern Europe, cf. the overview of Walter Daugsch, 'Balkanföderation, Balkankriege und Internationale: Sozialdemokratie in Südosteuropa 1908–1914', in Sandrine Mayoraz, Frithjof Benjamin Schenk and Ueli Mäder (eds), *Hundert Jahre Basler Friedenskongress (1912–2012): Die erhoffte 'Verbrüderung der Völker'* (Basel/Zürich: Schweizerisches Sozialarchiv, 2015), 109–18.

28 'Naša balkanska politika' [Our Balkan Politics], *Zarja*, no. 514, 20 February 1913; cf. Franc Rozman, 'Stališče slovenske socialne demokracije do Balkanskih vojn' [The Opinion of Slovene Social Democrats on the Balkan Wars], *Zgodovinski Časopis* [Historical Journal] 42(4) (1988), 517–24.

29 'Naša balkanska politika' [Our Politics in the Balkans], *Zarja*, 20 February 1913.

30 'Mars pleše kankan' [Mars Dances Cancan], *Zarja*, no. 513, 19 February 1913.

31 'Novi Balkan' [The New Balkans], *Zarja*, no. 564, 23 April 1913. This stance amounts to a Slovene variant of the general, if controversial, advancement of the Balkan socialists (and not only them) of the idea of a Balkan federation; cf. John A. Mazis, 'The Idea of an Eastern Federation: An Alternative to the Destruction of the Ottoman Empire', in Lucien J. Frary and Mara Kozelsky (eds), *Russian-Ottoman Borderlands: The Eastern Question Reconsidered* (Madison, WI: The University of Wisconsin Press, 2014), 251–79.

32 Ivan Cankar, 'Slovenci in Jugoslovani' [Slovenes and Yugoslavs], *Zbrano delo* [Collected Works] 25 (1976), 228–38, here 235–36.

33 Arhiv Republike Slovenije, Fond SI AS 307: Deželno sodišče v Ljubljani [Provincial Court in Ljubljana], Kazenski spis Ivana Cankarja [Ivan Cankar's Proceedings] (Spis Vr 445/13), 13 April–19 September 1913, Court Decision of 13 August 2013, p. 2.

34 Albin Prepeluh-Abditus, 'Slovenci ali Jugoslovani' [Slovenes or Yugoslavs], *Naši Zapiski. Socialistična Revija* [Our Notes. Socialist Review], 10 (1913), 137–40, here 138.

35 '50 000 žrtev' [50,000 Victims], *Zarja*, no. 626, 8 July 1913.

36 For details, cf. Rutar, *Kultur – Nation – Milieu*.

37 Cf. Ziemann, *Front und Heimat*, 4. Ziemann focuses on rural experiences of the First World War in Bavaria, and assesses the lack of analogous 'urban studies'.

38 Adolfo Leghissa, *Trieste che passa, 1884–1914* [Trieste As It Goes By] (Trieste: Liberia internazionale Italo Svevo, 1971), 36. Leghissa's account of 'the life of Trieste's poor' is highly detailed and valuable, and definitely entertaining to read because of the author's impressionistic ethnographic narration and strong sympathy for his objects of study. Accordingly, the numbers are to be read as impressionistic ones as well, that is, as rough estimates and not to be taken at face value.

39 'Il primo maggio a Trieste' [May Day In Trieste], *Il Lavoratore*, no. 2173, 3 May 1911.
40 Archivio di Stato di Trieste, Lugotenenza del Litorale, Atti Presidiali, b. 365: Scioperi e movimento operaio; Dimostrazioni per il rincaro del pane; per l'università italiana a Trieste; manifestazioni per Francesco Ferrer; Partito socialdemocratico jugoslavo [Strikes and workers' movement; Demonstrations over the increased price of bread; for an Italian university in Trieste; public manifestations for Francisco Ferrer; Yugoslav Social Democratic Party], Polizeidirektion an Statthalterei-Präsidium, Betreff: Inaugurations-Feier des neuen Arbeiterheims, 16 September 1912. Edmondo Puecher (1873–1954), mentioned in the quote, was a lawyer and one of the protagonists of Trieste's Austro-Italian socialist party.
41 'Shod proti vojni' [Gathering against the War], *Zarja*, no. 438, 19 November 1912.
42 'Na predvečer Balkanske vojne' [On the Eve of the Balkan war], *Zarja*, no. 398, 2 October 1912.
43 'Vojna ali mir? Balkanska kriza' [War or Peace? The Balkan Crisis], *Zarja*, no. 399, 3 October 1912; 'Delavstvu vseh narodov v Avstriji!' [To the Workers of All Peoples in Austria!], *Zarja*, no. 408, 14 October 1912.
44 'Vojna nevarnost na Balkanu: Položaj v Srbiji' [Danger of War in the Balkans: The Situation in Serbia], *Zarja*, no. 400, 4 October 1912.
45 'Velikanska draginja v Sofiji' [Huge Price Rise in Sofia], *Zarja*, no. 401, 5 October 1912.
46 'Pismo iz Sofije' [Letter from Sofia], *Zarja*, no. 479, 10 January 1913.
47 Rozman, 'Stališče slovenske socialne demokracije do Balkanskih vojn', 518.
48 'Il nostro Primo Maggio' [Our First of May], *Il Lavoratore*, no. 1935, 5 May 1909.
49 'La solenne manifestazione proletaria di Primo Maggio' [Our Solemn Proletarian Manifestation of the First of May], *Il Lavoratore*, 4 May 1912.
50 'Il manifesto di Primo Maggio del Partito Socialista Italiano' [The May Day Manifest of the Italian Socialist Party], *Il Lavoratore*, no. 2410, 30 April 1913.
51 'Primo Maggio 1913' [May Day 1913], *Il Lavoratore*, no. 2411, 30 April 1913. Cf. the analogous report of the Slovenian-language Social Democratic Party newspaper, 'Praznujmo prvi maj!' [Let's Celebrate the First of May!], *Zarja*, no. 570, 30 April 1913.
52 'Zblazeni šovinizem' [Insane Chauvinism], *Zarja*, no. 628, 10 July 1913.
53 'Mir, ki ni mir' [The Peace That Is No Peace], *Zarja*, no. 657, 13 August 1913.
54 Elio Apih, 'Valentino Pittoni fra Austria e Italia' [Valentino Pittoni between Austria and Italy], in Elio Apih (ed.), *Il socialismo italiano in Austria: Saggi* [Italian Socialism in Austria: Essays] (Udine: Del Bianco Editore, 1991), 35–100, 62f.
55 Letter from Valentino Pittoni to his brother Silvio, 26 January 1915, in ibid., 88–89.
56 Letter from Valentino Pittoni to Viktor Adler, 14 May 1915, in Italian translation (from the German original), in ibid., 91–92. Interestingly, Pittoni, like Adler in his preceding invitation letter, still believed that a war between Italy and Austria could be prevented.
57 Apih, 'Valentino Pittoni fra Austria e Italia', 66.

58 Archivio di Stato di Trieste, I.R. Lugotenenenza, Atti Presidiali,. b. 421. On Trieste during the war and the tensions in the city due to both anti-Italian violence and the general scarcity of provisions, see Lucio Fabi, *Trieste 1914– 1918: Una città in guerra* [Trieste 1914–1918: A City at War] (Trieste: MGS Press, 1996).
59 Apih, 'Valentino Pittoni fra Austria e Italia'; 'Valentino Pittoni', in Franco Andreucci and Tommaso Detti (eds), *Il movimento operaio italiano: Dizionario biografico 1853–1943* [The Italian Workers' Movement: Biographic Dictionary], Vol. IV (Rome: Editori riuniti, 1978), 181–83.
60 'Michele Susmel', in Andreucci and Detti, *Il movimento operaio italiano*, Vol. IV, 713–14.
61 'Angelo Vivante', in Andreucci and Detti, *Il movimento operaio italiano*, Vol. V, 249–52; cf. Anna Millo, *Storia di una borghesia: La famiglia Vivante a Trieste dall'emporio alla guerra mondiale* [History of a Middle Class: The Vivante Family in Trieste from the Merchant City to the World War] (Gorizia: Libreria Editrice Goriziana, 1998).
62 For a detailed overview, cf. Rolf Wörsdörfer, 'Julische Slowenen und Kroaten im Exil', in Wörsdörfer, *Krisenherd Adria*, 281–313. The story of demographic changes in this border region continued until the mid 1950s, when, after the Second World War, the majority of Italians left the then Yugoslav Istria. Cf. Rolf Wörsdörfer, 'Der Auszug der Italiener aus den adriatischen Provinzen', in Wörsdörfer, *Krisenherd Adria*, 522–60.
63 The reference here is to Reinhart Koselleck, '"Erfahrungsraum" und "Erwartungshorizont" – zwei historische Kategorien', in Reinhart Koselleck (ed.), *Vergangene Zukunft: Zur Semantik geschichtlicher Zeiten* (Frankfurt/M.: Suhrkamp, 1989), 349–75.
64 Angelo Vivante, *Irredentismo adriatico: Contributo alla discussione sui rapporti austro-italiani* [Adriatic Irredentism: A Contribution to the Discussion about the Austrian-Italian Relations] (Florence: Libreria de La Voce, 1912), 213.
65 Andreas Helmedach, *Das Verkehrssystem als Modernisierungsfaktor: Straßen, Post, Fuhrwesen und Reisen nach Triest und Fiume vom Beginn des 18. Jahrhunderts bis zum Eisenbahnzeitalter* (Munich: Oldenbourg, 2002), 40–41.
66 Ziemann, *Front und Heimat*, 1.
67 Cf. Viktor Adler's speech in the Basel Cathedral in November 2012: Bernard Degen, 'Basel im Zentrum der Friedensbewegung', in Degen et al., *Gegen den Krieg*, 30–41, here 37–38.
68 Cf. Pamela Ballinger, *History in Exile: Memory and Identity at the Border of the Balkans* (Princeton, NJ/Oxford: Princeton University Press, 2003), with a focus on Italian-language Istrians; Theodora Dragostinova, *Between Two Motherlands: Nationality and Emigration among the Greeks of Bulgaria, 1900–1949* (Ithaca, NY: Cornell University Press, 2011), with a focus on Bulgarians and Macedonians; Peter Thaler, 'Fluid Identities in Central European Borderland', *European History Quarterly* 31(4) (2001), 519–48, with a focus on Germans and Poles; Till van Rahden, *Juden und andere Breslauer: Die Beziehungen zwischen Juden, Protestanten und Katholiken in einer deutschen Großstadt von 1860 bis 1925* (Göttingen: Vandenhoeck & Ruprecht, 2000), with a focus on German Jews, Protestants and Catholics in Breslau, today's Wrocław in Poland.

Bibliography

Afflerbach, Holger. *Der Dreibund: Europäische Großmacht- und Allianzpolitik vor dem Ersten Weltkrieg*. Vienna/Cologne/Weimar: Böhlau, 2002.

Andreucci, Franco, and Tommaso Detti (eds). *Il movimento operaio italiano: Dizionario biografico 1853–1943* [The Italian Workers' Movement: Biographic Dictionary]. 6 Vols. Rome: Editori riuniti, 1975–1979.

Apih, Elio. 'Valentino Pittoni fra Austria e Italia' [Valentino Pittoni between Austria and Italy], in Elio Apih (ed.), *Il socialismo italiano in Austria: Saggi* [Italian Socialism in Austria: Essays] (Udine: Del Bianco Editore, 1991), 35–100.

Ballinger, Pamela. *History in Exile: Memory and Identity at the Border of the Balkans*. Princeton, NJ/Oxford: Princeton University Press, 2003.

Becker, Jean-Jacques. *Comment les français sont entrés dans la guerre*. Paris: Presses de la Fondation Nationale des Sciences Politiques, 1977.

Biagini, Antonello. *L'Italia e le guerre balcaniche* [Italy and the Balkan Wars]. 2nd ed. Rome: Edizioni Nuova Cultura, 2012 [1st ed. 1990].

Biber, Dušan. 'Jugoslovanska ideja in slovensko narodno vprašanja v slovenski publicistiki med balkanskimi vojnami v letih 1912–1913' [The Yugoslav Idea and the Slovene National Question in the Slovene Media during the Balkan Wars in the Years 1912–1913]. *Istorija XX veka* [History of the 20th Century] 1 (1959), 285–324.

Biondich, Mark. 'Eastern Borderlands and Prospective Shatter Zones: Identity and Conflict in East Central and Southeastern Europe on the Eve of the First World War', in Jochen Böhler, Włodzimierz Borodziej and Joachim von Puttkamer (eds), *Legacies of Violence: Eastern Europe's First World War* (Europas Osten im 20. Jahrhundert, 3) (Berlin: De Gruyter, 2014), 25–50.

Boeckh, Katrin. *Von den Balkankriegen zum Ersten Weltkrieg: Kleinstaatenpolitik und ethnische Selbstbestimmung auf dem Balkan*. Munich: Oldenbourg, 1996.

Callahan, Kevin J. 'The International Socialist Peace Movement on the Eve of World War I Revisited: The Campaign of "War against War!" and the Basle International Socialist Congress in 1912'. *Peace & Change* 29(2) (2004), 147–76.

Cankar, Ivan. 'Slovenci in Jugoslovani' [Slovenes and Yugoslavs]. *Zbrano delo* [Collected Works] 25 (1976), 228–38.

Cattaruzza, Marina. *La formazione del proletariato urbano: Immigrati, operai di mestiere, donne a Trieste dalla metà del secolo XIX alla prima guerra mondiale* [The Formation of the Urban Proletariat: Immigrants, Workers, Women in Trieste from the Second Half of the 19th Century to the First World War] (Teoria e storia di classe, 13). Turin: Musolini, 1979.

———. *Socialismo adriatico: La socialdemocrazia di lingua italiana nei territori costieri della monarchia asburgica, 1888–1915* [Adriatic Socialism: Italian-Language Social Democracy in the Littoral Territories of the Habsburg Monarchy]. 2nd ed. Manduria: P. Lacaita, 2001.

———. *L'Italia e il confine orientale, 1866–2006* [Italy and Its Eastern Border]. Bologna: Il Mulino, 2007.

———. *Italy and Its Eastern Border, 1866–2016*. New York: Routledge, 2017.

Childs, Timothy W. *Italo-Turkish Diplomacy and the War over Libya, 1911–1912* (Social, Economic, and Political Studies of the Middle East, 42). Leiden: Brill, 1990.

Clark, Christopher. *The Sleepwalkers: How Europe Went to War in 1914*. London: Penguin, 2013.
Damianova, Jivka. 'La fédération contre l'alliance militaire: les socialistes balkaniques et les guerres balkaniques 1912–3'. *Le Mouvement Social* 147 (1989), 69–85.
Daugsch, Walter. 'Balkanföderation, Balkankriege und Internationale: Sozialdemokratie in Südosteuropa 1908–1914', in Sandrine Mayoraz, Frithjof Benjamin Schenk and Ueli Mäder (eds), *Hundert Jahre Basler Friedenskongress (1912–2012): Die erhoffte 'Verbrüderung der Völker'*. Basel/Zürich: Schweizerisches Sozialarchiv, 2015, 109–18.
De Grand, Alexander. *The Hunchback's Tailor: Giovanni Giolitti and Liberal Italy from the Challenge of Mass Politics to the Rise of Fascism, 1882–1922*. Westport, CT: Praeger, 2001.
Degen, Bernard. 'Basel im Zentrum der Friedensbewegung', in Bernard Degen et al. (eds), *Gegen den Krieg: Der Basler Friedenskongress 1912 und seine Aktualität* (Basel: Christoph Merian, 2012), 30–41.
——. 'Die europaweite Ausstrahlung des Kongresses', in Bernard Degen et al. (eds), *Gegen den Krieg: Der Basler Friedenskongress 1912 und seine Aktualität* (Basel: Christoph Merian, 2012), 141–50.
Despot, Igor. *Balkanski ratovi 1912.–1913. i njihov odjek u Hrvatskoj* [The Balkan Wars and Their Echoes in Croatia]. Zagreb: Nova Plejada, 2013.
Detrez, Raymond. 'Pre-national Identities in the Balkans', in Roumen Daskalov and Tchavdar Marinov (eds), *Entangled Histories of the Balkans*, Vol. 1: *National Ideologies and Language Policies* (Balkans Studies Library, 9) (Leiden: Brill, 2013), 13–65.
Dragostinova, Theodora. *Between Two Motherlands: Nationality and Emigration among the Greeks of Bulgaria, 1900–1949*. Ithaca, NY: Cornell University Press, 2011.
Fabi, Lucio. *Trieste 1914–1918: Una città in guerra* [Trieste 1914–1918: A City at War]. Trieste: MGS Press, 1996.
Finzi, Roberto, Loredana Panariti and Giovanni Panjek (eds). *Storia economica e sociale di Trieste 1719–1918* [Economic and Social History of Trieste 1719–1918], Vol. 2, *La città dei traffici* [The City of Trade]. Trieste: LINT, 2003.
Finzi, Roberto, and Giovanni Panjek (eds). *Storia economica e sociale di Trieste 1719–1918* [Economic and Social History of Trieste 1719–1918], Vol. 1, *La città dei gruppi* [The City of Groups]. Trieste: LINT, 2001.
Greiner, Bernd, et al. (eds). *Angst im Kalten Krieg*. Hamburg: Hamburger Edition, 2009.
Hall, Richard C. *The Balkan Wars 1912–1913: Prelude to the First World War*. London/New York: Routledge, 2000.
Hannig, Alma. 'Angst und die Balkanpolitik Österreich-Ungarns vor dem Ersten Weltkrieg', in Patrick Bormann, Thomas Freiberger and Judith Michel (eds), *Angst in den internationalen Beziehungen* (Bonn: Bonn University Press, 2010), 93–113.
——. 'Die Balkanpolitik Österreich-Ungarns vor 1914', in Jürgen Angelow (ed.), *Der Erste Weltkrieg auf dem Balkan: Perspektiven der Forschung* (Berlin: be.bra, 2011), 35–56.

Haumann, Heiko, and Laura Polexe. 'Debatten um Krieg und Frieden in der Zweiten Internationale', in Bernard Degen et al. (eds), *Gegen den Krieg: Der Basler Friedenskongress 1912 und seine Aktualität* (Basel: Christoph Merian, 2012), 133–40.

Helmedach, Andreas. *Das Verkehrssystem als Modernisierungsfaktor: Straßen, Post, Fuhrwesen und Reisen nach Triest und Fiume vom Beginn des 18. Jahrhunderts bis zum Eisenbahnzeitalter*. Munich: Oldenbourg, 2002.

Herrmann, David G. *The Arming of Europe and the Making of the First World War*. Princeton, NJ: Princeton University Press, 1966.

Keisinger, Florian. *Unzivilisierte Kriege im zivilisierten Europa: Die Balkankriege und die öffentliche Meinung in Deutschland, England und Irland 1876–1913*. Paderborn: Schöningh, 2008.

Koselleck, Reinhart. '"Erfahrungsraum" und "Erwartungshorizont" – zwei historische Kategorien', in Reinhart Koselleck (ed.), *Vergangene Zukunft: Zur Semantik geschichtlicher Zeiten* (Frankfurt/M.: Suhrkamp, 1989), 349–75.

Leghissa, Adolfo. *Trieste che passa, 1884–1914* [Trieste As It Goes By]. Trieste: Liberia internazionale Italo Svevo, 1971.

Macdonald, John, and Željko Cimprić. *Caporetto and the Isonzo Campaign: The Italian Front, 1915–1918*. Barnsley: Pen & Sword Military, 2011.

Mazis, John A. 'The Idea of an Eastern Federation: An Alternative to the Destruction of the Ottoman Empire', in Lucien J. Frary and Mara Kozelsky (eds), *Russian-Ottoman Borderlands: The Eastern Question Reconsidered* (Madison, WI: The University of Wisconsin Press, 2014), 251–79.

Melik, Vasilij. *Slovenci v času Cankarjevega predavanja* [The Slovenes at the Time of Cankar's Lectures]. Maribor: Založba Obzorja, Izdaja Univerza v Mariboru in Zgodovinsko društvo Maribor, 1986.

Millo, Anna. *Storia di una borghesia: La famiglia Vivante a Trieste dall'emporio alla guerra mondiale* [History of a Middle Class: The Vivante Family in Trieste from the Merchant City to the World War]. Gorizia: Libreria Editrice Goriziana, 1998.

Monticone, Alberto. *La battaglia di Caporetto* [The Battle of Caporetto]. Udine: Gaspari editore, 1999.

Neitzel, Sönke. *Blut und Eisen: Deutschland im Ersten Weltkrieg*. Zürich: Pendo Verlag, 2003.

Plamper, Jan. 'Fear: Soldiers and Emotion in Early Twentieth-Century Russian Military Psychology'. *Slavic Review* 68(2) (2009), 259–83.

Prepeluh-Abditus, Albin. 'Slovenci ali Jugoslovani' [Slovenes or Yugoslavs]. *Naši Zapiski. Socialistična Revija* [Our Notes. Socialist Review] 10 (1913), 137–40.

Prijevec, Jože. *'Trst je naš!' Boj Slovencev za morje (1848–1954)* ['Trieste Is Ours!' The Struggle of the Slovenes for the Sea (1848–1954)]. Ljubljana: Nova revija, 2007.

Rahden, Till van. *Juden und andere Breslauer: Die Beziehungen zwischen Juden, Protestanten und Katholiken in einer deutschen Großstadt von 1860 bis 1925*. Göttingen: Vandenhoeck & Ruprecht, 2000.

Rajšp, Vincenc (ed.). *Soška fronta 1915–1917: Kultura spominjanja / Isonzofront 1915–1917: Die Kultur des Erinnerns* [The Isonzo Front, 1915–1917: The Culture of Remembrance]. Ljubljana: Založba ZRC, ZRC SAZU, 2010.

Rauchensteiner, Manfred. *Der Erste Weltkrieg und das Ende der Habsburgermonarchie 1914–1918*. Vienna/Cologne/Weimar: Böhlau, 2013 [rev. ed. 1993].
Reinschedl, Manfred. *Die Aufrüstung der Habsburgermonarchie von 1880 bis 1914 im internationalen Vergleich: Der Anteil Österreich-Ungarns am Wettrüsten vor dem Ersten Weltkrieg* (Beiträge zur Neueren Geschichte Österreichs, 16). Frankfurt/M.: Peter Lang, 2001.
Rogel, Carol. *The Slovenes and Yugoslavism, 1890–1914*. Boulder, CO: East European Quarterly, 1977.
Rozman, Franc. 'Ob sedemdesetletnici Tivolske resolucije' [70 Years since the Tivoli Resolution]. *Kronika. Časopis za slovensko krajevno zgodovino* [Chronicle. Journal for Slovene Regional History] 27 (1979), 180–84.
——. 'Stališče slovenske socialne demokracije do Balkanskih vojn' [The Opinion of Slovene Social Democrats on the Balkan Wars]. *Zgodovinski Časopis* [Historical Journal] 42(4) (1988), 517–24.
Rutar, Sabine. *Kultur – Nation – Milieu: Sozialdemokratie in Triest vor dem Ersten Weltkrieg*. Essen: Klartext, 2004.
Stergar, Rok. 'Fragen des Militärwesens in der slowenischen Politik 1867–1914'. *Österreichische Osthefte* 46(3) (2004), 391–422.
——. *Slovenci in vojska, 1867–1914: Slovenski odnos do vojaških vprašanj od uvedbe dualizma do začetka 1. svetovne vojne* [The Slovenes and the Military: The Slovene Attitude to Military Questions from the Introduction of Dualism to the Beginning of the First World War]. Ljubljana: Oddelek za Zgodovino Filozofske Fakultete, 2004.
Stevenson, David. *Armaments and the Coming of War: Europe 1904–1914*. Oxford: Clarendon Press, 1996.
Thaler, Peter. 'Fluid Identities in Central European Borderland'. *European History Quarterly* 31(4) (2001), 519–48.
Vivante, Angelo, *Irredentismo adriatico: Contributo alla discussione sui rapporti austro-italiani* [Adriatic Irredentism: A Contribution to the Discussion about the Austrian-Italian Relations]. Florence: Libreria de La Voce, 1912.
Wendel, Hermann. 'Der türkisch-italienische Krieg'. *Die neue Zeit: Wochenschrift der deutschen Sozialdemokratie* 30, 1(3) (20 October 1911), 65–72.
Wörsdörfer, Rolf. 'Der Auszug der Italiener aus den adriatischen Provinzen', in Rolf Wörsdörfer, *Krisenherd Adria 1915–1955: Konstruktion und Artikulation des Nationalen im italienisch-jugoslawischen Grenzraum* (Paderborn: Schöningh, 2004), 522–60.
——. 'Habsburgisch-venezianisches Erbe und großer Krieg: Zweierlei nationale Einigung – Italien 1860, Südslawien 1918', in Rolf Wörsdörfer, *Krisenherd Adria 1915–1955: Konstruktion und Artikulation des Nationalen im italienisch-jugoslawischen Grenzraum* (Paderborn: Schöningh, 2004), 35–69.
——. 'Julische Slowenen und Kroaten im Exil', in Rolf Wörsdörfer, *Krisenherd Adria 1915–1955: Konstruktion und Artikulation des Nationalen im italienisch-jugoslawischen Grenzraum* (Paderborn: Schöningh, 2004), 281–313.
Ziemann, Benjamin. *Front und Heimat: Ländliche Kriegserfahrungen im südlichen Bayern 1914–1923*. Essen: Klartext, 1997.
Zweig, Stefan. *Die Welt von gestern: Erinnerungen eines Europäers*. Berlin: Insel Verlag, 2013 [orig. 1942].

11

THE PLIGHT OF THE MUSLIM POPULATION IN SALONICA AND SURROUNDING AREAS

Vera Goseva and Natasha Kotlar-Trajkova

The Young Turk Revolution of 1908, the Italo-Turkish War and the Albanian rebellion, both of 1911, led to changes within the Balkan peninsula and the Ottoman Empire, prompting the governments of Belgrade and Sofia to form an alliance to drive the Ottomans from the Balkans. Talks held in early October 1911 paved the way for the Serbian-Bulgarian Treaty of Friendship and Alliance, but did not lead to the immediate signing of the document. There were disagreements over the partitioning of the disputed zone – the area of Macedonia within the Ottoman *Vilayet* of Monastir/Bitola – which delayed its signing by almost six months. In order to prevent the talks from failing and to encircle Austria-Hungary politically through the establishment of a Balkan League, Russian diplomacy entered these negotiations through its ambassadors in Belgrade (Nikolai Hartwig) and Sofia (Anatoli Nekliudov).[1] Initially, Serbia and Bulgaria were both intransigent, but as a result of the direct intervention of Russia in the negotiations, the pressure exerted by Great Britain and France, as well as the Ottoman Empire's refusal to meet Bulgarian demands in the separate negotiations between these two countries, they drew closer in their positions. The 'Treaty of Friendship and Alliance between Bulgaria and Serbia' was stipulated on 29 February 1912, and a secret annex regulated both the partition of Macedonia and Russian arbitration regarding the dividing line.[2]

The conclusion of the agreement between Serbia and Bulgaria provided Bulgarian diplomacy with the opportunity to carry out certain activities that aimed at concluding a similar agreement with Greece. The Bulgarian government had rejected similar Greek proposals in 1891 and 1897. In 1910, Greece's prime minister, Eleftherios Venizelos, had once again proposed to conclude a political alliance with Bulgaria, but to no avail. Bulgaria could not agree with the Greek proposal to cede Kavala and Serres (in the *Vilayet* of Salonica), as well as Voden, Kostur and Lerin (in the *Vilayet* of Monastir/Bitola) to Greece. In the following year, a group of public figures and politicians, among them then finance minister Lambros Koromilas and the former Greek consul in Istanbul, Ion Dragoumis, drafted a memorandum in Athens, stating that it was 'of the highest importance that spheres of influence be determined'.[3] The Bulgarian government was not keen, however, to determine spheres of influence in Macedonia, as it did not wish Salonica to be ceded to Greece. It had not explicitly stated that the city should be included within the borders of Bulgaria, as this would have prevented any possibility of renewed talks with the government in Athens. The progress of the Bulgarian–Serbian negotiations at the beginning of February 1912 created an opportunity for the Bulgarian government to request that the government in Athens resubmit its previous proposals via diplomatic channels. To this Bulgarian request the Greek government replied on 14 April 1912 with a draft agreement for a defensive alliance, which avoided any mention of Macedonia. The deterioration of Bulgarian–Ottoman relations, as well as the bombardment of the Straits of Otranto by Italy, however, brought the two sides to seek a compromise. A defensive alliance agreement was finally reached on 16 May 1912 and signed in Sofia by the Bulgarian prime minister Ivan E. Geshov and Dimitri Panas, a senior ambassador in the Greek Foreign Ministry.[4] Thus, a Balkan military power was created that would significantly impact the destiny of the Balkan peoples, especially their political relations and the state borders between them.

The Conquest of Salonica

This chapter examines hitherto scarcely used British and Austrian documents to investigate the plight of the second-largest community in the city of Salonica, the Muslim community, during the Balkan Wars (1912–13).[5] Salonica was an important trading, cultural and sociopolitical centre of the Ottoman Empire at the turn of the twentieth century, a multicultural city of some 118,000 inhabitants. According to an 1890 statistical assessment, the population included 55,000 Jews (46.6 per cent),[6] 26,000 Turks or members of other ethnic communities who declared their religious affiliation as Muslim (22.3 per cent), 16,000 Greeks or members of other ethnic communities whose religious affiliation was with the Patriarchate of Constantinople (13.6 per cent),

10,000 Bulgarians or members of other ethnic communities whose religious affiliation was with the Bulgarian Exarchate (8.4 per cent), 2,500 Roma and 8,500 people of other ethnic affiliations.[7] At that time the city of Salonica, which had a large port, was an administrative, economic, commercial and transportation centre. It was without doubt the second city of the Empire after Istanbul.

While the Balkan League was evolving, Salonica played a pivotal role in the ongoing political and military negotiations between Greece and Bulgaria. As no agreement was reached on the defensive alliance, the question of which state would win the city of Salonica from the Ottoman Empire was an open issue at the outbreak of the First Balkan War.[8] Even before the outbreak of the war, both sides intended to advance their armies towards Salonica in the hope of conquering the city and assimilating it within their new state borders.[9]

In the course of the war, the situation on the ground indicated that Greece stood a greater chance of achieving this goal. After the Greek victory in the Battle of Sarantaporos on 23 October 1912 over the Ottoman forces led by the city's military commander, Hasan Tahsin Paşa, the road for the Greek army's advance to Salonica was clear. Negotiations for the surrender of the city began on 7 November 1912, two weeks after the battle. The terms put forward by the Greeks included the demand that the Turkish forces were to lay down their weapons and to be detained in suitable locations, while the Turkish police were to keep their jobs until they were replaced by Greek counterparts. General Hasan Tahsin Paşa instead sought different conditions. His attempt to gain time by prolonging the negotiations proved unsuccessful when Greek forces entered the city on the following afternoon (8 November 1912) without encountering meaningful resistance.

Negotiations on the terms of surrender of Salonica were again held on the same night and completed the following morning between representatives of the Greek Crown Prince Constantine and Hasan Tahsin Paşa. The Protocol of Capitulation – which was almost identical to the one previously offered – was signed at 6 a.m. on 9 November 1912. According to these terms, the Turkish forces were to hand over their weapons for storage in military warehouses held by the Greek army. The disarmed forces were then to be detained in Zeytinlik and in Kara-Bouroum, as well as in other places where they would remain under Greek control. Their disarmament was to be carried out within forty-eight hours. The officers were to be allowed to keep their weapons and to be treated temporarily as captives, while the city officials as well as the police were allowed to retain their weapons and their freedom and to continue their duties until further notice. Most of the terms for capitulation had, however, already been carried out, provoking complaints by the Turks.¹⁰ A frequent complaint has been made about the treatment of the Turkish military forces. Even though it had been agreed that they would not be treated as prisoners of war, the officers were in fact guarded by the Greek army and some were even placed in camps established west of the city.¹¹ On 19 November 1912, Hasan Tahsin Paşa sent a memorandum to Prince Nicholas of Greece. In the memorandum, Tahsin Paşa objected to 'the acts and proceedings which have been and are being permitted in violation of the agreements signed between the two parties'.¹²

Crown Prince Constantine was already in Salonica by 4 a.m. on 10 November 1912, the reason for his haste being the speed with which the Bulgarian army was advancing towards the city.¹³ Thus, the Greek forces achieved their aim of establishing their position as the first and, as such, sole conquerors of Salonica. The vanguard of the Bulgarian forces, which entered the city later that morning, was received by Crown Prince Constantine, who had already appointed Periklis Argyropoulos (a former prefect of Larissa) as prefect of the city.

Despite attempts at the swift establishment of Greek authority,¹⁴ the British consul-general in Salonica, Harry H. Lamb, reported on 12 November 1912 that the situation in the city was increasingly tense and disquieting. The tension was caused by an intensification of rivalry between the Greeks and the Bulgarians over who should control the city.¹⁵ The arrival of King George I on 11 November was aimed at strengthening the Greek position in Salonica. The king entered the city with a military force of twenty thousand men, an entrance timed to coincide with the entrance of Prince Boris of Bulgaria, who was escorted by five thousand Bulgarian soldiers after having been granted consent to do so by Crown Prince Constantine.

Over the following days, Lamb recorded continuing tensions and clashes between Bulgarian and Greek soldiers. Describing the events of 14 November, for example, the British consul-general wrote that 'the two parties nearly two times came to blows over the possession of the Mosque of St. Sophia, over which the Bulgarians have hoisted their national flag'.¹⁶

The Plight of the Muslim Population

The number of Bulgarian and Greek soldiers and members of irregular units (*komitadjis* and *andartes*, respectively)¹⁷ in the city was constantly increasing: in the first days after the capitulation, the number of

Greek and Bulgarian soldiers in Salonica was almost identical.[18] Their intolerance of each other was manifested primarily in their treatment of civilians. A British diplomat noted the shamelessness with which both sides conducted themselves, carrying out searches and robbing people and their property in and around the city.[19] The Bulgarian army had already displayed cruelty in its treatment of the local civilian population, including the Muslim population, as it was advancing towards Salonica. The Bulgarians handed over villages they passed through to the local *komitadjis*.[20] The irregular units disarmed all Muslims and distributed their weapons to the Christian population. They then robbed the Muslim landowners, stealing their cattle and their wheat reserves before setting fire to 'everything that could not be taken along'.[21] As Sir Gerard Lowther, the British ambassador in Constantinople, wrote to the British foreign secretary Sir Edward Grey, according to Lamb 'the Mussulmen notables in the towns were then forced to pay large sums for a few days' respite, after which their houses were plundered and they only too often killed. ... In many districts there is only too good reason to believe that organised massacre has been resorted to'.[22]

According to the same source, the village of Jajladzik, near Salonica, was completely destroyed by the Bulgarian army and the estate of Suleiman Paşa was burnt to the ground. While the event in itself was confirmed by Henry Noel Brailsford, the British member of the Carnegie Commission, he reported, however, that this destruction had been committed by the 'Greek army and the people from the nearby Greek villages'.[23]

The British documents also give an account of how the Greek authorities in Salonica brutally violated the terms of the Protocol for Capitulation. A large number of Turkish officers, who were supposed to be treated only temporarily as prisoners of war, were arrested and boarded onto steamships for deportation to Turkish ports. Among those arrested were Dr Nazim Bey, the former secretary general of the Committee of Union and Progress and then director of the Red Crescent hospital in Salonica, as well as two former political party leaders from the city and a number of police officers, including their commander.[24]

The situation in the city grew even more critical as the number of its inhabitants had grown by 50 per cent. Military operations in other parts of Macedonia resulted in the arrival in the city of large numbers of refugees, mostly Muslims, from territories from which the Ottoman army was withdrawing. According to a report by the British consul, dated 26 October 1912, more than five thousand civilian refugees had arrived in Salonica from the interior of the country.[25] Under the general conditions of chaos and fear, people were heading towards Salonica considering it safer, having insufficient knowledge about the current situation in the city. The following day, the same source reported that the number of refugees had already reached ten thousand.[26] On 1 November 1912, their number was estimated at forty thousand,[27] and by 16 December it had risen as high as fifty thousand.[28]

As an important urban and administrative centre of the Ottoman state, Salonica was considered a safe haven by the Muslim civilian population, seeking refuge from the military actions of the Balkan alliance forces. Numerous demoralized and defeated Ottoman soldiers had the same opinion. According to Lamb's report of 7 November 1912:

> During these two days, deserters from Hasan Tahsin's force poured in an almost continuous stream into Salonica, where they were mostly collected and sent back, after refitting, to the front. They took no pains to conceal either their unwillingness to continue the war, their complete indifference to its results, or their supreme contempt for the greater number of their officers. Their only idea seemed to be to get into Salonica, where they looked forward to receiving food and a night's rest. Many declared that they had been three or even four days without bread, and it is officially admitted that the commissariat arrangements of a whole division broke down for forty-eight hours.[29]

For the defeated Ottoman soldiers, the city was a place where they could get help and support,[30] which is why their numbers reached thirty or forty thousand towards the end of October 1912.[31] This was how the situation had been until the Protocol of Capitulation was signed, at which time the twenty-five thousand Turkish soldiers present in the city surrendered.

In the first few weeks of the Balkan Wars, the Muslim population had become victim to various retaliatory and criminal actions committed by their Christian fellow citizens and the Balkan alliance forces. Forced to flee their homes, Muslims seeking refuge in Salonica helped to swell the city's population from '150,000 inhabitants to some 310,000'.[32] The refugees who fled to the city were housed in mosques, churches and vacant buildings. Many, however, including women and children, were forced to spend the cold winter nights in the open.[33] Until the capitulation of Salonica, bread was provided for the refugees by the city's mayor, Osman Sait Bey. After the arrival of the Greek and Bulgarian armies, food provision arrangements for the refugees deteriorated dramatically. Many of the Muslim refugees died of starvation. In an attempt to alleviate this grave situation, the French Sisters of Mercy provided the refugees with all the food they could spare. Despite these efforts, the refugees were so starved that they scavenged for leftovers from the military ships docked in the harbour.[34]

On 13 November 1912, the minister of justice, Konstantinos Raktivan, was appointed by royal edict as administrator of the Greek-occupied Macedonian regions. Prince Nicholas was appointed military governor of Salonica.[35] However, it was difficult to establish 'any settled form of government' in the city.[36] Theft and violence perpetrated by members of the armies went unpunished.[37] This was particularly characteristic of the first few weeks after the surrender of Salonica. British diplomatic reports registered a number of such cases. Not even important representatives of the Ottoman authorities in the city were safe from crime, including Hasan Tahsin Paşa himself and the mayor Osman Sait Bey.[38] Hasan Tahsin Paşa's son and his nephew were robbed in the family house under the pretext that they were in possession of weapons without permission. Bulgarian soldiers entered the house of Osman Sait Bey by force, threatened the mayor with their bayonets and forced him to hand over all the money in the house, including his wife's jewellery and many rare pieces of art.[39]

There is also a document containing information about the misconduct of Greek soldiers. A typical example is the case of a Turkish officer abused in broad daylight on one of the main streets of the city: after shaving his head and covering him in mud from head to toe, Greek soldiers stole the officer's money and his watch. With the intent of humiliating the religious and national feelings of the Muslim population, Greek soldiers abused anyone wearing a fez.[40] No ethnic group was spared from these offences, including foreigners living in the city.[41]

The position of the Muslim population was even worse in the areas surrounding the city. Many Muslim villages were burnt to the ground, and many instances were recorded of Muslims being robbed, raped and murdered. These atrocities were confirmed by a report of the Carnegie Commission referring to crimes committed by Bulgarian paramilitary units in the villages of Rayanovo, Planitsa and Kukurtovo. The report contains vivid descriptions of how men, women and children were executed.[42] Such actions were also confirmed by diplomatic representatives of other European countries.[43]

Such lawlessness was possible because local authority in the settlements around Salonica was largely left 'in the hands of notorious bandits'.[44] Therefore, it is not surprising that the Muslim population called for the establishment of an international commission to investigate and expose the numerous crimes being committed.[45] This request was received by the Austrian and German consuls in Salonica[46] but was never acted upon.[47] The same fate was shared by a request of 2 December 1912 from Cheri Paşa, a member of the Red Cross mission, calling on the British government for protection of the Muslim population against the destructive actions of the allied military units.[48]

The re-establishment of any administrative authority in Salonica and the surrounding areas was a slow and difficult process. In some cases, this process took six weeks after the elimination of Ottoman rule.[49] The numerous cases of violence, troublesome incidents and uncertainty persuaded many Muslim refugees to leave for the cities of Izmir and Istanbul.[50]

After the Second Balkan War and the signing of the Peace Treaty of Bucharest on 10 August 1913, the flow of emigrants from Thrace and Macedonia, including Salonica and its surrounding areas, intensified even further. This wave of emigration involved large numbers not only of Muslim, but also of Christian and Jewish emigrants. According to Austrian diplomatic reports, some 140,000 emigrants left Salonica and its surroundings after the end of the Second Balkan War, of which 'at least half' were Muslims.[51] Almost all of the refugees were intent on fleeing to territories under Ottoman rule. A special 'Muslim Transport Committee'[52] was established to organize the transfer of refugees to Asia Minor. This emigration acquired such intensity that the Turkish minister of internal affairs, Mehmed Talât Paşa (1913–17), sent a message to the Salonica *mufti*, informing him that 'the authorities of Smyrna will no longer allow anchoring of any further ships with immigrants'. As justification for this decision, he pointed out that the *Vilayet* of Aydın had already received seventy-five thousand refugees and that hygienic conditions there were 'degenerating'.[53] The refugees, he added, were now being 'diverted to Constantinople, Mudanya [Bursa], and most of them to Mershina [Mersin], Alexandretta [İskenderun], and Antakya'.[54] A chronicler of the city of Salonica, Mark Mazower, states that Mustafa Kemal's mother, sister and cousin were among those who fled to the refugee camps in Istanbul. The last governor of Salonica, Nazim Paşa, shared the same fate.[55]

Consequences and Conclusions

The Balkan Wars dramatically altered the position of various ethnic and religious groups in the Balkans – and that of the Muslim population in particular. What characterized these wars was the cruelty perpetrated upon the civilian population: this cruelty resulted in great loss of life, systematic extermination of civilians who were seen as belonging to the enemy side, a large number of annihilated villages and the destruction of entire regions. An immense demographic change took place within a short space of time, creating new political, economic and cultural conditions in the Balkans. With regard to Salonica in particular, the census carried out in 1913 by the Greek government registered the total population of the city at 157,889 inhabitants, of whom close to 40,000 were registered as Greeks, 45,867 were registered as 'Ottomans' (i.e. people of Muslim affiliation who were also Ottoman citizens), 61,439 as Jews,[56] and others. One year later, in May 1914, the German consul in Salonica noted that:

> Salonica will probably soon change its Judeo-Turkish appearance. The Greek language is heard a lot more than it used to be, and it seems that everyone is trying to learn this official language. King Constantine says that he had been going over the submitted plans for redecorating for some time and asserts that they shall be carried out soon in order for the city to lose its Turkish appearance.[57]

We can conclude that the Balkan Wars satisfied the ambitions of nationalist circles in the Balkan states. That these circles enjoyed the backing of the great powers became clear at two conferences which took place in London at the same time: the Ambassadors' Conference and the Peace Conference of the warring Balkan states.[58]

The victories won by the Balkan allies on the battlefield were not complete until the spoils of war were divided among them.[59] Dividing the newly conquered territories proved difficult, however. Demarcation lines became the subject of discussion at the London Peace Conference, which took place at the same time as the Ambassadors' Conference of the great powers. At the Ambassadors' Conference, the acting mediators 'agreed that it is not possible to restore the previous conditions and that the Balkan states should determine their future borders by way of an agreement'.[60] This development additionally deepened the disagreements among the Balkan allies (Bulgaria on one side, Serbia and Greece on the other) regarding the distribution of the territory of Macedonia. Serbia and Greece refused to relinquish the territories conquered by their respective armies. The excuse for such behaviour was found in the territories in Albania that they had lost and for which they had to be compensated in Macedonia. The peace agreement between the Balkan allies (according to the Treaty of London, 30 May 1913) was signed under a great deal of pressure exerted by the great powers. The Balkan ambassadors were forced, or rather blackmailed, into either signing the agreement or leaving the peace negotiations.[61]

Eighty years after these wars, a new war threatened the Balkans and was waged with familiar cruelty on the territory of the former Yugoslavia. Reflecting on this phenomenon from today's perspective, we may conclude that the historical lessons taught by the Balkan Wars of 1912–13 have not been learnt.

Vera Goseva is Professor at the Institute of National History in Skopje, and Head of the Department for the Period between 1912 and 1941. She is Editor-in-Chief of the *Glasnik / Bulletin* of the Institute of National History (2013), and author of the monographs *Ilindenskata organizaciia (1921–1947)* [The Ilinden Organization (1921–1947)], Institute of National History (2004) and *Misho Shkartov*, Ss. Cyril and Methodius University, Faculty of Philisophy, Skopje (2016). Between 2007 and 2011, she was a member of the Presidency of the Association of the Historians of the Republic of Macedonia.

Natasha Kotlar-Trajkova is Professor at the Institute of National History in Skopje. Her latest monographs are *Iane Sandanski*, Ss. Cyril and Methodius University, Faculty of Philisophy, Skopje (2016) and *Voivodata Nikola Petrov Rusinski* [Voivode Nikola Petrov Rusinski], Menora, Skopje (2013). She co-authored, with Todor Chepreganov et al., *Svedovshtva za makedonskiot identitet (XVIII–XX)* [Testimonies for the Macedonian Identity, 18th–20th Centuries], Institute of National History, Skopje (2010). Since 2011 she has been President of the Association of Historians of the Republic of Macedonia.

Notes

1 Serbia and Bulgaria had already reached a secret agreement in 1904, in which they had committed themselves to mutual solidarity in defending the principle of 'the Balkans to the Balkan peoples', as well as in opposing any intrusion into the territory of the Ottoman Balkans. The agreement singled out the four Balkan *vilayets* – Kosovo, Monastir/Bitola, Adrianople and Salonica (i.e. most of Macedonia) – as the areas of possible future disputes and decreed the Russian emperor as the final arbiter in eventual negotiations. Besides Russia, France and Britain were also privy to the details contained in the 1904 agreement. See Aleksandar Hristov and Jovan Donev, *Makedoniia vo meg'unarodnite dogovori 1875–1919, zbornik na dokumenti* [Macedonia in the International Treaties 1875–1919, Collection of Documents] (Skopje: Arhiv na Makedoniia, Matitsa Makedonska, 1994), 153–54.

2 Ibid., 162–66; Richard C. Hall, *The Balkan Wars 1912–1913: Prelude to the First World War* (London/New York: Routledge, 2000), 11.

3   G'org'i Abadzhiev, *Balkanskite voini i Makedoniia* [The Balkan Wars and Macedonia] (Skopje: Institut za natsionalna istoriia, 1958), 33.
4   Hristov and Donev, *Makedoniia vo meg'unarodnite dogovori 1875–1919*, 167–69.
5   These documents are from *Drzhaven Arhiv na Republika Makedoniia* [State Archive of the Republic of Macedonia], hereafter: DARM.
6   According to Ottoman data for 1902, 49 per cent of the city's inhabitants were Jews: see Mark Mazower, *Solun grad na duhovi: Hristiiani, Muslimani i Evrei 1430–1950* [Salonica City of Ghosts: Christians, Muslims and Jews, 1430–1950] (Skopje: Az-Buki, 2008), 192.
7   Vasil Kûnchov, *Izbrani proizvedeniia* [Selected Works], Vol. II (Sofia: Izdatelstvo i izkustvo, 1970), 440.
8   Abadzhiev, *Balkanskite voini i Makedoniia*, 46.
9   Hall, *The Balkan Wars 1912–1913*, 12, 59–62, 75.
10 Foreign Office (FO), 371/1507/51111 [DARM, mf. 1966], His Britannic Majesty's Consul-General Harry H. Lamb, Salonica, 19 November 1912.
11 FO, 371/1508/53714 [DARM, mf. 1966], Commander Keane to Commander in Chief, Mediterranean, 16 December 1912.
12 FO, 371/1507/51111 [DARM, mf. 1966], His Britannic Majesty's Consul-General Harry H. Lamb, Salonica, 19 November 1912.
13 Greece fielded two armies during the First Balkan War. The Army of Thessaly, commanded by Crown Prince Constantine, was the main force of the Greek army. Its objective was to occupy Thessaly and specifically to take Salonica before the Bulgarians arrived there. The secondary Greek force was the Army of Epirus, which was under the command of General Constantine Zapundzakis. Its objective was the southern Albanian town of Ioánnina/Janina.
14 FO, 371/1507/50525 [DARM, mf. 1966], His Britannic Majesty's Consulate General, Salonica, 15 November 1912, Official Notice of the Occupation of Salonica by the Greek Troops.
15 Lamb wrote: 'The most disquieting feature in the present situation is the growing ill-feeling between the Greeks and Bulgarians'; FO, 371/1507/50526 [DARM, mf. 1966], Consul-General Lamb to Sir Gerard Lowther, Salonica, 15 November 1912; see also FO, 371/1507/50521 [DARM, mf. 1966], Consul-General Lamb to Sir Gerard Lowther, Salonica, 12 November 1912.
16 FO, 371/1507/50526 [DARM, mf. 1966], Consul-General Lamb to Sir Gerard Lowther, Salonica, 15 November 1912.
17 The *komitadjis* were irregular units that had an auxiliary role in favour of the Bulgarian army and the *andartes* were irregular units that had an auxiliary role in favour of the Greek forces.
18 FO, 371/1507/50526 [DARM, mf. 1966], Consul General Lamb to Sir Gerard Lowther, Salonica, 15 November 1912. This trend continued, and in December 1912 the number had risen to forty-five thousand Greek soldiers and forty thousand Bulgarian soldiers: FO, 371/1508/53714 [DARM, mf. 1966], Commander Keane to Commander in Chief, Mediterranean, 16 December 1912.
19 FO, 371/1507/50278 [DARM, mf. 1965], Sir G. Lowther to Sir Edward Grey, Constantinople, 21 November 1912.

20 FO, 371/1507/51709 [DARM, mf. 1966], Sir G. Lowther to Sir Edward Grey, Constantinople, 29 November 1912.
21 Ibid.
22 Ibid.
23 *Poraneshnite balkanski voini (1912–1913): Izveshtai na Karnegievata balkanska komisiia* [The Other Balkan Wars: A 1913 Carnegie Endowment Inquiry] (Skopje: Kultura, 2000), 327.
24 The Greek authorities justified this particular action with the excuse that an uprising of the Muslim population had been in preparation: FO, 371/1507/51709 [DARM, mf. 1966], Sir G. Lowther to Sir Edward Grey, Constantinople, 29 November 1912.
25 Ibid.
26 FO, 371/1505/47817 [DARM, mf. 1965], Sir G. Lowther to Sir Edward Grey, Constantinople, 3 November 1912.
27 FO, 371/1506/48282 [DARM, mf. 1965], Sir G. Lowther to Sir Edward Grey, Constantinople, 8 November 1912.
28 FO, 371/1508/53714 [DARM, mf. 1966], Commander Keane to Commander in Chief, Mediterranean, 16 December 1912.
29 FO, 371/1506/48282 [DARM, mf. 1965], Consul-General Lamb to Sir Gerard Lowther, Salonica, 7 November 1912.
30 FO, 371/1506/48964 [DARM, mf. 1965], Sir G. Lowther to Sir Edward Grey, Constantinople, 14 November 1912.
31 FO, 371/1506/48282 [DARM, mf. 1965], Sir G. Lowther to Sir Edward Grey, Constantinople, 8 November 1912.
32 FO, 371/1508/53714 [DARM, mf. 1966], Commander Keane to Commander in Chief, Mediterranean, 16 December 1912,
33 Ibid.
34 Ibid.
35 FO, 371/1507/50525 [DARM, mf. 1966], His Britannic Majesty's Consulate General, Salonica, 15 November 1912.
36 FO, 371/1507/51709 [DARM, mf. 1966], Sir G. Lowther to Sir Edward Grey, Constantinople, 29 November 1912.
37 Ibid.
38 Osman Sait Bey remained mayor from 1912 to 1916 and held the position again from 1920 to 1922.
39 FO, 371/1507/50521 [DARM, mf. 1966], Consul-General Lamb to Sir Gerard Lowther, Salonica, 12 November 1912.
40 Ibid.; Mazower, *Solun grad na duhovi*, 285.
41 FO, 371/1507/53264 [DARM, mf. 1966], Sir G. Lowther to Sir Edward Grey, Constantinople, 9 December 1912. Instances included the robbing of an Italian citizen and of the Persian consul.
42 *Poraneshnite balkanski voini*, 104.
43 Ibid., 106.
44 FO, 371/1507/50695 [DARM, mf. 1966], His Britannic Majesty's Consul-General Lamb to Sir Edward Grey, Salonica, 27 November 1912.
45 Ibid.
46 FO, 371/1507/52380 [DARM, mf. 1966], His Britannic Majesty's Consul-General Lamb to Sir Edward Grey, Salonica, 8 December 1912.

47 *Poraneshnite balkanski voini*, 104.
48 FO, 371/1507/51479 [DARM, mf. 1966], Mohamed Cheri Paşa to Sir Edward Grey, Pera, 2 December 1912.
49 *Poraneshnite balkanski voini*, 104.
50 Mazover, *Solun grad na duhovi*, 283.
51 On 12 September 1913, the Austrian consul in Salonica informed his superior that 'the emigration of Muslims should not be seen as a consequence of the Second Balkan War and is undiminished in those areas that, in accordance with the Peace Treaty of Bucharest, remained under Bulgaria. It has undoubtedly gotten a new sudden stimulus, but it has been present since the beginning of the First Balkan War, as Your Excellence has already been informed. ... The Muslim Committee has been making assessments of it since the end of October, i.e. since the strike on Kumanovo; maybe the assessment is too high – that it is about 100,000 – and the Committee believes that in the coming period it shall increase (twofold) in size': DARM, Ministry of Foreign Affairs of Austria-Hungary (MFA-AH), Microfilm (M-316 (XV/177/34–38), An Seine Exzellenz den Hochgeborenen Herrn Leopold Grafen Berchtold, 12 September 1913.
52 DARM, Ministry of Foreign Affairs of Austria-Hungary (MNR-AU), M-316 (XV/177/31–33), An Seine Exzellenz den Hochgeborenen Herrn Leopold Grafen Berchtold, Salonich, 30 August 1913.
53 DARM, MNR-AU, M-316 (XV/177/34–38), An Seine Exzellenz den Hochgeborenen Herrn Leopold Grafen Berchtold, Salonich, 12 September 1913.
54 Ibid. Regarding the size of the wave of emigration, the fact that the city of Izmir in 1900 had a population of 150,000 inhabitants, while in 1914 that number had increased to 300,000, speaks volumes. See Donald Quataert, *The Ottoman Empire, 1700–1922* (Cambridge: Cambridge University Press, 2000), 114.
55 Mazower, *Solun grad na duhovi*, 285.
56 Ibid., 257.
57 Hans-Lothar Steppan, *Makedonskiot iazol: Identitetot na Makedontsite prikazhan na primerot na Balkanskiot soiuz 1878–1914* [The Macedonian Knot: The Identity of the Macedonians as Revealed in the Development of the Balkan League 1878–1914] (Skopje: Az-Buki, 2005), 357.
58 The armistice for the cessation of the First Balkan War was signed on 3 December 1912 at the London Peace Conference, composed of delegates from the Balkan alliance, including Greece, who had not signed the armistice, and the Ottoman Empire. Its first meeting was held on 16 December 1912. At the same time, the Ambassadors' Conference, consisting of Sir Edward Grey and the London representatives of the great powers, was also in session. The sessions of the Ambassador's Conference also began on 16 December 1912 and ended on 23 January 1913, on the day when the Young Turks' *coup d'état* took place in the Ottoman Empire. On that day, the Young Turks, led by Enver Bey, again seized power in Constantinople. Enver Bey was at the time the chief of staff of the Strategic Reserve in Constantinople. The assumption that the Ottoman grand vizir, Kamil Paşa, was preparing to concede Adrianople to the Bulgarians was a major motivating factor for this action. The Young Turks were determined to continue the war and to

save Adrianople by whatever means possible. They forced Kamil Paşa to resign, and a non-political soldier, Mahmut Şevket Paşa, a former minister of war, became grand vizir. His task was to do everything possible to retain Adrianople. On 30 May 1913, the London Peace Conference ended with the signing of the Treaty of London, an agreement under which the Ottoman Empire would give up all territory west of the Enos-Midia line. See Hristov and Donev, *Makedoniia vo meg'unarodnite dogovori 1875–1919*, 176–79.

59 Österreichisches Staatsarchiv (ÖSTA), Haus-, Hof- und Staatsarchiv (HHStA) Wien, Politisches Archiv (PA) I, Fasz. 1114, Diplomatische Aktenstücke, Dok. 60, pp. 36–37 [DARM, 1.1369, M-1305]; ÖSTA, HHStA Wien, PA I, Fasz. 1114, Diplomatische Aktenstücke, Dok. 153, pp. 80–81 [DARM, 1.1369, M-1305]; ÖSTA, HHStA Wien, PA I, Fasz. 1114, Diplomatische Aktenstücke, Dok. 166, pp. 87–90 [DARM, 1.1369, M-1305/192–94].

60 Stevan Pavlović, *Istorija Balkana 1804–1945* [History of the Balkans 1804–1945], 2nd ed. (Belgrade: Clio, drugo izd. 2004), 290.

61 Hristov and Donev, *Makedoniia vo meg'unarodnite dogovori 1875–1919*, 177; Pavlović, *Istorija Balkana 1804–1945*, 291.

Bibliography

Abadzhiev, G'org'i. *Balkanskite voini i Makedoniia* [The Balkan Wars and Macedonia]. Skopje: Institut za natsionalna istoriia, 1958.

Hall, Richard C. *The Balkan Wars 1912–1913: Prelude to the First World War.* London/New York: Routledge, 2000.

Hristov, Aleksandar, and Jovan Donev. *Makedoniia vo meg'unarodnite dogovori 1875–1919, zbornik na dokumenti* [Macedonia in the International Treaties 1875–1919, Collection of Documents]. Skopje: Arhiv na Makedoniia, Matitsa Makedonska, 1994.

Kûnchov, Vasil. *Izbrani proizvedeniia* [Selected Works]. Vol. II. Sofia: Izdatelstvo i izkustvo, 1970.

Mazower, Mark. *Solun grad na duhovi: Hristiiani, Muslimani i Evrei 1430–1950* [Salonica City of Ghosts: Christians, Muslims and Jews, 1430–1950]. Skopje: Az-Buki, 2008.

Pavlović, Stevan. *Istorija Balkana 1804–1945* [History of the Balkans 1804–1945]. 2nd ed. Belgrade: Clio, 2004.

Poraneshnite balkanski voini (1912–1913): Izveshtai na Karnegievata balkanska komisiia [The Other Balkan Wars: A 1913 Carnegie Endowment Inquiry]. Skopje: Kultura, 2000.

Quataert, Donald. *The Ottoman Empire, 1700–1922.* Cambridge: Cambridge University Press, 2000.

Steppan, Hans-Lothar. *Makedonskiot iazol: Identitetot na Makedontsite prikazhan na primerot na Balkanskiot soiuz 1878–1914* [The Macedonian Knot: The Identity of the Macedonians as Revealed in the Development of the Balkan League 1878–1914]. Skopje: Az-Buki, 2005.

12

CLEANSING THE NATION
War-Related Demographic Changes in Macedonia
Iakovos D. Michailidis

> The main feature had been (as it was
> always evident that, in a Balkan war, it
> would be) the sacrifice of non-combatants.
> —Noel Buxton, *With the Bulgarian Staff*

The Road to War

The Balkan Wars (1912–13) represented the first armed conflict between the allied newborn Balkan states and the Ottoman Empire. Hostilities started at the beginning of the twentieth century, when nationalism within the Balkan states reached an aggressive level.[1] Irredentist visions, such as the 'Great Idea' for Greeks, the 'San Stefano Bulgaria' for Bulgarians and the 'Great Serbia' for Serbs, led the Balkan states to fight each other as well as the Ottoman Empire in order to expand their national borders.

At the same time, the same states worked to achieve national homogeneity. Homogenization in linguistic, religious and ethnic terms emerged as a high-priority policy and a major demand during the last quarter of the nineteenth century, when it became clear that the decline of the Ottoman Empire opened the way towards a change in the status quo in the Balkans.[2] But national purity was by no means consistent with the actual ethnic make-up of the Balkan nation-states, all of which had emerged from the dissolution of the Ottoman Empire, where religion was the major criterion used to classify populations.

Paradoxically, the ideal of national purity conflicted with the national irredentist agenda of all the Balkan states. In Greece, for example, national expansion was based on the dogma of the superiority of Greek culture. The aim was to give all individuals the chance to join the Greek side and become members of the Greek nation, regardless of their linguistic preference or affiliation.³ The same goal can be detected in Bulgaria and Serbia, which used a linguistic criterion and fought for the incorporation of all Slavophone populations, underestimating the strength of their possible national affiliations.

There is likely no better example to illustrate the policy of national purity than the case of Macedonia, a geographical area that was administratively divided during the Ottoman period into the *vilayets* of Salonica, Monastir and Kosovo. Populated by approximately two million people, half of them Muslims and half of them Christians,⁴ Macedonia was the irredentist dream of all the Balkan states because it was a fertile area and a strategic trade centre with ports on the Aegean.⁵ Macedonia became an 'apple of discord' after 1878, when the Treaty of San Stefano temporarily resulted in a 'Greater Bulgaria',⁶ a creation annulled a few months later by the Treaty of Berlin.⁷ Shortly afterwards, Greece, Bulgaria and Serbia started a fierce educational, religious and armed debate to promote their interests in the region of Macedonia, a debate that lasted until the military movement of the Young Turks in 1908.⁸

During the Balkan Wars, the participants attempted to achieve their political, diplomatic and military goals. These efforts were all too often accompanied by attempts to eliminate the populations deemed enemies in ethnic and religious terms. It is worth noting that the Balkan national armies, in some cases, acted without regard to international law and exterminated not only armed opponents but also non-combatants. Irregular armed groups acted concurrently, probably in full cooperation with their national armies or at least with their permission.⁹ Such groups consisted of former fighters, Bulgarian and Serbian *komitadjis* and Greek *andartes*, who had already fought each other during the years before the wars, especially in the years 1904–8, when the battle for Macedonia was at its peak. In the Balkan Wars, these irregular groups were found in the rear areas of operation, where they undertook a reckoning with their opponents.

It should be noted that most of the information on the military campaigns of the various Balkan armies is available through the writings of European war correspondents and diplomatic missions, as well as the testimonies and memoirs of some of the Balkan actors, including politicians and members of the armed forces. It is still difficult to access the military archives of several Balkan states. As a result, there is considerable hesitation in drawing final conclusions about the conflict. Moreover, the wide use of propaganda during the Balkan Wars forces researchers to maintain a critical distance from what was reported via different sources. The only detailed source on the atrocities committed during the Balkan Wars remains the much-cited report of the Carnegie Endowment for International Peace,[10] but this document can hardly be considered unbiased.[11]

In this chapter, I offer insights into the demographic engineering in geographical Macedonia through re-examination of the available historical sources, such as documents from the archives of the German Ministry of Foreign Affairs, memories of some protagonists, diaries of some war correspondents and the extensive bibliography on the issue. It is worth underlining that the research on the topic is still in progress, with new archival material being realized, especially in Turkey. As a general remark, it could be argued that geographical Macedonia was one of the core battlefields of the Balkan Wars. Bounded by Greece, Serbia, Albania and Bulgaria, Ottoman Macedonia suffered greatly from the intensity of the armed conflicts. Non-combatants faced many dangers, and the Muslims in particular found themselves in the 'eye of the storm'. Numerous sources examine their fate. Although many Muslims were forced to emigrate to Asia Minor, many others remained in their motherland. In fact, the behaviour of the combatants during the Balkan Wars cannot be generalized or summarized in terms of ethnicity and religion.

The Balkan Wars were not the end of the efforts to purify the Balkan nations. In geographical Macedonia, the policy of homogenization lasted until the end of the 1920s. The campaign against minorities continued during the First World War; indeed, the forced exchange of populations between Greece and Turkey was ratified at Lausanne in 1923. The catastrophe of the Greek army in Asia Minor in 1922 led to the final abandonment of the respective minorities.

Christian minorities in the Balkan states – Greeks and Bulgarians, for example – also suffered massive violence not only during the Second Balkan War, but also during the First World War, as well as after the signing of the Treaty of Neuilly (1919), which provided for the reciprocal exchange of the 'racial, linguistic and religious' minority populations between Greece and Bulgaria.

Muslim Fatalities

During the First Balkan War, the major target was the Muslim population.[12] There is no doubt that murders, uprooting, starvation and migration were the fate of Muslim populations, especially in the northern provinces of Macedonia occupied by the Bulgarian and Serbian armies.

In southern Macedonia, in areas occupied by the Greek army, the situation seemed to be characterized by greater tolerance.[13] One of the best-known incidents of Greek violence is a massacre in Greek western Macedonia, where Greek soldiers destroyed the entire Muslim sector of the small town of Serfidje.[14] This slaughter is confirmed by many sources,[15] which agree that the incident was a reprisal for the massacre of seventy-two local Greek notables by the Ottomans.[16] The British-Greek lawyer D.J. Cassavetti, who wrote on the Balkan Wars in an effort to highlight the differences in the Greek and Bulgarian policies towards the Ottoman population, emphasizes the following:

> Unfortunately the Greek staff was not provided with cameras, and the evidence of the massacre has not been perpetuated. It may be because they were diffident as to the way in which things would go, or that, unlike the Bulgarians, they did not value self-advertisement highly enough; but no correspondents were allowed to be present to describe the battle, and the staff had no cameras or cinematographs for the purpose of putting on record their own performances or the Turkish lapses. If Bulgarians had been victims of the Serfidje massacre, the illustrated papers in all European countries would have been full of photographs of it.[17]

Cassavetti was not an isolated advocate of the Greek assertions. Crawfurd Price, the *Times* correspondent on the battlefields, described the massacre of the Greek notables as an 'unnecessary' event that destroyed any sympathy for the Turks.[18]

In contrast to what happened in the south, things turned out differently in the rest of Macedonia. Hundreds of years of Ottoman domination were ended by a bloody campaign. Hundreds of thousands of Muslims were killed or forced to emigrate as a result of the armed conflicts. National and private archives, memoirs and testimonies are full of evidence regarding a massive anti-Muslim campaign undertaken by the Christian Balkan states.[19] The anti-Muslim attitude and the desire for vengeance were widespread in the Balkan capitals, as was noted by numerous war correspondents in the area. Reporting from Sofia a few days before the outbreak of the war, Philip Gibbs, a London *Graphic* special correspondent with the Bulgarian army, wrote:

> The Bulgarians had not forgotten the old blood-feuds between Turks and Christians, nor the days of their own subjection to the Moslem rule; and though they found the individual Turk a harmless fellow in their own country, their hate was as active as ever against the Mohammedan Power in Europe. 'This will be a cruel war,' said a Bulgarian officer, as he sat at my table in one of the cafes at Sofia. 'There will be no non-combatants

and no quarter.' Are not all wars cruel? Even before a shot had been fired there was misery in the Balkans, for all the supplies of life had been requisitioned for the army; the horses, the bullocks and the carts had been taken from the farms; and in the villages of Bulgaria the women and children were staring at the desolation of their homes.[20]

Soon reports from the front line confirmed Philip Gibbs' predictions. In the *vilayet* of Monastir (Bitola), 80 per cent of the Muslim villages were destroyed by the Serbian army. In the town of Skopje, the irregular Serbian *četniks* (chetniks) burned the Albanian part of the city and killed many Albanian citizens. In the area of Kilkis, in three Muslim villages, the Bulgarian Vojvode Dontsev and his armed group burned non-combatants alive. Most of the mosques in the town of Kilkis were also destroyed. The Carnegie Commission argues that the measures taken by the Bulgarian government to protect Muslim populations were adequate but belated. Muslim villages outside Salonica were burned by Greek troops. The commission also refers to a systematic proscription of Muslims in southeastern Macedonia.[21]

In the discriminatory policy against the Muslims adopted by the Balkan states during the Balkan Wars, the political priorities of the Committee of Union and Progress (CUP) must be included. As Fuat Dündar has proved, the leaders of the CUP systematically pressed the Muslim population of the whole Balkan region to emigrate. Since, after the defeat in the First Balkan War, they lost the chance to create a nation-state in the Balkans, the leaders of the CUP found that the only reliable solution was to establish it in Asia Minor. In that framework, they worked for the creation of ethnic clear areas, transferring to Anatolia the Muslim populations from the Balkans and simultaneously deporting the Christians and the other minorities from the same places.[22]

The German consulate in Salonica observed in November 1912 that the majority of Muslims in the areas controlled by the Bulgarian army had been executed. The German consul believed that the Bulgarian government was fully aware of the event but made no attempt to stop the activities of Bulgarian irregular bands.[23] Similar information was received day after day by foreign diplomatic missions and war correspondents. Crawfurd Price, writing about the Bulgarian campaign in Macedonia, noted the 'hideous atrocities committed principally by the Bulgarian irregulars who accompanied the regular army into Macedonia', and remarked that 'it is difficult to imagine why the Bulgarian Government found it necessary to play into the hands of these blood-stained auxiliaries and hand over the administration of the conquered territories to their tender mercies'.[24] As confirmation of his allegations, Price recounts the regime established by the Bulgarian forces in the city of Kavala. One of the most eminent *komitadjis*, Christo Chernopeev, was appointed governor of the city. Chernopeev started his administration with promises to respect the lives and honour of all citizens, but very soon he ordered the imprisonment and then the execution of many Muslims.[25]

In February 1913, the Austro-Hungarian consulate in Belgrade observed that the Serbian army had executed the entire Albanian population of the villages of Ljbiste, Gjulekar, Cabashi and Topetza. In most cases, no mercy was shown, even to women and children.[26]

Leon Trotsky, at that time a military correspondent in the area for the Russian newspaper *Kievskaia Mysl'*, describes in detail the painful and catastrophic events:

> In all these areas a strong ... cyclone destroyed and turned to ashes anything created by human labour and killed the new generation ... the Turks burned as they left. The native Christians found the opportunity to burn and slaughter, as the allied armies were approaching. The soldiers killed all the wounded men ... the rebels who followed close behind looted all they found.[27]

Although it is difficult to determine the precise number of Muslim civilian victims during the First Balkan War, a figure of several thousand seems likely. It is also worth emphasizing that most of the great powers of the time showed no interest in stopping the massacres. Sir Gerald A. Lowther, the British ambassador in Constantinople, noted that the Foreign Office fully supported the Balkan allies. 'Although we know that in this case Bulgarians and Greeks have been offenders against Turks in the way of massacres, not a word is said in our press against them', he wrote.[28]

The Bulgarian aggression against the Muslims could possibly be explained as a result of the vivid memories of the Bulgarians regarding atrocities committed by Ottomans against their compatriots. The massacre in Batak (1876) and the Ottoman retaliation after the Ilinden uprising in 1903 may have led many of the Bulgarian irregular combatants to take revenge on their Ottoman neighbours:

> Every Bulgarian village in northern Macedonia had its memory of sufferings and wrongs. For a generation the insurgent organization had been busy, and the normal condition of these villages had been one of intermittent revolt. The inevitable Turkish reprisals had fallen now on one village and now on another. Searches for arms, beatings, tortures, wholesale arrests, and occasional massacres, were the price, which these peasants paid for their incessant struggle toward self-government. In all these incidents of repression, the local Moslems had played their part, marching behind the Turkish troops as bashi-bazouks and joining in the

work of pillage and slaughter. Their record was not forgotten when the Bulgarian victories brought the chance of revenge.[29]

Similarly, the Serbian campaign in northwest Macedonia against the Muslim population was possibly influenced by the Ottoman reaction against the Serbian inhabitants during the period of the Eastern Crisis (1875–78). In contrast, Greek memories of the Ottoman domination of geographical Macedonia were much more favourable, because the Ottoman administration generally facilitated the Greek campaign against the Bulgarians in the armed battle for Macedonia (1904–8). In addition, many of the Muslims in the area incorporated in the Greek side during the First Balkan War were Greek-speakers (*valaades*), and they had much in common with the Greek combatants.

Waves of Refugees

Crawfurd Price, the *Times* correspondent, describes the entrance of the Greek army into the city of Giannitsa in central Greek Macedonia. The Greek soldiers destroyed the Muslim district, and the Muslim population of the city was obliged to seek shelter in nearby Salonica. Yet along the way, death was everywhere:

> Then came a troop of barefooted Moslem peasants leading donkeys upon which were piled mattress and quilt and coffee-pot, all they had saved in the rush from Yenidje, when the Greek guns set fire to the rude huts they called home. Then a richer home. Two weedy oxen were dragging a creaky wooden wagon, which threatened to break asunder at every dip in the road. The worldly goods and chattels of these fugitives – beds, mats, the inevitable prayer rug, the shallow copper utensil which serves alike as cooking pan and salver even now as it did in Biblical times, a dozen unhappy ducks strung by their webbed feet to the frame – were piled high on the conveyance, and on top of this conglomeration of household effects sat wives and mothers, their sorrowful faces hidden from the sight of man, weeping and wailing as they ineffectually tried to comfort aged parents or to hold suckling babies to their breasts ... Farther along the highway were the corpses of two women who, driven from their sick-beds, had breathed their last during the cold of the bitter November night; and anon I passed at a canter, for I dared not stay to look, the small frail body of a little child, its lifeless eyes gazing wistfully up to the heavens.[30]

Salonica was the major port, and the majority of the Muslims fled there. The rapid advance of the allied Balkan forces and the power vacuum left by the collapse of the Ottoman regime were responsible for an essential lack of information about the refugees' movements. Some data can be found in reports written by the European consular network in the city. According to the German consulate, more than 50,000 Muslim refugees were gathered in Salonica in early November 1912,[31] and the number reached 140,000 a few weeks later.[32] Fifty persons died as a result of dreadful weather conditions, according to the same reports,[33] yet the newly arrived Greek authorities made no attempt to help them. Only a few days later, with the stabilization of the Greek administration in Macedonia, did humanitarian relief for the refugees begin to be offered.[34]

Simultaneously, the process of transferring the majority of the refugees to Asia Minor began. In May 1913, the German consul in Salonica noted that the Muslim population of the city had been reduced to fewer than 6,000 persons. About 2,000 Muslim refugees had been sent to Antalya (Attaleia) with the Greek steamboat *Themistoklis*;[35] another 3,500 had been moved to Smyrna (Izmir).[36] The Greek authorities in Salonica stated that 17,478 Muslims moved through the city to the Ottoman Empire in the period from August to December 1913.[37]

International missions that visited the Balkans during the Balkan Wars described the extermination policies on the battlefields and the frustration in the refugee camps. The Carnegie Commission recorded:

> At Salonica the Commission visited one of these camps, and made inquiries of the Islamic Committee, whose business it was to transport the refugees to Anatolia. They were Turkish emigrants. Some of them had left their villages several weeks ago; they came from all parts of Macedonia, from Soundja, Djoumaya-Bala, Nevrocope, Petritche, Razlogue, Tchakova, Demir-Hissar, Osmanie, Berovo, Radovitch. At the beginning of September, when the Commission made its inquiry, about 135,000 emigrants had passed through Salonica since the beginning of the second war. Each steamer starting for Anatolia carried some 2,500 bound for Mersina, Antakya or Iskenderoum.[38]

It has been alleged that approximately 400,000 Muslims left the Balkans as victims of the armed conflicts,[39] a number that seems exaggerated. Using statistical data provided by the Ottoman consulate in Salonica, the Greek administration estimated that the number of Muslim refugees from November 1912 to March 1914 was 243,807.[40]

The waves of desperate refugees who arrived in Ottoman cities created a painful spectacle that infuriated the Ottoman public. Refugees who lived under difficult circumstances in barracks and were helpless against disease populated Istanbul and other Ottoman cities.[41] The refugee drama was described in the correspondence of Western journalists who gathered in the Balkan peninsula during the war. Lieutenant Colonel Reginald Rankin, who followed the national armies during the Balkan Wars, was dismayed by the misery of the Muslim refugees arriving in Constantinople:

> The streets of Constantinople during the last day or two have presented worse sights than ever. Refugees are still crowding into the city. Of those remaining here 1,500 are lying ill in their filthy carts and tents with cholera and dysentery. The conditions are appalling, and a serious menace to the health of the city. It is impossible to estimate exactly the rate of mortality, but it must be frightfully high.[42]

The circumstances of refugees in the Ottoman cities were a disappointment both for the refugees themselves, who had hoped for a better future, and for the Ottoman authorities, who felt unprepared to handle the influx. The *Express* correspondent in the Ottoman capital paid a visit to the Sultan when the news about the flood of newcomers and their plight arrived. The dialogue between them reveals the confusion among Ottoman leaders:

> I pointed out to His Majesty that thousands of wounded soldiers from the army were mingled amongst the hordes of villagers. All are starving, I said, men, women, and children, for no food of any kind is available. It was impossible for me to describe adequately the misery and suffering of the refugees. I impressed on His Majesty the urgent need for some prompt organisation of relief measures, unless these hordes of famished and terror-stricken people were literally to starve to death at the gates of the capital. The Sultan was visibly much troubled as he heard my story.
>
> When at the close I told the Sultan that I intended describing the conditions I had seen to the readers of the *Express*, His Majesty grasped my hand and thanked me personally with great warmth. I learn this evening that efforts are to be made to ship as many as possible of the fugitives to Asia, but there is a great lack of organisation. Already the starving hordes that are surrounding the city have brought dysentery with them, and unless something is done immediately a famine on a scale never before experienced will result. With the army itself unfed, it is impossible to feed the fugitives, and myriads must starve to death.[43]

'Christian Monsters'

The atrocities of the First Balkan War continued during the Second Balkan War, only now the targets were not Muslims but Christians, for Greeks and Serbs fought against their former allies, the Bulgarians, for the formerly Ottoman lands of the Balkans. At first glance, it seems difficult to understand why the former allies turned against each other. Yet, after 1870, when the Bulgarian Exarchate was established and became detached from the spiritual supremacy of the Ecumenical Patriarchate, Greeks, Bulgarians and Serbs had spared no effort to prevail in Macedonian territories. Priests, notables and teachers had been the main victims of this ethnic and religious controversy. In fact, the First Balkan War was an exception to the longstanding suspicion existing among the Christian allies, a necessary step before the final reckoning.

Many reports vividly depict mutual hostilities, including the atrocities during the Battle of Kilkis. 'They burn the Greek villages, and we burn the Bulgarian ones', a Greek soldier wrote in his diary. 'This is a real war', added another, 'we are walking from day to night and we have burned all the villages'. Such testimonies are proof of an organized armed policy, very close to ethnic 'cleansing'.[44] The city of Kilkis was totally destroyed, wrote Albert Trapman: 'Between three and four hundred natives were killed'.[45] In Kilkis the bloody armed campaign was started by the Greek army, but both sides, Greeks and Bulgarians, were responsible for the terror that followed. Mutual suspicion did not arise from nowhere. As previously noted, the mutual hostilities between Greeks and Bulgarians were a result of the Bulgarian nationalization process and the struggle for domination in Macedonia. For that matter, four decades before the Balkan Wars, the image of Bulgarians in the Greek press had been negative. Bulgarians were not described as ordinary human beings, but rather as something close to criminals and monsters, as the Carnegie Commission Report indicates:

> Day after day the Bulgarians were represented as a race of monsters, and public feeling was roused to a pitch of chauvinism which made it inevitable that war, when it came, should be ruthless. In talk and in print one phrase summed up the general feeling of the Greeks toward the Bulgarians, '*Dhen einai anthropoid!*' [They are not human beings]. In their excitement and indignation the Greeks came to think of themselves as the appointed avengers of civilization against a race which stood outside the pale of humanity.[46]

In this context, the military campaigns of both the Greek and the Bulgarian armies during the Second Balkan War were aggressive. Kilkis, a town in central Greek Macedonia, an area that was mostly populated by Bulgarians, suffered greatly from the actions of the Greek soldiers.[47] About forty villages in the area, more than 4,725 houses, were burned by the Greek army, and approximately fourteen to fifteen thousand native Bulgarians were forced to emigrate from central Greek Macedonia. Another twenty thousand emigrated from eastern Greek Macedonia.[48]

For its part, the Bulgarian army destroyed many places in eastern Greek Macedonia, an area mostly populated by Greeks. Nigrita, Serres, Doxato and Melnik, four of the most famous Greek cities, were burned by Bulgarian soldiers, and more than five hundred Greeks in these towns were killed. Additionally, more than fifty thousand Greeks were forced to emigrate from Bulgarian territories under difficult circumstances. The Serbian population from the Bulgarian areas were similarly obliged to leave their homes for safer places.

Back to the Future?

It is evident that international law was violated on the battlefields of the Balkan Wars. These were mainly wars against the 'others', intended to achieve national ambitions and interests. Various categories of atrocities, including killing, looting and burning, were used as weapons. The atrocities left a distressing legacy in the Balkans. By the end of the first quarter of the twentieth century, the multiethnic character of Macedonia was replaced by nation-states that were close to 'pure' in ethnic and religious terms. Similarly, the waves of Muslim refugees created what Kemal Karpat has described as the 'islamization and turkification of Anatolia',[49] and also heightened a sense of isolation and xenophobia in the Ottoman Empire.[50] Greek, Bulgarian and Serbian refugees added their tragic experiences to the general history of Balkan refugee movements of the nineteenth and twentieth centuries.[51] Finally, the former refugees hindered and complicated the improvement of diplomatic relations among the Balkan states.[52] Attempts to establish liberal states in the Balkans failed. It is hardly surprising that the wars that dissolved Yugoslavia almost eight decades after the Balkan Wars gave rise to many recollections of ethnic 'cleansing' by various local national and religious groups.[53] The cultivation of hostility towards neighbours in the former Yugoslavia was perceived by many observers as the third Balkan War,[54] which is indicative of the prejudices still existing in the Balkans.

Iakovos D. Michailidis is Associate Professor of Modern and Contemporary History in the Department of History and Archaeology, Aristotle University of Thessaloniki, and head of the university's research centre 'Society for Macedonian History'. His research focuses on population movements, the status of minorities, and interventions from outside powers in Southeastern Europe. He represented Aristotle

University in the three-part European network 'A New History Agenda for a Growing Europe' (www.clioh.net and www.cliohres. net), organized by forty-five European universities. He co-edited (with Steven Ellis) *Regional and Transnational History in Europe: A Cliohworld Reader* (PLUS-Pisa University Press, 2011).

Notes

1. On the Balkan Wars, see the comprehensive analysis of Richard C. Hall, *The Balkan Wars 1912–1913: Prelude to the First World War* (London/New York: Routledge, 2000); see also William Miller, *The Ottoman Empire and Its Successors, 1801–1927* (Cambridge/London: Cambridge University Press, 1936), 498–522; Katrin Boeckh, *Von den Balkankriegen zum Ersten Weltkrieg: Kleinstaatenpolitik und ethnische Selbstbestimmung auf dem Balkan* (Munich: Oldenbourg, 1996); Feroz Ahmad, *The Making of Modern Turkey* (London/New York: Routledge, 1993), 37–38. On the military operations from the Turkish perspective in particular, see Edward J. Erickson, *Defeat in Detail: The Ottoman Army in the Balkans, 1912–1913* (Westport, CT: Praeger, 2003).
2. On the nationalistic ideas that spread through the Balkans, see Paschalis Kitromilides, *Enlightenment, Nationalism, Orthodoxy: Studies in the Culture and Political Thought of Southeastern Europe* (London: Variorum, 1994); see also Maria Todorova (ed.), *Balkan Identities: Nation and Memory* (London: Hurst & Co, 2004).
3. John S. Koliopoulos and Thanos Veremis, *Modern Greece: A History since 1821* (Oxford: Wiley-Blackwell, 2010), 1–8.
4. It is almost impossible to find accurate statistical data. According to Daniel Panzac, the balance between Muslims and Christians in Macedonia was 42 per cent to 55.7 per cent; see Daniel Panzac, *Population et Santé dans l'Empire Ottoman (XVIIIe –XXe siècles)* (Istanbul: Isis, 1996), 185.
5. On the boundaries of geographical Macedonia during the Ottoman period and the identities of its inhabitants, see Ioannis D. Stefanidis, Vlasis Vlasidis and Evangelos Kofos (eds), *Macedonian Identities through Time* (Thessaloniki: Epikentro, 2010).
6. On the political and diplomatic background of the Treaty of San Stefano, see Evangelos Kofos, *Greece and the Eastern Crisis, 1875–1878* (Thessaloniki: Institute for Balkan Studies, 1975).
7. On the Treaty of Berlin and its consequences, see the classical study by W.N. Medlicott, *The Congress of Berlin and After: A Diplomatic History of the Near East Settlement, 1878–1880* (London: Archon Books, 1938); see also Peter Sluglett and Hakan Yavuz (eds), *War and Diplomacy: The Russo-Turkish War of 1877–1878 and the Treaty of Berlin* (Salt Lake City: University of Utah Press, 2011).
8. These conflicting interests are illustrated with the case of Salonica in the chapter in this volume by Goseva and Trajkova.
9. Alexandre Toumarkine, *Les Migrations des Populations Musulmanes Balkaniques en Anatolie (1876–1913)* (Istanbul: Isis, 1995), 43.

10 Carnegie Endowment for International Peace, *Report of the International Commission to Inquire into the Causes and Conduct of the Balkan Wars* (Washington, DC: The Endowment, 1914).
11 The Serbs and Greeks in particular accused some members of the Carnegie Commission of being biased in favour of the Bulgarians. For a critical analysis of the mission of the Carnegie Commission in Macedonia, see Iakovos D. Michailidis, 'The Carnegie Commission in Macedonia, Summer 1913', http://www.macedonian-heritage.gr/Contributions/contr_Carnegie_1.html (accessed 5 February 2013).
12 Noel Buxton, *With the Bulgarian Staff* (New York: The Macmillan Company, 1913), 90.
13 The differential treatment of Muslim populations by Greeks, Bulgarians and Serbs has been confirmed by Justin McCarthy in his study *Death and Exile: The Ethnic Cleansing of Ottoman Muslims 1821–1922* (Princeton, NJ: The Darwin Press, Inc., 1995), 139, 141–52.
14 Filippou Stef. Dragoumi, *Imerologio: Valkanikoi Polemoi 1912–1913* [Diary of the Balkan Wars 1912–1913], ed. Ioannis K. Mazarakis-Ainian (Athens/Ioannina: Dodoni, 1988), 103; see also Spirou Mela, *Oi polemoi 1912–1913: Makedonia-Ipeiros-Aigaion. O polemos tis diplomatias* [The Wars 1912–1913: Macedonia-Epirus-Aegean. The War of Diplomacy] (Athens: Adelfoi Vlassi, 1972), 111–12.
15 It has also been reported in many Western newspapers. See, for example, *Poverty Bay Herald*, no. 12942, 28 December 1912; *Colonist*, no. 13564, 4 November 1912.
16 Petros Papapolyviou (ed.), *Ipodouloi Elefterotai adelfon alitroton: Epistoles, polemika imerologia kai antapokriseis Kiprion ethelonton apo tin Ipeiro kai ti Makedonia toy 1912–1913* [Enslaved Liberators, Unredeemed Brothers: Letters, War Diaries, and Correspondence of Cypriot Volunteers from Epirus and Macedonia in 1912–1913] (Nicosia: Kentro Epistimonikon Erevnon, 1999), 218, 349; see also Theodorou Pagkalou, *Apomnimoneumata 1897–1918* [Memoirs 1897–1918], Vol. I (Athens: Kedros, 1959), 174.
17 Demetrius John Cassavetti, *Hellas and the Balkan Wars* (London: T.F. Unwin, 1914), 84.
18 Walter Harrington Crawfurd Price, *The Balkan Cockpit* (London: T.W. Laurie Ltd., 1914), 66.
19 The destructive activities of irregular Bulgarian and Serbian troops have been recounted in Greek memoirs and testimonies. See, for example, Dragoumi, *Imerologio: Valkanikoi Polemoi*, 164, 169.
20 Philip Gibbs and Bernard Grant, *The Balkan War: Adventures of War with Cross and Crescent* (Boston, MA: Small, Maynard and Co., 1913), 35.
21 Carnegie Endowment for International Peace, *Report of the International Commission*, 72–78.
22 In his Ph.D. dissertation, Dündar makes extensive use of cypher telegrams of the CUP government. See Fuat Dündar, *Modern Türkiye'nin Şifresi: İttihat ve Terakki'nin Etnisite Mühendisliği (1913–1918)* [The Code of Modern Turkey: The Committee of Union and Progress's Ethnic Engineering (1913–1918)] (Istanbul: İletişim Yayınları, 2008). See also Elçin Macar, 'The Muslim Emigration in Western Anatolia', *Cahiers balkaniques* 40 (2012), 1–7.

23 Politisches Archiv des Auswärtigen Amtes, Berlin (PA AA), R 14274, Balkankrieg 1912–13: Walter to Bethmann-Hollweg, Salonica, 15 November 1912, no. 21027.
24 Price, *The Balkan Cockpit*, 175–76.
25 Ibid., 177.
26 PA AA, R 14274, Balkankrieg 1912–13: Griesinger to Bethmann-Hollweg, Belgrade, 22 February 1913, no. 3993.
27 Leon Trotsky, *Ta Valkania kai oi Valkanikoi Polemoi 1912–1913* [Balkans and the Balkan Wars 1912–1913], Greek translation (Athens: Themelio, 1993), 376.
28 Joseph Heller, *British Policy towards the Ottoman Empire* (London: Frank Cass, 1983), 76.
29 Carnegie Endowment for International Peace, *Report of the International Commission*, 71.
30 Price, *The Balkan Cockpit*, 97–99.
31 A different number, of approximately 10,000 Muslim refugees, is given by the Greek authorities. See Stathis Pelagidis, *Prosfigiki Ellada (1913–1930): O ponos kai i doksa* [Refugee Greece (1913–1930): The Pain and the Triumph] (Thessaloniki: Kyriakidis, 1997), 124.
32 Giannis Gklavinas, *Oi mousoulmanikoi plithismoi stin Ellada (1912–1923): Antilipseis kai praktikes tis ellinikis dioikisis. Sxeseis me Xristianous, gigeneis kai prosfiges* [The Muslim Population in Greece (1912–1923): Aspects and Practices of the Greek Administration. Relations with Christians, Natives and Refugees], Ph.D. dissertation (Thessaloniki: University of Thessaloniki, 2008), 54.
33 PA AA, R 14223, Balkankrieg 1912–13; Schwörbel to Bethmann-Hollweg, Salonica, 6 November 1912, no. 3375; see also PA AA, R 14274, Balkankrieg 1912–13: Walter to Bethmann-Hollweg, Salonica, 15 November 1912, no. 21027.
34 Cassavetti, *Hellas and the Balkan Wars*, 111.
35 PA AA, R 14311, Balkankrieg 1912–13: Report of unknown sender to Bethmann-Hollweg, Salonica, 10 May 1913, no. 84.
36 Ahmet Halaçoğlu, *Balkan Harbi Sirasinda: Rumeli'den Türk Göçleri (1912–1913)* [Turkish Migrations from the Balkans during the Balkan Wars (1912–1913)] (Ankara: Turkish Historical Society, 1995), 55.
37 Pelagidis, *Prosfigiki Ellada*, 129.
38 Carnegie Endowment for International Peace, *Report of the International Commission*, 151.
39 McCarthy, *Death and Exile*, 161. Using statistical data from the Ottoman Refugee Commission, McCarthy gives a total number of 413,922 Muslim refugees, most of them established in the *vilayets* of Aydin and Edirne. The same number, of 400,000 Muslim refugees from the Balkans during the Balkan Wars, has been reprinted in many essays, e.g. Berna Pekesen, 'Expulsion and Emigration of the Muslims from the Balkans', http://www.ieg-ego.eu/en/threads/europe-on-the-road/forced-ethnic-migration/berna-pekesen-expulsion-and-emigration-of-the-muslims-from-the-balkans (accessed 18 February 2014). See also Erik Jan Zürcher, 'Greek and Turkish Refugees and Deportees 1912–1924', Turkology Update Leiden Project

Working Papers Archive, Department of Turkish Studies, University of Leiden, http://www.transanatolie.com/english/turkey/turks/ottomans/ejz18.pdf (accessed 19 February 2014).
40   Gklavinas, *Oi mousoulmanikoi plithismoi*, 51.
41   Erik Jan Zürcher, *Sigxroni istoria tis Tourkias* [Contemporary Turkish History], trans. Vangelis Kechriotis (Athens: Aleksandreia, 2004), 164–65. See also Mustafa Aksakar, *The Ottoman Road to War in 1914: The Ottoman Empire and the First World War* (Cambridge/New York: Cambridge University Press, 2008), 23.
42   Reginald Rankin, *The Inner History of the Balkan War* (London: London Constable, 1914), 312.
43   Ibid., 292–93.
44   Iakovos D. Michailidis, *Metakiniseis slavofonon plithismon (1912–1913): O polemos ton statistikon* [Movements of Slavophone Populations (1912–1930): The War of Statistics] (Athens: Kritiki, 2004), 81.
45   Albert Henry Trapman, *O polemos Ellados kai Voulgarias* [The War between Greece and Bulgaria], Greek translation (Athens, 1914), 37.
46   Carnegie Endowment for International Peace, *Report of the International Commission*, 97.
47   Ioannis Tsagkaridis, a Greek Cypriot who fought as a volunteer in the Balkan Wars, wrote in his memoirs: 'We destroyed everything belonging to Bulgarians, they are doing the same'. Papaolyviou, *Ipodouloi elefterotes*, 361.
48   Michailidis, *Metakiniseis slavofonon plithismon (1912–1913)*, 81, 85, 88.
49   Kemal H. Karpat, *Ottoman Population 1830–1914: Demographic and Social Characteristics* (Madison, WI: The University of Wisconsin Press, 1985), 58. See also Ebru Boyar, *Ottomans, Turks and the Balkans: Empire Lost, Relations Altered* (London/New York: I.B. Tauris, 2007), 109.
50   Feroz Ahmad, *From Empire to Republic: Essays on the Late Ottoman Empire and Modern Turkey*, Vol. II (Istanbul: Bilgi University, 2009), 265.
51   On the ethnic cleansing policies during the First World War, see Dominik J. Scaller and Jürgen Zimmerer (eds), *Late Ottoman Genocides: The Dissolution of the Ottoman Empire and Young Turkish Population and Extermination Policies* (London/New York: Routledge, 2009).
52   Vasilis Gounaris and Iakovos Michailidis (eds), *Prosfiges sta Valkania: Mnimi kai Ensomatosi* [Refugees in the Balkans: Memory and Integration] (Athens: Patakis, 2004).
53   It is interesting to notice, for example, that Misha Glenny, the BBC's correspondent in Yugoslavia at the time of the dissolution, entitled his book on the Yugoslav Wars *The Fall of Yugoslavia: The Third Balkan War* (New York: Penguin Books, 1992). Moreover, Paul Mojzes in his book *Balkan Holocaust and Ethnic Cleansing in the Twentieth Century* (Lanham, MD: Rowman & Littlefield Publishers, Inc, 2011) argues on p. 1 that 'if there were "bragging rights" for being a genocidal and ethnic cleansing area, the Balkans could claim championship status'.
54   Linking the war in Yugoslavia directly with the Balkan Wars of 1912–13, the Carnegie Endowment for International Peace reissued its original report of 1913 with a new introduction by George Kennan, the former US ambassador to the Soviet Union, known as the author of the 'Long

Telegraph' of 1946, under the title *The Other Balkan Wars: A 1913 Carnegie Endowment Inquiry in Retrospect* (Washington, DC: Brookings Institution Publications, 1993). In his preface, Kennan found a lot of similarities between the Balkan Wars of 1912–13 and the war in Yugoslavia. See Predrag Simic, 'Balkans and Balkanisation: Western Perceptions of the Balkans in the Carnegie Commission's Reports on the Balkan Wars from 1914 to 1996', *Perceptions* 18(2) (2013), 113–134, http://sam.gov.tr/wp-content/uploads/2013/09/Predrag_Simic.pdf (accessed 13 September 2017), 123. See also Lene Hansen, 'Past as Preface: Civilizational Politics and the "Third" Balkan War', *Journal of Peace Research* 37(3) (2000), 345–62.

Bibliography

Ahmad, Feroz. *The Making of Modern Turkey*. London/New York: Routledge, 1993.

——. *From Empire to Republic: Essays on the Late Ottoman Empire and Modern Turkey*. Vol. II. Istanbul: Bilgi University, 2009.

Aksakar, Mustafa. *The Ottoman Road to War in 1914: The Ottoman Empire and the First World War*. Cambridge/New York: Cambridge University Press, 2008.

Boeckh, Katrin. *Von den Balkankriegen zum Ersten Weltkrieg: Kleinstaatenpolitik und ethnische Selbstbestimmung auf dem Balkan*. Munich: Oldenbourg, 1996.

Boyar, Ebru. *Ottomans, Turks and the Balkans: Empire Lost, Relations Altered*. London/New York: I.B. Tauris, 2007.

Buxton, Noel. *With the Bulgarian Staff*. New York: The Macmillan Company, 1913.

Carnegie Endowment for International Peace. *Report of the International Commission to Inquire into the Causes and Conduct of the Balkan Wars*. Washington, DC: The Endowment, 1914.

Cassavetti, Demetrius John. *Hellas and the Balkan Wars*. London: T.F. Unwin, 1914.

Dragoumi, Filippou Stef. *Imerologio: Valkanikoi Polemoi 1912–1913* [Diary of the Balkan Wars 1912–1913]. Ed. Ioannis K. Mazarakis-Ainian. Athens/Ioannina: Dodoni, 1988.

Dündar, Fuat. *Modern Türkiye'nin Şifresi: İttihat ve Terakki'nin Etnisite Mühendisliği (1913–1918)* [The Code of Modern Turkey: The Committee of Union and Progress's Ethnic Engineering (1913–1918)]. Istanbul: İletişim Yayınları, 2008.

Erickson, Edward J. *Defeat in Detail: The Ottoman Army in the Balkans, 1912–1913*. Westport, CT: Praeger, 2003.

Gibbs, Philip, and Bernard Grant. *The Balkan War: Adventures of War with Cross and Crescent*. Boston, MA: Small, Maynard and Co., 1913.

Gklavinas, Giannis. *Oi mousoulmanikoi plithismoi stin Ellada (1912–1923): Antilipseis kai praktikes tis ellinikis dioikisis. Sxeseis me Xristianous, gigeneis kai prosfiges* [The Muslim Population in Greece (1912–1923): Aspects and Practices of the Greek Administration. Relations with Christians, Natives and Refugees]. Ph.D. dissertation. Thessaloniki: University of Thessaloniki, 2008.

Glenny, Misha. *The Fall of Yugoslavia: The Third Balkan War*. New York: Penguin Books, 1992.

Gounaris, Vasilis, and Iakovos Michailidis (eds). *Prosfiges sta Valkania: Mnimi kai Ensomatosi* [Refugees in the Balkans: Memory and Integration]. Athens: Patakis, 2004.

Halaçoğlu, Ahmet. *Balkan Harbi Sirasinda: Rumeli'den Türk Göçleri (1912–1913)* [Turkish Migrations from the Balkans during the Balkan Wars (1912–1913)]. Ankara: Turkish Historical Society, 1995.

Hall, Richard C. *The Balkan Wars 1912–1913: Prelude to the First World War*. London/New York: Routledge, 2000.

Hansen, Lene. 'Past as Preface: Civilizational Politics and the "Third" Balkan War'. *Journal of Peace Research* 37(3) (2000), 345–62.

Heller, Joseph. *British Policy towards the Ottoman Empire*. London: Frank Cass, 1983.

Karpat, Kemal H. *Ottoman Population 1830–1914: Demographic and Social Characteristics*. Madison, WI: The University of Wisconsin Press, 1985.

Kitromilides, Paschalis. *Enlightenment, Nationalism, Orthodoxy: Studies in the Culture and Political Thought of Southeastern Europe*. London: Variorum, 1994.

Kofos, Evangelos. *Greece and the Eastern Crisis, 1875–1878*. Thessaloniki: Institute for Balkan Studies, 1975.

Koliopoulos, John S., and Thanos Veremis. *Modern Greece: A History since 1821*. Oxford: Wiley-Blackwell, 2010.

Macar, Elçin. 'The Muslim Emigration in Western Anatolia'. *Cahiers balkaniques* 40 (2012), 1–7.

McCarthy, Justin. *Death and Exile: The Ethnic Cleansing of Ottoman Muslims 1821–1922*. Princeton, NJ: The Darwin Press, Inc., 1995.

Medlicott, W.N. *The Congress of Berlin and After: A Diplomatic History of the Near East Settlement, 1878–1880*. London: Archon Books, 1938.

Mela, Spirou. *Oi polemoi 1912–1913: Makedonia-Ipeiros-Aigaion. O polemos tis diplomatias* [The Wars 1912–1913: Macedonia-Epirus-Aegean. The War of Diplomacy]. Athens: Adelfoi Vlassi, 1972.

Michailidis, Iakovos D. *Metakiniseis slavofonon plithismon (1912–1913): O polemos ton statistikon* [Movements of Slavophone Populations (1912–1930): The War of Statistics]. Athens: Kritiki, 2004.

———. 'The Carnegie Commission in Macedonia, Summer 1913'. http://www.macedonian-heritage.gr/Contributions/contr_Carnegie_1.html (accessed 5 February 2013).

Miller, William. *The Ottoman Empire and Its Successors, 1801–1927*. Cambridge/London: Cambridge University Press, 1936.

Mojzes, Paul. *Balkan Holocaust and Ethnic Cleansing in the Twentieth Century*. Lanham, MD: Rowman & Littlefield Publishers, Inc, 2011.

Pagkalou, Theodorou. *Apomnimoneumata 1897–1918* [Memoirs 1897–1918]. Vol. I. Athens: Kedros, 1959.

Panzac, Daniel. *Population et Santé dans l'Empire Ottoman (XVIIIe –XXe siècles)*. Istanbul: Isis, 1996.

Papapolyviou, Petros (ed.). *Ipodouloi Elefterotai adelfon alitroton: Epistoles, polemika imerologia kai antapokriseis Kiprion ethelonton apo tin Ipeiro kai ti Makedonia toy 1912–1913* [Enslaved Liberators, Unredeemed Brothers: Letters, War Diaries, and Correspondence of Cypriot Volunteers from Epirus and Macedonia in 1912–1913]. Nicosia: Kentro Epistimonikon Erevnon, 1999.

Pekesen, Berna. 'Expulsion and Emigration of the Muslims from the Balkans'. http://www.ieg-ego.eu/en/threads/europe-on-the-road/forced-ethnic-migration/berna-pekesen-expulsion-and-emigration-of-the-muslims-from-the-balkans (accessed 18 February 2014).

Pelagidis, Stathis. *Prosfigiki Ellada (1913–1930): O ponos kai i doksa* [Refugee Greece (1913–1930): The Pain and the Triumph]. Thessaloniki: Kyriakidis, 1997.

Price, Walter Harrington Crawfurd. *The Balkan Cockpit*. London: T.W. Laurie Ltd., 1914.

Rankin, Reginald. *The Inner History of the Balkan War*. London: London Constable, 1914.

Scaller, Dominik J., and Jürgen Zimmerer (eds). *Late Ottoman Genocides: The Dissolution of the Ottoman Empire and Young Turkish Population and Extermination Policies*. London/New York: Routledge, 2009.

Simic, Predrag. 'Balkans and Balkanisation: Western Perceptions of the Balkans in the Carnegie Commission's Reports on the Balkan Wars from 1914 to 1996'. http://sam.gov.tr/balkans-and-balkanisation-western-perceptions-of-the-balkans-in-the-carnegie-commissions-reports-on-the-balkan-wars-from-1914-to-1996/ (accessed 19 February 2014).

Sluglett, Peter, and Hakan Yavuz (eds). *War and Diplomacy: The Russo-Turkish War of 1877–1878 and the Treaty of Berlin*. Salt Lake City: University of Utah Press, 2011.

Stefanidis, Ioannis D., Vlasis Vlasidis and Evangelos Kofos (eds). *Macedonian Identities through Time*. Thessaloniki: Epikentro, 2010.

The Other Balkan Wars: A 1913 Carnegie Endowment Inquiry in Retrospect. Washington, DC: Brookings Institution Publications, 1993.

Todorova, Maria (ed.). *Balkan Identities: Nation and Memory*. London: Hurst & Co, 2004.

Toumarkine, Alexandre. *Les Migrations des Populations Musulmanes Balkaniques en Anatolie (1876–1913)*. Istanbul: Isis, 1995.

Trapman, Albert Henry. *O polemos Ellados kai Voulgarias* [The War between Greece and Bulgaria]. Greek translation. Athens, 1914.

Trotsky, Leon. *Ta Valkania kai oi Valkanikoi Polemoi 1912–1913* [Balkans and the Balkan Wars 1912–1913]. Greek translation. Athens: Themelio, 1993.

Zürcher, Erik Jan. *Sigxroni istoria tis Tourkias* [Contemporary Turkish History]. Trans. Vangelis Kechriotis. Athens: Aleksandreia, 2004.

———. 'Greek and Turkish Refugees and Deportees 1912–1924'. Turkology Update Leiden Project Working Papers Archive, Department of Turkish Studies, University of Leiden, 2003. http://www.transanatolie.com/english/turkey/turks/ottomans/ejz18.pdf (accessed 19 February 2014).

 13

Jewish Philanthropy and Mutual Assistance
Between Ottomanism and Communal Identities

Eyal Ginio

With the modernization of warfare in the nineteenth century, the ensuing increase in the targeting of civilian populations and the widespread acceptance of the concept of general mobilization, philanthropy on behalf of war victims became a major activity for civilians.[1] For non-combatant members of society – women, children, 'left-at-home' men[2] – giving aid to those who were deemed deserving victims of war became a significant way to demonstrate their loyalty and their attachment and contribution to the national cause, and thus to proclaim and affirm their status as active participants in the national community. While some donors contributed to private initiatives, many others took part in collective enterprises that shaped the home front and created an infrastructure of civilian preparedness outside the state military apparatus. The various activities of civilian benefactors and volunteers reflected a new understanding of the bond between the state and its citizens. Their philanthropy also created a new way for the well-off elites to show their commitment to the less fortunate members of the community while keeping social boundaries and hierarchies intact.[3]

The historical investigation of beneficence, Amy Singer states, is an integral part of the interpretation of any society or culture of the past.[4] Indeed, ideas and practices of philanthropy and communal identities relate to one another in various ways. Beneficence during wartime takes many forms and is shaped and affected by various agents – such as individuals, communities, institutions and the state itself – all of which operate as benefactors of those who are deemed to deserve assistance. The key concept of *deserving* is also understood and articulated in different ways. Therefore, philanthropy can never be removed from its political, cultural, social and economic contexts.

In this chapter, I examine the many forms of Jewish philanthropy during the Balkan Wars (1912–13) and their relation to different identities assumed by Ottoman Jews and foreign Jews during the conflicts in the Balkans. I argue that Jewish philanthropy during the Balkan Wars was generally offered by three groups of donors reflecting different agendas. The first group consisted of Ottoman Jews who engaged in philanthropy to assist the Jewish victims of the war and the general Ottoman cause. The second, *Sephardi*, group was made up of Jews who traced their origins to the Iberian peninsula. The network included both older Sephardi communities in the Ottoman Empire and in the former Ottoman provinces of the Balkan peninsula, and newer Sephardi communities in the Western diaspora. The old communities had been established under Ottoman rule in the sixteenth century by Jews emigrating from Spain and Portugal; the newer ones were established in the New World and in the European colonies in Africa and the Far East in the late nineteenth century, by Sephardi Jews emigrating from the Ottoman Empire. The third group sprang from the global Jewish diaspora and consisted of Western Jews who offered philanthropy to Jewish victims of the Balkan Wars, for purposes of both Jewish solidarity and civilizing mission. Needless to say, this division into three different categories is somewhat artificial, as the boundaries among the three groups of Jewish benefactors were not always clear-cut. However, the proposed distinctions can help us to understand Jewish philanthropy at the beginning of the twentieth century in a time of war.

The Local Dimension: The Philanthropy of Ottoman Jews

Distributing charity is a significant way to delineate one's community. In her study on welfare policy in premodern European societies, Katherine Lynch demonstrates the close connection between charity for the poor and construction of community. By deciding who among the poor were deserving of charity and by excluding others, the members of the community marked its boundaries: 'People created and maintained bonds of community in large part by entitling those who were or became members to those benefits. Providing relief to the poor thus proved essential to the formation of communities themselves'.[5] Furthermore, the language of patriotic service could override previous distinctions of religion, ethnicity or class. Examining the experiences of Jews in Germany in the First World War, Christhard

Hoffmann argues that 'history shows that wartime treats minorities and marginalized social groups in a paradoxical way'. War, he asserts, often offers new opportunities for integration where few had previously existed. However, war, and especially defeat, may also cause questioning of minorities' loyalty and result in their greater alienation and marginalization.[6] These two observations are germane to my discussion, for a study of the philanthropy of Jews during the Balkan Wars can shed light on the position of the Jewish communities of the Ottoman Empire as a religious minority in a multi-religious empire in wartime.[7]

There were two different arenas in which Jewish donors – both Ottoman and foreign – were active during the Balkan Wars. The first was the local, Jewish one, where assistance was offered to Jewish victims of the war, among them Jewish refugees who came from Eastern Thrace to Istanbul or from Macedonia to Salonica; Jewish prisoners of war, both Ottoman and Jewish soldiers serving in the armies of the Balkan states; and families of recruited soldiers. Indeed, Istanbul and Salonica became the main destinations for desperate Jewish refugees, thanks to their existing infrastructure of Jewish relief organizations and institutions and the size of their Jewish communities.

The other arena was state-defined; it consisted of military and civilian entities selected by the Ottoman state and its agencies for philanthropic activities. Among such entities were Ottoman semi-voluntary associations, like the Ottoman Red Crescent Society (Osmanlı Hilâl-i Ahmer Cemiyeti), and the local branches of the Committees for National Defence (Müdafaa-i Milliye Cemiyeti). This arena also included Jewish relief institutions, such as Jewish hospitals, which opened their doors to non-Jews as well. It should be noted that these two different arenas of philanthropy, the local Jewish one and the general, state-defined Ottoman one, were perceived by Jewish donors as complementary rather than contradictory. In both cases, providing assistance was depicted as serving the national cause.

To understand the shaping of local Jewish philanthropy during the Balkan Wars, it is necessary to examine the effects of the *tanzimat* reforms in the Ottoman Empire. The reforms clearly transformed the non-Muslim communities of the Ottoman Empire, including the Jewish communities. Although these reforms were long perceived as a top-down state project, recent studies indicate that local non-Muslims and other groups were not merely passive recipients but responded to them with efforts to secure their own interests and to adapt to the new order. This new understanding of the *tanzimat* dynamics suggests that one may view the reforms as 'a series of interactions between the central government and local societies'.⁸ Philanthropy was one of the arenas in which Ottoman Jews could pursue their own agenda of modernization and promote communal identity. As early as the Greco-Ottoman War of 1897, Jewish donors had contributed to the Ottoman war effort, thus marking their support for the project of Ottoman imperial citizenship.⁹

Modern relief institutions and discourses appeared in the Ottoman Empire during the second half of the nineteenth century. The new institutions often served new elites eager to build up their own legitimacy. Yet, as shown by Nadir Özbek,[10] Nora Şeni and Sophie Le Tarnec,[11] Meropi Anastassiadou[12] and others, many of these institutions followed traditional patterns of charity by concentrating their efforts in keeping with old communal boundaries. Indeed, Esther Benbassa and Aron Rodrigue observe that even after the 1908 revolution, 'the only truly legitimate political area for Ottoman Jews remained their community'.[13]

Therefore, it may not be surprising that the first appeals for assistance for Jewish war victims appeared in the thriving Judeo-Spanish press, clearly a medium accessible exclusively to Jewish audiences.[14] An example, *El Nuevo Avenir* [The New Future],[15] a Ladino daily published in Salonica, reported in its issue of 27 November 1912 on a missing child aged four or five, a son of Jewish refugees from İştip (now Štip, in the Republic of Macedonia). The daily explained that about twenty-five Jewish families, the majority of the small Jewish community living in İştip before the outbreak of the Balkan Wars, had arrived in Salonica at the end of October. It asked persons with information on the missing child's whereabouts to contact the central Jewish school, 'Talmud Torah', where many Jewish refugees from the interior had found shelter.[16]

This story exemplifies the role of the Jewish press in coordinating the relief efforts. More generally, it also testifies to the turmoil that the Balkan Wars brought upon refugee families. The strategies adopted by the family to cope with its misfortune are significant: the family members opted to ask for shelter from the Jewish community of Salonica. In their desperate search for the missing child, they approached a Ladino journal, probably the most efficient way at the time to reach a large Jewish audience. They clearly searched for assistance amidst the Jewish community.

Generally speaking, the assistance that the Jewish communities of Istanbul and Salonica, the two major centres of Ottoman Jewry in the Balkans, were able to extend to the refugees was limited to providing temporary shelter and some basic provisions. Helping Jewish victims was presented as a patriotic duty. After the outbreak of the war, *El Tyémpo*, a leading Jewish journal in Istanbul,[17] reported on a local initiative by various Jewish clubs in Salonica to assist Jewish families whose breadwinners, whether husbands or sons, had been mobilized for service at the front. Promoting this effort with patriotic messages and slogans ('[by joining the army's ranks] they fulfil the most sacred obligation of every citizen'), they clearly saw the Jewish victims of the war as the objects of their charity.[18]

Chief Rabbi of the Ottoman Empire Haim Nahum (1872–1960), an eminent Jewish public figure of the time, did his best to integrate Jewish philanthropy into the general mobilization for the war effort. On his well-publicized visits to hospitals, he invited reporters from the general press to write about his donations to injured soldiers, including non-Jews, who were being treated in Jewish hospitals.[19] Indeed, opening Jewish hospitals to wounded soldiers was one of the contributions made by the Jewish communities in Istanbul and Salonica. Towards the end of October 1912, the governor-general of Salonica announced that because the city would serve the needs of three different fronts, seven thousand beds would be put at the disposal of the Ottoman army, among them five hundred in the Hirsch Hospital, a Jewish institution opened in 1908. The remaining beds were allocated as follows: 1,000 beds in the Military Hospital, 500 beds in the Municipal Hospital and 500 beds in the Greek Hospital. The other 4,500 beds would be placed in various schools.[20] While this assignment of beds was the result of governmental orders, it was depicted in the Jewish press as symbolic of the Jews' contribution to the war effort.

The contributions of non-Muslims, including Jews, to the Ottoman Red Crescent are an example of participation in joint philanthropic activity during the war and an illustration of the Jews' understanding of their civic obligations towards the general community of Ottomans. Names of Jewish donors, whether acting as individuals or representing Jewish communities such as neighbourhoods, schools or associations, were often listed in the Jewish press as contributors to Ottoman relief organizations. Such lists in the Turkish-language press and official publications, as well as reports in the Turkish-language press of the presence of Ottoman officials in meetings and ceremonies organized by Jewish organizations on behalf of the Ottoman army, indicate that the discourse of general Ottoman mobilization for the war effort was welcomed and promoted by the Ottoman authorities.[21]

However, while it is true that prominent Jews took part in Ottoman relief organizations that sought to ease the suffering of war victims, their charity was dispensed very much according to sectarian needs. The Jews were not unique in their decision to channel most of their charity work into their own community; the Muslim and Christian communities did the same. This phenomenon may suggest that philanthropy in the late Ottoman period, even if portrayed as a display of Ottoman patriotism, was still very much provided by and based upon the traditional religious infrastructure; it may also testify to the prevailing communal affinities. Non-Muslim refugees arriving in the capital or in Salonica were taken care of exclusively by their respective religious organizations.

It can be thus observed that while slogans of Ottoman patriotism were often declaimed, the beneficiaries of most Jewish philanthropy were the Jewish victims of war. The wars presented Ottoman Jewry with several major difficulties. Jews had to endure all the usual problems of a mobilized society at war – the impoverishment of families whose breadwinners had been conscripted, the need to take care of injured soldiers and the necessity of providing assistance to bereaved families.[22] Furthermore, following the Ottoman army's retreat, Jews, as well as Muslims, were often singled out as targets for vengeance. Consequently, Jewish civilians fled hastily, along with the retreating Ottoman army. The Jewish community of Istanbul had to handle an influx of refugees from all over the occupied territories, but mainly from nearby Thrace.[23] Local Jewish benevolent committees were founded in Istanbul to assist Jewish refugees who had fled from the Balkans, mainly from Edirne and its surrounding region. The temporary shelters and material assistance offered to Jewish refugees from Kırkkilise (now Kırklareli) in the community's schools and synagogues illustrate this mobilization for the benefit of Jewish victims of war.[24] Interestingly, the Jewish communities of Bulgaria offered their assistance to the far fewer Jews who preferred to stay put in Eastern Thrace, in the areas that were now named 'New Bulgaria'. Like their coreligionists in Istanbul, they used patriotism to connect their assistance to Jewish victims of the war to the national Bulgarian cause.[25]

The Jewish community of Istanbul tried to develop effective forms of relief for the refugees. It organized itself promptly to alleviate the sufferings of Jewish victims and to prevent the outbreak and proliferation of disease among them. It had at its disposition the functioning committee of assistance for Jewish victims of the recent earthquake in Çorlu and Gallipoli in August 1912. In the earthquake, which devastated several localities in Eastern Thrace, eighty homes and forty stores belonging to Jews in Çorlu were destroyed; 150 Jewish families were made destitute; and two million francs were lost.[26] The Jewish community of Istanbul anticipated that the committee had the necessary experience to deal with a similarly grave crisis.

The Jewish community of Istanbul designated groups of individuals in neighbourhoods where Jews lived to assist those in distress. The chosen individuals were largely women and mainly those of the 'leisured class', the wives and daughters of Jewish public figures. This function was their designated role on the home front. Like other Ottoman women, Jewish women were encouraged, for the first time, to take active part in the war effort. To be sure, their contribution was channelled to specific tasks on the home front that were socially acceptable for middle-class women: bringing relief to the destitute and to war victims – refugees, wounded soldiers or families of conscripts. It was thought that they would use their innate feminine and maternal skills to assist those in need.[27] One example of a women's association was the *komité de la chika chanta del soldado* (The Committee of the Small Bag for the Soldier), which collected small packages with much-coveted treats and items for the soldiers at the front. The packages could include soap, needles, pins, sewing thread, jam, tobacco, matches, writing paper, pens, tea, sugar and coffee.[28]

Providing religious services for Jewish soldiers at the front was another area of charitable activity. Thus, for example, *El Tyémpo* informed its readers that the 150 Jewish soldiers who were serving on the Çatalca front line and in Istanbul at the end of March 1913 would receive several days of leave (*konjero*) for Passover. The Grand Rabbinate would arrange their lodging among Jewish families and would provide each soldier some money and three *okkas* of *matzah* (unleavened bread traditionally eaten by Jews during the week-long Passover holiday).[29]

As can be seen above, we learn about the activities of charitable committees through their own publications and through press reports. The publication of booklets depicting Jewish suffering was often meant to rouse the readers to donate money and provisions to Jewish war victims. Like their Muslim fellow citizens, Jews viewed religious festivals as an opportunity to raise such contributions.[30] Thus, for example, Eliya Elgazi published the 'Refugees' Haggadah' (*Haggadah de los Muhadjires*) in Istanbul just before Passover in 1913. His version connected the Jewish past and the Ottoman present in order to emphasize the shared destiny of Jews and Muslims. The author, himself a refugee from Selyvria (Selivri), moulded his description of recent events on the story of the Passover Haggadah read at the Seder table. In his version, the Ottomans in general, and the Jews in particular, took the place of the ancient Israelites, while the Balkan states represented the ancient Egyptians, the Jews' principal adversaries from the past. Potential buyers were asked to purchase the booklet for the amount they saw fit, based on their goodwill. All revenues were dedicated to assisting the refugees. Particular praise in this text was given to besieged Edirne and its defender, Şükrü Paşa.[31]

The traditional leadership of the community – the spiritual leadership and the neighbourhood organizations that developed around the synagogues – were the organizers and directors of this assistance. In this regard, Jewish mobilization to ease the suffering of the war victims largely resembled the Muslims' benevolent activity to aid their own. The necessity of assisting those in need was a major reason for the creation of charitable organizations that defined the Jewish public space during the Balkan Wars.

Following the capitulation of Edirne to its Bulgarian besiegers in March 1913, many refugees wished to return to their homes, now under Bulgarian administration. This desire probably reflected a wish to restore normality after several months of life as refugees. Here again, the community's assistance was needed. Thus, for example, *El Tyémpo* reported in May 1913 that a first group of 320 Jewish refugees had boarded an Austrian Lloyd ship destined for Burgas, from whence they would be sent to Edirne, Kırkkilise, Cisr-i Mustafa Paşa (now Svilengrad in Bulgaria), Vize and Lüle Burgas, their places of origin. The Jewish leadership in Istanbul encouraged the return of the refugees, and the Istanbul community took it upon itself to finance the journey and assist those who sought to regain their homes.[32]

From the description of local Jewish philanthropy during the Balkan Wars in the press and official publications, it may appear that assistance was a well-organized project initiated from above. However, we can imagine that, in such times of unprecedented defeat and chaos, much was left to individual initiative, personal and familial connections and luck, all accounts of which are generally absent from official documents. One example can illustrate an individual search for assistance. Roza Behmoiras, who was born in Edirne in 1895, remembered in old age that while the city was under Bulgarian occupation, she could cope with the constant shortages, thanks to the assistance of her aunt, Victoria Behmoiras-Aroyo, who was living in Sofia. Her aunt sent her packages with all kinds of vital provisions. Roza Behmoiras also remembered that the Bulgarian clerk at the post office demanded that she speak to him in Bulgarian and write her name in Bulgarian, a language that she did not know, to acknowledge receipt of the package.[33]

Jewish victims of the war were the first recipients of local Jewish philanthropy during the Balkan Wars. Jewish refugees' decision to seek assistance among Jewish communities and the tendency of local Jews to offer their assistance to coreligionists fleeing from the Balkans reflected the traditional modes of charity in the Ottoman Empire, in which assistance was channelled through local communities using religious entities and an associated understanding of charity.

Philanthropy during the Balkan Wars and the 'Sephardi' Dimension

The Ottoman context and tradition can explain the tendency of Ottoman Jews to concentrate their philanthropy on fellow Jews. However, another dimension of Jewish philanthropy during the Balkan Wars was the mobilization of Sephardi Jews living outside the Ottoman realm on behalf of the Jewish victims of war and, sometimes, in support of the Ottoman cause.

Sephardi identity, based on common origins in the Iberian peninsula and the use of Judeo-Spanish or another form of Ibero-Romance language, was one of the major cultural identities among Jews at the beginning of the twentieth century.[34] In this part of the chapter, I will demonstrate that Sephardi identity played a major part in the philanthropy extended by Jews during the Balkan Wars. In a world in which national identity played a growing role, the Sephardi identity enabled the various Jewish communities in the Ottoman Empire and in its rivals, the Balkan states, to communicate with each other and to offer information and assistance to Jewish prisoners of war (POWs). Their mutual assistance was channelled through traditional modes: the mediation of religious leaders and the abundant publications in Judeo-Spanish. Another dimension of Sephardi philanthropy was identification with the Ottoman cause in the Sephardi diaspora in Western Europe, the Americas and the colonial world.

The significance of 'Sephardi' assistance in the Balkans is visible in the treatment of Jewish POWs. The magnitude of the POW problem during the Balkan Wars is evident in the contemporary Jewish and general press alike. The death by starvation of thousands of Ottoman POWs in Edirne became one of the main symbols of Bulgarian atrocities.[35]

It is true that in the second half of the nineteenth century, legislators representing the European powers attempted to create a set of international and binding provisions that would limit destruction and human suffering in warfare. Their assumption was that warfare should be governed by rules reflecting the progress and morals prevailing in European and North American societies. By the outbreak of the Balkan Wars, a corpus of international law had emerged to codify what was considered permissible in modern warfare and what was deemed impermissible. This process of legislation reached its apex with the negotiation of the Hague Conventions of 1907, which included provisions regarding the treatment of POWs.[36] However, as discussed below, it seems that the ability of international organizations to offer help to POWs during the Balkan Wars was quite limited.

Our information about the conditions and experiences of captives in the Balkan Wars is still limited. Reports in the press shed some light on the misery of many POWs. Books and memoirs by former POWs, mostly officers, provide additional information. Bahri, an Ottoman officer who was held prisoner by the Serbian army, estimated that the number of Ottoman POWs incarcerated in Serbian camps was between four and five thousand; this figure included about 140 officers. However, not all prisoners in Serbian camps were Ottoman soldiers. The Serbian army put into these camps all those who were found on the battlefields: soldiers, but also *başıbozuk* (irregulars), Muslims and Christians. Among this diverse population, he recalled, one could find Turks, Albanians and Bulgarian civilians, and even lads no older than seventeen or eighteen years.[37] His verdict regarding the Serbian treatment of those POWs was clear: they treated their prisoners with harshness reminiscent of the Middle Ages.[38] International organizations were present in the Balkan Wars. On 16 November 1912, the International Committee of the Red Cross (ICRC) announced the opening in Belgrade of an international relief agency under the supervision of the Swiss consul. Its main task was to centralize information on the wounded and prisoners of war. The agency drew up a list of all Ottoman military personnel who were held captive in Serbia. Delegates representing the ICRC visited the camps and sought to learn the whereabouts of soldiers who were wounded or missing. The Ottoman Red Crescent, through its POWs' Commission (*Üsera Komisyonu*), which was established in November 1912, contacted the ICRC centre in Belgrade to deliver assistance to Ottoman POWs and to gather information. In return, the commission provided the ICRC in Belgrade with information on Bulgarian POWs held by the Ottoman army.[39] However, according to the ICRC, the Bulgarian Red Cross did not receive any information on captured Ottoman soldiers, and it obtained a list of them only after the fighting was over. The Ottoman authorities, moreover, did not provide any information on the prisoners they held. In addition, two delegates of the ICRC visited the different fronts in November–December 1912, and again in the spring of 1913, in an attempt to collect the wounded on the battlefield, to identify them and to organize relief at the rear.[40] For its part, the Ottoman Red Crescent could assist Ottoman POWs only after the conclusion of peace, in the aftermath of the Second Balkan War (August 1913).[41] For example, a delegation of the Red Crescent went to Rusçuk (Ruse) after news reached Istanbul that many prisoners were dying of contagious disease or medical neglect. In October 1913, the delegation left Sirkeci station, and arrived in Rusçuk via Sofia on 29 November.[42] Previously, according to the Ottoman press, the Ottoman

POWs in Rusçuk had been forced to rely on provisions supplied by the Muslim community of the city.[43]

Notwithstanding the presence of the ICRC in Belgrade, it seems that the Jewish POWs and their worried families relied mostly on Jewish networks to provide or collect information on their loved ones and to offer them basic assistance. Full names of Jewish POWs and letters written by Jewish POWs appeared regularly in the Jewish press in the Ottoman state and in the Balkan states. The Jewish press served as a source of information that could overcome the barriers between the belligerents. Consider the following example: the Salonican *El Nuevo Avenir* published, in its issue of 31 December 1912, a letter signed by Rabbi Yitzhak Yosef Ha-Levy, the rabbi of Niš in Serbia. The letter provided the full names of thirty-seven Jewish POWs from Salonica who were detained in a camp in Niš. In addition, it mentioned that there were also five prisoners from Istanbul, one from Çatalca, three from Gallipoli, eight from Urla (a suburb of Izmir) and four from Monastir (Bitola). The letter aimed to inform the families in Salonica of the whereabouts of their loved ones and to let them know that all the detainees were in good health and that their needs were being taken care of by the Jewish community of Niš. The letter arrived with the help of several persons. First, Rabbi Yitzhak Yosef Ha-Levy sent the letter through a person whose identity the journal chose to conceal, calling him *uno de nuestros amigos* (one of our friends). He was later identified as Eliezer Modiano, an employee in the branch of the Banka de Saloniko in Üsküb (Skopje). The messenger travelled with the letter via Üsküb to Salonica. There he entrusted it to the chief rabbi of Salonica, who delivered it to the journal.[44]

One week later, another letter arrived from Niš, this time carried by a certain Moshe Haim Venezia, who was returning from Serbia. This time the letter was signed by Jewish POWs from various places in Anatolia and Thrace. Extolling the assistance received from the local Jewish community in general and from Mr Venezia in particular, who provided each of them with one franc and a packet of tobacco, the POWs nevertheless felt themselves to be in a deplorable situation and asked the Jewish community of Salonica to come to their aid. The directors of *El Avenir* responded to this cry for help by using the services of Yosef Pinto of Belgrade to dispatch forty undershirts, forty pairs of underpants and forty pairs of socks.[45]

A certain 'coreligionist' (*uno korelijionario*), arriving from Greece, reported the names of five Jewish prisoners from Salonica who were being held in Larisa. Eliyahu Avraham Shalem, Daniel Shmuel Mano, Yosef Shmuel Estrog, Avraham Yosef Hanukah and Pinhas Haim Naar were all said to be in good health. The Jewish community of Larisa was taking care of all their needs and endeavouring to ensure that these POWs would not be transferred elsewhere.[46]

Another example of the role played by Jewish organizations in providing assistance to Jewish POWs comes from Edirne. As early as December 1912, *El Nuevo Avenir* sent a request to Haim Bejarano, the chief rabbi of Edirne, asking for information about the Jewish soldiers from Salonica who were serving in the besieged city. Bejarano was able to respond to the request only four months later, when Edirne capitulated to the Bulgarian army. He reported that no Jews from Salonica were among the fallen soldiers during the siege. He further notified the readers of *El Avenir* that following several weeks of captivity, the Salonican POWs, previously Ottoman soldiers but now assumed citizens of Greece, an ally of Bulgaria, had all been liberated and sent back to their homes in Salonica, although some of them had preferred to stay in Edirne in the meantime.[47] The ability of Sephardi Jewish communities in the Balkans to gain information through a network based on personal relations, connections and the Judeo-Spanish press thus met the sheer necessity to provide some information on missing soldiers and to extend assistance to them.

Jewish philanthropy during the Balkan Wars reveals yet another ingredient of a 'Sephardi' identity based on affiliation and identification with the Ottoman state. On 1 November 1912, when the First Balkan War had just begun, the daily *El Tyémpo* reported on a public gathering that had taken place the previous Saturday in the 'Fortifikasyones synagogue'[48] in Antwerp, Belgium. Nissim Roditi Bey, the consul-general representing the Ottoman Empire in Antwerp and one of the few Jews to reach such an elevated post in the Ottoman Foreign Office, organized public prayers in the synagogue, asking for Ottoman victory in the ongoing combat in the Balkans. In addition, *El Tyémpo* informed its readers that Nissim Roditi Bey presided over a new philanthropic committee, established to collect donations for the Ottoman Red Crescent to help it carry out humanitarian activities at the front on behalf of Ottoman victims of the fighting. The committee was composed of local Jewish, Muslim and Armenian merchants in Antwerp. These volunteers represented what *El Tyémpo* defined as the local 'Kolonia Ottomana', the Ottoman colony, in Antwerp. Finally, the Jewish daily reported, 'according to our information, our Ottoman coreligionists of Antwerp who always demonstrated their patriotic sentiments are doing their best to positively respond to the public call made by the committee and have already collected more than 10,000 francs'.[49]

We can only speculate about the decision of the Ottoman Ministry of Foreign Affairs to appoint a Jew as its consul-general in Antwerp. We may assume that the presence of well-established and affluent Jewish merchants of Sephardi origin in this major Belgian port contributed to the decision. In fact, as long ago as the 1850s, the Ottoman Ministry of Foreign Affairs had named another Jew, B.J. Posno, to represent the Ottoman state in Antwerp.[50] Indeed, it is clear that Roditi was motivated to use the 'Sephardi' link to boost the image of the Ottoman Empire in the city.[51]

However, the connection between the Sephardim of Antwerp and the Ottoman Empire was not especially evident. Unlike the Judeo-Spanish-speaking Sephardim of the Ottoman Empire, many of the Sephardim of Antwerp, who were mainly Portuguese Jews, did not originate in the Ottoman realm, nor were the majority of them descendants of Jews from the Ottoman Empire. While the Portuguese community did receive some Jewish emigrants from the Ottoman state in the second half of the nineteenth century, the lion's share of the Sephardi merchants of Antwerp, like their coreligionists living in Amsterdam and other port cities in northern Germany, England and the New World, were part of what is now labelled 'the Western Sephardi communities'. These were much smaller communities of Jews, some of them former *conversos*, who left the Iberian peninsula for Western Europe rather than the Ottoman Empire or northern Africa, as the Ladino-speaking Jews of the East had done.[52] Established in Antwerp since the first half of the sixteenth century, the city's 'Portuguese' community had its own synagogue, the Synagogue Israélite du Rite Portugais (inaugurated in 1898), and its own rabbi. On the basis of their rituals separating them from the other Jewish communities in Antwerp, the Sephardi Jews demanded and obtained from the state a separate status of *personalité civile*.[53] The only cultural link that could connect the affluent merchants of Antwerp to their brethren in the Ottoman Empire was a common Iberian origin. We may infer that claiming an affiliation with the Ottoman state would emphasize their particular origin and justify their separate organization among the Ashkenazi Jews of Antwerp. Roditi was determined to use this motivation to benefit the Ottoman war effort. According to the Judeo-Spanish Jewish press of Istanbul, he was successful.

The case of the Portuguese community of Antwerp was not unique. Similar initiatives were undertaken in places around the globe, such as distant Salisbury, the capital of Rhodesia (now Zimbabwe), where Ottoman Jewish immigrants from the island of Rhodes and Muslim Indians who had settled in the British colony organized joint subscriptions to benefit the Ottoman war effort. In their case, offering donations to the Ottoman Empire in the name of an imagined attachment to the distant Ottoman motherland could reinforce solidarity and develop a shared image of an Ottoman affiliation, probably viewed as an asset in the context of colonial Africa.[54]

Indeed, it is worth mentioning that in colonial Africa, philanthropy was not the only way to demonstrate affiliation with the Ottoman nation. The South African jurist and historian Nathan Manfred (1875–1945) wrote an interesting description of the *seraglio*, the residence of Henri Bettelheim, the Ottoman consul in Johannesburg in the 1890s. Bettelheim was an Ashkenazi Jewish merchant and an Ottoman citizen before he settled in South Africa. His residence in Doornfontein, the first residential suburb of Johannesburg, was festooned with an onion dome and golden crescent to create a fantasy of Ottoman residential architecture.[55]

A report published in *El Tyémpo* provides another example of the mobilization of a Sephardi diaspora in support of the Ottoman war effort. The report informs its readers about the subscription that was opened in Seattle, 'where many Jews who originate from Turkey are found and who are always attached to their motherland from which they came'. Shmuel Alkhadef, the president of the subscription committee, notified Chief Rabbi Haim Nahum that the sum of $214 was collected on behalf of the Jewish refugees who arrived in Istanbul. By December 1912, the committee sent a cheque for $1,000 via B'nai B'rith to assist the refugees. B'nai B'rith, an international Jewish social and cultural organization established in 1843 in New York to promote mutual aid, social services and philanthropy among Jews,[56] opened its first lodge in Istanbul in 1911.[57]

The creation of relief committees among Ottoman émigrés may suggest an attempt to construct an Ottoman diaspora built around a common Ottoman identity shared by Muslims, Christians and Jews. The recruitment of Ottoman émigrés abroad for philanthropic activity in wartime in the name of shared Ottoman identity may also indicate a close relation between philanthropy and the shaping of communities and their boundaries. However, as stated above, in many other cases of philanthropy reported in the Jewish press, the choice of beneficiaries for relief activity demonstrates the continuity of old patterns of charity that prevailed in Ottoman societies long before the Ottoman reforms of the 'long nineteenth century'.

Jewish Philanthropy and the Global Jewish Dimension: The Role of the 'Prosperous and Enlightened' Diaspora

Philanthropic Jewish associations from abroad joined forces to found a unified organization that would assist the Jewish victims of the Balkan Wars. Of course, providing charity to Jewish religious institutions and personnel in the Holy Land, especially in Jerusalem, Safed, Hebron and Tiberias, the Four Holy Cities of Judaism, was one of the main features of relations between the Jewish diaspora and the small Jewish communities in Ottoman Palestine/Eretz Israel. Since the mid nineteenth century, however, individual benevolent and Jewish philanthropic associations from Western Europe had distributed philanthropy to Jewish communities in the Ottoman Empire for other special reasons: Jewish solidarity and the proclaimed obligation of the enlightened Jewish communities of the West to assist their 'less fortunate' and 'backward' brethren in the Orient. These philanthropic projects were part of the wider European Jewish movement of *Haskalah*, or Jewish Enlightenment.[58] The aim was to achieve a better integration of the Jews of the Islamic lands by reforming Jewish society and culture in accordance with modern European civilization. Organizations like the Alliance Israélite Universelle (AIU), founded in Paris by French Jews in 1860, established and supported the activities of various Jewish educational, health, vocational training and beneficent institutions in the Ottoman Empire so that Jews there could become more productive members of their states. Philanthropy was likewise intended to counter and resist the growing activities of Christian missionaries in the Ottoman Empire in the fields of education and health. In 1912, every Ottoman Jewish community of around a thousand souls possessed at least one Alliance school. Some of these schools were situated in the small communities of Eastern Thrace. The directors and teachers of these schools were thus eyewitnesses to the agonies of those communities during the Balkan Wars and were able to convey their difficulties to the Alliance directors in Paris.[59]

Offering assistance on behalf of their brethren of the Orient when in crisis or danger was another major philanthropic opportunity for the emancipated Jews of Europe. The Balkan Wars resulted in a flood of Jewish refugees, most of whom settled in Salonica and Istanbul, and such an emergency called for swift action. Indeed, the *American Jewish Year Book 5674* (1912–13) described this mobilization as 'the prompt and generous response of the prosperous Jewries in Western Europe and America to the Balkan distress, and the effort to secure a guarantee for the civil and political liberty and equality of the Jews in the conquered territory'.⁶⁰

It is impossible to present here a unified 'diaspora Jewish' response to the Balkan Wars, for at the beginning of the twentieth century, very different and often contradictory ideological currents and perceptions divided the Jewish world into different ideological and political groups. This diversity of ideologies resulted in manifold opinions regarding any aspect of the main contemporary dilemmas and debates then faced by Jewish readers. Also, the scope of this chapter is too narrow to offer a discussion of the attitudes of the contemporary Jewish press with regard to the Balkan Wars. Suffice it to say, for present purposes, that the Jewish press outside the Ottoman Empire keenly followed the news from the Ottoman Empire, probably because of the significance of Ottoman Palestine/Eretz Israel for its Jewish readers. Another reason for the particular interest of the Jewish press of Central and Eastern Europe in the news arriving from the Balkans was the implications of the conflict for the Austro-Hungarian Empire.

Some of the Jewish journals quoted news from the Turkish-language press or received regular reports from their agents living in Istanbul. As one example, Yaakov Perahia, a Jewish journalist residing in Istanbul, dispatched regular reports on the Balkan Wars and the Ottoman Jews to *Ha-Mitzpe*, a Hebrew weekly published in Cracow.⁶¹ An advertisement headed *Der Balkan-Krieg und die Kriegsgefahr zwischen Österreich-Ungarn un[d] Serbien* [The Balkan War and the Danger of War between Austria-Hungary and Serbia], which called upon readers of German to follow the news in the Jewish *Allgemeine Jüdische Zeitung* of Budapest, also attests to this interest.⁶² Furthermore, the general enmity of the Jewish press towards Tsarist Russia, due to its constant oppression and harassment of its numerous Jewish subjects, often prompted identification with the Ottoman Empire, which was perceived as another victim of Russia's bigotry, perpetrated through its Slavic client states in the Balkans.⁶³ The identification with an Islamic Sultanate coming under Christian military pressure could also stem from the outlook of certain Jewish intellectuals of the late nineteenth century, many of them Orientalists by profession, who spoke of a Judeo-Islamic world, reflected in medieval Andalusia, in which a vibrant Jewish culture could flourish, as opposed to the oppression of Jews and their culture in the Christian world.⁶⁴

In December 1912, representatives of the eight major Jewish philanthropic institutions centred in France, the United States, the United Kingdom, Germany and Austria met in Brussels to promote joint action for the relief of Balkan Jews. The outcome of this meeting was the establishment of the Union des Associations Israélites, an umbrella organization that assessed the needs of the various Balkan and Ottoman Jewish communities and supervised the assistance offered to them. Its activities were later described in a booklet.[65] For its part, the Judeo-Spanish press followed the activities of the major Jewish philanthropic organizations and reported their activities with respect to the Jewish communities in the Balkans.[66] Referring to the philanthropy offered by these organizations representing 'World Jewry', *El Nuevo Avenir* proclaimed: 'Jewish solidarity is not an empty word!'[67]

A summary of these philanthropic activities appeared in the *American Jewish Year Book 5674*. It revealed the scope of humanitarian aid during the First Balkan War and its aftermath, and its distribution among the different Balkan Jewish communities: Approximately $175,000 was contributed by the Jews in Europe and America. Of this amount, $58,000 came from the United States. The greatest distress was in Istanbul. Here, $65,000 was expended for relief and repatriation of the refugees. Though not a scene of occupation and displacement in the First Balkan War, Bulgaria required assistance to the extent of $25,000. Even more was needed to meet the distress in Edirne during and after the siege. Salonica, Janina and Serres together required the expenditure of $25,000. In İştip and other places occupied by the Bulgarians, $10,000 was spent. In Monastir, Üsküb and other places taken by Serbia, a little less than $2,000 was used. These amounts were expended before war broke out among the allies. The distress following the Second Balkan War exhausted the funds of the Brussels committee, and made necessary a further appeal to the generosity of the Jews.[68]

The AIU organization, which was part of the Union des Associations Israélites, also used its vast network of schools, situated all over the Ottoman lands, in North Africa and Iran,[69] to propound the Ottoman case and to collect donations for the benefit of the war victims. One illustration concerns an Alliance school serving a small community in Iran. The Unionist daily *Tanin* reported on donations to the Ottoman Red Crescent that arrived through the Ottoman consulate in Karamanşah in Iran. Among the donors appeared the name of Lucio Franko (?), the director of the Alliance school in the city, who donated 100 qiran to the Ottoman war effort. The list included the names of other local Jews, among them a merchant, a banker and an artisan.[70] The efforts of global Jewish philanthropic organizations to alleviate the suffering of Balkan Jews could be promoted and then realized through the networks of the Jewish press and schools. Their unified response combined the traditional principle of Jewish solidarity with the perception of the obligation of the 'more progressed' Jews in the West to assist their 'backward' brothers living under Islamic rule.[71]

Conclusions

Coordinating and managing philanthropy was one of the major forms of communal work during the Balkan Wars. Alongside active military service and self-sacrifice on the front lines, patriotic service by non-combatants on the home front demonstrated not only that Jews had civic duties and responsibilities but also that they would carry them out. For Jewish social and economic elites, the discourse around the Balkan Wars was an ideal avenue for entry into the new age of Ottoman civic patriotism: it enabled them to speak the language of community, of equality, of sacrifice and of communal responsibility and care in the name of patriotism. Yet, while the Jewish discourse of serving the Ottoman cause in the Balkan Wars dovetailed with the Ottomanist discourse that appeared in the Turkish-language press, it is important to note that Jewish assistance to Jewish war victims was channelled through networks of Jewish charitable organizations that were overwhelmingly distinct from those established by Ottoman Muslims or Christians.

In her study of child welfare during the First World War in the Bohemian lands of the Habsburg Empire, Tara Zahra asserts that the First World War represented a watershed in the expansion of the welfare state, due to the state's increasing responsibility to provide assistance to the war's victims. However, as the Austrian empire (of which the Bohemian lands were part), nation and state were not coterminous, Austrian officials entrusted private nationalist associations with the management of the wartime welfare state. Accordingly, German and Czech nationalists significantly expanded their authority over children and the family.[72]

The Ottoman situation during the Balkan Wars looks similar. The inability to form genuine state-sponsored charitable organizations that would assist all Ottomans probably kept communal boundaries intact in a period in which an inclusive Ottoman identity still prevailed in formal declarations and in the press. The growing significance and organization of Jewish philanthropy during the Balkan Wars is evident. As Jewish nationalism (Zionism) was still marginal in the central Ottoman lands, we cannot claim that the activities of prolific Jewish philanthropic organizations promoted Jewish national awareness among Ottoman Jews. On the contrary, the activities of such organizations strengthened the status of traditional roles and institutions inside the community, such as the central and local rabbinates, and enabled them to assert that they were servants of modernity and patriotism. An illustration is provided by the public activities of Haim Nahum, the chief rabbi of the

Ottoman Empire during the Balkan Wars. Regarded by Zionist activists in the Ottoman lands as a steadfast opponent of the Zionist movement, Nahum was probably the major Jewish figure who coordinated and controlled many of the philanthropic activities in favour of Ottoman Jews. His vital connections with the Ottoman authorities and with international Jewish organizations, in combination with his formal authority over Ottoman Jewish communities, placed him at the centre of the assistance activities offered to Jewish victims of the Balkan Wars. For Nahum, this was an opportunity to promote his political agenda of strengthening the bonds connecting the Jews, as a community, with the Ottoman nation.[73]

The support and succour of global Jewish organizations enabled these entities to promote the concept of Jewish solidarity. While such activities did not contradict the Ottomanist discourse promoted by the state – and indeed Ottoman officials supported the activities of local and foreign Jewish philanthropic organizations during the Balkan Wars – more than anything else, they asserted communal Jewish awareness and identity in the framework of the Ottoman state. Therefore, I argue, the philanthropy offered during the Balkan Wars in the name of Ottoman patriotism actually strengthened communal identities and boundaries. This was probably the case among other Ottoman communities as well.[74]

Eyal Ginio is Associate Professor in the Department of Islam and Middle Eastern Studies at the Hebrew University of Jerusalem and the Director of the Ben-Zvi Institute for the Study of the Jewish Communities of the East, also in Jerusalem. His research focuses on the social history of the Ottoman Empire with a particular emphasis on the Balkan Wars (1912–13). His recent publications include *The Ottoman Culture of Defeat: The Balkan Wars and Their Aftermath* (Hurst and Oxford University Press, 2016) and, co-edited with Karl Kaser, *Ottoman Legacies in the Contemporary Mediterranean: The Balkans and the Middle East Compared* (The Hebrew University of Jerusalem, the forum for European Studies, 2013).

Notes

1 Jean H. Quataert, 'Mobilizing Philanthropy in the Service of War: The Female Rituals of Care in the New Germany, 1871–1914', in Manfred F. Boemeke, Roger Chickering and Stig Förster (eds), *Anticipating Total War: The German and American Experiences, 1871–1914* (Washington, DC: German

Historical Institute; Cambridge: Cambridge University Press, 1999), 217–38, here 224–27.
2   This term is taken from Maureen Healy, *Vienna and the Fall of the Habsburg Empire: Total War and Everyday Life in World War I* (Cambridge: Cambridge University Press, 2004), 262–72.
3   There is a growing body of literature on civilians during the age of total war and on the shaping of the home front. See, for example, Richard Wall and Jay Winter (eds), *The Upheaval of War: Family, Work and Welfare in Europe 1914–1918* (Cambridge: Cambridge University Press, 1988); Jay Winter and Antoine Prost, *The Great War in History: Debates and Controversies, 1914 to the Present* (Cambridge: Cambridge University Press, 2005), chapter 7.
4   Amy Singer, *Constructing Ottoman Beneficence: An Imperial Soup Kitchen in Jerusalem* (Albany, NY: State University of New York Press, 2002), 13.
5   Katherine Lynch, *Individuals, Families, and Communities in Europe, 1200–1800: The Urban Foundations of Western Society* (Cambridge: Cambridge University Press, 2003), 103.
6   Christhard Hoffmann, 'Between Integration and Rejection: The Jewish Community in Germany, 1914–1918', in John Horne (ed.), *State, Society and Mobilization in Europe during the First World War* (Cambridge: Cambridge University Press, 1997), 89–104, here 89.
7   On the Ottoman Jews during the Balkan Wars and their mobilization to assist the Ottoman war effort, see Eyal Ginio, '*El Dovér al mas Sànto* – The Mobilization of the Ottoman Jewish Population during the Balkan Wars (1912–1913)', in Nathalie Clayer, Hannes Grandits and Robert Pichler (eds), *Social Integration and National Turn in the Late and Post-Ottoman Balkan Societies (1839–1914)* (London: I.B. Tauris, 2011), 157–81.
8   Masayuki Ueno, '"For Fatherland and the State": Armenians Negotiate the Tanzimat Reforms', *International Journal of Middle East Studies* 45 (2013), 93–109, here 94.
9   Julia Phillips-Cohen, 'Between Civic and Islamic Ottomanism: Jewish Imperial Citizenship in the Hamidian Era', *International Journal of Middle East Studies* 44 (2012), 237–55, here 245–47.
10 Nadir Özbek, 'The Politics of Poor Relief in the Late Ottoman Empire 1876–1914', *New Perspectives on Turkey* 21 (1999), 1–33.
11 Nora Şeni and Sophie Le Tarnec, *Les Camondo ou l'éclipse d'une fortune* (Arles: Actes Sud, 1997), 43–67.
12 Meropi Anastassiadou, 'La protection de l'enfance abandonnée dans l'Empire ottoman au XIXe siècle: Le cas de la communauté grecque orthodoxe de Beyoglu (Istanbul)', *Südost-Forschungen* 59/60 (2000/2001), 272–323.
13 Esther Benbassa and Aron Rodrigue, *The Jews of the Balkans: The Judeo-Spanish Community, 15th to 20th Centuries* (Oxford: Blackwell, 1995), 87.
14 It should be mentioned here that the Jewish press in the Ottoman state served as an important platform to promote the notion of Ottoman patriotism among its Jewish readers. See Michelle U. Campos, *Ottoman Brothers: Muslims, Christians, and Jews in Early Twentieth-Century Palestine* (Stanford, CA: Stanford University Press, 2011), 67.

15 This journal appeared under the title of *El Avenir* until November 1912. The adding of the word *Nuevo*, meaning 'new', and the addition of a transliterated title in Greek letters next to the title in Hebrew letters (used for writing Judeo-Spanish until the Second World War), at the expense of Arabic letters, reflect the wish of the journal's editors to adapt to the changed circumstances following the Greek takeover of Salonica.

16 'En Saloniko' [In Salonica], *El Nuevo Avenir*, 27 November 1912. On the small Jewish community of İştip and its flight to Salonica, see *The American Jewish Year Book 5674* (Philadelphia, PA: The Jewish Publication Society of America, 1913), 192.

17 On *El Tyémpo* and its cultural and political significance, see Sarah Abrevaya-Stein, *Making Jews Modern: The Yiddish and Ladino Press in the Russian and Ottoman Empires* (Bloomington, IN: Indiana University Press, 2003).

18 'Por las famiyas de los soldados djidios de Salonica' [For the Families of the Jewish Soldiers from Salonica], *El Tyémpo*, 28 October 1912.

19 Esther Benbassa, *Un Grand Rabbin Sepharade en politique 1892–1923* (Paris: Presses du CNRS, 1990), 224–25. See also 'El Gran Rabbinu de Turkía visita los soldados feridos' [The Chief Rabbi of Turkey Visits the Wounded Soldiers], *El Tyémpo*, 1 November 1912; 'Soldados feridos en el Ospital Or Ha-Hayim' [Wounded Soldiers in the Hospital Or Ha-Hayim], *El Tyémpo*, 8 November 1912.

20 *El Nuevo Avenir*, 18 October 1912; *El Nuevo Avenir*, 23 October 1912.

21 See, for example, 'Musevi Vatandaşlarımız' [Our Jewish Co-citizens], *Tanin*, 25 January/7 February 1913.

22 See, for example, 'En Ayúda de las famiyas de los militáres' [Assisting the Soldiers' Families], *El Tyémpo*, 25 October 1912.

23 The number of Jewish refugees who were registered in the community was estimated at 3,545 in April 1913. See 'Por los refujiados djidios en Konstantinopla' [For the Jewish Refugees in Istanbul], *El Tyémpo*, 18 April 1913. Other examples are: 'Los emigrádos djidios del teátro de la gerra' [The Jewish Immigrants from the War Zone], *El Tyémpo*, 1 November 1912; 'La Komisyón de Sokurros por la sinistrados de la gerra' [The Assistance Commission for War Victims], *El Tyémpo*, 3 January 1913; 'La Óvra de la Komisyón de Sokurros i los emigrados' [The Activity of the Assistance Commission and the Immigrants], *El Tyémpo*, 18 December 1912. On the plight of Muslim refugees during the Balkan Wars, see Ahmet Halaçoğlu, *Balkan Harbi sırasında Rumeli'den Türk Göçleri (1912–1913)* [Turkish Immigrants from Rumeli during the Balkan War (1912–1913)] (Ankara: Türk Tarih Kurumu, 1995).

24 I discuss this particular community during the Balkan Wars in Eyal Ginio, 'Balkan Savaşları Döneminde Kırkkilise (Kırklareli) Musevi Cemaati' [The Jewish Community of Kırkkilise (Kırklareli) during the Balkan Wars], in Kenan Gültürk and S. Bilal Nur (eds), *Balkan Savaşlarının 100. Yılı* [The Centenary of the Balkan Wars] (Bağcılar: Kültür Yayınları, 2012), 554–63.

25 On the activities of the Komité Central de Sokurros (The Central Committee of Assistance) to assist the Jews of 'New Bulgaria' as well as the families of conscripted Jewish soldiers, see Avraham Tadžir, *Notas Istórikas sovre los Djidios de Bulgaría i la Kommunita de Sofia* [Historical Notes Regarding

the Jews of Bulgaria and the Community of Sofia] (Sofia: Nadezna, 1932), 180–83.
26 Ibid., 344.
27 See, as examples, 'Gran Rabinato de Turkía – una Yamada' [The Chief Rabbinate of Turkey: A Call], *El Tyémpo*, 11 November 1912; 'Yamada a las mujeres djudías' [A Call to Jewish Women], *El Tyémpo*, 11 November 1912. On the Balkan Wars as a catalyst for the founding of women's organizations, see Ellen L. Fleischmann, 'The Other "Awakening": The Emergence of Women's Movements in the Modern Middle East, 1900–1940', in Margaret L. Meriwether and Judith E. Tucker (eds), *A Social History of Women and Gender in the Modern Middle East* (Boulder, CO: Westview, 1999), 89–134, here 103. See also Fatma Müge Göçek, 'From Empire to Nation: Images of Women and War in Ottoman Political Cartoons, 1908–1923', in Billie Melman (ed.), *Borderlines – Genders and Identities in War and Peace 1870–1930* (New York/London: Routledge, 1998), 47–72, here 50–51.
28 'Yamada a las mujeres djudías' [A Call to Jewish Women], *El Tyémpo*, 11 November 1912.
29 'Los soldados Israélitas i la Paskua' [The Jewish Soldiers and the Passover Holiday], *El Tyémpo*, 18 April 1913.
30 See, for example, the calls in the Turkish-language press to celebrate the Festival of Sacrifice (Kurban Bayramı) by collecting donations, instead of the traditional sacrifice of sheep (*kurban bedeli*), for the benefit of the soldiers serving at the front: 'Donanma-yi Osmanı Muavenet-i Milliye Cemiyeti Merkez-i Umumisinden' [From the General Centre of the Association of National Assistance to the Ottoman Navy], *Ranin* [*Tanin*], 18/31 October 1912.
31 Eliya Elgazi, *Haggadah de los Muhadjires* [The Refugees' Haggadah] (Istanbul: Emprimería Ardity i Kastro, 5673 [1913]). For another example of a Haggadah that depicted the Balkan Wars through the story of the biblical Exodus, see Rabbi Yotfata [sic], *Haggadah echa apropyada por la anyada de la gerra del anyo 5673* [A Haggadah Adapted for the War of the Year 5673] (Istanbul: Emprimería Ardity i Kastro, 1913), 2–3. I would like to thank Dr Dov HaKohen and Dr Avner Peretz for providing me with copies of these *haggadot*.
32 'El Repatriamyento de los refujiados de Israélitas' [The Repatriation of the Jewish Refugees], *El Tyémpo*, 6 May 1913.
33 Interview with Roza's granddaughter, Malka Dvir, Jerusalem, 3 February 2009.
34 For a general introduction to the different dimensions of Sephardi identities, see the various chapters in Zion Zohar (ed.), *Sephardic and Mizrahi Jewry: From the Golden Age of Spain to Modern Times* (New York: New York University Press, 2005).
35 See, for example, the description of the misery experienced by Ottoman POWs in Raif Necdet, *Ufûl* [The Extinction] (Istanbul: Resimli Matbaası, November 1329 [1913]), 159. On this book, see Halûk Harun Duman, *Balkanlara Veda* [A Farewell to the Balkans] (Istanbul: Duyap, 2005), 288. On Ottoman POWs during the Balkan Wars, see Uğur Özcan, 'Ottoman Prisoners of War and Their Repatriation Challenge in the Balkan Wars', in

Aleksandar Rastović (ed.), *Prvi balkanski rat 1912/1913. godine: Društveni i civilizacijski smisao. Povodom stogodišnjice oslobođenja Stare Srbije i Makedonije 1912* [The First Balkan War, 1912–1913: Social and Cultural Meaning. On the Occasion of the 100th Anniversary of the Liberation of Old Serbia and Macedonia in 1912], Vol. I (Niš: The University of Niš, 2013), 159–82, https://www.academia.edu/4722022/Ottoman_Prisoners_of_War_and_their_Repatriation_Challenge_in_Balkan_Wars_P_1912_1913._._1912._V._I_The_University_of_Nis_Ed_Prf._Dr._Aleksandar_Rastovic_Nis_2013 (accessed 5 December 2013).

36 Alon Rachamimov, *POWs and the Great War: Captivity on the Eastern Front* (Oxford: Berg, 2002), 71–78.

37 Yüzbaşı Selânikli Bahri, *Balkan Harbinde Sırb Ordusu* [The Serbian Army during the Balkan War] (Istanbul: Tanin Matbaası, 1329 [1913]), 65.

38 Ibid.

39 *Osmanlı Hilâl-i Ahmer Cemiyeti 1329–1331 Salnamesi* [The Yearbook of the Ottoman Red Crescent 1329/1331 (1913)] (Istanbul: Ahmed İhsan ve Şürekâsı Matbaacılık Osmanlı Şirketi, n.d.), 231.

40 International Committee of the Red Cross, 'The Balkan Wars (1912–1913)', http://www.icrc.org/eng/resources/documents/misc/57jnvy.htm (accessed 16 June 2013).

41 See *Osmanlı Hilâl-i Ahmer Cemiyeti*, 231–36; Seçil Karal Akgün and Murat Uluğtekin, *Hilâl-i Ahmer'den Kızılay'a* [From the *Hilâl-i Ahmer* to the *Kızılay*]. (Ankara: Beyda Basımevi, 2000), 130–33.

42 Besim Ömer [Akalın], *Hanımlar Efendilere Hilâl-ı Ahmere dair konferans* [A Conference for Women on the Red Crescent] (Istanbul: Ahmet İhsan, 1330 [1913/14]), 68.

43 *Tanin*, 8/21 October 1913.

44 'Letra de Niš' [A Letter from Niš], *El Nuevo Avenir*, 31 December 1912. See also *El Nuevo Avenir*, 25 December 1912.

45 'Letra de soldados djidios de Niš' [A Letter from Jewish Soldiers of Niš], *El Nuevo Avenir*, 5 January 1913.

46 *El Nuevo Avenir*, 5 November 1912.

47 'Letra de Gran Rabbinu de Edirne' [A Letter from the Chief Rabbi of Edirne], *El Nuevo Avenir*, 13 April 1913.

48 In 1888, a new synagogue was established on 'Fortifications Street' in Antwerp. Named Ahavas Sholem, it served the Jewish community until the interwar period, when it was moved to Van Diepenbeeckstraat. I would like to thank Daniel Dratwa, the curator of the Musée Juif de Belgique, for providing me with this information.

49 'En la kolonía djudía Otomána de Anversa' [In the Jewish Ottoman Colony of Antwerp], *El Tyémpo*, 1 November 1912. According to the yearbook published by the Ottoman Red Crescent, Nissim Roditi, the deputy [*sic*] consul in Antwerp, provided the organization with donations of 4,735 kuruş in 1328 [1912/13]. Other individual donations that arrived through the Ottoman consulate in Antwerp included the different sums of 574 kuruş, 831 kuruş and 35 santim, 844 kuruş and 375 santim, 475 kuruş and 5,927.75 kuruş. Dr Armand Bloch, the chief rabbi of Belgium, donated 861 kuruş and 875 santim. A certain Mr Herman from Antwerp donated the

considerable sums of 8,750.50 and 1,119.50 kuruş. See *Osmanlı Hilâl-i Ahmer Cemiyeti*, 398–401. On the donations, mostly linens and clothes provided by the 'big shops' of Brussels and Antwerp, which Nissim Roditi sent to the Chief Rabbinate of Istanbul to assist Jewish refugees in Istanbul, see 'En favor de los refujiados de gerra djidios en Konstantinopla' [On Behalf of the Jewish War Refugees in Istanbul], *El Tyémpo*, 28 February 1913.

50 Ephraim Schmidt, *L'Histoire des juifs à Anvers (Antwerpen)* (Antwerp: Excelsior, 1969), 87.

51 The Centre for Political History at the University of Antwerp is currently preparing a digitalization project on Ottoman Diplomats to Belgium, 1848–1914. The Ottoman archives hold the correspondence between Nissim Roditi, the consul-general in Antwerp, and the Ottoman Ministry of Foreign Affairs. All of Roditi's letters were written in French. I would like to thank Houssine Alloul of the University of Antwerp for providing me with this information and for enabling me to consult the letters written by Nissim Roditi.

52 For a general introduction to the Western Sephardi diaspora, see Yosef Kaplan, 'The Sephardim in North-Western Europe and the New World', in Haim Beinart (ed.), *The Sephardi Legacy*, Vol. II (Jerusalem: The Magness Press, 1992), 240–87.

53 Schmidt, *L'histoire des juifs à Anvers*, 10–34.

54 'Patriotismo de djidios Otomanos' [Patriotism of Ottoman Jews], *El Tyémpo*, 26 May 1913. According to the annual of the Ottoman Red Crescent, the Muslims of South Africa donated 13,211 Ottoman lira to the Red Crescent. This contribution placed the Muslims of South Africa in the fourth rank of donors during the Balkan Wars, after India, the Muslims of Russia, and Algiers. See *Osmanlı Hilâl-i Ahmer Cemiyeti*, 312, 395.

55 'The only building in the town which had any pretensions to architectural appearance was the house of Henri Bettelheim, the Turkish Consul, known as "Bettles", in Beit Street, Doornfontein. It was Oriental, with a dome and a balustrade front. What need there was for a Turkish Consul I have yet to learn, as I don't suppose there were three Turks on the whole Rand. The place was known as the "seraglio"; but I fancy the odalisques hailed from Seven Dials, and had never seen (or smelt) the Bosphorus. The house was consecrated, in the main, to poker.' Nathan Manfred, *Not Heaven Itself: An Autobiography* (Durban: The Knox Publishing Company, 1944), 70. I would like to thank my colleague Dr Louise Bethlehem for providing me with this reference. On the establishment of the Ottoman consulate in Johannesburg and the appointment of Bettelheim (Beytülham in Ottoman documents) as the second consul, see Ahmet Uçar, *140 Yıllık Miras: Güney Afrika'da Osmanlılar* [140 Years of Legacy: The Ottomans in South Africa] (Istanbul: Tez Yayınları, 2000), 310–11.

56 'En ayuda de los refujiados de gerra djidios en Konstantinopla' [In Assistance of the Jewish War Refugees in Istanbul], *El Tyémpo*, 2 April 1913. According to the American Jewish Year Book of 5674 (1913–14), there were about six hundred Levantine Jews living in Seattle in 1912, most of them originating from Rhodes and Gallipoli. This was the biggest Sephardi community in the United States outside of New York City. See

The American Jewish Year Book 5674, 211–12. On the B'nai B'rith Association, see Edward E. Grusd, *B'nai B'rith – The Story of a Covenant* (New York: Appleton-Century, 1966).

57 Esther Benbassa, *Ha-Yahadut Ha-Othmanit beyn Hitma'arvut le-Tzionut 1908–1920* [Ottoman Judaism between Westernization and Zionism 1908–1920] (Jerusalem: Zalman Shazar, 1996), 124–26.

58 Benbassa and Rodrigue, *Jews of the Balkans*, 83.

59 Thus, for example, Angela Guéron, a teacher at the local Alliance school for girls in Edirne, compiled a diary that describes in detail her experiences during the siege of that city. Her diary was kept for decades in the archives of the Alliance Israélite in Paris. It was discovered and published in part by Avigdor Levy in Hebrew and English, edited by Rifat Bali and published in its original French: Angela Guéron, *Journal du siège d'Andrinople, 30 Octobre 1912–26 Mars 1913* (Istanbul: The Isis Press, 2002).

60 *The American Jewish Year Book 5674*, 221.

61 See, for example, *Ha-Mitzpe*, vol. 8, 21 February 1913.

62 See, for example, the advertisement that appeared in *Ha-Mitzpe*, vol. 7, 7 February 1912.

63 For different interpretations of the Balkan Wars and their ramifications for the Ottoman Empire, its Jewish communities and the future of Zionism, see, as a random example, *Ha-Shiloah* (a Zionist monthly published in Odessa), vol. 27 (Av 5672–Tevet 5673 [August 1912–December 1913]).

64 For the writings of nineteenth-century Jewish Orientalists on the Islamic-Jewish cultural symbiosis in the medieval period, see the articles in Martin Kramer (ed.), *The Jewish Discovery of Islam* (Tel Aviv: Tel Aviv University Press, 1999).

65 Paul Nathan, Elkan Adler and Bernhard Kahn, *Bericht über das Balkanhilfswerk* (Berlin: Union des Associations Israélites, 1913).

66 See, for example, 'Gran Rabinato de Turkía' [The Chief Rabbi of Turkey], *El Tyémpo*, 3 January 1913.

67 'La solidaridad djudía' [Jewish Solidarity], *El Nuevo Avenir*, 12 January 1913.

68 *The American Jewish Year Book 5674*, 195.

69 On the Alliance and its 'civilizing mission' regarding the Jewish communities of the Islamic World, see Aron Rodrigue, *Jews and Muslims: Images of Sephardi and Eastern Jewries in Modern Times* (Seattle, WA: University of Washington Press, 2003).

70 'İanât: Hilâl-i Ahmer için' [Assistance: In Favour of the Red Crescent], *Tanin*, 3/18 March 1913. On the small Jewish community of Karamanshah (about 1,400 at the beginning of the twentieth century) and the proposal to establish an Alliance school in the city, see M. Bassan, 'Israélites de Perse', *Bulletin de l'Alliance Israélite Universelle* (1 January 1903), 132–37.

71 An illustrative example of the attitude prevailing among Jewish donors in the West with regard to the backwardness of Ottoman Jews living in the European provinces can be gleaned from the following description, published in the *American Jewish Year Book* of 1913 after the Balkan Wars: 'The Balkan Jew is a man without needs. He lacks the energy and the intense ambition which animates even the poorest of the Eastern Jews. The

striving to better his lot is not so powerful. ... The middle class lives more in accord with European style, but it too has few wants. There are Jews of wealth only in a few of the large cities. Most striking is the absence of what may be called an "intelegenzia", a professional class. ... In spite of the poverty and misery in which the mass of Balkan Jews live, they have seldom sought assistance from their more fortunate brothers in Europe. Having few needs, they are content with a hand-to-mouth existence. Only in great disasters, like the Russo-Turkish War of 1878, the earthquake last year, and great conflagrations, have they made appeals to the charity of the European Jewry' (*The American Jewish Year Book 5674*, 202–3).

72 Tara Zahra, '"Each Nation Only Cares for Its Own": Empire, Nation, and Child Welfare Activism in the Bohemian Lands, 1900–1918', *American Historical Review* 111 (2006), 1378–402.

73 On the role of Rabbi Haim Nahum during the Balkan Wars, see also Benbassa, *Un Grand Rabbin Sepharade*, 36–39, 47.

74 For studies exploring the relations between non-Muslim communities and the Young Turk Revolution and their impacts on the shaping of communal identities through the Ottoman framework, see Vangelis Kechriotis, 'Greek-Orthodox, Ottoman Greeks or Just Greeks? Theories of Coexistence in the Aftermath of the Young Turk Revolution', *Études Balkaniques* 1 (2005), 51–71; Bedross Der Matossian, 'Administrating the Non-Muslims and the "Question of Jerusalem" after the Young Turk Revolution', in Yuval Ben-Bassat and Eyal Ginio (eds), *Late Ottoman Palestine: The Period of Young Turk Rule* (London: I.B. Tauris, 2011), 211–39.

Bibliography

Abrevaya-Stein, Sarah. *Making Jews Modern: The Yiddish and Ladino Press in the Russian and Ottoman Empires*. Bloomington, IN: Indiana University Press, 2003.

Akgün, Seçil Karal, and Murat Uluğtekin. *Hilâl-i Ahmer'den Kızılay'a* [From the Hilâl-i Ahmer to the Kızılay]. Ankara: Beyda Basımevi, 2000.

The American Jewish Year Book 5674. Philadelphia, PA: The Jewish Publication Society of America, 1913.

Anastassiadou, Meropi. 'La protection de l'enfance abandonnée dans l'Empire ottoman au XIXe siècle: Le cas de la communauté grecque orthodoxe de Beyoglu (Istanbul)'. *Südost-Forschungen* 59/60 (2000/2001), 272–323.

Bahri, Yüzbaşı Selânikli. *Balkan Harbinde Sırb Ordusu* [The Serbian Army during the Balkan War]. Istanbul: Tanin Matbaası, 1329 [1913].

Bassan, M. 'Israélites de Perse'. *Bulletin de l'Alliance Israélite Universelle* (1 January 1903), 132–37.

Benbassa, Esther. *Un Grand Rabbin Sepharade en politique 1892–1923*. Paris: Presses du CNRS, 1990.

———. *Ha-Yahadut Ha-Othmanit beyn Hitma'arvut le-Tzionut 1908–1920* [Ottoman Judaism between Westernization and Zionism 1908–1920]. Jerusalem: Zalman Shazar, 1996.

Benbassa, Esther, and Aron Rodrigue. *The Jews of the Balkans: The Judeo-Spanish Community, 15th to 20th Centuries*. Oxford: Blackwell, 1995.

Campos, Michelle U. *Ottoman Brothers: Muslims, Christians, and Jews in Early Twentieth-Century Palestine*. Stanford, CA: Stanford University Press, 2011.

Der Matossian, Bedross. 'Administrating the Non-Muslims and the "Question of Jerusalem" after the Young Turk Revolution', in Yuval Ben-Bassat and Eyal Ginio (eds), *Late Ottoman Palestine: The Period of Young Turk Rule* (London: I.B. Tauris, 2011), 211–39.

Duman, Halûk Harun. *Balkanlara Veda* [A Farewell to the Balkans]. Istanbul: Duyap, 2005.

Elgazi, Eliya. *Haggadah de los Muhadjires* [The Refugees' Haggadah]. Istanbul: Emprimería Ardity i Kastro, 5673 [1913].

Fleischmann, Ellen L. 'The Other "Awakening": The Emergence of Women's Movements in the Modern Middle East, 1900–1940', in Margaret L. Meriwether and Judith E. Tucker (eds), *A Social History of Women and Gender in the Modern Middle East* (Boulder, CO: Westview, 1999), 89–134.

Ginio, Eyal. '*El Dovér al mas Sànto* – The Mobilization of the Ottoman Jewish Population during the Balkan Wars (1912–1913)', in Nathalie Clayer, Hannes Grandits and Robert Pichler (eds), *Social Integration and National Turn in the Late and Post-Ottoman Balkan Societies (1839–1914)* (London: I.B. Tauris, 2011), 157–81.

——. 'Balkan Savaşları Döneminde Kırkkilise (Kırklareli) Musevi Cemaati' [The Jewish Community of Kırkkilise (Kırklareli) during the Balkan Wars], in Kenan Gültürk and S. Bilal Nur (eds), *Balkan Savaşlarının 100. Yılı* [The Centenary of the Balkan Wars] (Bağcılar: Kültür Yayınları, 2012), 554–63.

Göçek, Fatma Müge. 'From Empire to Nation: Images of Women and War in Ottoman Political Cartoons, 1908–1923', in Billie Melman (ed.), *Borderlines – Genders and Identities in War and Peace 1870–1930* (New York/London: Routledge, 1998), 47–72.

Grusd, Edward E. *B'nai B'rith – The Story of a Covenant*. New York: Appleton-Century, 1966.

Guéron, Angela. *Journal du siège d'Andrinople, 30 Octobre 1912–26 Mars 1913*. Istanbul: The Isis Press, 2002.

Halaçoğlu, Ahmet. *Balkan Harbi sırasında Rumeli'den Türk Göçleri (1912–1913)* [Turkish Immigrants from Rumeli during the Balkan War (1912–1913)]. Ankara: Türk Tarih Kurumu, 1995.

Healy, Maureen. *Vienna and the Fall of the Habsburg Empire: Total War and Everyday Life in World War I*. Cambridge: Cambridge University Press, 2004.

Hoffmann, Christhard. 'Between Integration and Rejection: The Jewish Community in Germany, 1914–1918', in John Horne (ed.), *State, Society and Mobilization in Europe during the First World War* (Cambridge: Cambridge University Press, 1997), 89–104.

Kaplan, Yosef. 'The Sephardim in North-Western Europe and the New World', in Haim Beinart (ed.), *The Sephardi Legacy*. Vol. II (Jerusalem: The Magness Press, 1992), 240–87.

Kechriotis, Vangelis. 'Greek-Orthodox, Ottoman Greeks or Just Greeks? Theories of Coexistence in the Aftermath of the Young Turk Revolution'. *Études Balkaniques* 1 (2005), 51–71.

Kramer, Martin (ed.). *The Jewish Discovery of Islam*. Tel Aviv: Tel Aviv University Press, 1999.
Lynch, Katherine. *Individuals, Families, and Communities in Europe, 1200–1800: The Urban Foundations of Western Society*. Cambridge: Cambridge University Press, 2003.
Manfred, Nathan. *Not Heaven Itself: An Autobiography*. Durban: The Knox Publishing Company, 1944.
Nathan, Paul, Elkan Adler and Bernhard Kahn. *Bericht über das Balkanhilfswerk*. Berlin: Union des Associations Israélites, 1913.
Necdet, Raif. *Ufûl* [The Extinction]. Istanbul: Resimli Matbaası, November 1329 [1913].
Ömer [Akalın], Besim. *Hanımlar Efendilere Hilâl-ı Ahmere dair konferans* [A Conference for Women on the Red Crescent]. Istanbul: Ahmet İhsan, 1330 [1913/14].
Osmanlı Hilâl-i Ahmer Cemiyeti 1329–1331 Salnamesi [The Yearbook of the Ottoman Red Crescent 1329/1331 (1913)]. Istanbul: Ahmed İhsan ve Şürekâsı Matbaacılık Osmanlı Şirketi, 1329 [1913].
Özbek, Nadir. 'The Politics of Poor Relief in the Late Ottoman Empire 1876–1914'. *New Perspectives on Turkey* 21 (1999), 1–33.
Özcan, Uğur. 'Ottoman Prisoners of War and Their Repatriation Challenge in the Balkan Wars', in Aleksandar Rastović (ed.), *Prvi balkanski rat 1912/1913. godine: Društveni i civilizacijski smisao. Povodom stogodišnjice oslobođenja Stare Srbije i Makedonije 1912* [The First Balkan War, 1912–1913: Social and Cultural Meaning. On the Occasion of the 100th Anniversary of the Liberation of Old Serbia and Macedonia in 1912]. Vol. I (Niš: The University of Niš, 2013), 159–82. https://www.academia.edu/4722022/Ottoman_Prisoners_of_War_and_their_Repatriation_Challenge_in_Balkan_Wars_P_1912_1913._._1912._V._I_The_University_of_Nis_Ed_Prf._Dr._Aleksandar_Rastovic_Nis_2013 (accessed 5 December 2013).
Phillips-Cohen, Julia. 'Between Civic and Islamic Ottomanism: Jewish Imperial Citizenship in the Hamidian Era'. *International Journal of Middle East Studies* 44 (2012), 237–55.
Quataert, Jean H. 'Mobilizing Philanthropy in the Service of War: The Female Rituals of Care in the New Germany, 1871–1914', in Manfred F. Boemeke, Roger Chickering and Stig Förster (eds), *Anticipating Total War: The German and American Experiences, 1871–1914* (Washington, DC: German Historical Institute; Cambridge: Cambridge University Press, 1999), 217–38.
Rachamimov, Alon. *POWs and the Great War: Captivity on the Eastern Front*. Oxford: Berg, 2002.
Rodrigue, Aron. *Jews and Muslims: Images of Sephardi and Eastern Jewries in Modern Times*. Seattle, WA: University of Washington Press, 2003.
Schmidt, Ephraim. *L'Histoire des juifs à Anvers (Antwerpen)*. Antwerp: Excelsior, 1969.
Şeni, Nora, and Sophie Le Tarnec. *Les Camondo ou l'éclipse d'une fortune*. Arles: Actes Sud, 1997.
Singer, Amy. *Constructing Ottoman Beneficence: An Imperial Soup Kitchen in Jerusalem*. Albany, NY: State University of New York Press, 2002.

Tadžir, Avraham. *Notas Istórikas sovre los Djidios de Bulgaría i la Kommunita de Sofia* [Historical Notes Regarding the Jews of Bulgaria and the Community of Sofia]. Sofia: Nadezna, 1932.

Uçar, Ahmet. *140 Yıllık Miras: Güney Afrika'da Osmanlılar* [140 Years of Legacy: The Ottomans in South Africa]. Istanbul: Tez Yayınları, 2000.

Ueno, Masayuki. '"For Fatherland and the State": Armenians Negotiate the Tanzimat Reforms'. *International Journal of Middle East Studies* 45 (2013), 93–109.

Wall, Richard, and Jay Winter (eds). *The Upheaval of War: Family, Work and Welfare in Europe 1914–1918*. Cambridge: Cambridge University Press, 1988.

Winter, Jay, and Antoine Prost. *The Great War in History: Debates and Controversies, 1914 to the Present*. Cambridge: Cambridge University Press, 2005.

Yotfata [sic], Rabbi. *Haggadah echa apropyada por la anyada de la gerra del anyo 5673* [A Haggadah Adapted for the War of the Year 5673]. Istanbul: Emprímería Ardity i Kastro, 1913.

Zahra, Tara. '"Each Nation Only Cares for Its Own": Empire, Nation, and Child Welfare Activism in the Bohemian Lands, 1900–1918'. *American Historical Review* 111 (2006), 1378–402.

Zohar, Zion (ed.). *Sephardic and Mizrahi Jewry: From the Golden Age of Spain to Modern Times*. New York: New York University Press, 2005.

14

THE ASSISTANCE OF THE BRITISH RED CROSS TO THE OTTOMAN EMPIRE

Oya Dağlar Macar

This chapter investigates the medical aspect of the Balkan Wars from the viewpoint of the doctors, surgeons, nurses and other medical staff who assisted the Ottomans either under the umbrella of the British Red Cross or as individual volunteers. This group primarily consisted of well-educated British citizens of the middle and upper classes who worked in various ranks in the medical professions. They represented a small number of people who witnessed the war from a non-military perspective. Because of their education and their social position, many of them wrote in magazines and newspapers about their experiences after their return. Some of them also published memoirs. These texts give us the opportunity to examine this period from a different perspective, approaching it from the viewpoint of a 'history of experience' (*Erfahrungsgeschichte*). Their writings and assessments carry great importance in that they tell us from a medical standpoint about the health problems they encountered during the war, the treatments they applied, the Ottoman soldiers' reactions to these treatments and how all of the above influenced the war's outcome. The texts also shed a historical light on how this group, which until now has not received much of a voice, perceived the war. By examining medical sources, this study should be seen as a first step towards a more comprehensive investigation of the Balkan Wars and fills a gap in the existing scholarship. Scholarly studies on the experiences, observations and assessments of medical teams, not only in the Ottoman Empire but also in other countries involved in the Balkan Wars, will bring to light a different dimension of the conflict.

The British Red Cross and Red Crescent Corps in the Ottoman Empire

At the beginning of the First Balkan War, the British Red Cross, based on the First Geneva Convention (1864), decided to send aid units to the five Balkan countries involved: the Ottoman Empire, Bulgaria, Serbia, Greece and Montenegro. In order to be able to offer the Balkan countries assistance in the framework of the Geneva Convention, the British Red Cross Fund was established, together with a special committee that would ensure the correct administration and usage of the fund.[1] Following the fund's establishment, the director of the British Red Cross, Nathaniel Lord Rothschild, issued a public call for donations. Because the existing budget was not sufficient to put together medical teams, he asked for financial support from the British people,[2] many of whom contributed financially. With the approval of the countries involved, the British Red Cross began to form several medical corps.

The call issued by the Red Cross was not limited to financial assistance, however. In order to form medical corps, there was also a great need for volunteer doctors and medical personnel, because the warring countries were not organized enough to provide health services to the military, and there was an extreme scarcity of personnel and medical supplies. The British Red Cross published newspaper announcements calling for volunteers wishing to go to the Near East.[3] The organization received a tremendous response and established a number of corps. In the end, the British Red Cross sent four medical corps to the Ottoman Empire during the Balkan Wars. Before their departure, volunteers received lessons in various basic subjects.[4] Each of them was provided with medical equipment, including surgical tools, medicine and supplies. The director of these four corps was Major Doughty Wylie.[5] The first three corps, consisting of fifty-six persons, arrived in Istanbul on 5 November 1912, the fourth on 5 December of the same year.[6]

Throughout the war, the British Red Cross corps offered their services in Istanbul in the School of Fine Arts (Sanayi-i Nefise Mektebi) on the Alibey Farmstead in Çatalca and in the hospitals they established in Beykoz, Kalikratya and Ayastefanos/San Stefano (Yeşilköy). Some of them also worked in the Clemow Hospital in Şişli. In addition, Muslims of Indian origin living in Britain sent medical corps to the Ottoman Empire. This aid was provided under the banner of the British Medical Mission led by Amer Ali, one of India's foremost political leaders, who resided in London. This corps, named the Committee of the British Red Crescent Society, was under the directorship of Colonel Sortie.[7] The British Red Crescent issued a call in the British newspapers on 12

October 1912. The Muslims of Great Britain, India and other British colonies requested support in order to help those injured in the war, the sick and the needy. Mirroring the establishment of the British Red Cross Fund, the British Red Crescent Fund was brought into existence.[8]

A British Red Crescent corps consisting of fifteen persons arrived in Istanbul immediately after the outset of the war and first settled down in the building of the Rüştiye Mektebi in Üsküdar,[9] which had been turned into a hospital. Hospital beds and other basic needs were met by the Ottoman Red Crescent Society.[10] However, because a ceasefire was announced shortly thereafter and because transporting patients to Üsküdar proved difficult, the corps left this hospital and moved to San Stefano. The Health Administration moved the British Red Crescent's team to the European part of Istanbul, where it was stationed in the barracks of Ayastefanos, which had been established for cholera patients, and there they treated the sick. For their services, the corps received twenty Turkish lira per week from the Ottoman Red Crescent.[11]

The British Red Cross and Aid Contributions

Why did the Red Cross and its many corps provide aid to the Ottomans? Generally, there were two different groups of medical staff. First, there was the group who came as part of the British Red Cross or Red Crescent's efforts. One of the foremost reasons for the provision of aid by the Red Cross was legal in nature. When Great Britain signed the Geneva Convention in 1864, it guaranteed that it would send humanitarian and medical aid to warring countries by means of the Red Cross's neutral humanitarian organization.[12] Hence, the Red Cross had a legal obligation. The second group was not connected to any national or international organization and volunteered purely for personal reasons, the most obvious being moral in nature – to provide humanitarian aid. Still, outside of these two groups we can observe other individual or collective reasons. Foremost among these was a curiosity and interest in the East. From an Orientalist viewpoint, this war was an opportunity to see the mysterious East, maybe even the best way to experience and understand Islam. For example, A. Duncan Johnstone, who came to Istanbul with the British Red Cross corps and worked as stretcher-bearer in various camps and hospitals, explained similar sentiments in the following words:

> Ever since I was a small boy I have had a great desire to see the East. In fact, this passion once induced me to go into the head-master's study at a preparatory school and take a Koran off one of the shelves, for which I

remember getting a good licking. On the outbreak of the Balkan War this desire reawoke in me, and I tried in various ways to get out to Turkey, my idea being to serve as a volunteer with the Turkish forces; but owing to the proclamation of neutrality by England, this was impossible. One morning, happening to read in the Daily Telegraph that volunteers were urgently needed for the Red Cross work in the Near East, I quickly made up my mind, and that afternoon, leaving my work early, I rushed home to change preparatory to going down to Victoria Street.[13]

Volunteers also went to the Ottoman Empire to acquire professional experience. The war promised those working in war surgery that they would see many diverse cases, be able to apply theoretical knowledge in practice, and gain expertise. One cannot over-emphasize the importance and value of this motivation. In fact, we know that medical professionals responded in great numbers to the newspaper announcements of the Red Cross searching for corps volunteers.

Yet those who wanted to volunteer for medical positions were not limited to the Red Cross. Many also personally contacted British consulates in the Balkan countries. Large numbers of applications from doctors, surgeons, medical students and other medical personnel are found in the Prime Ministry's Ottoman Archives. In a document that was sent from the British embassy on 15 October 1912 to the Ottoman Foreign Ministry, for instance, we learn that various British citizens applied to the British embassy, stating that they would like to serve in the Ottoman army as surgeons and certified nurses. The British embassy requested that the Ottoman government or the Ottoman Red Crescent Society directly notify these persons of the answer, whether positive or negative.[14] Another telegram that Tevfik Pasha (1845–1936), the Ottoman ambassador to London, sent to the Foreign Ministry on 8 October 1912 states that during the Balkan War, British doctors and surgeons applied to serve in military hospitals.[15] There are many more such examples.

Slogans such as 'patriotism' and 'service to the motherland' were also used to ensure the public's contributions to the campaign in Great Britain. Even the Red Cross was co-opted for this. For instance, in the Red Cross's newspaper call for medical personnel, the director of the British Red Cross, Lord Rothschild, emphasized that although the conditions would be difficult, it was important that 'the young generations serving their own country' help with the war efforts in order to gain experience. His statement continued:

The details of medical practice, as learned in the schools and practised in civil life, form only a small part of the work that necessarily falls to the lot of a military medical officer on active service. The remainder can be properly learned only in war, and experience has shown that the most well-meaning and competent medical man, until he has acquired that knowledge, is almost as much of an encumbrance as a help. Further, these qualities of discipline, command and subordination, and of organisation are, in themselves, of the utmost value, not only in war, but in any time of public calamity, such as earthquakes, rioting, mining and other disasters on a large scale; and in the trend of modern medical practice will undoubtedly prove a valuable asset to their possessor.[16]

As can be expected, another motivation for the Red Cross was that, by going abroad and helping another country, it would introduce both the Red Cross and the Red Crescent internationally and also examine where its own strengths and weaknesses lay. During the Russian-Japanese War (1904–5), for example, the excellent organization of the Japanese Red Cross as well as its efficient administration of human and material resources very much impressed its British counterpart.[17] The British Red Cross's experiences in the Boer War (1899–1902) had brought to light its shortcomings; furthermore, these experiences added much medical knowledge in general. In fact, it was no coincidence that many British Red Cross doctors constantly compared the Balkan Wars to the Russian-Japanese and Boer Wars.[18] One of these British Red Cross doctors was Doughty Wylie, who served in the hospital in the art school in Istanbul. Another was Professor Dr Jacques-Ambroise Monprofit, whom the Greek Red Cross appointed as the director of the surgical society at Thessaloniki. In his position, Monprofit had the opportunity to personally observe developments in Athens, Thessaloniki, Skopje and Belgrade; he emphasized that the knowledge that the military surgeons had gained in the Boer War in South Africa and in the Russian-Japanese War had been proven right in the most stunning way.[19]

Another reason for sending medical aid during the Balkan Wars was the increasing effort to modernize. Since the nineteenth century, wars had constituted a field of experimentation and implementation for medical, scientific and technological innovations. From the use of X-ray machines to bacteriological tests, experiments with new medicines to trying out antiseptics, many innovations were employed to save soldiers' lives during wars. The Balkan Wars constituted a very important event in which Western medical professionals could showcase their expertise and new findings. In fact, some of the doctors who came to the Ottoman Empire during the war gained a name for themselves in their fields. At the beginning of the war, a doctor from the Indian public health administration with expertise in treating cholera, for example, arrived in the empire. In another instance, a bacteriologist specializing in tropical diseases served during the Balkan Wars. Some of them came as volunteers while others were brought by the Ottoman government based on specific needs. These experts gave Ottoman medical professionals the opportunity to witness various innovations and the chance to modernize in turn. Apart from their destructive impact, wars also compelled modernization and medical progress.

Finally, there is the possibility that the willingness to provide aid was based on certain religious expectations. Indeed, Dr Muhammad Ensari, who served with the Egyptian Red Crescent, claimed that British Red Cross doctors conducted missionary work in hospitals during the Balkan Wars. Even though this claim was never proven, it caused an uproar among Muslims in Great Britain and India, provoking serious reactions against Great Britain and leaving the British government in a difficult position.[20]

The British Red Cross and War Surgery

The expectation that they would gain professional knowledge was certainly one of the primary motivations of British doctors who brought medical aid to the Balkan countries. In fact, most of them shared their experiences in writing after their return home. For example, one can find articles by many doctors and surgeons about the Balkan Wars in *The Lancet* and the *British Medical Journal*, two of Britain's foremost medical publications. Moreover, there are many articles published by Red Cross doctors in various newspapers, such as *The Manchester Guardian*, *The Observer*, *The Advance* and *The Times*. Even though their number is much smaller, many who served with the Red Cross also wrote their memoirs. These texts contain much valuable information and important observations, especially in terms of war surgery and medicine.

The principle observation was the high mortality rate at the beginning of the war. Dr C. Max Page and Dr Sydney Vere Appleyard, who worked in the museum hospital in Istanbul, drew attention to the great decrease in the mortality rate over the duration of the war.[21] For instance, of the first 130 patients who arrived at that hospital, fifty-four died, thus the mortality rate was as high as 41.6 per cent. In the following 448 cases, however, the mortality rate fell to 4 per cent.[22] What could have been the reason for this change? The first answer that comes to mind is the violence of the battles and the extensive injuries caused by weapons. Yet, according to the published information, the reasons can be found in ineffective first aid early in the war, the delayed transportation of patients to hospitals, starvation, contagious diseases, cold weather, a demoralized attitude and unhygienic conditions.[23]

Although some of the wounded soldiers could have been easily treated with basic interventions, many ended up needing surgery, simply because they had not received proper first aid and were left without medical treatment under terrible conditions. As a consequence, many could not be saved even by surgical intervention. According to Wylie's explanations, the first arriving soldiers were malnourished both before and after injury.[24] Reports in *The Lancet* supported Wylie in his assessment: starvation was the biggest problem of all. Many of the injured soldiers who arrived in the hospital had not eaten anything for two or three days. Some of them had eaten only grass and wild herbs for as much as a week.[25] Thus, their immune system had declined and could no longer fight diseases.

In the first months of the war, patient transport did not function properly either. Much of this was because preparations had not been completed during the short mobilization period. The weather and the poor road conditions were equally an important factor. The Balkan Wars began in the winter months, and therefore transportation would have been very difficult even under normal circumstances. Heavy rains made for even worse conditions. The bad weather only contributed to the occurrence of epidemics such as cholera. Once all these negative factors coalesced, the already insufficient transportation system and health services collapsed completely.[26]

The first soldiers brought to the hospitals of Istanbul had mostly been wounded in the battles of Kırklareli and Lüleburgaz and arrived in the city after eight to twelve days. Most of the patients were not only injured, but also stricken with dysentery, cholera or various gastrointestinal ailments.[27] These ailments were accompanied by anaemia, anasarca and ascites,[28] complications that often led to death. Hence, most of the injured who were brought to the hospital did not die of their wounds, but of other causes.[29] The above-mentioned stretcher-bearer Johnstone described in detail what he saw when he went to the Haydarpaşa train station to collect patients:

> We found that most of the wounded were from Kirk-Kilise three weeks earlier. Many had not been attended to since the first field dressing after the battle, and were almost starving. The wounds were horrible to look at, and had grown twice their size through neglect. They were also full of maggots and earth-worms, which had to be scraped out with the fingers. One man had had some wooden splinters behind his eye for twelve days without any attention; the smell in the hospital was dreadful. It appeared to us at the time that the Turkish Medical Service and the Ottoman Red Crescent seemed to be absolutely disorganised, no provision of any sort being made for the men.[30]

Soldiers who arrived after some weeks in the war were more fortunate. The provisioning and medical services for the soldiers on the Çatalca front were reorganized after some time, and the condition of the soldiers improved both morally and physically. Wounded soldiers were now transported to Istanbul within one to four days. With this came a major change in the appearance of the soldiers, who in the first months of battle had been exhausted, sickly and left to their fate. The mortality rate decreased considerably.[31]

The second observation discussed by British surgeons in their writings was related to the importance of first aid. Doctors had learned about the importance of first aid in treating gunshot injuries during the Boer War. During the Balkan Wars, however, the Turkish first aid and the medical services on the home front were worse than the British during the Boer War. Broken bones became irritated and infected due to the disorganized patient transport and insufficient immobilization and cast techniques. Most of the patients reaching hospitals had not received any dressings for their injuries. Those with broken bones were often merely bandaged, and had not been fitted with proper fixation apparatuses. All these deficiencies made even simple fractures a serious problem.[32]

Comparing Turkish soldiers with those from other Balkan countries, Professor Octave Laurent, of Brussels, observed that Turkish soldiers experienced surgical problems arising from wound infection at a much higher rate. One of the primary reasons was the lack of aseptic dressing, which was not applied very often, patient transport was very slow and hospital conditions were insufficient. All these problems resulted once again in the defeat and demoralization of the otherwise sturdy, stoic Turkish soldiers. In contrast, the first aid services of other Balkan countries were much better organized. For instance, France supplied first aid material for the Greek army, and the Netherlands did the same for the Bulgarian and Serbian armies. According to Monprofit, it was obvious that first aid material at the front was life-saving. Every Greek and Serbian soldier carried a small bag with dressings and knew how to apply them in case no surgeon was available. A Serbian surgeon reported to Monprofit that the wounds of the eight hundred injured soldiers he saw close to Bitola had all been dressed within a very short time span.[33]

The widespread occurrence of gangrene among Ottoman soldiers was also widely reported. In an article published in *The Manchester Guardian* on 11 December 1912, a British surgeon who arrived in Istanbul with the British Red Cross wrote that there were many patients with gangrene in the cholera hospital that had been established in the

Greek school in Ayastefanos/San Stefano.[34] The number of gangrene cases was also elevated in the museum hospital. The British Red Cross doctors distinguished between three types of gangrene: limb gangrene, emphysematous gangrene and symmetrical gangrene. Among these, the latter, which affected multiple limbs – if there was gangrene afflicting one leg, it would also appear on the other – had not been significantly observed before the Balkan Wars, but now there was a great increase in this type. According to the observations of the British Red Cross doctors, there were six patients with this disease in the museum hospital, three in the hospital in Beykoz and many more in Ayastefanos/San Stefano. Dr Lothar Dreyer reported thirty-one cases in the German hospital in Istanbul. It was Dr McClean who had great success in treating this type of gangrene.[35]

Wounds that were not treated in time and soldiers left in cold, wet trenches for long periods contributed to the spread of gangrene. A British surgeon who worked in the cholera hospital in Ayastefanos/San Stefano explained:

> I have chosen the patients for the tent hospital chiefly out of the cholera barracks. Most of them have also badly inflamed and gangrenous feet and there has been no attempt of any kind made by the Turks either to clean or dress them, much less amputate and save them. A man tonight told me he was walking forty days through the freezing mud without any shoes, and his leg needing amputation. Most of them give a history of sleeping all night in the trenches in the rain and very cold weather, and waking up with feet numb and swollen. The pressure of their puttees cuts off the circulation, and their feet become frost-bitten. Many of them have dysentery as well. The various diseases which roughly have been drafted here as cholera are in reality a mixture of typhoid, dysentery, typhus, inanition, gangrene, septic disease, and cholera.[36]

The boots traditionally worn by the Turkish soldiers also provoked the widespread occurrence of gangrene. The boots were tightly wrapped around the legs with laces, obstructing blood circulation and causing blood clots. The extremities of the exhausted soldiers froze when they were exposed to the cold, wet air, and the disrupted blood vessel function turned the symptoms of exposure into gangrene. The best-known treatment for light cases was to keep the toes dry. If the gangrene had not spread too quickly, the limb was amputated. If it had spread and the symptoms of blood poisoning had appeared, the disease was equivalent to a death sentence.[37]

Surgeons serving in the Balkan Wars also drew attention to the way different kinds of firearms led to diverse types of injuries. Principally, the doctors realized that injuries caused by bullets and shrapnel differed significantly. For instance, during the eleven weeks he worked in the British hospital in Şişli, the British Red Cross surgeon Dr Sidney Smith treated 110 Turkish soldiers who had been wounded by bullets and shrapnel. Afterwards, he published in *The Lancet* his observations on soldiers with chest wounds. He distinguished between two types of injuries: wounds caused by rifle bullets and shrapnel wounds. Smith reported that bullet wounds were relatively harmless and generally healed without serious complications. If the injury was caused by a Mannlicher bullet from a close distance and at great speed, this could entail serious problems; if not, then the bullet went straight through. Only in two cases did the bullet remain in the body. Shrapnel wounds, however, were much more serious. Again, Smith distinguished two kinds: those caused by shrapnel exploding close to the body and entering the bones, which generally led to sepsis, and injuries from shells exploding close by. The shells were usually called spherical bullets because of their rounded tips, causing serious injuries.[38] Wylie made similar observations. Turkish soldiers used Mauser rifles bought from the Germans; a bullet from these rifles entering the body at great speed did not do much damage, causing only a small entrance wound. But shrapnel, which entered the body at a lower speed, did much greater damage, thrusting the torn uniform fabric into the flesh and causing infection.[39]

According to Monprofit's observations, bullet wounds also led to fewer casualties. The Mannlicher bullets that the Turks used in the Balkan Wars were a long type of bullet and caused clean entry wounds, with the tissue closing quickly. Aseptic measures helped a great deal, so that barely a scar remained. Even in injuries to bones or the thorax, few complications occurred. Monprofit also emphasized that shrapnel wounds were very different. He observed that there was a steady decrease in infantry fire, but an increase in the usage of artillery, meaning that instead of being wounded in man-to-man combat, soldiers were now more often injured by artillery shells launched from a distance. Shrapnel wounds were always more dangerous, as bones were smashed to pieces, ribs broken and fatal wounds dealt.[40] Finally, Dr Samuel Osborn's information largely confirmed the knowledge of Wylie, Smith and Monprofit. According to Osborn, bullet wounds were not as serious as they had been in the Boer War, when soft-nosed bullets were employed. The bullets used in the Balkan Wars only caused small open wounds and few serious injuries.[41] Rather, most serious injuries resulted from shrapnel.

The mortality rate of the wounded represented another shared observation concerning war surgery. Sources offer different statistics, resulting from the fact that doctors only gave numbers related to the hospitals in which they worked. For example, Wylie emphasized that in the museum hospital the mortality rate among surgical cases was very high – 13.1 per cent.[42] He reported that the gunshot wounds brought to his hospital were caused by rifle bullets in 60 per cent of the cases, and by shrapnel in 40 per cent.[43] Professor Laurent stated that bullet wounds were five times more likely to occur than shrapnel wounds, but that most soldiers on the front died from shrapnel injuries.[44] The numbers given by Professor Dr Antoine Depage of Brussels diverge yet again: among the Turks, 80 per cent of the wounds were caused by shrapnel. Another 10 per cent were due to rifle fire, and the remaining 10 per cent caused by bayonets and swords. In comparison, among the Allied forces shrapnel wounds accounted for 15 per cent, bullet wounds for 80 per cent, and bayonet and sword wounds from man-to-man combat for 5 per cent. Depage concluded that a much higher proportion of Turkish soldiers were rendered *hors de combat* than their counterparts in the Balkan Allies. The Allied forces, then, used more artillery against the Turks, leading to serious injuries among the Turkish soldiers and decimating the Turkish forces. It is noteworthy that Depage was able to draw such a comparison because he shared information about the cases he encountered, the treatments he applied, the recovery and the mortality rates with Monprofit, who worked for the Greek side. Depage was also a pioneer in another undertaking: with the help of the Imperial Society of Surgery in Istanbul, he started a protest movement against what he saw as the inhumane use of shrapnel. Monprofit did not believe that Depage would be successful in this endeavour, since the artillery skills of the Allied forces were more developed than those of the Turks.[45]

However, statistical information regarding the real causes of death among soldiers – apart from statistics given by doctors – was rarely collected or evaluated. The lack of autopsies due to religious objections prevented a sound evaluation of the causes of death,[46] and medical records remained incomplete.[47] This information would have offered important data not only for the British medical profession, but for medicine in general. Nevertheless, we can reasonably assume that the knowledge and experience acquired in the Balkan Wars were used efficiently in World War I, which followed closely on its heels.

General Observations about the Ottomans

The relations between Ottoman soldiers and medical professionals represented another common issue in the writings of the Red Cross medical staff. Interestingly, this dynamic manifested itself predominantly in the medical corps members' many critical comments about foreign journalists reporting on the war. Most Red Cross doctors and surgeons thought that the journalists held prejudices against Ottoman soldiers, that they made incorrect generalizations and offered interpretations that did not fit with the realities of war. One instance was related to the use of anaesthesia. Several war correspondents wrote that Turkish soldiers refused anaesthesia; however, British doctors vehemently denied this claim. For example, Osborn emphasized that the information given in a European newspaper about Turkish soldiers refusing anaesthesia for religious reasons was completely unfounded.[48] Instead, he said that Turkish soldiers never refused chloroform, but that when doctors had to perform surgery on them without chloroform because it was unavailable, they endured the pain with admirable bravery.[49] He thought that the terrible defeat of the Turkish army on the front was not due to a lack of courage or poor battle tactics, but rather the army's unpreparedness.[50] In contrast to such general newspaper claims, medical corps members reported that Turkish soldiers were grateful for the chloroform, and Turkish as well as Red Cross doctors usually operated on patients under anaesthesia.[51]

There are nevertheless several related observations for which all sources provide unanimous evidence. For instance, Turkish soldiers vehemently refused amputation, and they would not change their minds even when being told their wounds would be lethal otherwise. Some of the injured lost their lives because of their refusal to undergo amputation.[52] The above-mentioned stretcher-bearer Johnstone wrote that '[m]any of the wounded showed a curious aversion to operations of any kind. Whether it was that they mistrusted us, or that the loss of a limb minimised their chances of paradise, I don't know'.[53]

Another often-repeated observation was that Turkish soldiers endured even the worst injuries without complaint, expressing pain or excessive emotion, and that they awaited death in a quiet and dignified manner. This behaviour drew the attention of many foreign doctors; while some of them related it to the Turkish people's bravery and endurance, others thought it was rooted in a resignation to one's fate stemming from their religious beliefs. Osborn reported that not a single soldier had complained about his wounds or the lengthy duration of the treatment.[54]

In a similar manner, Dr Frank G. Clemow, the director of the British hospital in Şişli and personal doctor of the British embassy personnel, summarized his experiences in a lecture he gave on 26 April 1913, before he returned to his home country. Of the approximately two hundred patients they treated in five and a half months, he stated, all of the soldiers behaved respectfully.⁵⁵ Wylie, too, gave a lecture on 26 April 1913, in which he remembered the Ottoman soldiers with great appreciation, declaring that it was impossible not to love an Ottoman soldier if one got to know him.⁵⁶ Johnstone claimed also that in spite of the awful conditions, the patients were quiet, showed great strength of character and did not move or speak; this greatly impressed and surprised the entire corps.⁵⁷

In contrast to the generally positive opinion about the Ottoman soldiers, however, Ottoman medical professionals were seen in a completely different light. British doctors and medical professionals who worked together with Turkish medical staff were of the opinion that they did not like to work. For instance, Wylie observed that, although there were many Turkish staff members in the museum hospital, only a few did their job well. He continued with the observation that only a small number of the trained male nurses and Turkish staff members running the wards accomplished their tasks successfully.⁵⁸ Another British doctor wrote that there were also Turkish doctors and medical personnel in the hospital in the Greek school, but that they were disorganized and could not complete their work in a timely fashion.⁵⁹ Johnstone observed that Turkish medical staff would never refuse to do a specific duty, but that they would always procrastinate, and therefore various jobs were constantly impeded. According to the British Red Cross staff, one of the words the Turks most often used was 'tomorrow', and the most often proffered statement was that 'apart from the sun rising in the East and setting in the West nothing is certain'. This attitude was seen as a characteristic derived from the Turks' fatalism.⁶⁰ While Red Cross medical staff cared for a limited number of Ottoman patients and medical professionals, they generalized their experiences as a reflection of all Turks, suggesting that they looked down on native medical professionals.

The Indian Red Crescent and the British Red Cross

Another question that deserves consideration is whether the British Red Cross corps sent to the Ottoman Empire during the Balkan Wars were considered a vehicle of British politics. In other words, did British politics have any influence over the Red Cross, which was known as a humanitarian aid organization? This question cannot be easily answered. Nevertheless, the criticism of the Indian Red Crescent, which came from one of the biggest, most important British colonies, did to a certain extent influence Great Britain's Balkan politics. During the

Balkan Wars, Muslims in Great Britain – foremost among them Indians – openly sided with the Ottoman Empire. They attempted to cast this war as a 'Crusade' and to secure every possible type of support for the Ottomans against the Balkan countries. The extensive assistance by the Muslims of London and India and the medical aid of the Indian Red Crescent corps strengthened the relations between the Ottoman Empire and India to an unprecedented extent. Moreover, Muslims wrote to various newspapers asking for political, financial and moral support for the Ottomans, gave lectures and organized meetings. According to a news item from Reuters, 'Orientals' in England arranged a gathering in Oxford under the leadership of Seyyid Haydar Riza, where participants swore their allegiance to the caliphate, condemning the inhumane attack against Turkey. On the other hand, they wished Britain would intervene and negotiate an end to the war.[61] When they did not see any developments in this direction, they began to criticize the British government.

The criticism by the Red Crescent official Ensari against the Red Cross only added to the tensions. Ensari published an article in the newspaper *Comrade* on 8 February 1913, stating that the work done by the German Red Cross hospital in Turkey, the British Red Cross hospitals and the French Red Cross hospitals was ineffective. According to this article, the doctors working in these hospitals deliberately mistreated patients who would have been curable with regular intervention, intentionally removed organs where unnecessary, and left their patients disabled.[62] Ensari contended that British doctors were less effective than bone-setters. As soon as the article appeared, many Indian Muslims began to protest. Although the British government warned that it would take legal steps if Ensari continued his accusations, he did not retract. When news about British doctors doing missionary work was added to these accusations, tensions between the British government and the Indian Red Crescent came to a head and left British politicians uneasy.[63] None of these accusations were proven to be true, but anti-Christian sentiments among Indian Muslims escalated even further. Various interpretations of the events appeared in the Indian press, claiming that Britain felt sympathy for Christians in the Balkans and that it supported the dismantling of the Ottoman Empire.[64] These developments had a lasting political influence: they left the British government in a difficult position, leading to its adoption of a negative stance towards the Ottomans during and at the end of the Balkan Wars.[65]

Conclusion

During the Balkan Wars, the Ottoman Empire received aid from many foreign Red Cross and Red Crescent organizations that emerged from the Geneva Convention. Great Britain was one of the many countries that sent medical assistance. Many doctors, surgeons, nurses and other medical professionals came to the Ottoman Empire as part of the British Red Cross and the British Red Crescent, which assisted wounded, sick soldiers by establishing hospitals in Istanbul and on the front. Apart from these organizations, many British medical professionals also individually came to Istanbul as volunteers. Regardless of where they came from and in addition to humanitarian motives, volunteers embarked on the mission for various reasons: a personal interest in the Orient, to acquire professional experience in different medical fields, to find opportunities to apply the newest medical innovations of the day, and especially to gain new knowledge in war surgery. In fact, after the end of the war, returning doctors shared their newly acquired knowledge with their colleagues by writing articles and books. One of the most significant points that doctors and surgeons drew attention to was the opportunity to compare the Balkan Wars with the Russo-Japanese War and the Second Boer War. By using the knowledge and experience gained in the Balkan Wars, they may have saved the lives of tens of thousands of soldiers in World War I.

Important know-how was also gained in terms of the organization of medicine, its administration and operation by the British Red Cross and Red Crescent during the Balkan Wars. There is no doubt about the significance of learning how to administer a medical corps effectively, to use medical supplies and to correctly organize logistics under exceptional war conditions. Having understood where their shortcomings lay, the British Red Cross and Red Crescent were able to improve and perfect their operations.

Oya Dağlar Macar is Professor in the Political Science and International Relations Department of Istanbul Commerce University, Istanbul. She is interested in the history of medicine and the social history of the late Ottoman Empire. Her monographic works are *War, Epidemics and Medicine in the Late Ottoman Empire (1912–1918)* (SOTA, 2008), *Balkan Savaşlari'nda Salgin Hastaliklar ve Saglik Hizmetleri* [Infectious Diseases and Medicine in the Balkan Wars] (Libra, 2009) and *Beyaz Rus Ordusu Turkiye'de* [The White Russian Army in Turkey] (with Elçin Macar; Libra 2010). She is a member of the Turkish Society for the History of Medicine.

Notes

1 'British Red Cross Balkan Fund', *The Lancet* 180(4,652) (1912), 1,179.
2 'Surgeons Needed for the Balkan War', *The Lancet* 180(4,652) (1912), 1,168.
3 Ibid.
4 A. Duncan Johnstone, *With the British Red Cross in Turkey: The Experience of Two Volunteers, 1912–1913* (London: James Nisbet, 1913), 6.
5 The following doctors were members of these corps. First corps: C.M. Page (from among the surgeons of the Hospital of St. Thomas), Dr H.L. Mann, Dr L.G. Bourdillon; second corps: Dr E.D. Anderson, Dr F.R. Thornton, Dr R. Ogier Ward; third corps: Dr S.V. Appleyard, Dr E.L. Steele, Dr M.C. Gardner; fourth corps: Captain J.H. Horton I.M.S. D.S.O., Captain A.B. Smallman R.A.M.C., Captain Lloyd Jones R.A.M.C.: Red Crescent Archive (Ankara/Turkey), box no. 21, document no. 13.
6 Red Crescent Archive (Ankara/Turkey), box no. 21, document no. 13. There are some inconsistencies between the documents in the Prime Ministry's Ottoman Archives in Istanbul (Başbakanlık Osmanlı Arşivi, hereafter: BOA) and those in the Red Crescent Archive regarding the arrival dates in Istanbul and the size of the first mission of the British Red Cross. The documents in the BOA show that a well-equipped British Red Cross mission under the leadership of Wylie and his wife arrived in Istanbul on 4 November 1912. The corps consisted of a total of sixty-six persons, among them twelve doctors, eleven assistants and forty-three nurses. See BOA, HR SYS 2025/5. In this case, the information recorded by the British Red Cross officials themselves can be considered more reliable.
7 BOA, İ. MBH, no.13/20.B. 1331; BOA, BEO, no. 4174/313007.
8 'The British Red Crescent Society and the War', *The Manchester Guardian*, 12 October 1912, 5.
9 The names of the British Red Crescent corps members are as follows: Director Colonel Sortie, surgeon Dr Calthrop, surgeon Dr Baylin, intern Mr Wylie and intern Mr Stavela, nurse and pharmacist Knapland, and three male and six female nurses, accounting for a total of fifteen people: Red Crescent Archive, folder no. 211.
10 *1329–1331 Salnamesi* [The Ottoman Red Crescent Yearbook, 1913–1915] (Istanbul: Ahmet İhsan ve Sürekası Matbaası, 1915), 188–89.
11 Ibid.; Seçil Karal Akgün and Murat Uluğtekin, *Hilal-i Ahmer'den Kızılay'a* [From Ottoman Red Crescent to Kızılay], Vol. I (Ankara: Kızılay, 2000), 410.
12 Angela Bennett, *The Geneva Convention: The Hidden Origins of the Red Cross* (Stroud: Sutton Publishing, 2006), 212.
13 Johnstone, *With the British Red Cross in Turkey*, 3–4.
14 BOA, HR SYS 2025/5, 45.
15 BOA, HR SYS 2025/5, 19.
16 'Surgeons Needed for The Balkan War', *The Lancet* 180(4,652) (1912), 1,168.
17 John F. Hutchinson, *Champions of Charity: War and the Rise of the Red Cross* (Boulder, CO: Westview Press, 1996), 248.
18 'Medical and Surgical Experience in the Balkan War', *The Lancet* 182(4,691) (1913), 240.

19 'Surgery in the Balkans War', *British Medical Journal* 1(2,725) (1913), 623–24, here 624.
20 Azmi Özcan, *Pan-İslamizm: Osmanlı Devleti Hindistan Müslümanları ve İngiltere, 1877–1924* [Pan-Islamism: Ottoman Empire, Indian Muslims and Britain, 1877–1924] (Ankara: Türkiye Diyanet Vakfı, 1997), 191–211.
21 'The British Red Cross in the Balkan War', *The Lancet* 182(4,691) (1913), 235.
22 'Medical and Surgical Experience in the Balkan War', *The Lancet* 182(4,690) (1913), 164.
23 'Medical and Surgical Experience in the Balkan War', *The Lancet* 182(4,691) (1913), 237; 'The British Red Cross in the Balkan War', *The Lancet* 182(4,691) (1913), 235.
24 'Medical and Surgical Experience in the Balkan War', *The Lancet* 182(4,690) (1913), 163–64.
25 'Cholera and War in the Near East', *The Lancet* 181(4,668) (1913), 485.
26 'Constantinople, the War, Cholera, Disease, Privation', *The Lancet* 180(4,656) (1912), 1,470.
27 'Medical and Surgical Experience in the Balkan War', *The Lancet* 182(4,690) (1913), 163.
28 'Cholera and War in the Near East', *The Lancet* 181(4,668) (1913), 485.
29 'Medical and Surgical Experience in the Balkan War', *The Lancet* 182(4,690) (1913), 163.
30 Johnstone, *With the British Red Cross in Turkey*, 29–30.
31 'Medical and Surgical Experience in the Balkan War', *The Lancet* 182(4,690) (1913), 163–64.
32 'Medical and Surgical Experience in the Balkan War', *The Lancet* 182(4,691) (1913), 240.
33 'Surgery in the Balkans War', *British Medical Journal* 1(2,725) (1913), 624.
34 'The Cholera Camp at San Stefano', *The Manchester Guardian*, 11 December 1912, 9.
35 'Medical and Surgical Experience in the Balkan War', *The Lancet* 182(4,691) (1913), 238.
36 'The Cholera Camp at San Stefano', *The Manchester Guardian*, 11 December 1912, 9.
37 'Medical and Surgical Experience in the Balkan War', *The Lancet* 182(4,691) (1913), 239.
38 Sidney Smith, 'Some Surgical Experiences during the Balkan War', *The Lancet* 181(4,683) (1913), 1,547–49, here 1,547–48.
39 'Medical and Surgical Experience in the Balkan War', *The Lancet* 182(4,691) (1913), 237.
40 'Surgery in the Balkans War', *British Medical Journal* 1(2,725) (1913), 624.
41 'Beleaguered Constantinople', *The Lancet* 180(4,657) (1912), 1,529.
42 'Medical and Surgical Experience in the Balkan War', *The Lancet* 182(4,690) (1913), 164.
43 'Medical and Surgical Experience in the Balkan War', *The Lancet* 182(4,691) (1913), 237.
44 'Surgery in the Balkan War', *British Medical Journal* 2(2,857) (1915), 505.
45 'Surgery in the Balkans War', *British Medical Journal* 1(2,725) (1913), 624.

46 There is no definition for Muslims regarding autopsy in Islam. For detailed information, see Üveis Maskar, 'İslâmda ve Osmanlılarda Otopsi Sorunu Üzerine Bir Etüd' [A Study on Autopsy Problems in Islam and the Ottoman Empire], *Patoloji Bülteni* 3(3) (1976), 259–74, http://www.turkjpath.org/pdf/pdf_PB_245.pdf (accessed 26 February 2014); and Hayrettin Karaman, 'İslâm Otopsi Meselesi' [Islam-Autopsy Problem], http://www.hayrettinkaraman.net/kitap/helalharam/0255.htm (accessed 26 February 2014).
47 'Medical and Surgical Experience in the Balkan War', *The Lancet* 182(4,691) (1913), 237.
48 'Constantinople, the War, Cholera, Disease, Privation', *The Lancet* 180(4,656) (1912), 1,471.
49 'Beleaguered Constantinople', *The Lancet* 180(4,657) (1912), 1,529.
50 'Constantinople, the War, Cholera, Disease, Privation', *The Lancet* 180(4,656) (1912), 1,471.
51 'Medical and Surgical Experience in the Balkan War', *The Lancet* 182 (4,691) (1913), 238.
52 Ibid.
53 Johnstone, *With the British Red Cross in Turkey*, 37.
54 'Beleaguered Constantinople', *The Lancet* 180(4,657) (1912), 1,529.
55 *1329–1331 Salnamesi*, 252.
56 Ibid., 254.
57 Johnstone, *With the British Red Cross in Turkey*, 33.
58 'Medical and Surgical Experience in the Balkan War', *The Lancet* 182(4,690) (1913), 163.
59 'The Cholera Camp at San Stefano', *The Manchester Guardian*, 11 December 1912, 9.
60 Johnstone, *With the British Red Cross in Turkey*, 132.
61 Ali Fuat Örenç, 'Bulgar Kuşatması Döneminde Edirne'de Kolera Salgını ve Hindistanlı Fatma Hanımefendi'nin Faaliyetleri' [Cholera Outbreak in Edirne during the Bulgarian Siege and the Activities of Lady Fatma of India], in İbrahim Sezgin, Cengiz Fedakar and Hasan Demiroğlu (eds), *Uluslararası Edirne'nin Fethi'nin 650. Yılı Sempozyumu Bildiriler Kitabı, 4–6 Mayıs 2011* [Proceedings of the International Symposium for the 650th Anniversary of the Conquest of Edirne] (Edirne: Trakya University, 2012), 385–402, here 395–96.
62 Red Crescent Archives, box no. 18, document no. 52.2.
63 Özcan, *Pan-İslamizm*, 191–211.
64 This claim was not only made by Indian Muslims. The British Orientalist Edward G. Browne wrote in a letter that he sent to the editor of *The Manchester Guardian* on 8 June 1913: 'Whatever may be said as to the official attitude of Great Britain towards Turkey, I still believe that nowhere in Europe do the Turks count more genuine friends and well-wishers than in this country': 'The Distress in Turkey, Browne's Appeal', *The Manchester Guardian*, 16 June 1913, 12.
65 Özcan, *Pan-İslamizm*, 191–211.

Bibliography

1329–1331 Salnamesi [The Ottoman Red Crescent Yearbook, 1913–1915]. Istanbul: Ahmet İhsan ve Sürekası Matbaası, 1915.

Akgün, Seçil Karal, and Murat Uluğtekin. *Hilal-i Ahmer'den Kızılay'a* [From Ottoman Red Crescent to Kızılay]. Vol. I. Ankara: Kızılay, 2000.

Bennett, Angela. *The Geneva Convention: The Hidden Origins of the Red Cross.* Stroud: Sutton Publishing, 2006.

Hutchinson, John F. *Champions of Charity: War and the Rise of the Red Cross.* Boulder, CO: Westview Press, 1996.

Johnstone, A. Duncan. *With the British Red Cross in Turkey: The Experience of Two Volunteers, 1912–1913.* London: James Nisbet, 1913.

Karaman, Hayrettin. 'İslâm Otopsi Meselesi' [Islam-Autopsy Problem]. http://www.hayrettinkaraman.net/kitap/helalharam/0255.htm (accessed 26 February 2014).

Maskar, Üveis. 'İslâmda ve Osmanlılarda Otopsi Sorunu Üzerine Bir Etüd' [A Study on Autopsy Problems in Islam and the Ottoman Empire]. *Patoloji Bülteni* 3(3) (1976), 259–74. http://www.turkjpath.org/pdf/pdf_PB_245.pdf (accessed 26 February 2014).

Örenç, Ali Fuat. 'Bulgar Kuşatması Döneminde Edirne'de Kolera Salgını ve Hindistanlı Fatma Hanımefendi'nin Faaliyetleri' [Cholera Outbreak in Edirne during the Bulgarian Siege and the Activities of Lady Fatma of India], in İbrahim Sezgin, Cengiz Fedakar and Hasan Demiroğlu (eds), *Uluslararası Edirne'nin Fethi'nin 650. Yılı Sempozyumu Bildiriler Kitabı, 4–6 Mayıs 2011* [Proceedings of the International Symposium for the 650th Anniversary of the Conquest of Edirne] (Edirne: Trakya University, 2012), 385–402.

Özcan, Azmi. *Pan-İslamizm: Osmanlı Devleti Hindistan Müslümanları ve İngiltere, 1877–1924* [Pan-Islamism: Ottoman Empire, Indian Muslims and Britain, 1877–1924]. Ankara: Türkiye Diyanet Vakfı, 1997.

Smith, Sidney. 'Some Surgical Experiences during the Balkan War'. *The Lancet* 181(4,683) (1913), 1,547–49.

15

WAR NEUROSIS AND PSYCHIATRY IN THE AFTERMATH OF THE BALKAN WARS

Heike Karge

In the spring of 1914, not long before the start of the First World War, the Croatian medical journal *Liječnički vjesnik* [Medical Journal] published an article addressing the low incidence of mental illness among Serbian, Bulgarian, Montenegrin and Greek troops during the Balkan Wars.[1] I open this chapter with a detailed account of this short piece, as it displays some constitutive features of the discourse on the mental illnesses that afflicted soldiers in the wake of the Balkan Wars and the First World War in what would become Yugoslavia in 1918.

The author of the article, M.F., outlines the results of an analysis conducted by Dr Vojslav M. Subotić, secretary of the Serbian Red Cross. During the Balkan Wars, Dr Subotić was the administrator of the Royal Serbian Institute for the Mentally Disturbed (Kraljevski Srpski Zavod za umobolne) in Belgrade and the 5th Red Cross Auxiliary Hospital, and he thus had insight into the issue that interested him: the relationship between war and mental illness. The data concerning Serbia were taken from the hospital records of the Belgrade Institute for the period from November 1912 until November 1913. The data pertaining to other states were sent to him by colleagues in the other warring states.

According to Dr Subotić, during the period analysed, 102 servicemen were admitted to the Belgrade Institute: seven officers, six non-commissioned officers and 84 enlisted men, all 97 of whom were serving in the Serbian army; two Turkish prisoners of war; and three Albanian prisoners of war. Before arriving at the Belgrade Institute, all had been treated in other hospitals for maladies such as typhus, malaria and cholera. Only nine of the 102 admitted had suffered physical injuries, most of which were not severe.[2] Their mental disorders, according to Dr Subotić, did not develop during combat or immediately thereafter, but rather in the course of the hospital treatment of their respective physical injuries or infectious diseases. The author of the journal article provides the specific diagnoses of these patients: most frequent was *mania*, followed in descending order by *melancholia, dementia praecox, dementia paralytica* and epilepsy. Least common, affecting only one patient, was alcoholism. On the basis of this sample, Dr Subotić concluded, 'It follows that in the Serbian army, alcohol was not abused'.[3]

Dr Subotić further reported that patients who recovered were in most cases unable to give any meaningful account of the origin of their mental disorder. Some of them blamed the cold weather, others the wet conditions. Only four of the patients reported having had hallucinations provoked by fear. If we disregard epileptic and paralytic patients, because they might have suffered from their maladies before serving in the army, as well as patients who were not serving in the Serbian army at all, then, according to Dr Subotić, we arrive at the conclusion that in the Serbian military population, which comprised 400,000 troops, the incidence of afflicted soldiers during the wars was seventy-four, or 0.0185 per cent.[4]

Very similar findings could be derived from the records of other nations.[5] In Greece, according to M.F., only twenty-nine enlisted men and officers – 0.0097 per cent of an army of 300,000 – were referred to clinics and hospitals as being mentally disturbed.[6] Montenegro had an army of 50,000 and only five cases of mental illness, a rate of 0.01 per cent.[7] Only in Bulgaria were the numbers somewhat higher. In its army of 500,000, there were 165 soldiers and officers with mental disorders, that is, 0.033 per cent.[8]

Dr Subotić then compared these statistics with the data on the incidence of mental disorders in other armies, for example among Russian soldiers after the Russo-Japanese War, English troops after the Boer Wars and Prussian forces after the Franco-German War of 1870–71. In all these armies, the percentage of mentally ill soldiers was much higher. Dr Subotić therefore concluded:

> ... this time the expectation we had for a long time did not come true, the expectation that in modern warfare – and the Balkan Wars were, no doubt, modern – the rate of mental illness will significantly rise. The cause of that is to be ascribed to the resilience of the Balkan peoples. Fortunately, in the Balkans alcohol was not abused. Therein lays one of the reasons for such a negligible number of disorders.[9]

According to my research, this article, only three pages long but tightly focused, is the only contemporary material dealing with the question of mental illness in the military during the Balkan Wars. In what once was Yugoslavia, the topic of mental injuries from war – starting with the Balkan Wars and ending with the Second World War – has yet to be investigated.[10] During those wars and even now, the topic was and is marginalized in both Yugoslavia and its successor states, not only in literature and research in the field of (military) medicine but also, and to an even greater extent, in historiography inspired by the field of cultural studies. As a result, the analysis offered here of the treatment of mentally ill soldiers in the wake of the Balkan Wars and the First World War in Serbia, Croatia-Slavonia and later in the Kingdom of Yugoslavia has scarcely any body of literature on which to draw.[11] The following discussion should therefore be understood as merely an introduction to a topic that is being investigated more broadly each day in Western and Central Europe.[12]

This chapter examines, for the most part, contemporary source materials. I have systematically analysed three journals. Two of them, *Liječnički vjesnik* in the Kingdom of Croatia-Slavonia and *Srpski arhiv za celokupno lekarstvo* [Serbian Archive for Medicine] in Serbia, were published by the Croatian and the Serbian Associations of Physicians, respectively, and thus were leading medical journals.[13] The third is the military-medical journal *Vojnosanitetski glasnik* [Military-Sanitary Gazette], published from 1930 until 1939. In addition, I refer to several documents from the Military Archive in Belgrade, articles from the war years 1912–18 in the *Wiener Klinische Wochenschrift* [Vienna Medical Weekly], and contemporary monographs and brochures.

Why tackle a topic so neglected by both contemporaries and later researchers? What could we possibly discover if we try to go beyond the assertions of Dr Subotić? Inquiry into the perception of the mental illnesses that afflicted soldiers in Serbia and Croatia during the Balkan Wars and the First World War is relevant for three reasons, I believe.

First, this topic allows us to enter terrain in which we can inspect not merely how mentally ill soldiers were treated, but also how the disturbed, the mentally ill and other persons whose behaviour was regarded as deviant were perceived in Serbia and Croatia in the late nineteenth and early twentieth centuries. Who was considered 'insane', and when did this label come to imply a medical diagnosis? What was the role of cultural, political and social traditions in the perception of the 'weak' and the mentally disturbed, and how did these traditions influence the way these individuals were perceived? At what point in time did the 'mad', the 'insane' or the mentally disturbed in general begin to be hospitalized? And how did these social traditions affect the discourses in the wake of the Balkan Wars and the First World War?

Although the topic of mentally injured soldiers in the Balkan Wars was undoubtedly marginalized, the few existing discussions nevertheless demonstrate – and here we see the second reason for which this inquiry is relevant – that political, national and what we now call *orientalizing* discourse inscribed itself in the discourse on mental illness in war. During the Balkan Wars, and because of them, this inscribing was not limited to Serbia. It was also the doing of the Croatian physicians who offered their medical services to the warring nations through Red Cross missions and later published, both in Croatia and abroad, copious accounts of their experiences. Like the analysis by Dr Subotić, these materials suggest that by the early twentieth century, military medicine and psychiatry, both as a science and as an institution slowly emerging in Serbia and Croatia at the time, were closely connected to European scientific and medical discourses. It thus appears that before the First World War, the Balkan Wars had offered an opportunity for an intense transfer of knowledge and practices in the sphere of health and illness.

Finally, developments in the field of social politics are always both slowed and accelerated by warfare. Hence the notions of health and illness, poverty and welfare benefits are always shaped and reshaped by warfare. The literature concerning the cultural history of gender and violence has repeatedly rejected the idea that war is a caesura,[14] and therefore the psychiatric concepts of health and illness, as shaped by war, are also open to discussion. Croatian physicians participated early on in the discourse concerning what was probably the most important issue with respect to the perception of mental disorder in war, not only in Croatia but throughout Europe: the issue of social policy. After the First World War broke out, the early twentieth-century diagnoses of 'shell shock', trauma and combat fatigue initiated a discourse that centred on social policy, and Croatian physicians took part in that discourse. On every battlefield of the First World War, soldiers diagnosed with shell shock, hysteria, trauma or combat fatigue presented a uniquely visible and serious problem. There was a threat that enormous sums would have to be spent on soldiers injured in service, so that psychiatric notions of health and illness, as well as sociopolitical conceptions of welfare, pensions and disability, were re-examined during those years. As a part of the Austro-Hungarian Empire, Croatia-Slavonia engaged in these discourses. In addition, because the empire had been gradually implementing a social security system since the end of the nineteenth century, a great number of requests for compensation for mental injuries due to war could be expected. This was not the case for Serbia, as the country did not have a system of social security. In Yugoslavia, social policy inspired medical and military-medical discussions of shell shock only in the interwar period, and at that time the debates adopted and built on the existing discourses in Western and Central Europe.

Background

What was the background of the social, psychiatric and military approaches to mental injuries at the beginning of the twentieth century in Serbia and Croatia? First, it could be argued that in the southeastern regions of Europe, in comparison with Western and Central Europe, pre-state practices of confining mentally ill patients, as well as pre-medical practices of treating them, continued for a longer period of time. A gradual abandoning of these practices had begun in the western parts of Europe by the end of the eighteenth century, while in Croatia-Slavonia and Serbia it was not until one hundred years later, in the late nineteenth century, that two large state institutions were founded. The Kingdom of Croatia-Slavonia was then a part of the Hungarian half of the Austro-Hungarian Monarchy. As mental institutions were being created throughout the empire, the Royal State Institute for the Mentally Ill for Croatia-Slavonia (Kraljevski zemaljski zavod za umobolne za Hrvatsku i Slavoniju) opened its doors in 1879, in Stenjevec, near Zagreb. In Serbia, a Home for the Unsound of Mind (Dom za s uma sišavše) had been founded in 1861, in Guberevac near Belgrade, by a Prince's Decree. The establishment of these institutions marked a turning point in both nations for their emerging public health and welfare systems. These institutions were the first, and for a long time the only, psychiatric institutions. There was also a series of institutional and legislative innovations. The first professional association of doctors, the Serbian Medical Society (Srpsko lekarsko društvo), was founded in 1872. In 1881, the Home for the Unsound of Mind in Guberevac was renamed and became the Hospital for Mental Illnesses (Bolnica za duševne bolesti). In a concurrent development in Croatia-Slavonia, the Croatian Medical Association (Zbor liječnika Hrvatske) was founded in 1874. The processes of establishing state institutions and establishing the profession went hand in hand, except for one minor detail: at the time, Serbia and Croatia had no psychiatrists. In the nineteenth century, Croats and Serbs studied medicine in Vienna and Graz, Padua and Prague, but they did not study psychiatry.[15] Medical schools at the university level opened in Zagreb and Belgrade only in 1918 and 1923, respectively. Initially, therefore, neither institution was headed by trained psychiatrists but rather by family and general practitioners.[16]

However, the founding of the two large hospitals was the first step in a gradual process that eventually led to a perception that insane persons were sick. Modern clinical diagnostics were introduced after the Belgrade asylum was turned into a hospital, and from then on, the diagnostics practised there were virtually indistinguishable from diagnostics in Stenjevec. In Stenjevec, around 1880, the majority of the diagnoses coincided with those common in Vienna, Budapest and Graz: *'mania'*, *'melancholia'* or *'partial insanity'*.[17] From the moment when doctors working in these institutions were sent to study, train and further their education in Feldhof or Graz – that is, from 1880 onwards – more sophisticated diagnostics began to emerge. At the end of the century, Dr Ivan Žirovčić, at the time the head of the institute in Stenjevec, published a series of articles in *Liječnički vjesnik*, which since 1877 had been the professional monthly journal of the Croatian Medical Association.[18] The series was titled 'On Naming and Classifying Mental Disorders'.[19] Dr Žirovčić not only mentioned *dementia paralytica* (chronic inflammation of nervous tissue during a late stage of syphilis), which he described as a 'real scourge of our times',[20] but also identified alcoholism as one of the most common causes of mental disorders in Croatia-Slavonia.

Despite these developments, and despite the pervasive optimism that marked the dominant outlook in institutions and among scientists, it is a fact that the problems of the mentally ill and psychiatry itself, both as a science and as an institutionalized practice, occupied a social position that could only be designated as marginal. Psychiatry lagged behind the flourishing medical sciences of the time. Even the highest position in a psychiatric hospital was not considered prestigious by medical professionals.[21] It is thus not surprising that no new hospitals for the mentally ill were founded until the end of the First World War. Also, military psychiatry did not exist, even in the most rudimentary form. In the early 1930s, Dr Djuro Vranešić, a Zagreb neurologist, maintained in a popular scientific journal that psychiatry had been neglected at the time it was institutionalized and that it remained neglected. Dr Vranešić claimed that local physicians were interested, insofar as they were interested in anything, only in the nerves and organic functions, and not in the mentally ill.[22] Gradually, psychiatry began to develop, but the mentally ill were still regarded, by psychiatry and also by the wider society, as a burdensome evil.

The Balkan Wars

In view of the marginal position of psychiatry, it is not greatly surprising that the statistics of Dr Subotić included such a small number of mentally injured soldiers in the wake of the Balkan Wars. Rather, given the marginalization of the topic and even of the suffering patients themselves, it is astounding that such statistics were compiled in the first place. During the Balkan Wars, both domestic and foreign doctors working in the Balkans focused on an entirely different set of problems. Combat injuries, especially shrapnel and bullet wounds, had to be treated primarily by surgical procedures, and therefore the medical reports in *Wiener Klinische Wochenschrift* and *Liječnički vjesnik* addressed primarily surgical issues. Besides the treatment of rampant infectious diseases like typhus, tuberculosis, malaria and syphilis, these issues were the primary concern of doctors.[23]

The authors in both journals were mostly doctors from the Dual Monarchy, surgeons who came to the Balkans with the Red Cross missions. They worked for weeks or months in the military and auxiliary hospitals in Serbia and in hospitals of the other nations involved in the conflict. *Liječnički vjesnik*'s reports, however, mostly concerned their work in Serbia.[24] *Wiener Klinische Wochenschrift* included a number of reports from Bulgaria and Montenegro. The help that the Red Cross provided in the surgical care of combat casualties proved to be of vital importance in view of the few domestic physicians who participated. Milan Figartner, a Croatian physician who was decorated by the Serbian king for his medical and surgical achievements, reported that all available doctors in Serbia were brought to the military and auxiliary hospitals, but there were only three hundred such doctors.[25] And in Serbia, as elsewhere, trained orderlies and nursing staff were in short supply.[26]

It is not surprising, therefore, that the number of hospitalized Serbian soldiers who succumbed to disease almost matched the number of those who were killed in combat.[27] The treatment of patients with infectious diseases and the performance of surgical procedures on those with shell and bullet wounds were the issues that primarily concerned the doctors and nursing staff. Mental injuries held a very insignificant place.

This neglect was not a phenomenon limited to Southeastern Europe. In the rest of Europe, mental afflictions among combat troops were recognized to a much lesser degree than after the First World War broke out. However, the first pertinent statistical data, which were also discussed in medical circles, stem from the Russo-Japanese War (1904–5). It was the first modern war in which mentally ill combatants, Russians in particular, were treated by psychiatrists. Military psychiatric institutions were a prerequisite for that kind of treatment, and Russia had had such institutions since the end of the 1860s.[28] In Croatia-Slavonia and Serbia, however, at the time of the Balkan Wars no such establishments existed. Not until 1932 did the main military hospital in Belgrade open a psychiatric ward.[29] Psychiatry and the military thus began to collaborate in the whole of Europe only after the Balkan Wars, or, more precisely, after the beginning of the First World War. The term 'war neurosis' (*Kriegsneurose*) was coined before the First World War by the German internist Georg Honigmann, who treated Russian officers in 1905–6, after the Russo-Japanese War, but the diagnosis of battle fatigue or shell shock became relevant only in 1914 and 1915.[30]

It follows, then, that according to the data compiled by Dr Subotić, soldiers and officers in the Belgrade hospital were treated not for war neurosis but rather for mental illnesses typically diagnosed at the time, *mania* and *melancholia*. According to the 1912 records, there were 770 patients in the hospital, and 474 of them, more than half, were men.[31] In 1913, the hospital held 900 patients, and again more than half were men (553).[32] The single most frequent diagnosis during both years was paralytic dementia, which can be either a late stage of untreated syphilis or a paralysis that results from alcoholism. For every female patient, there were more than two male patients. The other most frequent diagnoses were *mania, melancholia, paranoia* und *folia alcoholica*. These results were in line with contemporary diagnostic practice, and we find the same disorders in the records from hospitals in Croatia-Slavonia. In 1912, *Liječnički vjesnik* published the records of public hospitals in several towns, Sremska Mitrovica in Vojvodina, Vinkovci in Eastern Croatia, and Nova Gradiška on the border with Bosnia and Herzegovina. Croatia-Slavonia was not at war either in 1912 or in the preceding decade, so these psychiatric diagnoses – *dementia, mania, psychosis, neurasthenia, hysteria* and others – are part of an entirely civilian medical and psychiatric discourse.[33] And so, too, are the diagnoses from Dr Subotić's records, although Serbia was at war.

Besides these data, which Dr Subotić compiled only after the Balkan Wars, the Serbian Military Archive in Belgrade has very few contemporary patient records of Serbian soldiers and officers. A great deal of material was destroyed during the Balkan Wars and the subsequent two world wars. It is also likely that under wartime conditions, the dispatching of patient records from field hospitals was not regular and the data were not always accurate. Moreover, even the small amount of data preserved from civilian hospitals in Serbia in 1912 cannot be considered completely reliable. In the journal *Srpski arhiv za celokupno lekarstvo*, an anonymous author claimed that the data from Serbian hospitals were often incomplete, because they were compiled by hospital accountants rather than doctors.[34] We must therefore be cautious when drawing conclusions. However, one thing may be stated with a fair degree of certainty: we need not look for the diagnosis of 'war neurosis' or 'traumatic neurosis' in patient records during the Balkan

Wars to learn whether combatants suffered mental injuries stemming from war, that is, whether such injuries were recognized and treated.

The patient records from a field hospital of the Drina Division for the period from September 1912 to September 1913 contain virtually no psychiatric cases. The sole exceptions are a case of epilepsy, often called 'falling sickness' and traditionally considered a mental defect, and a relatively small number of cases of 'soldier's heart'.[35] The latter might be an indication of a neurotic reaction, the one later labelled war neurosis, as it had no somatic basis. The negligible number of psychiatric diagnoses allows us to assume that mentally ill soldiers in the Balkan Wars often were not recognized as such, and that, lacking somatic causes for their complaints, they were treated, if at all, for general 'weakness'. In a memorandum from the medical department of the Serbian High Command, dated March 1913, shortly before the end of the First Balkan War, military hospitals are criticized for being filled with people who should not be there, people who 'are not sick at all, but only weak and have not had enough rest, or are exhausted and weary because of the strains and exertions they have had to endure'.[36]

During the Balkan Wars, there were patients with diagnoses of *mania*, *melancholia* or *hysteria*, and there were the weak and the exhausted. The latter were not considered ill at all, in contrast to patients suffering from 'soldier's heart', a very rare diagnosis. This was the opinion of both Serbian and Croatian doctors. A Croatian doctor who treated wounded Serbian soldiers and officers at a Red Cross mission in Kragujevac after the battle of Kumanovo in October 1912 reported:

> There were a lot of soldiers who suffered from the consequences of shock because a shell exploded in their proximity, knocked them to the ground, and they got showered with dirt; some of them stayed like that for hours, unconscious. These soldiers complained about a variety of neurasthenic syndromes and recovered much more slowly than the ones who were really injured. Many of them gave the impression of degenerated neuropathic individuals.[37]

The presence of a genuine disease, identified a few years later as shell shock, and having the same aetiology (a result of a shock, a nearby shell explosion, and 'neurasthenic' complaints with no somatic explanation), was dismissed by the Croatian doctors as well.

The second contention that could be made with a fair degree of certainty is that during the Balkan Wars, soldiers did suffer from mental illnesses. However, it was not thought that war acted as their cause. Rather, it was believed that the origin of these illnesses, or the process of their generation, was unrelated to warfare. This viewpoint is implicit not only in the diagnoses stemming from the civilian psychiatric discourse, but also in the Croatian doctor's derogatory statement about degeneration and his suggestion that the patient had mental abnormalities even before the war.[38] Clear evidence of this viewpoint is seen in the analysis by Dr Subotić, in which he explicitly emphasized that symptoms did not appear during battles or immediately after them, but only later, and as a result of patients' stays in other hospitals. The experience of shock during the war and the fear of battle, of the enemy or of death – none of that played any role, as yet, in the medical records and remarks concerning mentally disturbed Serbian soldiers. In his short analysis, Dr Subotić pointed out that even the soldiers themselves were not able to identify the causes of their illness, in their own opinion. Cold and dampness were mentioned. Only four soldiers spoke of hallucinations provoked by fear. Just four of seventy-four mentally ill Serbs spoke of fear, a number so small that the question whether the war was the cause of their illness was as good as answered.

However, the real question for Dr Subotić was not whether the war was responsible for mental illness, but what factors were responsible for the purportedly low incidence of mental injuries in the armies of the warring Balkan nations. He proposes two factors: resilience and low alcohol consumption. Now we can understand why he mentions the negligible number of 'frightened' patients. He aimed to demonstrate that the statistics attested to the prevalence of a tenacious and robust spirit among Serbian soldiers and soldiers of other Balkan nations. From this moment on, if not before, the medical and psychiatric discourse was in the service of politics. All the armies of the anti-Ottoman Balkan League are thus portrayed by Dr Subotić as healthy, tough and not prone to alcohol consumption. True, Dr Subotić does not mention the Turkish army, but he does refer to mentally ill soldiers in earlier wars fought by Germany, Britain and Russia. The considerably higher incidence of mentally ill soldiers among the armed forces of these three nations served Dr Subotić as a foil, a means to make his data seem even more impressive. The argument based on the resiliency of the Balkan peoples offers a key to the real purpose of Dr Subotić's analysis. A purely medical interest might have guided him, given that he was an outstanding physician, yet his analysis had a distinctly patriotic cast. One cannot overlook his pride in the notion that inherent physical hardiness and psychological flexibility enabled the Balkan peoples to withstand the stress of war, especially modern warfare. Dr Subotić's approach marks the beginning of an instrumentalization of psychiatry, a hitherto and subsequently socially marginalized field. This trend towards use of psychiatry as an instrument to achieve other ends would become even more pronounced after the First World War as discussions on social policy in the Kingdom of Yugoslavia intensified, but the first steps had already been taken in the context of the Balkan Wars. Even more striking was the custom of using not only psychiatry, but also other fields of medical expertise as a patriotic vehicle, as was done in reports on alcohol abuse during the Balkan Wars. After the Second Balkan War, Serbian medical journals suddenly began to publish reports and booklets that noted a marked difference between Serbian and Bulgarian soldiers regarding their respective attitudes towards alcohol and hygiene.

These reports are interesting because Dr Subotić was not the only observer to note the connection between the use of alcohol and mental illness. Psychiatrists, who were becoming established in the region at that time, had already recognized it as an important fact. In the late nineteenth century, Croatian psychiatrist Dr Ivan Žirovčić had pinpointed a relation between alcoholism and mental illness. In the early twentieth century, there were many hospitalized patients in Belgrade and Zagreb who suffered from paralytic dementia, a disorder that can be an attendant phenomenon of long-term alcohol abuse. The incidence of the disorder in this region suggests that alcohol was traditionally consumed in large quantities there.

The situation was virtually the same during the Balkan Wars, although an anonymous contributor to the newspaper *Narodno zdravlje* [National Health], a supplement to the journal *Srpski arhiv za celokupno lekarstvo*, claimed in January 1914 that during these wars, Serbian soldiers had consumed almost no alcohol. The Bulgarians, by contrast, had resorted to 'rakija', a popular alcoholic beverage in Southeastern Europe, to boost their strength and courage, and it cost them dearly in the end (the author alludes to the outcome of the Second Balkan War).[39] However, one tiny brochure, also published in 1914, explained that during the Balkan Wars, *hydrophobia* spread among Serbian soldiers like an infectious disease. He claimed that *hydrophobia*, the fear of drinking water that might be contaminated and an accompanying fear of cholera and other infectious diseases, was in large part responsible for the high alcohol intake during the Balkan Wars.[40]

Thus, there were differing perceptions of contemporaries concerning the use of alcohol among Serbian soldiers during the Balkan Wars. These differing perceptions may have been caused by military rules in the first instance, since in a gesture that was unique in the context of the Balkan Wars, the Serbian High Command stated in Paragraph 1,039 of the 'Rules of War Service [that] ... it is recommended to refrain completely from alcohol use during the war'.[41] Popović regrets only that this was merely a recommendation and not an order, but he insists that '[i]t is very important to say their superiors have not authorized any distribution of alcoholic drinks among healthy soldiers'.[42] To Bulgarian soldiers – and on this point the two reports described above agree – alcohol was distributed at all times, especially cognac and 'rakija'.

The brochure mentions not only the immoderate drinking of Bulgarian soldiers, but also their poor hygiene habits. Serbian soldiers, even in the restrictive conditions of military field camps, tried to stay clean; they dug wells and washed dishes. Bulgarians, on the contrary, were satisfied with the most primitive conditions and made no effort to improve them:

> For Bulgarian soldiers, and even their officers, a bit of straw and a most primitive mud shelter were good enough, but our soldiers would build whole settlements and, using even the most primitive materials, they tried to make more comfortable and pleasant surroundings.[43]

So the lack of hygiene and the alcohol abuse among Bulgarians was a perceived contrast to the undoubtedly more civilized and modern Serbian army, at least from the perspective of some contemporary observers. It is interesting that in the reports from the First Balkan War, when Serbia and Bulgaria were still allies, these differences were looked upon differently. Poor sanitary conditions were mentioned, but only in relation to medical facilities, and they were explained away by the inadequate equipment and insufficient supplies of the Red Cross in Bulgaria.

There are many reports about the First Balkan War in the *Wiener Klinische Wochenschrift*, and all of them point to the poor and inadequate first aid given to the wounded as the primary reason for the high rate of infectious diseases and death among soldiers. None of these reports mentions alcohol, but they do mention the lack of medical supplies, limited options for transport of the injured and shortage of nursing staff.[44]

In March 1913, not long before the end of the First Balkan War, *Srpski arhiv za celokupno lekarstvo* published several articles in which foreign authors discussed sanitary conditions during the war. The authors, one from the Netherlands, one from Bosnia and one from Croatia, made no mention at all of the poor hygiene of Bulgarians or their drinking habits. Instead, they criticized the hygienic conditions in the auxiliary hospitals in Belgrade[45] and the poor rate of wound healing among Bulgarians, for which they blamed ill-equipped and undersupplied Red Cross facilities.[46]

In short, only after the Second Balkan War were medicine and hygiene used to denounce Bulgarians, after their military defeat, as being uncivilized. Here we find the orientalizing discourse: on the one side there are modern Serbs, with healthy, hygienic habits, and on the other side, scruffy Bulgarians, habitually reaching for a drink. A part of this narrative is the Serbs' abstinence from alcohol, and here we find the source of Dr Subotić's explanation for the small number of mentally ill soldiers during the Balkan Wars.

As was noted at the outset, political subtleties played no role in Dr Subotić's statistics: he ascribed resiliency and abstinence from alcohol to all Balkan peoples. However, that analysis does not affect the contention that during the Balkan Wars, the psychiatric and medical sciences tried to be of service to the homeland. The expression of this desire varied according to the political allegiance of the given author, or as social and political circumstances changed, but the foundations for future forms of service were firmly laid.

Dr Subotić's statistics, I believe, represented more a political than a psychiatric or medical statement. Neither 'resilience' nor abstinence from alcohol as attributes of Serbian soldiers would hold up under scrutiny, and so neither factor could have had an effect on the incidence of mental illness in war. In the reports on the Bulgarians, we have seen that they suffered from the poor sanitary conditions that led to a high rate of infected wounds and death. The high rate of death from infectious diseases among Serbian soldiers could have led Dr Subotić to doubt their 'resilience'. And regarding alcohol abuse, it seems that in spite of the recommendation of the Serbian High Command, reality in the field was different. Popović mentions that although alcohol was not distributed, soldiers nevertheless did consume a great deal of it, as did officers and doctors, too: 'The only time they weren't drinking was when they had nothing to drink'.[47] It appears that the only difference between Serbs and Bulgarians was that the latter drank with the approval of their superiors, and deliberately before combat. Popović mentions the conditions in Serbian military and auxiliary hospitals and claims:

> Alcohol triumphantly invaded all hospitals; it poured in from all over. The Red Cross meted it out, as did private persons, our compatriots and foreigners alike. Patients, nurses, doctors, commissioners, guests, they all drank. Drinking binges were organized in many hospitals and sometimes the military authorities had to send someone to restore order and disperse merry crowds. ... If we keep all that in mind, we can see that this war also has shown and confirmed that alcohol has brought us nothing but harm. It had an adverse effect on discipline, health, surgery success rate, pride and dignity of individuals and of the army as a whole.[48]

The patient records from Belgrade Hospital for Mental Illnesses in 1912 and 1913 also attest to the immoderate consumption of alcohol during the Balkan Wars. In these records, paralytic dementia is the most frequent diagnosis. Later reports in *Liječnički vjesnik* attest that alcohol was heavily consumed by Serbs and Croats during the First World War.[49] Likewise, the reports from the period just before the Second World War give more than enough reason to conclude that during the entire period in question there was a close relation between alcohol abuse and mental illness in Serbia, and later in Yugoslavia:

> Many people ended up in asylums because of alcohol since alcohol drove them to insanity and mental retardation. Alcoholics make up about 30% of lunatics in asylums. Besides drunkards who suffer from delirium episodes, asylums and shelters are being filled with sick people who were driven to madness by alcohol. ... Neurological complications are the most important. Mental disorders sometimes manifest in such a way that the patient becomes paralysed.[50]

The low incidence of mentally ill soldiers and officers in Dr Subotić's statistics had nothing to do with alcohol consumption as a causal factor. In my opinion, alcohol is not an explanation, because relatively heavy and regular alcohol abuse, especially among men, was perfectly acceptable socially; alcoholics were admitted to hospital only after they had shown the first signs of paralysis. The causes for the low number of cases of mental illnesses are different. Among them are, notably, the limited capacity of facilities where such illnesses could be treated and the underdevelopment of military psychiatry in Serbia and Croatia. The situation remained essentially unchanged for at least thirty years after the Balkan Wars had ended. Even in 1946, the psychiatrist and neurologist Josip Dojč lamented the low standing of military psychiatry:

> In the state of war, the valid motto is 'Surgery and only surgery, above all! In time of war, only the physician who reports on the successes in war surgery, or at least on a wounded man or a wound, can raise his voice'. In the war clamour, even the best and the most modern psychiatrist must keep quiet.[51]

Perspective: After the Balkan Wars

The First World War brought about a noticeable increase in the number of patients admitted to mental institutions. When soldiers suffering from neurotic tremor and shell shock became an everyday occurrence throughout Europe, they appeared in Croatia-Slavonia and Serbia too, that is, in the newly formed Kingdom of Yugoslavia. After the First World War, the number of patients admitted to Guberevac doubled.[52] By the end of the war, about five hundred patients were admitted to Stenjevec, and in the late 1920s that number suddenly soared to almost 1,400.[53] The

First World War also brought to the region the diagnosis of 'trauma', shell shock. It is clear that the pertinent discussions on the nature of traumatic neurosis, the civilian precursor to shell shock, especially the discussions in the German Empire, were being followed attentively elsewhere.[54] After the war, the system of social security for workers was gradually introduced in Yugoslavia, and discussions followed, comparable to those in Germany, Great Britain and Switzerland. The discussions looked at shell shock from the perspective of social policy and medical and actuarial science.[55] This was the moment at which Yugoslav, that is, Serbian and Croatian, physicians and an increasing number of locally educated psychiatrists and neurologists made a leap into psychiatric modernity. The characteristic of this modernity in almost all of Europe after 1916 was the fact that medicine, actuarial science and psychiatry believed that the genesis of traumatic neurosis and shell shock responsibility lay particularly in the (ill-founded) intent and desire of patients to receive compensation.[56] Consequently, after 1916, the notions of 'shell shock' and 'war neurosis' were deleted from the English and German vocabulary of psychiatry and social medicine, and for a long time war neurosis was not considered grounds for receiving compensation.[57] In Yugoslavia too, use of non-somatic, psychological injuries incurred during the war as a basis for compensation was finally revoked in the amended Invalid Persons Act in 1929. In § 4 of this act, a war invalid is defined as

> [a combatant] who after the first clashes at the border after the war was declared, or after the beginning of clashes with the enemy and before the end of the war, 'was wounded, injured or hurt in a way that has functionally crippled a body part, and whose ability to perform economic activity is thus lost or diminished to such a degree that he can be, in accordance with the stipulations of this law, recognized as a war invalid'.[58]

From the moment this law came into effect, psychologically disturbed ex-soldiers were not considered to be war invalids and as a result were sent to mental institutions. Psychiatry followed in the footsteps of social policy. In 1930, only one year after the amended Invalid Persons Act was adopted, *Vojnosanitetski glasnik*, a Yugoslav journal for military medicine, published an article in which the authors, confirming and completely in agreement with the spirit permeating contemporary social policy, infer: 'Mental disorders among the injured who are in shock are manifested particularly among individuals with abnormal psychological constitutions (alcoholics and syphilitics)'.[59]

We can clearly see that the interwar period in Yugoslavia was marked by the interplay between the psychiatric discourse and the social policy discourse. This interaction was not a peculiarity of Southeastern

Europe or Yugoslavia, and it could be observed in most nations that participated in the First World War. The peculiarity of the region was the fact that during the Balkan Wars, psychiatry, as a science, was already colluding with politics. At the time, in 1912 and 1913, the nationalistic and patriotic tenor of psychiatry was stronger than its ties to social policy. However, it was a foreshadowing of what would come during and after the First World War and what would become a sign of the times both in Western Europe and in (South)Eastern Europe: the frighteningly strong political bias of the science of psychiatry, and its uncommon readiness to accommodate.

Heike Karge is Assistant Professor at the Chair for Southeast and East European History, University of Regensburg. She is the author of *Steinerne Erinnerung – versteinerte Erinnerung? Kriegsgedenken im sozialistischen Jugoslawien* (Harrassowitz, 2010), revised and translated into Serbocroatian as *Sećanje u kamenu – okamjeno sećanje?* (Biblioteka XX vek, 2014). Recently, she co-edited, with Friederike Kind-Kovacs and Sara Bernasconi, *From the Midwife's Bag to the Patient's File: Public Health in Eastern Europe* (CEU Press 2017). Currently, she is working on a book on *Mental Breakdown in War in the Yugoslav Area in the First Half of the 20th Century*.

Notes

1 M.F., 'Dr. V.M. Subotić: Duševna oboljenja u vojskama Srbije, Bugarske, Grčke i Crnegore za vrijeme i u posljetku balkanskih ratova 1912/13' [Dr V.M. Subotić: Mental Illness in the Serbian, Bulgarian, Greek and Montenegrin Armies during and after the Balkan Wars 1912/13], *Liječnički vjesnik* 36(4) (1914), 217–20, here 217.
2 Ibid., 218.
3 Ibid., 218.
4 The numbers of soldiers in the Serbian, Bulgarian, Montenegrin and Greek armies are given here as they are mentioned by M.F.
5 M.F., 'Dr. V.M. Subotić', 219.
6 Cf. Helen Gardikas-Katsiadakis, 'The Balkan Wars 1912–13: Their Effect on the Everyday Life of Civilians', in Council of Europe (ed.), *Crossroads of European Histories: Multiple Outlooks on Five Key Moments in the History of Europe* (Strasbourg: Council of Europe Publ., 2006), 89–100, here 90, for an assessment of the strength of the Greek army. She mentions an army of about 150,000 men. If this number were taken as a basis, the Greek percentage of mentally ill soldiers would be close to that of the Serbian and Montenegrin armies.

7   M.F., 'Dr. V.M. Subotić', 220.
8   Ibid., 219.
9   Ibid.
10 Few historians so far have dealt with the subject of psychiatry in Yugoslav cultural history. One of them is Ana Antić, who wrote her dissertation on the subject of psychiatry in Yugoslavia during the Second World War. Cf. Ana Antić, *Therapeutic Fascism Experiencing the Violence of the Nazi New Order* (Oxford: Oxford University Press, 2016).
11 One can at least partly draw on the research done by Ljubomir Petrović, who examined the situation of war invalids in interwar Yugoslavia. Cf. Ljubomir Petrović, *Nevidljivi geto – invalidi u Kraljevini Jugoslaviji: 1918–1941* [The Invisible Ghetto – Invalids in the Kingdom of Yugoslavia: 1918–1941] (Belgrade: Institut za savremenu istoriju, 2007).
12 For Austria and Germany, see Hans-Georg Hofer, 'Was waren "Kriegsneurosen"? Zur Kulturgeschichte psychischer Erkrankungen im Ersten Weltkrieg', in Hermann J.W. Kuprian and Oswald Überegger (eds), *Der Erste Weltkrieg im Alpenraum: Erfahrung, Deutung, Erinnerung* (Innsbruck: Universitätsverlag Wagner, 2006), 309–21. For other countries, see for instance Simon Wessely, 'Twentieth-Century Theories on Combat Motivation and Breakdown', *Journal of Contemporary History* 41(2) (2006), 268–86; George L. Mosse, 'Shell-Shock as a Social Disease', *Journal of Contemporary History* 35(1) (2000), 101–8. For the various terms for war neurosis, see Jay Winter, 'Shell-Shock and the Cultural History of the Great War', *Journal of Contemporary History* 35(1) (2000), 7–11.
13 I analysed the *Liječnički vjesnik* for the years 1904–17 and the *Srpski arhiv za celokupno lekarstvo* for the years 1912–46.
14 For the history of violence, see Dirk Schumann and Andreas Wirsching (eds), *Violence and Society after the First World War* (Munich: C.H. Beck Verlag, 2003); for the perspective of gender history, see Ute Daniel, 'Fiktionen, Friktionen und Fakten – Frauenlohnarbeit im Ersten Weltkrieg', in Wolfgang Michalka (ed.), *Der Erste Weltkrieg: Wirkung, Wahrnehmung, Analyse* (Munich: Piper, 1994), 530–62.
15 See Vladimir Dugački, 'Proces institucionalizacije hrvatske medicine do prvoga svjetskog rata' [The Process of Institutionalization of Croatian Medicine up to the First World War], *Acta Medico-Historica Adriatica* 7(1) (2009), 61–70. For Serbian medical students in Western and Central Europe in the nineteenth century, see Ljubinka Trgovčević, *Planirana Elita: O studentima iz Srbije na Evropskim univerzitetima u 19. veku* [The Planned Elite: Students from Serbia at European Universities in the 19th Century] (Belgrade: Istorijski Institut, 2003).
16 For Stenjevec, see Rudolf Herceg, 'Zavod za umobolne "Stenjevec" od 1879 do 1933' [The 'Stenjevec' Institute for the Mentally Ill from 1879 to 1933], in Društvo za socijalnu pomoć duševnim bolesnicima u Stenjevcu (ed.), *Stenjevec: Državna bolnica za duševne bolesti 1879–1933* [Stenjevec: State Hospital for Mental Diseases 1879–1933] (Zagreb: Zagrebačka Privredna Štamparija, 1933), 6–29, here 10. For Guberevac, see Jovan Danić and Mihailo Cvijetić, *Duševne bolesti u Srbiji: Statistika bolnice za duševne bolesti za prvih trideset godina (1861–1890)* [Mental Illness in Serbia: Statistics of the

Hospital for Mental Illness for the First Thirty Years (1861–1890)] (Belgrade: Državna štamparija Kraljevine Srbije, 1895), 21.
17 The author inspected the patient archives of the Hospital for Mental Diseases in Vrapče, the successor to the hospital in Stenjevec. The archival patient records date back to the year 1880.
18 For a long time, the journal *Liječnički vjesnik* was the only South Slav medical journal. The journal of the Serbian Medical Society, *Srpski Arhiv za celokupno lekarstvo*, began publication in 1895.
19 Ivan Žirovčić, 'O nazivlju i razdielbi duševnih bolesti' [On the Concept and Classification of Mental Diseases], *Liječnički vjesnik* 17(1) (1895), 1–5; continued under the same title, *Liječnički vjesnik* 17(2) (1895), 17–21; and *Liječnički vjesnik* 17(5) (1895), 89–93.
20 Žirovčić, 'O nazivlju i razdielbi', 1. In the Serbian hospital too, *dementia paralytica* was the most commonly diagnosed mental disease. See Danić and Cvijetić, *Duševne bolesti*, 48.
21 The Sanitary Act, adopted in 1881, downgraded the position of the administrator of the Belgrade hospital. It became no different from the position of an ordinary district physician. Cf. Danić and Cvijetić, *Duševne bolesti*, 24.
22 Đuro Vranešić, 'Neuroze (Neurastenija, histerija i ostali oblici živčane slabosti)' [Neuroses (Neurasthenia, Hysteria and Other Forms of Nervous Infirmity)], *Priroda* 21(7–8) (1931), 196–228, here 198.
23 Focusing on these aspects, see also Indira Duraković, 'Experimentierfeld Balkan: Ärzte am Schauplatz der Balkankriege 1912/13', *Südost-Forschungen* 68 (2009), 298–327.
24 I.H., 'Pod crvenim krstom' [Under the Red Cross], *Liječnički vjesnik* 34(12) (1912), 486–87; Vojslav Subotić, 'Pod crvenim krstom' [Under the Red Cross], *Liječnički vjesnik* 35(3) (1913), 109–13; Edo Šlajmer, 'Pod crvenim krstom' [Under the Red Cross], *Liječnički vjesnik* 35(4) (1913), 171–77; and Julius Budisavljević, 'Pod crvenim krstom: Liječnička iskustva iz drugog balkanskog rata' [Under the Red Cross: Medical Experiences from the Second Balkan War], *Liječnički vjesnik* 35(5) (1913), 223–29. See also Ivan Oražen, 'Medju ranjenom srpskom braćom' [Among the Injured Serbian Brothers], *Liječnički vjesnik* 35(9) (1913), 436–38; Vatroslav Florschütz, 'Iskustva iz ratne bolnice' [Experiences from the War Hospital], *Liječnički vjesnik* 36(1) (1914), 1–14; Julius Budisavljević, 'Pod crvenim križem: Liječnička iskustva iz drugog balkanskog rata' [Under the Red Cross: Medical Experiences from the Second Balkan War], *Liječnički vjesnik* 36(8) (1914), 382–89; continued under the same title, *Liječnički vjesnik* 36(9) (1914), 432–44.
25 Milan Figartner, 'Serbischer und bulgarischer Feldsanitätsdienst', *Srpski arhiv za celokupno lekarstvo* 19(3) (1913), 77–78, here 77.
26 [No author], 'Ranjenici i bolesnici u ratu' [The Injured and the Sick during Wartime], *Narodno zdravlje. Lekarske pouke narodu* 18(2) (1913), 25–27, here 26.
27 According to the aforementioned statistics, in the Balkan Wars Serbia lost thirteen thousand servicemen in combat and twelve thousand to disease. Cf. M.F., 'Dr. V.M. Subotić', 217.

28 Béla Révész, 'Psychiatrische Fürsorge auf dem Kriegsschauplatze', *Wiener Klinische Wochenschrift* 25(50) (1912), 1, 965–67.
29 Srđan Milovanović et al., 'The Historical Development of Psychiatry in Serbia', *Psychiatria danubina* 21(2) (2009), 156–65, here 160.
30 Klaus-Dieter Thomann and Michael Rauschmann, 'Die "posttraumatische Belastungsstörung" – historische Aspekte einer "modernen" psychischen Erkrankung im deutschen Sprachraum', *Medizin-Historisches Journal* 38(1) (2003), 103–38, here 113.
31 [No author], 'Godišnji izveštaj Bolnice za duševne bolesti za 1912 godinu' [Annual Report of the Hospital for Mental Diseases for the Year 1912], *Srpski arhiv za celokupno lekarstvo* 19(3) (1913), 81–82.
32 [No author], 'Godišnji izveštaj Bolnice za duševne bolesti za 1913 g.' [Annual Report of the Hospital for Mental Diseases for the Year 1913], *Srpski arhiv za celokupno lekarstvo* 20(1) (1914), 22–23.
33 Nikola Vujić, 'Godišnji izvještaji naših bolnica: Iskaz o gibanju bolesnika tečajem godine 1912. u općoj javnoj bolnici u Mitrovici' [Annual Report of Our Hospitals: List of the Sick for the Year 1912 in the General Public Hospital in Mitrovica], *Liječnički vjesnik* 35(16) (1913), 5–8; Leo Vrbanić, 'Godišnji izvještaji naših bolnica: Iskaz o gibanju bolesnika tečajem godine 1912. u javnoj sveopćoj bolnici u Vinkovcima' [Annual Report of Our Hospitals: List of the Sick for the Year 1912 in the Public Hospital in Vinkovci], *Liječnički vjesnik* 35(20) (1913), 1–6; and Kosta Mladenović, 'Godišnji izvještaji naših bolnica: Iskaz o gibanju bolesnika tečajem godine 1912. u javnoj sveopćoj gradskoj bolnici u Novoj Gradiški' [Annual Report of Our Hospitals: List of the Sick for the Year 1912 in the Public and General Municipal Hospital in Nova Gradiška], *Liječnički vjesnik* 35(27) (1913), 5–8.
34 [No author], 'Sanitetska izvešća' [Sanitary Information], *Srpski arhiv za celokupno lekarstvo* 18(3) (1912), 107.
35 Vojni Arhiv Beograd (VA), Fond Vojske Kraljevine Srbije (FVKS), Balkanski ratovi 1912/13 (P-2), k-63, f-1, d-1/1.
36 VA, FVKS, P-2, k-29, f-1, d-6/1.
37 I.H., 'Pod crvenim krstom', 487.
38 The term 'degeneration' is used also in [no author], 'Degeneracija bosansko-hercegovačkih vojnika' [Degeneration of Bosnian-Herzegovinian Soldiers], *Liječnički vjesnik* 34(11) (1912), 467. The author states that 214 Bosnian soldiers were admitted to the psychiatric ward of a Vienna hospital from 1897 to 1906. The author refers to studies showing that these soldiers more frequently fell ill and died in active service as a result of poor hygiene, widespread syphilis and heavy alcohol abuse.
39 [No author], 'Zdravlje u ratu' [Health in War], *Narodno zdravlje* 19(1) (1914), 15–19, here 17.
40 M.Đ. Popović, *Alkohol u Balkanskom ratu* [Alcohol during the Balkan War] (Belgrade: Štamparija Merkur, 1914), 14.
41 Ibid., 7.
42 Ibid.
43 [No author], 'Zdravlje u ratu', 19.
44 Alfred Exner, 'Kriegschirurgische Erfahrungen aus Bulgarien', *Wiener Klinische Wochenschrift* 26(6) (1913), 203–5, here 203–4. Similarly also, Hans

Heyrovsky, 'Chirurgische Erfahrungen aus dem Bulgarisch-Türkischen Krieg', *Wiener Klinische Wochenschrift* 26(6) (1913), 205–6; Johann Steiner, 'Feldärztliche Erfahrungen in der vordersten Hilfszone', *Wiener Klinische Wochenschrift* 26(9) (1913), 321–23.

45 F. Hijmans, 'Balkanski rat: Dva meseca u službi srpskog Crvenog Krsta' [The Balkan War: Two Months in the Service of the Serbian Red Cross], *Srpski arhiv za celokupno lekarstvo* 19(3) (1913), 76–77; Milivoj Kostić, 'Die chirurgischen Erfahrungen im Balkankriege', *Srpski arhiv za celokupno lekarstvo* 19(3) (1913), 78–79.

46 Figartner, 'Serbischer und bulgarischer Feldsanitätsdienst', 77–78.

47 Popović, *Alkohol u Balkanskom ratu*, 9.

48 Ibid., 16.

49 [No author], 'Alkoholna pića u ratu' [Alcoholic Beverages in Wartime], *Liječnički vjesnik* 36(12) (1914), 607.

50 Vladislav M. Bogdanović, 'Alkohol i njegov uticaj na naše fizičke i duševne osobine: Njegova socijalna štetnost' [Alcohol and Its Influence on Our Physical and Mental Properties: Its Negative Social Effects], *Srpski arhiv za celokupno lekarstvo* 42(11) (1940), 573–81, here 577.

51 Josip Dojč, 'Psihička trauma ranjenika i njezino lečenje' [The Mental Trauma of the Injured and Its Healing], *Vojnosanitetski pregled* 3(1) (1946), 24–27, here 24–25.

52 Cf. Milovanović, 'The Historical Development of Psychiatry', 160.

53 Herceg, 'Zavod za umobolne', 10.

54 Cf. the following book reviews: Č., 'Književne Vijesti [Literary News]: A. Silberstein, Kriegsinvalidenfürsorge, Würzburg 1916', *Liječnički vjesnik* 37(5) (1915), 105; Ljudevit Thaller, 'Književne Vijesti: Kurt Singer, Die Objektivierung nervöser Beschwerden im Kriege, Würzburg 1916', *Liječnički vjesnik* 38(8) (1916), 261–62; Ljudevit Thaller, 'Histerija i traumatska neuroza' [Hysteria and Traumatic Neurosis], *Liječnički vjesnik* 39(7) (1917), 259–63.

55 Laza Stanojević, 'Kako treba "rentne neuroze" shvatiti sa sudsko-medicinskog gledišta?' [How to Understand 'Pension Neurosis' from the Perspective of Forensic Medicine], *Vojnosanitetski glasnik* 2(3) (1931), 521–24; and Vranešić, 'Neuroze', 213, who states: 'However, it is a fact that we do not have any data on traumatic neurosis from the time before social security was introduced …'.

56 Thomann and Rauschmann, 'Die "posttraumatische Belastungsstörung"', 114.

57 Wessely, 'Twentieth-Century Theories', 272.

58 Đuro Šurmin, 'Invalidsko pitanje u Jugoslaviji' [The Problem of the Invalids in Yugoslavia], *Invalid* (1935), 38.

59 Gavrilo Petrović and Ivo Jovanović, 'O traumatičnom šoku: Mehanizam, simptomatologija i lečenje' [On the Traumatic Shock: Mechanism, Symptomatology and Healing], *Vojnosanitetski glasnik* 1(3–4) (1930), 193–206, here 198.

Bibliography

[No author]. 'Alkoholna pića u ratu' [Alcoholic Beverages in Wartime]. *Liječnički vjesnik* 36(12) (1914), 607.
[No author]. 'Degeneracija bosansko-hercegovačkih vojnika' [Degeneration of Bosnian-Herzegovinian Soldiers]. *Liječnički vjesnik* 34(11) (1912), 467.
[No author]. 'Godišnji izveštaj Bolnice za duševne bolesti za 1912 godinu' [Annual Report of the Hospital for Mental Diseases for the Year 1912]. *Srpski arhiv za celokupno lekarstvo* 19(3) (1913), 81–82.
[No author]. 'Godišnji izveštaj Bolnice za duševne bolesti za 1913 g.' [Annual Report of the Hospital for Mental Diseases for the Year 1913]. *Srpski arhiv za celokupno lekarstvo* 20(1) (1914), 22–23.
[No author]. 'Ranjenici i bolesnici u ratu' [The Injured and the Sick during Wartime]. *Narodno zdravlje. Lekarske pouke narodu* 18(2) (1913), 25–27.
[No author]. 'Sanitetska izvešća' [Sanitary Information]. *Srpski arhiv za celokupno lekarstvo* 18(3) (1912), 107.
[No author]. 'Zdravlje u ratu' [Health in War]. *Narodno zdravlje* 19(1) (1914), 15–19.
Antić, Ana. *Psychiatry at War: Psychiatric Culture and Political Ideology in Yugoslavia under the Nazi Occupation*. Columbia University Academic Commons, 2012. DOI: 10.7916/D8JS9NJC.
Bogdanović, Vladislav M. 'Alkohol i njegov uticaj na naše fizičke i duševne osobine: Njegova socijalna štetnost' [Alcohol and Its Influence on Our Physical and Mental Properties: Its Negative Social Effects]. *Srpski arhiv za celokupno lekarstvo* 42(11) (1940), 573–81.
Budisavljević, Julius. 'Pod crvenim križem: Liječnička iskustva iz drugog balkanskog rata' [Under the Red Cross: Medical Experiences from the Second Balkan War]. *Liječnički vjesnik* 35(5) (1913), 223–29.
———. 'Pod crvenim križem: Liječnička iskustva iz drugog balkanskog rata' [Under the Red Cross: Medical Experiences from the Second Balkan War]. *Liječnički vjesnik* 36(8) (1914), 382–89.
———. 'Pod crvenim križem: Liječnička iskustva iz drugog balkanskog rata' [Under the Red Cross: Medical Experiences from the Second Balkan War]. *Liječnički vjesnik* 36(9) (1914), 432–44.
Č. 'Književne Vijesti [Literary News]: A. Silberstein, Kriegsinvalidenfürsorge, Würzburg 1916'. *Liječnički vjesnik* 37(5) (1915), 105.
Danić, Jovan, and Mihailo Cvijetić. *Duševne bolesti u Srbiji: Statistika bolnice za duševne bolesti za prvih trideset godina (1861–1890)* [Mental Illness in Serbia: Statistics of the Hospital for Mental Illness for the First Thirty Years (1861–1890)]. Belgrade: Državna štamparija Kraljevine Srbije, 1895.
Daniel, Ute. 'Fiktionen, Friktionen und Fakten – Frauenlohnarbeit im Ersten Weltkrieg', in Wolfgang Michalka (ed.), *Der Erste Weltkrieg: Wirkung, Wahrnehmung, Analyse* (Munich: Piper, 1994), 530–62.
Dojč, Josip. 'Psihička trauma ranjenika i njezino lečenje' [The Mental Trauma of the Injured and Its Healing]. *Vojnosanitetski pregled* 3(1) (1946), 24–27.
Dugački, Vladimir. 'Proces institucionalizacije hrvatske medicine do prvoga svjetskog rata' [The Process of Institutionalization of Croatian Medicine up to the First World War]. *Acta Medico-Historica Adriatica* 7(1) (2009), 61–70.

Duraković, Indira. 'Experimentierfeld Balkan: Ärzte am Schauplatz der Balkankriege 1912/13'. *Südost-Forschungen* 68 (2009), 298–327.

Exner, Alfred. 'Kriegschirurgische Erfahrungen aus Bulgarien'. *Wiener Klinische Wochenschrift* 26(6) (1913), 203–5.

F., M. 'Dr. V.M. Subotić: Duševna oboljenja u vojskama Srbije, Bugarske, Grčke i Crnegore za vrijeme i u posljetku balkanskih ratova 1912/13' [Dr V.M. Subotić: Mental Illness in the Serbian, Bulgarian, Greek and Montenegrin Armies during and after the Balkan Wars 1912/13]. *Liječnički vjesnik* 36(4) (1914), 217–20.

Figartner, Milan. 'Serbischer und bulgarischer Feldsanitätsdienst'. *Srpski arhiv za celokupno lekarstvo* 19(3) (1913), 77–78.

Florschütz, Vatroslav. 'Iskustva iz ratne bolnice' [Experiences from the War Hospital]. *Liječnički vjesnik* 36(1) (1914), 1–14.

Gardikas-Katsiadakis, Helen. 'The Balkan Wars 1912–13: Their Effect on the Everyday Life of Civilians', in Council of Europe (ed.), *Crossroads of European Histories: Multiple Outlooks on Five Key Moments in the History of Europe* (Strasbourg: Council of Europe Publ., 2006), 89–100.

H., I. 'Pod crvenim krstom' [Under the Red Cross]. *Liječnički vjesnik* 34(12) (1912), 486–87.

Herceg, Rudolf. 'Zavod za umobolne "Stenjevec" od 1879 do 1933' [The "Stenjevec" Institute for the Mentally Ill from 1879 to 1933], in Društvo za socijalnu pomoć duševnim bolesnicima u Stenjevcu (ed.), *Stenjevec: Državna bolnica za duševne bolesti 1879–1933* [Stenjevec: State Hospital for Mental Diseases 1879–1933] (Zagreb: Zagrebaćka Privredna Štamparija, 1933), 6–29.

Heyrovsky, Hans. 'Chirurgische Erfahrungen aus dem Bulgarisch-Türkischen Krieg'. *Wiener Klinische Wochenschrift* 26(6) (1913), 205–6.

Hijmans, F. 'Balkanski rat: Dva meseca u službi srpskog Crvenog Krsta' [The Balkan War: Two Months in the Service of the Serbian Red Cross]. *Srpski arhiv za celokupno lekarstvo* 19(3) (1913), 76–77.

Hofer, Hans-Georg. 'Was waren "Kriegsneurosen"? Zur Kulturgeschichte psychischer Erkrankungen im Ersten Weltkrieg', in Hermann J.W. Kuprian, and Oswald Überegger (eds), *Der Erste Weltkrieg im Alpenraum: Erfahrung, Deutung, Erinnerung* (Innsbruck: Universitätsverlag Wagner, 2006), 309–21.

Kostić, Milivoj. 'Die chirurgischen Erfahrungen im Balkankriege'. *Srpski arhiv za celokupno lekarstvo* 19(3) (1913), 78–79.

Milovanović, Srđan, et al. 'The Historical Development of Psychiatry in Serbia'. *Psychiatria danubina* 21(2) (2009), 156–65.

Mladenović, Kosta. 'Godišnji izvještaji naših bolnica: Iskaz o gibanju bolesnika tečajem godine 1912. u javnoj sveopćoj gradskoj bolnici u Novoj Gradiški' [Annual Report of Our Hospitals: List of the Sick for the Year 1912 in the Public and General Municipal Hospital in Nova Gradiška]. *Liječnički vjesnik* 35(27) (1913), 5–8.

Mosse, George L. 'Shell-Shock as a Social Disease'. *Journal of Contemporary History* 35(1) (2000), 101–8.

Oražen, Ivan. 'Medju ranjenom srpskom braćom' [Among the Injured Serbian Brothers]. *Liječnički vjesnik* 35(9) (1913), 436–38.

Petrović, Gavrilo, and Ivo Jovanović. 'O traumatičnom šoku: Mehanizam, simptomatologija i lečenje' [On the Traumatic Shock: Mechanism, Symptomatology and Healing]. *Vojnosanitetski glasnik* 1(3–4) (1930), 193–206.

Petrović, Ljubomir. *Nevidljivi geto – invalidi u Kraljevini Jugoslaviji: 1918–1941* [The Invisible Ghetto – Invalids in the Kingdom of Yugoslavia: 1918–1941]. Belgrade: Institut za savremenu istoriju, 2007.

Popović, M.Ð. *Alkohol u Balkanskom ratu* [Alcohol during the Balkan War]. Belgrade: Štamparija Merkur, 1914.

Révész, Béla. 'Psychiatrische Fürsorge auf dem Kriegsschauplatze'. *Wiener Klinische Wochenschrift* 25(50) (1912), 1,965–67.

Schumann, Dirk, and Andreas Wirsching (eds). *Violence and Society after the First World War*. Munich: C.H. Beck Verlag, 2003.

Šlajmer, Edo. 'Pod crvenim krstom' [Under the Red Cross]. *Liječnički vjesnik* 35(4) (1913), 171–77.

Stanojević, Laza. 'Kako treba "rentne neuroze" shvatiti sa sudsko-medicinskog gledišta?' [How to Understand 'Pension Neurosis' from the Perspective of Forensic Medicine]. *Vojnosanitetski glasnik* 2(3) (1931), 521–24.

Steiner, Johann. 'Feldärztliche Erfahrungen in der vordersten Hilfszone'. *Wiener Klinische Wochenschrift* 26(9) (1913), 321–23.

Subotić, Vojslav M. 'Pod crvenim krstom' [Under the Red Cross]. *Liječnički vjesnik* 35(3) (1913), 109–13.

Šurmin, Ðuro. 'Invalidsko pitanje u Jugoslaviji' [The Problem of the Invalids in Yugoslavia]. *Invalid* (1935), 38.

Thaller, Ljudevit. 'Književne Vijesti: Kurt Singer, Die Objektivierung nervöser Beschwerden im Kriege, Würzburg 1916'. *Liječnički Vjesnik* 38(8) (1916), 261–62.

———. 'Histerija i traumatska neuroza' [Hysteria and Traumatic Neurosis]. *Liječnički vjesnik* 39(7) (1917), 259–63.

Thomann, Klaus-Dieter, and Michael Rauschmann. 'Die "posttraumatische Belastungsstörung" – historische Aspekte einer "modernen" psychischen Erkrankung im deutschen Sprachraum'. *Medizin-Historisches Journal* 38(1) (2003), 103–38.

Trgovčević, Ljubinka. *Planirana Elita: O studentima iz Srbije na Evropskim univerzitetima u 19. veku* [The Planned Elite: Students from Serbia at European Universities in the 19th Century]. Belgrade: Istorijski Institut, 2003.

Vranešić, Ðuro. 'Neuroze (Neurastenija, histerija i ostali oblici živčane slabosti)' [Neuroses (Neurasthenia, Hysteria and Other Forms of Nervous Infirmity)]. *Priroda* 21(7–8) (1931), 196–228.

Vrbanić, Leo. 'Godišnji izvještaji naših bolnica: Iskaz o gibanju bolesnika tečajem godine 1912. u javnoj sveopćoj bolnici u Vinkovcima' [Annual Report of Our Hospitals: List of the Sick for the Year 1912 in the Public Hospital in Vinkovci]. *Liječnički vjesnik* 35(20) (1913), 1–6.

Vujić, Nikola. 'Godišnji izvještaji naših bolnica: Iskaz o gibanju bolesnika tečajem godine 1912. u općoj javnoj bolnici u Mitrovici' [Annual Report of Our Hospitals: List of the Sick for the Year 1912 in the General Public Hospital in Mitrovica]. *Liječnički vjesnik* 35(16) (1913), 5–8.

Wessely, Simon. 'Twentieth-Century Theories on Combat Motivation and Breakdown'. *Journal of Contemporary History* 41(2) (2006), 268–86.

Winter, Jay. 'Shell-Shock and the Cultural History of the Great War'. *Journal of Contemporary History* 35(1) (2000), 7–11.

Žirovčić, Ivan. 'O nazivlju i razdielbi duševnih bolesti' [On the Concept and Classification of Mental Diseases]. *Liječnički vjesnik* 17(1) (1895), 1–5.

———. 'O nazivlju i razdielbi duševnih bolesti' [On the Concept and Classification of Mental Diseases]. *Liječnički vjesnik* 17(2) (1895), 17–21.

———. 'O nazivlju i razdielbi duševnih bolesti' [On the Concept and Classification of Mental Diseases]. *Liječnički vjesnik* 17(5) (1895), 89–93.

Conclusion

Bringing the Balkan Wars into Historiographic Debates

Katrin Boeckh and Sabine Rutar

The years 2012–13 marked the centennial of the Balkan Wars, which preceded the First World War and 'reshaped the map of south-eastern Europe'.[1] Given the complex, overlapping and multiethnic layers of historical agency, as well as the sheer quantity of settings, languages involved and, ultimately, canonical traditions to be challenged, our collectively written volume has proved to represent the proper, if not the only, format to examine the topic in a comprehensive, albeit specific way. In this volume, scholars from all over Europe and the US have offered expertise drawn from various academic backgrounds and have produced a multifaceted narrative that defies any (ex-post) nation-state framework. This volume's case studies communicate with one another through the common methodological intention of 'writing in' the Balkan Wars to integrate them better into the history of European warfare. In going beyond the exclusivity of the nation-state perspective, the authors have paved the way to further research that will broaden our knowledge in analogously comparative, if not entangled ways. At stake here has been the introduction of the potential to achieve a solid grip on the social history of early twentieth-century warfare, in the vein of the field of New Military History. Involving scholars from the (successor) states of all former belligerents, the book makes evident the conspicuously parallel experiences of all the societies engulfed in these wars. This entanglement of empirical research on these wars pursues a 'Europeanizing' and even a 'globalizing' effect.

The twentieth century's wars and violence are of pivotal relevance in the current debates on the proper interpretation of twentieth-century European history. Arguably most emblematic in this respect are Timothy Snyder's *Bloodlands: Europe between Hitler and Stalin* and Christopher Clark's *The Sleepwalkers: How Europe Went to War in*

1914, the latter representing precisely an effort to Europeanize, if not globalize, the history of the First World War.[2] Especially with reference to Clark's effort, our volume works towards the increased inclusion of the Balkans and Turkey in the ongoing debate.

Western scholars, if they have paid attention to the two Balkan Wars of 1912–13 at all, have tended to see them as a 'prelude' to the Great War; their interpretive frameworks place them merely 'in the shadow' of the subsequent global conflagration. Mostly, the Balkans have been treated as a peripheral historical region at the mercy of great power politics. In challenging this pervasive scholarly assumption, this volume strengthens an emerging field that examines the enmeshed and comparative histories of Southeastern Europe, represented for example by the recent four-volume work *Entangled Histories of the Balkans*[3] and by *Beyond the Balkans: Towards an Inclusive History of Southeastern Europe*, edited by Sabine Rutar.[4] Not least, our recent jointly edited volume, *The Balkan Wars from Contemporary Perception to Historic Memory*, assesses the mnemonic workings related to the Balkan Wars, clearly bringing to light their unduly neglected European dimensions.[5]

As this book shows, the Balkan Wars offer grounds for ambivalent and contradictory assessments. Whereas in the Balkan countries themselves they have long been generally glorified as 'wars of liberation', with little attention given to their violence and social consequences,[6] elsewhere in Europe the public and the historiography often described them almost exclusively via negative stereotypes, with familiar dialectical pillars: 'powder keg', 'rogue states', 'propensity towards violence' and 'Balkanization'. As Wolfgang Höpken convincingly shows in his contribution to this book, many considered the Balkan Wars to be 'traditional' and 'typically Balkan', while others, such as the military experts who travelled in great numbers to the Balkan battlefields, viewed them as a 'modern' event because they clearly saw in them a foreshadowing of what Europe would experience in the eventuality of war. To be sure, authors like Mark Mazower and Niall Ferguson have considered the violence of the Balkan Wars in the broader context of what happened in other parts of Europe during the 'age of extremes'.[7] Reflecting upon the Yugoslav wars of the 1990s, and trying to save the region and its people from the 'orientalist' accusation of being inherently violent, Mark Biondich has regarded the wars and violence in the Balkans to be an integral part of Europe's 'dark' twentieth century.[8] The Balkan Wars were hybrid in nature, blending traditional warfare with many characteristics of later twentieth-century European conflicts. The authors in this volume make evident these deeply ambivalent features. The wars were 'the last Turkish wars' in the tradition of the eighteenth- and nineteenth-century 'oriental question', but at the same time they went very much beyond the kind of warfare experienced in the region during the previous two centuries.[9]

In terms of the exercise of violence, the Balkan Wars and the First World War cannot be distinguished, and future researchers should commit themselves to comprehensive reading, to avoid the trap of cultural determinism.[10] The Balkan Wars were accompanied by a completely new dimension of general mobilization, and the number of prisoners of war was unprecedented in the region. Unsurprisingly, these prisoners' treatment became grounds for accusations made on all sides, whether justified or not. Yet, if mistreatment and even the killing of prisoners occurred, scholars would still need to assess them within the framework of other wars, not least the First World War, to adequately contextualize them.[11] Also, the phenomenon of ethnic 'cleansing' is often perceived as an idiosyncratic outgrowth of the nationalization processes of Southeastern Europe and its multiethnic patchwork. Yet, while events during the Balkan Wars certainly set a precedent for systematically exercised violence, there would be many parallels on the Eastern Front during the First World War, and this type of violence would become an intrinsic feature of the Second World War and extend well into its aftermath.[12]

Following Maria Todorova's influential paradigm of the 'imagining of the Balkans', scholars, not least in relation to the Balkan Wars, have warned against debating these wars in terms of 'a "typification" of differences between Europe and the Balkan "other"'.[13] Indeed, in placing the Balkan Wars within European war history, one should not exoticize them as 'un-European' wars that deviate from the traditions of 'regulated' European warfare. Rather, they should be seen in light of their deep vacillation between 'traditional' and 'modern' forms of modern armed conflict. Highly modernized armies and an unprecedented mobilization of manpower came up against the limited institutional and organizational capacities of 'premodern' states and societies. The destructive capabilities of 'modern' armies merged with a 'tradition' of warfare that made no clear distinction between 'regular' and 'irregular' actors. The result was a hitherto unknown level of violence and the overturning of experiences and skills that people had derived from the experiences of previous wars. In their ideological dimensions, the wars no less show their deeply ambiguous character, as they were fuelled not only by the 'traditional' romantic nationalism that surrounded the nineteenth-century 'oriental question' but also by the 'new', twentieth-century rhetoric of 'culturalism' and 'racism'. Conventional religious arguments may have legitimized these wars, but they also offered a field for new existential experiences, as even intellectuals grasped. If 'modernity and primitive archaism coexisted in the Great War', as Stéphane Audoin-Rouzeau and Annette Becker have remarked,[14] then the Balkan Wars surely are to be considered part and parcel of this history – *these* wars were the primordial experimental laboratory for modern warfare.

Besides this significance for European, if not global history, little is known in other areas of the world about these wars' importance for the history of the wider region in which they took place. In Southeastern Europe, the construction of the historical memory of the Balkan Wars throughout the twentieth century hovered around ideas of heroism and victimhood, aiming to solidify the respective nation-states. For the Ottoman Empire, the Balkan Wars inflicted a traumatic territorial loss. This trauma extended into the post-Ottoman republic; it strengthened Turkish nationalism and made it more aggressive. Also, it buried the last dreams of Ottomanism, in the sense of a cohabitation among communities tied together by their loyalty to the Ottoman state. Part and parcel of this remembrance recently has been a new form of Ottomanism, in the sense that the various unspoken memories of the defeat and the loss of European Turkey were finally expressed, including a reimagination of the *Pax Ottomanica* in the Balkans, the imperial rule in peace that the Ottomans had not been able to sustain. The dissonances in the official memories of the Balkan Wars thus abounded on several levels – and not least between their manifestations in Western and Eastern Europe. While Western Europe forgot about the Balkan Wars shortly after their end, in Southeastern Europe, and especially among the belligerents, remembering the wars has been of constitutional importance.

Western scholars have tended to perceive the Balkan Wars nearly exclusively in terms of their military actions. During the 1990s, in the face of the Yugoslav wars of dissolution – all too often erroneously labelled the 'new' Balkan wars – they renewed their focus on atrocities. The story of the exoticization of the Balkans thus comes full circle.[15] In each of the (successor) states of the former belligerents, on the other hand, remembering the Balkan Wars has entailed a quest for a smoothed-out, uncontested representation. Yet while the Western audience has not even been willing to differentiate the First from the Second Balkan War and acknowledge their differing alliances, Bulgarian historians have characterized the Second Balkan War as the 'inter-alliance war', whereas Turkish historians often enough spoke only of 'the' Balkan war, showing no reference whatsoever to the intra-Balkan conflict that ensued. Fragmentation on varying levels, thus, is evident.[16]

After the end of the organized military actions in 1913, no period of peace followed in the Balkans. On the contrary, while the new state borders were drawn, guerrilla fighting continued, with informal military groups terrorizing the civilian population and expelling those whom they perceived as 'non-natives' of their respective newly gained territories. On the state level, the Balkan governments introduced propaganda campaigns accusing the other former belligerents of war crimes. Alas, the large number of pamphlets, reports and leaflets documenting the atrocities committed during *and* after the wars by all sides involved did not reach the diplomats of the great powers, whose decisions about the future of the former Ottoman territories reckoned only with their own interests.[17]

One of the main reasons for the East–West gap in perceptions is the differing meanings of the Great War. In Western Europe, it has come to be perceived as *the* defining catastrophe of the twentieth century. Beyond the collapse of the imperial 'world of yesterday',[18] this conflagration planted the seeds of revenge and further destruction, indeed of another world war. But in Southeastern Europe, the Great War cemented the *status quo ante* that had resulted from the Balkan Wars. Thus here, the 'preluding' regional wars, rather than the subsequent global conflagration, have been perceived as defining a threshold of national histories. To be sure, one aspect is common to all historiographies, in (South-)East and West alike: hardly any of the scholarly debate has been pluri-dimensional. On one side, nation-building efforts dictated historiographic pursuits, while on the other there was simply no interest in doing anything other than affirm stereotypes. Our volume, we are confident, enhances, differentiates and entangles such perspectives – and transcends them.

Katrin Boeckh is Senior Researcher at the Leibniz Institute for East and Southeast European Studies in Regensburg and Professor for East and Southeast European History at the LMU Munich. She is the author of a volume on the Balkan Wars (*Von den Balkankriegen zum Ersten Weltkrieg: Kleinstaatenpolitik und ethnische Selbstbestimmung auf dem Balkan*, Oldenbourg, 1996) and co-editor, with Sabine Rutar, of *The Balkan Wars from Contemporary Perception to Historic Memory* (Palgrave, 2017). Her further monographs cover the political history of Ukraine and of Serbia.

Sabine Rutar is Senior Researcher at the Leibniz Institute for East and Southeast European Studies in Regensburg. She is Editor-in-Chief of the quarterly *Südosteuropa. Journal of Politics and Society*; author of *Kultur – Nation – Milieu: Sozialdemokratie in Triest vor dem Ersten Weltkrieg* (Klartext, 2004); and editor of several academic collections, including *Violence in Late Socialist Public Spheres* (special issue of *European History Quarterly*, 2015) and *Beyond the Balkans: Towards an Inclusive History of Southeastern Europe* (Lit, 2014). Recently, she co-edited (with Katrin Boeckh) *The Balkan Wars from Contemporary Perception to Historic Memory* (Palgrave, 2017).

Notes

1 'The Balkan Wars: Reshaping the Map of South-Eastern Europe', *The Economist*, 9 November 2012, http://www.economist.com/blogs/easternapproaches/2012/11/balkan-wars.
2 Timothy Snyder, *Bloodlands: Europe between Hitler and Stalin* (New York: Basic Books, 2010); Christopher Clark, *The Sleepwalkers: How Europe Went to War in 1914* (London: Penguin, 2012).
3 *Entangled Histories of the Balkans*. Vol. 1: *National Ideologies and Language Policies*, ed. Roumen Daskalov and Tchavdar Marinov (Leiden: Brill, 2013); Vol. 2: *Transfers of Political Ideologies and Institutions*, ed. Roumen Daskalov and Diana Mishkova (Leiden: Brill, 2014); Vol. 3: *Shared Pasts, Disputed Legacies*, ed. Roumen Daskalov and Alexander Vezenkov (Leiden: Brill, 2015); Vol. 4: *Concepts, Approaches, and (Self-)Representations*, ed. Roumen Daskalov, Diana Mishkova, Tchavdar Marinov and Alexander Vezenkov (Leiden: Brill, 2017). None of the volumes focus much on wars, let alone the history or the mnemonic threads pertaining specifically to the Balkan Wars.
4 Sabine Rutar (ed.), *Beyond the Balkans: Towards an Inclusive History of Southeastern Europe* (Vienna: Lit, 2014).
5 Katrin Boeckh and Sabine Rutar (eds), *The Balkan Wars from Contemporary Perception to Historic Memory* (Basingstoke: Palgrave, 2017).
6 In the case of the Bulgarian historiography, for example, Ivan Ilchev concludes that communist rule did not have a great impact on the interpretation of the Balkan Wars, nor did the end of communism 'change the scope of scholarly interest' much, despite the emergence of some new questions raised by younger scholars. There remained 'a general inability to let go of pomp and traditional rhetoric'. Ivan Ilchev, 'The Balkan Wars in Recent Bulgarian Historiography and Textbooks', in Council of Europe (ed.), *Crossroads of European Histories: Multiple Outlooks on Five Key Moments in the History of Europe* (Strasbourg: Council of Europe Publ., 2006), 111–18. Cf. also Svetlozar Eldarov and Bisser Petrov, 'Bulgarian Historiography on the Balkan Wars 1912–13', in Boeckh and Rutar, *The Balkan Wars from Contemporary Perception to Historic Memory*, 219–48.

7 Cf., for example, Mark Mazower, *Dark Continent: Europe's Twentieth Century* (New York: Vintage, 1998) or Niall Ferguson, *The War of the World: Twentieth-Century Conflict and the Descent of the West* (London: Penguin, 2007).

8 Mark Biondich, *The Balkans: Revolutions, Wars and Political Violence since 1878* (Oxford: Oxford University Press, 2011).

9 Cf. Fikret Adanır, 'Ethnonationalism, Irredentism, and Empire', in Boeckh and Rutar, *The Balkan Wars from Contemporary Perception to Historic Memory*, 13–56.

10 Cf., to give but one example, Joanna Bourke, *An Intimate History of Killing: Face-to-Face Killing in 20th Century Warfare* (London: Granta, 1999), which is *not* focused in any way on the Balkans. How would her account have differed had she included them? It seems to be, in fact, the gaze *towards* the Balkans from aloof locations that accounts for a mostly unreflective 'interpretive automatism' with regard to their historic role.

11 Cf. the contributions in Sibylle Scheipers (ed.), *Prisoners in War* (Oxford: Oxford University Press, 2010), especially Stephen C. Neff, 'Prisoners of War in International Law: The Nineteenth Century', 57–74; Alan Kramer, 'Prisoners in the First World War', 75–90; Isabel V. Hull, 'Prisoners in Colonial Warfare: The Imperial German Example', 157–72.

12 Hans Mommsen, 'Anfänge des ethnic cleansing und der Umsiedelungspolitik im Ersten Weltkrieg', in Eduard Mühle (ed.), *Mentalitäten – Nationen – Spannungsfelder: Studien zu Mittel- und Osteuropa im 19. und 20. Jahrhundert, Festschrift für Hans Lemberg* (Marburg: Verlag Herder-Institut, 2001), 147–62; István Deák, 'The Worst of Friends: Germany's Allies in East Central Europe – Struggles for Regional Dominance and Ethnic Cleansing 1938–1945', in Marina Cattaruzza, Stefan Dyrhoff and Dieter Langewiesche (eds), *Territorial Revisionism and the Allies of Germany in the Second World War: Goals, Expectations, Practices* (New York: Berghahn Books, 2013), 17–29; as well as other chapters in the volume.

13 Enika Abazi, 'Between Facts and Interpretations: Three Images of the Balkan Wars of 1912–1913', in James Pettifer and Tom Buchanan (eds), *War in the Balkans: Conflict and Diplomacy before World War I* (London/New York: Tauris, 2016), 203–25, here 218.

14 Stéphane Audoin-Rouzeau and Annette Becker, *14–18: Understanding the Great War* (New York: Hill and Wang, 2002), 59.

15 Cf. Eugène Michail, 'The Balkan Wars in Western Historiography, 1912–2012', in Boeckh and Rutar, *The Balkan Wars from Contemporary Perception to Historic Memory*, 319–40.

16 Comprehensively, on the constructions of (official) remembrance pertaining to the Balkan Wars, cf. Boeckh and Rutar, *The Balkan Wars from Contemporary Perception to Historic Memory*.

17 Katrin Boeckh, *Von den Balkankriegen zum Ersten Weltkrieg: Kleinstaatenpolitik und ethnische Selbstbestimmung auf dem Balkan* (Munich: Oldenbourg, 1996), 365–70.

18 In the sense of Stefan Zweig, *The World of Yesterday: An Autobiography* (Lincoln: University of Nebraska Press, 1964) [German original: *Die Welt von gestern: Erinnerungen eines Europäers* (Stockholm: Bermann-Fischer, 1942)].

Bibliography

Abazi, Enika. 'Between Facts and Interpretations: Three Images of the Balkan Wars of 1912–1913', in James Pettifer and Tom Buchanan (eds), *War in the Balkans: Conflict and Diplomacy before World War I* (London/New York: Tauris, 2016), 203–25.

Adanır, Fikret. 'Ethnonationalism, Irredentism, and Empire', in Katrin Boeckh and Sabine Rutar (eds), *The Balkan Wars from Contemporary Perception to Historic Memory* (Basingstoke: Palgrave, 2017), 13–56.

Audoin-Rouzeau, Stéphane, and Annette Becker. *14–18: Understanding the Great War*. New York: Hill and Wang, 2002.

'The Balkan Wars: Reshaping the Map of South-Eastern Europe'. *The Economist*, 9 November 2012. http://www.economist.com/blogs/easternapproaches/2012/11/balkan-wars.

Biondich, Mark. *The Balkans: Revolutions, Wars and Political Violence since 1878*. Oxford: Oxford University Press, 2011.

Boeckh, Katrin. *Von den Balkankriegen zum Ersten Weltkrieg: Kleinstaatenpolitik und ethnische Selbstbestimmung auf dem Balkan*. Munich: Oldenbourg, 1996.

Boeckh, Katrin, and Sabine Rutar (eds). *The Balkan Wars from Contemporary Perception to Historic Memory*. Basingstoke: Palgrave, 2017.

Bourke, Joanna. *An Intimate History of Killing: Face-to-Face Killing in 20th Century Warfare*. London: Granta, 1999.

Clark, Christopher. *The Sleepwalkers: How Europe Went to War in 1914*. London: Penguin, 2012.

Deák, István. 'The Worst of Friends: Germany's Allies in East Central Europe – Struggles for Regional Dominance and Ethnic Cleansing 1938–1945', in Marina Cattaruzza, Stefan Dyrhoff and Dieter Langewiesche (eds), *Territorial Revisionism and the Allies of Germany in the Second World War: Goals, Expectations, Practices* (New York: Berghahn Books, 2013), 17–29.

Eldarov, Svetlozar, and Bisser Petrov. 'Bulgarian Historiography on the Balkan Wars 1912–13', in Katrin Boeckh and Sabine Rutar (eds), *The Balkan Wars from Contemporary Perception to Historic Memory* (Basingstoke: Palgrave, 2017), 219–48.

Entangled Histories of the Balkans. Vol. 1: *National Ideologies and Language Policies*. Ed. Roumen Daskalov and Tchavdar Marinov. Leiden: Brill, 2013.

Entangled Histories of the Balkans. Vol. 2: *Transfers of Political Ideologies and Institutions*. Ed. Roumen Daskalov and Diana Mishkova. Leiden: Brill, 2014.

Entangled Histories of the Balkans. Vol. 3: *Shared Pasts, Disputed Legacies*. Ed. Roumen Daskalov and Alexander Vezenkov. Leiden: Brill, 2015.

Entangled Histories of the Balkans. Vol. 4: *Concepts, Approaches, and (Self-) Representations*. Ed. Roumen Daskalov, Diana Mishkova, Tchavdar Marinov and Alexander Vezenkov. Leiden: Brill, 2017.

Ferguson, Niall. *The War of the World: Twentieth-Century Conflict and the Descent of the West*. London: Penguin, 2007.

Hull, Isabel V. 'Prisoners in Colonial Warfare: The Imperial German Example', in Sibylle Scheipers (ed.), *Prisoners in War* (Oxford: Oxford University Press, 2010), 157–72.

Ilchev, Ivan. 'The Balkan Wars in Recent Bulgarian Historiography and Textbooks', in Council of Europe (ed.), *Crossroads of European Histories: Multiple Outlooks on Five Key Moments in the History of Europe* (Strasbourg: Council of Europe Publ., 2006), 111–18.

Kramer, Alan. 'Prisoners in the First World War', in Sibylle Scheipers (ed.), *Prisoners in War* (Oxford: Oxford University Press, 2010), 75–90.

Mazower, Mark. *Dark Continent: Europe's Twentieth Century*. New York: Vintage, 1998.

Michail, Eugène. 'The Balkan Wars in Western Historiography, 1912–2012', in Katrin Boeckh and Sabine Rutar (eds), *The Balkan Wars from Contemporary Perception to Historic Memory* (Basingstoke: Palgrave, 2017), 319–40.

Mommsen, Hans. 'Anfänge des ethnic cleansing und der Umsiedelungspolitik im Ersten Weltkrieg', in Eduard Mühle (ed.), *Mentalitäten – Nationen – Spannungsfelder: Studien zu Mittel- und Osteuropa im 19. und 20. Jahrhundert, Festschrift für Hans Lemberg* (Marburg: Verlag Herder-Institut, 2001), 147–62.

Neff, Stephen C. 'Prisoners of War in International Law: The Nineteenth Century', in Sibylle Scheipers (ed.), *Prisoners in War* (Oxford: Oxford University Press, 2010), 57–74.

Rutar, Sabine (ed.). *Beyond the Balkans: Towards an Inclusive History of Southeastern Europe*. Vienna: Lit, 2014.

Scheipers, Sibylle (ed.). *Prisoners in War*. Oxford: Oxford University Press, 2010.

Snyder, Timothy. *Bloodlands: Europe between Hitler and Stalin*. New York: Basic Books, 2010.

Zweig, Stefan. *The World of Yesterday: An Autobiography*. Lincoln: University of Nebraska Press, 1964. [German original: *Die Welt von gestern: Erinnerungen eines Europäers*. Stockholm: Bermann-Fischer, 1942.]

Index

Abazi, Enika, 19
Abdülhamid II, Sultan of the Ottoman Empire, 168
Abdullah Paşa/Pasha, 171–72, 174, 193, 196
Adanır, Fikret, 174
Adler, Viktor, 297
Adrianople, 23, 33, 44, 104, 150, 190–95, 197, 199–200, 261, 360. *See also* Edirne
Adriatic Sea, 115, 299
Aegean Sea, 94, 97–98, 103–05, 169, 192, 211, 327
Africa, 10, 206, 209, 218, 294, 345, 356–57, 360, 377
Agadir Crisis, 137–38, 143–44, 147, 150, 154
Albania, 3, 36, 41, 93–101, 104, 105, 115, 118–19, 122, 124, 138, 144, 146, 150–51, 163, 192, 213, 217, 261, 268, 271–72, 291–92, 312, 320, 328, 330–31, 353, 392
Albanian question/issue, 93, 97, 101, 104–05
Albanian uprisings/rebellion, 96, 99–100, 312
Albanians, 36, 62, 70, 94–96, 100, 105, 108, 144, 213, 261, 271, 278, 292, 353
alcohol abuse, 393, 401–06, 410
alcoholism, 393, 397, 399, 402
Alexander III of Macedon (Alexander the Great), 211
Alexandretta, 319
Ali, Amer, 374
Alkhadef, Shmuel, 357
Allgemeine Jüdische Zeitung (newspaper), 359
Alliance Israélite Universelle (AIU), 358, 360, 368

ambassadors' conference, 9, 104–05, 117–19, 125, 132, 147, 320, 324
America, 10, 295, 352, 358, 360
American Civil War, 164
Amsterdam, 356
Anatolia, 36, 39, 167, 169, 173–74, 178, 192, 199, 243, 330, 333, 336, 354
Andalusia, 359
andartes, 73, 327, 315, 322
Andonyan, Aram, 171
Angelescu, Constantin, 246
Anglo-German relations, 115, 118, 124
  cooperation, 117–18, 126
  détente, 117–18, 122–23
Ankaran/Ancarano, 297
annexation
  of Bosnia and Herzegovina, 93, 287, 295, 305
  of Crete, 97–98
  of Trieste and Istria, 298
Antakya, 319
Antalya/Attaleia, 333
anti-militarism, 293–94, 296, 287
anti-nationalism, 299
anti-war declarations, 295
  gathering, 9, 294, 301–02
  rhetoric, 287
  speech, 296
Antwerp, 10, 355, 356
Apak, Rahmi, 171
Appleyard, Sydney Vere, 378
Arabs, 169, 173
Arbeiter-Zeitung (socialist newspaper), 298
Arbon, 247
Archangelsk, 248
Argeş, river, 245
Argyropoulos, Periklis, 315
armament industry, 293

Armenians, 171, 174, 355
armistice, 104, 144, 198, 200, 324
army
  Bulgarian, 22, 24, 27, 29, 30, 32, 40,
    53–54, 72, 76, 102, 165, 191–200,
    241, 272, 315–17, 322, 329–30,
    335–36, 355
    Greek, 7, 23, 44, 53, 70, 165, 213–15,
      217, 273, 314–17, 322, 328–29,
      332, 335, 380, 407
    Montenegrin, 24, 165, 407
    Ottoman, 8, 21, 25–26, 29, 33, 35, 52,
      60–61, 73, 103, 165–167, 171–73,
      177, 190, 193, 196–97, 201, 213,
      217, 268, 270, 276, 278, 316, 348–
      49, 353, 376
    Romanian, 6, 240–45, 248–49, 253
    Serbian, 7, 20–22, 24–26, 28, 32, 70,
      122, 165, 195, 260, 263, 266, 269–
      72, 329–31, 353, 380, 392–93, 403
Asia Minor, 207–08, 319, 328, 330, 333
Athens, 99, 122, 207–09, 313, 377
atrocities, 7, 9–11, 19, 36, 38, 42–45,
  68–73, 208, 214, 217–18, 228, 231–
  32, 249, 252, 318, 328, 330–31,
  334–36, 352, 419, 420
Audoin-Rouzeau, Stéphane, 37, 46,
  419
August-Erlebnis (August experience),
  39, 65
Austria, 6, 9, 24, 26, 29–30, 32–34,
  39–40, 42–44, 93, 94–97, 99–100,
  104, 113–16, 118–120, 122, 139,
  142, 145, 151, 242–43, 263, 265–
  66, 285–93, 295, 297–99, 312–13,
  318–19, 351, 359, 361. *See also*
  Austro-Hungary
Austrians, 42, 96–97, 100, 104, 109,
  142, 242, 288, 291
Austro-Hungary, 6, 9, 93, 97, 99–101,
  104, 113–26, 137–39, 146–47, 177,
  243, 245, 247, 250, 263–66, 269,
  285, 287, 289–90, 298–99, 312,
  359. *See also* Austria
Averescu, Alexandru, 245
Ayastefanos/San Stefano/Yeşilköy,
  29, 326–27, 374–75, 381
Aydin, 319
Azmanov, Dimităr, 33
Azot, 267–69

Baberowski, Jörg, 43
Babuna, mountain, 267–68, 270
Baghdad, 171
Balchik, 242
Baldwin, Herbert, 34
Balkan alliance, 24, 93–94, 97–99, 100,
  105, 165–67, 169, 317, 324
Balkan League/confederation, 93,
  102, 114–15, 118, 122, 125, 139,
  291, 293–94, 296, 305, 312, 314,
  401
Ballhausplatz, 113, 115, 121–25
Basel, 9, 286, 288–89, 294
bashi-bazouks (*başıbozuk*), 261, 268,
  271, 276, 331, 353
Batak, 331
Battle
  of Chataldzha/Çatalca, 172,
    191,197–201
  of Kilkis, 220, 335
  of Kırkkilise/Lozengrad, 172,
    190–97, 200
  of Kosovo, 36, 38
  of Lüleburgaz-Pınarhisar/
    Liuleburgas-Bunar Hisar, 195–
    97, 200
  of Sarantaporos, 314
Bavaria, 25
Becker, Annette, 37, 46, 419
bedel (exemption fee), 168, 173, 181
Behmoiras, Roza, 351
Behmoiras-Aroyo, Victoria, 351
Bejarano, Haim, 355
Belgium, 214, 228, 355
Belgrade/Beograd, 29, 39–40, 95, 113,
  119, 122, 260, 265–68, 274, 295,
  312, 331, 353–54, 377, 392, 394,
  396, 398–99, 402–04, 408
Belić, Aleksandar, 36
Benbassa, Esther, 347
Berchtold, Leopold von, 94, 98–100,
  103, 105, 113–14, 116–23, 125–26
Berkovitsa, 242
Berlin, 8, 93, 96, 102–05, 113–16,
  118–26, 139–40, 142, 144–45, 242,
  261, 327
Berntsen, Klaus, 143, 149, 152–53
Berovo, 333
Bethmann Hollweg, Theobald von,
  114–19, 123, 126

Bettelheim, Henri, 357
Beykoz, 374, 381
Biondich, Mark, 20, 417
Bitola, 261, 271, 312–13, 330, 354, 380. *See also* Monastir; Manastır
Black Sea, 190, 198–99
Blagojević, Aca, 264–65
Blondel, Camille, 249
Blondel, Yvonne, 249
B'nai B'rith (Jewish organization), 357
Boletini, Isa, 96
borders, 3–4, 100, 104–105, 115, 118, 141, 145, 148–49, 192–93, 210, 242–44, 246, 251, 262, 267, 269–70, 278, 285, 287, 292–93, 299–300, 307, 313–14, 320, 326, 399, 406, 420
Boris, Prince of Bulgaria, 315. *See also* Boris III, King of Bulgaria
Boris III, King of Bulgaria, 315
Bosnia, 93, 116, 263, 265, 287, 290–91, 295, 399, 403
Bosphorus, 247
Bourke, Joanne, 45, 228
Brailovo, 271
Brailsford, Henry Noel, 316
Brătianu, Ion C., 242, 245
Britain, 24, 116–17, 119–20, 122, 124, 126, 137–39, 144–47, 150–54, 170, 209, 292, 312, 374–76, 378, 385–87, 401, 406. *See also* England
British Intelligence Bureau, 290
Brown, Keith, 37
Brussels, 359–60, 380, 383
brutalization, 208, 217–19
Bucharest, 113, 116, 120, 122, 125, 241–42, 244, 246, 249–50, 272, 296, 319
Budapest, 242, 244, 247, 288, 359, 397
Bulgaria, 3, 6, 7–8, 20, 22–40, 44–45, 93–99, 101–02, 104, 113, 115, 119–25, 138–40, 144, 150, 165, 167, 174, 190–201, 210, 215, 218, 240–46, 248–50, 261–62, 264–66, 269, 272–73, 295, 312–18, 320, 326–32, 334–36, 349, 351–53, 355, 360, 374, 380, 392–93, 398, 402–04, 419

Bulgarians, 8, 44, 74, 94, 96, 98, 101–02, 150, 174, 191–201, 210, 215, 218, 240–42, 244, 248–49, 265, 272, 314–16, 322, 324, 326, 328–29, 331–32, 334–35, 338, 340, 360, 402–04
Burgas, 32, 351
Bursa, 319
Buxton, Noel, 326
Byzantine Empire, 218

Callaghan, Sir George, 146–47, 154
Çanakkale, 171
Cancicov, Vasile Th., 244
Cankar, Ivan, 292
Caporetto/Kobarid/Karfreit, 301
Capşa, 244
Carnegie Commission, 76, 316, 318, 330, 333, 335, 338
 Endowment for International Peace, 10–11, 14, 41, 207, 328, 340
Carol I, King of Romania, 120, 122
Carpathians, 243–44, 250
Catalça/Chataldzha, 40, 144, 172, 190, 197–201, 350, 354, 374, 380
Catholic, 100, 214, 243
centenary, 4–5, 416
Central Powers. *See* great powers
Cetinje, 29
Chernopeev, Christo, 331
chetniks, 258–59, 262–65, 267–74, 330
Chickering, Roger, 34
cholera, 29, 57, 75, 198–99, 246–48, 334, 375, 377, 379, 380–81, 393, 402
Christian, 29, 36, 39, 43, 47, 61, 94, 96–97, 102, 107, 139, 209, 215, 224, 258, 261, 267, 317, 319, 327–31, 334–35, 337, 353, 357, 359, 361, 386
 Communities, 94, 100, 348
 Missionaries, 358 (*see also* Christian – Orthodox)
 Orthodox, 7, 10, 190, 228, 243, 271
 population 74, 173, 316
Christian, Crown Prince of Denmark, 143. *See also* Christian X, King of Denmark
Christian X, King of Denmark, 143
Churchill, Winston, 140, 151–53, 206

Circolo di studi sociali, 285, 287, 289, 298
civilian, 6–7, 10, 26, 28, 34, 38, 42–44, 72, 144, 147–48, 164, 207–08, 212–13, 215–18, 221–22, 227, 272, 283, 285, 293, 295, 316–17, 319, 331, 344, 346, 349, 353, 363, 399–400, 406, 420
Clark, Christopher, 5, 416–17
Clemow, Frank G., 384
Committee of the Small Bag for the Soldier, 350
Committee of Union and Progress (CUP), 99, 175, 316, 330
conscription, 21–24, 40, 164, 166–68, 170, 173, 175–78, 180
Constantine, Crown Prince, 213–14, 314–15, 320. *See also* Constantine I, King of Greece
Constantine I, King of Greece, 213–14, 314–15, 320
Constantinople, 94, 99–100, 123, 138, 140, 142, 144, 146, 190, 192, 195, 197–98, 201, 261, 299, 313, 316, 319, 331, 334. *See also* Istanbul
conversos (Jewish converts to catholic Christianity), 356
Copenhagen, 137, 143–44, 149, 152
Corabia, 242
Çorlu, 349
Cracow, 359
Cretan issue, 93–94, 97, 99, 104
Crete, 97–98, 100, 104, 106
Crimean War, 31, 38, 150
Crnička Reka, 268
Croatia, 262, 265, 290–91, 392, 394–407
Croats, 263, 286, 298, 405
Culcer, Ion, 242
Cvijić, Jovan, 36, 260
Cyrenaica, 289
Czechoslovakia, 290
Czechs, 286
Czernin, Ottokar, Count, 122

Dalmatia, 290
Damascus, 171
Danev, Stojan, 24
Danube, river, 241–44, 246, 248–49, 266
Daras, Dimitrios, 217
Dardanelles, 247
defection, 299
demographic engineering, 328
Denmark, 137–38, 142–43, 149–50, 154
Depage, Antoine, 383
deportation, 316
desertion, 167, 172–74, 178, 180
Desovo, 271
Detrez, Raymond, 7
di San Giuliano, Antonino, 100–01, 289
Dimitriev, Radko, 31, 191, 196, 198–99
Dimitrijević-Apis, Dragutin, 261
Diner, Dan, 19
disarmament, 146, 314
 agreement, 118, 130
displacement, 4, 6, 11
Djokić, Milan, 266–68
Djordjević, Vladan, 28, 36
Dobrich, 242
Dobruja, 3, 242–44, 250
doctors, 10, 28–29, 30–32, 42–44, 56–57, 71, 215, 246, 273, 374, 376–78, 380–88, 396–400, 404
Dodecanese, 94, 98–99, 105
Dodona, 211
Dojč, Josip, 405
Dolgać, Jovan, 272
Doornfontein, 357
Doxato, 336
Dragoumis, Filippos, 211, 215
Dragoumis, Ion, 209, 313
Dreyer, Lothar, 381
Dual Monarchy, 113, 115–16, 120–21, 123–25, 150, 288, 290, 398
Dučić, Nićifor, 263
Dündar, Fuat, 330
Dupnitsa, 269
Dürres/Durrësi/Durazzo/Dıraç, 144
dysentery, 334, 379, 381

Ecumenical Patriarchate, 98, 335
Edirne, 150, 174, 190, 261, 349–52, 355. *See also* Adrianople
El Nuevo Avenir (newspaper), 347, 354–55, 360
El Tyémpo (newspaper), 347, 350–51, 355, 357
Elassona, 214

Elgazi, Eliya, 350
Endres, Franz Carl, 25–26
England, 117, 126, 356, 376, 386. *See also* Britain
Ensari, Muhammad, 378, 386
Enver Pasha, Ismail, 175
Epirus, 105, 211–12, 215, 218, 220–23, 225
Eretz Israel, 358–59. *See also* Holy Land; Palestine
Erzincan, 171
Estrog, Yosef Shmuel, 354
ethnic cleansing, 42, 45, 335–36, 340, 418
Etropole, 242
Exner, Alfred, 29
expansion (territorial), 28, 100–01, 114–15, 118–20, 124–25, 145, 167, 209, 290, 361

Farrar, Jr., Lancelot L., 39
fascism, 298, 300
fear of war, 10, 285, 290, 292–94, 296
Feldhof, 397
Fényes, Ladislaus von, 39, 44
Ferdinand I., Tsar of Bulgaria, 36, 95, 101, 195–96, 198
Ferguson, Niall, 417
Fichev, Ivan, 191, 195–96, 198–99
Figartner, Milan, 398
Figes, Orlando, 31
Finland, 141
first aid, 30, 378–80, 403
First Balkan War, 3, 6, 8–9, 24, 27, 36–37, 40, 47, 50, 93, 115, 117, 120, 124, 137–38, 190–91, 200, 206, 271, 291–92, 294–96, 314, 322, 324, 330–32, 334–35, 355, 360, 366, 371, 374, 400, 403, 419
First World War, 3–8, 10, 19–20, 31–34, 36–38, 40, 45–46, 63–64, 67, 120, 122, 125–26, 137–38, 150, 153, 164, 176–80, 197, 199–01, 207, 214, 220, 223, 227–28, 240, 242, 285–87, 290, 299, 301, 328, 340, 345, 361, 392, 394–95, 397–99, 401, 405–07, 416–20
Flămânda, 245, 249
foreign policy, 95, 114–15, 120–21, 123–24, 126, 142, 190, 260–61

of Austria 113–14, 120–21, 123–24, 291
of Italy, 290
Fox, Fred, 30, 38
Fragiskos, Isidoros, 215
France, 22–25, 114, 116–17, 119–20, 126, 140, 144–45, 148, 151, 154, 177, 209, 228, 247, 249, 292, 312, 359, 380
Franz Ferdinand, Archduke of Austria, 116–17, 120, 122–23, 127, 290
Franz Joseph, Emperor of Austria, 118
Frederik VIII, King of Denmark, 143
Freundlich, Leo, 41
Fries-Skene, Alfred Freiherr von, 298
Fussell, Paul, 228

Gaćinović, Vladimir, 264
Galicia, 116
Gallipoli, 201, 349, 354
gangrene, 380–81
Geneva Convention (1864), 374–75, 387
George I, King of Greece, 36, 315
George V, King of the United Kingdom, 140
German Military Mission (in the Ottoman Empire, 1913), 175
German Wars of Unification, 164
Germany, 9, 22–25, 97, 113–27, 137–39, 141–47, 149–54, 177, 245, 247, 250, 289, 292, 297, 299, 345, 356, 359, 401, 406
Geshov, Ivan, 95, 99, 101–02, 313
Gevgelia, 272
Giannitsa, 213, 332
Giers, Mikhail, 198
Gibbs, Philip, 329–30
Ginio, Eyal, 7, 10, 35, 344, 362
Giolitti, Giovanni, 289
Gothenburg, 148, 152
Gotland, 142
Graz, 396–97
great powers, 9, 93, 99, 100–01, 103–06, 114–19, 121–23, 125–26, 128, 131, 133, 137–41, 149, 170, 194, 260, 286–87, 292, 297, 301, 320, 324, 331, 420

Great War. *See* First World War
Greater Serbia, 113, 326
Greco-Ottoman war, 40, 209, 261, 347
Greece, 3, 6, 8, 20, 22–24, 26–27, 31, 35–36, 40, 93, 95, 97–98, 104, 106, 119–21, 124, 139, 167, 190, 207–13, 219, 221, 227, 241, 262, 312–15, 320, 326–28, 354–55, 374, 393
Greeks, 8, 97–98, 174, 209–15, 217, 219, 222, 225, 227–28, 265, 313–15, 320, 326, 328, 331, 334–36, 338, 369
Grey, Sir Edward, 95, 104–05, 118–19, 139, 316
Guberevac, 396, 405
guerrilla warfare, 6, 8, 10, 23, 258, 261, 263, 315–16, 322, 420

Hague Convention (1907), 150, 352
haiduchia, 258–62, 273
Hakkı Pasha, Hafız, 175
Haldane, Lord Richard, 146–47
Ha-Levy, Yitzhak Yosef, 354
Hall, Richard, 6, 8, 34, 138, 190, 201
Hamburger, Josef, 30
Hamidiye Cavalry Regiments, 168
Hamit, Ercan, 171
Ha-Mitzpe (newspaper), 359
Hannig, Alma, 6, 9, 113, 127, 285
Hanukah, Avraham Yosef, 354
Hârjeu, Constantin N., 245
Hartwig, Nikolai, 312
Haskalah (Jewish Enlightenment), 358
hate 44, 329
  speech, 293
Hatzioannou, Evangelos, 221
Haydarpaşa, 379
Hebron, 358
Heimroth, Richard, 43–44
Heligoland, 140, 147
Hellenism, 104, 209, 211, 213
Helmedach, Andreas, 299
heroism, 8, 11, 37, 196, 219, 220, 222, 228, 259, 294–95, 419
Herzegovina, 93, 263, 291, 295, 305, 399
Herzfeld, Max von, 33
Hikmed Bey, Fuad, 95
Hilmi Paşa, Hüseyin, 96

Hochwächter, Gustav von, 171
Hoffmann, Christhard, 346
Hohenlohe, Gottfried zu, Prince, 116, 127, 290
Hohenlohe-Schillingsfürst, Konrad, 289
Holy Cross, 226
Holy Land, 358. *See also* Palestine; Eretz Israel
Honigmann, Georg, 399
Honour, 30, 143, 208, 223–24, 226, 248, 331
Hopman, Albert, 139, 144–45, 151
Horne, John, 45, 228
Hospital for Mental Illnesses (*bolnica za duševne bolesti*), 396, 404
Hötzendorf, Franz Conrad von, 116–17, 120
Howard, Michael, 19
Howell, Philip, 24–25, 46
Hoyos, Alexander, Count, 123
Hristofidis, Kostadinos, 210
Hristov, Kyrill, 35, 37
humanitarian aid, 360, 375, 385
Hungary, 6, 9, 93, 97, 99–101, 104, 113–26, 137–39, 146–47, 177, 243, 245, 247, 250, 263–66, 269, 285, 287, 289–90, 298–99, 312, 359. *See also* Austro-Hungary
hunger, 27, 76, 212, 216, 218, 222, 246, 295
hygiene, 319, 378, 402–04, 410
hysteria, 395, 399–400

Iberian Peninsula, 345, 352, 356
İhsan Sâbis, Ali, 173
Il Lavoratore (socialist newspaper), 288
Iliescu, Dumitru, 245
Ilinden uprising, 331
Ilustracija Svetlina, 39
Ilustrovana ratna kronika, 38
IMRO (Internal Macedonian Revolutionary Organisation), 101
independence
  of Albania, 3, 96, 100, 104, 144
  of Bulgaria, 93–95
  of Greece, 23
  of the Serbian principality, 263

India, 26, 374–75, 377–78, 385–86
intellectuals, 35–38, 46, 209, 227, 292–93, 298–99, 359, 419
intelligentsia (*inteligencija*), 23, 39, 260
internationalism. *See* socialism
Internationalist Socialist Congress (Basel, November 1912), 286, 288, 294
Invalid Persons Act (1929), 406
Iran, 360
irredentism, 61, 98–99, 209, 228, 288, 297, 326–27
irregular units. *See* guerrilla warfare
Islam, 7, 173, 209, 214, 301, 358–59, 360, 375, 390
Islamic Committee, 333
Isonzo, river, 286, 301
Istanbul/İstanbul, 5, 39, 171, 178, 313–14, 319, 333, 346–51, 353–54, 356–60, 374–75, 377–81, 383, 387. *See also* Constantinople
Istria, 289, 298, 307
İştip/Štip, 347, 360
Italian Socialist Party, 289, 295
Italians, 96–97, 99–100, 104–05, 109, 287, 289–90, 307
Italo-Turkish war, 114, 312
Italy, 99–102, 104–05, 114, 118, 126, 139, 177, 247, 286, 288–90, 292, 294, 297–300, 313
Ivanov, Nikola, 191, 195
Izmir, 171, 319, 333, 354. *See also* Smyrna
Izvol'skii, Aleksandr, 104
İzzet Paşa/Pasha, Ahmed, 95, 169, 193

Jagow, Gottlieb von, 113, 119, 123, 126
Jajladžik, 316
Janina/Ioannina/Joannina/Yanya, 44, 100, 104, 200, 214, 291, 360
Jerusalem, 358, 362
Jewish
  community, 346–49, 351–52, 354–56, 358, 360, 362, 366
  diaspora, 345, 352, 357, 358–59, 367
  identity, 352, 355, 362
  philanthropy, 7, 345–46, 348–49, 351–52, 355, 358–62
  prisoners of war, 352, 354–55
  press, 347–48, 352, 354, 356–57, 359–60, 363
  refugees, 346–47, 349, 351, 357–58, 364, 367
  victims of war, 345–52, 358, 361–62
  women, 350
Jews, 10, 243, 307, 313, 320, 322, 345–52, 355–64, 367–69
Johannesburg, 357
Johnstone, A. Duncan, 375, 379, 384–85
Jovkov, Jordan, 37
Judeo-Spanish
  language, 352
  press, 347–48, 355, 360
  publications, 352
jugoslovenstvo. *See* Yugoslavism
Jünger, Ernst, 37
Jurišić-Šturm, Pavle, 271

Kailaria, 217
Kalikratya, 374
Kamburov, Stojan Christov, 44
Kamil Paşa, Mehmed, 95, 99, 102–03
Kara-Bouroum, 314
Karadjordjević, Peter I, King of Serbia, 36
Karadžić, Vuk, 263
Karamanşah, 360
Karlskrona, 142, 148
Karpat, Kemal, 336
Kaser, Karl, 39, 362
Kastelanos, Giorgos, 226
Kavala, 313, 331
Kazazis, Neoklis, 209–10
Keegan, John, 19
Keisinger, Florian, 286
Kemal, Mustafa (Atatürk), 319
Kennan, George, 207
Kiderlen-Wächter, Alfred von, 114–16, 118–19, 125–26, 139
Kiel, 145, 147
Kievskaia Mysl' (Russian newspaper), 331
Kilkis, 220, 330, 335
Király, Béla 31
Kırkkilise/Kırklareli/Lozengrad, 34, 40, 172, 190–97, 200, 292, 349, 351, 379
Kiustendil, 242, 269

Kokanović, Dragitun, 264
komitadjis/komitadži, 26, 74, 315–16, 322, 327, 331
Konopiště, 122
Koromilas, Lambros, 313
Koselleck, Reinhart, 7, 45
Kosovo, 35–38, 95–96, 100–01, 105, 192, 261, 269, 327
Kostur, 313
Kouvelis, Aristotelis, 210
Kozani, 214
Kragujevac, 273, 400
Kramer, Alan, 45, 227–28
Kriva Palanka, 269
Krobatin, Alexander von, 117
Ktenaveas, Stratis, 216, 225
Kukurtovo, 318
Kumanovo, 40, 269–70, 292, 400
Kurds, 167–68, 169, 173
Kursumlija, 269
Kutinchev, Vasil, 191
Kutschbach, Albin, 32
Kyustendil, 242, 269

labour battalions (in the Ottoman Army), 8, 177
Lamb, Harry H., 315–17
Larisa/Larissa, 315, 354–55
Lascarov-Moldovanu, Alexandru, 246
Laurent, Octave, 380, 383
Lausanne, 328
L'Avanti! (Italian socialist newspaper), 289
Lavras, 222
Laz, 169
Le Tarnec, Sophie, 347
Lerin, 313
Lexa von Aehrental, Alois, 98
Libya, 105, 114, 163
Lichnowsky, Karl Max, Prince, 117–18
Lidorikis, Miltiadis, 212
Liječnički vjesnik (Croatian medical journal), 392, 394, 397–99, 405, 409
Ljubljana, 288, 292
London, 9, 102–06, 117–18, 122, 125, 140, 144, 147, 151, 200, 329, 374, 376, 386

London Peace Conference, 320, 324–25
Lossow, Otto von, 26
Lowther, Sir Gerard, 316, 331
Lukovit, 242
Lüle Burgas/Lüleburgaz/Liuleburgas, 32, 192, 195–97, 200, 351, 379
Luxemburg, 126
Lynch, Katherine, 345

Macedonia, 3, 6, 8, 26, 35, 42, 93–96, 98–102, 106, 165, 169, 190–92, 194–95, 211–13, 215, 217–18, 221–23, 241, 251 261–66, 269, 271–72, 274, 312–13, 316, 318–21, 326–33, 335–36, 346–47
Macedonian question, 63, 93, 95
Mach, Richard von, 22, 41
Mackensen, August von, 243
Mahmud II, Sultan of the Ottoman Empire, 167
Maidovski, Rajcho, 33
Malliaros, Antonios, 213
Manastır, 261. *See also* Bitola; Monastir
Manfred, Nathan, 357
Mano, Daniel Shmuel, 354
Maribor, 292
Marijanović, Alimpij, 269
Marmara, Sea of, 190, 198–99
Martinov, Evgenii, 264
martyrdom, 209, 222, 224–26
masculinity, 216, 220, 222–23, 226, 228
Matscheko, Franz von, 123
Mavroyeni, Alexandre, 94
May Day, 294–96
Mazower, Mark, 45, 209, 319, 417
Mazzini, Giuseppe, 292
medical staff, 7, 375, 383, 385
Mediterranean Sea, 140, 146, 151, 362
medrese students, 168
Melnik, 336
mental illness, 9, 298–99, 392–96, 399–02, 404–05
mental injuries, 393, 395–96, 398, 400–01
Mershina, 319
Middle East, 167, 178, 206, 362

migration, 34, 95, 100, 176, 288, 298, 319, 324, 328–30, 333, 335–36, 345, 356
Milan/Milano, 298
military
　education, 21–2, 24, 26
　experts, 19, 22, 25, 30, 32, 50, 417
　history, 4–6, 10, 13, 19, 163, 194, 274, 276, 416
　psychiatry, 395, 397–98, 405
　reform(s), 20, 23–24, 101
　technology, 7, 25, 30, 52
Miller, William, 213
Milojević, Miloš, 263
Milovanović, Milan, 266
Milovanović-Pilac, Milan, 266
Mišić, Živojin, 22
mobilization, 27, 34–35, 38–39, 44, 46, 53, 102, 115, 119, 139, 141–42, 144–46, 149, 153–54, 163–73, 175–78, 193, 241–42, 245–46, 267, 269, 293, 295, 300, 344, 348–49, 351–52, 357–58, 363, 379, 418
Modiano, Eliezer, 354
Mokreni, 267–68
Moldavia, 245
Moltke, Helmuth von, 117, 145, 147
Monastir, 95–96, 100, 261, 271, 312–13, 327, 330, 354, 360, 380. *See also* Bitola; Manastır
Monprofit, Jacques-Ambroise, 377, 380, 382–83
Montenegro, 3, 8, 26, 29, 40, 95, 105, 118, 126, 139, 144, 150, 157, 190, 269, 374, 393, 398
morale, 173–75, 194, 219, 222, 227
Morava, 269
mortality rate, 334, 378, 380, 382–83
Moscow, 299
Mudanya, 319
Mukhtar/Muhtar Paşa/Pasha, Mahmud, 36, 172, 174, 193–96
Mukhtar/Muhtar Paşa, Gazi Ahmed, 99, 101–02
Mukos, 270
Müller, Georg Alexander, 117
multiethnicity, 173, 299, 336, 416, 418
Muslim Committee, 319, 324
Muslims, 37, 43–44, 100, 107, 243, 261, 272, 316–19, 324, 327–34, 337, 349–51, 353, 357, 361, 367, 374–75, 378, 386, 390

Naar, Pinhas Haim, 354
Naby Bey, Mehemmed, 99
Nahum, Haim, Chief Rabbi of the Ottoman Empire, 348, 357, 361–62
Narodna vojska (people's army), 21, 26, 260
Nazim Bey, Mehmed, 316
Nazim Paşa, Huseyin, 193, 319
Near East, 374, 376
Neitzel, Sönke, 287
Nekliudov, Anatoli, 312
Netherlands, 380, 403
New York, 247, 357
Nicholas, Prince of Greece and Denmark, 315, 318
Nigrita, 336
Niš, 44, 247, 354
non-Muslims, 35, 168, 173–174, 176–178, 346, 348, 369
Noradunkyan, Gabriel Efendi, 102–03
Nova Gradiška, 399
Novi Pazar/Novibazar, 95, 101, 270

Obrenović, Aleksandar, King of Serbia, 5, 266
Obrenović, Milan, King of Serbia, 263
Odrin, 190, 261
Oriental Question, 20, 46, 418
Orhanie, 242, 246, 248
Osborn, Samuel, 382, 384
Ottoman Empire, 93, 163, 373
Ottoman-Italian war, 101, 105, 139, 163, 179, 287, 289
Ottoman military service law (1886), 168, 170, (1909) 168, 173, 176, (1914) 176
Ottoman Ministry of Foreign Affairs, 99, 106, 355–56, 367, 376
Ottoman War College, 171
Ottomans, 9, 20, 35, 94, 97, 99–105, 115, 165, 167–69, 173–74, 176, 178, 191–201, 263, 267, 286, 289, 292, 312, 320, 329, 331, 348, 350, 361, 373, 375, 386, 419
Otranto, Straits of, 313

434 • Index

outbreak of war, 5, 8–9, 25, 35–36, 39, 61, 103, 122, 191–92, 206, 286–88, 294–95, 297, 299, 314, 329, 347, 352, 376
Özbek, Nadir, 347

Padua, 396
Page, C. Max, 378
Palestine, 358–59. *See also* Eretz Israel; Holy Land
Pallavicini, Johann von, 100
Panas, Dimitri, 313
pan-Slavism, 104, 124, 299
Papaioannou, Stefan, 42, 44–45
Papavasileiou, Ippokratis, 223
Paprikov, Stefan, 95
Paraskevopoulos, Giorgios, 213
Paraskevopoulos, Leonidas, 214, 220–22
Paris, 103–04, 358
Pašić, Nikola, 265
Patriarchate of Constantinople, 313
Pauli, Carl, 41
Pazardjik, 243
peace, 9–10, 38, 94, 99, 102, 113–15, 117–18, 120, 124–26, 139–40, 198, 200, 207, 219, 241–42, 250, 270, 272, 286, 289, 292, 295–97, 301, 319–20, 324–25, 328, 340, 353, 419–20
Peć/Ipek, 95–96
Pella, 211
Petimezas, Nikolaos, 212, 216, 220, 222, 225
Petrović, Veljko, 36
Philippopolis, 242
Pigasios, Ioannis, 215
Pınarhisar/Bunar Hisar, 195–97, 200
Pinto, Yosef, 354
Pittoni, Valentino, 295, 297
Plamper, Jan, 285
Planica, 318
Pleven, 195, 242
Plovdiv. *See* Philippopolis
Poincaré, Raymond, 99
Popov, Ivan, 30
Popović, Vuk, 270–72
Poreče, 268–69
Porter, Patrick, 225, 227
Portugal, 345

Posno, B.J., 256
post-traumatic stress disorder, 9, 298–99
Poulopoulos, Alexandros, 210
powder keg, 4, 11, 286, 417
Prague, 288, 396
Prakhovo, 247
Prepeluh, Albin, 293
Price, Crawfurd, 329–30, 332
Prilep, 268, 270–72
Princip, Gavrilo, 265
prisoners of war (POWs), 44–45, 75–76, 194, 197, 208, 215, 216, 217, 218, 227, 249, 315–16, 331, 346, 352–55, 392, 418
Prizren, 291
Prokuplje 265
propaganda, 7, 38, 40, 95, 227, 248, 273, 286, 290, 296, 298, 327, 420
  anti-militarist, 296
  for peace, 286
  Islamic, 173
  pro-armament, 286
  social democratic, 298
  war, 9, 36–37
Protestant, 214, 243
Prussia, 25, 28, 393
Puecher, Edmondo, 294, 296
Putnik, Radomir, 269, 272

Raktivan, Konstantinos, 318
Rankin, Reginald, 38, 333
Ranković, Svetolik, 260
Rayanovo, 318
recruitment, 6, 35, 149, 166–70, 173, 267, 301, 357
Red Crescent
  British, 374–75, 387–88
  Egyptian, 378
  Indian, 385–86
  Ottoman, 346, 353, 355, 360, 366–67, 375–76, 379
Red Cross
  British, 7, 29, 347–75, 373–78, 380–88
  Bulgarian, 353, 403
  Greek, 377
  International, 29, 45, 353–54
  Japanese, 377
Reder, Bertold, 32

refugees, 29, 40, 67, 316–17, 319, 332–34, 336, 339, 346–47, 349–51, 357–58, 360, 364, 367
  Muslim, 176, 316–17, 319, 333–34, 336, 339
Regent, Ivan, 294
Reichsrat (Viennese parliament), 293–94, 301
Renner, Karl, 285–87, 296
reserve system, 170–72, 175–76
Rhine, river, 243
Rhodes, 356
Rhodesia/Zimbabwe, 356
Rifaat Paşa, Ahmad, 103–05
Riza, Seyyid Haydar, 386
Roditi Bey, Nissim, 355–56
Rodrigue, Aron, 347
Romania, 3, 6, 8, 37, 98, 115–16, 118–24, 126–27, 145, 240–50
Rome, 119
Rosen, Georg, 260
Rosetti, Radu R., 245
Ross, Colin, 32–33
Rothschild, Nathaniel Lord, 374, 376
Royal Navy 140, 144–47, 151–52
Royal Serbian Institute for the Mentally Disturbed (*Kraljevski Srpski Zavod za umobolne*), 392
Royal State Institute for the Mentally Ill for Croatia-Slavonia (*Kraljevski zemaljski zavod za umobolne za Hrvatsku i Slavoniju*), 396
Rusçuk/Ruse, 353–54
Russia, 8, 10, 22–23, 25, 28, 34, 96–97, 99, 101, 103–04, 114–16, 118–26, 137–39, 141–42, 145, 149, 152, 177, 192, 195, 197–98, 209, 243, 248, 250, 262–64, 273–74, 292, 299, 312, 331, 359, 377, 387, 393, 398–99, 401
Russian-Ottoman war, 8, 190
Russian-Japanese war, 22, 27, 29, 32, 38, 43, 46, 114, 164, 273, 377, 387, 393, 398–99
Russo-Turkish war, 93, 369
Rüştiye Mektebi, 375

Safed, 358
Said Paşa, Mehmed, 99
Sait Bey, Osman, 317–18
Salisbury/Harare, 356
Salonica/Thessaloniki/Thessalonica, 6, 95, 115, 144, 171, 247, 261, 312–20, 327, 330, 332–33, 336, 346–49, 354, 355, 358, 360, 377
Sanders, Liman von, 123, 175
Sarantaporo, 314
Şark *Ordusu* (Eastern Army), 165–66
Savov, Mihail, 192, 196, 198–200
Sazonov, Sergey, 99, 101–103
Schemua, Blasius, 116
Schlieffen Plan, 200
Schliep, Ludwig, 32
Schmitt, Carl, 37
Scutari, 32, 100, 150
Seattle, 357
Second Balkan War, 3, 6–7, 9, 24, 31, 33, 37, 40, 44, 50, 54, 68, 113, 120, 128, 215, 218, 240, 272, 289, 293, 301, 319, 324, 328, 333–35, 353, 360, 402–03, 419
Second Boer War, 29, 209, 377, 380, 382, 387, 393
Second International, 186, 301
Second World War, 4, 13, 138, 227, 307, 364, 393, 405, 408, 418
Sekulić, Isidora, 37
Selyvria/Selivri, 350
Şeni, Nora, 347
Serbia, 3–8, 12, 20–28, 31–33, 35–40, 42–43, 94–95, 97–102, 104–05, 113, 115–16, 118–26, 138–39, 144, 150, 165, 167, 174, 190, 195, 217, 241, 245, 247, 258–74, 290–91 295, 312–13, 320, 326–32, 336, 353–54, 359–60, 374, 380, 392–96, 398–406, 420
Serbian-Bulgarian Treaty of Friendship and Alliance, 312
Serbian-Bulgarian war (1885/86), 8
Serbian uprising, 21, 263
Serbs, 8, 35, 57, 95–96, 99–100, 105, 174, 195, 243, 263, 271, 286, 291, 326, 334–35, 338, 396, 401, 404–05
Serfidje, 329
Serres, 336, 360
Seton-Watson, Robert William, 290
Shalem, Eliyahu Avraham, 354
shell shock 31, 395, 399–400, 405–06

Sicily, 289
Silistra, 242–43
Sinaniotis, Labros, 224
Singer, Amy, 344
Şişli, 374, 382, 384
Sisters of Mercy, 317
Skagerrak, 148
Skátula, Emanuel, 34
Skopje, 42, 266, 269, 321, 330, 354, 377. *See also* Üsküb
Skopska Crna Gora, 269
Skutari, 119
Slavonia, 266, 394–99, 405
Slovenes, 286–87, 289–92, 294, 298
Smith, Sidney, 382
Smyrna, 319, 333. *See also* Izmir
Snyder, Timothy, 416
social democrats. *See* socialism
socialism, 141, 209, 219, 285–99
Sofoulis, Emannouil, 221
Soglje, 268–70
soldiers, 6–7, 9–10, 21–34, 36–40, 43–45, 53–54, 58, 61, 65–67, 73–75, 101, 148, 155, 161, 164, 173–74, 198–99, 206–08, 210–29, 241, 245–49, 252, 268, 270, 273, 276, 285, 293, 295, 300, 315, 317–18, 322, 325, 329, 331–32, 334–36, 346, 348–50, 353, 355, 364–66, 373, 377–85, 387, 392–95, 397–407
Soulis, Hristos, 221
Sound, the (Öresund), 142, 148, 149
South Slavs, 115, 291–92, 299
Sozos, Hristodoulos, 212
Spanish Civil War, 138
Sremska Mitrovica, 399
Srpski arhiv za celokupno lekarstvo (Serbian medical journal), 394, 399, 402–03
St. Petersburg, 9, 103, 116, 118, 122, 152
Staaff, Karl, 141
Stambulov, Stefan, 22
Stanojević, Stanoje, 35
starvation, 317, 328, 352, 378–79
Stenjevec, 396–97, 405
Stepanović, Stepa, 195
Stobart, Claire, 29, 33
Stockholm, 137, 142, 152

Stratigopoulos, Anastasios, 210–11, 223
Subotić, Vojslav M., 392–95, 397, 399, 401–02, 404–05
Sudetenland Crisis, 138
Şükrü Paşa, Mehmed, 350
Susmel, Michele, 298
Svilengrad/Cisr-i Mustafa Paşa, 351
Sweden, 137–38, 141–43, 148, 150, 153–54
Switzerland, 39, 353

Tahsin Paşa, Hasan, 314–15, 317–18
Talât Paşa, Mehmed, 319
Tanin (Ottoman newspaper), 360
Tankosić, Vojislav, 265, 270
Tantilov, Petŭr, 193
Tanzimat, 167, 346
Teodorescu, Constantin, 243
Teovo, 267–68
Tevfik Paşa, Ahmet, 102
The Express (British newspaper), 334
The Graphic (British newspaper), 329
The Times (British newspaper), 38, 329, 332, 378
Thrace, 26, 32, 35, 39, 139, 150, 165, 190–94, 200, 261, 319, 346, 349, 354, 358
Tiberias, 358
Timok, river, 260
Tirpitz, Alfred von, 117, 139
Tisza, István, 121
Todorova, Maria, 19, 45, 206, 418
Toshev, Stefan, 243
total war, 20, 31, 34–35, 163–64, 243, 363
Transylvania, 122, 243–44, 246
traumatic neuroses, 32, 399, 406, 411
Trbić, Vasilije, 266–67, 268–72
Treaty of Berlin (1878), 9, 93, 96, 102–05, 327
Treaty of London (1913), 178, 320, 325
Treaty of Neuilly, 328
Treaty of San Stefano, 327
Trieste/Trst/Triest, 6, 9, 285–90, 292–95, 297–300, 304–06
Trifunović, Ilija, 271
Triha, Lydia, 207
Triple Alliance, 116, 118, 122–23, 125, 126, 139, 289–90

Tripolitania, 289
Trotsky, Leon, 41, 174, 331
Tsigaridis, Ioannis, 216–18, 225
Turco-Italian war. *See* Ottoman-Italian war
Turkey, 3, 5, 6, 99, 102–03, 245, 263, 265, 296, 328, 357, 376, 386–87, 417, 419
Turkhan Paşa, Arnavut, 103
Turkish National Struggle (1919–1922), 163, 179
Turks, 37, 150, 174, 194, 197, 210, 213, 215, 265–67, 269, 271–72, 313, 315, 329, 331, 353, 367, 381–83, 385, 390
Turnu Măgurele, 242
Turnu Severin, 247
Tutrakan, 240, 242–44, 246, 249–50
Tyrol, 288, 294

Union des Associations Israélites, 359–60
United States, 139, 201, 259, 359, 360
Unity or Death (Serbian society), 261, 264–66
Üsküb, 42–44, 354, 360. *See also* Skopje
Üsküdar, 375

Vacirca, Vincenzo, 289
Vaina, Michele, 289
valaades, 332
Vardar, 3, 269, 272
Vasić, Milan, 266, 269, 271
Vasos, Konstadinos, 211
Vazov, Ivan, 35, 37
Veles, 266–70, 272
Venezia, Moshe Haim, 354
Venizelos, Eleftherios, 98, 210, 312
Verdun, 243
Vidin, 248
Vienna/Wien, 40, 94, 98, 100, 113–15, 118–27, 140, 210, 242, 287–88, 290, 294, 298, 394, 396–97
vilayet
  of Aydin, 319, 339
  of Kosovo, 95, 100, 202, 261, 321, 327
  of Monastir/Bitola, 100, 202, 261, 312–13, 321, 327, 330
  of Salonica, 202, 321, 327, 361, 313
Vinkovci, 399
violence, 6–7, 11, 14–15, 19–20, 27, 30, 32, 37, 41–46, 70–73, 125, 206–07, 215, 217, 225, 227–29, 232, 260–61, 272–73, 298–301, 307, 318–19, 328–29, 378, 395, 408, 416–18
  against civilians, 42–43, 72, 207, 227
  sexual, 42
  systematic political, 298
Vischer, Alfred, 39
Vivante, Angelo, 298–99
Vize, 351
Vladivostok, 248
Vlorë/Vlora, 144
Voden, 313
Vojnosanitetski Glasnik (Yugoslav military medical journal), 394, 406
volunteers, 28, 35, 67, 73, 168, 208, 210, 213, 215, 218, 221, 226, 263, 265, 269, 272, 312, 344, 355, 373–74, 376–77, 387
Vranešić, Djuro, 397
Vranje, 265, 269
Vratsa, 242, 248
Vzajemnost (cultural association), 292

Wagner, Felix, 39
Waldmann, Anton, 30
Wallachian Plain, 244
war
  council (*Kriegsrat*), 117, 147, 151, 154, 253
  crimes, 10–11, 38, 41, 45, 273, 274, 420
  European, 4–5, 8, 25, 45–46, 106, 117, 126, 137, 142, 229, 295, 327
  effort, 163–64, 209, 247, 347–48, 350, 356–57, 360, 376
  neurosis, 7, 392, 399–400, 406
  plans, 118, 154, 225
  preparations, 9, 36, 38–39, 55, 116–17, 137–38, 145, 147, 154
  risk, 118, 124, 142, 146
  surgery, 376, 378, 382, 387
Watson, Alexander, 225, 227
West, Rebecca, 206

Wiener Klinische Wochenschrift (Austrian medical journal), 394, 398, 403
Wilhelm II, German Emperor and King of Prussia, 115, 119–20, 122, 139, 145–47
Wilhelmshaven, 145–46, 148
workers, 7, 42, 286, 293–95, 406
Wylie, Doughty, 374, 377, 379, 382–83, 385

X-ray machines, 377

Yemen, 163, 168–69
Young Turk revolution (1908), 93–94, 168, 173, 312, 324, 369
 ultimatum, 102, 122
Young Turks, 95–97, 173, 324, 327
Yugoslav Social Democratic Party (JSDS) 292
Yugoslav wars of the 1990s, 4, 11, 14, 20, 69, 207, 286, 320, 336, 340–41, 417, 419
Yugoslavia, 207, 274, 290, 298, 320, 336, 392–95, 402, 405–07

Yugoslavism, 288, 290–91

Zagreb, 265, 396–97, 402
Zahra, Tara, 361
Zaionchikovski, Andrei Medardovitovich, 243, 250
Zarja (socialist newspaper), 291, 294–95
Zemun, 265
Žeraić, Bogdan, 264
Zeytinlik, 314
Ziemann, Benjamin, 299
zionism, 361, 368
Žirovčić, Ivan, 397, 402
Zografos, Andreas, 223
Zumakov, 242
Zweig, Stefan, 6, 11, 287, 299

www.ingramcontent.com/pod-product-compliance
Lightning Source LLC
Chambersburg PA
CBHW072140100526
44589CB00015B/2023